Assessing Policy Landscapes in Taxation Dynamics

Ana Arromba Dinis
Research Centre on Accounting and Taxation, Polytechnic Institute of Cávado and Ave, Portugal

Fátima David
Research Centre on Accounting and Taxation, Polytechnic Institute of Cávado and Ave, Portugal

Liliana Pereira
Research Centre on Accounting and Taxation, Polytechnic Institute of Cávado and Ave, Portugal

Sara Luís Dias
Research Centre on Accounting and Taxation, Polytechnic Institute of Cávado and Ave, Portugal

IGI Global
Publishing Tomorrow's Research Today

Vice President of Editorial — Melissa Wagner
Managing Editor of Acquisitions — Mikaela Felty
Managing Editor of Book Development — Jocelynn Hessler
Production Manager — Mike Brehm
Cover Design — Phillip Shickler

Published in the United States of America by
IGI Global Scientific Publishing
701 East Chocolate Avenue
Hershey, PA, 17033, USA
Tel: 717-533-8845
Fax: 717-533-8661
E-mail: cust@igi-global.com
Website: https://www.igi-global.com

Library of Congress Cataloging-in-Publication Data

Names: Dinis, Ana Cristina dos Santos Arromba, editor. | David, Fátima, 1968- editor. | Pereira, Liliana, 1978- editor. | Dias, Sara Luís, 1985- editor.
Title: Assessing policy landscapes in taxation dynamics / edited by Ana Dinis, Fátima David, Liliana Pereira, Sara Dias.
Description: Hershey, PA : Information Science Reference, [2025] | Includes bibliographical references and index. | Summary: "Assessing Policy Landscapes in Taxation Dynamics book is intended to contribute to the evaluation of fiscal policy and to broaden the scope for the systematic study and evaluation of fiscal policy in order to enhance informed debate on these issues"-- Provided by publisher.
Identifiers: LCCN 2024045915 (print) | LCCN 2024045916 (ebook) | ISBN 9798369339084 (hardcover) | ISBN 9798369350935 (paperback) | ISBN 9798369339091 (ebook)
Subjects: LCSH: Fiscal policy. | Taxation.
Classification: LCC HJ192.5 .A87 2025 (print) | LCC HJ192.5 (ebook) | DDC 339.5/2--dc23/eng/20241227
LC record available at https://lccn.loc.gov/2024045915
LC ebook record available at https://lccn.loc.gov/2024045916

British Cataloguing in Publication Data
A Cataloguing in Publication record for this book is available from the British Library.

Editorial Advisory Board

Table of Contents

Preface xvii

Chapter 1
A Financial Model for Optimizing Savings by Indirect Tax Rate Convergence ... 1
Guillermo Peña, Universidad de Zaragoza, Spain

Chapter 2
Assessing Tax Policies for Urban Rehabilitation: The Role of Tax Incentives on Sustainability 33
André Carvalho, Research Centre on Accounting and Taxation, Polytechnic University of Cávado and Ave, Portugal
Ana Dinis, Research Centre on Accounting and Taxation, Polytechnic University of Cávado and Ave, Portugal
Liliana Pereira, Research Centre on Accounting and Taxation, Polytechnic University of Cávado and Ave, Portugal

Chapter 3
Challenges and Opportunities of the Autonomous Communities Financing Reform in Spain 71
Mónica García Freiría, University of Vigo, Spain

Chapter 4
Concordat Between the Portuguese Republic and the Holy See: Exploring Tax Interpretation 115
Hélder Lopes, Pontificio Collegio Portoghese, Roma, Italy
Fátima David, Guarda Polytechnic Institute, Portugal
Maria Helena Martins Pernadas, Tax and Customs Authority, Portugal

Chapter 5
Fat Tax: Impact on Consumption and Health 141
Sérgio Ravara Cruz, University of Aveiro, Portugal
Nina Santos Damas, University of Aveiro, Portugal

Chapter 6
Green and Inclusive Taxation Towards a Sustainable Model That Strengthens the Colombian Economy 171
Franz Esteban Rodríguez Franky, Fundación Universitaria Compensar, Colombia

Chapter 7
Green Taxation and Sustainable Tourism Destinations: A Bibliometric Analysis 211
Vânia Costa, Polytechnic Institute of Cávado and Ave, Portugal
Raquel Pereira, Polytechnic Institute of Cávado and Ave, Portugal

Chapter 8
Regulatory Impact Assessment of Tax Policies in the Legislative Procedure of the State Budget: The Case of the Tax Benefit Granted to "Non-Habitual Residents" in Portugal 247
Ricardo Sousa da Cunha, Polytechnic Institute of Cávado and Ave, Portugal
Sara Luís Dias, Polytechnic Institute of Cávado and Ave, Portugal

Chapter 9
Significance of Tax Reforms as a Solution of Economic Problems 273
Saurabh Chandra, Bennett University, India
Bhumika Muchan, Independent Researcher, India

Chapter 10
Sustainable Economies: Government Measures for Integrating Green Taxation in Higher Education Curricula 303
Sílvia Coutinho Santos, SDRI, Technological University of the Shannon, Ireland & CICF, Polytechnic University of Cávado and Ave, Portugal
Ana Arromba Dinis, Research Centre on Accounting and Taxation, Polytechnic University of Cávado and Ave, Portugal
Liliana Pereira, Research Centre on Accounting and Taxation, Polytechnic University of Cávado and Ave, Portugal
Shane O'Sullivan, Sustainable Development Research Institute, Technological University of the Shannon, Ireland

Chapter 11
Tax on Urban Property and Land (IPTU) and Tax Benefits in the Municipality of Salvador/Bahia, Brazil 329
Tânia Cristina Azevedo, State University of Feira de Santana, Brazil & Federal University of Bahia, Brazil
José Renato Sena Oliveira, State University of Feira de Santana, Brazil
Mirian Gomes Conceição, State University of Feira de Santana, Brazil

Chapter 12
Tax Policy Responses to Economic Crises: The Case of Post-COVID-19 Reform in Morocco (2023-2026).. 359
Rida Belahouaoui, Cadi Ayyad University, Marrakesh, Morocco
El Houssain Attak, Cadi Ayyad University, Marrakesh, Morocco

Chapter 13
Taxation of the Non-Profit Sector in Portugal: In the Light of the Recent Developments in the European Union 387
Ana Paula Rocha, ISCAP, Instituto Politécnico do Porto, Portugal

Chapter 14
Taxation on Online Gaming Industry and Allied Stakeholders: An Elusive Policy?.. 409
Siddharth Kanojia, O.P. Jindal Global University, India

Chapter 15
Transfer Pricing for Baseline Distribution Structures: Assessing the Simplified and Streamlined Approach of Pillar One – Amount B.................... 423
Pascal René Marcel Kubin, University of Speyer, Germany

Chapter 16
A Measure to Prevent Tax Evasion 453
Susana Cristina Rodrigues Aldeia, Independent Researcher, Portugal
Anna Białek-Jaworska, University of Warsaw, Poland

Chapter 17
Trends and Perspectives on Tax Benefits Research: A Bibliometric Analysis .. 473
Carlos Lucas, University of Aveiro, Portugal
Sérgio Ravara Cruz, University of Aveiro, Portugal
Cecília Rendeiro Carmo, University of Aveiro, Portugal

Chapter 18
What We Can Learn From Flat Tax Research 515
Paulo Jorge Dias, Instituto Universitário de Lisboa, Portugal
Miguel Tavares, ISCTE, Portugal

Compilation of References 565

About the Contributors 639

Index 647

Detailed Table of Contents

Preface.. xvii

Chapter 1
A Financial Model for Optimizing Savings by Indirect Tax Rate Convergence ... 1
Guillermo Peña, Universidad de Zaragoza, Spain

This chapter discusses and affirmatively concludes the suitability of directly including financial services in the utility function—as usually done for non-financial products. This implies applying the same Value Added Tax (VAT) rate on them as the standard rate on most of goods and services. It avoids distortions in intertemporal households' decisions on savings substitution. The VAT rate divergence between general goods and services and financial services is associated with different shifts on economic variables, using panel data techniques for a sample of 33 countries for 1960-2019. This tax-induced anomaly in prices also Granger-causes a deficit on savings over GDP.

Chapter 2
Assessing Tax Policies for Urban Rehabilitation: The Role of Tax Incentives on Sustainability... 33
André Carvalho, Research Centre on Accounting and Taxation, Polytechnic University of Cávado and Ave, Portugal
Ana Dinis, Research Centre on Accounting and Taxation, Polytechnic University of Cávado and Ave, Portugal
Liliana Pereira, Research Centre on Accounting and Taxation, Polytechnic University of Cávado and Ave, Portugal

The urgent need to transform buildings into sustainable energy-efficient spaces is driven by the environmental impact of construction activities. This study examine the impact of tax incentives on urban rehabilitation among Portuguese companies using data from the Portuguese Tax Authority Portal (2015-2022) and the Sabi Database. Employing SPSS for descriptive analysis and Pearson correlation, the authors examine the tax incentives and urban rehabilitation indicators, including Municipal Property Tax, Municipal Property Transfer Tax, energy consumption, greenhouse gas emissions, and municipal environmental expenditures. The findings reveal significant positive correlations between tax incentives, higher reconstruction rates, and increased municipal environmental expenditures. However, these incentives also correlate with higher energy consumption and GHG emissions, highlighting the need for stricter environmental criteria in tax policies. This study offers valuable insights for policymakers on enhancing sustainable urban development through effective tax incentives.

Chapter 3
Challenges and Opportunities of the Autonomous Communities Financing Reform in Spain 71
Mónica García Freiría, University of Vigo, Spain

This chapter describes the main features of the current financing model of the Autonomous Communities of the common system in Spain. The Spanish lawmaker progressively promoted an increased fiscal co-responsability of the Autonomous Communities, in order that they could be provided with significant own resources enabling them to achieve their financial autonomy and sufficiency. However, the latest fundamental reform has proven to be inefficient and unfair. Thus, the current social and economic environment requires a deep reformulation of the existing legal framework of autonomous financing, in view to determine the scope and content of the asymmetrical fiscal power within a supranational integration system, such as the European Union. In this context is necessary to propose an amendment of the current financing model of the Autonomous Communities from the perspective of the public revenues which makes it compatible with the requirements of EU law in tax and budget matters.

Chapter 4
Concordat Between the Portuguese Republic and the Holy See: Exploring Tax Interpretation.. 115
Hélder Lopes, Pontificio Collegio Portoghese, Roma, Italy
Fátima David, Guarda Polytechnic Institute, Portugal
Maria Helena Martins Pernadas, Tax and Customs Authority, Portugal

This chapter aims to contribute to the interpretation, regulation, and implementation of the tax part of the Concordat established in 2004 between the Portuguese Republic and the Holy See. On the one hand, the legal framework of the different religions will be sought, underlining their positive externalities and enumerating the process that grants them legal personality, which is the reason for the tax benefits given to each religion. On the other hand, the tax framework of the religions in the Portuguese tax regime will be analyzed, examining the normative set emanating from the Constitution of the Portuguese Republic, the Religious Freedom Law, the Concordat, the Agreements with the Ismaili Imamat, and other relevant statutory norms. Thus, faced with the complex Portuguese landscape of tax laws, helpful clarifications will emerge for religious entities, particularly for many private social solidarity institutions associated with them, enabling better allocate of resources and improving their community impact.

Chapter 5
Fat Tax: Impact on Consumption and Health 141
Sérgio Ravara Cruz, University of Aveiro, Portugal
Nina Santos Damas, University of Aveiro, Portugal

The objectives of this study are to analyze whether the fat tax stimulates a reduction in the consumption of taxed products and to assess whether the fat tax has led to an improvement in the population's health. The main conclusion of the study was that there was an increase in consumption of goods subject to the tax between 2016 and 2023. It also showed that the health of the Portuguese population in general has not improved with the implementation of the tax. The contributions of this article have made it possible to deepen our knowledge of fat tax consumption in the Portuguese population, and to study the perception of the level of health of the Portuguese after the implementation of the tax, something that previous studies had not addressed.

Chapter 6
Green and Inclusive Taxation Towards a Sustainable Model That Strengthens the Colombian Economy 171
Franz Esteban Rodríguez Franky, Fundación Universitaria Compensar, Colombia

This chapter proposes to analyze green and inclusive taxation as a tool for the construction of a sustainable economic model in Colombia. The need for a change in the Colombian tax system is addressed, incorporating practical environmental and social criteria that are adjusted to MSMEs and SMEs, which allow promoting a fairer and more equitable economic development, in harmony with the environment. The Chapter analyzes the need for a green and inclusive tax reform, in which the economic and social impact is evaluated; issues related to the challenges for the implementation of green and inclusive taxation in Colombia are addressed, including the strategies that should be implemented and how these progressive taxes can benefit vulnerable populations and the targeting of public spending, which is key to reducing inequalities. "An equitable tax system strengthens social cohesion".

Chapter 7
Green Taxation and Sustainable Tourism Destinations: A Bibliometric Analysis.. 211
Vânia Costa, Polytechnic Institute of Cávado and Ave, Portugal
Raquel Pereira, Polytechnic Institute of Cávado and Ave, Portugal

This research aims to analyse the evolving literature of green taxation or tourist taxes and the development of sustainable tourism destinations. Using the PRISMA Method, this study is based on a bibliometric analysis of articles published in SCOPUS and Web of Science. The study analyses all publications over time, with the keywords "taxes", "tourism destinations" and "sustainability" in titles, keywords and abstracts. Tourism taxation is a public policy instrument applied to solve externalities caused by tourism and serves as a means of financing the maintenance and continuous improvement of services and infrastructures that directly and indirectly support tourism activity. The main contribution of our research is therefore to identify the evolving literature concerning tourism taxes and destinations, as well as to explore public strategies that contribute to rethinking, revitalizing and increasing the sustainability of tourism destinations through conceptual frameworks based on the integration of sustainable management practices in the planning processes of tourism destinations.

Chapter 8
Regulatory Impact Assessment of Tax Policies in the Legislative Procedure of the State Budget: The Case of the Tax Benefit Granted to "Non-Habitual Residents" in Portugal 247
Ricardo Sousa da Cunha, Polytechnic Institute of Cávado and Ave, Portugal
Sara Luís Dias, Polytechnic Institute of Cávado and Ave, Portugal

The quality of the legislation is one of the foundations of the principle of the rule of law and a condition for a more effective implementation. This is even more relevant for tax legislation, one of the birthplaces of modern Constitutions and probably the field of law most directly affecting the daily life of citizens. Assessing the regulatory impact of an important contemporary tax policy in Portugal, such as the taxation of non-habitual residents, reveals the virtues and limitations of this procedure - as recently confirmed by the creation of a governmental technical unit for the evaluation of tax policies (U-TAX) on the back of the conclusions of the Working Group on Tax Benefits. This is part of a methodological exercise that demands the same degree of argumentative "justification" from the legislator as from the judge - Legisprudence. In this paper the possibilities of extending this exercise to the tax policy options that are part of the State Budget are discussed.

Chapter 9
Significance of Tax Reforms as a Solution of Economic Problems 273
Saurabh Chandra, Bennett University, India
Bhumika Muchan, Independent Researcher, India

The latest changes to India's taxes have had an impact on recent economic development and growth. To really understand what those changes meant, it's necessary to grasp a thorough understanding of them—something this qualitative study seeks to attain in order to evaluate the GST and corporate tax rate revisions comprehensively. The research investigates how the changes may affect key sectors like agriculture, industry, services, and international trade—that is, any ramifications they may have on fostered economic expansion via these sectors. Using current literature, the study considers how the changes might affect investment patterns, company performance, and income distribution; it also takes a look at the potential opportunities and challenges associated with implementing tax reform—including compliance issues and administrative capacity. It concludes that the tax system in India remains a substantial impediment to improvement, despite eight years of reforms.

Chapter 10
Sustainable Economies: Government Measures for Integrating Green Taxation in Higher Education Curricula 303
Sílvia Coutinho Santos, SDRI, Technological University of the Shannon, Ireland & CICF, Polytechnic University of Cávado and Ave, Portugal
Ana Arromba Dinis, Research Centre on Accounting and Taxation, Polytechnic University of Cávado and Ave, Portugal
Liliana Pereira, Research Centre on Accounting and Taxation, Polytechnic University of Cávado and Ave, Portugal
Shane O'Sullivan, Sustainable Development Research Institute, Technological University of the Shannon, Ireland

The protection of the environment is a matter of global concern that effects the population and endangers future generations. Consequently, the implementation of measures such as green taxation (also referred to in the international literature as environmental taxation and environmental law) is significant to effect behavioural change. In this context, the role of Higher Education Institutions (HEIs) is utmost importance in terms of sustainability and economic growth. This study aims to critically analyse the courses offered in the field of green taxation at the top 100 universities in the Shanghai Ranking, 2023. This analysis will contribute to the body of knowledge about the progress made in teaching green taxation and the measures that have been put in place by governments to this end. The study revealed that in European Union and China, the teaching of science and technology continues to be a dominant force.

Chapter 11
Tax on Urban Property and Land (IPTU) and Tax Benefits in the Municipality of Salvador/Bahia, Brazil 329
Tânia Cristina Azevedo, State University of Feira de Santana, Brazil & Federal University of Bahia, Brazil
José Renato Sena Oliveira, State University of Feira de Santana, Brazil
Mirian Gomes Conceição, State University of Feira de Santana, Brazil

This chapter aims to explore in detail the Tax on Urban Property and Land (IPTU, in portuguese), a Brazilian tax of municipal jurisdiction, specifically the tax benefits. For this purpose, the panorama of this tax, its context, and characteristics were approached and possibilities of tax benefits and incentives that have been used in the city of Salvador, capital of the state of Bahia, Brazil, were presented. This study brings the discussion of possible ecological and sustainable tax incentives in the city from the perspective of an urban development that contributes to the environmental, social, economic, cultural, and educational dimensions, and to the integration into the commitments of the 2030 Agenda of Sustainable Development Goals (SDGs). As for the methodological procedures, this is a case study, supported by bibliographical and documentary research. The research results bring possibilities of urban policy tax instruments in the matter of the IPTU, that can be associated with incentives aimed at the sustainable development.

Chapter 12
Tax Policy Responses to Economic Crises: The Case of Post-COVID-19 Reform in Morocco (2023-2026) 359
Rida Belahouaoui, Cadi Ayyad University, Marrakesh, Morocco
El Houssain Attak, Cadi Ayyad University, Marrakesh, Morocco

This chapter explores Morocco's tax policy responses to the economic crises induced by the COVID-19 pandemic, focusing on the comprehensive tax reform initiatives implemented between 2023 and 2026. It examines how these reforms aim to balance the need for increased fiscal revenue with the principles of tax equity and efficiency amidst the economic disruptions caused by the pandemic. The chapter discusses the background of Morocco's tax system, the objectives and strategies of the reforms, and their implementation and outcomes. It also addresses the challenges faced and lessons learned during the reform process. The chapter concludes by reflecting on the significance of Morocco's tax policy response in enhancing fiscal sustainability and economic resilience, while suggesting areas for future research and policy development.

Chapter 13
Taxation of the Non-Profit Sector in Portugal: In the Light of the Recent Developments in the European Union 387
Ana Paula Rocha, ISCAP, Instituto Politécnico do Porto, Portugal

The encouragement and development of the social economy sector are recognized as values of general interest in Portugal. Therefore, the promotion of the social economy by the Portuguese public authorities is legally foreseen, namely through the provision of a more favorable tax status for the non-profit entities. However, the need to rethink and (perhaps) update the Portuguese tax legislation applicable to the social economy sector has often been discussed, namely, to guarantee that the tax benefits in force truly respect the most important tax principles. Moreover, the need to rethink the tax legislation applicable to the social economy sector have also been recognized at the European Union' level. Accordingly, and with the use of the legal methodology, the objective of our work is to identify and analyze the major opinions and recommendations that have been issued in this context by several European' organisms, in order to understand whether the Portuguese tax system is already upon those recommendations or, on the contrary, needs to be amended to keep up with them.

Chapter 14
Taxation on Online Gaming Industry and Allied Stakeholders: An Elusive Policy? 409
Siddharth Kanojia, O.P. Jindal Global University, India

The online gaming industry in India has undergone remarkable growth in the recent years. According to few reports, the industry envisaged to reach a market size of INR 290 billion by end of the year 2025 i.e., approximately USD 4 billion, growing at a CAGR of 21.4% from 2020 to 2025. Wherein, the mobile gaming segment is the prodigious and burgeoning segment in Indian online gaming market, accounting for nearly 85% of the market share. Whereas, e-sports market is expected to grow rapidly in the coming years, with the potential to reach a market size of INR 11 billion (approximately USD 150 million) by 2025 (Arora 2019). Accordingly, In light of the ever increasing popularity of online gaming, the government of Indian government has proposed to include specific clauses pertaining the taxability of online games in the Finance Bill of year 2023. Hence, this chapter shall explore the connotation of imposing taxes on online gaming industry in India.

Chapter 15
Transfer Pricing for Baseline Distribution Structures: Assessing the Simplified and Streamlined Approach of Pillar One – Amount B..................... 423
Pascal René Marcel Kubin, University of Speyer, Germany

Baseline distribution transactions are relatively simple yet frequently occurring transactions within multinational enterprises. However, from a transfer pricing perspective, they are often associated with high compliance costs and substantial uncertainties for taxpayers. Against this background, the OECD/G20 Inclusive Framework on BEPS has introduced the Simplified and Streamlined Approach (SSA) under Pillar One - Amount B. By providing standardized, arm's length return on sales margins for the wholesale distribution of goods, the SSA intends to reduce compliance costs and increase tax certainty. This chapter initially presents the key aspects of the approach, before critically assessing their implications. The analysis particularly indicates that an incongruent implementation of the SSA across jurisdictions may undermine the intention of simplifying transfer pricing. Moreover, the narrow price range of the SSA could increase the importance of software solutions for controlling transfer prices.

Chapter 16
A Measure to Prevent Tax Evasion 453
Susana Cristina Rodrigues Aldeia, Independent Researcher, Portugal
Anna Białek-Jaworska, University of Warsaw, Poland

This research project is focused on examining the impact of transfer pricing regulations on preventing tax evasion, specifically within the context of Portuguese jurisdiction. To accomplish this, the study utilizes a legal research methodology. Extensive examination of both national and international data sources was conducted, with particular attention given to scrutinizing the corporate income tax law and related tax documents at the national level. Additionally, thorough analysis of the OECD guidelines and reports on transfer pricing was undertaken at the international level.

Chapter 17
Trends and Perspectives on Tax Benefits Research: A Bibliometric Analysis .. 473
Carlos Lucas, University of Aveiro, Portugal
Sérgio Ravara Cruz, University of Aveiro, Portugal
Cecília Rendeiro Carmo, University of Aveiro, Portugal

Reducing taxation is a relevant and cross-cutting issue in society, at the level of governments, companies and citizens. There are currently a large number of scientific publications on this subject. The aim of this study is to present a mapping of scientific production on the subject of tax benefits, which will make it possible to understand the evolution and trends of research in this area. A bibliometric analysis was carried out using the Bibliometrix tool, based on the documents available on the Scopus and Web of Science platforms. The results show that the greatest growth in research on this topic has occurred from the beginning of this century to the present day. The use of dominant expressions is also observed, resulting in two clusters that separate research into tax benefits at a company level from those at an individual level. This result suggests the need for future studies to deal separately with corporate and personal tax benefits.

Chapter 18
What We Can Learn From Flat Tax Research 515
Paulo Jorge Dias, Instituto Universitário de Lisboa, Portugal
Miguel Tavares, ISCTE, Portugal

This chapter explores the increasing academic and political interest in the "Flat Tax" system, particularly inspired by the outcomes observed in countries with proportional taxation. By analyzing a sample of 109 scientific articles from the Scopus platform using bibliometric indicators, the chapter provides a comprehensive overview of the research trends and key findings in this area. The study reveals a significant rise in publications and citations over the last few decades, with a strong focus from European researchers, though the USA shows the highest interest. The findings indicate that the topic spans various disciplines, resulting in diverse and sometimes conflicting conclusions. This chapter underscores the importance of continued investigation into the flat tax to better understand its broader implications.

Compilation of References 565

About the Contributors 639

Index 647

Preface

As editors of this reference book, we are delighted to present the culmination of a collaborative effort that delves into the intricate dynamics of taxation and its role in addressing key economic, social, and environmental challenges.

In an increasingly complex global landscape, where fiscal policies are central to driving sustainable development, the need for innovative tax reforms has never been more critical. Governments, businesses, and policymakers are recognizing the power of taxation as a tool for fostering economic equity, environmental sustainability, and long-term resilience.

This book offers an in-depth exploration of taxation strategies, shedding light on how they can shape a more sustainable and inclusive future.

Taxation policies play a pivotal role in shaping economies, driving sustainable development, and addressing societal inequities. In the face of global challenges, tax systems must adapt to promote growth, ensure fairness, and respond to the socio-economic needs of diverse populations. This collection of studies, Assessing Policy Landscapes in Taxation Dynamics, delves into various dimensions of tax policy from multiple international perspectives, providing invaluable insights into the evolving landscapes of taxation across the globe.

This book brings together a diverse array of research, examining topics ranging from the implementation of Value Added Tax (VAT) on financial services to the intricacies of tax incentives for urban rehabilitation and sustainability. The studies also explore critical issues such as tax reform in response to economic crises, the role of green taxation in promoting environmental sustainability, and the implications of transfer pricing regulations in preventing tax evasion. Each chapter offers a unique perspective on the dynamic relationship between taxation policies and economic, social, and environmental outcomes.

The work presented here is a collaborative effort of scholars and practitioners dedicated to expanding our understanding of how tax policy can be leveraged as a tool for development and social progress. As editors, we are proud to present these contributions, which are grounded in rigorous research and aimed at informing policymakers, academics, and practitioners alike.

We hope that this book will serve as a valuable resource for those seeking to understand and influence the future of taxation policy in an ever-changing world.

Chapter 1 explores the potential benefits of applying the same VAT rates to financial services as other goods and services. The chapter uses panel data from thirty-three countries (1960-2019) to demonstrate how VAT rate divergence can distort savings behavior and cause economic imbalances.

Chapter 2 focuses on the role of tax incentives in promoting urban rehabilitation and sustainability in Portugal. The study finds positive correlations between tax incentives and higher reconstruction rates but also notes adverse effects like increased energy consumption and greenhouse gas emissions.

Chapter 3 critiques Spain's current regional financing model, arguing it inadequately provides for fiscal autonomy and fairness. The chapter advocates for a reform that aligns fiscal responsibilities with EU tax and budget standards, ensuring a more balanced distribution of financial resources.

Chapter 4 analyzes the tax benefits granted to religious entities under the 2004 Concordat between Portugal and the Vatican. The chapter examines how tax laws and religious frameworks intersect, offering recommendations to improve resource allocation and the social impact of religious institutions.

Chapter 5 investigates whether the implementation of the fat tax in Portugal has reduced the consumption of unhealthy foods and improved public health. The results show increased consumption of taxed items and limited health improvements, raising questions about the tax's overall effectiveness.

Chapter 6 proposes a green tax reform in Colombia that incorporates environmental and social criteria. The chapter emphasizes that such reforms can promote equitable development, particularly for MSMEs and SMEs, and reduce inequalities through progressive taxation and targeted public spending.

Chapter 7 conducts a bibliometric analysis of green taxation literature related to sustainable tourism. The chapter highlights how tourism taxes can help mitigate negative externalities, support environmental protection, and improve infrastructure in tourist destinations.

Chapter 8 focuses on the taxation of non-habitual residents in Portugal, discussing the strengths and limitations of regulatory impact assessments (RIA) in shaping tax policy. The chapter underscores the importance of RIAs in enhancing legislative transparency and effectiveness.

Chapter 9 reviews recent tax reforms in India, including GST and corporate tax rate adjustments, and their effects on sectors like agriculture, industry, and trade. The chapter also addresses challenges in compliance and administration, highlighting areas for future reform to stimulate economic growth.

Chapter 10 analyzes green taxation courses offered by top universities, focusing on their role in driving sustainable development. The study underscores the need for more comprehensive education in environmental taxation, particularly considering global sustainability goals.

Chapter 11 examines the Urban Property and Land Tax (IPTU) in Salvador, Brazil, and its potential for supporting sustainable urban development. The chapter discusses how IPTU tax incentives can promote ecological and social improvements, aligning with the UN's Sustainable Development Goals (SDGs).

Chapter 12 explores Morocco's tax policy reforms in response to the COVID-19 crisis, focusing on balancing fiscal sustainability with fairness. The chapter reviews strategies for enhancing tax equity and efficiency while reflecting on the lessons learned from Morocco's economic recovery efforts.

Chapter 13 analyzes the Portuguese tax framework for non-profit entities, evaluating the need for updates to ensure tax benefits are aligned with EU standards. The chapter examines potential improvements to better support the social economy sector and enhance public interest initiatives.

Chapter 14 discusses the rapid growth of India's online gaming industry and the government's efforts to regulate it through taxation. The chapter explores the implications of these taxes for industry stakeholders and the broader economy, particularly regarding compliance and market dynamics.

Chapter 15 analyzes the OECD's Simplified and Streamlined Approach (SSA) for transfer pricing of baseline distribution transactions in multinational enterprises. The chapter critiques the SSA's narrow price range and its potential to increase reliance on software solutions for compliance.

Chapter 16 investigates the role of transfer pricing regulations in preventing tax evasion within Portuguese jurisdiction, using national and international data. The study also evaluates Portugal's alignment with OECD guidelines and the effectiveness of these regulations in curbing tax avoidance.

Chapter 17 conducts a bibliometric analysis of tax benefits research, mapping the growth and trends in this field. The chapter identifies key areas of focus, such as corporate vs. personal tax benefits, and suggests directions for future studies on the socio-economic impacts of tax reductions.

Chapter 18 Provides a comprehensive review of flat tax research, highlighting the increasing interest in proportional taxation models. The chapter analyzes research trends and outcomes from countries with flat tax systems, noting the complex and sometimes contradictory conclusions drawn from the literature.

We extend our sincere gratitude to all the contributors for their thoughtful and engaging analyses, and to the many professionals and institutions whose support made this book possible. We also want to thank the readers for engaging with this critical discourse and for contributing to the ongoing conversation on the role of taxation in shaping a more equitable and sustainable future.

In conclusion, we hope this reference book serves as a valuable resource for academics, professionals, and policymakers, inspiring meaningful action, and dialogue to address the complexities of taxation in shaping economic and social outcomes. By exploring effective and innovative tax strategies, we aim to contribute to the development of policies that promote growth and equity.

The Editors,

Ana Arromba Dinis

Research Centre on Accounting and Taxation, Polytechnic University of Cávado and Ave

Fátima David

Research Centre on Accounting and Taxation, Polytechnic University of Guarda

Liliana Pereira

Research Centre on Accounting and Taxation, Polytechnic University of Cávado and Ave

Sara Luís Dias

Polytechnic University of Cávado and Ave

Chapter 1
A Financial Model for Optimizing Savings by Indirect Tax Rate Convergence

Guillermo Peña
Universidad de Zaragoza, Spain

ABSTRACT

This chapter discusses and affirmatively concludes the suitability of directly including financial services in the utility function—as usually done for non-financial products. This implies applying the same Value Added Tax (VAT) rate on them as the standard rate on most of goods and services. It avoids distortions in intertemporal households' decisions on savings substitution. The VAT rate divergence between general goods and services and financial services is associated with different shifts on economic variables, using panel data techniques for a sample of 33 countries for 1960-2019. This tax-induced anomaly in prices also Granger-causes a deficit on savings over GDP.

1. INTRODUCTION

The current exemption of financial services under the Value Added Tax (VAT) in most countries leads to distortions on agents' behavior (Poddar and English, 1997). Furthermore, prices are currently rising, with one the biggest raises of interest rates since the last decades. This raise of the official interest rates could also lead to financial corrections towards the equilibrium. For solving these frictions and reaching a more neutral and efficient—and not over-dimensioned—financial

DOI: 10.4018/979-8-3693-3908-4.ch001

system, it is crucial to achieve a correct taxation of this sector (IMF, 2010)—even more in taxes as VAT where its pass from an income tax is associated with higher growth (Şen and Kaya, 2023). The aforementioned exemption is mainly provoked because of technical—but also theoretical—difficulties, since the optimal taxation of financial services is an unconcluded debate (Christiansen, 2017). In addition, the European Commission is recently studying how to modernize the value added taxation of insurance and financial services (EC, 2020; López-Laborda and Peña, 2022). The optimal taxation of the financial sector is an essential topic for understanding the uniform taxation of all goods and services (Christiansen and Smith, 2021), also taking into account specific banking services as payment services (Lockwood & Yerushalmi, 2019) or insurance services (Altenburguer, 2022).

This paper theoretically discusses whether all these services directly yield the consumer utility, and provides empirical panel data evidence showing that the differentiated tax regime of the financial sector leads to shifts in intertemporal decisions of households, concretely, involving savings choices. For solving this fact and allowing a uniform taxation without distortions, fully levying explicit and implicit fees as Peña (2019) proposes may be a good reason for directly including financial services in the utility function in wider models of optimal taxation as those of Boadway and Keen (2003) and Christiansen (2017). Nonetheless, Baydur & Yilmaz (2021) recently show that passing financial services from being exempt to levied under VAT only reports welfare gains with low VAT rates. After this introduction, Section 2 reviews the optimal taxation literature in brief and shows the conceptual debate whereas Section 3 provides the theoretical model. Section 4 analyzes the empirical data, Section 5 illustrates an empirical exercise, Section 6 performs a robustness check and determines possible factors on the tax rate divergence, while Section 7 discusses the results. Finally, Section 8 concludes.

2. OPTIMAL TAXATION LITERATURE

An issue to address is that financial services have not been incorporated yet directly in the utility function for indirect taxation in modern financial models. They can be considered as final goods for instance when they are consumed directly by households. In this case, they are final goods and should be directly included in the utility function, but it is not the case when the customer is a business. The literature has slightly discussed regarding these issues. For instance, Auerbach and Gordon (2002) find the need to tax them at the same VAT rate as other products to avoid distortions, but without including these services in the utility function. Indeed, they do not even consider financial services as final products in their model, only as an intermediary service to firms. To the author's knowledge, no authors are explicitly in favor of directly including financial services in this function for taxation purposes. For instance, Christiansen (2017, p.3) asserts that "a recurring argument [...] is that financial services are not consumption goods that directly yield the consumer utility". Other authors consider that many items are taxed even though they seem not to be final objects of utility (Boadway and Keen, 2003).

In spite of the words of Tobin (1980, p.86) stating that "the practice of putting money stocks in the utility function is reprehensible," the money-in-the-utility function (MUF) is popular outside public finance (Poterba and Rotemberg, 1986; Croushore, 1993). Some authors have recently considered this kind of model (Lagos et al., 2017). Nonetheless, all these authors are aware that inclusion is a controversial issue, and some others include money-in-the-utility function indirectly but not directly. There are many reasons for considering money—and, therefore, savings and borrowing—in the utility function. Some authors even suggest that financial assets directly yield the consumer utility (Poterba and Rotemberg, 1986), and there are even welfare effects other than deferred consumption, which may be relevant in reducing poverty (Sherraden, 1990). Among other reasons, since durable goods can provide utility to agents, money could do it as well (Croushore, 1993). The previous author observes that money, in particular, actually provides the service of liquidity.

There is also empirical literature confirming the presence of utility provided to consumers by banking institutions: satisfaction surveys can outline the consumer benefits of these products. Krishnan et al. (1999) find that the supply of financial products by the banks is one of the main drivers of overall consumer satisfaction. According to the empirical results of Montfort et al. (2000), the performance level of these services has a significant positive direct effect on consumer satisfaction. Maddern et al. (2007) find that the technical aspects of the service also play an important role in consumer satisfaction. Recent studies highlight the importance of satisfaction stemming from financial entities providing complete information (Sivesan, 2019). Therefore, all these empirical results suggest that financial intermediation institutions provide some differential benefits with respect to a world without them. Specifically, satisfying the following needs could provide utility to households: offering financial product variety, friendly service and more highly prepared personnel answering questions and solving problems, and banking staff addressing technical issues when households cannot do it on their own—reducing search costs. Additionally, in the case where financial services are provided to households, these services can be considered as final product, since there are no intermediaries through non-financial companies, so they cannot be considered as input. As final product, it may be considered that the households buy and consume this service because it provides utility.

Given all the previous reasons, financial services could also be directly included in the utility function, as money and assets. They also provide liquidity, nearly complete financial information and product variety to agents, and maintenance and security of on-line and off-line financial services (Allen et al., 2018). Furthermore, the insatiability premise is fulfilled: the more financial services people have, the more money people may obtain, and the more satisfied people will be. This premise is even clearer with low-income households. Banks provide intertemporal and inter-agent intermediation, thus allowing intertemporal trade (Jack, 2000) by reducing transaction costs. They also provide services related to money safety, the reduction of uncertainty and risk, and services that allow availability or increase of money. Nevertheless, households will naturally have to pay a price, which is the value added of the financial service per unit. This is the microeconomic view, considering the utility function. The same case can also be considered for welfare at a macroeconomic level: the higher degree of use of financial services, the more economical the generated activity will be. Another issue is controlling the size of this sector and of the economic activity, but this paper only seeks the neutrality of households' behavior when applying value-added taxes—or taxes on financial services. If efficiency is sought, then Pigouvian taxes have to be considered—or taxes on financial transactions, (Poledna and Thurner, 2016)—to avoid financial crises or negative externalities.

3. THE MODEL

This section compares a model in a second best by applying a lump-sum tax where there is no intertemporal distortion in the decision of investing. The only distortion could be with leisure but not with consumption. The second model applies a VAT rate to all financial and real services in order to see whether the neutrality in the above-mentioned second-best way is maintained by observing that the fraction between the marginal utilities respect to consumption are kept.

3.1. Lump-Sum Tax

Section 4 is based on the theoretical models by Christiansen (2017) and Boadway and Keen (2003), following the modelling steps and notation of the former author. N consumers are considered as the total population, divided into L households that save money and M consumers who borrow. Each household earns an exogenous income Y^n_k, where n represents an individual consumer (l and m represent an individual that saves and borrows, respectively) and k is a point in time (k=1,2). According to this author, in the first period, exogenous income can be used for 'real' consumption

C_1^n and for positive or negative savings, positive savings are represented by S and negative savings are reflected by borrowing, B. The aggregate budget constraint at period 1 is:

$$\sum_{n=1}^{N} Y_1^n - NT_1 + B = \sum_{n=1}^{N} C_1^n + S + NK$$

According to Christiansen (2017), consumers are charged with an explicit fee K in period 1 and Q in period 2, when consumers take out deposit accounts or apply for a loan. Consumers also pay a lump-sum tax in period k, denoted by T_k. The use of the lump-sum tax is to see whether the intertemporal utilities with this tax are also kept by using VAT. The budget constraints for the savers (Figure 2) and borrowers (Figure 3) are equal to, following accountant identities:

$$\sum_{l=1}^{L} Y_1^l = \sum_{l=1}^{L} C_1^l + L(K + T_1) + S$$

$$\sum_{m=1}^{M} Y_1^m = \sum_{m=1}^{M} C_1^m + M(K + T_1) - B$$

There is a fixed return to capital in the world market. The interest rate of borrowing is ρ_B and the lump-sum tax is T_k. Consumer preferences over goods and services are given by a utility function that depends on the total consumption of both periods. The aggregate budget constraint at period 2 is:

$$S(1 + i) + \sum_{n=1}^{N} Y_2^n - B(1 + i) - NT_2$$

$$= \sum_{n=1}^{N} C_2^n + S(i - \rho_s) + B(\rho_B - i) + NQ$$

Where ρ_S is the saving interest rate, i is the world market return to capital, considered equivalent to the pure interest in this paper: for each borrowing/saving interest rate there is a value added that constitutes part of the value added of the loan/deposit, and the rest, the pure interest, constitutes the capital return, so $\rho_B = i + K_B$, $\rho_B = i + K_S$, $\rho_S = i - K_S$, where K_B and K_S are the profits and salary costs—value added—of the bank service per unit of, respectively, borrowing and savings, where the sum constitutes the financial margin. In this paper, terms K_B and K_S are substituted by the expression they are equal to, that is, $\rho_B - i$ and $i - \rho_S$. This follows a cash flow with a TCA system for calculating the value added of financial services (Poddar and English, 1997). These variables can be generalized to financial cash flows by considering B and S as, respectively, the outflows and inflows of capital amounts; where ρ_B and ρ_S can be considered the input and output flows of capital interests. Substituting B and S of Figures 2 and 3 in the capital gain of expression (Figure 4)—in other words, the capital amount plus pure interests—the interests without the value-added components, and rearranging terms, the intertemporal budget constraint leads to:

$$\sum_{n=1}^{N} Y_2^n + (1+i)\sum_{n=1}^{N} Y_1^n = (1+i)\sum_{n=1}^{N} C_1^n + \sum_{n=1}^{N} C_2^n + S(i-\rho_S)$$
$$+B(\rho_B - i) + (1+i)N(K+T_1) + N(+T_2 \rightarrow \sum_{n=1}^{N} Y_1^n$$
$$= (1+i)\left(\sum_{n=1}^{N} C_1^n + \sum_{n=1}^{N} C_1^f\right) + \sum_{n=1}^{N} C_2^n + \sum_{n=1}^{N} C_2^f$$

In this paper, the utility function involves consuming real goods and financial services, and it is defined as 'total consumption' $\left(C_t^T\right)$ of the global economy, for each period. Thus, the quantities and prices of the 'financial consumption' $\left(C_t^f\right)$ are, respectively, *S,B,N*—the number of customers for the explicit fees and commissions, EFC—and i–ρ_S, ρ_B–i, *K/Q*—in the last case of EFC, depending on whether we are on the first or second periods. Therefore, the intertemporal utility margins can be considered:

$$\frac{U_1}{U_2} = 1 + i$$

Where, for notational simplicity as in Christiansen (2017), $U_k = \partial U / \partial C_k^T \rightarrow \partial Y / \partial C_k^T \left(k = 1{,}2\right)$. It is easy to see that the equilibrium would be the same without taxes.

The main difference with the previous author is considering the market interest—inter-banking or pure interest—instead of the borrowing/saving interest for each case since this paper follows Peña's (2019) treatment of banking services, where financial consumption is considered, the value added of financial services, leading to a consumer discount rate for customers equal to the pure interest rate. Thus, capital income, in the strict sense of the term, according to the previous author, is driven by the interest rate without fees and risk, in other words, the market interest rate given by the 'pure' interest rate. Value added or financial consumption comes from the respective difference between this 'pure' interest and the borrowing or deposit interest, where the rest constitutes the consumer's capital return, as explained above.

Besides incorporating Peña's (2019) efficient treatment of banking services in a context of optimal taxation of financial services, this model generalizes the proposals of Boadway and Keen (2003) and Christiansen (2017) by considering explicit and implicit fees for savings and borrowing at the same time. Nonetheless, the main methodological novelty is the direct incorporation of financial services into the utility function in the dynamic model, as will be seen and discussed below.

3.2. Non-Financial and Financial VAT

Now, financial services and real goods are levied by a VAT rate τ. Then, the budget constraints of period 1 for all the consumers and for savers and borrowers are equal to:

$$\sum_{n=1}^{N} Y_1^n + B = (1+\tau)\sum_{n=1}^{N} C_1^n + S + N(1+\tau)K$$

$$\sum_{l=1}^{L} Y_1^l = (1+\tau)\sum_{l=1}^{L} C_1^l + L(1+\tau)K + S$$

$$\sum_{m=1}^{M} Y_1^m = (1+\tau)\sum_{m=1}^{M} C_1^m + M(1+\tau)K - B$$

The intertemporal budget constraint yields, with savings and borrowing substituted and terms rearranged:

$$\sum_{n=1}^{N} Y_2^n + (1+i)\left[\sum_{n=1}^{N} Y_1^n - (1+\tau)\sum_{n=1}^{N} C_1^n - N(1+\tau)K\right]$$

$$= (1+\tau)\sum_{n=1}^{N} C_2^n + (1+\tau)S(i-\rho_S) + (1+\tau)B(\rho_B - i) + N(1+\tau)Q$$

The term $S(i{-}\rho_S)$ can be considered the value added from savings, and $B(\rho_B{-}i)$ from borrowing, identified with the profits and salary costs of the financial services, as explained above, where the sum is financial consumption. After rearranging:

$$\sum_{n=1}^{N} Y_2^n + (1+i)\sum_{n=1}^{N} Y_1^n$$

$$= (1+i)(1+\tau)\sum_{n=1}^{N} C_1^n + (1+\tau)\sum_{n=1}^{N} C_2^n + (1+\tau)S(i-\rho_S) + (1+\tau)B(\rho_B - i)$$

$$+(1+i)(1+\tau)NK + (1+\tau)NQ \rightarrow \sum_{n=1}^{N} Y_2^n + (1+i)\sum_{n=1}^{N} Y_1^n$$

$$= (1+i)(1+\tau)\left(\sum_{n=1}^{N} C_2^n + \sum_{n=1}^{N} C_2^f\right)$$

As in the previous section, the utility function involves consuming real and financial goods and services. Therefore, the intertemporal utility margins are considered:

$$\frac{U_1}{U_2} = \frac{(1+i)(1+\tau)}{(1+\tau)} = 1+i$$

The above expression applies the efficient treatment of banking services proposed by Peña (2019) to the proposed model. Therefore, in equation (10) the intertemporal discount rate is now the pure interest rate instead of the borrowing or saving rate in contrast to other authors. Derived from the explicit inclusion of the financial services in the utility function, it is necessary to tax at the same tax rate real and financial goods as in expression for being neutral to intertemporal decisions and to relative prices, according to expression. This result is similar as in Peña (2019) concerning the consideration of the spend of income for providing the financial services and also similar as in Peña (2022), where an endogenous and static model is applied instead of an exogenous and dynamic one.

4. PROPERTIES OF THE MODEL

4.1. Relevance of Directly Including Financial Consumption in the Utility

The distinction between real and financial consumption is key for achieving expression and, so, reaching economic efficiency. By including financial consumption as part of total consumption, we are considering some facts that are would not be addressed otherwise and would lead to misperceptions of economic inefficiency. It is also relevant that the savings and borrowings, respectively, S and B, are decided in t=1 but for t=2 they are already a given datum for the decisions of the respective economic agent. Otherwise, if we substitute their respective values from expressions and we introduce them by additionally only considering real—without financial—consumption as it is currently common in the literature—so, considering financial services only an indirect consumption, being indirectly included in the utility function by this way—, we have:

$$\sum_{n=1}^{N} Y_2^n + (1+i)\sum_{n=1}^{N} Y_1^n - (1+\tau)\left[(i - \rho_S \sum_{n=1}^{L} Y_1^l - (\rho_B - i)\sum_{n=1}^{M} Y_1^m\right]$$

$$-(1+i)(1+\tau)NK + (1+\tau)^2\left[(i-\rho_S)LK - (\rho_B - i)MK\right]$$

$$=(1+\tau)\sum_{n=1}^{N} C_2^n + (1+i)(1+\tau)\sum_{n=1}^{N} C_1^n - (1+\tau)^2\left[(i-\rho_S)\sum_{n=1}^{L} C_1^l - (\rho_B - i)MK\right]$$

$$=(1+\tau)\sum_{n=1}^{N} C_2^n + (1+i)(1+\tau)\sum_{n=1}^{N} C_1^n - (1+\tau)^2\left[(1-\rho_S)\sum_{n=1}^{L} C_1^l - (\rho_B - i)\sum_{n=1}^{M} C_1^m\right]$$

in this case, as previously commented, only real consumption is considered. For achieving the former expression of economic efficiency, there is a need of annulling the differences that are multiplied by the square of the tax rate plus a unit. This can only be obtained when—after considering $\beta_{mi}\{\beta_m := \sum_{n=1}^{M} C_1^n, \beta_{mEFC} := M/N\}$

$$i = \rho_B\beta_{mi} + \rho_S(1 - \beta_{mi}) \xrightarrow{if\ S=B,L=M} i = \frac{\rho_B + \rho_S}{2}$$

Therefore, it would only be achieved if the pure interest rate is a weighted sum of the deposit and lending interest rates. After providing the same assumptions as in López-Laborda and Peña (2018) of equality of the capital amounts, and additionally of the number of lenders and savers, the only pure interest rate that would allow to economic efficiency as in expression would be the mid-price of the interest rates (Peña, 2020). Nonetheless, the mid-price is only compatible with the explicit expression of pure interest provided in the former authors[1] $i=2\rho_B\rho_S/(\rho_B+\rho_S)$ when the proportion of lending interest rates are equal to the deposit interest rates, or, in general, when:

$$\beta_{mi} = \frac{\rho_S(\rho_B - \rho_S)}{\rho_B^2 - \rho_S^2} = \frac{\rho_S}{\rho_B + \rho_S}, 1 - \beta_{mi} = \frac{\rho_B(\rho_B - \rho_S)}{\rho_B^2 - \rho_S^2} \rightarrow \frac{\beta_{mi}}{1 - \beta_{mi}} = \frac{\rho_S}{\rho_B}$$

The previous expression means that the proportion of loans over deposits has to be equal to the proportion of deposit interest rates over lending rates, which is impossible in practice —or never seen in the most common banking practice, since loans usually hold higher amounts than deposits and it is the same relationship for their rates. Therefore, the only possibility of considering taxing financial services and the rest of goods and services at the same tax rate would be by explicitly considering the financial consumption, and so, directly including the financial services under the utility function. The next section will show whether there is a gain in economic efficiency by taxing real and financial goods and services at the same rate—seen by the impact of the tax rate divergence on national income and economic growth, in addition to several other variables, as savings.

4.2. Optimization of Savings by Tax Rate Convergence

If the proposed case of expression is considered, then the reduction on savings due to a raise on the tax rate would be lower than distinguishing between real and financial tax rates, with the traditional lower tax rate on financial services. Considering the expression for savings obtained from equation (Figure 2), we have that the impact of the tax rate on savings is:

$$\frac{\partial S}{\partial \tau} > \frac{\partial S}{\partial \tau_G} + \frac{\partial S}{\partial \tau_f} \leftrightarrow -(1 + \tau)(2 + i)2L > -(2 + i)gL(1 + \tau_G)$$

$$+(f + 1)L(1 + \tau_f - b) \leftrightarrow 0 > -(f + 1)b$$

where τ_G is the general VAT rate, τ_f the financial one and g and f are, respectively, the proportion of real goods and services and financial services over the total consumption, between 0 and 1, as well as the reduction in the financial VAT rate respect to the standard VAT rate is also between 0 and 1 and is b. Expression is always fulfilled since all the parameters have positive values.

Therefore, the previous expression shows that a way for optimizing savings is applying the model proposed inn this paper by including financial services into the utility function and taxing non-financial—real—goods and services and financial services with a same general VAT rate. This allows a lower reduction on savings rather than keeping lower VAT rates on financial services.

5. DESCRIPTIVE EVIDENCE

This section is going to analyze the behavior of the difference in absolute value between the Value Added Tax (VAT) rates from the 36 OECD countries[2] and the financial VAT rate of the countries where the exemption of financial services under VAT has already been eliminated. The descriptive statistics and sources will be provided in the next section. Figure 1 shows the temporal evolution of that variable, *devsfrates*, from 1960 to 2019, country by country. Above from each graph it appears the country code from the World Bank. It can be observed a raising or steady behavior of the deviation, with the exceptions of Denmark, with a sharp decline at the beginning of the period, and France, with a steady decrease in the full period. Figure 2 represents the distribution functions by density of the same variable for each country. Figure 3 shows the outliers per country.

It can be observed the nonpresence of outliers in most countries, whereas Denmark, Estonia, France, United Kingdom, Hungary, Ireland, Israel, Korea, Mexico, the Netherlands, Sweden, and Turkey only present a few outliers, later than 1978. Finally, Figure 4 shows the analysis of outliers for the full sample (left, above), with 1983 and 1984 as the main outliers, and the temporal disposition of the outliers by World Bank's code also for the full sample, showing a high value of the deviation around 1980 in Ireland (right, above).

Figure 1. Temporal evolution of devsfrates country by country

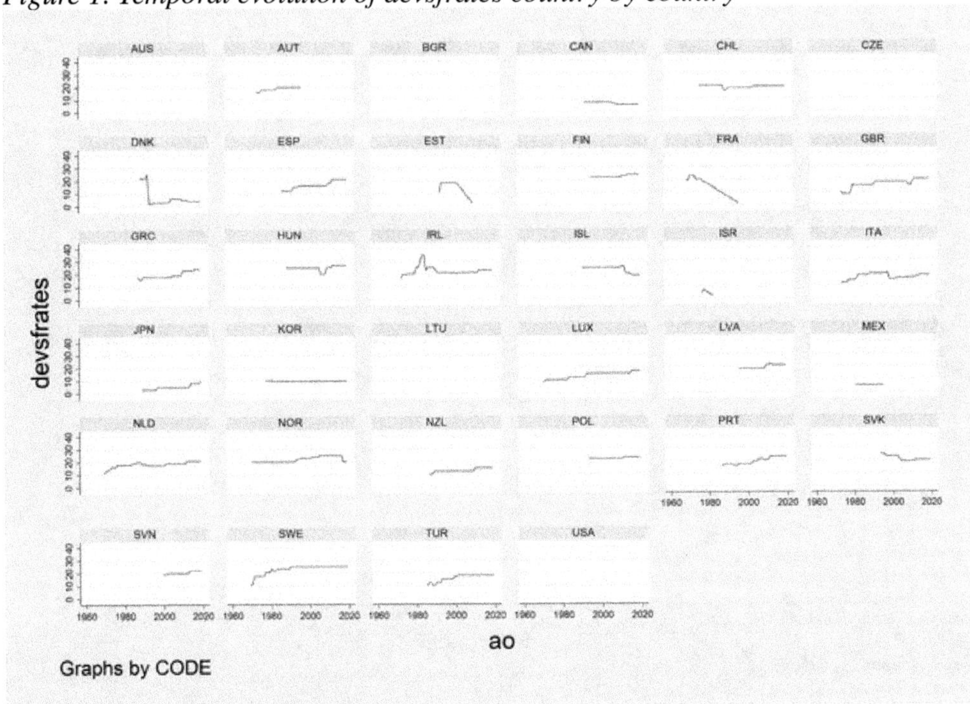

Figure 2. Density of devsfrates for each country

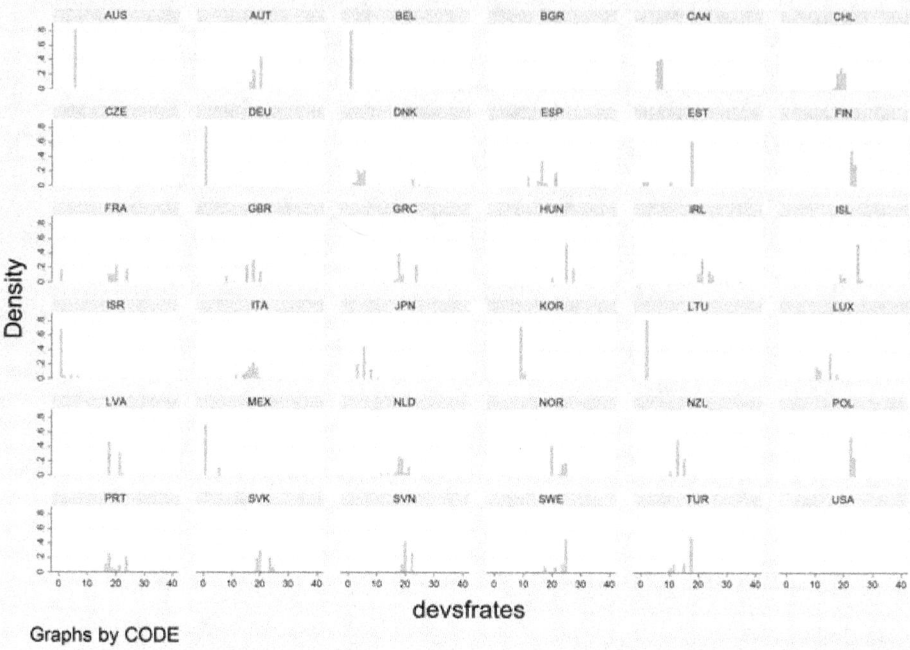

Figure 3. Analysis of outliers for devsfrates per country

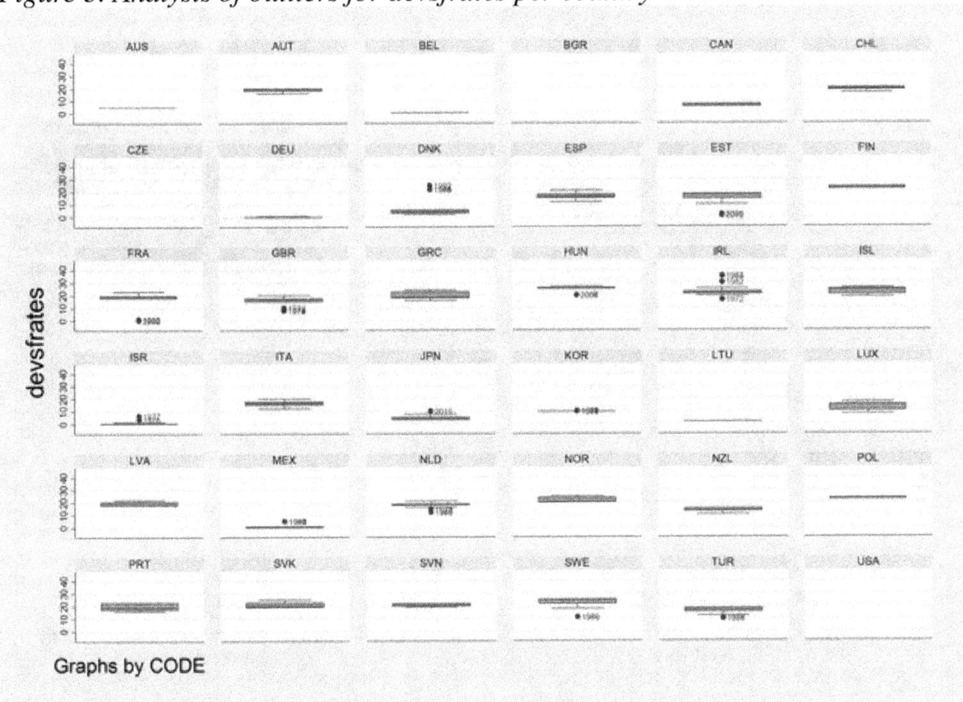

Figure 4. Analysis of outliers (above) and density function (below) for the full sample

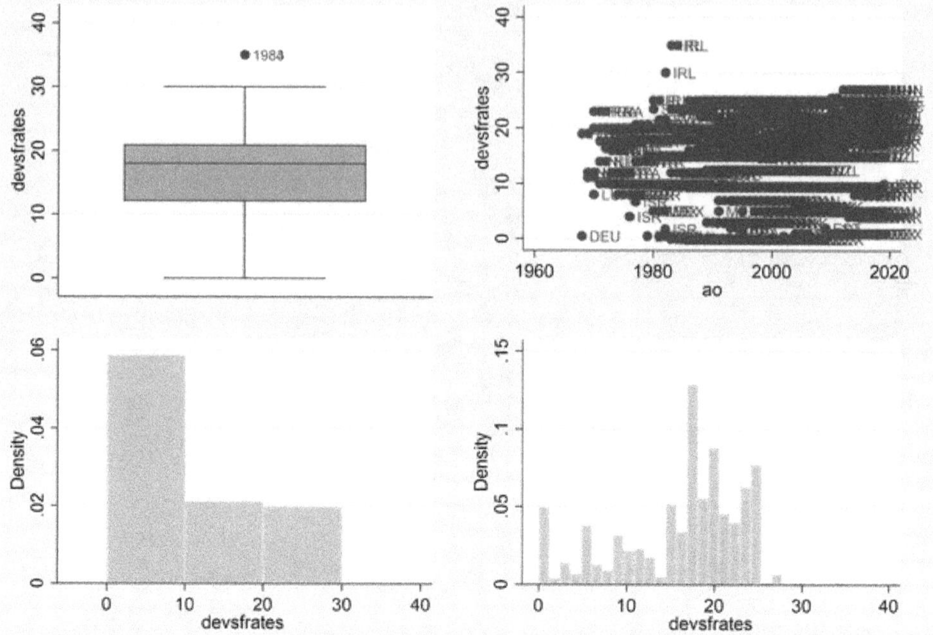

The two graphs below show the density function of the *devsfrates* variable both for all the data with a bandwidth of 10 (left, below), and for the cases when there is a positive value for *devsfrates* with a bandwidth of 0 (right, below). It can be observed that the higher density is around a deviation of 20 percent points. In the second outliers' analysis for the full sample, it is seen that the vast majority of values of the variable are below the 30 percent value, as it can also be observed in the density function for positive values of the variable. Map 1 shows the geographical representation of *devsfrates* variable in 2019.

Figure 5. Geographical representation of the devsfrates in 2019

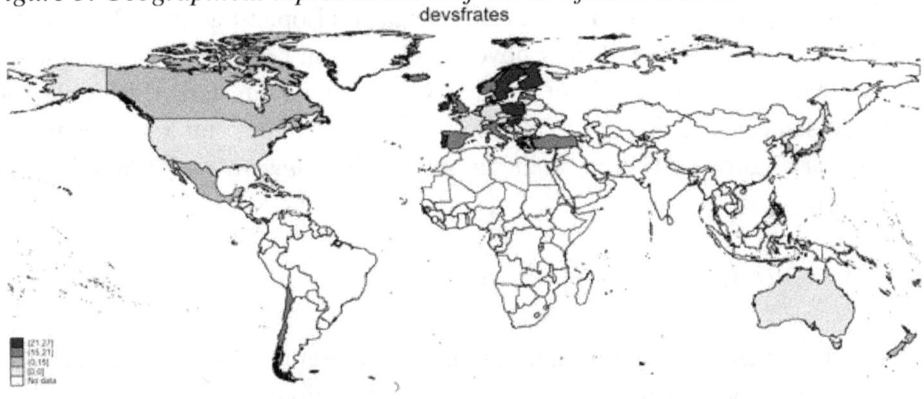

The previous Map 1 reflects a higher tax rate deviation on the East, and the West, of Europe, with less deviation in the center of the continent. These features could explain why some countries have this difference and not others, as we will see in the empirical section when the determinants of *devsfrates* will be found.

6. DATA SAMPLE AND EMPIRICAL STRATEGY AND EVIDENCE

An unbalanced panel dataset is handled, using a full sample of 33 countries for the period 1960-2019, as Table 1 shows. Furthermore, as the novel Granger Causality technique with panel data used in this paper only allows for balanced datasets, the table also includes the two reduced—but balanced—samples for the two variables where a consistent and significant Granger Causality is obtained. The null hypothesis is that one variable does not Granger-cause (GC) another.

Table 1. Data samples

Full database: unbalanced panel data of 33 countries for annual data of the 1960-2019 period		
Australia-Hungary-Netherlands-Austria-Ireland-New Zealand-Belgium-Iceland-Norway-Canada-Israel-Poland-Chile-Italy-Portugal-Denmark-Japan-Slovak Republic-Estonia-Korea, Rep.-Slovenia-Finland-Luxembourg-Spain-France-Latvia-Sweden-Germany-Mexico-Turkiye-Greece-Lithuania-United Kingdom		
Balanced Sub-samples for GC:	2006-2019 for *savsgdp, gdpgr* and *gdppcgr*, same country-level sample	1995-2018 for *invest*, same country-level sample but without Lithuania

The selected countries are those with non-empty data in the two main databases joined in this paper —the OECD (2022) and Peña and López-Laborda (2022) databases. The reason is the use of their novel databases on, respectively, the standard VAT and financial services indirect tax rates for designing our 'target' variable, the Euclidian distance—the difference in absolute values—of both tax rates according to expression (Figure 1). Therefore, the target variable, *devsfrates*, follows the next specification:

$$devsfrates := d(\tau, \tau_{fs}) = |\tau - \tau_{fs}|$$

Where the general VAT rate is τ and τ_{ft} is the VAT rate applied to financial services. The methodology is the usual univariate OLS specification for panel data—pool—, or, alternatively, the fixed or random effects methodology:

$$y_{it} = \beta \bullet devsfrates_{it} + \alpha + u_{it}$$

The dependent variables are efficiency, sufficiency, financial development and equity variables, to check the main economic principles of the Public Finance. The β is the coefficient of the target variable, α is the constant and the perturbation for country i and time t is μ_{it}. The following Table 2 shows all the variables used in the empirical section with their main descriptive statistics and the expected sign.

The efficient variables include the Gross Domestic Product (GDP) growth in levels and per capita, respectively, *gdp* and *gdppc*, both in current amounts in dollars, the *inflation* variable as the growth rate of the Consumer Price Index (CPI), the investment per capita is represented by the *invest* variable, and the savings over GDP by the *savsgdp* variable. The expected effect of the deviation of expression (16), collected in the variable *devsfrates* of expression (Figure 2), is negative, since a distortion in the economy produced by these differences is expected. Other authors as Baydur & Yilmaz (2021) consider that passing financial services from exempt to levied by VAT only reports welfare gains with low VAT rates. The variables of sufficiency reflect the effect on the suitability for the public administration of paying the public services with its available revenues. The remarkable variables used in the estimations are the *pexp* variable, which measures the share of public spending over total GDP and the *taxpress* variable, as the percentage of tax revenues over total GDP. We expect a lower sufficiency when general and financial services rates are different, due to the lack of tax collection.

Table 2. Descriptive statistics of the selected variables

Variable	Source	Observations	Mean	Standard Deviation	Minimum	Maximum
gdpgr	World Bank Indicators	1,596	3.421061	3.375954	-14.8386	25.1762
gdppcgr		1,597	2.671734	3.282805	-14.4643	23.9991
inflation		1,786	12.32687	55.82339	-4.478103	1281.443
bankconc		1,498	62.22645	52.06565	5.275254	484.9275
dcreditgdp		920	79.29796	46.96523	0.1861699	304.5751
pcreditgdp		1,602	66.33437	42.08526	5.629829	304.5745
pexp		1,269	33.53557	9.874457	10.0885	78.86197
invest		1,583	4684.999	4464.017	11.91169	34470.06
taxpress		1,261	20.49002	5.410517	7.091172	37.61462
gini		554	32.67653	6.016402	22.2	57.2
intrate		441	9.187801	7.608269	0.5	59.43167
vafins	OECD Database	1,012	5.395333	3.59912	1.505103	29.64303
savsgdp	World Bank Indicators	1,144	23.11576	5.675137	1.55834	42.22535
	Peña and López-Laborda (2022)	1,936	3.139096	6.861446	0	25
	OECD (2022)	1,980	11.11226	9.491514	0	35
devsfrates	Own elaboration	1,936	8.388342	9.584459	0	35

The financial development variables show whether the target variable is neutral, prejudicial or beneficial for the size and development of the financial sector. The selected variables are the *dcreditgdp* and *pcreditgdp* variables, which are measured as, respectively, the percentage of domestic/private credit over GDP, or the *vafins* variable, representing the share of value added of the financial sector. A positive effect of the target variable on financial development is expected since the rate differentiation may sort the financial sector more attractive for investing, and then, there will be a higher development. The lending interest rate is included in the *intrate* variable.

Finally, the last principle to take into account is the equity principle, where the Gini Index collected in the *gini* variable provides a faithful measure of income inequality. As high-income people are the most often users of the financial services (Huizinga, 2002), then, a positive effect on inequality is expected since these services are being encouraged due to their lower VAT rate. Thus, a main policy derived from this paper—the taxation of all financial and non-financial goods and services by a uniform tax rate—could serve as a benefit for financial inclusion. Therefore, the proposal could be useful as a guideline for developing countries as China, where, recently, a tax reform for settling up the VAT has been performed (Ahmad, 2018). This financial inclusion has additional positive effects on financial stability by reducing Non-Performing Loans (NPLs) and the probability of a bank default (Morgan and Pontines, 2018).

The empirical estimates are as follows. Table 3 includes the results for applying OLS, fixed effects (FE) and random effects (RE) to the main variables. After that, the variables with significant and robust effect are assessed according to the Granger Causality test. A reduced balanced panel is elaborated for each one of these variables. Table 4 collects the lower p-value of the null hypothesis that states *devsfrates* variable does not Granger-causes (GC) another variable, for the *invest* variable—Test A. Additional variables are empirically checked, as consumption—without robust results, dropping it from the results and from the descriptive statistics for this reason—or *savsgdp* variables, additionally showing the results for this last variable in Table 4—the OLS, FE and RE models in Models B and rejecting that *devsfrates* does not GC *savsgdp* in Test C.

A novel econometric approach for panel data is employed for checking whether the tax rate divergence (*devsfrate*) GC any of the previous dependent variables. Concretely, the method proposed by Juodis et al. (2021) and developed in Xiao et al. (2023), where they solve the well-known 'Neville bias'. As previously said, it is only useful for balanced panels, using the balanced panels of Table 1.

Table 3. Main panel data estimates

Method	OLS	RE	FE	OLS	RE	FE	OLS	RE	FE
Variable		*gdpgr*			*gdppcgr*			*inflation*	
devsfrate	-0.042***	-0.069***	-0.083***	-0.020*	-0.050**	-0.065**	-0.428***	-0.793*	-0.931*
	(0.009)	(0.02)	(0.023)	(0.008)	(0.019)	(0.021)	(0.116)	(0.352)	(0.419)
Constant	3.825***	4.158***	4.234***	2.854***	3.278***	3.301***	15.429***	19.912***	20.032***
	(0.121)	(0.305)	(0.229)	(0.117)	(0.282)	(0.211)	(2.156)	(6.031)	(3.837)
N	1588	1588	1588	1589	1589	1589	1774	1774	1774
R^2 adj.	0.0143	0.0029	0.0304	0.0036	0.016	0.0196	0.0069	0.0293	0.0209
Variable		*bankconc*			*dcreditgdp*			*pcreditgdp*	
devsfrate	0.525***	1.553**	1.589**	0.793***	2.879***	3.173***	1.050***	2.086***	2.154***
	(0.096)	(0.515)	(0.523)	(0.146)	(0.569)	(0.608)	(0.099)	(0.374)	(0.382)
Const	57.447***	46.806***	47.202***	70.831***	45.936***	45.436***	56.350***	45.457***	45.535***
	(1.351)	(5.069)	(5.041)	(2.175)	(9.053)	(6.493)	(1.379)	(6.467)	(3.736)

continued on following page

Table 3. Continued

Method	OLS	RE	FE	OLS	RE	FE	OLS	RE	FE
N	1489	1489	1489	920	920	920	1593	1593	1593
R^2 adj.	0.0097	0.02	0.1075	0.0286	0.0159	0.1947	0.0592	0.0275	0.1998
Variable		*pexp*			*invest*			*taxpress*	
devsfrate	0.276***	0.316*	0.316*	98.768***	159.212***	168.394***	0.127***	0.08	0.079
	(0.028)	(0.137)	(0.139)	(12.239)	(44.893)	(47.212)	(0.016)	(0.067)	(0.067)
Constant	30.289***	30.179***	29.817***	3698.318***	2891.646***	2986.786***	18.976***	19.154***	19.546***
	(0.496)	(2.29)	(1.629)	(137.864)	(589.853)	(482.479)	(0.293)	(1.241)	(0.801)
N	1260	1260	1260	1574	1574	1574	1252	1252	1252
R^2 adj.	0.0721	0.0825	0.107	0.0455	0.0036	0.0814	0.0507	0.0548	0.0348
Variable		*gini*			*intrate*			*vafins*	
devsfrate	-0.088**	0.014	0.02	0.066	-0.340*	-0.484*	0.033***	0.028	0.028
	(0.026)	(0.05)	(0.053)	(0.041)	(0.16)	(0.166)	(0.006)	(0.016)	(0.016)
Constant	33.850***	32.782***	32.405***	8.450***	12.704***	14.617***	4.989***	5.207***	5.065***
	(0.454)	(1.3)	(0.71)	(0.573)	(3.063)	(1.861)	(0.099)	(0.682)	(0.21)
N	554	554	554	441	441	441	1003	1003	1003
R^2 adj.	0.0199	0.0342	0.0012	0.0066	0.045	0.0833	0.0196	0.0065	0.0196

Note: ***, ** and * indicate statistical significance at 0.1%, 1% and 5% level, respectively. Standard errors in parenthesis.

The results of Table 3 show that the price anomalies derived from the tax rate divergence are significantly and robustly associated with lower economic growth and inflation (Das, 2017), and higher bank concentration, size of the financial sector, public expenditure and investment. Finally, Table 4 shows that the null of hypothesis that the divergence on VAT rate does not GC *savsgdp* is rejected with a significant level of 0.1% and additionally shows a negative, significant and robust association of the target and *savsgdp* variable.

Table 4. Granger causality tests and further panel data estimates

Test A	**H_0: *devsfrates* does not Granger-cause *invest***			
	Wald test	3.4602	p-value	0.0629
Model B	Variable	*savsgdp*		
	Method	**OLS**	**RE**	**FE**
	devsfrates	-0.079***	-0.156***	-0.159**
		(0.017)	(0.059)	(0.06)
	Constant	24.129***	24.803***	25.089***
		(0.202)	(0.869)	(0.719)
	N	1135	1135	1135
	R^2 adj.	0.0174	0.0405	0.0466
Test C	**H_0: *devsfrates* does not Granger-cause *savsgdp***			
	Wald test	7.3162	p-value	0.0068

Note: ***, ** and * indicate statistical significance at 0.1%, 1% and 5% level, respectively. Standard errors in parenthesis.

As Table 4 shows, the theoretical expectance of expression (16) of a tax rate divergence associated with lower savings over GDP is empirically confirmed in the Model B of the previous Table 4. Furthermore, it cannot be accepted the null hypothesis that the tax rate divergence does not GC the percentage of savings over GDP, showing that one variable statistically may lead the other.

7. ROBUSTNESS CHECK AND DETERMINANTS OF THE TAX RATE DEVIATION

This section provides a robustness check of the influence of the tax rate deviation on economic efficiency by applying Instrumental Variable (IV) models and analyzes the determinants of this deviation by considering different socio-economic variables and by applying pool, Fix Effects (FE) and System (SYS) and Differences (DIF) Generalized Method of Moments (GMM) methods. The empirical specification for the GMM models, following Arellano and Bond (1991), Arellano and Bover (1995) and Blundell and Bond (1998), is:

$$devsfrates_{it} = ydevsfrates_{it-1} + X_{it}\beta + u_{it}$$

Where γ is the coefficient of the lag of the dependent variable, X is the regression matrix of possible determinant variables and β is the vector of their coefficients. Table 5 collects the main descriptive statistics of the new selected variables. Table 6 shows the results.

The data sample is the full one of Tables 1 and 2, but additionally includng new variables collected in Table 5 from the World Bank database. They are the *gdp* variable as the Gross Domestic Product (GDP), and the rest are potential determinants of the deviation between financial and standard rates. This deviation mainly appears because the presence of the exemption of financial services under VAT is still in force. We include some variables regarding economic development, technological progress and institutional stability as potential influence on the deviation. Another reason for considering its determinants is to provide the best instrumental variable for *devsfrates*.

Table 5. Descriptive statistics of the new selected variables

Variable	*Obs*	*Mean*	*Std. dev.*	*Min*	*Max*
gdp	1,740	4.54E+11	8.53E+11	2.48E+08	6.20E+12
electricity	1,654	6267.461	5892.719	92.31101	54799.18
rdexp	735	1.71048	0.9974154	0.25067	5.13983
polstab	693	0.7123976	0.6649284	-2.009063	1.760102
mobiles	1,096	65.51238	52.84689	0.0007281	172.1218
ruleoflaw	693	1.24434	0.6295855	-0.726646	2.12967
secondary	1,414	96.82916	20.99548	21.7265	163.935
urbanity	1,980	72.00048	13.21282	27.71	98.041
bcrisis	1,584	0.0883838	0.283942	0	1

Table 6. Panel data estimates for the determinants of devsfrates

devsfrates	**(1)**	**(2)**	**(3)**	**(4)**	**(5)**	**(6)**
VARIABLES	Static Pool	Static FE	Dynamic Pool	Dynamic FE	SYS GMM	DIF GMM
Lag t-1 devsfrates			1.001***	1.001***	0.999***	0.810**
			(0.00413)	(0.00342)	(0.0289)	(0.343)

continued on following page

Table 6. Continued

devsfrates	(1)	(2)	(3)	(4)	(5)	(6)
electricity	0.000472***	-8.34e-05***	2.85e-06	2.85e-06	2.12e-05	-2.54e-05
	(7.05e-05)	(2.17e-05)	(6.01e-06)	(4.48e-06)	(1.97e-05)	(4.79e-05)
rdexp	-3.293***	0.0941	-0.0440	-0.0440	-0.231	0.0342
	(0.488)	(0.579)	(0.0414)	(0.0445)	(0.176)	(0.335)
polstab	1.194	1.043	-0.253**	-0.253**	-0.530***	-0.456*
	(0.854)	(0.689)	(0.115)	(0.101)	(0.187)	(0.267)
mobiles	0.0211*	-0.00340	0.00276**	0.00276***	0.00467	0.00547
	(0.0118)	(0.00985)	(0.00108)	(0.000925)	(0.00372)	(0.00570)
ruleoflaw	0.817	-5.137**	0.226*	0.226**	0.821**	-0.233
	(1.156)	(2.469)	(0.118)	(0.101)	(0.324)	(0.797)
secondary	-0.0176	0.0493	0.00797**	0.00797***	0.00405	0.00395
	(0.0353)	(0.0320)	(0.00349)	(0.00296)	(0.00576)	(0.00941)
urbanity	-0.163***	0.315**	-0.00890*	-0.00890**	-0.0197*	-0.0626
	(0.0493)	(0.157)	(0.00502)	(0.00421)	(0.0116)	(0.151)
bcrisis	2.000*	0.657**	0.241	0.241	0.182	0.147
	(1.022)	(0.273)	(0.155)	(0.156)	(0.116)	(0.174)
constant	24.80***	-9.800	-0.531*	-0.531*		
	(3.880)	(10.44)	(0.281)	(0.313)		
Observations	444	444	443	443	443	331
R-squared	0.244		0.986			
Number of i		33		33	33	30
Sargan p-value					0.885	0.451
A-B (2nd order p-value)					0.587	0.666

Robust standard errors in parentheses, *** indicates p-value (p)<0.01, ** p<0.05, * p<0.1

Among the potential factors of influence, we have included *electricity* as the electric power consumption (kWh per capita), *rdexp* represents the expenditure in research and development as an indicator of economic development as percentage of GDP, *polstab* reflects the political stability and absence of violence/terrorism with 0 as the lowest rank and 100 the maximum, *mobiles* reflect the number of mobile cellular s subscriptions per 100 inhabitants as an indicator of technological development that allows solving the technical difficulties in adapting an indirect tax on financial services, *ruleoflaw* as the rule of law that "captures perceptions of the extent to which agents have confidence in and abide by the rules of society, and in particular the quality of contract enforcement, property rights, the police, and the courts, as well as the likelihood of crime and violence", it ranges from -2.5 to 2.5. Other variables are the gross enrollment on secondary school, addressed by the *secondary* variable, the percentage of urban population over the total by *urbanity* and the presence of a systemic banking crisis by *bcrisis*.

All the determinants are jointly included in the models (1-6) of Table 6, showing, respectively, static pool and FE models, dynamic pool and FE models and System and Differences GMM models. It can be noted that for SYS GMM model 5, which intrinsically considers exogenous instruments, the best determinant for the presence of a deviation on financial and standard rates is the low political stability. Therefore, this variable will be used as instrument for looking for a robustness check of the influence of the *devsfrates* variable on economic efficiency measured by the *gdp* variable.

Finally, Table 7 shows the robustness check where, using *polstab* as instrumental variable, it is shown the pernicious influence of tax rate heterogeneity on economic efficiency (model 2). Additionally, it has been observed that the endogeneity test of considering devsfrates as exogenous for the dependent variables is not rejected for *gdp*, *gdpgr* and *gdppcgr* (the two last ones shown in the previous Table 3) with a p-value of, respectively, 0.694, 0.244 and 0.9449, so IV models were not necessary for those variables.

Table 7. Instrumental Variables (IV) estimates for the economic efficiency of devsfrates

Model	**(1)**	**(2)**
Methodology	OLS	IV OLS
VARIABLES	*gdp*	
devsfrates	-5.306e+09***	-4.379e+10***
	(1.620e+09)	(1.578e+10)
Constant	5.040e+11***	1.371e+12***
	(3.061e+10)	(2.083e+11)
Observations	1,731	688
R-squared	0.004	0.098
Endogeneity test (p-value)	0.694	

Therefore, this confirms the lack of economic efficiency of the current divergence between tax rates on financial and real goods and services. As policy implication, a homogeneous treatment of all goods and services by applying the standard VAT rate would improve national income, economic growth, and so, economic efficiency. Therefore, there is a need of directly including financial services in the utility function for achieving the theoretical efficiency according to expression (12) and to Section 3.3, but also empirically as this section illustrates.

8. DISCUSSION OF THE RESULTS

The full VAT taxation of all real (non-financial) goods and financial services, including both implicit and explicit fees, is not distortionary, or at least, it is less distortionary than the exemption of these services on the tax. This taxation is equivalent to a lump-sum tax. This fact is observed after directly incorporating the consumption of financial services in the utility function—as other authors have considered with money or with financial assets—as a result of consumer satisfaction with the provision of financial services, as studied in the empirical literature.

The taxation of financial services and all other kinds of consumption under VAT has turned out to be neutral to households' intertemporal choice, compared to a lump-sum tax. Another issue is to consider whether the taxation of financial services could discourage working hours. Boadway and Gahvari (2006) show that when the time spent consuming is considered and this time is a substitute for leisure, then the classical optimal tax system remains intact, thus avoiding this optimal commodity taxation problem, but when consumption is a substitute of labor (as financial services) it affects the optimal tax structure of a Ramsey tax framework, needing to be taxed with a lower tax rate. According to Sepulveda (2021, p. 2): "Boadway and Gahvari (2006) allow for home labor to be either a leisure-substitute, in which case consumption time has no opportunity cost because it is enjoyable (like leisure), or a labor-substitute, in which case consumption time is not enjoyable and thus faces the opportunity cost of not working". There are two possible roles of financial services in the leisure-labor allocation.

First, the consumption of financial services could be considered a time substitute for working hours, because when consumers are informed about the financial services that the banking sector provides and employ time in buying the financial service, households avoid working since, instead of working, they substitute this time to acquire information about this kind of services or to displace to the banking branch. Second, the strict obtainment of capital income from financial services (after the contract) could be considered neutral between labor and leisure, given that when people buy a financial service, the mere loss of time generates value added for the household, since this product is consumed at the same time as the household is working or enjoying free time. This is the same case for other kinds of services providing some kind of security, for example public goods such as national defense, which are consumed at any time. Therefore, the taxation of financial services, not only the consumption, but also taxing the mere pass of time (the pure interest) would mitigate the labor-discouraging effect of taxing some real—non-financial—goods and services, thus attaining a higher tax optimal situation than with the full or partial exemption of financial services under VAT. Nonetheless, the research about this issue could be an extension of this paper for future research.

Finally, the divergence on the last previous result necessarily implies robust and statistically significant negative effects on efficiency and equity, and not robust for sufficiency and financial development, after applying OLS panel data models to a sample of 36 EU and OECD countries for the 1960-2019 period.

This paper sheds further light on the descriptive and analytical debate of the optimality of the indirect taxation of financial services. The paper discusses whether financial services directly yield the consumer utility—e.g. by reducing search costs (Shen et al., 2021). It necessarily implies the convergence in the VAT rates among all goods and services in order to achieve efficiency. In addition to other factors for lower savings rate —e.g. financial illiteracy or lack of self-control (Gathergood, 2012)—, this paper provides conceptual evidence for rethinking the not direct inclusion of financial services in the utility function and, subsequently, exempting these services under VAT. Not applying the same tax rate to financial services as other goods and services can be considered a determinant on shifting the households' decisions on savings.

9. CONCLUSIONS

The contributions of the paper are several. First, this paper sheds further light on the descriptive and analytical debate of the optimality of the indirect taxation of financial services. The paper discusses whether financial services directly yield the consumer utility—e.g. by reducing search costs (Shen et al., 2021). It necessarily implies the convergence in the VAT rates among all the goods and services in order to achieve efficiency. Second, a new proposal of variable shows a tax anomaly in prices of financial services respect to other goods and services closely attributed the non-direct inclusion of these services in the utility function. The variable addresses this issue by calculating the Euclidean distance between the standard VAT rate and the indirect tax rate on financial services, providing a new dataset for this new variable for 33 countries from 1960 to 2019. Finally, there is a novel empirical checking of the implications of the tax rate divergence, applying recent panel data methodologies of Granger-causality for balanced datasets. In addition to other factors for lower savings rate—e.g. financial illiteracy or lack of self-control (Gathergood,

2012)—, this paper provides empirical evidence of not directly including financial services under VAT as a determinant on decisions on savings.

After explicitly seen that the theoretical expectations and previous empirical evidence support directly including financial services in the utility function, this paper contributes by empirically checking a direct consequence of this fact. It is the distortion in intertemporal households' decisions of differentiating the VAT rates of financial services and the rest of goods and services, and so, its correspondent anomaly in prices. As obtained in this paper, the divergence on VAT rates is associated with lower savings over GDP. Furthermore, it is observed that the tax rate divergence associated to the previous anomaly in prices Granger-causes (GC) the decrease on savings. Hence, as different treatment of financial services respect to other goods under VAT GC changes in the household behavior regarding the decision on substitution of savings, these services may be levied under VAT and treated in the utility function in the same way as any other good.

The previous Granger Causality and estimates obtained mean that the recommendable policy is taxing the financial margin and explicit fees and commissions of financial services under the standard VAT rate (Peña, 2019), as well as directly considering them in the utility function in financial models—which is closely associated to that. The proposed model of applying the same VAT rate to financial services as well as to the rest of non-financial—here denominated "real"—goods and services can be considered an encouragement or contributor for optimizing savings by tax rate convergence.

REFERENCES

Allen, D. W., Berg, C., & Novak, M. (2018). Blockchain: An entangled political economy approach. *Journal of Public Finance and Public Choice*, 33(2), 105–125. DOI: 10.1332/251569118X15282111163993

Altenburger, O. A. (2022). Applying VAT to financial services: Is the new mobile-ratio method adequate for insurance?. *Zeitschrift für die gesamte Versicherungswissenschaft*, 111(3), 353-360.

Arellano, M., & Bond, S. (1991). Some tests of specification for panel data: Monte Carlo evidence and an application to employment equations. *The Review of Economic Studies*, 58(2), 277–297. DOI: 10.2307/2297968

Arellano, M., & Bover, O. (1995). Another look at the instrumental variable estimation of error-components models. *Journal of Econometrics*, 68(1), 29–51. DOI: 10.1016/0304-4076(94)01642-D

Auerbach, A. J., & Gordon, R. H. (2002). Taxation of Financial Services under a VAT. *The American Economic Review*, 92(2), 411–416. DOI: 10.1257/000282802320191714

Baydur, I., & Yilmaz, F. (2021). VAT Treatment of the Financial Services: Implications for the Real Economy. *Journal of Money, Credit and Banking*, 53(8), 2167–2200. DOI: 10.1111/jmcb.12780

Blundell, R., & Bond, S. (1998). Initial conditions and moment restrictions in dynamic panel data models. *Journal of Econometrics*, 87(1), 115–143. DOI: 10.1016/S0304-4076(98)00009-8

Boadway, R., & Gahvari, F. (2006). Optimal taxation with consumption time as a leisure or labor substitute. *Journal of Public Economics*, 90(10-11), 1851–1878. DOI: 10.1016/j.jpubeco.2006.05.002

Boadway, R., & Keen, M. (2003). Theoretical perspectives on the taxation of capital income and financial services: a survey. In Honohan, P. (Ed.), *Taxation of Financial Intermediation: Theory and Practice for Emerging Economies* (Vol. 27). World Bank and Oxford University Press.

Christiansen, V. (2017). Indirect Taxation of Financial Services, Working paper. CESifo area conferences on Public Sector Economics. Munich, April 27-29 2017.

Christiansen, V., & Smith, S. (2021). *Economic Principles of Commodity Taxation (Elements in Public Economics)*. Cambridge University Press., DOI: 10.1017/9781009004497

Croushore, D. (1993). Money in the utility function: Functional equivalence to a shopping-time model. *Journal of Macroeconomics*, 15(1), 175–182. DOI: 10.1016/0164-0704(93)90060-Y

Das, S. (2017). Some concerns regarding the goods and services tax. *Economic and Political Weekly*, 52(9), 107–124.

EC (European Commission) (2020). Revue of the VAT Rules for Financial and Insurance Services. Combined Evaluation Roadmap/Inception Impact Assessment, Ares (2020)5770956.

European Commission. (2022). https://taxation-customs.ec.europa.eu/taxation-1/value-added-tax-vat_en

Gathergood, J. (2012). Self-control, financial literacy and consumer over-indebtedness. *Journal of Economic Psychology*, 33(3), 590–602. DOI: 10.1016/j.joep.2011.11.006

IMF (2010). A fair and substantial contribution by the financial sector. *Financial Sector Taxation: The IMF's Report to the G-20 and Background Material.*

Jack, W. (2000). The treatment of financial services under a broad-based consumption tax. *National Tax Journal*, 53(4), 841–851. DOI: 10.17310/ntj.2000.4.03

Juodis, A., Karavias, Y., & Sarafidis, V. (2021). A homogeneous approach to testing for Granger noncausality in heterogeneous panels. *Empirical Economics*, 60(1), 93–112. DOI: 10.1007/s00181-020-01970-9

Krishnan, M. S., Ramaswamy, V., Meyer, M. C., & Damien, P. (1999). Customer satisfaction for financial services: The role of products, services, and information technology. *Management Science*, 45(9), 1194–1209. DOI: 10.1287/mnsc.45.9.1194

Lagos, R., Rocheteau, G., & Wright, R. (2017). Liquidity: A new monetarist perspective. *Journal of Economic Literature*, 55(2), 371–440. DOI: 10.1257/jel.20141195

Lockwood, B., & Yerushalmi, E. (2019). How should payment services be taxed? *Social Choice and Welfare*, 53(1), 21–47. DOI: 10.1007/s00355-019-01178-6

Lompo, M. L., & Ouoba, M. M. (2024). Taxes and social instability: How large corporations and wealthy taxpayers hide taxable money? *Economic Analysis Letters*, 3(1), 36–45. DOI: 10.58567/eal03010005

López-Laborda, J., & Peña, G. (2018). A new method for applying VAT to financial services. *National Tax Journal*, 71(1), 155–182. DOI: 10.17310/ntj.2018.1.05

López-Laborda, J., & Peña, G. (2022). Financial VAT may improve trade openness. *Applied Economics*, 54(19), 2148–2160. DOI: 10.1080/00036846.2021.1985072

Maddern, H., Maull, R., Smart, A., & Baker, P. (2007). Customer satisfaction and service quality in UK financial services. *International Journal of Operations & Production Management*, 27(9), 999–1019. DOI: 10.1108/01443570710775838

Montfort, K. V., Masurel, E., & Rijn, I. V. (2000). Service satisfaction: An empirical analysis of consumer satisfaction in financial services. *Service Industries Journal*, 20(3), 80–94. DOI: 10.1080/02642060000000033

OECD. (2022). https://www.oecd.org/tax/consumption/vat-gst-rates-historical-tax-database.xlsx

Peña, G. (2019). Efficient treatment of banking services under VAT. *Economics and Business Letters*, 8(2), 115–121. DOI: 10.17811/ebl.8.2.2019.115-121

Peña, G. (2020). A new trading algorithm with financial applications. *Quantitative Finance and Economics*, 4(4), 596–607. DOI: 10.3934/QFE.2020027

Peña, G. (2022). Optimal VAT on Financial Services: A Theoretical Model of Financial VAT. In Handbook of Research on Challenges in Public Economics in the Era of Globalization (pp. 279-318). IGI Global.

Peña, G., & López-Laborda, J. (2022). Financial VAT may improve trade openness, Harvard-Dataverse, DOI: 10.7910/DVN/WEW6EU

Poddar, S., & English, M. (1997). Taxation of Financial Services under a Value-Added Tax: Applying the Cash-Flow Approach. *National Tax Journal*, 50(1), 89–111. DOI: 10.1086/NTJ41789244

Poledna, S., & Thurner, S. (2016). Elimination of systemic risk in financial networks by means of a systemic risk transaction tax. *Quantitative Finance*, 16(10), 1599–1613. DOI: 10.1080/14697688.2016.1156146

Poterba, J. M., & Rotemberg, J. J. (1986). Money in the utility function: An empirical implementation, *NBER Working Papers*.

Şen, H., & Kaya, A. (2023). Do revenue-neutral tax swaps boost growth? *Journal of Economic Policy Reform*, •••, 1–20.

Sepulveda, C. F. (2021). Time-saving goods, time inequalities and optimal commodity taxation. *International Tax and Public Finance*, •••, 1–26.

Shen, J., Wei, B., & Yan, H. (2021). Financial intermediation chains in an over-the-counter market. *Management Science*, 67(7), 4623–4642. DOI: 10.1287/mnsc.2020.3687

Sherraden, M. (1990). Stakeholding: Notes on a theory of welfare based on assets. *The Social Service Review*, 64(4), 580–601. DOI: 10.1086/603797

Sivesan, S. (2019). Impact of Service Quality on Customer Satisfaction in Life Insurance Companies in Sri Lanka. *Global Journal of Management and Business Research: E-Marketing*, 19(5), 50–55.

Tobin, J. (1980). Discussion. In Kareken, J. H., & Wallace, N. (Eds.), *Models of Monetary Economies*. Federal Reserve Bank of Minneapolis.

Xiao, J., Karavias, Y., Juodis, A., Sarafidis, V., & Ditzen, J. (2023). Improved tests for Granger noncausality in panel data. *The Stata Journal*, 23(1), 230–242. DOI: 10.1177/1536867X231162034

KEY TERMS AND DEFINITIONS

Financial Value Added Tax (VAT): Application of VAT to financial services.

Generalized Method of Moments (GMM): In econometrics and statistics, the generalized method of moments (GMM) is a generic method for estimating parameters in statistical models.

Optimal taxation: Concerns the question of how several forms of taxation should be designed in order to maximize a standard social welfare function subject to a revenue constraint.

Organization for Economic Cooperation and Development (OECD): Forum and knowledge hub for data, analysis and best practices in public policy. We work with over 100 countries across the world to build stronger, fairer and cleaner societies - helping to shape better policies for better lives.

Value Added Tax (VAT): Tax levied on sales or supplies of services. VAT is paid by consumers when paying for goods or services supplied. The seller or service provider receives the VAT and then pays it to the Tax and Customs Authority (AT).

Value Added Tax (VAT) Exemption: VAT exemption can refer to either goods and services that are not subject to VAT or to organizations that cannot register for VAT. When the VAT rate is zero for that product there is no recoverable input VAT.

Value Added Tax (VAT) Rate: Each EU country has a standard rate which applies to the supply of most goods and services. This cannot be less than 15%.

ENDNOTES

1 The formula is directly obtained by them from a proposed system of equations, given by:

$$\rho\rho_B = \rho_B - i; \rho\rho_S = i - \rho_S \rightarrow i = \frac{2\rho_B\rho_S}{\rho_B + \rho_S}; \rho = \left(\rho_B - \rho_S\right)/\left(\rho_B + \rho_S\right).$$

where each one of the two first expressions represents the value added of the financial services, the right size is the financial margin or implicit fee according to Poddar and English (1997) and the left hand reflects the proportion of value added over lending and deposit interest rates, respectively, adapting the meaning and notation for this paper. So, p represents the unitary value added—called as “mobile ratio” by them.

2 In some of the graphs, only a representation of these countries appears.

Chapter 2
Assessing Tax Policies for Urban Rehabilitation:
The Role of Tax Incentives on Sustainability

André Carvalho
https://orcid.org/0000-0002-7896-0947
Research Centre on Accounting and Taxation, Polytechnic University of Cávado and Ave, Portugal

Ana Dinis
https://orcid.org/0000-0003-3945-5726
Research Centre on Accounting and Taxation, Polytechnic University of Cávado and Ave, Portugal

Liliana Pereira
https://orcid.org/0000-0002-0211-6205
Research Centre on Accounting and Taxation, Polytechnic University of Cávado and Ave, Portugal

ABSTRACT

The urgent need to transform buildings into sustainable energy-efficient spaces is driven by the environmental impact of construction activities. This study examine the impact of tax incentives on urban rehabilitation among Portuguese companies using data from the Portuguese Tax Authority Portal (2015-2022) and the Sabi Database. Employing SPSS for descriptive analysis and Pearson correlation, the authors examine the tax incentives and urban rehabilitation indicators, including Municipal Property Tax, Municipal Property Transfer Tax, energy consumption, greenhouse gas emissions, and municipal environmental expenditures. The findings reveal significant positive correlations between tax incentives, higher reconstruction

DOI: 10.4018/979-8-3693-3908-4.ch002

rates, and increased municipal environmental expenditures. However, these incentives also correlate with higher energy consumption and GHG emissions, highlighting the need for stricter environmental criteria in tax policies. This study offers valuable insights for policymakers on enhancing sustainable urban development through effective tax incentives.

INTRODUCTION

Urban regeneration has been identified as an essential component of sustainable development practices, particularly in the context of greenhouse gas (GHG) reduction and energy efficiency innovation (Liu et al., 2023; McGreal et al., 2002). The construction sector, which is one of the biggest contributors to uncontrolled GHG emissions and energy consumption, has also been identified as an area for implementing tax policies aimed at promoting sustainability (Zhang et al., 2023). In this context, environmental sustainability should act as the basis for legislative policy action (Glass & Newig, 2019). Sustainable development strategies should focus on energy consumption and the emission of environmentally harmful gases to achieve climate neutrality, seen as a pillar policy of the European Union's sustainable agenda (Kluza et al., 2024).

From the perspective of national governments, there is a need to align public policies to achieve carbon neutrality mutually. Conversely, it is within this context that environmental taxes become more interesting, reducing taxation in the energy, transport, and pollution sectors (Dinis et al., 2023; Sackitey, 2023). When these tax policies are effectively implemented, can significantly improve the environmental effects of each country (Chung & Yoon, 2023).

Nowadays, every government advocates linking environmental policy with tax law policy as a strategic component that could transform the tax system (Dinis et al., 2023). It is an important objective to guide the economy towards better use of existing resources, reduce energy consumption to foster business and social innovation, reduce the ecological footprint and emissions of harmful gases into the environment, and promote long-term sustainability (Akdag & Yildirim, 2020; Delgado et al., 2022; Han & Lee, 2023).

In the Portuguese case, tax incentives have been strategically implemented to promote urban regeneration in Portuguese cities, with the main goal of aligning economic growth with existing sustainable development objectives (Dinis, 2024; Picas et al., 2021).

This chapter aims to contribute to the existing tax literature by showing the main previous studies on environmental taxation in the business sector and evaluating environmental tax policies as effective measures. The main objectives of this chapter are: (i) To emphasize the relevance of green taxation for environmental sustainability; (ii) To assess the Portuguese tax incentive policies that promote urban regeneration in Portugal; (iii) To discuss and provide, based on the Portuguese experience, recommendations for strengthening the international results of tax incentives for urban regeneration.

This study reveals that there is an urgent need to integrate environmental criteria to mitigate the prominent levels of energy consumption and greenhouse gas emissions. By clarifying the role of tax incentives in promoting urban regeneration in Portuguese cities, this study contributes to a wider discussion on the need for efficient sustainable urban development. It provides necessary observations for political decision-makers on the effectiveness of public tax spending policies and presents some recommendations in this direction.

The structure of this chapter is as follows. First, section one examines the main concepts of energy consumption and greenhouse gas emissions in the international context and presents a general discussion of the problem in countries' urban regeneration agendas. The second section presents the contribution of environmental taxation and its important role in promoting sustainable urban development. Then, the third section analyses the policy of tax incentives for urban regeneration as a measure to fight climate change. The main results obtained are presented, analyzed and discussed in section four. Finally, section five presents the future research directions, and the main conclusions of the study are presented.

BACKGROUND

The notable economic strides witnessed in emerging economies are undeniably linked to significant energy consumption, consequently increasing the threat of environmental harm (Heide et al., 2023). This underlines the critical need for a firm commitment to environmental sustainability in the current government agenda. Strategic initiatives for sustainable development especially those directed at decreasing energy emissions and GHG levels to achieve climate neutrality, are recognized as fundamental policies within the European Union (EU) climate Framework (Yassaghi & Hoque, 2019).

Cities, responsible for 60% to 80% of global energy consumption and 70% of human-induced GHG emissions, play a significant role in this scenario (IPCC, 2023). The construction sector, contributing 40% of total energy consumption and approximately 36% of global GHG emissions, emerges as a major contributor to carbon emissions (Zhang et al., 2023).

The critical need to convert buildings into sustainable energy-efficient spaces is underscored by the imperative to mitigate the environmental impact of construction activities (Hafez et al., 2023).

This urgency is further intensified by the ongoing energy crisis and the European Green Deal`s strategic emphasis on long-term energy efficiency in buildings (Run et al., 2023; Economidou et al., 2020). Existing buildings are significant contributors to energy consumption and GHG emissions in developed economies (Cai et al., 2023; Dadzie et al., 2018). This global recognition underscores the substantial concern, emphasizing the necessity for sustainable practices in both the construction and operation of buildings (Silva et al., 2024).

This has led to an essential shift towards sustainability in building practices, highlighting the critical need for proactive measures in the building sector to address climate-related challenges (Heide et al., 2023). Acknowledging the environmental implications of construction activities, urban rehabilitation is advocated as a pivotal paradigm for sustainable development within the building sector (Chen & Duan, 2022). This recognition emphasizes the necessity for a transformative approach to address environmental concerns and aligns with the broader goal of fostering sustainability in the construction industry (Kim et al., 2021).

The increasing demand for energy efficiency and thermal quality in buildings is driven by several factors, including population growth, elevated living standards, and the significant challenges posed by climate change (Yassaghi & Hoque, 2019). This focus outlined the importance of addressing building energy consumption and the associated GHG emissions in the context of sustainable urban development (Zhang et al., 2023). Recognizing thermal quality as a key strategy is instrumental in decreasing energy consumption (Raimundo et al., 2023).

Integrating energy-efficient practices and the green building movement aligns perfectly with the need to improve thermal quality, thus advancing both sustainability and environmental goals in the construction sector. Achieving low energy consumption is a fundamental aspect of designing energy-efficient buildings, alongside providing high thermal quality standards.

Recent years have seen the introduction of the Energy Performance Certificate policy, which advocates for benchmarking the building stock to identify structures that require rehabilitation (Heidenthaler et al., 2023). This policy is a crucial instrument in reducing energy consumption and GHG emissions from the building sector (Ji et al., 2022). The growing concern about climate change and the environmental impact of energy consumption has led to significant research and policy developments aimed at improving energy efficiency in buildings.

For instance, in Lithuania, energy, performance certificates (EPCs) are mandatory for both new and existing buildings, providing essential data for energy management and planning (Jonkutė et al., 2021). Qiu and Kahn (2019) argue that credible estimates of energy savings from green buildings are essential for policymakers to evaluate the cost and benefits of incentives designed to encourage green building practices, emphasizing that energy efficiency is a crucial public tool, helping to reduce greenhouse gas emissions and improve grid reliability. Similarly, Nunes et al. (2013) discuss the importance of energy efficiency in buildings as part of international climate and energy objectives. In Europe, building energy performance improvements are central to reducing energy dependency and achieving carbon emissions targets, with energy certification and labelling being key policy instruments (Hafez et al., 2023).

In Portugal, the Buildings Energy Certification System (SCE) was established through Decree-Law 78/2006, mandating energy certificates for all residential and service buildings from January 1, 2009 (Vaguero, 2020). Despite the system's intentions, inconsistencies have emerged over time. Vaquero (2020) highlights that energy efficiency indicators have changed significantly, with final energy consumption for certified buildings in 2013 being 37% lower than those in 2009, but CO2 emissions quadrupling, raising concerns about the true performance of certified buildings.

This system helps identify the most energy-consuming buildings, aiding efforts to reduce CO2 emissions and improve energy performance. Green building certifications have been shown to influence energy performance significantly.

Several policies and regulations have been enacted to enhance building energy efficiency. The European Union's Energy. Performance of Buildings Directive (EPBD) 2002/91/EC and its recast, Directive 2010/31/EU, set the framework for energy performance standards and zero-energy buildings (NZEB) (Jonkute et al., 2021). These directives require member states to implement minimum energy performance standards and promote energy-efficient renovations. The Building Energy Efficiency Certificate (BEEC) is presented as a vital tool for reducing energy consumption and greenhouse gas emissions in the building sector (Ji et al., 2022). Despite the progress made, several challenges remain in achieving energy efficiency in buildings. Heidenthaler et al. (2023) address the ambitious targets set forth in the European Green Deal, including the objective of reducing greenhouse gas emissions by 60% by 2030, which include strategies for decarbonizing the building stock. Berg and Donarelli (2019) explore the refurbishment of historic buildings to reduce energy dependency and enhance energy efficiency, highlighting the role of energy performance certificates in promoting energy-efficient refurbishments, which are crucial for meeting national and international climate goals.

Additionally, several governments are implementing innovative measures to promote energy efficiency and sustainability within the building sector. These measures include the introduction of environmental taxation and incentive schemes designed to support building rehabilitation efforts.

For example, the Portuguese government has introduced measures such as the Green Taxation Reform to promote environmental sustainability through tax policies. These incentives were designed to support building rehabilitation efforts, aligned with broader environmental and sustainability goals (Dinis, 2024). This reform includes several tax incentives for urban rehabilitation, aimed at encouraging the rehabilitation of existing buildings and promoting sustainable practices within the construction industry.

DRIVING SUSTAINABILITY: THE ROLE OF ENVIRONMENTAL TAXATION

The concept of environmental taxes can be traced back to the early 20th-century work by Cannan and Pigou in "Welfare Economics" (1921). They proposed that polluters should be responsible for the costs associated with pollution through taxation, although they did not outline specific mechanisms. Tullock (1967) expanded on this idea by introducing the "double dividend" effect of environmental taxes. The double dividend hypothesis suggests that environmental tax reform can improve economic efficiency by shifting the tax burden from more distortionary taxes to less distortionary ones, thereby achieving both economic and environmental benefits (Noubissi Domguia, 2023). Allan et al. (2017) have shown that using carbon tax revenue to reduce income taxes could enhance the double dividend effect. Other studies, such as those by Lei et al. (2022), Abdullah and Morley (2014), and Walid Oueslati (2014), found a positive causal relationship between environmental taxes and enterprise performance, suggesting that such taxes can stimulate economic growth and technological innovation.

Moreover, evidence from Feng et al. (2022) supports the presence of a double dividend effect under a low-carbon tax policy. Dagar et al. (2022) suggested that shifting GDP growth towards greener and more technologically advanced sectors could reduce environmental degradation over the long term. This is consistent with the findings by Adamou et al. (2012) and Liu et al. (2022), who argued that under certain conditions, environmental taxes do not negatively impact enterprises. In Portugal, evidence from Dinis et al. (2024) and Dinis et al. (2023) supports the positive effects of environmental taxation policies. These studies demonstrate that green tax incentives in Portugal have successfully encouraged companies to adopt more sustainable practices, supporting both environmental protection and economic growth.

The concept of environmental inequalities extends beyond social justice, encompassing the latest problems and populations related to environmental issues (Noubissi Domguia, 2023). To address the negative effects of human activities on the environment and environmental inequalities, many governments have implemented environmental taxes (Yang & Tang, 2023). To contextualize the debate on the socio-economic impacts of environmental taxes, it is essential to review existing research on this subject. Table 1 provides an overview of studies exploring the effects of environmental taxes across several regions, highlighting both the environmental and economic outcomes observed in these studies.

Table 1. Overview of research on environmental taxes and economic impact

Study	Region	Main Conclusion
Ghazouani et al. (2020)	Developed nations (Denmark, Finland, Sweden, Netherlands, Norway)	Carbon tax reforms improve environmental quality by reducing carbon emissions.
Guo et al. (2022)	China	Environmental tax reform significantly reduces urban air pollution with positive spatial spillover effects.
Hassan et al. (2020)	31 OECD countries	Environmentally related tax revenues negatively impact economic growth, but higher GDP per capita can mitigate this effect.
Jiang et al. (2020)	China	Tax reform has a limited influence on reducing the tax burden in the iron ore industry. Namely, at higher tax rates, it may negatively impact GDP and overall welfare.
Li and Zhou (2022)	China	Inverted U-shaped relationship between financial expenditure and carbon emissions.
Loganathan et al. (2014)	Malaysia	Cointegration between economic growth and CO2 emissions; Bidirectional causal relationship suggests the need for alternative pollution control instruments.
Mardones (2022)	Chile	Replacing royalties on copper mining with Pigouvian taxes reduces mining activity and emissions but impacts income for productive factors.
Mardones and Baeza (2018)	Brazil, Mexico, Chile	Different effects of CO2 tax rates on sectoral prices and emissions depending on electricity generation carbonization.
Meireles et al. (2021)	Europe	The transport sector is the largest contributor to CO2 emissions in Europe. Implementing CO2-based vehicle taxation can help reduce these emissions.
Mitić et al. (2023)	Western Balkan countries	There is a long-term cointegration between CO2 emissions and GDP per capita, highlighting the need for policies that simultaneously promote economic growth and environmental sustainability.
Ivanovic & Golusin, (2012)	Serbia	Environmental taxes are significant for sustainable development.

The studies presented in Table 1 support the conclusion that carbon tax reforms and other forms of ecological taxation can reduce pollutant emissions and enhance environmental quality, as observed in both developed and developing nations. However, the socio-economic impacts of these taxes remain a topic of debate. While some studies indicate that environmental taxes can negatively impact economic growth and intensify inequalities (Hassan et al., 2020; Jiang et al., 2020), others suggest that these taxes can create a more equitable tax system by reducing other distortionary taxes (Mitić et al., 2023; Guo et al., 2022; Ghazouani et al., 2020). This dual advantage outlined the importance of well-designed environmental tax policies in achieving sustainable development goals, reducing greenhouse gas emissions, and fostering green technology innovation (Tetiana et al., 2023).

According to Ceko and Cakrani (2023), environmental taxation functions as a critical economic and environmental policy tool, fostering sustainable practices, and promoting the efficient use of natural resources. In this regard, environmental taxation aims to promote sustainability by incorporating environmental costs into the decision-making of companies and individuals (Albrecht, 2006), through taxation, fees, or the granting of tax incentives (Shen & Zhang, 2022). By promoting sustainable practices and minimizing ecological footprints, green taxation helps to protect the environment and develop a more resilient and equitable economy (Su et al., 2023), supporting the transition to a greener economy and mitigating the negative impacts of human activities on the environment (Nobanee & Ullah, 2023).

Initially, the compulsory environmental taxes drive the cost of doing business, especially for heavily polluting industries, resulting in short-term losses and limited flexibility in tax implementation (Wang et al., 2022). These enterprises should anticipate higher production costs and reduced capacity due to stringent requirements for energy conservation, emission reduction, and technological innovation. However, overall, environmental taxes positively influence the economic features of enterprises (Dinis et al., 2024; Dinis et al., 2023; Yi et al., 2021). Similarly, enterprises that invest in technology research and development can reduce their tax burdens through reduced costs associated with improved production efficiency (Zhang et al., 2020). The innovation compensation effect of environmental regulations further offsets compliance costs, enhancing productivity and performance (Dinis et al., 2023; Qiu et al., 2018). Green tax reforms can be achieved through complementary measures such as introducing new taxes or restructuring existing ones, like those on transportation or energy, to better reflect the environmental impact of the taxed activities or goods (OECD, 2001). Traditionally, taxes are collected to finance public expenditures, serving financial purposes. However, environmental taxes are used for broader objectives beyond just financial purposes. When it comes to the contribution of green taxation, tax incentives are emerging as a climate policy instrument (Dinis et al., 2023; Mpofu, 2022). Several authors have drawn upon their countries' specific experiences to justify and highlight the relevance of government environmental protection policies. For instance, Deyganto (2022) notes that tax incentives have fostered corporate sustainability, even during times of crisis. Furthermore, Qi et al. (2023) conducted a study demonstrating that tax policies under environmental law, including tax reductions via investment tax incentives, can lead to a reduction in GHG emissions. Similarly, Yang et al. (2022) argue that sustainable companies achieve higher levels of economic profitability. Consequently, sustainable companies tend to be more tax-compliant and contribute more to income tax (Saka et al., 2020). Additionally, they exhibit higher levels of financial sustainability, characterized by lower debt ratios (He & Liu, 2023), higher solvency ratios (Aziz et al., 2021), and raised equity ratios (Gonçalves et al., 2022). Previous studies have also shown that companies reply more effectively to tax incentives compared to subsidies (Wu et al., 2023). Green tax incentives are a helpful tool not only because of their direct effect on reducing the tax burden but also because they address the emerging concern for environmental protection given the impact of pollution on environmental sustainability. A case in point is the experience of Portugal, which will be presented in the following section.

The Green Taxation Reform in Portugal: short background note

In Portugal, several tax policies have been introduced to facilitate the shift towards a greener and more sustainable economy (Dias & Ribeiro, 2023). These policies encompass the taxation of activities with higher pollution levels, the provision of tax incentives for investments in renewable energy, energy efficiency, and sustainable transportation, and the imposition of fees on natural resource consumption and waste generation. Such measures outlined a commitment to sustainable development and environmental conservation, while encouraging greener and more responsible practices (Dinis et al., 2023).

Before the comprehensive green taxation reform introduced by Law No. 82-D/2014 on December 31, Portugal's approach to environmental taxation was characterized by fragmentation and early-stage development. Although certain measures and policies were implemented, the tax framework concerning environmental issues was still maturing. Until the end of 2014, Portugal's environmental taxation focused on three main aspects: taxation based on the environmental impact of consumed products, waste taxation, and environmental tax incentives. However, these measures were neither widely applied nor uniformly developed across all economic sectors.

Aligning with OECD recommendations, the Portuguese government introduced the Green Taxation Reform in 2015 through Law no. 82-D/2014, aiming to foster innovation and resource-efficient use. Law No. 82-D/2014 marked a significant reform, introducing and restructuring a range of environmental tax norms across several sectors in Portugal. This law impacts the business sector, affecting the Corporate Income Tax Code (CIT), Value Added Tax Code (VAT), and the Tax Benefits Statute (TBS). The law aimed to promote more sustainable behaviors in the production, consumption, and use of natural resources while penalizing polluting activities (Dinis et al., 2023; Rodríguez et al., 2019). Key areas covered by this law included energy and emissions, transport, water, waste, and biodiversity. Portugal, as a member state of the EU, follows the European Regulations and instructions related to green taxation and the measures to address the effects of climate change and to promote sustainability and the consumption of resources with more efficiency and less impact on the environment. The importance of green taxation is also highlighted by the revenue it generates. According to the Portuguese National Statistics Institute (2022), environmental taxes reached approximately five billion euros in 2021. This value constituted 6.6% of total revenue from taxes and social contributions, representing an increase of 6.3% compared to 2020. However, it is important to note that there was a 7.5% decrease compared to 2021, which can be attributed to a decrease in fuel tax revenue. This decrease may have been caused by the mitigation of fuel price increases (directly in taxation).

This law reviewed and implemented environmental tax measures across sectors such as energy and emissions, transport, water, waste, land planning, forests, and biodiversity. Most changes involved adding new rules to existing taxes to integrate environmental considerations into their application. The literature has extensively analyzed environmental taxation reforms (Halim & Rahman, 2022). The primary environmental goal of these reforms is to encourage more ecologically responsible behaviors among taxpayers (Tetiana et al., 2023). By imposing taxes on activities that cause substantial environmental harm, such as greenhouse gas emissions or excessive waste generation, these reforms seek to dissuade such behaviors and promote the adoption of sustainable practices (Nobanee & Ullah, 2023). Consequently, this contributes to environmental conservation and efforts to mitigate climate change.

Tax Incentives in Portugal for Urban Rehabilitation

The main Portuguese tax benefits in the context of urban rehabilitation are primarily related to Value Added Tax (VAT), Municipal Property Tax (MPT), Municipal Property Transfer Tax (MPTT), Personal Income Tax (PIT), and Corporate Income Tax (CIT). The Tax Benefits Statute (TIS) presents several tax incentives; however, this chapter will focus exclusively on the tax incentives related to MPT and MPTT. Notable adjustments, particularly in the context of urban rehabilitation, are made in the Portuguese Tax Incentives Statute under Article 45.

Before December 2014, Article 45 of the TIS stipulated that urban properties undergoing urban rehabilitation were exempt from MPT for two years from the year of issuance of the respective municipal license. Additionally, acquisitions of urban properties intended for urban rehabilitation were exempt from the MPTT provided the rehabilitation works commenced within two years from the date of acquisition. Urban rehabilitation was defined as the process of transforming urbanized land, including construction, reconstruction, alteration, expansion, demolition, and conservation works aimed at improving usability while preserving the fundamental character of the buildings.

In December 2017, changes extended the MPT exemption period for urban properties undergoing urban rehabilitation to three years from the year of issuance of the respective municipal license. The period to initiate rehabilitation works for MPTT exemption was similarly extended to three years from the date of acquisition. Additionally, for these tax benefits to apply, the rehabilitated property had to achieve an energy certification of A or improve its energy class by at least two levels.

By June 2022, further clarifications and conditions were introduced in Article 45 of the TIS. Urban properties or autonomous units completed more than 30 years ago or located in urban rehabilitation areas became eligible for incentives, provided they met specific cumulative conditions. The properties had to undergo rehabilitation by the Urban Rehabilitation Legal Framework or exceptional regimes. Following the intervention, the property's state of conservation had to improve by at least two levels and achieve a minimum 'good' rating, meeting energy efficiency and thermal quality standards. The MPT exemption period remained three years, with the possibility of a five-year renewal for properties used for permanent housing or rental. Furthermore, exemptions from MPTT were extended to the first transmission after rehabilitation if the property was used for permanent housing or located in an urban rehabilitation area. Furthermore, the fees for the evaluation of the conservation state were reduced by 50%. Regarding Value Added Tax (VAT), urban rehabilitation works benefit from a reduced VAT rate of 6% under item 2.23 of List I annexed to the VAT Code, in conjunction with Article 18(a) of the same code. This reduced rate applies to rehabilitation works in urban rehabilitation areas and public spaces within legally defined rehabilitation areas or recognized national public interest projects. In terms of Personal Income Tax (PIT), property owners can deduct 30% of the expenses incurred in the rehabilitation of properties, up to a limit of €500. This benefit applies to properties located in urban rehabilitation areas and rehabilitated according to respective strategies or properties subject to phased rent updates under the New Urban Lease Regime and undergoing rehabilitation[1]. These expenses must be on file and certified by the management body of the rehabilitation area or the municipal arbitration commission, as applicable.

These benefits collectively aim to incentivize and support urban rehabilitation efforts, promoting the enhancement and preservation of urban areas while ensuring energy efficiency and improved living conditions.

Over time, the tax benefit stipulated in Article 45 of the TIS has undergone significant amendments aimed at better aligning the tax incentive with the evolving needs for urban rehabilitation and sustainability.

The progressive changes to Article 45 demonstrate the Portuguese legislative body's growing responsiveness to the need for sustainable urban development. The introduction and tightening of energy efficiency criteria highlight a clear policy direction aimed at reducing the environmental footprint of rehabilitated buildings. By extending benefit periods and easing initial requirements, the Portuguese legislative body has made these incentives more accessible, fostering a more conducive environment for sustainable urban rehabilitation.

These amendments reflect a balanced approach, addressing both the practical challenges faced by property owners and developers and the broader societal goal of promoting sustainability. The evolution of Article 45 represents a proactive legislative effort to align tax incentives with sustainable development objectives, ensuring that urban rehabilitation projects contribute meaningfully to environmental conservation and energy efficiency.

Study on the Portuguese Companies That Have Accessed Tax Incentives for Urban Rehabilitation: Research Methodology and Results

This study employs an exploratory analysis of tax incentives for urban rehabilitation within the context of Portuguese companies. By using publicly available data from the Portuguese Tax Authority Portal (2015-2022) and the Database of Financial Analysis of Portuguese and Spanish Companies (SABI), a comprehensive dataset emerges. This dataset includes aggregated values for Municipal Property Tax and Municipal Property Transfer Tax. Additionally, to include relevant indicators related to urban regeneration policies, it was essential to collect data from the Portuguese National Statistics Institute and the Portuguese Environment Agency. Analytical approach uses SPSS software for descriptive analysis and Pearson correlation to explore the relationships within the dataset. This methodology allows for the understanding of the tax incentives and their correlation with urban rehabilitation indicators. Table 2 shows the data sources, including the Portuguese Tax Authority Portal, covering the period from 2015 to 2022, and the Database of Financial Analysis of Portuguese and Spanish Companies (SABI). These sources provided detailed information on Municipal Property Tax and Municipal Property Transfer Tax. Furthermore, data from the Portuguese National Statistics Institute and the Portuguese Environment Agency were referenced to enrich the dataset with relevant indicators of urban rehabilitation policies.

Table 2. Data sources

Variables	Sources
Region	*Database of Financial Analysis of Portuguese and Spanish Companies*
District	*Database of Financial Analysis of Portuguese and Spanish Companies*
Municipality	*Database of Financial Analysis of Portuguese and Spanish Companies*
Main Economic Activity	*Database of Financial Analysis of Portuguese and Spanish Companies*
Secondary Economic Activity	*Database of Financial Analysis of Portuguese and Spanish Companies*
Number of Companies	*Portuguese Tax Authority Portal*
Total amount of tax incentive	*Portuguese Tax Authority Portal*
Reconstructions Completed per 100 New Constructions (%)	*Portuguese National Statistics Institute*
Total Electrical Energy Consumption (TEC) (kWh)	*Portuguese National Statistics Institute*
Greenhouse Gas Emissions (GHG) (kt CO_2eq)	*Portuguese Environment Agency*
Total Municipal Expenditures on Environment (TMEE) (€)	*Portuguese National Statistics Institute*

The variable "*Region*" is used to categorize the different geographical areas of the study, while "*District*" is employed to specify administrative subdivisions within these regions. "*Municipality*" identifies the most detailed local units, which is the basis for the analysis of the database used in this study. The "*Main Economic Activity*" highlights the predominant sector driving the local economy, while the "*Secondary Economic Activity*" indicates other significant sectors. The "*Number of Companies*" indicates the number of business entities that took advantage of the tax incentive under study in each municipality. The "*Total Amount of Tax Incentive*" reveals the total amount of tax incentives to stimulate urban rehabilitation activities. The variable "*Reconstructions Completed per 100 New Constructions (%)*" measures the proportion of reconstruction projects relative to new constructions per municipality, reflecting the dynamics of urban rehabilitation development. "*Total Electrical Energy Consumption (TEC) (kWh)*" provides data on energy usage per municipality, and "*Greenhouse Gas Emissions (GHG) (kt CO_2eq)*" quantifies the environmental impact in terms of emissions per municipality. Lastly, the variable "*Total Municipal Expenditure on the Environment (TMEE) (€)*" indicates the amount of municipal spending on environmental initiatives and policies. Collectively, these variables provide a comprehensive insight into the economic, environmental, and administrative characteristics of the areas under study.

Table 3 presents descriptive statistics related to the municipalities where companies that took advantage of the tax incentives for urban rehabilitation are based.

Table 3. Municipal descriptive statistics of urban rehabilitation tax incentives

Descriptive Statistics					
Municipality	*N*	*Minimum*	*Maximum*	*Mean*	*Std. Deviation*
Companies	66	1	130	5	16.66
Tax Incentives (2015-2022)		4.82 €	1,732,573.76 €	52,891.18 €	221,964.23 €

Source: Output SPSS Statistics; Data extracted from https://www.portaldasfinancas.gov.pt

On the results achieved, the authors verify that during the analyzed period only 330 companies took advantage of this tax incentive. The study involves *sixty-six* municipalities, with the number of companies benefiting from the incentive varying between a minimum of one and a maximum of *130* per municipality where the companies that took advantage of the tax incentive under study are based. The average number of companies per municipality is *five*, indicating that, on average, each municipality had five entities that accessed the tax incentive between 2015 and 2022. The standard deviation of *16.66* suggests significant variability in the number of companies taking advantage of the tax incentive across different municipalities. The variable "*Tax Incentives 2015-2022*" shows that the tax incentives provided ranged from a minimum of *€4.82* to a maximum of *€1,732,573.76* per municipality. Table 4 exhibits the evolution of tax incentives for urban rehabilitation that the Portuguese companies took advantage of from 2015 to 2022.

Table 4. Evolution of tax incentives for urban rehabilitation that the Portuguese companies took advantage (2015-2022)

Year	**No**	**Tax Incentives 2015-2022**	**No (%)**	**Tax Incentives 2015-2022 (%)**
2015	27	78,776.33 €	8.18	2.26
2016	41	120,414.29 €	12.42	3.45
2017	60	273,188.00 €	18.18	7.83
2018	80	414,405.34 €	24.24	11.87
2019	105	513,074.35 €	31.82	14.70
2020	119	651,924.37 €	36.06	18.68

continued on following page

Table 4. Continued

Year	No	Tax Incentives 2015-2022	No (%)	Tax Incentives 2015-2022 (%)
2021	137	746,949.74 €	41.52	21.40
2022	147	692,085.56 €	44.55	19.83
TOTAL	330	3,490,817.98 €	100.00	100.00

Source: Carvalho et al. (2024)

Notes: Year- The year in which the tax incentive for urban rehabilitation was obtained; N- The number of companies that took advantage of the tax incentive; Tax Incentives 2015-2022- The total amount of tax incentives granted from 2015 to 2022; %N- The percentage of the number of companies that took advantage of the tax incentive relative to the total; %Tax Incentives 2015-2022- The percentage of the total amount of tax incentives that the Portuguese companies took advantage of 2015 to 2022 relative to the total.

Table 4 shows data on the tax incentives for urban regeneration that Portuguese companies took advantage of between 2015 and 2022. Over the period analyzed, it is possible to see an upward trend in the number of companies benefiting from these incentives, culminating in a total of *147* companies in 2022. Consequently, the total amount of tax incentives awarded has significantly increased, rising from *€78,776.33* in 2015 to *€692,085.56* in 2022. Exploring the percentage contribution relative to the overall total there is a marked increase. In 2015, this percentage was *8.18%,* which grew to *44.55%* by 2022. This indicates a substantial rise in the engagement of companies with the tax incentive over the years. The year 2021 is particularly noteworthy, in the number of beneficiary companies and the total amount of the tax incentive. The percentage variation highlights significant year-on-year growth, reflecting the increasing adoption of the tax incentive throughout the period under review. Table 5 presents an overview of the distribution of tax incentives among companies and municipalities from 2015 to 2022, categorized by different brackets of the tax incentives.

Table 5. Brackets of tax incentives: companies and municipalities overview

Tax Incentives 2015-2022	Companies	Municipalities
<1000 tax incentives	8	8
>1000 tax incentives <=5000	29	22
> 5000 tax incentives <= 10000	10	6
> 10000 tax incentives <= 20000	25	10

continued on following page

Table 5. Continued

Tax Incentives 2015-2022	**Companies**	**Municipalities**
> 20000 tax incentives	258	20
Total	330	66

Source: Output SPSS Statistics; Data extracted from https://www.portaldasfinancas.gov.pt

Following the methodology of Dinis & Pereira (2022), Table 5 reveals insights into the distribution of companies across several brackets of tax incentives based on values from 2015 to 2022. In the category of *<1000 tax incentives*, *8* companies were identified, dispersed across *8* municipalities. Moving to the bracket of *>1000 tax incentives <=5000*, 29 companies are spread across *22* municipalities. The next bracket, *>5000 tax incentives <=10000*, includes *10* companies with a presence in *6* municipalities. In the bracket of *>10000 tax incentives <=20000*, there are *25* companies spread across *10* municipalities. Finally, the bracket of *>20000 tax incentives* encompass *258* companies based in *20* municipalities. The diversity of municipalities where companies are based suggests a broad geographical distribution of tax benefits. However, concentration in some municipalities may point to specific regional development strategies. The distribution indicates that most companies that took advantage of substantial tax incentives (over 20.000 euros) are concentrated in a smaller number of municipalities (*20*), suggesting a concentration of larger or more tax-incentive-reliant businesses within these areas. On the other hand, smaller tax incentives are better balanced between companies and municipalities. This pattern may reflect ranging levels of economic activity and tax policy effectiveness across different regions.

Sample and Descriptive Statistics

This section provides an overview of the sample and presents the descriptive statistics used in this analysis of tax incentives for urban rehabilitation among Portuguese companies. These statistics provide an understanding of the distribution and central tendencies within the data, offering insights into the characteristics and behaviors of the companies that took advantage of these tax incentives. Through this approach, the study aims to present a clear and comprehensive picture of how tax incentives for urban rehabilitation have been used by Portuguese companies across different regions and company profile in Portugal. Table 6 details the concentration of companies and the average urban rehabilitation tax incentives across several regions, districts, and municipalities, as well as the main and secondary economic activities of these companies.

Table 6. Detail of companies that benefited from tax incentives for urban rehabilitation

Company Data	Percentage	Average urban rehabilitation tax incentives
Region: Lisboa and Vale do Tejo North Centre	**52.96** 31.66 7.69	**11,567.72** 9,361.81 6,579.93
District: Lisboa Porto Setúbal Braga	**48.22** 21.30 4.14 3.55	**12,221.40** 10,315.19 4,839.36 9,876.36
Municipality: Lisboa Porto Vila Nova de Gaia Cascais	**39.05** 13.61 2.66 2.37	**13,318.83** 11,945.54 2,973.03 4,267.03
Main Economic Activity: Purchase and sale of real estate Renting of real estate Furnished accommodation for tourists Building construction	**41.72** 7.69 6.80 6.80	6,916.61 **17,183.42** 6.117,69 2.805,12
Secondary Economic Activity: Property rental Purchase and sale of real estate Furnished accommodation for tourists Other short-term accommodation No secondary economic activity	**20.12** 15.38 7.40 5.30 15.38	9,342.77 8,576.67 4,756.09 6,308.57 **17,430.15**

Source: Output SPSS Statistics; Data extracted from https://www.portaldasfinancas.gov.pt

Table 6 shows a detailed analysis of the concentration of companies and tax incentives across different regions, districts, and municipalities, where the Portuguese companies are located and by economic activity. The Lisbon and Tagus Valley region holds the highest concentration of companies at *52.96%,* accompanied by the highest average urban rehabilitation tax incentive of *€11,567.72*. The North and Centre regions follow, with *31.66%* and *7.69%* of companies respectively, and correspondingly lower tax incentives. Lisbon district emerges as the dominant area with *48.22%* of companies, also with the highest average tax benefit of *€12,221.40*. This is followed by Porto, Setúbal, and Braga districts, which have lower concentrations of companies and average tax benefits. Lisbon municipality leads with *39.05%* of companies and the highest tax incentive of *€13,318.83*, followed by Porto, Vila Nova de Gaia, and Cascais. Exploring the main economic activities, the purchase and sale of real estate account for *41.72%* of companies, yet the renting of real estate, despite representing only *7.69%* of companies, enjoys the highest average tax benefit of *€17,183.42*. The secondary economic activities show that companies engaged in property rental have the highest concentration at *20.12%*, but companies with no secondary economic activity receive the highest average tax benefit of *€17,430.15*.

The results underline a clear concentration of companies in the Lisbon and Tagus Valley region, particularly in the city of Lisbon, with higher tax incentives. The analysis also highlights those specific activities, such as the renting of real estate, despite their lower prevalence, receive higher tax benefits. Additionally, the lack of multiplicity in economic activities appears to be advantageous in terms of tax benefits.

Results: Bivariate Analysis

This section presents the findings from the bivariate analysis conducted to explore the relation between key variables within the dataset on tax incentives for urban rehabilitation among Portuguese companies. Bivariate analysis allows to understand how these associations might influence urban rehabilitation efforts and sustainable urban development. This analysis focuses on the correlation between total urban rehabilitation tax incentives and several economic and demographic indicators. This includes the number of companies that took advantage of tax incentives, the total amounts of tax incentives granted, reconstructions completed per 100 new constructions (%), total electrical energy consumption (TEC) (kWh), greenhouse gas emissions (GHG) (kt CO_2eq), and total municipal expenditures on environment (TMEE) (€).

Table 7 presents the Pearson correlation coefficients (R) and significance levels (p) between the number of reconstructions completed per one hundred new constructions per municipality and two variables: the number of companies per municipality and the total amount of tax incentives that these companies took advantage of in each municipality, for selected years and the mean value.

Table 7. Impact of companies and tax incentives on reconstruction rates

Input	Correlation	*Reconstructions completed per 100 new constructions (%)*					
		Reconst_2015	*Reconst_2016*	*Reconst_2017*	*Reconst_2018*	*Reconst_2020*	*Reconst_mean*
	Coefficient	0.260*	0.666**	0.446**	0.325**	0.300*	0.403**
No of companies	Significance	0.035	<0.001	<0.001	0.008	0.014	<0.001
	Number	66	66	66	66	66	66
	Coefficient	0.285*	0.663**	0.426**	0.317**	0.312*	0.411**

continued on following page

Table 7. Continued

Input	Correlation	Reconstructions completed per 100 new constructions (%)					
		Reconst_2015	*Reconst_2016*	*Reconst_2017*	*Reconst_2018*	*Reconst_2020*	*Reconst_mean*
Total amount of tax incentive	Significance	0.02	<0.001	<0.001	0.01	0.011	<0.001
	Number	66	66	66	66	66	66

* Significant at 5%
** Significant at 1%
Source: Output SPSS Statistics; Data extracted from https://www.portaldasfinancas.gov.pt

For the number of companies per municipality, in 2015 the correlation coefficient was $R = 0.260$ with a significance level of $p = 0.035$, indicating a weak positive correlation that is statistically significant. In 2016, the coefficient was $R = 0.666$ with a significance of $p < 0.001$, demonstrating a strong positive correlation. In 2017, the coefficient was $R = 0.446$ with a significance of $p < 0.001$, indicating a moderate positive correlation. In 2018, the coefficient was $R = 0.325$ with a significance of $p = 0.008$, showing a moderate positive correlation. In 2020, the coefficient is $R = 0.300$ with a significance of $p = 0.014$, indicating a weak to moderate positive correlation. The mean correlation coefficient is $R = 0.403$ with a significance of $p < 0.001$, indicating a moderate positive correlation on average.

Regarding the total amount of tax incentives, in 2015 the correlation coefficient was $R = 0.285$ with a significance level of $p = 0.020$, indicating a weak positive correlation that is statistically significant. In 2016, the coefficient was $R = 0.663$ with a significance of $p < 0.001$, demonstrating a strong positive correlation. In 2017, the coefficient was $R = 0.426$ with a significance of $p < 0.001$, indicating a moderate positive correlation. In 2018, the coefficient was $R = 0.317$ with a significance of $p = 0.010$, showing a moderate positive correlation. In 2020, the coefficient is $R = 0.312$ with a significance of $p = 0.011$, indicating a weak to moderate positive correlation. The mean correlation coefficient is $R = 0.411$ with a significance of $p < 0.001$, indicating a moderate positive correlation on average.

The analysis indicates that municipalities with a higher number of companies and greater amounts of tax incentives to which companies have taken advantage tend to have a higher number of reconstructions completed per one hundred new constructions. These findings provide empirical support for the need for targeted tax policies to promote urban rehabilitation, as discussed by Chen and Duan (2022). The positive effect of tax incentives on reconstruction rates indicates that such policies are effective tools for fostering urban renewal and environmental sustainability, aligning with the broader goals of sustainable urban development.

Table 8 presents the Pearson correlation coefficients between total electrical energy consumption (TEC) in kilowatt-hours (kWh) and two variables: the number of companies per municipality and the total amount of tax incentives that these companies took advantage of in each municipality, across different years from 2015 to 2022.

Table 8. Correlation of energy consumption with business and tax incentives

Input	**Correlation**	*Total Electrical Energy Consumption (TEC) (kWh)*								
		TEC_2015	*TEC_2016*	*TEC_2017*	*TEC_2018*	*TEC_2019*	*TEC_2020*	*TEC_2021*	*TEC_2022*	*TEC_ Mean*
	Coefficient	0.745**	0.752**	0.746**	0.752**	0.751**	0.709**	0.711**	0.745**	0.740**
No of companies	Significance	<0.001	<0.001	<0.001	<0.001	<0.001	<0.001	<0.001	<0.001	<0.001
	Number	66	66	66	66	66	66	66	66	66
	Coefficient	0.716**	0.723**	0.717**	0.723**	0.722**	0.678**	0.679**	0.713**	0.710**
Total amount of tax incentive	Significance	<0.001	<0.001	<0.001	<0.001	<0.001	<0.001	<0.001	<0.001	<0.001
	Number	66	66	66	66	66	66	66	66	66

* Significant at 5%

** Significant at 1%

Source: Output SPSS Statistics; Data extracted from https://www.portaldasfinancas.gov.pt

Concerning the number of companies per municipality, the correlation coefficient for 2015 is $R=0.745$ with a significance level of $p<0.001$, indicating a strong positive correlation that is highly statistically significant. Similarly, for 2016, the coefficient is $R=0.752$ with a significance of $p<0.001$, demonstrating a strong positive correlation. This pattern continues for 2017 and 2018, with coefficients of $R=0.746$ and $R=0.752$ respectively, both with significance levels of $p<0.001$. In 2019, the correlation coefficient is $R=0.751$, and in 2020, it is $R=0.709$, both with significance levels of $p<0.001$, indicating strong positive correlations. For 2021 and 2022, the coefficients are $R=0.711$ and $R=0.745$ respectively, each maintaining a significance level of $p<0.001$. The mean correlation coefficient is $R=0.740$, with a significance level of $p<0.001$, suggesting a consistently strong positive correlation over the years.

Regarding the total amount of tax incentives, the correlation coefficient for 2015 is $R=0.716$ with a significance level of $p<0.001$, indicating a strong positive correlation that is statistically significant. This trend continues in 2016 and 2017, with coefficients of $R=0.723$ and $R=0.717$ respectively, both with significance levels of $p<0.001$. For 2018 and 2019, the coefficients are $R=0.723$ and $R=0.722$, respectively, again with high statistical significance. In 2020, the correlation coefficient is $R=0.678$, while in 2021 it is $R=0.679$, both showing significance levels of *p<0.001*. For 2022, the coefficient is *R=0.713*, and the mean coefficient over the years is *R=0.710*, both with significance levels of *p<0.001*. These values indicate strong positive correlations between the total amount of tax incentives and total electrical energy consumption. The analysis reveals that municipalities with a higher number of companies and a greater amount of tax incentives granted tend to have higher total electrical energy consumption. These findings highlight the importance of integrating energy-efficient practices in urban rehabilitation efforts, aligning with the strategic goals of the European Green Deal, which emphasizes long-term energy efficiency in buildings as a key policy (Economidou et al., 2020). The results highlight the necessity of balancing economic development with sustainable energy consumption practices, a critical point emphasized by Yassaghi and Hoque (2019) in their discussion on sustainable urban development. The results reinforce Heide et al. (2023) and Hafez et al. (2023), who underscored the need for enhancing energy efficiency in buildings to mitigate the environmental impact of urban development. Furthermore, following the study of Kim et al. (2021), the results highlighted the importance of integrating energy-efficient practices in urban rehabilitation to mitigate environmental impact.

Table 9 presents the Pearson correlation coefficients between greenhouse gas emissions (GHG) in kilotons of CO_2 equivalent (kt CO_2eq) and two variables: the number of companies per municipality and the total amount of tax incentives that these companies took advantage of in each municipality, across selected years 2015, 2017, and 2019, along with the mean value over these years.

Table 9. Statistical correlations of GHG emissions with number of companies and tax incentives

Input	**Correlation**	*Greenhouse Gas Emissions (GHG) (kt CO_2eq)*			
		GHG_2015	*GHG_2017*	*GHG_2019*	*GHG_Mean*
	Coefficient	0.605**	0.374**	0.602**	0.889**
No of companies	Significance	<0.001	0.002	<0.001	<0.001
	Number	66	66	66	66
	Coefficient	0.328**	0.245*	0.323**	0.872**
Total amount of tax incentive	Significance	0.007	0.047	0.008	<0.001
	Number	66	66	66	66

* Significant at 5%

** Significant at 1%

Source: Output SPSS Statistics; Data extracted from https://www.portaldasfinancas.gov.pt

For the number of companies per municipality, the correlation coefficient for GHG emissions in 2015 was *R=0.605* with a significance level of *p<0.001*, indicating a strong positive correlation that is statistically significant. In 2017, the coefficient was *R=0.374* with a significance of *p=0.002*, showing a moderate positive correlation. For 2019, the correlation coefficient is *R=0.602* with a significance of *p<0.001*, again indicating a strong positive correlation. The mean correlation coefficient across these years is *R=0.889* with a significance of *p<0.001*, suggesting an extremely strong positive correlation overall.

Regarding the total amount of tax incentives, the correlation coefficient for GHG emissions in 2015 is *R=0.328* with a significance level of *p=0.007*, indicating a moderate positive correlation that is statistically significant. In 2017, the coefficient was *R=0.245* with a significance of *p=0.047*, showing a weak positive correlation that is nonetheless statistically significant. For 2019, the coefficient is *R=0.323* with a significance of *p=0.008*, indicating a moderate positive correlation. The mean correlation coefficient is *R=0.872* with a significance of *p<0.001*, suggesting a strong positive correlation overall. The analysis indicates that municipalities with a higher number of companies and greater amounts of tax incentives which companies have taken advantage of tend to have higher greenhouse gas emissions. This emphasizes the study of Akdag and Yildirim (2020) who discussed the importance of sustainable mitigation approaches to reduce greenhouse gas emissions in the context of energy efficiency. The consistent significance of these variables across multiple years also follows the argument by Silva et al. (2024) that sustainable practices in building operations are essential for reducing greenhouse gas emissions and achieving climate neutrality. The findings highlight the concerns in defining the objectives of Portugal's National Energy and Climate Plan 2030, which aims to reduce GHG emissions by 45 to 55 per cent by 2030, compared to 2005 levels.

Table 10 presents the Pearson correlation coefficients between total municipal expenditures on the environment (TMEE) in euros and two variables: the number of companies per municipality and the total amount of tax incentives that these companies took advantage of in each municipality, across the years 2015 to 2022, as well as the mean values over these years.

Table 10. Correlation analysis of total municipal expenditures on the environment

Input	Correlation	*Total Municipal Expenditures on Environment (TMEE) (€)*								
		TMEE_2015	*TMEE_2016*	*TMEE_2017*	*TMEE_2018*	*TMEE_2019*	*TMEE_2020*	*TMEE_2021*	*TMEE_2022*	*TMEE_ Mean*
	Coefficient	0.911**	0.906**	0.920**	0.909**	0.901**	0.873**	0.793**	0.700**	0.889**
No of companies	Significance	<0.001	<0.001	<0.001	<0.001	<0.001	<0.001	<0.001	<0.001	<0.001
	Number	66	66	66	66	66	66	66	66	66
	Coefficient	0.889**	0.887**	0.902**	0.895**	0.889**	0.856**	0.779**	0.677**	0.872**
Total amount of tax incentive	Significance	<0.001	<0.001	<0.001	<0.001	<0.001	<0.001	<0.001	<0.001	<0.001
	Number	66	66	66	66	66	66	66	66	66

* Significant at 5%
** Significant at 1%
Source: Output SPSS Statistics; Data extracted from https://www.portaldasfinancas.gov.pt

For the number of companies per municipality, the correlation coefficient for TMEE in 2015 is *R=0.911* with a significance level of *p<0.001*, indicating a strong positive correlation that is statistically significant. This strong positive correlation persists in 2016 with a coefficient of *R=0.906*, in 2017 with a coefficient of *R=0.920*, and in 2018 with a coefficient of *R=0.909*, all with significance levels of *p<0.001*. The correlation remains robust in 2019 and 2020, with coefficients of *R=0.901* and *R=0.873*, respectively. In 2021, the correlation coefficient is *R=0.793*, and in 2022 it is *R=0.700,* both still indicating strong positive correlations. The mean correlation coefficient across these years is *R=0.889*, with a significance level of *p<0.001*, suggesting a consistently strong positive correlation over the years.

Regarding the total amount of tax incentives, the correlation coefficient for TMEE in 2015 is *R=0.889* with a significance level of *p<0.001*, indicating a strong positive correlation that is statistically significant. This strong correlation is consistent in 2016 with a coefficient of *R=0.887*, in 2017 with a coefficient of *R=0.902*, and in 2018 with a coefficient of *R=0.895*, all with significance levels of *p<0.001*. For 2019 and 2020, the coefficients are *R=0.889* and *R=0.856*, respectively, maintaining strong positive correlations. In 2021, the correlation coefficient is *R=0.779*, and in 2022 it is *R=0.677*, both indicating strong but slightly weaker positive correlations. The mean correlation coefficient over these years is *R=0.872*, with a significance level of *p<0.001*, indicating a consistently strong positive correlation. The analysis indicates that municipalities with a higher number of companies and greater amounts of tax incentives have taken advantage of tending to have higher Total Municipal Expenditures on the Environment. These findings highlight the critical role of tax policies in supporting environmental sustainability initiatives at the municipal level. The significant positive correlations between TMEE and tax incentives follow Hafez et al. (2023). Linking tax incentives to environmental expenditures can enhance the capacity to implement sustainable practices and infrastructure improvements. The results suggest that municipalities where the companies that took advantage of the tax incentive are located enhance their environmental expenditures, fostering sustainable urban development.

FINDINGS DISCUSSION

The findings reveal key insights into the effectiveness of tax policies in promoting sustainable urban development. Municipalities with higher levels of engagement in tax incentives tend to experience more active reconstruction activities. These findings align with the arguments presented by Chen and Duan (2022), who advocated for a transformative approach to sustainable development within the construction sector. The results also highlight the need to balance economic development with sustainable energy consumption practices, reinforcing the importance of government incentives in promoting sustainable development and energy efficiency.

Municipalities should consider incorporating measures such as energy-efficient building standards, incentives for renewable energy use, and requirements for reducing carbon footprints in projects receiving tax incentives. By doing so, they can mitigate the potential environmental impacts of increased economic activities, aligning with the goals of sustainable development.

The findings reflect the importance of well-designed tax incentives in promoting sustainable urban development suggesting that these tax policies are effective tools for fostering urban renewal, energy efficiency, and environmental sustainability.

Policymakers should consider enhancing the design of tax incentives to promote environmental sustainability. This includes incorporating energy efficiency standards and GHG reduction targets into the eligibility criteria for tax incentives. Additionally, raising awareness and providing guidance can encourage more companies to engage in sustainable practices. By aligning tax incentives with sustainability goals, policymakers can foster a more balanced approach to urban rehabilitation, promoting both economic growth and environmental protection. These findings contribute to broader discourse on the role of tax policies in achieving sustainable development and offer practical recommendations for enhancing the effectiveness of tax incentives in promoting urban rehabilitation.

FUTURE RESEARCH DIRECTIONS

Several areas warrant further exploration to improve the design and implementation of these tax policies.

Firstly, comparative studies across regions and countries would offer valuable insights. Conducting a comparative analysis between different regions within Portugal, as well as between Portugal and other countries with similar urban rehabilitation policies, could identify best practices and highlight differences in policy effectiveness due to regional economic conditions, administrative practices, and cultural factors. Secondly, exploring the impact of specific tax incentives on several economic activities is crucial. Future research could focus on how distinct types of tax incentives specifically affect several economic activities related to urban rehabilitation. Thirdly, analyzing environmental and social sustainability metrics in future analyses would provide a more holistic view. While this study focuses on economic and environmental indicators, incorporating metrics such as social equity, community engagement, and the impact on local employment could offer insights into how tax incentives for urban rehabilitation contribute to broader goals. Fourthly, researching the barriers to accessing tax incentives for urban rehabilitation could provide critical insights. Factors such as administrative complexity, lack of awareness, and the perceived burden of compliance could be significant factors. Fifthly, evaluating how tax incentives interact with other policy instruments, such as subsidies, grants, and regulatory measures, can provide a more comprehensive understanding of their effectiveness. Future research could analyze the synergies and potential conflicts between different policy tools, offering insights into how to design integrated policy frameworks that maximize the benefits of urban rehabilitation efforts. For instance, a comparative analysis of how environmental certification systems, such as LEED™ (Leadership in Energy and Environmental Design) and HQE (Haute Qualité Environnementale), are used to encourage sustainable construction practices across different countries. Specifically, this research could explore the intersection of these certifications with tax incentives and their subsequent economic impacts.

Lastly, understanding the perspectives of several stakeholders, including policymakers, and companies, is crucial for the effective implementation of tax incentives. Future research could employ qualitative methods such as interviews and focus groups to gather in-depth insights into stakeholder experiences and perceptions.

By exploring these future research directions, scholars and policymakers can increase a deeper understanding of the potential of tax incentives for urban rehabilitation. This could result in more companies adopting sustainable practices to remain competitive in the marketplace.

CONCLUSION

This chapter highlights the significant role of tax incentives in promoting urban rehabilitation among Portuguese companies, focusing on fostering sustainable development and environmental protection. Using SPSS software for descriptive analysis and Pearson correlations, this research analyses the correlations between tax incentives and their main indicators, such as the rate of reconstruction as a proportion of new construction, energy consumption, greenhouse gas emissions, and municipal environmental expenditure.

The findings highlight several key points. Firstly, there is a significant positive correlation between the number of companies per municipality, the total amount of tax incentives that these companies took advantage of in each municipality, and the rates of reconstruction activities. This suggests that tax incentives effectively stimulate reconstruction activities, aligning with sustainable development goals within the construction sector. Secondly, while tax incentives are associated with increased economic activities, they also relate to higher energy consumption. This emphasizes the need for municipalities to adopt energy-efficient practices and integrate sustainability criteria into urban rehabilitation efforts to balance economic growth with environmental sustainability.

Moreover, the study reveals a positive correlation between GHG emissions and both the number of companies and the total amount of tax incentives. This reinforces the necessity of incorporating stricter environmental criteria into tax policies to mitigate the environmental impact of increased economic activities. Additionally, there is a strong positive correlation between total municipal expenditures on the environment and the number of companies and tax incentives. This indicates that municipalities where companies that took advantage of the tax incentive are located with higher engagement in tax incentives tend to invest more in environmental initiatives, supporting sustainable urban development. The study emphasizes the need for well-designed tax incentives that promote both economic development and environmental sustainability. Policymakers should consider integrating energy efficiency standards and GHG reduction targets into the eligibility criteria for tax incentives.

This chapter contributes to the accounting field by offering valuable insights into how tax incentives can be strategically aligned with the Sustainable Development Goals (SDGs) to promote urban rehabilitation and environmental sustainability. By analyzing key indicators such as reconstruction rates, energy consumption, greenhouse gas emissions, and municipal environmental expenditure, this study provides a framework for integrating sustainability considerations into accounting practices. These findings encourage accounting professionals to incorporate environmental metrics into strategic tax planning, thereby supporting the broader global objectives of reducing environmental impact and fostering sustainable development within the corporate sector.

ACKNOWLEDGMENT

This work is financed by national funds through the FCT - Foundation for Science and Technology, I.P., under projects UIDB/04043/2020 and UIDP/04043/2020.

REFERENCES

Abdullah, S., & Morley, B. (2014). Environmental taxes and economic growth: Evidence from panel causality tests. *Energy Economics*, 42, 27–33. DOI: 10.1016/j.eneco.2013.11.013

Adamou, A., Clerides, S., & Zachariadis, T. (2012). Trade-offs in CO2-oriented vehicle tax reforms: A case study of Greece. *Transportation Research Part D, Transport and Environment*, 17(6), 451–456. DOI: 10.1016/j.trd.2012.05.005

Akdag, S., & Yıldırım, H. (2020). Toward a sustainable mitigation approach of energy efficiency to greenhouse gas emissions in the European countries. *Heliyon*, 6(3), e03396. DOI: 10.1016/j.heliyon.2020.e03396 PMID: 32154402

Albrecht, J. (2006). The use of consumption taxes to re-launch green tax reforms. *International Review of Law and Economics*, 26(1), 88–103. DOI: 10.1016/j.irle.2006.05.007

Allan, G. J., Lecca, P., McGregor, P. G., McIntyre, S. G., & Kim Swales, J. (2017). Computable General Equilibrium Modelling in Regional Science. In R. Jackson & P. Schaeffer (Eds.), *Regional Research Frontiers—Vol. 2* (pp. 59–78). Springer International Publishing. DOI: 10.1007/978-3-319-50590-9_4

Aziz, S., Rahman, M., Hussain, D., & Nguyen, D. K. (2021). Does corporate environmentalism affect corporate insolvency risk? The role of market power and competitive intensity. *Ecological Economics*, 189, 107182. DOI: 10.1016/j.ecolecon.2021.107182

Berg, F., & Donarelli, A. (2019). Energy Performance Certificates and Historic Apartment Buildings: A Method to Encourage User Participation and Sustainability in the Refurbishment Process. *The Historic Environment*, 10(2), 224–240. DOI: 10.1080/17567505.2019.1592836

Cai, K., Wang, H., Wang, J., Bai, J., Zuo, J., Chan, K., Lai, K., & Song, Q. (2023). Mitigating lifecycle GHG emissions of building sector through prefabricated light-steel buildings in comparison with traditional cast-in-place buildings. *Resources, Conservation and Recycling*, 194, 107007. DOI: 10.1016/j.resconrec.2023.107007

Carvalho, A., Dinis, A., & Pereira, L. (2024). Enhancing urban regeneration through digital transparency and open government. *19th Iberian Conference on Information Systems and Technologies (CISTI)*, Salamanca, Spain.

Ceko, E., & Cakrani, E. (2023). Environmental Tax Reform in Western Balkan Countries. In *Taking on Climate Change Through Green Taxation* (pp. 101–153). IGI Global., DOI: 10.4018/978-1-6684-8592-7.ch005

Chen, X., & Duan, J. (2022). What they talk about when they talk about urban regeneration: Understanding the concept 'urban regeneration' in PRD, China. *Cities (London, England)*, 130, 103880. DOI: 10.1016/j.cities.2022.103880

Chung, J., & Yoon, S. (2023). Effects of Tax Incentive Policies for Land Use on Local Socioeconomic Conditions: A Case of Tax Policies for Urban Regeneration Projects in Republic of Korea. *Land (Basel)*, 12(9), 1801. DOI: 10.3390/land12091801

Dadzie, J., Runeson, G., & Ding, G. (2018). Sustainable Technologies as Determinants of Energy Efficient Upgrade of Existing Buildings. *2018 International Conference on Smart Grid and Clean Energy Technologies (ICSGCE)*, 145–149. DOI: 10.1109/ICSGCE.2018.8556688

Dagar, V., Ahmed, F., Waheed, F., Bojnec, Š., Khan, M. K., & Shaikh, S. (2022). Testing the Pollution Haven Hypothesis with the Role of Foreign Direct Investments and Total Energy Consumption. *Energies*, 15(11), 4046. DOI: 10.3390/en15114046

Delgado, F. J., Freire-Gonzãlez, J., & Presno, M. J. (2022). Environmental taxation in the European Union: Are there common trends? *Economic Analysis and Policy*, 73, 670–682. DOI: 10.1016/j.eap.2021.12.019

Deyganto, K. O. (2022). The effect of tax incentives practices on the sustainability of micro, small and medium enterprises in Ethiopia during the outbreak of corona virus pandemic. *Journal of Innovation and Entrepreneurship*, 11(1), 8. DOI: 10.1186/s13731-022-00194-8 PMID: 35106268

Dias, S. L., & Ribeiro, J. S. (2023). Taxation Policies as an Environmental Protection Instrument: The Portuguese Case. In Taking on Climate Change Through Green Taxation (pp. 265–281). IGI Global. DOI: 10.4018/978-1-6684-8592-7.ch011

Dinis, A., Carvalho, A., & Pereira, L. (2024). Forest Protection Tax Policy in the Context of Portuguese Societies. *Portuguese Review of Regional Studies*, 68(68), 68. Advance online publication. DOI: 10.59072/rper.vi68.584

Dinis, A. A. (2024). Promoting Fiscal Incentives for Urban Regeneration: Local Government Digital Presence. In Rocha, Á., Adeli, H., Dzemyda, G., Moreira, F., & Poniszewska-Marańda, A. (Eds.), *Good Practices and New Perspectives in Information Systems and Technologies* (Vol. 990, pp. 335–343). Springer Nature Switzerland., DOI: 10.1007/978-3-031-60328-0_34

Dinis, A. A., Carvalho, A., & Dias, S. L. (2023). Sustainable Taxi Fleet: An Approach to the Contribution of Green Taxation. In A. A. Dinis, F. David, L. Pereira, & S. L. Dias (Eds.), *Taking on Climate Change Through Green Taxation* (pp. 241–264). IGI Global. DOI: 10.4018/978-1-6684-8592-7.ch010

Dinis, A. A., & Pereira, L. (2022). Tax Incentives for Tourism: The Case of Portuguese Municipalities. In Costa, V., & Costa, C. (Eds.), *Advances in Hospitality, Tourism, and the Services Industry* (pp. 95–118). IGI Global., DOI: 10.4018/978-1-7998-9285-4.ch004

Economidou, M., Todeschi, V., Bertoldi, P., D'Agostino, D., Zangheri, P., & Castellazzi, L. (2020). Review of 50 years of EU energy efficiency policies for buildings. *Energy and Building*, 225, 110322. DOI: 10.1016/j.enbuild.2020.110322

Feng, P., Lu, H., Li, W., & Wang, X. (2022). Tax Policies of Low Carbon in China: Effectiveness Evaluation, System Design and Prospects. *Frontiers in Environmental Science*, 10, 953512. DOI: 10.3389/fenvs.2022.953512

Ghazouani, A., Xia, W., Ben Jebli, M., & Shahzad, U. (2020). Exploring the Role of Carbon Taxation Policies on CO2 Emissions: Contextual Evidence from Tax Implementation and Non-Implementation European Countries. *Sustainability (Basel)*, 12(20), 8680. DOI: 10.3390/su12208680

Glass, L.-M., & Newig, J. (2019). Governance for achieving the Sustainable Development Goals: How important are participation, policy coherence, reflexivity, adaptation and democratic institutions? *Earth System Governance*, 2, 100031. DOI: 10.1016/j.esg.2019.100031

Gonçalves, T., Dias, J., & Barros, V. (2022). Sustainability Performance and the Cost of Capital. *International Journal of Financial Studies*, 10(3), 63. DOI: 10.3390/ijfs10030063

Guo, B., Wang, Y., Feng, Y., Liang, C., Tang, L., Yao, X., & Hu, F. (2022). The effects of environmental tax reform on urban air pollution: A quasi-natural experiment based on the Environmental Protection Tax Law. *Frontiers in Public Health*, 10, 967524. DOI: 10.3389/fpubh.2022.967524 PMID: 36033767

Hafez, F. S., Sa'di, B., Safa-Gamal, M., Taufiq-Yap, Y. H., Alrifaey, M., Seyedmahmoudian, M., Stojcevski, A., Horan, B., & Mekhilef, S. (2023). Energy Efficiency in Sustainable Buildings: A Systematic Review with Taxonomy, Challenges, Motivations, Methodological Aspects, Recommendations, and Pathways for Future Research. *Energy Strategy Reviews*, 45, 101013. DOI: 10.1016/j.esr.2022.101013

Halim, M. A., & Rahman, M. M. (2022). The effect of taxation on sustainable development goals: Evidence from emerging countries. *Heliyon*, 8(9), e10512. DOI: 10.1016/j.heliyon.2022.e10512 PMID: 36105472

Han, H., & Lee, T. (2023). Varieties of Green Stimulus Policies: Comparative Analysis of the Green Growth and Green New Deal Policies in South Korea. *Journal of Environment & Development*, 32(1), 61–82. DOI: 10.1177/10704965221139303

Hassan, M., Oueslati, W., & Rousselière, D. (2020). Environmental taxes, reforms and economic growth: An empirical analysis of panel data. *Economic Systems*, 44(3), 100806. DOI: 10.1016/j.ecosys.2020.100806

He, Y., & Liu, R. (2023). The impact of the level of green finance development on corporate debt financing capacity. *Finance Research Letters*, 52, 103552. DOI: 10.1016/j.frl.2022.103552

Heide, M., Dudka, K. M., & Hauschild, M. Z. (2023). Absolute sustainable CO2-limits for buildings should reflect their function. A case study of four building typologies. *Developments in the Built Environment*, 15, 100175. DOI: 10.1016/j.dibe.2023.100175

Heidenthaler, D., Deng, Y., Leeb, M., Grobbauer, M., Kranzl, L., Seiwald, L., Mascherbauer, P., Reindl, P., & Bednar, T. (2023). Automated energy performance certificate based urban building energy modelling approach for predicting heat load profiles of districts. *Energy*, 278, 128024. DOI: 10.1016/j.energy.2023.128024

Ivanovic, O. M., & Golusin, M. (2012). Environmental Taxation as a Tool for Sustainable Development Policy-State Comparison of Serbia and Application of Ecological Taxation Reform in European Union. *Economic Analysis*, 45, 32–44.

Ji, C., Hong, T., Kim, H., & Yeom, S. (2022). Effect of building energy efficiency certificate on reducing energy consumption of non-residential buildings in South Korea. *Energy and Building*, 255, 111701. DOI: 10.1016/j.enbuild.2021.111701

Jiang, H.-D., Hao, W.-T., Xu, Q.-Y., & Liang, Q.-M. (2020). Socio-economic and environmental impacts of the iron ore resource tax reform in China: A CGE-based analysis. *Resources Policy*, 68, 101775. DOI: 10.1016/j.resourpol.2020.101775

Jonkutė, G., Norvaišienė, R., Banionis, K., Monstvilas, E., & Bliūdžius, R. (2021). Analysis of carbon dioxide emissions in residential buildings through energy performance certification in Lithuania. *Energy Sources. Part B, Economics, Planning, and Policy*, 16(2), 198–215. DOI: 10.1080/15567249.2020.1773581

Kim, K., Križnik, B., & Kamvasinou, K. (2021). Between the state and citizens: Changing governance of intermediary organisations for inclusive and sustainable urban regeneration in Seoul. *Land Use Policy*, 105, 105433. DOI: 10.1016/j.landusepol.2021.105433

Kluza, K., Ziolo, M., & Postula, M. (2024). Climate policy development and implementation from the Sustainable Development Goals perspective. Evidence from the European Union countries. *Energy Strategy Reviews*, 52, 101321. DOI: 10.1016/j.esr.2024.101321

Lei, Z., Huang, L., & Cai, Y. (2022). Can environmental tax bring strong porter effect? Evidence from Chinese listed companies. *Environmental Science and Pollution Research International*, 29(21), 32246–32260. DOI: 10.1007/s11356-021-17119-9 PMID: 35013959

Li, Z., & Zhou, Z. (2022). Research on the Impact Mechanism of Fiscal and Tax Policies on Carbon Emissions under the Dual Carbon Goals. *Frontiers in Business. Economics and Management*, 6(2), 32–37. DOI: 10.54097/fbem.v6i2.2637

Liu, Y., Sang, M., Xu, X., Shen, L., & Bao, H. (2023). How Can Urban Regeneration Reduce Carbon Emissions? A Bibliometric Review. *Land (Basel)*, 12(7), 1328. DOI: 10.3390/land12071328

Loganathan, N., Shahbaz, M., & Taha, R. (2014). The link between green taxation and economic growth on CO2 emissions: Fresh evidence from Malaysia. *Renewable & Sustainable Energy Reviews*, 38, 1083–1091. DOI: 10.1016/j.rser.2014.07.057

Mardones, C. (2022). Pigouvian taxes to internalize environmental damages from Chilean mining–A computable general equilibrium analysis. *Journal of Cleaner Production*, 362, 132359. DOI: 10.1016/j.jclepro.2022.132359

Mardones, C., & Baeza, N. (2018). Economic and environmental effects of a CO2 tax in Latin American countries. *Energy Policy*, 114, 262–273. DOI: 10.1016/j.enpol.2017.12.001

McGreal, S., Berry, J., Lloyd, G., & McCarthy, J. (2002). Tax-based Mechanisms in Urban Regeneration: Dublin and Chicago Models. *Urban Studies (Edinburgh, Scotland)*, 39(10), 1819–1831. DOI: 10.1080/0042098022000002975

Meireles, M., Robaina, M., & Magueta, D. (2021). The Effectiveness of Environmental Taxes in Reducing CO2 Emissions in Passenger Vehicles: The Case of Mediterranean Countries. *International Journal of Environmental Research and Public Health*, 18(10), 5442. DOI: 10.3390/ijerph18105442 PMID: 34069643

Mitić, P., Fedajev, A., & Kojić, M. (2023). Exploring the Economy – Environment Interactions in the Western Balkans. *Economic Analysis*, 56(1), 43–56. DOI: 10.28934/ea.23.56.1.pp43-56

Mpofu, F. Y. (2022). Green Taxes in Africa: Opportunities and Challenges for Environmental Protection, Sustainability, and the Attainment of Sustainable Development Goals. *Sustainability (Basel)*, 14(16), 10239. DOI: 10.3390/su141610239

Nobanee, H., & Ullah, S. (2023). Mapping green tax: A bibliometric analysis and visualization of relevant research. *Sustainable Futures : An Applied Journal of Technology, Environment and Society*, 6, 100129. DOI: 10.1016/j.sftr.2023.100129

Noubissi Domguia, E. (2023). Taxing for a better life? The impact of environmental taxes on income distribution and inclusive education. *Heliyon*, 9(11), e21443. DOI: 10.1016/j.heliyon.2023.e21443 PMID: 38027993

Nunes, P., Lerer, M. M., & Carrilho da Graça, G. (2013). Energy certification of existing office buildings: Analysis of two case studies and qualitative reflection. *Sustainable Cities and Society*, 9, 81–95. DOI: 10.1016/j.scs.2013.03.003

OECD. (2001). *Environmentally Related Taxes in OECD Countries: Issues and Strategies*. OECD., DOI: 10.1787/9789264193659-

Oueslati, W. (2014). Environmental tax reform: Short-term versus long-term macroeconomic effects. *Journal of Macroeconomics*, 40, 190–201. DOI: 10.1016/j.jmacro.2014.02.004

Picas, S., Reis, P., Pinto, A., & Abrantes, J. L. (2021). Does Tax, Financial, and Government Incentives Impact Long-Term Portuguese SMEs' Sustainable Company Performance? *Sustainability (Basel)*, 13(21), 11866. DOI: 10.3390/su132111866

Qi, Y., Zhang, J., & Chen, J. (2023). Tax incentives, environmental regulation and firms' emission reduction strategies: Evidence from China. *Journal of Environmental Economics and Management*, 117, 102750. DOI: 10.1016/j.jeem.2022.102750

Qiu, L. D., Zhou, M., & Wei, X. (2018). Regulation, innovation, and firm selection: The porter hypothesis under monopolistic competition. *Journal of Environmental Economics and Management*, 92, 638–658. DOI: 10.1016/j.jeem.2017.08.012

Qiu, Y., & Kahn, M. E. (2019). Impact of voluntary green certification on building energy performance. *Energy Economics*, 80, 461–475. DOI: 10.1016/j.eneco.2019.01.035

Raimundo, A. M., Sousa, A. M., & Oliveira, A. V. M. (2023). Assessment of Energy, Environmental and Economic Costs of Buildings' Thermal Insulation–Influence of Type of Use and Climate. *Buildings*, 13(2), 279. DOI: 10.3390/buildings13020279

Rodríguez, M., Robaina, M., & Teotónio, C. (2019). Sectoral effects of a Green Tax Reform in Portugal. *Renewable & Sustainable Energy Reviews*, 104, 408–418. DOI: 10.1016/j.rser.2019.01.016

Run, K., Cévaër, F., & Dubé, J.-F. (2023). Does energy-efficient renovation positively impact thermal comfort and air quality in university buildings? *Journal of Building Engineering*, 78, 107507. DOI: 10.1016/j.jobe.2023.107507

Sackitey, G. L. (2023). Do environmental taxes affect energy consumption and energy intensity? An empirical analysis of OECD countries. *Cogent Economics & Finance*, 11(1), 2156094. DOI: 10.1080/23322039.2022.2156094

Saka, C., Oshika, T., & Jimichi, M. (2020). Does Tax Avoidance Diminish Firms' Sustainability? *Journal Global Policy and Governance*, 8(2). Advance online publication. DOI: 10.14666/2194-7759-8-2-005

Shen, Y., & Zhang, X. (2022). Study on the Impact of Environmental Tax on Industrial Green Transformation. *International Journal of Environmental Research and Public Health*, 19(24), 16749. DOI: 10.3390/ijerph192416749 PMID: 36554630

Silva, B. V. F., Holm-Nielsen, J. B., Sadrizadeh, S., Teles, M. P. R., Kiani-Moghaddam, M., & Arabkoohsar, A. (2024). Sustainable, green, or smart? Pathways for energy-efficient healthcare buildings. *Sustainable Cities and Society*, 100, 105013. DOI: 10.1016/j.scs.2023.105013

Su, S., Qamruzzaman, M., & Karim, S. (2023). Charting a Sustainable Future: The Impact of Economic Policy, Environmental Taxation, Innovation, and Natural Resources on Clean Energy Consumption. *Sustainability (Basel)*, 15(18), 13585. DOI: 10.3390/su151813585

Tetiana, V., Samusevych, Y., Babenko, V., Bestuzheva, S., Bondarenko, S. A., & Nesterenko, I. (2023). Environmental Taxation: Role in Promotion of the Pro-Environmental Behaviour. *WSEAS Transactions On Business And Economics*, 20, 410–427. DOI: 10.37394/23207.2023.20.38

Tullock, G. (1967). The welfare costs of tariffs, monopolies, and theft. *Economic Inquiry*, 5(3), 224–232. DOI: 10.1111/j.1465-7295.1967.tb01923.x

(2023). Urban Systems and Other Settlements. InIntergovernmental Panel On Climate Change (IPCC) (Ed.), *Climate Change 2022—Mitigation of Climate Change* (1st ed., pp. 861–952). Cambridge University Press., DOI: 10.1017/9781009157926.010

Vaquero, P. (2020). Buildings Energy Certification System in Portugal: Ten years later. *Energy Reports*, 6, 541–547. DOI: 10.1016/j.egyr.2019.09.023

Wang, Z., Zhu, N., Wang, J., Hu, Y., & Nkana, M. (2022). The impact of environmental taxes on economic benefits and technology innovation input of heavily polluting industries in China. *Frontiers in Environmental Science*, 10, 959939. DOI: 10.3389/fenvs.2022.959939

Wu, W., Hu, Y., & Wu, Q. (2023). Subsidies and tax incentives - Does it make a difference on TFP? Evidences from China's photovoltaic and wind listed companies. *Renewable Energy*, 208, 645–656. DOI: 10.1016/j.renene.2023.03.080

Yang, L., Zhou, Y., Meng, B., Li, H., Zhan, J., Xiong, H., Zhao, H., Cong, W., Wang, X., Zhang, W., Lakshmanan, P., Deng, Y., Shi, X., Chen, X., & Zhang, F. (2022). Reconciling productivity, profitability and sustainability of small-holder sugarcane farms: A combined life cycle and data envelopment analysis. *Agricultural Systems*, 199, 103392. DOI: 10.1016/j.agsy.2022.103392

Yang, X., & Tang, W. (2023). Additional social welfare of environmental regulation: The effect of environmental taxes on income inequality. *Journal of Environmental Management*, 330, 117095. DOI: 10.1016/j.jenvman.2022.117095 PMID: 36584467

Yassaghi, H., & Hoque, S. (2019). An Overview of Climate Change and Building Energy: Performance, Responses and Uncertainties. *Buildings*, 9(7), 166. DOI: 10.3390/buildings9070166

Yi, Y., Wei, Z., & Fu, C. (2021). An optimal combination of emissions tax and green innovation subsidies for polluting oligopolies. *Journal of Cleaner Production*, 284, 124693. DOI: 10.1016/j.jclepro.2020.124693

Zhang, Y., Sun, J., Yang, Z., & Wang, Y. (2020). Critical success factors of green innovation: Technology, organization and environment readiness. *Journal of Cleaner Production*, 264, 121701. DOI: 10.1016/j.jclepro.2020.121701

Zhang, Y., Teoh, B. K., & Zhang, L. (2023). Exploring driving force factors of building energy use and GHG emission using a spatio-temporal regression method. *Energy*, 269, 126747. DOI: 10.1016/j.energy.2023.126747

Zhou, Z., Zhang, W., Pan, X., Hu, J., & Pu, G. (2019). Environmental Tax Reform and the "Double Dividend" Hypothesis in a Small Open Economy. *International Journal of Environmental Research and Public Health*, 17(1), 217. DOI: 10.3390/ijerph17010217 PMID: 31892259

ADDITIONAL READING

Alonso-Martinez, D., De Marchi, V., & Di Maria, E. (2021). The sustainability performances of sustainable business models. *Journal of Cleaner Production*, 323(129145), 129145. Advance online publication. DOI: 10.1016/j.jclepro.2021.129145

Antón, Á. (2022). EU energy taxation framework revision in the context of the green deal. *International Visual Culture Review, 9*(Monográfico), 1–13. DOI: 10.37467/revvisual.v9.3670

Li, Y., Mao, J., Chen, S., & Yang, D. (2022). Tax-reducing incentive and corporate green performance: What we learn from China. *Renewable Energy*, 199(April), 791–802. DOI: 10.1016/j.renene.2022.07.128

Mosquera Valderrama, I., & Balharová, M. (2021). *Tax Incentives in Developing Countries: A Case Study—Singapore and Philippines*. 119–147. DOI: 10.1007/978-3-030-64857-2_7

Panarello, D., & Gatto, A. (2023). Decarbonising Europe – EU citizens' perception of renewable energy transition amidst the European Green Deal. *Energy Policy*, 172, 113272. Advance online publication. DOI: 10.1016/j.enpol.2022.113272

Papadakis, N., & Al Katsaprakakis, D. (2023). A Review of Energy Efficiency Interventions in Public Buildings. *Energies*, 16(17), 6329. DOI: 10.3390/en16176329

Rahman, M. M. (2022). The effect of taxation on sustainable development goals: Evidence from emerging countries. *Heliyon*, 8(9), e10512. DOI: 10.1016/j.heliyon.2022.e10512 PMID: 36105472

Saad, N. (2014). Tax Knowledge, Tax Complexity and Tax Compliance: Taxpayers' View. *Procedia: Social and Behavioral Sciences*, 109, 1069–1075. DOI: 10.1016/j.sbspro.2013.12.590

Shafi, M., Ramos-Meza, C. S., Jain, V., Salman, A., Kamal, M., Shabbir, M. S., & Rehman, M. (2023). The dynamic relationship between green tax incentives and environmental protection. *Environmental Science and Pollution Research International*, 30(12), 32184–32192. DOI: 10.1007/s11356-023-25482-y PMID: 36723845

Uche, E., Narasingha, D., & Ngepah, N. (2024). Green environments reimagined through the lens of green finance, green innovations, green taxation, and green energies. Wavelet quantile correlation and rolling window-based quantile causality perspective. *Renewable Energy*, 120650, 120650. Advance online publication. DOI: 10.1016/j.renene.2024.120650

KEY TERMS AND DEFINITIONS

Climate Changes: A long-term alteration in global or regional climate patterns, primarily driven by human activities such as the burning of fossil fuels, deforestation, and industrial processes, which increase concentrations of greenhouse gases in the atmosphere, leading to changes in temperature, precipitation, and the frequency and intensity of extreme weather events.

Energy Consumption: The total amount of energy used by individuals, businesses, and industries to perform several activities and operations. This includes energy utilized for heating, cooling, transportation, manufacturing, and electricity generation.

Environmental Tax: A fiscal policy instrument designed to promote environmental sustainability by imposing levies on activities and products that cause environmental harm. This type of tax aims to internalize the external costs of environmental damage, incentivize the reduction of pollution, encourage the efficient use of natural resources, and support the transition to a greener economy. Examples include carbon taxes, energy taxes, and waste disposal fees.

Green Building: A structure designed, constructed, and operated to minimize environmental impacts and reduce energy consumption, often incorporating sustainable materials and energy-efficient technologies.

Greenhouse Gas (GHG) Emissions: Gases released into the atmosphere from human activities, such as carbon dioxide and methane, which contribute to global warming and climate change.

Sustainable Development: A holistic approach to growth and progress that aims to meet the needs of the present without compromising the ability of future generations to meet their own needs. It encompasses three interconnected pillars: economic growth, social inclusion, and environmental protection.

Taxation: The process by which a government imposes financial charges or levies on individuals, businesses, and other entities to generate revenue for public expenditures, including infrastructure, social services, and administrative functions. This system includes several forms of taxes, such as income tax, corporate tax, property tax, and value-added tax, which are essential for the functioning and development of a country's economy and society.

Urban Rehabilitation: The process of revitalizing and renewing urban areas that have experienced decline or deterioration. This involves a range of activities such as renovating buildings, improving infrastructure, enhancing public spaces, and promoting economic and social development.

ENDNOTES

1 Recognition of the rehabilitation intervention to apply the provisions of Article 45 of the TIS must be requested with the prior communication or the application for a license for the urban development operation. It is the responsibility of the competent municipal council or, where appropriate, the urban rehabilitation management entity to communicate this recognition to the tax office in the area where the building or fraction is located, within a maximum of 20 days from the date of determination of the state of repair resulting from the works or the issue of the respective energy certification.

Chapter 3
Challenges and Opportunities of the Autonomous Communities Financing Reform in Spain

Mónica García Freiría
https://orcid.org/0000-0002-6580-1787
University of Vigo, Spain

ABSTRACT

This chapter describes the main features of the current financing model of the Autonomous Communities of the common system in Spain. The Spanish lawmaker progressively promoted an increased fiscal co-responsability of the Autonomous Communities, in order that they could be provided with significant own resources enabling them to achieve their financial autonomy and sufficiency. However, the latest fundamental reform has proven to be inefficient and unfair. Thus, the current social and economic environment requires a deep reformulation of the existing legal framework of autonomous financing, in view to determine the scope and content of the asymmetrical fiscal power within a supranational integration system, such as the European Union. In this context is necessary to propose an amendment of the current financing model of the Autonomous Communities from the perspective of the public revenues which makes it compatible with the requirements of EU law in tax and budget matters.

DOI: 10.4018/979-8-3693-3908-4.ch003

INTRODUCTION

This paper aims to develop the essential lines that should be taken into consideration with respect to a future reform of the autonomous financing system in Spain.

With this objective, it will be carried out a general analysis of the main problems that can be found in the current financing system of the Autonomous Communities of the general regime. Specifically, there are several aspects of the current financing system that present some relevant problems: the financial balance between the State and the Autonomous Communities and the need for coordination between the different Treasurys; the impact of EU Law on the financing of the Autonomous Communities; the litigation around the tax resources of the Autonomous Communities; the difficulties when transferring certain tax figures from the State to the Communities and the impact of the shared taxes on tax competition; and, ultimately, the impact that the funds of the regional financing system have on the necessary financial balance between Autonomous Communities.

Therefore, the current social and economic environment requires a deep reformulation of the existing legal framework of autonomous financing, in view to determine the scope and content of the asymmetrical fiscal power within a supranational integration system, such as the European Union.

And, on the other hand, in this context is necessary to propose an amendment of the current financing model of the Autonomous Communities from the perspective of the public revenues which makes it possible to achieve a proper balance between the fiscal co-responsibility and the constitutional principles of tax justice and inter-territorial solidarity, compatible also with the requirements of EU law in tax and budget matters.

In this sense, each of the different problematic aspects will be analysed to provide possible solutions and recommendations for a future fiscal reform in Spain.

BACKGROUND

The last general review of the regional financing system occurred in 2009 with the approval of Law 22/2009. Since then, the political and economic context of Spain has changed. Therefore, the need to address a substantial reform of the regional financing system is currently an objective shared by various political and academic sectors.

Currently every five years the *Consejo de Política Fiscal y Financiera* assumes the role of updating the model to adapt it to the financial needs of the Autonomous Communities, which has normally led to the formulation of a new system of distribution every five years. Given this panorama, some authors consider necessary to establish a definitive distribution model of taxing powers.

In 2022, a report by a group of experts (known as the "White Book on tax reform" or *"Libro Blanco sobre la reforma tributaria"*)[1], proposed different measures to adapt the Spanish tax system to the 21st century. Its objective was to serve as the basis for a reform of the tax system that guarantees the sustainability of public finances so that it can respond to the financing of public expenses, contributing to reducing the structural deficit and the maintenance of the Welfare State.

With the imminent approval of a new model for regional financing in Spain, old and new reflections and proposals are gaining importance. This issue has a complex solution. However, as some authors have warned (González González, 2018, p. 177), the new reform of regional financing must pivot between financial sufficiency and tax autonomy.

Initially, with the Spanish Constitution of 1978, the main purpose of the financing system was to guarantee a sufficient level of income for the regional treasuries. In the beginning, the financing system of the regions in the common regime was based on lump-sum general grants. But, as some authors warned (López Laborda, Martínez Vázquez & Monasterio Escudero, 2023, p. 350), this approach had two very clear weaknesses. First, it tended to perpetuate whatever differences existed across regions under the centralized provision of services before their devolution to the regional governments. Thus, the approach did not guarantee an equal provision of public services. Second, the complete reliance on grants, as opposed to own taxes, meant that regional governments had practically no revenue autonomy. This blunted the greater efficiency and accountability benefits typically associated with fiscal decentralization. However, from the 1990s onwards, the need to also achieve fiscal co-responsibility was raised.

The financing model of the Autonomous Communities has undergone successive reforms. This makes it an open and flexible model but lacking in stability. Furthermore, these reforms have been accompanied by greater decentralization of income and an increase in revenues. In fact, with the advancement of the decentralization process, tax revenues have increased considerably. According to the OECD, the tax-to-GDP ratio in Spain has increased from 33.0% in 2000 to 37.5% in 2022. Spain ranked 13th out of 38 OECD countries in terms of the tax-to-GDP ratio in 2022. In 2022, Spain had a tax-to-GDP ratio of 37.5% compared with the OECD average of 34.0% (OECD, 2023).

But since 2009, when the current regional financing system came into force, a new model has not been approved. In 2017, the report known as *"Informe de la Comisión de Expertos sobre la reforma del sistema de financiación autonómica"* indicated that the main deficiencies of the financing system of the Autonomous Communities in force since 2009 were the following: i) the distribution of financing per inhabitant is unequal; ii) there is not enough fiscal responsibility for the CCAA; iii) there is no mechanism for vertical levelling of resources between Administrations; iv) the regulation of transferred taxes is defective; v) and there are problems in the collection of traditional transferred taxes (2017, p. 12). In addition, there are two other general problems such as the insufficient resources of the Autonomous Communities to maintain spending on public services and, on the other hand, the lack of responsibility of them in meeting stability objectives and controlling the public deficit (2017, p. 32).

As Menéndez Moreno (2023, p. 15) recognizes, these problems, despite having been warned in 2017, are fully current. And, following Lago Peñas (2019, p. 52), the OECD's effective measurement of tax autonomy places Spain first within the EU. This suggests that the focus should not be on increasing the extent of tax decentralisation in Spain but redesigning the context in which tax autonomy is exercised. To accomplish this, it is vital to tighten the so-called 'soft budget constraint' in the regional sphere and fine-tune most of the taxes transferred.

Furthermore, the impact of EU integration and the adoption of EU law on the tax system of the Member States and on the model of distribution of financial powers is evident. Specifically, two apparently opposing logics can be seen. On the one hand, the economic and market unity pursued by the EU. And, on the other, the fiscal decentralisation of some States such as Spain. In practice, the plurality of sources and the variable distribution of authority between the European Union and the Member States, and between the latter and their own sub-central entities, such as Autonomous Communities in Spain, give rise to different assumptions and levels of incidence of the limits envisaged by European Union Law (Ruíz Almendral, 2022b, p. 39). In this context, what is relevant is to determine the current legal contours within which the tax systems of Member States can develop. In fact, the 2022 White Book for tax reform has also stressed the need to better coordinate the exercise of tax powers in a multilevel setting. And this is a challenge for Spain in the coming years.

THE CONSTITUTIONAL FRAMEWORK OF THE FINANCIAL SYSTEM OF AUTONOMOUS COMMUNITIES IN SPAIN

As Ferreiro Lapatza (1984, pp. 326-327) stated, the expression "financing of the Autonomous Communities" refers to the system or set of means with which the Autonomous Communities that are part of the Spanish State obtain the necessary resources to carry out the tasks entrusted to them according to the plan reflected in a public budget. In a scheme where there is a central State, as well as autonomous territories with their own financial power, each of such entities must have their own resources. However, the specific forms of distribution of financial autonomy are very different. It is possible to distinguish at least two opposite systems: the separation system, or the union system.

In the first case, the different taxes are distributed between the central State and the autonomous territories, each one of them have its own taxes, and they are also independent to manage their own budget. On the contrary, in the union system, the central State has the exclusive competence to establish equal taxes throughout the national territory, as well as to collect them. In this way, the budgets of the autonomous territories must follow the guidelines of the central State. Likewise, between one model and another it is possible to identify mixed systems.

Within financial sovereignty, four fundamental elements are distinguished: legislative sovereignty, sovereignty over collection, administrative sovereignty regarding income and budgetary sovereignty. Different models emerge from the combination of these four elements depending on who they are attributed to.

It should be noted that the Spanish system can be described as mixed because it combines elements of the union system and the separation one.

The Spanish Constitution of 1978 recognizes in its article 2 the right to autonomy of nationalities and regions. Apart from the central State, Spain is organized territorially into Autonomous Communities and local corporations. Both central State and the Autonomous Communities have legislative power and competence to enact their own taxes. On the contrary, local corporations do not have legislative power and therefore require the State to provide for the specific framework of their resources.

After a decentralizing process, 17 Autonomous Communities were created, some belonging to the general regime and others to the special regime. This work will focus only on the first group. Although the Spanish Constitution does not contain any reference to the system of the State (centralised, unitary, federal, or regional), the level of decentralization of public expenditures and the taxation powers, is like that of many federal States. Given this multi-level structure, it should be noted that treasury issues are not the same in the framework of a federal State as in the framework of an unitary State.

In any case, and given the structure of the Spanish State, it is possible to affirm that it is included within the States that follow the scheme of fiscal federalism. According to Vanistendael (2011, p. 584), fiscal federalism is a concept which covers many ways of distributing taxing and spending power between various levels of government. In fact, there is no single model of fiscal federalism and there are also contradictory movements and many different stages in fiscal federalism. Moreover, federal fiscal powers include the power to tax, the power to expend, the power to coin money and the power to borrow. Spanish system includes all of them.

The overriding issue in fiscal federalism is referred to as the assignment problem, that is, the assignment of different relevant fiscal responsibilities to different orders of government (Tremblay, 2023, p. 7).

On the other hand, the financial power of the different entities refers to the power to emanate legal acts in the financial field and the power to apply them (Pita Grandal, 2003, p. 151). In particular, articles 148 and 149 of the Spanish Constitution delimit the financial power of the State and the Autonomous Communities.

The essence of any regional financing system is that spending needs are financed with two sources: resources from the country's own tax capacity and the equalization transfers of the central government. Therefore, describing the financing system requires knowing these elements.

Following Lago Peñas (2019, p. 54), on the expense side, only Canada, Switzerland, the US and Mexico are more decentralised than Spain. On the revenue side, Spain ranks sixth, just behind Australia and further behind Canada, Switzerland, Germany and the US[2]. In the European Union, Spain is currently the leader in effective tax decentralisation.

However, all countries falling under this category follow a similar structure which covers key questions on the structure of government and allocation of expenditure responsibilities, taxation responsibilities, intergovernmental fiscal transfers and revenue sharing, macroeconomic management, and ongoing challenges to their structure of fiscal federalism (Tremblay, 2023, p. 8). Likewise, there are many common challenges to fiscal federalism systems. Most importantly perhaps, achieving and maintaining fiscal balance, both vertically and horizontally, is a constant concern in most of the countries (Tremblay, 2023, p. 471).

An important feature of this state model is its asymmetry. This asymmetry is both *de facto* and *de jure* and explains the key role played by political agreements (Ruíz Almendral, 2002, p. 468).

Basic principles of the autonomic financial system

As Blasco Delgado (1996, p. 257) stated, every financing system must be inspired by basic principles that mark its trajectory and whose fulfilment it must aim for.

The 1978 Spanish Constitution establishes some general principles that refer to the relationship between the financial powers of the central State and Autonomous Communities and local governments. First, article 143 determines the recognition of financial autonomy for autonomous regions and nationalities, while articles 140 and 142 recognize the autonomy of municipalities and their financial sufficiency. Concretely, the exercise and recognition of the autonomy of Autonomous Communities is implemented by the approval of their Statutes of Autonomy[3], including the financial competences assumed by them. Otherwise, and following the article

138.1, the central State will guarantee the effective realization of the principle of solidarity among regions and nationalities[4]. And article 139 recognizes in section 1 the equality of rights and obligations for Spaniards in any part of the State. Its second section forbids public measures that hinder the free movement and establishment of persons or public measures that are against the free movement of goods throughout the territory. Concerning financial relationships between central and Autonomous Communities and local governments, article 149.1.14 establishes the exclusive competence of the central State on general financial affairs and matters of State debt. Specifically, article 133.1 recognizes the original power of the central State to establish taxes through law, while its second section recognizes that Autonomous Communities and local corporations may establish and require taxes according to the Constitution and laws. Likewise, article 138 of the Constitution recognizes the principle of solidarity among regions and nationalities.

Regarding the autonomous financing system of the Spanish State, both in the Constitution and in the Organic Law on Financing of the Autonomous Communities (*Ley Orgánica de Financiación de las Comunidades Autónomas* -LOFCA-), emphasis is placed on the following principles: financial sufficiency; financial autonomy; non-interference in the allocation of resources and in the national economy; and finally, that of solidarity.

The principle of financial sufficiency implies that each Autonomous Community must have sufficient resources to meet its expenses. This principle is included in article 2.1.d of the LOFCA when it provides that the financial activity of the Autonomous Communities will be carried out in coordination with the State Treasury.

Regarding the principle of financial autonomy, this implies that Communities must have certain sources of financing and the capacity to allocate the resources from these sources to certain objectives. This principle, contained in article 156 of the Spanish Constitution and article 1.1 of the LOFCA, supposes autonomy in income and expenses. García Prats (2011, 373) points out that financial autonomy entails the assumption of legislative power and administrative competences to enable its own system of resources and expenses to be set up. However, financial autonomy is linked to the material competences attributed to Autonomous Communities and is therefore considered to be instrumental.

From the point of view of the expenses, the Constitutional Court recognizes that financial autonomy encompasses the freedom of the governments of the Autonomous Communities to decide the destiny and orientation of the public expenses, and the quantification and distribution of the expenses within the framework of their competences[5]. While, and regarding resources, financial autonomy implies the ability to establish and require taxes, and to have access to a sufficient system of resources to attain the competences attributed to the Autonomous Communities, considering the real possibilities of the economic structure of the country as a whole. However, there are certain limits that must be followed[6].

In general terms, financial power of the Autonomous Communities extends to both their income and their expenses. LOFCA grants them the competence over the elaboration, analysis, approval and control of their own budget; the establishment and amendment of their own taxes, fees, and special contributions; the establishment and amendment of surcharges on state taxes, carrying out credit operations with certain restrictions and limitations; and the development of their own taxes. In this sense, autonomy has been understood as autonomy in spending and autonomy in income, without it being clear from the Constitution in which of these areas the greatest weight of the level of autonomy should fall (Pita Grandal, 2003, p. 162).

The principles of financial autonomy and sufficiency are closely connected. As Pita Grandal (1987, p. 141) pointed out, if one of the characteristics of financial autonomy is the existence of own resources and decision-making capacity over the use of these resources, the principle of sufficiency guarantees the realization of the content of financial autonomy.

Furthermore, and as Lago Peñas (2019, p. 52) acknowledges, significant vertical imbalances between decentralised expenses and revenue sources undermine fiscal stability and generate higher public deficits. Given this situation, and as Ruíz Almendral (2012, p. 98) recognizes, the problem must be resolved, and the allocation of resources must be "re-balanced". Vertical Fiscal Imbalance can be solved either through transfers from the State or through a reassignment of taxation powers. In practice, a mix of the two will be used, so that most sub-national governments receive financing in the form of both transfers and own taxes. Likewise, there may also be horizontal fiscal imbalance, but it is much harder to solve than the vertical one. Because an increase of sub-national taxation systems will normally make horizontal fiscal imbalance more obvious -richer regions also have higher taxing capacity- (Ruíz Almendral, 2012, p. 99).

As regards the principle of non-interference in the allocation of resources in the national economy, it means that the financing system of the Autonomous Communities will not foster the existence of economic and social privileges, either fiscal barriers that prevent the free movement of people and productive factors throughout the national territory. This principle is regulated in the article 157.2 of the Spanish Constitution and in the article 2.1.a) of LOFCA.

Likewise, the principle of solidarity means, on the one hand, the existence of a balance between the different territories that make up the State, as well as equality in the provision of services in those territories. This is stated in the article 158 of the Constitution and in the article 2.1, sections b) and c) of the LOFCA.

However, according to García Prats (2011, pp. 376-377), the limits to the exercising of the financial competences of Autonomous Communities derive from the principles of instrumentality, solidarity, and unity of the Nation. First, instrumentality principle imposes a link between the financial competences and the material competences of each Autonomous Community, which requires exercising the financial competences, mainly on the expenses side, within the framework of material competences. But also recognizes such competence as a basic guarantee of the exercise of political autonomy. Meanwhile, the resources side is achieved through the impulse of the sufficiency principle. In second place, solidarity principle entails that Autonomous Communities must refrain from adopting decisions or acts that may harm the general interest. But it also entails the obligation of the central state to adopt measures to ensure the redistribution of wealth among the different Autonomous Communities and the provision of basic or essential public services on equal levels. Finally, unity principle serves the purpose of counterbalancing the right of autonomy and loyalty to the State.

And, as Calvo Ortega (2008, pp. 10-13) points out, the principles of article 31 of the Constitution also have a guiding function for autonomic financing system. In particular, the principle of economic capacity, the principle of tax equality and the principle of legality.

On the other hand, article 156 of the Constitution includes the principle of coordination which constitutes a requirement derived from the existence of several tax powers in the same territory. With this objective, LOFCA created different bodies for the coordination of budgetary policy and fiscal measures like the so-called *Consejo de Política Fiscal y Financiera*.

The regional financing system has evolved over the years following a decentralizing process and in which several stages are differentiated. However, and following some authors, the different reforms on the financing model have been superficial. According to García Prats (2011, p. 374), the evolution has been from a "system of transfers from the central state to the autonomous communities" to a system that is more oriented towards so-called "fiscal joint responsibility" or "fiscal co-responsibility" (*corresponsabilidad fiscal*).

Through fiscal co-responsibility, the aim is to promote the responsibility of the Autonomous Communities over their own sources of income, which over time should lead to a balance between their income and expenses and, therefore, a reduction in the deficit (García Novoa, 1998, p. 126).

However, it has been said that the reason that explains why deep reforms in Spain have not been that the Autonomous Communities do not have the same point of view regarding the need to increase their degree of fiscal joint responsibility (Blasco Delgado, 1996, p. 264). In the same way that the Autonomous Communities enjoy a wide margin in relation to spending decisions, it is necessary to increase their decision-making possibilities in relation to sources of income and graduate their contribution to their respective treasuries. Specifically, this concept refers to the correspondence between the decision-making capacity over income and the decision-making capacity over expenses. In short, increasing fiscal joint responsibility means that Communities are not passive in obtaining resources to finance their expenses, that is, that they stop being recipients of State income and adopt a dynamic role in obtaining income. In fact, there are different ways to increase the degree of fiscal joint responsibility of the Autonomous Communities: (i) increase the scope of their yielded taxes; (ii) increase their own taxes; or (iii) attribute to them a part of the income from some state taxes in their territories -surcharges on state taxes and participation on state resources-. For example, from Blasco Delgado's point of view, the third way would be the most appropriate to increase the degree of fiscal joint responsibility (1996, p. 266).

However, as Menéndez Moreno (2023, p. 16) recognizes, fiscal co-responsibility has advantages since it provides transparency. But it also has drawbacks since the greater regulatory capacity of the CCAA makes the system more complex and generates territorial inequalities.

In general terms, the most important reform of the financial system occurred in 2009, which involved an increase in the percentages of yielded taxes, an expansion of the regulatory capacity over yielded taxes, as well as the modification of some state funds aimed at compensating the inequalities of resources of the different Autonomous Communities. Most Communities employed their newly enlarged taxing powers to establish tax deductions and thus lowered the tax pressure in their territories.

Any tax reform must consider its impact and consequences on subnational entities based on the principles of cooperation and coordination between the State and the Autonomous Communities[7]. In this way, financial autonomy as well as the high decentralization of public income and expenditure in Spain require that the proposed tax reform consider the current distribution of powers. It is not, however, a comprehensive reform of the current system but rather improving the levelling mechanisms and modifying some of the tax resources of the Autonomous Communities. Any reform proposal revolves around two axes: attributing greater importance to the tax revenues of the Autonomous Communities or, on the contrary, to transfers or allocations from the State.

In short, when establishing new measures to reform the regional financing system, the principle of financial sustainability must be kept in mind. The new system must aim to achieve vertical financial balance between the three levels of government: state, regional and local (Ramos Prieto *et al.*, 2019, p. 11). This implies evaluating the overall distribution of spending between the different Treasurys if an equitable distribution of economic resources is to be achieved, and reviewing the current model of distribution of powers and, therefore, public spending.

Despite the financial autonomy of the Autonomous Communities, the principles of coordination and solidarity act as limits to this autonomy. According to Ramos Prieto *et al.* (2019, pp. 13-14), an important aspect of the reform of the financing system would be to define the levelling mechanisms that guarantee the principle of solidarity. In accordance with this principle, it is up to the State to carry out spending actions that erode possible interterritorial economic imbalances. Furthermore, this principle requires financial levelling between the different autonomous treasuries, so the resource system of the Autonomous Communities must be configured in such a way that, whatever their fiscal capacity, they can provide a similar level of public services. In relation to this aspect, there are two possibilities: a total levelling that covers all public services or, on the contrary, a partial levelling limited to fundamental public services such as health, education, or social services. On the other hand, solidarity implies that the Communities must refrain from adopting decisions or acts that harm the general interest, that is, the goal is to avoid unfair tax competition between them.

The financial and tax powers of the Autonomous Communities of common regime: resources

The article 157.1 of the Spanish Constitution sets out a general composition of the resources of Autonomous Communities: yielded state taxes, surcharges on state taxes, other participations in state resources, own taxes (classified as taxes, fees, and special contributions[8]), and other assignations on account of the general state budget, wealth revenue, private law income, credit/debit income[9], fees from penalties and sanctions and public fees, and attribution of income in the general budget and transfers from an interterritorial compensation fund (among others). As Tejerizo López (2004, p. 22) stated, the Spanish Constitution established a financing system based on taxes (*"tributos"*), while other sources of financing such as property income or credit have much less importance in sustaining public needs.

On the other hand, the second section of the same constitutional provision delimits the financial power of the Autonomous Communities by pointing out that they will not be able to adopt tax measures on goods located outside their territory or that represent an obstacle to the free movement of goods or services.

Finally, the third section of the article recognizes the harmonizing power of the State and establishes the possibility for an organic act to regulate the exercise of the financial powers derived from article 157. In fact, this possibility has been become a reality through the so-called LOFCA (*Ley Orgánica de Financiación de las Comunidades Autónomas*) that was originally approved by Organic Law 8/1980, but this has been subsequently amended by Organic Laws 3/1996, 7/2001 and 3/2009. LOFCA establishes the general criteria to which the Autonomous Communities of the general regime must submit in relation to their incomes and their expenses. Nevertheless, this Law leaves aside the relationship with the Communities that enjoy a specific charter regime (known as *fueros*).

As the Spanish Constitutional Court has recognized, the State is competent to regulate not only its own taxes, but also the general framework of the entire tax system and the delimitation of the financial powers of the Autonomous Communities[10].

On the other hand, article 158.1 of the Constitution establishes that in the General Budgets of the State an allocation may be established to the Autonomous Communities based on the volume of state services and activities that they have assumed, and the guarantee of a minimum level in the provision of fundamental public services throughout the Spanish territory.

According to Ferreiro Lapatza (1984, p. 331), articles 157 and 158 of the Constitution establish a system of financing the autonomies that it can described as mixed since it combines elements of the union system and the separation one.

Own taxes

The Autonomous Communities have regulatory powers for the establishment, regulation, modification, and elimination of their own taxes, as well as the administrative powers for their application (management, collection and inspection), administrative review, the exercise of sanctioning power and the ownership of performance -Articles 17. b), 19. Uno and 20. Uno of LOFCA-.

The exercise by the Autonomous Communities of its own competence in establishing taxes is subject to various limits. According to article 9 of LOFCA there are two limitations: (i) it is not possible to tax assets located, or income originated, or expenses made outside the territory of the respective Autonomous Community; and (ii) it will not be possible to tax business, acts or facts celebrated or performed outside the territory of the respective Autonomous Community. Moreover, article 6 of LOFCA prohibits double taxation derived from the exercise of the tax power by the Autonomous Communities regarding state taxes and local taxes[11].

Article 6.3 of LOFCA[12] points out that the taxes established by the Autonomous Communities may not fall on taxable facts taxed by local taxes. But it immediately points out that the Autonomous Communities may establish and manage taxes on the matters that the Local Regime legislation reserves for local Corporations. In any case, appropriate compensation or coordination measures must be established in favour of those Corporations, so that the income of such Local Corporations is not diminished or reduced in their possibilities of future growth. Likewise, regional taxes cannot be levied on taxable events already taxed by the State. For its part, the state tax jurisdiction does not have these limitations, so it may dictate state taxes with taxable events like those of regional taxes.

As Lasarte López (2017, p. 180) has pointed out, the interpretation of this article continues to generate controversies that are raised before the Constitutional Court.

However, and in order not to economically harm the regional coffers, the State must compensate the Autonomous Communities. Specifically, two requirements must be met to activate the compensation clause: on the one hand, the previous regional tax must have a taxable event like that of the new state tax and, on the other hand, the suspension of the pre-existing regional tax must imply a decrease in income of the Autonomous Community. Although the compensation clause has been incorporated into the LOFCA since its inception, until 2012 there was no need to use it. Many state taxes that are activating the compensation clause have ecological connotations and try to align with the environmental objectives of the EU. Following Salassa Boix (2023, p. 227), the minimal legislative details on how to apply the compensation clause of the LOFCA in favour of the regional treasury and the limited jurisprudential interpretation, because of its lack of application, place us before an uncertain and challenging legal scenario for the coming years.

Although LOFCA recognizes the possibility of creating its own taxes, this category is residual from an economic point of view and generates too many conflicts from a legal point of view (Lago Montero, 2017, pp. 15-16). These taxes have very little collection capacity since most of the potential taxable facts are already taxed by local authorities or by central authorities (income, consumption, ownership of assets and traffic of goods and services). And its effectiveness in terms of environmental policy is also highly questionable (López Díaz, 2013, p. 243). Specifically, the tax revenues corresponding to the Autonomous Communities of the common regime barely amount to 2% of the total regional revenues. The taxes of the Autonomous Communities refer to different matters such as the environment, the betting, gaming and lotteries sector, the water or water pollution and other polluting activities, different energy uses, etc[13]. Specifically, these are taxes at the service of social and economic policy objectives.

However, many of these taxes have been declared unconstitutional by the Constitutional Court[14] which affects the legal security of taxpayers. Likewise, the greatest collection importance in the respective budgets of the Autonomous Communities falls on taxes (*impuestos*) and fees (*tasas*), since special contributions (*contribuciones especiales*) are a figure very rarely used at the autonomic level. Finally, the surcharges on state taxes have not been successful since they currently do not exist in any Community (especially due to the taxpayer's resistance to its acceptance). Instead, the cases of yielded taxes have increased, and the Communities have assumed more regulatory powers over some state taxes[15].

The situation described has led to a multi, disorderly, and unsystematic imposition. For this reason, some authors (Lago Montero, 2017, p. 22) have offered two possible solutions: a) that the State renounces the taxable spaces occupied by the Communities, but with a design in the LOFCA that regulates the structural elements of these taxes and that the Communities will be able to develop with their own acts creating new taxes but harmonized on a state basis; or b) that the Autonomous Communities withdraw from these taxable areas and the State exercises its tax power creating state taxes that then transfer the collection or management, including certain regulatory power, to Communities and local entities. From the point of view of a certain sector of doctrine (Ramos Prieto *et al.*, 2019, p. 25), the best solution would be to homogenize regional environmental taxation by establishing state tax figures in which collection is transferred, but with limited regulatory powers for the Autonomous Communities. This would reduce the risks of possible lack of coordination.

As the most important doctrine recognized, the same taxable fact should not be subject to multiple taxation. The criterion of rationality that permeates the entire tax system opposes this, as well as the need for an equitable distribution of the tax burden among taxpayers (Lasarte, 1979, p. 431). However, currently the Spanish system is characterized by a certain lack of coordination of the different tax powers.

The conclusion that must be reached is that a power to create taxes with limitations on the choice of taxable facts does not determine the creation of an autonomous tax system, but rather an unconnected series of very different figures. Thus, the situation in Spain is very different from that of the United States where a clear distribution of tax figures is established between the Federation and the States (García Novoa, 2008, p. 424).

The problem is that the State began to legislate taxes decisively environmental, that is, with an indisputable extra-fiscal purpose. This complicates the regional initiatives to legislate ecological taxes with facts similar to state ones. As Salassa Boix (2022, p. 75) recognizes, there is a danger of extinction of the tax jurisdiction of the Autonomous Communities. Therefore, it is easy to imagine that environmental taxation in Spain will be marked by a majority presence of state taxes in the future (Salassa Boix, 2022, p. 103).

This is why some authors consider that the State should free certain taxable matters so that they could be taxed by the Autonomous Communities (Ribes Ribes, 2018, p. 219). This would involve strengthening the regulatory capacity of the Autonomous communities.

At the present, there is a need for a clearer design of the taxable space for the Autonomous Communities in which it does not conflict with either the State or local entities. This should be kept in mind for a future reform of the financing system in Spain. In fact, this need for coordination between the State and the CCAA was also highlighted in the report of the Committee of Experts for the Reform of the Spanish tax system (2022, p. 218).

Despite the situation, we agree with Ribes Ribes (2018, p. 213) that greater autonomy should be granted in the income of autonomous entities.

Yielded taxes

In practice, the tax autonomy of the Autonomous Communities has been developed to a greater extent through the transfer of taxes. Yielded taxes are originally taxes enacted and established by the State which are transferred to Autonomous Communities. The transfer can be total or partial and, therefore, there are fully yielded taxes and partially yielded taxes. Apart from the administrative competences and the collection of the amount of tax, Autonomous Communities were entitled to introduce certain normative amendments in the regulation of the yielded taxes in accordance with the Yielded Taxes Act of 30 of December (*Ley 14/1996 de Cesión de Tributos*), enabling Communities to establish their own rates and deductions for some important taxes. However, the concretion of the yielded taxes corresponds exclusively to the central State, which, according to the Constitutional Court, implies that the formulation of a list of yielded taxes by a Statute of Autonomy has no binding effect on the State.

On the other hand, it is necessary to determine what the concept of yield means in Spanish context. As Lasarte (1979, pp. 421-422) has stated, this concept refers to taxes created by a state act, managed by the central administration, whose collection is transferred to the Autonomous Communities by the own State in compliance with its duty to protect their financial autonomy. However, the State can also transfer not only the collection, but also the management. Although it is also possible that yielded taxes involve the exercise of certain normative competences on the tax structure.

Nowadays the exercise of these regulatory powers represents the main manifestation of the tax power of the Autonomies. Articles 19.2 LOFCA and 45 to 53 of Law 22/2009 establish the limits within which this competence will be exercised. The percentage of the collection that is transferred is established, in general, for each tax, in articles 30 to 44 of Law 22/2009. Along with the scope of the transfer, the connection points (or connecting factors) are also established, which are objective criteria that determine which Autonomous Community exercises the transferred regulatory competence and to which the collection is attributed. For example, the Communities have exercised regulatory powers in personal income tax, inheritance and gift tax and wealth tax. In these years, not only has the number of taxes transferred increased, but also the percentage of transfers. In Spain, the gambling tax, the inheritance and gift tax, the wealth tax, the onerous property transfers tax, or the tax on electricity are totally transferred taxes. Meanwhile, personal income tax, VAT, or special taxes are partially transferred. The taxes that have not been transferred are corporate tax, non-resident income tax, insurance premium tax and customs duties.

What must be clear is that a greater transfer of taxes is not incompatible with the fact that the Autonomous Community makes solidarity contributions (Rodríguez Márquez, 2009, p. 245). In fact, the principle of solidarity not only projects its demands in the relations between the State and the Autonomous Communities, but also in their relations with each other.

In particular, the expansion of these regulatory powers has allowed a greater development of the financial autonomy of the Communities, but at the same time poses the challenge of the greater need for coordination. In this sense, regulatory harmonization has even been proposed, as well as the creation of a commission to control regional tax regulations, by the expert committee for the reform of the regional financing system of 2017. However, many Autonomous Communities (such as Andalucía, Madrid, Murcia, Galicia, or Castilla y León) have opposed restricting the current scope of their regulatory powers in the wealth tax and the inheritance and gift tax.

Following Menéndez Moreno (2010, p. 7), since that Autonomous Communities have expanded their financial powers, it is logical that they need more resources to cover their own expenses. However, the increase in the percentages of transfer of State taxes is not linked to the higher expenses of each Community, but rather to their political pressure on the central government. In addition, and since the Communities hardly have their own taxes, the consequence is that the regional administrations provide the services and the central State covers the cost of them, making it difficult to achieve egalitarian public services throughout the Spanish territory.

As Ramos Prieto *et al.* (2019, p. 25) state, there is an increasing tendency to establish regional tax incentives in favour of cultural, sports or scientific patronage. To avoid a lack of coordination within the system, greater control over its collection costs would be desirable so that citizens are aware of the economic effects of such measures.

Furthermore, and regarding the future of yielded taxes, some authors have wondered if these should be classified as own taxes, converting some taxes totally transferred to the Autonomous Communities, such as taxes on gambling, into own taxes (Ramos Prieto *et al.*, 2019, p. 29). In fact, as Ribes Ribes (2018, p. 217) states, this proposal would contribute to increasing the financial autonomy of the regional governments in terms of income. However, and given that the current taxes have a very important redistributive effect, it would be advisable to maintain them as yielded taxes since they could always be recovered by the State if any Community decided to derogate them (Calvo Ortega, 2008, p. 16).

On the other hand, it is also asked whether it would be convenient to establish the partial transfer of corporate tax to the Communities becoming a shared collection tax. In this case, the competence could be attributed to the Community where the company has its domicile. In this sense, Autonomous Communities could attract investments to their territories, but this solution would be problematic from the perspective of solidarity principle (Calvo Ortega, 2008, p. 22). Therefore, and although a potential transfer of the tax would increase the resources of the regional treasuries due to its collection potential, it could generate numerous problems. Furthermore, there would be difficulties in establishing simple, objective distribution criteria that do not generate distortions. Regarding customs imposition, the transfer would not be possible since it is the EU that establishes the common customs tariff. And, finally, in the income tax of non-residents there are also difficulties in transferring its collection since certain criteria would have to be established, which is not easy. And there could also be harmful tax competition between Communities, as occurs in the inheritance tax.

Finally, there is a structural problem to which some doctrine has referred, which is the lack of fiscal responsibility demonstrated by Autonomous Communities. The autonomies have generally been reluctant to use their taxing powers to raise revenue, and instead relied on government transfers or public debt, thereby avoiding the political cost of increasing tax pressure (Ruíz Almendral, 2013, p. 199). In fact, many Autonomous Communities have amended their tax benefits in the inheritance and gift tax, even with 99% bonuses in the quota, in a race to the bottom that shows the tax competition between them. And, regarding the personal income tax, the regulatory power of the Autonomous Communities has led to the creation of numerous deductions on the quota that reduce collection and harm the principles of tax justice.

In short, practice shows that the Autonomous Communities continue to depend on the State, since they have not used their greater autonomy to solve their financial insufficiency problems but have reduced direct taxes and increased indirect taxes. And this is not a reasoned exercise of its regulatory powers with the aim of achieving fiscal co-responsibility, but rather a short-term approach (Ribes Ribes, 2018, pp. 212-213).

Therefore, neither through the transferred taxes nor through their own taxes has a true co-responsibility been achieved. On the contrary, the transferred taxes have been used to grant tax benefits, generating fiscal competition to the downside. On the other hand, the Autonomous communities tend to increase their spending, demanding resources from the central State or resorting to indebtedness (González González, 2018, p. 187).

Surcharges on state taxes

From the beginning, the surcharges opened an interesting avenue for the development of financial autonomy and fiscal co-responsibility of the regional treasuries, allowing them to obtain additional revenues. The establishment of surcharges constitutes the upward modification of the rate or tax rate of a tax over which the Autonomous Community has recognized regulatory competence, except for the special excise duty on retail hydrocarbon sales. For VAT and other excise duties, the possibility is only recognized on those taxes for which the Autonomous Community has tax competences on the regulation of the tax rates.

Nowadays, Autonomous Communities have not normally used this possibility. Furthermore, the collection capacity of these tax resources is very limited. Nevertheless, some doctrine considers that if these had become the most important source of financing for the Autonomous Communities, the Spanish tax system would be less complex (Tejerizo López, 2004, p. 32).

However, as Ribes Ribes (2018, p. 218) states, the actions of the Autonomous Communities through the establishment of surcharges can distort the structure of these taxes. For example, in the case of personal income tax there could be an increase in progressivity.

Funds

Since Organic Law 6/2009, the funds foreseen in LOFCA are the following: (i) Interterritorial Compensation Fund (*Fondo de Compensación Interterritorial*); (ii) Fund for the Guarantee of Fundamental Public Services (*Fondo de Garantía de Servicios Públicos Fundamentales*); (iii) Global Sufficiency Fund (*Fondo de Suficiencia Global*); and (iv) Autonomous Convergence Funds (*Fondos de Convergencia Autonómica*). The aim of the first one is to correct inter-territorial economic imbalances and make the principle of solidarity effective, by financing investment projects, and its resources will be provided annually by the State in its General Budget. The second one establishes a guarantee of a basic equivalent level of financing for fundamental public services (education, health, and essential social services). The third fund covers the difference between the expense requirements and the tax capacity of each Autonomous Community and the transfers of the previous fund, trying to ensure their sufficient financing. Its purpose is to guarantee the *statu quo* clause. The fourth fund aims to reinforce the equity and efficiency of the financing system reducing the per capita attribution of resources to each Autonomous Community, discouraging the race to the bottom as regards tax competition.

Finally, in 2012 two extraordinary financing mechanisms were created: the Fund for Financing Payments to Suppliers (*Fondo para la Financiación de los Pagos a Proveedores*) and the Regional Liquidity Fund (*Fondo de Liquidez Autonómica*). The objective of these funds was to provide liquidity to the territorial Administrations, reducing the cost of resorting to public debt. However, and due to the degree of interference of the State in the autonomous financial autonomy, the doctrine is in favour of cancelling the debt assumed by the regional Treasury with the State and eliminating these funds so that the Communities can finance themselves.

The Fundamental Public Services Guarantee Fund responds to the principle of interterritorial financial solidarity. This fund is endowed each year with 75% of the tax capacity of each of the Autonomous Communities and with an additional contribution from the State equivalent to 5% of the total resources of the Fund. The remaining 25% of the collection from transferred taxes obtained by each Community is not subject to contribution to the fund and belongs to the corresponding Autonomous Community. The fund is distributed among the different Autonomous Communities based on a series of criteria such as population, surface area, geographical dispersion, population over 65 years of age, etc. Thus, when the need for financing fundamental public services is greater than its tax capacity, the Autonomous Community will receive a transfer for the difference. On the other hand, if the difference is negative, the Autonomous Community will have to make a transfer to the fund.

As some doctrine has warned, the fund presents three problems: firstly, and because of the economic crisis that began in 2008, there was a significant decrease in the collection of yielded taxes; secondly, the criteria are not always the most appropriate; and, thirdly, the Autonomous Communities with a special regime (País Vasco and Navarra) should also provide resources to the fund.

Regarding the Global Sufficiency Fund, it presents two problems: the *statu quo* clause perpetuates the financing differences between Autonomous Communities that already existed in the past and, on the other hand, the fund distorts the distribution criteria of the Fundamental Public Services Guarantee Fund, by equalizing spending needs with tax capacity plus transfers of the first fund, increasing the differences between Communities.

Among the regional convergence funds are the Competitiveness Fund and the Cooperation Fund. The first of them is provided with additional resources by the State and tries to guarantee that those Communities whose resources per capita are lower than the average, considering the fiscal capacity of the Autonomous Communities, increase their resources. It aims to prevent the Autonomous Communities with greater fiscal capacity from being underfinanced. The Cooperation Fund seeks to balance and harmonize regional development but has been highly criticized because it distorts the convergence achieved with the Fundamental Public Services Guarantee Fund.

Finally, the Interterritorial Compensation Funds are of great importance in the financing of the Autonomous Communities, since they pursue the development of the least favoured with respect to investment in public goods and services, increasing their rent per capita and approaching them closer to the average of the Autonomous Communities as a whole. The funds are intended for investment expenses in comparatively less developed territories.

The problems they raise are mentioned in the 2017 Report (*"Informe de la Comisión de Expertos sobre la reforma del sistema de financiación autonómica"*). Firstly, the economic under-provision of the funds; secondly, the distribution criteria between Autonomous Communities are not correctly weighted; and, thirdly, greater coordination is necessary between the EU's regional development policies through the different European funds and the objectives of the Interterritorial Compensation Funds.

However, the impact that the State's assumption of regional debt may have in the medium and long term should be reflected on.

As González González (2018, p. 187) has warned, the operation of the different funds with which the system was provided has made it more complex, lacking transparency and has not managed to solve all the problems for which it was created.

In 2018, Spain exited the EU's Excessive Deficit Procedure, as its deficit was below the European reference value of 3% of GDP. However, several regional governments are still excessively dependent on the Regional Liquidity Fund and should reduce their high level of indebtedness, due to the high-interest rate risk they will face when the ECB proceeds to normalize interest rates, with the consequent effect on the cost of debt (López Laborda, Martínez Vázquez & Monasterio Escudero, 2023, p. 376). From the point of view of macroeconomic management, the Fund for Financing Autonomous Communities should be reformed to stop financing deficit deviations.

These references to the Constitution have been intended to reflect the constitutional framework of the financial power of the Autonomous Communities. Next it is convenient to make a reference to the conditions imposed by European integration.

THE AUTONOMIC FINANCIAL SYSTEM AND THE RESTRAINTS IMPOSED BY EUROPEAN INTEGRATION

According to Vanistendael (2011, p. 586), in a structure of multi-level government, attention will be paid to (i) the assignment of expenditures among different levels of government in providing public goods and services (defence, education and research, public health, social protection, infrastructure, etc); (ii) the financing of expenditures through taxes and the corresponding assignment of revenue raising responsibility to different levels of government; (iii) the inter-governmental transfers in the form of revenue sharing, conditional and unconditional grants, and the related problems of horizontal and vertical equity of the (re-)distribution of inter-governmental transfers; (iv) the multi-level administrative control on expenditures; and (v) the role of central and sub-central borrowing in the financing expenditures. In fact, this is particularly relevant in the EU context if we want to understand the relationship between the Member States and the EU.

No tax system is any more strictly national since the interdependence of States is increasing. In particular, Spain is integrated into a globalized economy, has a highly decentralized structure of distribution of powers and is part of the EU. Furthermore, the tax system must adapt to the continuous development of European regulations.

As Tejerizo López (2015, 24-25) has stated, the limits of the taxing power of the Autonomous Communities come from the Spanish Constitution and the rules of the European Union. Although it is true that are the Member States, and not the sub-central entities or regions, that are directly bound by European Law, the impact of EU Law on the Autonomous Communities is evident. Among the limits on taxation power arising from EU law are the freedom of movement of goods, the freedom of movement of persons, the freedom of establishment, the freedom to provide services and the freedom of movement of capital. As Ruíz Almendral (2022b, p. 45) states, the EU taxation legal framework is particularly permeated by the four fundamental freedoms.

From the analysis of the Spanish public revenue system, it can be seen that it is influenced by the construction of the EU internal market based on provisions such as the prohibition of tariffs; the prohibition of establishing discriminatory taxes on production; the limits derived from the harmonization Directives of some indirect taxes; the prohibition of state aid, etc. However, the deep decentralization of spending means that still exists a wide imbalance between income and expenses in the public budget of the Autonomous Communities.

Thus, and following Tejerizo López (2015, 26), the Autonomous Communities cannot create taxes that restrict the freedoms recognized by EU Law. In fact, a possible increase in the tax power of the Autonomous Communities, through their own taxation or through regulatory powers in the transferred taxes, could increase the potential situations of state aid incompatible with EU Law. Although it is true that article 107.3 of the TFEU admits that selective regional aid may be compatible if its objective is to compensate for regional differences.

In short, the limitations on the taxation powers of the Autonomous Communities derive not only from the freedoms mentioned, but also from the tax harmonisation of the Directives, and from the prohibition of adopting measures that imply harmful tax competition (Tejerizo López, 2015, 62). The most tangible consequence of tax harmonisation is the requirement for Member States to establish harmonised taxes in their territory, as well as the impossibility of establishing taxes equivalent to them (Ruíz Almendral, 2022b, p. 51).

There are three key elements in the reform of the financing system in a multilevel context like the Spanish one: the international context, the integration into the EU and the internal decentralization of the Spanish system.

Therefore, the reform proposed must consider both the limitations and opportunities arising from the European context. On the other hand, the intense decentralization of public income and expenditure in Spain requires that the tax reform consider the current distribution of powers.

Tax harmonization and tax autonomy of the Autonomous Communities in Spain: the prohibition of State aid.

As Calvo Ortega has stated, the authorization of article 93 of the Constitution for a Treaty to attribute to an international organization (like the European Union) the exercise of powers has effects on the system of the Communities. Firstly, Autonomous Communities are prohibited from granting tax exemptions or benefits that could be classified as State aid. And, secondly, regarding harmonized taxes, it is not possible to attribute regulatory capacity by the State to the Communities, therefore, only a shared collection system is possible (Calvo Ortega, 2008, p. 14).

As many authors have warned, the State Aid regime constitutes a limit to the tax power of sub-central entities (Ruíz Almendral, 2017, p. 92).

The distribution of powers within a State, even though it is an internal matter, cannot hinder or impede the effectiveness of European Union Law. And this statement can be extended to the financing system. For this reason, the provisions of the Communities referring to their financing system may also contradict EU Law. According to García Novoa (2008, p. 446), we are referring to the question of whether, in the exercise of their own tax power, the Communities could grant certain tax advantages that constitute state aid prohibited by EU law[16]. The Commission shall, in cooperation with Member States, keep under constant review all systems of aid existing in those States. If, after giving notice to the parties concerned to submit their comments, the Commission finds that aid granted by a State or through State resources is not compatible with the internal market, or that such aid is being misused, it shall decide that the State concerned shall abolish or alter such aid (*ex*-article 108 TFEU).

As Merino Jara (2017, p. 228) states, the concept is built on four elements: a) that the measure confers an advantage to its recipients; b) that is attributable to the Member State (or its sub-state entities); c) which distorts or threatens to distort competition; and d) that is selective or specific due to the fact that it favours certain companies or productions.

In this sense, state aid constitutes an important limit in the exercise of the tax power of the Autonomous Communities through measures such as the establishment of exemptions and other tax benefits. However, for exemptions from an autonomic tax to constitute state aid, they must favour certain companies or productions, excluding *a priori* others (García Novoa, 2008, p. 448). In fact, the Commission has considered regional tax measures to be selective, unless they constitute an exception to the rule of incompatibility of State aid. For the first time in 2006, the Court confronted the phenomenon of territorial selectivity with the existence of regional autonomies. It was about assessing a tax regime different from that of the rest of the State that implied or made possible the existence of a lower tax pressure regarding taxes existing in the national territory. The Court noted that *"in order to determine whether the measure at issue is selective it is appropriate to examine whether, within the context of a particular legal system, that measure constitutes an advantage for certain undertakings in comparison with others which are in a comparable legal and factual situation. The determination of the reference framework has a particular importance in the case of tax measures, since the very existence of an advantage may be established only when compared with 'normal' taxation. The 'normal' tax rate is the rate in force in the geographical area constituting the reference framework (…) It is possible that an infra-State body enjoys a legal and factual status which makes it sufficiently autonomous in relation to the central government of a Member State, with the result that, by the measures it adopts, it is that body and not the central government which plays a fundamental role in the definition of the political and economic environment in which undertakings operate. In such a case it is the area in which the infra-State body responsible for the measure exercises its powers, and not the country as a whole, that constitutes the relevant context for the assessment of whether a measure adopted by such a body favours certain undertakings in comparison with others in a comparable legal and factual situation, having regard to the objective pursued by the measure or the legal system concerned"*[17].

In short, for a general tax measure applicable in a part of the territory of a Member State to not be selective aid, it must meet three requirements: i) the regional authority that adopts it must enjoy political and administrative autonomy; ii) it must have the possibility to adopt these fiscal measures without the central government intervening directly; and iii) regional institutions must assume the financial and political consequences of the modification of the tax levy that applies to companies located in their territory. As Rodríguez Márquez (2009, p. 243) stated, in the case of the Autonomous Communities of the common regime, these three requirements are not met. In particular, there is no economic autonomy because they receive numerous transfers from the central State.

The decision has had great relevance for Spain since it is one of the most decentralized States in Europe. In particular, the attribution of regulatory powers over some state taxes (yielded taxes) must be taken into account. According to Calderón Carrero & Ruíz Almendral (2006, pp. 3-4) certain interpretive problems arise regarding the concept of *selectivity*. The question is whether the limitation of the effects of a regional measure, as happens whenever it has been established by a region, is in itself an indication of that selectivity because, according to the Court, measures that represent a deviation from the country's normal taxation system will be selective. The Court introduces an element to examine such deviation: the degree and type of autonomy of the entity when establishing the measure that is the object of the conflict. Therefore, the greater the degree of autonomy, the less likely the measure will be to be considered contrary to the European Law as long as the measure does not introduce additional elements that make it selective (like limiting its application to companies in a certain sector or that carry out a certain activity). Following these authors, integration into the European Union influences the internal model of distribution of powers and may even have a centralizing effect on the regulatory powers of the general regime Communities. This situation could lead to a reconfiguration of the current model, centralizing in the State the jurisdiction over taxes that fall within the scope of application of State aid and decentralizing the tax jurisdiction over tax figures that are outside that regime in the sub-state entities (Calderón Carrero & Ruíz Almendral, 2006, pp. 9-10).

Definitely, it would be necessary to increase the control over regional regulations as much as possible in order to avoid uncertainties regarding the compatibility of this type of measures with EU Law.

Other problematic issues arising from European integration in the context of the financing of the Autonomous Communities

As Ruíz Almendral (2017, pp. 83-84) acknowledges, there are no specific or explicit limits in EU law for the creation of own taxes by sub-central entities. In fact, the CJEU has recognised the neutrality of this law with respect to the system of distribution of internal powers as regards direct taxation. However, EU law must be respected in all cases.

There are different internal limits to the financial power of the Autonomous Communities, but they must also respect the principles of European tax harmonization. From Lago Montero's point of view, an example of lack of coordination is the disorderly proliferation of environmental taxes that leads to companies to situations of unequal competitiveness (Lago Montero, 2017, p. 18). An obvious risk in the field of state aid is the current development of uncoordinated environmental taxation at the regional level, through own taxes instead of transferred state taxes (Ramos Prieto *et al.*, 2019, p. 23). Following the CJEU, a tax with a theoretical environmental purpose must justify any difference in treatment on those environmental grounds, since if any activity or company is excluded without said justification, incompatible State aid would be produced. It is precisely in environmental matters where collisions can occur between European and regional regulations. However, and as Manzano Silva (2005, p. 92) recognizes, if there is a conflict between the financial provisions of the EU and the national or regional ones, it should be resolved in favour of European regulations, which constitute a limit to the regulatory capacity of both the State and the Autonomous Communities. All based on the principles of direct effectiveness and primacy of EU Law.

Likewise, the financing system may not affect the establishment in Spain, and therefore in the Autonomous Communities, of nationals of any Member State. Nor can the financing system entail restrictions on capital movements between States. For this reason, and as García Novoa (1998, p. 125) affirms, every Spanish citizen will see his right to the free movement of people, goods or services protected in the face of a certain organization of regional financing, not only from article 157.2 of the Constitution and 9 c) of the LOFCA, but also from EU Law. However, fiscal co-responsibility can collide with fiscal harmonization and with the freedoms already mentioned. In fact, article 19.2 of the LOFCA establishes that the powers attributed to the Autonomous Communities in relation to transferred taxes will be exercised by the State when necessary to comply with the regulations on tax harmonization of the European Union. This rule is aimed at guaranteeing the effectiveness of EU Law. This reassignment of powers could force the reform, and even the abolition, of regulations issued by the Autonomous Communities. Without a doubt, the aspect that implies the greatest potential for generating situations of contradiction with EU Law is the transfer of regulatory powers to the Autonomous Communities (García Novoa, 1998, p. 132).

Another problematic issue that deserves special interest is the one pointed out by Pita Grandal which refers to the possible lack of coordination of the tax systems of the Communities within the EU framework. In her opinion, since if the new financing system of the Communities was articulated based on financial autonomy in spending, with reduced or discouraged autonomy in income, the problems of coordination of the territorial treasuries in relation to European policies will be less (Pita Grandal, 2003, p. 155). This would mean moving towards a more centralized system in Spain. However, this opinion is not unanimously shared by the doctrine. It is true that today there are numerous frictions between the EU legal system and national systems and one of the challenges of the EU is the integration of the different regions that are part of each State.

Specifically, three aspects of friction can be identified between the financial autonomy of the Autonomous Communities and the financial power of the EU (Pita Grandal, 2003, pp. 162-168).

Firstly, from the perspective of normative production, the principle of legality has been affected. EU policies have undergone a great expansion that in tax matters has translated into the need to expand the scope of tax harmonization. In fact, the structure of each State and its distribution of powers cannot prevent the implementation of EU policies, and particularly the primacy of European law.

Secondly, and from the perspective of the resources of the Communities, European tax policies have an enormous influence over them. In particular, the scope of the transfer of regulatory powers in yielded taxes is limited by European law. This is because, in relation to VAT, the *"Ley de Financiación de las Comunidades Autónomas*" does not recognize these regulatory powers in relation to this tax. To protect the neutrality of this tax, the European Union does not allow the existence of different types of tax rates within the same State. VAT is the main mechanism used by the EU to develop the tax harmonization policy in all States. And, with respect to Special taxes, it is not possible to introduce differentiated tax rates. The explanation is that these are harmonized taxes and, in accordance with European law, Member States cannot block the free movement of goods or the proper functioning of the internal market. Therefore, the transfer and its scope are determined by EU Law. Regarding own taxes, two assumptions must be differentiated. On the one hand, to establish taxes on taxable facts not regulated by state taxes, the limits derived from European community policies come into play. And, on the other hand, Spain can create new national taxes on tobacco and hydrocarbons with the condition that they must have an objective other than the budgetary one and that the tax is levied at the time of consumption. In addition, the Autonomous Communities will not be able to establish different tax rates applicable to tobacco and hydrocarbons.

Third, from the perspective of public spending, the budgetary stability objectives from the European Union affect the development of the financial power of the Autonomous Communities. Spain, like other States, must comply with the rules of the European Stability and Growth Pact which is a set of rules designed to ensure that countries in the European Union pursue sound public finances and coordinate their fiscal policies. In September of 2011, Article 135 of the Spanish Constitution was amended for the purpose of introducing deficit and debt rules[18]. And, consequently, in 2012, Organic Law 2/2012 on Budgetary Stability and Financial Sustainability (*Ley de Estabilidad Presupuestaria y Sostenibilidad Financiera*) was approved to this end.

This Law had the primary objective of coordinating the deficit in what in practice is a highly decentralized country, since the Spanish regions, currently manage 35% of public spending, while local entities are in charge of 13%. Section 1 and 2 of Article 135 enshrine the principle of stability for all public administrations as regulated in EU Law, which makes it easier to impose these limits to sub-national entities without the constant claim that it may limit the financial autonomy of the Communities. The reform also limited the public debt (section 3), not just the deficit. Subsequently, Autonomous Communities began to approve their own laws regulating the stability obligations. As stated Ruíz Almendral (2013, p. 196), this reform changed the previous Spanish legal environment of debt and deficit limitation and had consequences on the Spanish "quasi-federal" model of Autonomous Communities. In fact, the main change was the substantial limitation on the leeway of the Autonomous Communities to incur indebtment and deficit, after decades of legal reforms increasing both their taxing powers and financial autonomy. As a result of EU impositions, there was an increase in the powers of the central government to curb the deficit and the debt. Likewise, article 10.3 of the Law 2/2012 empowers the central government to establish any measure necessary to ensure the full coordination of the budgetary policies of the Communities, the municipalities, and the central government.

According to Ruíz Almendral (2013, p. 200), the lack of fiscal responsibility of Autonomous Communities is a problem for debt and deficit because when subnational governments receive financing almost exclusively in the form of transfers, an incentive to overspend those moneys is created. In her words, *"it is easier to spend revenue when, a) one does not withstand the political burden of having to raise it (…), and b) there is no need to explain the relationship between revenue raised and spent to voters/taxpayers. The situation creates a lack of accountability that fosters the increase of debt and deficit"*. However, the stability rules are facilizing the re-centralization of the powers of Autonomous Communities, which have lost all leeway to propose their own debt limits. Furthermore, Communities' control over their own budgets has substantially decreased. Hence, there is still a need to improve the culture of budgetary stability in Spain (Ruíz Almendral, 2022a, p. 13).

Another of the main problems identified in the regional financing system is that the EU has powers to harmonize indirect taxation, fundamentally that which affects the consumption of goods and services. Although all tax regulations emanating from these entities must, in general, be in accordance with EU Law. In Spain, the Autonomous Communities of the common regime continue to depend to a high degree on transfers or participation in VAT and special taxes, over which they do not have tax autonomy.

The harmonisation of indirect taxation is a clear example of integration into the EU. The consequence of this process is not only the obligation to establish and develop harmonised taxes as set out in the Directives, but also the impossibility for Member States and their sub-central bodies to create similar taxes (Ruíz Almendral, 2017, p. 87).

Therefore, the possible transfer of VAT to the Autonomous Communities would have, as Manzano Silva (2005, pp. 73-74) has warned, multiple drawbacks. On the one hand, those derived from the nature of the tax and its implementation in a certain phase, depending on the content of the LOFCA and of the Statutes of Autonomy. And, on the other hand, many obstacles derived from the European harmonization process. Therefore, the delegation of management powers would be very problematic since it would cause technical problems that would affect the application of the tax. And, in addition, the transfer of regulatory powers to the Autonomous Communities, allowing the existence of multiple types of tax within the same State, would put the neutrality of the tax at risk. This would also cause distortions in competition between different territories of a Member State. As García Martínez & Herrera Molina (2001, p. 179) have stated, regulatory diversity could conflict with EU freedoms and, on the other hand, regional diversity would make progress towards a harmonizing process more difficult. Without a doubt, regarding the transfer of VAT performance, this is the one that poses the least problems. This explains why VAT is currently a state-owned tax partially transferred to the Autonomous Communities for 50% of its product, but over which they do not have regulatory powers. Following García Martínez & Herrera Molina (2001, p. 192), theoretically, it would be possible to attribute certain regulatory powers without harming the constitutional and European framework, but such powers would be so limited that they would not contribute to fiscal co-responsibility. And with respect to special taxes, the CJEU has also ruled against recognizing regulatory powers to the Autonomous Communities.

Furthermore, regarding taxes on those who enjoy tax autonomy (inheritance and gift tax, wealth tax and property transfer tax) present certain problems: state regulations over these taxes are obsolete, and the decentralization of property taxation (inheritance and gift tax or wealth tax) can generate the mobility of tax bases and other negative fiscal externalities. In fact, the Court of Justice of the EU has declared some regional regulatory provisions incompatible with European law, both with respect to own taxes and taxes transferred from the State to the Communities[19].

Regarding the Inheritance and Gift Tax, there are various problems related to the recognition of certain tax benefits. It is necessary to analyse whether these measures are compatible with the freedom of establishment and the free movement of capital. In Spain there is significant tax competition between Autonomous Communities to attract taxpayers. Thus, as Adame Martínez states, the regional governments use their regulatory capacity in the Inheritance and Gift Tax to attract taxpayers (2015, p. 85).

This situation has led to the tax being different depending on the territory. For this reason, the 2014 Report (*Informe de la Comisión de expertos para la reforma del sistema tributario*, 2014, pp. 252-253) has proposed establishing a single minimum exemption set by the State for the entire territory.

Furthermore, the measures approved by the Autonomous Communities in relation to this tax and which may be incompatible with the freedoms of EU law are: i) tax benefits related to the transfer of the habitual residence; ii) tax benefits related to the transfer of companies and agricultural holdings; iii) and other tax benefits (Adame Martínez, 2015, p. 90). However, many regional measures are clearly contrary to the EU legal framework, but this has not provoked a sufficient coordinated reaction (Ruíz Almendral, 2022b, p. 37).

As Adame Martínez (2015, p. 108) has pointed out, the tax benefits established by the Autonomous Communities in relation to the tax and which only apply when the goods or activities are located in the territory of an Autonomous Community are not compatible with the jurisprudence of the Court of Justice of the EU. Thus, they affect the freedom of establishment and the free movement of capital. And for the Court these differences would only be possible if there were a reasonable justification based on the general interest.

Specifically, when recognising such tax benefits, the regional governments have established territorial criteria requiring that the assets be linked to a specific territory or that they be maintained for a long period of time, or even the hiring of workers residing in a certain territory. Indeed, there are numerous tax benefits that affect personal income tax, inheritance and gift tax, or tax on onerous property transfers. However, as Lucas Durán (2020, pp. 173-174) points out, in many cases the limitation of the freedoms of movement, establishment and movement of capital that such tax benefits imply is not proportionate to the aims that they seek to achieve. And in some cases, it is not proportionate from the perspective of domestic law either.

Regarding the wealth tax, and as Ruíz Almendral (2022b, p. 73) states, the wealth tax regime applicable to non-residents no longer appears to be flagrantly contrary to EU law, although it cannot be ruled out that, in its practical application, it could lead to higher taxation of a non-resident.

In this sense, two limits are identified by EU Law on the tax power of the Autonomous Communities: the necessary respect for the fundamental freedoms of movement of goods, people, services, and capital, as well as the freedom of establishment (*ex*-articles 26 and 49 of the TFEU); and the prohibition of state aid. Following the Court, a provision will be contrary to the free movement of capital when it is arbitrary, that is, when it recognizes differential treatment that is not justified by reasons of general interest or, if justified, generates disproportionate consequences.

In short, and as Ribes Ribes (2015, p. 266) recognises, the greatest restrictions on regional financial policy come from both EU law and the case law of the CJEU. The CJEU is carrying out what is known as "negative harmonisation". This is particularly noticeable in indirect taxes. However, in the absence of true harmonisation, uncertainty remains (Merino Jara, 2017, p. 232). And it leads to numerous asymmetries (Ruíz Almendral, 2017, p. 101).

On the other hand, direct taxation is not subject to harmonisation. The only directly harmonising measures with an impact on direct taxation are not strictly tax measures. However, it has been direct taxation that has been most influenced by EU law, through a process often referred to as indirect or improper harmonisation, which has taken place mainly through the case law of the ECJ, with the support of the European Commission (Ruíz Almendral, 2022b, p. 60). The creation of special regimes, incentives and various tax benefits, as well as the introduction of specific anti-avoidance measures, have accentuated the differences in treatment between residents and non-residents. But this model has been progressively eroded on the basis of the fundamental freedoms of the EU.

In short, and as Ruíz Almendral (2022b, p. 37) recognizes, given the confluence of many of the European rules that are relevant to tax matters and the limits derived from the Spanish Constitution, it would be possible to advance towards greater coordination that would not entail a reduction in financial autonomy and that would in fact increase fiscal co-responsibility. In any case, the problems posed by fiscal decentralisation in a context of EU integration require an increased focus.

SOLUTIONS AND RECOMMENDATIONS

Next, the main lines of reform of the current financing system of the Autonomous Communities will be explained.

First of all, it is not about reforming the system as a whole, but about introducing adjustments that guarantee the principles of financial autonomy, solidarity, coordination, budgetary stability and financial sustainability. In addition, the reform must be carried out in order to last over time. Within the new scheme, the distribution model of public expenses and revenues between the State and the Autonomous Communities must be clear with the aim of guaranteeing a vertical financial balance.

In second place, not all the tax resources of the Autonomous Communities contribute in the same way to their financial autonomy (own taxes or yielded taxes with more or less regulatory and administrative powers). In this sense, the system that was designed should consider the greater collection weight of each tax figure. In any case, nothing prevents the autonomous region from maintaining its regulatory capacity (Ribes Ribes, 2018, p. 213).

In third place, the financial autonomy of the Autonomous Communities must respect the limits derived from European integration. To avoid a violation of the free movement of capital, the connection points that are used to attribute to the Autonomous Communities regulatory powers to establish tax benefits or to regulate the calculation of the quota in state taxes transferred totally or partially (IRPF -Personal income tax-, IP - Wealth tax-, ISD - Inheritance and gift tax-, etc.) cannot imply a more unfavourable situation for non-residents in Spain, unless justified by general interest (Ramos Prieto *et al.*, 2019, p. 24). These circumstances must be taken into account when establishing connection points by the central State. And, on the other hand, prior control mechanisms should be established over regional measures to avoid incurring prohibited state aid.

However, as some authors have warned, it seems that there is no tax room left for sub-central entities because of the strong harmonisation process arising from the EU (Ruíz Almendral, 2017, p. 117).

In fourth place, regarding to own taxes, it would be desirable to establish a system of prior and extrajudicial resolution of possible disputes between the State and the Autonomous Communities with the aim of guaranteeing the conformity of regional taxes with the Constitution and EU Law. Likewise, the LOFCA should also specify the characteristics that regional taxes must have to avoid the collision of taxable events. On the other hand, a series of taxable matters could be reserved by law for the State to avoid conflicts; although this delimitation cannot be excessively detailed nor excessively generic (Ramos Prieto *et al.*, 2019, pp. 28-29; Menéndez Moreno, 2023, p. 13). It would even be possible to assume own taxes of the Autonomous Communities (like the tax on sugary drinks) and, later, transfer their collection by the State to them. This would allow its regulation to be harmonized to limit distorting territorial differences. Although this position is not unanimously shared. Specifically, there are authors (Salassa Boix, 2022, p. 103) who consider that an alternative would be to transfer all state environmental taxes, not only with respect to its collection, but also with regard to the regulatory powers, but always respecting minimums set by the State to guarantee coordination.

Specifically, the best way to resolve tax overlaps between the State and the Autonomous Communities is for the new state taxes that suspend the effects of their own regional taxes to be expressly incorporated into the list of taxes assignable to the Autonomous Communities. Therefore, the Autonomous Communities should be granted not only the management and collection of the tax, but also the regulatory powers so that they can modify the quantification elements within minimum and maximum limits. Following Salassa Boix (2023, p. 260), the economic compensation should not be indefinite but should be operational until the Autonomous Communities have the possibility of modifying the elements of quantification of the state tax once regulatory powers are transferred.

Fifth, and regarding possible reforms related to yielded taxes, it would be desirable to include recently created taxes by the State within this list, even if this would imply emptying the central State of economic resources. In this sense, the following taxes could be transferred totally or partially to the Autonomous Communities: tax on gambling activities; tax on deposits from credit institutions; tax on fluorinated greenhouse gases; tax on the value of extraction of gas, oil, and condensate; tax on the value of electrical energy production; tax on the production of nuclear fuel, etc. Along with this measure, another formula would be to increase the resources of the Communities through the expansion of the percentages of collection that correspond to them from the state taxes partially transferred.

However, in taxes such as personal income tax or VAT it would not be convenient since they would increase taxation differences between territories and lead to situations of tax competition. Meanwhile, in special taxes an increase in the transfer percentage would be plausible. The transfer of the insurance premium tax would also be possible (Ramos Prieto *et al.*, 2019, pp. 30-39). Regarding corporate tax, this should not be included among the transferred taxes since, given its characteristics, it is difficult to establish that its income has been generated in a specific territory. For this reason, its management must continue to be state-owned (Tejerizo López, 2004, p. 37).

On the contrary, with respect to other taxes such as wealth tax or inheritance and gift tax, the regulation, collection, and management powers of the Autonomous Communities could be expanded.

Following the expert committee (2022, pp. 730-733), when reforming the framework for the transfer of regulatory powers in the wealth tax and in the inheritance and gift tax transferred to the Autonomous Communities of the common regime, four possibilities are identified: (i) first, on the same taxable object, taxes could be established by both a state law and by regional laws, but the regional quota would reduce the state one; (ii) second, the State and the Autonomous Communities could independently regulate, based on a single tax base, the exempt minimum, the rate, the deductions and bonuses applicable respectively to the state and regional sections, although the collection would correspond only to the Communities; (iii) third, the State would regulate all the elements of the tax up to the tax base and a maximum limit would be established for the increase of the exempt minimum, a minimum for the reduction of the state rate and a maximum limit for the deductions and bonuses of the full quota; and (iv) fourth, to establish ranges for the exempt minimum, the rate and the deductions and bonuses so that the Communities could not raise taxation above a certain threshold. These four options appear ordered from least to greatest limitation of autonomy but all of them would require an extensive reform of the regional financing system. Even among the doctrine there are positions that are in favour of the elimination of both taxes.

From the point of view of the Commission, the third option should be chosen, maintaining the regulatory powers of the Communities on the exempt minimum, the tax scales, and possible deductions in the quota, maintaining the coordination of the tax base in the State. In addition, a series of limits are proposed: regarding the exempt minimum, a maximum percentage increase over that established in the

State provision is recommended; regarding the tax scales, a maximum percentage reduction of the state rate; and as for deductions, a maximum joint limit.

Sixthly, and with respect to the Guarantee Fund for fundamental public services, not only should some of the distribution criteria be reviewed, but its resources should also be increased with contributions from the Autonomous Communities of the special regime, increasing the percentage of the tax capacity that each Community contributes to the fund and increasing the additional resources contributed by the State.

Regarding the Global Sufficiency Fund, this should be maintained as a closing clause of the system but linked to the financing of other spending needs not covered by the previous fund.

As for the Competitiveness Fund and the Cooperation Fund, their elimination could be considered as long as the Guarantee Fund for Fundamental Public Services as well as the Interterritorial Compensation Funds are strengthened.

After referring to the problems linked to the Interterritorial Compensation Fund, the following reforms should be proposed: increase the allocation of these funds, review and update the distribution criteria, and improve coordination with the different European funds for regional development.

Finally, guaranteeing financial sufficiency and autonomy and, at the same time, encouraging fiscal co-responsibility of the Autonomous Communities continues to be the objective to be achieved (González González, 2018, p. 188).

FUTURE RESEARCH DIRECTIONS

Since 2017, there has been talk of reforming the financing system of the Autonomous Communities in Spain. However, in recent decades its complexity has been increasing, leading to enormous legal uncertainty, as well as many territorial inequalities. The proposals that have just been presented are hardly viable because they require profound socio-political changes, as well as changes in legal systems of the State and the Autonomous Communities.

What is clear is that the principles and criteria that must guide the review of the financing system are: the principles of solidarity, sufficiency, equity, transparency, fiscal co-responsibility, financial balance and guarantee of citizen access to public services.

However, any possible reform will imply two options: a better articulate system within the current context, or on the contrary, a complete modification of the current context. And this means increasing the financial autonomy of the Autonomous Communities or, on the contrary, reducing it. Thus, the two possible scenarios differ in the degree of autonomy of the revenues and expenses of the subnational entities. In short, the current reform of the system will move between two extremes, that is, continuing with the decentralization of the State or returning towards a centralized State.

CONCLUSION

It can be concluded that the system currently in force does not satisfy the financing needs of the Autonomous Communities and, therefore, a modification of the current system would be necessary.

In this sense, it would be advisable to propose an amendment of the current financing model of the Autonomous Communities from the perspective of the public revenues which makes possible to achieve a proper balance between the fiscal joint responsibility and the constitutional principles of tax justice and inter-territorial solidarity. Furthermore, this reform must make fair and balanced financing of the Autonomous Communities compatible with the requirements of EU law in fiscal and budgetary matters.

Finally, the reform of the regional financing system is an opportunity to bet on the efficiency, rationality, and growth of the Spanish economy.

ACKNOWLEDGMENT

This work is part of the Research Project "Los desafíos de la reforma de la financiación autonómica en el marco jurídico de la Unión Europea", funded by the Ministerio de Ciencia, Innovación y Universidades (PID2023-146377NB-I00).

REFERENCES

Adame Martínez, F. (2015). La compatiblidad de diversas medidas adoptadas por las Comunidades Autónomas con el Derecho europeo. In *Patón García, G. (dir.), Libertades comunitarias, autonomía tributaria y medio ambiente* (pp. 83–109). CEF.

Blasco Delgado, C. (1996). La financiación de las Comunidades Autónomas y la corresponsabilidad fiscal. In Sánchez Domingo, R. (Coord.), *Estudios sobre el ordenamiento jurídico español: libro conmemorativo del X aniversario de la Facultad de Derecho, Universidad de Burgos* (255-272). Universidad de Burgos, Facultad de Derecho: Caja de Burgos.

Calderón Carrero, J. M., & Ruíz Almendral, V. (2006). Autonomía financiera de las CC.AA. *vs*. Derecho Comunitario (la doctrina del TJCE en el caso Azores). *Jurisprudencia Tributaria Aranzadi*, 24, 21261–21269.

Calvo Ortega, R. (2008). Financiación de las Comunidades Autónomas y Constitución. *Nueva Fiscalidad*, 1, 9–24.

Ferreiro Lapatza, J. J. (1984). Financiación de las Comunidades Autónomas. In González Encinar, J.J. (Coord.), *Diccionario del sistema político español* (326-337). Akal.

García Martínez, A., & Herrera Molina, P. M. (2001). Europa: El Derecho comunitario como límite a la cesión del IVA a las Comunidades Autónomas. *Revista Valenciana de Economía y Hacienda*, 2, 167–195.

García Novoa, C. (1998). Financiación autonómica y Derecho Comunitario. *Crónica Tributaria*, 85, 119–144.

García Novoa, C. (2008). Reflexiones sobre los impuestos propios de carácter medioambiental en el ámbito de la tributación autonómica. In Aneiros Pereira, J. (Coord.), *La financiación autonómica en los Estatutos de Autonomía* (411-461). Marcial Pons.

García Prats, F. A. (2011). Spain. In Bizioli, G. & Sacchetto, C. (Coords), *Tax Aspects of Fiscal Federalism. A Comparative Analysis* (361-402). IBFD.

González González, A. I. (2018). Una nueva reforma de la financiación autonómica: Entre la suficiencia financiera y la autonomía tributaria. *Documentos-Instituto de Estudios Fiscales*, 12/2018, 177–189.

Instituto de Estudios Fiscales. (2022). *Libro Blanco sobre la Reforma Tributaria*, Ministerio de Hacienda y Función Pública. https://www.ief.es/docs/investigacion/comiteexpertos/LibroBlancoReformaTributaria_2022.pdf

Lago Montero, J. M. (2017). Los impuestos propios en el sistema de financiación autonómica. In *Sanz Gómez, R. (coord.), Tributos propios de las Comunidades Autónomas* (pp. 15–43). Tirant lo Blanch.

Lago Peñas, S. (2019). Tax decentralisation in Spain: Significant progress and remaining challenges. *Funcas SEFO, Vol. 8, N. 5,* 51-58. https://www.funcas.es/wp-content/uploads/Migracion/Articulos/FUNCAS_SEFO/045art07.pdf

Lasarte Álvarez, F. J. (1979). La financiación de las Comunidades Autónomas. *Documentación Administrativa*, 181, 413–443.

Lasarte López, R. (2017). Principios y límites rectores en la creación de tributos propios tras la modificación del artículo 6 de la LOFCA. In Sanz Gómez, R. (Coord.), *Tributos propios de las Comunidades Autónomas* (179-205). Tirant lo Blanch.

López Díaz, A. (2013). Tributación medioambiental en España a nivel subcentral: CCAA y CCLL. *Dereito*, 22, 225–244.

López Laborda, J., Martínez Vázquez, J., & Monasterio Escudero, C. (2023). Spain. In Tremblay, J.-F. (Ed.), *The Forum of Federations Handbook on Fiscal Federalism* (pp. 341–382). Palgrave Macmillan. DOI: 10.1007/978-3-030-97258-5_9

Lucas Durán, M. (2020). Beneficios fiscales con requisitos territoriales, normativa tributaria autonómica y libre circulación de personas y capitales: Reflexiones desde el derecho de la UE, la constitución española y el bloque de constitucionalidad. *Nueva Fiscalidad*, 3, 127–177.

Manzano Silva, E. (2005). Proceso de integración europea *versus* autonomía financiera autonómica. *Nueva Fiscalidad*, 1, 47–102.

Menéndez Moreno, A. (2010). La nueva financiación de las Comunidades Autónomas. *Lex nova: La revista, 59,* 7.

Menéndez Moreno, A. (2023). ¿Qué fue de la reforma del sistema de financiación de las Comunidades Autónomas? *Quincena Fiscal*, 9, 9–20.

Merino Jara, I. (2017). Los impuestos autonómicos sobre grandes establecimientos comerciales desde la perspectiva de las libertades de la Unión Europea y del régimen de ayudas de Estado. In Sanz Gómez, R. (Coord.), *Tributos propios de las Comunidades Autónomas* (207-232). Tirant lo Blanch.

Ministerio de Hacienda y Función Pública. (2021). *Las Haciendas Autonómicas en cifras*. https://www.hacienda.gob.es/CDI/Sist%20Financiacion%20y%20Deuda/Informaci%C3%B3nCCAA/Las-Haciendas-Autonomicas-en-cifras-2021.pdf

OECD. (2023). *Revenue Statistics 2023 – Spain*. https://www.oecd.org/content/dam/oecd/en/topics/policy-sub-issues/global-tax-revenues/revenue-statistics-spain.pdf

Pita Grandal, A. M. (1987). Reflexiones en torno a los límites de la previsión contenida en el art. 6,3 de la LOFCA. *Impuestos: Revista de doctrina, legislación y jurisprudencia. Year*, 3(2), 136–146.

Pita Grandal, A. M. (2003). Incidencia del Derecho comunitario europeo en el poder financiero autonómico. In Pita Grandal, A.M. (Dir.), *Hacienda autonómica y local. III Seminario Iberoamericano de Derecho Tributario* (149-168). Tórculo Edicións.

Ramos Prieto, J. (2017). La importancia presupuestaria de los tributos propios de las Comunidades Autónomas. Análisis comparativo. In Sanz Gómez, R. (Coord.), *Tributos propios de las Comunidades Autónomas* (45-82). Tirant lo Blanch.

Ramos Prieto, J., García Martínez, A., Martín Rodríguez, J.M. & Macarro Osuna, J.M. (2019). A propósito de la reforma del sistema de financiación de las Comunidades Autónomas de régimen general. Problemas y propuestas. *Documentos- IEF, 2,* 1-51.

Ribes Ribes, A. (2015). Capacidad normativa autonómica y límites derivados del Derecho y la jurisprudencia europeos: especial referencia al Impuesto sobre las Ventas Minoristas de Determinados Hidrocarburos. In *Patón García, G. (dir.), Libertades comunitarias, autonomía tributaria y medio ambiente* (pp. 265–288). CEF.

Ribes Ribes, A. (2018). Los retos del nuevo modelo de financiación autonómica: Reflexiones y propuestas. *Documentos-Instituto de Estudios Fiscales*, 12/2018, 209–221.

Rodríguez Márquez, J. (2008). Aspectos controvertidos en el futuro sistema de financiación autonómica. In Aneiros Pereira, J. (Coord.), *La financiación autonómica en los Estatutos de Autonomía* (239-257). Marcial Pons.

Ruíz Almendral, V. (2002). Fiscal Federalism in Spain: The Assignment of Taxation Powers to the Autonomous Communities. *European Taxation*, 42(11), 467–475.

Ruíz Almendral, V. (2012). Sharing Taxes and Sharing the Deficit in Spanish Fiscal Federalism. *eJournal of Tax Research, Vol. 10, No. 1*, 88-125.

Ruíz Almendral, V. (2013). The Spanish Legal Framework for Curbing the Public Debt and the Deficit. *European Constitutional Law Review*, 9(2), 189–204. DOI: 10.1017/S1574019612001113

Ruíz Almendral, V. (2017). La imposición propia autonómica ante el Derecho de la Unión Europea. In Sanz Gómez, R. (Coord.), *Tributos propios de las Comunidades Autónomas* (83-118). Tirant lo Blanch.

Ruíz Almendral, V. (2022a). Una reforma tributaria para España. *Actualidad Jurídica Uría Menéndez*, 58, 7–26.

Ruíz Almendral, V. (2022b). Tax decentralization and tax reform in the EU context. *Revista General de Derecho Europeo*, 57, 3.

Salassa Boix, R. (2022). Los impuestos autonómicos propios: ¿una especie en peligro de extinción? *Crónica Tributaria*, 187(2), 67–105. DOI: 10.47092/CT.23.2.3

Salassa Boix, R. (2023). Cláusula de compensación en favor de las Comunidades Autónomas: Desafíos de una medida excepcional cada vez más habitual. *Nueva Fiscalidad*, 2(2-2023), 227–262. DOI: 10.14679/2089

Tejerizo López, J. M. (2005). La financiación de las Comunidades Autónomas. Notas para un balance. In Varona Alabern, J.E. (Ed.), *25 años de financiación autonómica* (21-38). Editorial de la Universidad de Cantabria.

Tejerizo López, J. M. (2015). Las libertades comunitarias como límite al ejercicio del poder tributario de las regiones. In *Patón García, G. (dir.), Libertades comunitarias, autonomía tributaria y medio ambiente* (pp. 23–64). CEF.

Tremblay, J.-F. (2023). *The Forum of Federations Handbook on Fiscal Federalism*. Palgrave Macmillan., DOI: 10.1007/978-3-030-97258-5

Vanistendael, F. (2011). The European Union. In Bizioli, G. & Sacchetto, C. (Coords), *Tax Aspects of Fiscal Federalism. A Comparative Analysis* (581-646). IBFD.

VV.AA. (2014). *Informe de la Comisión de Expertos para la reforma del sistema tributario español. Ministerio de Hacienda y Administraciones Públicas.*https://www.hacienda.gob.es/es-ES/Prensa/En%20Portada/2014/Documents/Informe%20expertos.pdf

VV.AA. (2017). *Informe de la Comisión de Expertos para la revisión del modelo de financiación autonómica.* Ministerio de Hacienda y Función Pública._https://www.hacienda.gob.es/CDI/sist%20financiacion%20y%20deuda/informaci%C3%B3nccaa/informe_final_comisi%C3%B3n_reforma_sfa.pdf

ADDITIONAL READING

Abril Abadín, E., & Zurdo Ruíz-Ayúcar, J. (1979). Los límites internacionales a las autonomías tributarias. *Revista Hacienda Pública Española*, 59, 239–256.

Beteta Barreda, A. (2015). La financiación de las Comunidades Autónomas y la reforma fiscal: Una perspectiva desde los Fondos de financiación a las Comunidades Autónomas. *Economistas*, 145, 61–67.

Cuenca García, A. (2015). Reforma de la financiación autonómica. *Economistas*, 145, 79–85.

De la Fuente, Á. (2018). La liquidación de 2016 del sistema de financiación de las comunidades autónomas de régimen común. *Estudios sobre la Economía Española, 18/11*, 1-41.

Pérez Royo, F. (2008). Cuestiones sobre el poder tributario de las CCAA: la relación entre las disposiciones sobre financiación en los Estatutos y la Ley orgánica del artículo 157.3. In Aneiros Pereira, J. (Coord.), *La financiación autonómica en los Estatutos de Autonomía* (231-238). Marcial Pons.

Pita Grandal, A. M. (2008). La organización de la gestión tributaria en los Estatutos de Autonomía. In Aneiros Pereira, J. (Coord.), *La financiación autonómica en los Estatutos de Autonomía* (201-228). Marcial Pons.

Rubio Guerrero, J. J. (2023). El sistema de financiación local en España: fortalezas y debilidades. Líneas de reforma. In *VV.AA., Retos de la financiación territorial en tiempos de postpandemia. Un homenaje a Alfonso Utrilla de la Hoz* (pp. 287–303). IEF.

Rubio Guerrero, J. J., & Álvarez García, S. (2015). Sistema de financiación autonómica: Problemas de funcionamiento y perspectivas de reforma. *Economistas*, 145, 69–78.

Ruíz Almendral, V. (2022). Reformas tributarias en un entorno multinivel y un siglo XXI incierto. *Revista Española de Derecho financiero, Nº 194,* 17-48.

Ruíz Almendral, V., & Cuenca García, A. (2014). Estabilidad presupuestaria en las Comunidades Autónomas: Más allá de la reforma de la Constitución. *Cuadernos de Información Económica*, 241, 35–44.

KEY TERMS AND DEFINITIONS

Autonomous Community: A territorial entity that, within the current constitutional legal system, is endowed with autonomy, with its own institutions and representatives and certain legislative, executive, and administrative powers, which in many aspects assimilates it to federated entities.

Connecting factors: The elements used to establish the competence of each Autonomous Community to the corresponding amount of tax collected which is handed over on one hand, and the criteria that set the rules that are applicable for determining the amount of tax to be paid by the taxpayers on the other.

Fiscal Federalism: It refers to the distribution of financial and fiscal resources among various political entities within a country. In general terms, it implies that financial and fiscal power is distributed between the central government and regional or local governments.

Horizontal Fiscal Imbalance: The situation that arises when there are significant differences in income and thus public resources among sub-national governments.

LOFCA: the Organic Law on Financing of the Autonomous Communities establishes the basic lines of the financing system and the general features of the sources of income of the Autonomous Treasury.

Own Taxes: A source of financing for the Autonomous Communities which have regulatory powers for the establishment, regulation, modification, and elimination of their own taxes, as well as the administrative powers for their application (management, collection and inspection), administrative review, the exercise of sanctioning power and the ownership of performance.

Tax Power: Power to approve laws in relation to the different sources of financing of a certain entity, especially through the creation of new taxes.

Vertical Fiscal Imbalance: The situation that arises when one tier of government – usually the Central Government – has a greater power to obtain revenues than it needs for the exercise of its assigned level of authority, while the other – usually sub-national governments – is in the opposite situation.

Yielded taxes/ shared taxes/ transferred taxes: Are originally taxes enacted and established by the State which are transferred to Autonomous Communities total or partially.

ENDNOTES

1 See Instituto de Estudios Fiscales (2022). *Libro Blanco sobre la Reforma Tributaria*, Ministerio de Hacienda y Función Pública.

2 It is possible to consult the data referring to these issues in the author's work. In that work data is collected on the percentage of public expenditure in the hands of regional governments in OECD nations and the percentage of tax collection in the hands of regional governments in OECD nations.

3 The Statutes of Autonomy are the basic institutional norm of each of the Autonomous Communities. They contain the identification of the community, the institutions of self-government, and the powers assumed within the constitutional framework.

4 For this purpose, a fund has been created, known as *Fondo de Compensación Interterritorial* aimed at correcting imbalances between Communities.

5 See STC 13/1992 of 6 February.

6 See STC 135/1992.

7 For example, *vid.* STC 204/2011; STC 53/2014; STC 217/2016; or STC 65/2020.

8 This classification of taxes is defined by the General Tax Act 58/2003 in its article 2.2. In section a) it states that *"tasas"* will be required for the private use or special use of the public domain, the provision of services or the performance of activities under public law that refer to, affect or benefit in a particular way the taxpayer, when the services or activities are not requested or received voluntarily by the taxpayers or are not provided or carried out by the private sector. Meanwhile, section b) states that *"contribuciones especiales"* will be required for the taxpayer obtaining a benefit or an increase in the value of their assets because of the performance of public works or the establishment or expansion of public services. Finally, section c) states that the taxable fact of *"impuestos"* is constituted by businesses, acts or events that reveal the economic capacity of the taxpayer.

9 Anyway, the product of credit operations is only a support but does not constitute an ordinary financing system for the budget of the Communities, as happens in the budgets of the State and local entities. The use of credit should be limited to meeting treasury needs, extraordinary expenses and, in general, investment expenses (Lasarte, 1979, p. 419).

10 See STC 192/2000 of 13 July.

11 Similarly to Autonomous Communities, article 142 of the Spanish Constitution recognizes the need for the local public treasuries to have sufficient funds available to perform the functions assigned by law to the local municipalities,

which shall mainly be financed by their own taxes and by their share of state taxes and those provided by the Autonomous Communities. In fact, local municipalities do not have legislative power, so the central State must establish the general framework of resources that enable local municipalities to guarantee the sufficiency principle. The regulation of the financial competences of local corporations has been made through the so-called *Texto Refundido de la Ley Reguladora de las Haciendas Locales* of 5 March. Therefore, Autonomous Communities can create taxes *ex novo*, while local corporations can only apply taxes already created and determined in their essential elements by a state or autonomous law.

12 A more detailed study of this article can be seen in Pita Grandal, A.M. (1987). Reflexiones en torno a los límites de la previsión contenida en el art. 6,3 de la LOFCA. *Impuestos: Revista de doctrina, legislación y jurisprudencia, Year 3, nº 2,* 136-146.

13 There are the following regional taxes, among others: impuesto sobre el bingo; impuesto sobre emisión de gases a la atmósfera; impuesto sobre vertidos a las aguas litorales; impuesto sobre depósitos de residuos radioactivos; canon de saneamiento; canon eólico; impuesto sobre grandes establecimientos comerciales; impuesto sobre determinadas actividades que inciden sobre el medio ambiente; canon sobre la disposición de residuos; impuesto sobre aprovechamientos cinegéticos; impuesto sobre las estancias en establecimientos turísticos; impuesto compensatorio minero; impuesto sobre las bolsas de plástico de un solo uso; impuesto sobre bebidas azucaradas envasadas; impuesto sobre los embalses de agua, etc.

14 For example, *vid.* STC 49/1995; STC 60/2013; STC 110/2014; STC 30/2015; and STC 74/2016.

15 For a detailed analysis of the quantitative differences between own taxes and yielded taxes in the Autonomous Communities see: Ramos Prieto, J. (2017). La importancia presupuestaria de los tributos propios de las Comunidades Autónomas. Análisis comparativo. In Sanz Gómez, R. (Coord.), *Tributos propios de las Comunidades Autónomas* (45-82). Tirant lo Blanch.

16 Specifically, the article 107.1 of the Treaty on the Functioning of the European Union establishes that *"Save as otherwise provided in the Treaties, any aid granted by a Member State or through State resources in any form whatsoever which distorts or threatens to distort competition by favouring certain undertakings or the production of certain goods shall, in so far as it affects trade between Member States, be incompatible with the internal market"*.

17 See ECJ Azores Case (C-88/03, of 6 September 2006).

18 This article reads as follows: *"1. All public administrations will conform to the principle of budgetary stability. 2. The State and the Self-governing Communities may not incur a structural deficit that exceeds the limits established by the European Union for their member states. An Organic Act shall determine the maximum structural deficit the State and the Self-governing Communities may have, in relation to its gross domestic product. Local authorities must submit a balanced budget. 3. The State and the Self-governing Communities must be authorized by Act in order to issue public debt bonds or to contract loans. Loans to meet payment on the interest and capital of the State's Public Debt shall always be deemed to be included in budget expenditure and their payment shall have absolute priority. These appropriations may not be subject to amendment or modification as long as the conform to the terms of issue. The volume of public debt of all the public administrations in relation to the State's gross domestic product may not exceed the benchmark laid down by the Treaty on the Functioning of the European Union (...)".*

19 See ECJ Case 127/14, of 3 September 2014 in which a regulatory provision gave different treatment to residents and non-residents in Spain in the inheritance and gift tax. Also, see ECJ Persche Case 318/07 of 27 January 2009 or the ECJ Case 10/10 of 16 June 2011.

Chapter 4
Concordat Between the Portuguese Republic and the Holy See:
Exploring Tax Interpretation

Hélder Lopes
Pontificio Collegio Portoghese, Roma, Italy

Fátima David
https://orcid.org/0000-0001-7075-5159
Guarda Polytechnic Institute, Portugal

Maria Helena Martins Pernadas
https://orcid.org/0009-0002-3915-8596
Tax and Customs Authority, Portugal

ABSTRACT

This chapter aims to contribute to the interpretation, regulation, and implementation of the tax part of the Concordat established in 2004 between the Portuguese Republic and the Holy See. On the one hand, the legal framework of the different religions will be sought, underlining their positive externalities and enumerating the process that grants them legal personality, which is the reason for the tax benefits given to each religion. On the other hand, the tax framework of the religions in the Portuguese tax regime will be analyzed, examining the normative set emanating from the Constitution of the Portuguese Republic, the Religious Freedom Law, the Concordat, the Agreements with the Ismaili Imamat, and other relevant statutory norms. Thus, faced with the complex Portuguese landscape of tax laws, helpful clarifications will emerge for religious entities, particularly for many private social solidarity institutions associated with them, enabling better allocate of resources

DOI: 10.4018/979-8-3693-3908-4.ch004

and improving their community impact.

INTRODUCTION

Two decades after the signing of the significant 2004 Concordat between the Portuguese Republic and the Holy See, there remains a need for clarity regarding its fiscal provisions. This chapter seeks to enhance the understanding and implementation of the Concordat's fiscal aspects, particularly concerning taxation and tax exemptions for the Catholic Church in Portugal. It analyzes the provisions outlined in Law No. 16/2001, of June 22 (AR, 2001), known as the Religious Freedom Law (Portuguese acronym: LLR), alongside the stipulations of the Concordat signed on 18 May 2004 (MPP, 2004). However, examining the broader religious landscape must provide a comprehensive historical, legal, and fiscal context. Thus, the research will not only focus on the tax status of the Catholic Church but will also include other religious denominations. A comparative analysis will evaluate the legal frameworks governing taxation for the significant religious entities in Portugal.

The main objectives of this chapter are as follows: to understand the tax regulations governing religious entities in Portugal; to clarify the tax rights and obligations applicable to these entities; to enhance understanding of fiscal and tax regulations by elucidating and differentiating specific tax terms within this domain; and to facilitate a clearer understanding of the implementation of tax regulations by both religious entities and the Tax and Customs Authority (Portuguese acronym: AT). Through this comprehensive analysis, the chapter aims to shed light on the complexities of the tax system concerning religious organizations, ensuring that both the entities and the regulatory authorities are well-informed and aligned in their interpretations and applications of the law. Additionally, this chapter seeks to contribute to the ongoing discourse on the intersection of religion and taxation, providing valuable insights that can inform future policy development and implementation.

The chosen methodology is qualitative and descriptive (Maxwell, 1992; Sandelowski, 2000; Mack et al., 2005; Sandelowski, 2010; Nassaji, 2015; Manjunatha, 2019; Elliott & Timulak, 2021; Cropley, 2022), involving a thorough review of the legality of religious phenomena and the taxation of religious entities in Portugal, with a particular emphasis on the Catholic Church. This approach, chosen for its ability to provide a detailed examination of the legal frameworks and tax regulations governing religious organizations, will allow for a comprehensive understanding of the tax system concerning religious organizations. By focusing on the Catholic Church, which holds significant prominence and influence in Portugal, the research aims to comprehensively understand how these regulations are applied and their broader implications. Additionally, this methodology will facilitate a comparative analysis of different religious entities, highlighting similarities and differences in their tax treatment under Portuguese law.

The remainder of this chapter is organized as follows. The second section will present the legal framework of the religious phenomenon in Portugal, examining the legislative texts that govern this domain, including the LLR, the Concordat, and the Agreements with the Ismaili Imamat (AII). In addition, it will detail the conditions and processes for the legal recognition of the legal personality of religious entities, providing a comprehensive understanding of the legal status and rights of these organizations. The third section will contextualize the relationship between religions and society, highlighting the positive externalities of religions and exploring how religious practices and institutions contribute to social cohesion, community support, and cultural enrichment. The fourth section, dedicated to presenting the tax framework of religions in the Portuguese tax regime, analyzes the specific tax regulations that apply to religious entities, covering the various tax obligations, exemptions, and benefits available to these organizations under Portuguese law. The fifth section delves into the specificities of the tax framework, offering a detailed examination of the particular tax terms and conditions that apply to different religious entities, differentiating the various types of religious organizations and the unique tax considerations for each. The final section will summarize the findings and conclusions of the chapter. It will discuss the application of tax regulations outlined in the Concordat and other relevant legal frameworks, aiming to provide clarity and efficacy in implementing these regulations. This discussion will contribute to a better understanding of the intersection of religion and taxation in Portugal, offering insights for future policy development and practical implementation. Through this structured approach, the chapter seeks to provide a thorough analysis of the legal and tax aspects of religious entities in Portugal to enhance clarity and compliance in this complex regulatory environment.

LEGAL FRAMEWORK OF THE RELIGIOUS PHENOMENON

Introductory remarks

The separation of churches and other religious communities from the state has historically been understood and implemented in two distinct ways. On one hand, it can be seen as irrelevance, contempt, opposition to religion, or confinement of religion to the private sphere. On the other hand, it can be viewed as the non-identification of the state with any religion, out of respect for individual freedom. The first interpretation aligns with the concept of secularism, characterized by a strict division where the state disregards religious influences entirely. The second interpretation aligns with secularity, which allows for a more nuanced relationship where the State maintains its independence from religious institutions while recognizing its role in society. The Constitution of the Portuguese Republic (Portuguese acronym: CRP) leans towards this second understanding, emphasizing secularity over secularism. If it followed secularism, the state would ignore the religious experiences present in society and the significant social functions that religious organizations play in areas such as education, solidarity, and social inclusion. This would mean a strict separation where religious contributions to public life are dismissed or undervalued.

Conversely, from the perspective of secularity, the state does not adopt religious purposes, endorse any religion, or subject any church to an administrative regime. However, this does not imply that the State considers religion irrelevant or refuses to cooperate with religious organizations. Instead, the State acknowledges these organizations' importance and potential contributions to the common good. Thus, the state remains neutral in religious matters, ensuring freedom of belief while fostering a collaborative environment where religious institutions can contribute positively to societal development. This balanced approach aims to respect and protect individual freedoms while promoting collective well-being through possible cooperation with religious communities when beneficial.

Indeed, the Portuguese State declares itself non-denominational and upholds the separation between the state and religious institutions. The foundation of secularism is enshrined in Article 41 of the CRP, which states that "*freedom of conscience, religion, and worship is inviolable*" and that "*churches and other religious communities are separated from the State and are free in their organization and in the exercise of their functions and worship*" (AR, 2005).

However, the State also must guarantee the freedoms necessary for the practice of faith. It is essential to understand that secularism does not equate to an alienation from religious matters. On the contrary, ignoring religious concerns does not ensure all citizens' freedom of conscience, religion, and worship. Therefore, the State must balance its non-denominational stance with active support for religious freedom, recognizing the role of religious communities in society while maintaining its neutrality. This approach ensures that all citizens can freely practice their faith without state interference, upholding the principles of freedom and respect for individual beliefs.

According to Miranda (2000: 409), religious freedom "*consists in the State allowing or enabling those who follow a certain religion to fulfill the duties that arise from it – in matters of worship, family, or education, for example - in reasonable terms*". This means that the State can facilitate the fulfillment of religious duties without imposing specific obligations on citizens, thereby safeguarding their freedom of conscience and worship. Therefore, the legal framework governing religions in Portugal must be well-regulated and clearly defined. This ensures that religious practices can be carried out freely and respectfully, within the bounds of the law, while maintaining the principles of individual liberty and State neutrality (Miranda, 2023).

The Constitution of the Portuguese Republic

The CRP (AR, 2005) does not define religion, nor could it, under penalty of infringing on the core of freedom itself. The problem arises, however, when it is necessary to define religion to address its collective and institutional dimensions. This issue requires legislative interventions to establish distinctions and border areas. For example, the constitutional text uses terminology with historical-cultural significance, sometimes referring to 'Churches and religious communities' (paragraph 4 of Article 41), sometimes to 'confessions' (paragraph 5 of Article 41 and paragraph 4 of Article 55), and sometimes simply to 'Churches' (paragraph 3 of Article 51 and Article 288).

In a systematic analysis of the constitutional text, it is worth distinguishing various levels of the content of religious freedom:

- Freedom of religion implies the freedom to manifest one's religion or convictions, alone or in a community, both in public and private, through teaching, practice, worship, or rituals, and to change religion or convictions (Article 18);
- Its guarantees include: no one can be persecuted, deprived of rights, or exempted from obligations or civic duties because of their beliefs or religious practices, which upholds the principle of equality (Article 13, paragraph 2); individuals cannot be questioned by any authority about their religious beliefs or practices, except for the collection of non-individually identifiable statistical data, nor can they be penalized for refusing to respond (paragraph 3 of Article 35);
- At the institutional level, according to Article 38, it is ensured that: Churches and other religious communities are separated from the State and are accessible in their organization (paragraph 4); Churches and other religious communities are free to exercise their functions and worship (paragraph 4); freedom to teach any religion practiced within the scope of the respective confession is guaranteed (paragraph 5); the use of social media outlets belonging to religious denominations is guaranteed for the pursuit of their activities (paragraph 5) and, therefore, journalists who work in them cannot intervene in their editorial guidance (paragraph 2);
- Related or complementary to religious freedom are several rules established in particular: the right to reserve the privacy of private life (paragraph 1 of Article 26); the diversity of forms of celebrating marriage, with requirements

and effects regulated by law (paragraph 2 of Article 36) forms should facilitate the celebration of marriage in harmony with the beliefs and convictions of the bride and groom; the right and duty of parents to educate their children (paragraph 5 of Article 36), including religious education; the State cannot impose educational and cultural programs based on any religious guidelines (paragraph 2 of Article 43). It must uphold religious pluralism and refrain from interfering with choices and guidelines of a religious nature that manifest themselves in education and culture; and

- Interferences with other rights or the delimitation of the scope of religious freedom in light of other rights also include: political parties cannot use denominations that contain expressions directly related to any religions or Churches, nor emblems that can be confused with religious symbols, without prejudice to the philosophy or ideology inspiring their program (paragraph 3 of Article 51 and Article 205); and trade union associations are independent of religious denominations (paragraph 4 of Article 55).

The Religious Freedom Law

Considering Article 41 of the CRP (AR, 2005), the LLR, approved through Law No. 16/2001, of June 22 (AR, 2001), guarantees that freedom of conscience, religion, and worship is inviolable in Portugal, granting separation from the State and freedom to religions in their organization and exercise of their functions and worship. The LLR (AR, 2001) outlines individuals' rights and powers (Article 8 et seq.), including:

- Professing one's belief, seeking new believers, freely expressing and disseminating thoughts on religious matters;
- Joining the Church or religious community of one's choice and participating in its internal life and communal religious rites;
- Receiving requested religious assistance;
- Celebrating marriage with the rites of one's religion;
- Publicly observing religious festivals;
- Being buried with the rites of one's religion;
- Informing and being informed about religion, learning and teaching religion;
- Gathering, demonstrating and associating with others according to religious convictions;
- Choosing proper names from their children's onomastics of the professed religion;
- Being exempt from work, classes, and exams on days required by their religion;

- Not being obliged to practice or attend acts of worship, receive religious assistance, or be subjected to religious propaganda;
- Not being coerced to join, remain in, or leave a religious association, Church, or religious community; and
- Not being required to take a religious oath.

To further guarantee the institutional freedom of religious confessions, the LLR (AR, 2001) enshrines specific norms for ministers of worship or individuals considered as such and certified according to the norms of their respective confession, as well as for members of institutes of consecrated life (Articles 15 and paragraph 5 of 16). These include religious secrecy, whereby they cannot be compelled by magistrates or other authorities to divulge information obtained through their ministry (paragraph 1 of Article 16); consideration of their ministry as a professional activity when it provides them with means of support (paragraph 3 of Article 16), which implies subjection to income tax; fulfillment of military obligations in the religious assistance, health, and social services of the Armed Forces (Article 17); and the possibility of requesting exemption from serving as jurors (Article 18).

To determine the legal regime, under Article 21 of the LLR (AR, 2001), "*religious purposes are defined as those involving worship and rituals, religious assistance, training of ministers of worship, mission work, and the propagation of the professed confession, as well as the teaching of religion*". And "*non-religious purposes include activities such as assistance and charity, education and culture, as well as commercial and profit-driven endeavors*", regardless of whether they are claimed to be religious by the respective confessions themselves. It is this legal framework that determines that "*activities with non-religious purposes are subject to the legal and tax regulations applicable to such activities*".

The Concordat between the Portuguese Republic and the Holy See

Portugal has maintained a privileged historical relationship with the Holy See since May 23, 1179. Noteworthy events in the chronology of relations between Portugal and the Holy See include:

- The opening of the Nunciature in Lisbon in 1513;
- The signing of the first contractual Concordat in 1738, during the reign of Dom João V;
- The signing of a new Concordat during the reign of D. Maria I in 1778 and in 1857, following the break-in institutional relations between 1834 and 1841;

- The reestablishment of diplomatic relations on July 9, 1918, after severing diplomatic ties with the Holy See during the First Republic on July 1, 1911;
- The Concordat and Missionary Agreement was signed on May 7, 1940; and
- The elevation of the Portuguese Legation to the Holy See to an Embassy, making it the fourth abroad after London, Rio de Janeiro, and Madrid (MNE, 2024).

The Concordat signed on May 18, 2004, is in force. It was approved by Resolution of the Assembly of the Republic No. 74/2004 on September 30 and by Presidential Decree No. 80/2004 on November 16 (MPP, 2004). Through the Concordat, the Portuguese State recognizes the legal personality of the Catholic Church, as a supranational institution and international subject represented by the Holy See, recognizing two types of legal persons: on the one hand, the Portuguese Episcopal Conference (Article 8) and the dioceses, parishes and other ecclesiastical jurisdictions (paragraph 1 of Article 9); and on the other, the canonical legal entities created by those entities.

The Portuguese Episcopal Conference and the dioceses, parishes, and other ecclesiastical jurisdictions are entities with unquestionably religious purposes, recognized by the Portuguese State, following paragraph 1 of Article 2 of the Concordat. Other canonical legal entities created by these organizations may or may not pursue religious purposes. If, in addition to religious purposes, they engage in activities of assistance and solidarity, they operate under the legal regime established by Portuguese law and enjoy the rights and benefits granted to private legal entities with similar objectives (Article 12).

The 2004 Concordat, like the 1940 Concordat, is a proper international treaty, possessing the binding force of such agreements, which prevail over domestic law as constitutionally recognized. As a repository of legal norms, the Concordat must be interpreted considering the meaning and origin of the canonical concepts it expresses, reflecting their significance in the documents of the Catholic Church. The tax qualification of the facts must consider their canonical conceptualization, as the Canon Law of the Church is constitutionally recognized as a prior and necessary legal order for their framework.

The Agreements between the Portuguese Republic and the Ismaili Imamat

Over the past four decades, the Portuguese State has signed six agreements with leaders of the Ismaili Muslim community. The relationship between the Ismaili Imamat and the Portuguese State began in 1983, when the Aga Khan Foundation was recognized as a collective entity of public utility (Articles 1 and 3 of Decree-

Law No. 130/83, of March 16 – PCM, 1983). The Aga Khan Foundation (AKF) and the AKF Portugal are part of the Aga Khan Development Network (AKDN), established and directed by the Ismaili Imamat, which encompasses several institutions that conduct development support activities in various regions of the world.

On December 19, 2005, through Decree No. 11/2006 (MNE, 2006), the Portuguese Government and the Ismaili Imamat signed a cooperation protocol in Lisbon aimed at providing the AKDN with better conditions to carry out its activities in Portugal (paragraph 2 of Article 2). With significant legal-international relevance, the Portuguese government committed to conferring on a personal representative appointed by the Ismaili Imamat for Portugal, prerogatives equivalent to those defined in the Vienna Conventions on Diplomatic Relations and Consular Relations (Articles 3 and 5), and to guarantee tax exemptions for the representative and their family, as well as for goods imported by the AKDN (Articles 3, 5, and 12).

The legal-international nature of the cooperation protocol adopted in 2005 was further underscored by the international agreement signed on May 8, 2009, between Portugal and the Ismaili Imamat (AR, 2009). This agreement, considered an instrument similar to the Cooperation Protocol, had a non-religious scope. It was justified by the unique institutional configuration of the Ismaili community, which is institutionally represented by the Ismaili Imamat, a supranational entity, due to its lack of a formal autonomous local or national religious authority in each country.

This framework paved the way for a broader agreement, culminating in the AII, signed in Lisbon on June 3, 2015 (AR, 2015). Through this agreement, the Portuguese Republic recognizes the legal personality and capacity of the Ismaili Imamat to act in international relations. It welcomes the Imam's decision to establish the international headquarters of the Ismaili Imamat in Portugal (Article 2). This development underscores Portugal's commitment to fostering strong diplomatic and cooperative relationships with diverse religious communities, enhancing its role as a center for international dialogue and development.

Legal personality is at the core of tax personality, which, according to the Portuguese General Tax Law, in Article 15, "*susceptibility to being the subject of tax legal relations*" (AT, 2024a). Entities without legal personality also lack tax personality. However, there can be cases where an entity possesses legal personality but not tax personality. In such cases, it is not subject to tax relations because it has no income or assets, does not carry out taxable acts, or because the law expressly excludes it from such subjection. Table 1 presents the legal regulations by which the Portuguese State recognizes the legal personality of religious entities.

Table 1. Recognition of the legal personality of religious legal entities

Normative	Religious Legal Entities	Recognition of Legal Personality
2001 - Religious Freedom Law	• Churches and religious communities at a national, regional or local level. • Organizations representing believers residing in national territory. • Institutes of consecrated life. • Other Institutes with the nature of associations or foundations.	Registration in the Register of Religious Legal Entities (LLR, Article 33)
2004 - Concordat between the Portuguese Republic and the Holy See	• Holy See. • Catholic church. • Portuguese Episcopal Conference.	*De jure* Concordat, Articles 1 and 8)
	• Dioceses. • Parishes. • Other ecclesiastical jurisdictions.	Notification to the competent State organ (Concordat, paragraph 2 of Article 9)
	• Other canonical legal entities. • Institutes of consecrated life. • Societies of apostolic life, constituted and participated before December 18, 2004.	Registration in the Register of Religious Legal Entities (LLR, paragraph 3 of Article 10)
2015 - Agreements with the Ismaili Imamat	• Ismaili Imamat.	*De jure* (AII, paragraph 1 of Article 2)

Source: Adapted from Panzina (2016).

RELATIONSHIP BETWEEN RELIGIONS AND SOCIETY

The importance of the religious phenomenon also can be gauged by the relevance given to it in legal instruments, such as the Universal Declaration of Human Rights (UDHR), particularly Articles 2, 18, 19 and 20 (UN, 1948); the International Covenant on Economic, Social and Cultural Rights (ICESCR), Article 13 (UN, 1967a); the International Covenant on Civil and Political Rights (ICCPR), Articles 18, 20, 24 and 26 (UN, 1967b); the Declaration on the Elimination of All Forms of Intolerance and Discrimination Based on Religion or Belief (UN, 1981); the Rome Statute of the International Criminal Court, Articles 7 and 8 (ICC, 2021); the European Convention on Human Rights, for the Projection of Human Rights and Fundamental Freedoms (ECHR), Articles 9 and 10 (TEDH, 1950); the Treaty on the Functioning of the European Union (TEEC), Article 10 (EU, 2012); or the Charter of Fundamental Rights of the European Union (CFR), Articles 10, 21 and 22 (EU, 2000). These instruments underscore the significance of religious freedom and the protection of religious rights globally, establishing a legal framework that supports the free practice of religion, combats discrimination, and promotes tolerance and understanding across different faiths and beliefs.

The religious phenomenon extends beyond the exercise of individual rights and manifests as a communal experience that impacts various aspects of life in society. It contributes to the integral development of the human being, human fraternity, the preservation of culture and identity, ecology, interreligious dialogue, and peace. As noted by Miranda (2000: 405), the religious phenomenon "*penetrates the most intimate spheres of human consciousness and, simultaneously, manifests itself in large collective movements, and has always had an important political and legal-political projection. It has constantly influenced not only cultural history but also political history. No Constitution fails to consider it, affecting International Law*".

Religion's influence spans history, continually shaping humanity, families, and individuals. Consequently, religion is deeply embedded in the organizational structures and guiding values of States. Weninger (2009: 72) observes, "*the Church, society, and the State are not separate entities, but necessarily interdependent, although each with its characteristics*". The concept of secularism within States is both a product and a desire of religion, offering reciprocal advantages. This interdependence underscores religion's pivotal role in shaping societal values and governance, highlighting its enduring significance in the modern world.

Some economists argue that economics is fundamentally atheistic, asserting that religious beliefs, practices, and behaviors do not play a relevant role in the life of '*homo economicus*'. However, this perspective may be overly simplistic. Religion and economy are interrelated, and "*one can even speak of an economy of religion, which buries two myths: that of homo economicus as a creature without the need or capacity for pity, and that of homo religious as a regression to pre-rational times*" (Iannaccone, 2023: 257-258).

While a specific non-empirical Freudian tradition seeks to blame religion for prejudice and authoritarianism, empirical studies consistently find that "*high rates of religious commitment and activity are associated with better mental health, reduced stress, and increased satisfaction with life*" (Iannaccone, 2023: 240). This evidence suggests that the religious phenomenon produces positive externalities, such as improved mental health and overall well-being.

These potential positive externalities form the basis for the tax benefits granted to religious organizations. These benefits can take various forms, including the exclusion of tax liability, exemption from paying taxes, or the refund of certain taxes. By recognizing the beneficial societal impacts of religious commitment and activity, such tax benefits aim to support the continued contribution of religious entities to the common good. This intertwining of economic and religious considerations highlights the importance of religion in shaping personal lives and broader economic and social policies.

Acts of production or consumption that generate benefits are called 'positive externalities,' while 'negative externalities' generate losses. For example, pollution caused by certain industries or generated by car traffic is considered a negative externality. Conversely, public education and vaccination are considered positive externalities due to the benefits they bring to society. Activities associated with positive externalities can be supported through a subsidy, equal to the external marginal benefit. An implicit form of subsidy is "*the granting of tax benefits through which a company or consumer is taxed less than they should be in the absence of that exceptional tax measure, given that their activity is associated with positive external effects*" (Pereira et al., 2016: 61-62). The opposite also applies, as activities associated with negative externalities can be taxed to ensure producers internalize the external marginal cost of their activity, such as the taxation of tobacco or sugary products.

In this sense, the religious phenomenon, understood as a type of 'consumer good' that satisfies certain individual and collective needs, can be associated with benefits classified as positive externalities. Given that these benefits are useful and desired by society, some economists argue that State intervention is justified to stimulate these effects. Examples include the defense of human dignity and fundamental rights, the social, educational, and health dimensions, the defense of the common good, and the promotion of universal fraternity and peace. Society benefits from the message that religions transmit to their believers, which values the good of the person and defends their fundamental rights.

However, it is also essential to acknowledge that sometimes negative externalities are associated with certain abusive religious phenomena, such as extremist groups that misuse religion to justify their terrorist, extremist, and ideological acts. In these cases, it is crucial to recognize that religion is being misused, contrary to its more profound sense of fraternity, communion, common good, and peace. Proper regulation and oversight are necessary to distinguish between the positive contributions of religious activities and the potential harms caused by their misuse. This nuanced understanding ensures that the positive externalities of religious phenomena are supported and maximized while negative impacts are mitigated.

Positive externalities provide a rationale for extending benefits and privileges without compromising the principle of equality. This principle applies broadly across society, prompting the question of how the State might acknowledge and support the positive externalities generated by religions. One approach could involve earmarking specific tax revenues collected by the State for allocation to Churches. This model is observed in several Islamic nations and certain European countries such as Germany, Austria, and Switzerland, where an ecclesiastical tax known as 'kirschensteuer' exists. Another method could be for the State to assume certain financial obligations that aid Churches, such as directly funding salaries for clergy. This practice is notably prevalent in regions where the Orthodox Church holds a majority. Additionally, governments may grant tax incentives to religious organizations, as seen in Portugal. While this approach does not entail levying a dedicated tax nor imply state interference in Church affairs, it effectively functions as indirect support since forgoing taxes equates to a form of subsidy.

TAX FRAMEWORK OF RELIGIONS

Introductory Remarks

The State finances its services and infrastructure through taxes and fees on taxpayers' assets and income. However, it provides tax exemptions or deductions to non-profit entities - such as religious organizations, cooperatives, and foundations - that contribute to the common good, particularly in areas like social services, education, or health. The aim is to acknowledge the social value of these organizations and support their activities, which benefit society as a whole. Consequently, churches and other religious communities, as integral parts of the social sector, are subject to the same legal and tax provisions that apply to social economy organizations, enabling them to access these incentives while carrying out their religious and community-oriented roles. Additionally, certain types of heritage and income with cultural, historical, or devotional significance are also eligible for these exemptions.

Article 2 of the Portuguese Tax Benefits Code (Portuguese acronym: EBF) considers exemptions, rate reductions, deductions from the tax base and tax collection, accelerated amortizations and reinstatements, and other tax measures to be tax benefits (AT, 2024b).

In the context of Personal Income Tax (Portuguese acronym: IRS) paragraph 1 of Article 37 of the EBF (AT, 2024b) exempts the staff of diplomatic and consular missions from this tax on their remuneration, provided there is applicable international law or reciprocity. This applies to the Apostolic Nuncio of the Catholic Church and the Imam, his family, and other diplomatic representatives of the Ismaili Imamat recognized by the Portuguese State. Also, Article 63 of the EBF specifies that donations made to churches, religious institutions, or non-profit entities associated with or established by religious denominations are IRS deductible, with their value considered at 130% of the donation amount. This provision encourages charitable contributions and provides substantial fiscal incentives to support religious and related non-profit organizations, highlighting the Government's commitment to fostering philanthropy and supporting the financial sustainability of entities that play a crucial role in social and community services.

Regarding tax benefits related to property, Article 44 of the EBF (AT, 2024b) states as exemptions from IMI:

- Properties used as diplomatic or consular representations of foreign states, provided there is reciprocity, i.e., the Apostolic Nunciature for the Catholic Church and to the international headquarters, Imam's residences, and other diplomatic buildings for the Ismaili Imamat;
- Temples or buildings of religious associations or organizations exclusively used for worship or related non-economic purposes. This applies to all legally recognized religions in Portugal; and
- Properties classified as national monuments or individually classified as of public or municipal interest, i.e., religious temples, particularly Catholic, classified as monuments due to their age or heritage value.

Concerning donations, Article 62 of the EBF (AT, 2024b) specifies that, for determining taxable profit, costs are considered in amounts corresponding to:

- 140% of the total, when intended exclusively to achieve social purposes;
- 120%, if intended exclusively for environmental, sporting and educational purposes; and
- 130% of the total, when allocated under multi-year contracts for specific purposes that define the objectives pursued by the beneficiary entities and the amounts contributed by the taxpayers.

The preceding Article holds particular significance for the Catholic Church, given that most Portuguese Private Institutions of Social Solidarity (Portuguese acronym: IPSS) are associated with dioceses and parishes. Additionally, it is noteworthy that the Ismaili Imamat similarly benefits from the exemptions outlined in this Article, as the Aga Khan Portugal Foundation functions as a non-governmental development organization.

Also, under the scope of Value Added Tax (Portuguese acronym: IVA), Decree-Law No. 20/90, of January 13 (MF, 1990), provides certain VAT exemptions to the Catholic Church and other Religious Communities based in Portugal. These exemptions, in line with the Concordat between the Holy See and the Portuguese Republic (MPP, 2004) and the Religious Freedom Law (AR, 2001), allow for the refund of VAT paid on specific imports and purchases of goods and services. Similarly, the Ismaili Imamat is entitled to a refund of the amounts corresponding to VAT paid on certain goods and services acquired or imported for its official use (AR, 2015).

The Religious Freedom Law

Articles 31 and 32 of the LLR (AR, 2001) outline the taxation applied to religious entities in Portugal. In Article 31, the tax-exempt contributions are identified:

"1 - Churches and other religious communities may freely, without being subject to any tax:

a) receive contributions from believers for the exercise of worship and rites, as well as donations for the achievement of their religious purposes, either on a regular or occasional basis.
b) conduct public collections, particularly inside or at the entrance of places of worship, as well as buildings or places belonging to them.
c) distribute religious publications with statements, notices, or instructions for free and post them in places of worship.

2 - The provisions of the previous paragraph do not include the price of training, therapy, or spiritual counselling services offered commercially."

Thus, religious entities are exempt from any tax on contributions, donations, and public collections conducted for religious purposes. However, training, therapy, or spiritual counselling activities offered commercially are not eligible for tax exemption. In this sense, Article 32 establishes the legal framework for tax benefits, such as:

- Paragraph 1 enumerates the properties exempt from any tax or contribution, specifically Municipal Property Tax (Portuguese acronym: IMI);
- Paragraph 2 outlines the situations exempt from any tax or contribution, specifically Municipal Property Transfer Tax (Portuguese acronym: IMT);
- Paragraph 3 specifies the deductible bonus granted to individuals who make donations to religious legal entities;
- Paragraph 4 grants taxpayers the option to choose the Church or religious community that may benefit from a percentage of their tax paid to the State;
- Paragraph 5 explains that this process is always conducted exclusively through the State Treasury, which collects taxes and redistributes them according to the expressed wishes of taxpayers; and
- Paragraph 6 expands the range of potential beneficiaries of this individual taxpayer choice, allowing charitable, assistance, humanitarian, or social institutions to also benefit from this percentage of tax collected by the State.

The Concordat between the Portuguese Republic and the Holy See

Articles 10, 12 and 26 of the Concordat (MPP, 2004) establish the fiscal framework applied to religious entities in Portugal. On the one hand, following paragraph 1 of Article 10, the Catholic Church in Portugal has the freedom to organize itself according to canon law norms and establish, modify, and dissolve canonical legal entities, which the State recognizes as possessing civil legal personality. On the other hand, Article 12 stipulates that those canonical legal entities that pursue purposes of assistance and solidarity in addition to religious objectives must conduct their activities by the legal regime established by Portuguese law.

These entities enjoy the rights and benefits granted to private legal entities with similar purposes. Thus, Article 26, similarly to Article 31 of LLR (AR, 2001), mandates that the Holy See, the Portuguese Episcopal Conference, dioceses and other religious entities are exempt, among others, from any:

- Tax on contributions, donations, and public collections conducted for religious purposes (paragraph 1);
- Municipal Property Tax, i.e. IMI (paragraph 2); and
- Municipal Property Transfer Tax, i.e. IMT (paragraph 3).

Therefore, the 2004 Concordat established a new tax regime for religious entities within the Catholic Church. This regime is characterized and justified by the nature of these religious entities and their religious purposes. The basis of this new regime is the nature of the legal entities it applies to and the religious aims they pursue through their activities. Under this regime, these entities are exempt from taxes on services, donations, public collections, and the free distribution of publications if they are for religious purposes. They are also exempt from any general, regional, or local taxes or contributions on properties, buildings, facilities, dependencies, gardens, yards, and movable assets used for religious purposes or by IPSS. Additionally, these entities are exempt from the Stamp Tax (Portuguese acronym: IS) and all taxes on the transfer of properties, whether real estate or other assets, or the establishment of foundations. In summary, 2004 adopted an exemption/objective taxation criterion, effectively linking tax exemptions to the assets and the activities conducted there.

Specificities of the tax framework

Table 2 addresses the topic of tax exemption from Corporate Income Tax (Portuguese acronym: IRC). This table presents Articles 31 (paragraphs 1 and 2) of the LLR (AR, 2001), 26 (paragraph 1) of the Concordat (MPP, 2004), and 11 (paragraphs 1, 2 and 3) of the AII (AR, 2009; 2015), in parallel. The income excluded from taxation is similar across the three regulations. However, some differences can be identified.

Table 2. Articles that exclude from subjection to IRC

Religious Freedom Law (Article 31)	**Concordat between the Portuguese Republic and the Holy See (Article 26)**	**Agreements with the Ismaili Imamat (Article 11)**
1 - Churches and other religious communities may freely, without being subject to any tax:	1 - The Holy See, the Portuguese Episcopal Conference, dioceses and other ecclesiastical jurisdictions, as well as other canonical legal entities recognized as civil entities under Articles 9 and 10, are not subject to any tax on:	1 - Donations, legacies, income (including capital gains), and assets related to the Ismaili Imamat or the Imam are exempt from all taxes, including income and property taxes.
a) Payments from believers for worship and rites, as well as donations for religious purposes.	a) Services for worship and rites by believers; b) Donations for religious purposes;	2 - Except for more favorable provisions granted by the Portuguese Republic to other religious institutions, paragraph 1 does not apply to:
b) Public collections, both inside and outside places of worship.	c) Proceeds from public collections for religious purposes;	a) Income derived from any business activity conducted directly in Portugal or assets related to such activity;
c) Free distribution and posting of religious publications in places of worship.	d) Free distribution and posting of religious publications with declarations, warnings, or instructions in places of worship.	b) Interest and other investment income, whether received or paid by residents of Portugal or effectively connected to the operations of a permanent establishment or fixed base in Portugal, as outlined in the Portuguese Corporate Income Tax Code.
2 - Corporate training, therapy, or spiritual counselling services are not tax-exempt.	---	3 - Income specified in paragraph 2(b), is subject to final withholding tax as per the IRC regulations of the Portuguese Republic.

Source: Adapted from Panzina (2016).

For example, concerning public collections, the LLR (paragraph 1(b) of Article 31) imposes a limitation not found in the Concordat. The LLR specifies that the exclusion from taxation on public collections is limited to those conducted "*inside or at the door of places of worship, as well as buildings or places belonging to them*" (AR, 2001), while the Concordat does not specify any geographical limitations.

Also, in Article 31 of the LLR, the legislator does not restrict public collections of Churches and religious communities to 'religious purposes', unlike the restriction established for the Catholic Church in the Concordat. According to Article 21 (paragraph 1(a)) of the LLR, 'religious purposes' include "*the exercise of worship and rites, religious assistance, training of ministers of worship, missionary and dissemination of the professed confession, and teaching of religion*" (AR, 2001).

On the other hand, paragraph 2 of Article 31 of the LLR, which excludes from tax exemption "*the price of training, therapy, or spiritual counselling services offered on a corporate basis*" (AR, 2001), has no equivalent in the Concordat.

In turn, the differences and the lack of equivalence are even more pronounced in the 2015 AII. Article 11 (paragraph 1) of the AII extends benefits not only to the legal entity, the Ismaili Imamat, but also to the natural person, the Imam, creating an exception unparalleled in the LLR and the Concordat.

Table 3 statements the topic of tax exemption from IMI, in which Articles 32 (paragraph 1) of the LLR (AR, 2001), 26 (paragraph 2) of the Concordat (MPP, 2004), and 11 (paragraph 4) of the AII (AR, 2009; 2015), are placed in parallel, to allow a transversal reading of the tax exemption on IMI.

Table 3. Articles that exclude from subjection to IMI

Religious Freedom Law (Article 32)	**Concordat between the Portuguese Republic and the Holy See (Article 26)**	**Agreements with the Ismaili Imamat (Article 11)**
1 - Registered religious legal entities are exempt from general, regional, or local taxes or contributions on:	2 - The Holy See, the Portuguese Episcopal Conference, dioceses and other ecclesiastical jurisdictions, as well as other canonical legal entities recognized as civil entities under Articles 9 and 10, are exempt from any general, regional or local tax or contribution, on:	4 - The Ismaili Imamat will be exempt from any local or national tax on real property concerning the Headquarters facilities.
a) Places of worship or other buildings intended directly for religious purposes;	a) Places of worship or other buildings directly intended for religious purposes;	
b) Facilities exclusively supporting activities for religious purposes;	b) Facilities exclusively supporting activities for religious purposes;	
c) Seminaries or establishments specifically for training ministers of worship or teaching religion;	c) Seminaries or establishments for ecclesiastical training or teaching the Catholic religion;	
d) Dependencies or annexes of the buildings in a) to c) for use by IPSS;	d) Dependencies or annexes of the buildings in a) to c) for use by IPSS;	
e) Gardens and public areas of the buildings in a) to d), provided they are not intended for profit.	e) Gardens and public areas of the buildings in a) to d), provided they are not intended for profit;	
---	f) Movable assets of a religious nature integrated into the properties mentioned above or as accessories thereto.	

Source: Adapted from Panzina (2016).

Thus, considering Article 26 of the Concordat (MPP, 2004), canonical legal entities that, in addition to their religious purposes, also engage in activities aimed at aiding and fostering solidarity, are immediately recognized and granted specific tax rights and benefits. These include exemptions and reductions, particularly in matters related to the IMI, facilitating their operations and enhancing their ability to contribute to social welfare.

In Table 4, a parallel is established between Articles 32 (paragraph 2) of the LLR (AR, 2001), 26 (paragraph 3) of the Concordat (MPP, 2004), and 11 (paragraphs 5 and 6) of the AII (AR, 2009; 2015), which specifically refer to IMT and IS exemption.

Table 4. Articles that exclude from subjection to IMT

<table>
<tr><th>Religious Freedom Law
(Article 31)</th><th>Concordat between the Portuguese Republic and the Holy See
(Article 26)</th><th>Agreements with the Ismaili Imamat
(Article 11)</th></tr>
<tr><td>2 - Registered religious legal entities are exempt from IMT, or any similar tax with patrimonial impact, regarding:</td><td>3 - The Holy See, the Portuguese Episcopal Conference, dioceses and other ecclesiastical jurisdictions, as well as other canonical legal entities recognized as civil entities under Articles 9 and 10, are exempt from IS and all taxes on the transfer of goods that affect:</td><td>5 - The Ismaili Imamat and Imam are exempt from IS and any other transaction taxes related to the acquisition or sale of movable or immovable property used or intended for their official functions.</td></tr>
<tr><td rowspan="2">a) Acquisitions of goods for religious purposes;</td><td>a) Purchases of real property for religious purposes, whether onerous or free;</td><td rowspan="3">6 - The Ismaili Imamat and Imam are exempt from taxes or duties on the purchase, ownership, registration, use, or sale of land, air, or sea vehicles, including spare parts and consumables, used for their official functions.</td></tr>
<tr><td>b) Acquisitions of goods for religious purposes without consideration;</td></tr>
<tr><td>b) Establishment acts of foundations, once registered as religious legal entities.</td><td>c) Acts establishing foundations, once registered in the State registry under Article 10.</td></tr>
</table>

Source: Adapted from Panzina (2016).

As observed in Tables 2, 3, and 4, paragraphs 5 and 6 of Article 11 of the AII (AR, 2009; 2015) show no parallelism with either the text or the spirit of the LLR and the Concordat and introduce significant inequality in the system of benefits provided to different religions. They exempt the Imam from paying IS and IMT to acquire real estate and furniture. They extend this exemption to other taxes related to the purchase, sale, ownership, registration, and use of vehicles, aircraft, and vessels. Attempting to justify this tax disparity, it appears that these differences might be understood only because the Imam, besides benefiting from the legal protections of these religious agreements, also enjoys the legal status accorded to diplomatic delegations. This dual religious and political coverage is the only plausible explanation. Otherwise, such provisions lack rational justification and distort the LLR principles.

CONCLUSION

The Portuguese context regarding religious freedom, ecumenical and inter-religious dialogue, peace, security, and religious education is highly positive and has served as an inspiration and example for other countries worldwide. The approval and implementation of the LLR (AR, 2001), which outlines the relationship between religions and the State, has significantly contributed to this favorable environment.

In Portugal, the foundation for recognizing the legal personality of religious entities is rooted in a legal framework that starts with the CRP (AR, 2005) itself and extends to other essential documents that elaborate on it, including the LLR (AR, 2001), the Concordat with the Holy See (MPP, 2004), and the Agreements with the Ismaili Imamat (AR, 2009; 2015). Such recognition is essential, as it forms the basis for the subsequent recognition and regulation of their tax personality. Acknowledging these religious entities' legal and tax personalities is crucial for fostering a healthy and fruitful relationship between the State and religious entities. This dual recognition facilitates compliance with tax obligations and enables religious entities to benefit from tax exemptions and other tax benefits. However, this analysis raises questions that require further clarification, whether concerning the obligation of maintaining organized accounting or the fulfillment of certain declarative tax obligations, the definition of the specific purposes of the Catholic Church, or the reference to Portuguese law for certain activities.

The parallelism established between the LLR (AR, 2001), the Concordat (MPP, 2004) and the AII (AR, 2009; 2015) highlights the discrepancies among these different regulations. This suggests the need for a comprehensive reflection on the potential benefits of revising these regulations to achieve more significant legal conciliation while respecting the specificities of each religion. Such a reflection could follow the recommended steps for drafting normative acts, helping to achieve more outstanding quality and transparency. Critical steps in this legal process include establishing the normative framework of the issue; defining the objectives to be achieved through legislative intervention, analyzing alternatives to legislative intervention, adopting the normative solution that best addresses the initial problem, and conducting a self-assessment of legality.

In conclusion, the Portuguese legal and fiscal governance model for religious entities is a notable example, offering insights and strategies that could benefit other countries. This approach highlights the significance of ongoing dialogue and collaboration between the State and the religious communities. It demonstrates how legal systems can accommodate religious diversity while ensuring social cohesion and equity. However, it is crucial to note that the research does not aim to resolve all issues definitively but aims to stimulate inquiry, propose solutions, foster critical thinking, and encourage societal engagement. The chapter aims to contribute meaningfully to the discussion of taxation and religious entities in Portugal by fostering critical thinking.

REFERENCES

AR - Assembleia da República. (2001). *Lei n.º 16/2001, 22.06.2001 - Lei da Liberdade Religiosa.* Available in: https://diariodarepublica.pt/dr/legislacao-consolidada/lei/2001-34483475 [Accessed in January 2024].

AR - Assembleia da República. (2005). *Lei Constitucional nº 1/2005, 12.08.2005 - Sétima da Constituição da República Portuguesa.* Available in: https://files.dre.pt/1s/2005/08/155a00/46424686.pdf [Accessed in January 2024].

AR - Assembleia da República. (2009). *Acordo com o Imamat Ismaili.* Available in: https://files.dre.pt/1s/2010/09/18700/0427104275.pdf [Accessed in January 2024].

AR - Assembleia da República. (2015). *Acordo com o Imamat Ismaili com vista ao estabelecimento da sua Sede em Portugal.* Available in: https://files.diariodarepublica.pt/1s/2015/10/21000/0924609253.pdf [Accessed in January 2024].

AT - Autoridade Tributária e Aduaneira. (2024a). *Lei Geral Tributária.* Available in: https://info.portaldasfinancas.gov.pt/pt/informacao_fiscal/codigos_tributarios/lgt/Pages/lei-geral-tributaria-indice.aspx [Accessed in January 2024].

AT – Autoridade Tributária e Aduaneira. (2024b). *Estatuto dos Benefícios Fiscais.* Available in: https://info.portaldasfinancas.gov.pt/pt/informacao_fiscal/codigos_tributarios/bf_rep/Pages/estatuto-dos-beneficios-fiscais-indice.aspx [Accessed in January 2024].

Cropley, A. J. (2022). *Qualitative research methods: A practice-oriented introduction.* Bucharest: Editura Intaglio. https://doi:DOI: 10.13140/RG.2.1.3095.6888/1

Elliott, R., & Timulak, L. (2021). Why a generic approach to descriptive-interpretive qualitative research? In Elliott, R., & Timulak, L. (Eds.), *Essentials of descriptive-interpretive qualitative research: A generic approach* (pp. 3–14). American Psychological Association., DOI: 10.1037/0000224-001

EU - European Union. (2000). *Charter of Fundamental Rights of the European Union.* Available in: https://www.europarl.europa.eu/charter/pdf/text_en.pdf [Accessed in January 2024].

EU - European Union. (2012). *Treaty on the Functioning of the European Union.* Available in: https://eur-lex.europa.eu/legal-content/EN/TXT/PDF/?uri=CELEX:12012E/TXT [Accessed in January 2024].

Iannaccone, L. (2023). *Introdução à economia da religião.* Available in: https://www.researchgate.net/publication/376014586_Introducao_a_economia_da_religiao [Accessed in January 2024].

ICC - International Criminal Court. (2021). *Rome Statute of the International Criminal Court.* Available in: https://www.icc-cpi.int/sites/default/files/2024-05/Rome-Statute-eng.pdf [Accessed in January 2024].

Mack, N., Woodsong, C., Macqueen, K. M., Guest, G., & Namey, E. (2005). *Qualitative Research Methods: A Data Collector's Field Guide.* Available in: https://www.fhi360.org/wp-content/uploads/2024/01/Qualitative-Research-Methods-A-Data-Collectors-Field-Guide.pdf [Accessed in January 2024].

Manjunatha, N. (2019). Descriptive Research. *Journal of Emerging Technologies and Innovative Research*, 6(6), 863–867. https://www.jetir.org/papers/JETIR1908597.pdf

Maxwell, J. A. (1992). Understanding and validity in qualitative research. *Harvard Educational Review*, 62(3), 279–300. DOI: 10.17763/haer.62.3.8323320856251826

MF - Ministério das Finanças. (1990). *Decreto-Lei n.º 20/90, 13.01.1990 – Prevê a restituição de IVA à Igreja Católica e às instituições particulares de solidariedade social.* Available in: https://files.diariodarepublica.pt/1s/1990/01/01100/01990201.pdf [Accessed in January 2024].

Miranda, J. (2000). *Manual de Direito Constitucional, Tomo IV, Direitos Fundamentais.* Coimbra Editora.

Miranda, J. (2023). Liberdade Religiosa e Constituição. In *Marujo, A. (2023). Os Caminhos da Liberdade Religiosa em Portugal. Catálogo da exposição na Assembleia da República.* Edições Assembleia da República.

MNE - Ministério dos Negócios Estrangeiros (2006). *Decreto n.º 11/2006, 11.03.2006 - Protocolo de Cooperação entre o Governo da República Portuguesa e o Imamat Ismaili e respectiva lista de compromissos existentes e iniciativas adicionais.* Available in: https://files.diariodarepublica.pt/1s/2006/03/053a00/18581870.pdf [Accessed in January 2024].

MNE - Ministério dos Negócios Estrangeiros (2024). *Relações de Portugal com a Santa Sé.* Available in: https://santase.embaixadaportugal.mne.gov.pt/pt/sobre-a-santa-se/relações-com-portugal [Accessed in January 2024].

MPP - Ministério Público Portugal. (2004). *Concordata entre a República Portuguesa e a Santa Sé.* Available in: https://gddc.ministeriopublico.pt/sites/default/files/documentos/instrumentos/concordata_santa_se.pdf [Accessed in January 2024].

Nassaji, H. (2015). Qualitative and descriptive research: Data type versus data analysis. *Language Teaching Research*, 19(2), 129–132. DOI: 10.1177/1362168815572747

Panzina, J. P. (2016). *Direito Fiscal das Religiões*. Available in: https://repositorio-aberto.up.pt/handle/10216/86804 [Accessed in January 2024].

PCM - Presidência do Conselho de Ministros. (1983). *Decreto-Lei n.º 130/83, 16.03.1983, Autoriza a Fundação Aga Kahn a desenvolver a sua actividade em Portugal.* Available in: https://files.diariodarepublica.pt/gratuitos/1s/1983/03/06200.pdf [Accessed in January 2024].

Pereira, P. T., Afonso, A., Arcanjo, M., & Santos, J. C. G. (2016). *Economia e Finanças Públicas*. Escolar Editora.

Sandelowski, M. (2000). Whatever Happened to Qualitative Description? *Research in Nursing & Health*, 23(4), 334–340. DOI: 10.1002/1098-240X(200008)23:4<334::AID-NUR9>3.0.CO;2-G PMID: 10940958

Sandelowski, M. (2010). What's in a name? Qualitative description revisited. *Research in Nursing & Health*, 33(1), 77–84. DOI: 10.1002/nur.20362 PMID: 20014004

TEDH - Tribunal Europeu dos Direitos do Homem (1950). *European Convention on Human Rights, for the Projection of Human Rights and Fundamental Freedoms*. Available in: https://gddc.ministeriopublico.pt/sites/default/files/convention_por.pdf [Accessed in January 2024].

UN - United Nations. (1948). *Universal Declaration of Human Rights.* Available in: https://www.un.org/en/about-us/universal-declaration-of-human-rights [Accessed in January 2024].

UN - United Nations. (1967a). *International Covenant on Economic, Social and Cultural Rights.* Available in: https://treaties.un.org/doc/Treaties/1976/01/19760103%2009-57%20PM/Ch_IV_03.pdf [Accessed in January 2024].

UN - United Nations. (1967b). *International Covenant on Civil and Political Rights.* Available in: https://treaties.un.org/doc/Treaties/1976/03/19760323%2006-17%20AM/Ch_IV_04.pdf [Accessed in January 2024].

UN - United Nations. (1981). *Declaration on the Elimination of All Forms of Intolerance and of Discrimination Based on Religion or Belief.* Available in: https://www.ohchr.org/en/instruments-mechanisms/instruments/declaration-elimination-all-forms-intolerance-and-discrimination [Accessed in January 2024].

Weninger, M. (2009). *Uma Europa sem Deus? A União Europeia e o diálogo com religiões, igrejas e comunidades confessionais*. Coimbra: Edições 70.

KEY TERMS AND DEFINITIONS

Agreements with the Ismaili Imamat: refer to formal agreements or arrangements made between governments or other entities and the Ismaili Imamat, which represents the spiritual leadership of the Ismaili Muslim community. These agreements often cover a range of areas, such as cultural, social, economic, and developmental initiatives. The agreements may outline specific rights, responsibilities, and privileges for the Ismaili Imamat within the context of the respective jurisdictions where these agreements are established.

Concordat: it is a treaty concluded between the Holy See and a State. The Holy See, headquartered in Vatican City-State, represents the Catholic Church and is considered its central government. Currently, the Holy See is internationally recognized as a sovereign entity and maintains full diplomatic relations with 184 States, 91 of which have established embassies to the Holy See, including Portugal.

Positive externalities: refer to the indirect beneficial effects that religious practices and institutions can have on society beyond the direct benefits to individual practitioners or members of religious communities. These impacts encompass contributions to social cohesion, community well-being, public morality, solidarity, volunteerism, and other positive social values that transcend the boundaries of religious communities.

Negative externalities: refer to the unintended adverse effects or consequences of religious practices or institutions on individuals, groups, or society, beyond the direct participants or adherents. These negative externalities encompass issues such as religious intolerance, conflict, discrimination, restrictions on individual freedoms, community divisiveness, and the marginalization of certain groups based on religious beliefs or practices.

Religious Freedom Law: refers to legislation designed to protect and uphold the rights of individuals and groups to practice their religion freely without interference or discrimination from the Government or other entities. This law typically guarantees freedom of belief, worship, assembly, and expression related to religion. It may also outline provisions for establishment and operation of religious organizations, as well as mechanisms to address religious discrimination or violations of religious rights.

Taxation of religions: refers to applying tax laws and regulations to religious organizations, institutions, or activities. This can involve determining whether religious entities are subject to taxes on income, property, or transactions, and if so, under what conditions and at what rates. This area of taxation often intersects with broader legal and constitutional principles regarding the separation of Church and State, religious freedom, and the regulation of non-profit entities.

Tax benefits: refer to advantages or privileges governments grant to individuals, businesses, or organizations through the tax system. These benefits typically involve exemptions, deductions, credits, or preferential rates that reduce the tax owed by the taxpayer. Tax benefits primarily aim to incentivize certain behaviors, activities, or investments deemed beneficial to society or the economy.

Tax exemption: is a legal provision that excludes certain individuals, organizations, or transactions from paying taxes on specific income, property, or transactions. This can be full or partial, depending on tax laws. Its purpose is to encourage activities deemed beneficial to society or the economy, like charitable donations, religious activities, or investments in sectors such as education or healthcare. Unlike deductions or credits, tax exemption avoids taxation rather than reducing taxable income or tax liability.

Tax obligations: are the legal duties that individuals, businesses, or organizations must meet according to tax laws. These duties usually involve filing accurate tax returns, reporting income correctly, calculating taxes owed, and paying taxes to the government punctually. The specifics of tax obligations depend on factors such as the taxpayer's type (individual or entity), the nature of income or transactions, and relevant tax laws and rates. Non-compliance with tax obligations can result in penalties, fines, or other legal actions from tax authorities.

Chapter 5
Fat Tax:
Impact on Consumption and Health

Sérgio Ravara Cruz
https://orcid.org/0000-0002-4454-2800
University of Aveiro, Portugal

Nina Santos Damas
University of Aveiro, Portugal

ABSTRACT

The objectives of this study are to analyze whether the fat tax stimulates a reduction in the consumption of taxed products and to assess whether the fat tax has led to an improvement in the population's health. The main conclusion of the study was that there was an increase in consumption of goods subject to the tax between 2016 and 2023. It also showed that the health of the Portuguese population in general has not improved with the implementation of the tax. The contributions of this article have made it possible to deepen our knowledge of fat tax consumption in the Portuguese population, and to study the perception of the level of health of the Portuguese after the implementation of the tax, something that previous studies had not addressed.

DOI: 10.4018/979-8-3693-3908-4.ch005

INTRODUCTION

There is a growing awareness of dietary concerns, from raising awareness of the consequences of consumption to taxing unhealthy foods and drinks. Poor diet has led to several health and lifestyle problems.

Drinks and sugary foods are less satiating, which leads to greater consumption of these goods. It should be noted that this can increase the risk of death. For example, consuming two or more glasses of sweetened drinks can increase the risk of premature death by 57%. In the case of sugary drinks, consumption of one or two glasses a day increases the risk of death by 59% (Albiero et al., 2021; Baptista et al., 2018; Mullee et al. 2019). In general, what distinguishes sweetened beverages from sugar-sweetened beverages is that the former include not only sugar-sweetened beverages but also diet drinks, i.e. those with sweeteners (Albiero et al., 2021).

Having said this, we consider it relevant to investigate the taxation of this type of product, internationally known as fat tax. The studies that have been carried out seek to study whether the tax has regressive characteristics (Hagenaars et al., 2017; Lin et al., 2011; Miao et al., 2011; Powell & Chaloupka, 2009). In 2018, a study was carried out to verify the impact of the excise tax on beverages (Baptista et al., 2018).

Thus, the choice of this topic is justified by the need to understand whether this taxation has had implications for the population, both in terms of consumption and health. We consider our research to be important because it focuses on an issue that is related to the population's quality of life, so we propose to make a modest contribution to research in this area, given that the topic of fat tax lacks scientific exploration, particularly in Portugal. The objectives of this research are: 1) To analyze whether the fat tax encourages a reduction in the consumption of the products subject to taxation; 2) To understand whether the fat tax has led to an improvement in the population's health. With the objectives defined, we drew up the following research questions: 1) Does the fat tax encourage a reduction in the consumption of taxed products? 2) What is the perception of the possibility of the fat tax inducing improvements in the population's health?

In terms of the structure of the work, the literature review presents the "state of the art", which includes an approach to tax measures applied in some countries, with an emphasis on Portugal. The empirical study is based on content analysis of data collected on the evolution of consumption of the products under study and interviews with health professionals. This information will be presented and interpreted to present the main conclusions.

BACKGROUND

Health

Over the years, measures have been taken to adopt a healthier lifestyle, thereby reducing the consumption of unhealthy foods and drinks that contain ingredients harmful to human health, such as sugar, fat, artificial sweeteners, and salt. These measures aim to reduce the high rates of overweight, obesity and other diet-related diseases (World Health Organization [WHO], 2015).

Table 1 shows, in descending order, the top ten causes of death worldwide in 2019 and in Portugal in 2021. Half of the causes of death and disease are related to nutrient-deficient diets and high intakes of, for example, products high in salt, fat, added sugars and artificial sweeteners (Hruby & Hu, 2015).

Table 1. Comparison of the ten main causes of death in the world and in Portugal

Main causes of death in the world (WHO, 2020)	Main causes of death in Portugal (Instituto Nacional de Estatísticas [INE], 2023)
1 - Ischemic heart disease	1 - Diseases of the circulatory system
2 - Stroke	2 - Malignant tumors
3 - Chronic obstructive pulmonary disease	3 - Diseases of the respiratory system
4 - Lower respiratory infections	4 - Cerebrovascular diseases
5 - Neonatal conditions	5 - Other heart diseases
6 - Cancer of the trachea, bronchi, and lungs	6 - Mental and behavioral disorders
7 - Alzheimer's and other dementias	7 - Diseases of the digestive system
8 - Diarrheal disease	8 - External causes of injury and poisoning
9 - Diabetes Mellitus	9 - Endocrine, nutritional, and metabolic diseases
10 - Kidney diseases	10 - Malignant tumor of the trachea, bronchi, and lung

Obesity is a bridge in the development of other diseases such as diabetes, hypertension, chronic respiratory diseases, muscle and bone complications, mental illnesses, kidney diseases, liver diseases, sleep apnea, cancer, and cardiovascular diseases, i.e. it develops some diseases that are present in the top 10 leading causes of death (Ferreira, 2023; WHO, 2022). Obesity (and excess weight) is fundamentally caused by the excessive consumption of high-calorie foods compared to what the individual spends throughout the day. These foods are often high in fat, salt, added sugars and other additives that are harmful to health (Hruby & Hu, 2015; Saw & Rajan, 1997; WHO, 2021). To reduce obesity and excess weight, priority should be given to healthier, lower-calorie foods and avoiding foods high in fat, salt and added sugar. Regular exercise should also be practiced encouraging calorie expenditure (Saw & Rajan, 1997; WHO, 2021). This context has led to a growing call from the WHO to tax unhealthy foods and drinks (Graça et al., 2016; Lopez et al., 2010; Lusa, 2016).

A study in the UK population found that a 40% reduction in sugars in sugary drinks over a five-year period would lead to an average reduction in energy intake of 38.4 kcal per day, resulting in an average weight loss in adults of 1.20 kg. In turn, this reduction will result in a 1% reduction in overweight and a 2.1% reduction in obesity. This study estimated that a 40% reduction in sugars in drinks should prevent more than 250,000 new cases of type 2 diabetes related to obesity. This effect will be greater in certain groups, particularly younger people, and those with lower socioeconomic status (Graça et al., 2016; Ma et al., 2016).

In Portugal, the weight of inadequate nutrition in 2019 accounted for 11.4% of deaths, including cardiovascular diseases, cancer, diabetes, and kidney disease (Portugal. Ministério da Saúde., 2022). Inadequate food consumption is characterized, in particular, by (Inquérito Alimentar Nacional e de Atividade Física [IAN-AF], 2016; Portugal. Ministry of Health, 2022): i) low consumption of vegetables and fruit; ii) daily consumption of soft drinks; iii) daily consumption of ultra-processed foods; iv) intake of free sugars in an amount greater than 10% of the WHO reference value; v) consumption of an amount of salt greater than 5g/day; vi) 30% of the total consumption of the Portuguese is based on goods that do not belong to the main sections of the food wheel.

In 2014, a study was carried out in Portugal to analyze food consumption in generation 21. It found that around 35% of two-year-olds consumed soft drinks at least once a week. This behavior was maintained by 88% of the children until they reached the age of four. This consumption worsened, i.e. more than half of the children aged four started drinking soft drinks every day. It was also concluded that the consumption of soft drinks by children is related to the level of schooling, being higher when this level is lower (Lopes et al., 2014; Portugal. Ministério da Saúde., 2022).

Recent research establishes the relationship between body mass index (BMI) and food choices, pointing out that during childhood and adolescence the prefrontal cortex, an area of the brain related to decision-making, is under development. For this reason, it is difficult for children with a higher BMI to resist the temptation of foods that alter serotonin (pleasure hormone) levels, making it difficult to choose healthy foods (Carvalho, 2021; Meer et al., 2019). It is emphasized that interventions aimed at changing the environment, promoting healthier behaviors among children, will be a more effective measure than leaving a freer environment in terms of food (Carvalho, 2021).

Graph 1 shows the annual human consumption of sugar per capita and Graph 2 shows statistics on the perception of health in Portugal.

Graph 1 shows the decrease in sugar consumption from 2015/2016 to 2022/2023. The decrease may indicate that when the fat tax came into force in Portugal, there was an awareness among the population and a consequent decrease in the consumption of sugary drinks.

Figure 1. Annual human consumption of sugar per capita in Portugal (Own elaboration based on data from INE (2024))

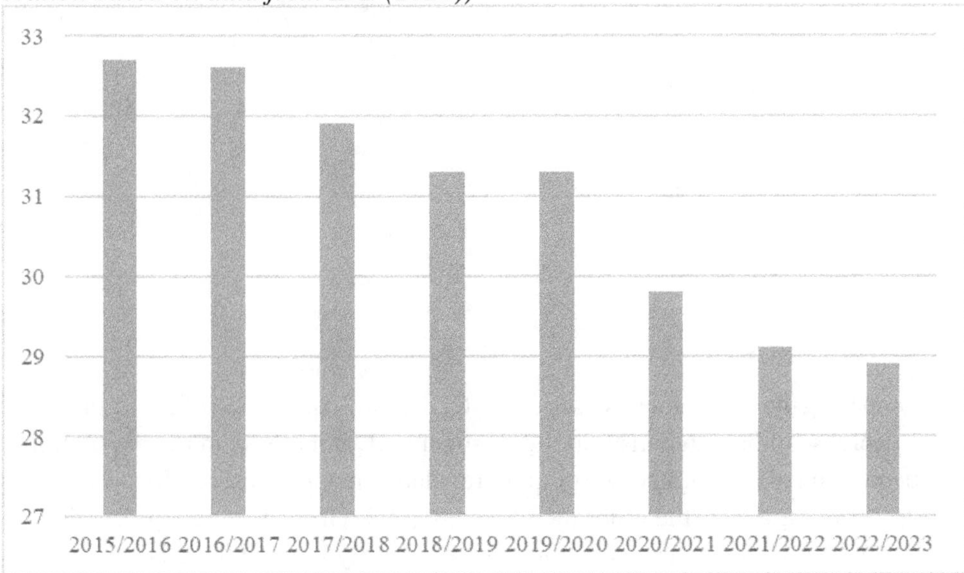

Graph 2 shows, as a percentage, the self-perceived health of the Portuguese population, including both sexes, those aged over 16 and all income groups. We can see that from 2015 to 2020 the population's self-perception increased and from 2020 to 2022 the opposite occurred. It then increased until 2023.

Figure 2. Self-perception of health in Portugal (Own elaboration based on Eurostat (2024) data)

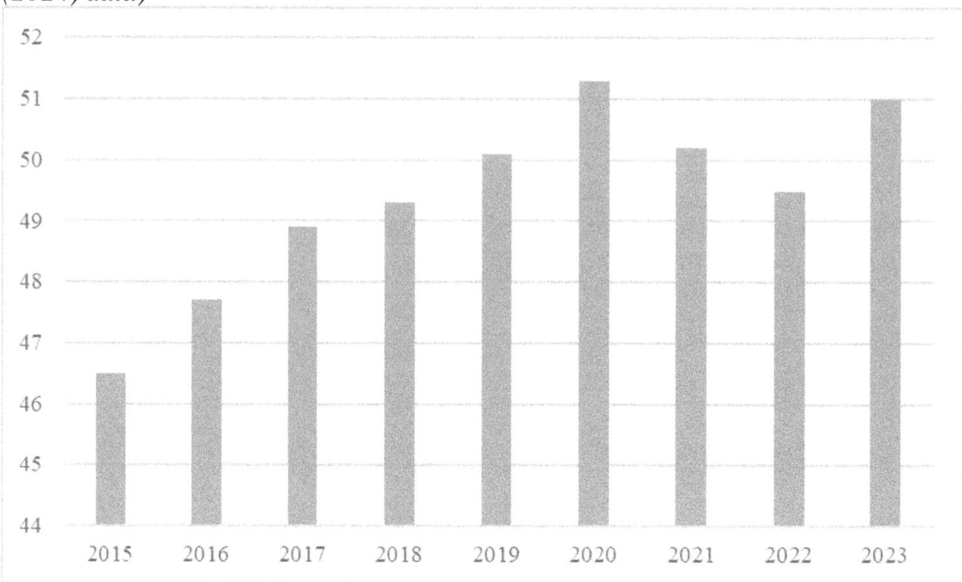

Comparing the two graphs, we see that after the implementation of the fat tax there was a decrease in human consumption of sugar and an increase in the population's self-perception of health. The two graphs are related in opposite directions, i.e. when one decreases, graph 1, the other increases, graph 2. Obviously, self-perception of health can be related to various factors, so we can only say that there is evidence of a relationship with sugar consumption by the Portuguese.

The marketing strategies used by the soft drinks industry are intense and have a high power to influence food consumption and are clearly more powerful than health promotion policies (Graça et al., 2016; Jacobson, 2005; Lopez et al., 2010). Regarding the ban on advertising, a study was carried out in May 2023 to assess Portuguese children's exposure to advertising and at the same time to see whether Law No. 30/2019 of April 23 by the Portuguese Parliament (limitations on food advertising) has had the intended effect. The authors concluded that children and young people who are overweight or obese have greater vulnerability when it comes to the influence of food marketing, and that more economically disadvantaged children are usually more exposed to this advertising (Figueira et al., 2023). This issue has deserved more attention from health policies, given that the digital environment has the power to amplify and use increasingly perceptive and persuasive strategies for young people. This study found that those aged between 3 and 16 are being exposed to advertisements while using social platforms, such as Instagram, which is the platform that provides the most advertisements of this kind. It was found that 1 in 12 were promoting food and drink, and of these, 80% were about unhealthy foods (Figueira et al., 2023). Finally, since the legislation was published, some adaptation strategies have been identified, such as the use of age verification systems to access the content of the websites of some food and drink brands. There has also been an increase in advertisements that refer to the brand rather than the specific food product (Figueira et al., 2023).

WEIGHTING FACTORS FOR APPLYING THE FAT TAX

Measures to adopt a healthier lifestyle incorporate a set of food policies that promote the adoption of a diet rich in healthy products. Policies can focus on prices, increasing them for unhealthy foods and drinks, and on the adoption of subsidies to support the consumption of fruit, vegetables, and others to replace harmful foods (Andreyeva et al., 2010; Andreyeva et al., 2011; Graça et al., 2016; Lin et al., 2011; Powell et al, 2013; Smith et al., 2010; WHO, 2015).

By imposing a tax on these goods, the state would, in most cases, act as a constraint on their consumption. In this case, tax measures should be seen as support for health promotion and not as a way for the state to collect more revenue, so that there is greater adherence from the population (Donaldson et al., 2015; Graça et al., 2016; WHO, 2015).

The WHO (2015) considers the following factors to be important for the development of pricing policy: 1) Price elasticity of demand; 2) The substitution effect; 3) Consumer subsidy; 4) The impact of socio-economic inequalities on health.

The price elasticity of demand is the influence that the price has on a given consumer and is measured by the percentage by which the consumer changes their choice of product if the price changes by 1%. A product is considered to have a high elasticity when there is a drastic reduction in consumption as the price rises. On the other hand, when there is a low elasticity of demand, it means that with a change in price there will only be a slight difference in consumption of the good (Lin et al., 2011; Thow, 2014; WHO, 2015). The elasticity of demand can vary according to consumers' predilections, habits developed throughout life and existing alternatives to products (WHO, 2015). Tamir et al. (2018) concluded that stakeholders in economic sectors estimate that taxation will reduce consumption, however they found that non-economists claim that the tax will not be accepted by consumers, i.e. the higher price will not reduce consumption.

The substitution effect shows the change that consumers make when prices change. In this case, the price policy must be as broad as possible, i.e. it must cover as many unhealthy products as possible, thus preventing the consumer substitution effect from being redirected towards more nutritionally precarious foods (WHO, 2015). Studies have concluded that there is no evidence that imposing taxes on unhealthy products has an undesirable effect, thus encouraging consumers to switch from taxed foods to others with a similar energy density (Finkelstein et al., 2013; Graça et al., 2016). Subsidies are important in this analysis, as they support consumers in buying healthier foods with a wider range of nutrients, such as fruit and vegetables (WHO, 2015).

As far as subsidies for the consumer are concerned, these would not be directly attributed, but indirectly, poured into the price of foodstuffs with higher nutrients and vitamins, leading consumers to choose these over those with a worse nutritional table, improving the productivity, health, and well-being of the population (Thow, 2014; WHO, 2015). This price would change in at least two ways: i) a measure similar to the one that took place, for example, in Portugal in 2023 could be implemented, with VAT being levied at a rate of 0% on these foods; ii) the use of a reduction in the price of the final product, leading the point of sale to declare the amount sold of the products subject to this subsidy, which would then be deducted from the business taxes that would be handed over to the state. A study carried out in the United States found that a 50% subsidy on fruit and vegetables would increase consumption of these goods by 25% (Thow, 2014).

As there are different socio-economic groups, a careful analysis is needed so that the most disadvantaged do not see their income fall (Cutler, 1995; Lin et al., 2011; Tamir, et al., 2018; WHO, 2015). The fat tax is a regressive tax, meaning that consumers with lower incomes will have to spend more of their income compared to consumers with higher incomes (Chaloupka, 2009; Hagenaars et al., 2017; Lin et al., 2011; Miao et al., 2011; Powell & Thow, 2014). According to Hagenaars et al. (2017), although the tax has regressive characteristics, it is offset by health benefits. This is to emphasize that although it is important to have this notion, not everything can be considered negative, i.e., when taxes are applied to unhealthy foods and drinks, consumers from a lower socio-economic group will make better choices and can thus have a significant improvement in their well-being. These taxes will be a strong ally in reducing health inequalities (WHO, 2015).

Advantages for the Consumer with the Taxation of Unhealthy Products

Although it is difficult to see any positive impact from this tax at first, the advantage can be seen in the increase in prices of unhealthy foods and drinks, which is expected to lead to a reduction in the consumption of these goods. In addition, taxation can reduce the impact that advertising these foods has on the population, motivating better health choices. As a result, consumers will benefit from better quality health, a better lifestyle and a reduction in health expenses, i.e. lower costs, particularly with health insurance, medical services, hospitalizations, and medicines (Cutler, 1995; Santos & Cordeiro, 2016).

Economically, taxing unhealthy food and drink can be considered a regressive measure, since it affects the poorest population, and they must spend a higher proportion of their income. However, this type of tax can be considered a progressive measure, since it is expected to redirect consumption, thus contributing to healthier diets and, consequently, to an improvement in the quality of health levels (Albiero et al., 2021; Santos & Cordeiro, 2016; WHO, 2015). We therefore believe that this is a tax whose main objective is not tax revenue, but to shape consumer behavior so that they make healthier choices, which will therefore reduce state spending on health.

Finally, another advantage may come from the need for the industry to create new products with a similar taste without the additives (which led to the tax burden of these goods), providing an increasing number of alternative healthy products available for the benefit of the consumer (Baptista et al., 2018).

Fat Tax

Table 2 shows the countries in which the fat tax system is in force. For the sake of simplicity, we have chosen to indicate only the year of implementation of the tax, excluding the years of modification. The last column shows the categories subject to the tax, based on the information collected up to the end of 2022. We have excluded Portugal from the table because it will be dealt with separately.

Table 2. Countries subject to fat tax

Geographical Space	Time of implementation	Product categories
America		
Barbados	August 2015	Sweetened drinks and foods
Bermuda	October 2018	Sweetened drinks and foods
Canada	British Columbia - April 2021	Carbonated and sweetened drinks
	Newfoundland and Labrador - April 2022	Sweetened drinks
Chile	October 2014	Sweetened drinks
Dominica	September 2015	Sweetened drinks and food
Ecuador	May 2016	Sweetened beverages

continued on following page

Table 2. Continued

Geographical Space	Time of implementation	Product categories
America		
United States of America	Albany, California- April 2017	Sugary drinks
	Berkeley, California- February 2015	Sugary drinks
	Boulder, Colorado- July 2017	Sweetened drinks
	Cook County, Illinois- August 2017	Sweetened drinks
	Philadelphia, Pennsylvania- January 2017	Sweetened drinks
	Navajo Nation, Arizona- April 2015	Sweetened beverages and food
	Okland, California- July 2017	Sweetened beverages
	San Francisco, California- January 2018	Sweetened drinks
	Seattle, Washington- January 2018	Sweetened beverages
Mexico	January 2014	Sugar-sweetened drinks and foods
Panama	November 2019	Carbonated drinks and sugary drinks
Peru	May 2018	Sweetened beverages
Africa		
South Africa	April 2018	Sugary drinks
Ethiopia	February 2020	Sugary drinks and food
Morocco	January 2019	Sugary drinks
Mauritius	January 2013	Sugary drinks
Nigeria	December 2021	Sugar-sweetened beverages
St. Helena	May 2014	Sugar-sweetened beverages
Seychelles	April 2019	Sugar-sweetened beverages
Middle East and Asia		
Saudi Arabia	June 2017	Sweetened drinks and energy drinks
Bahrain	December 2017	Carbonated drinks and energy drinks
Qatar	January 2019	Carbonated drinks and energy drinks
United Arab Emirates	October 2017	Sweetened beverages and energy drinks
India	July 2017	Sweetened beverages and food
Israel	January 2022	Sweetened beverages
Malaysia	July 2019	Sweetened drinks
Maldives	March 2017	Carbonated drinks, energy drinks and sports drinks
Oman	June 2019	Carbonated drinks, energy drinks and food

continued on following page

Table 2. Continued

Geographical Space	Time of implementation	Product categories
America		
Sri Lanka	November 2017	Sweetened beverages
Thailand	September 2017	Sweetened beverages
Geographical Space	**Time of implementation**	**Product categories**
Oceania		
Brunei	April 2017	Sweetened drinks
Fiji	2007	Sweetened drinks and foods
Fiji	January 2018	Sweetened drinks
Cook Islands	2013	Sweetened drinks
Kiribati	2014	Sweetened drinks
Marshall Island	2008	Carbonated drinks and sugary drinks
Northern Mariana Islands	1995	Sweetened beverages
Micronesia	2014	Sugar-sweetened beverages
Nauru	July 2017	Sweetened beverages and food
Niue	2016	Sweetened beverages
New Caledonia	2017	Sweetened drinks
Palau	September 2003	Carbonated drinks
French Polynesia	2002	Sweetened beverages and food
Kiribati	2003	Sweetened beverages
Samoa	1984	Carbonated drinks and food
Tonga	august 2013	Sweetened beverages and food
Tuvalu	2010	Sweetened beverages
Vanuatu	February 2015	Carbonated drinks
Wallis and Futuna	2017	Sweetened beverages
Europe		
Belgium	January 2016	Sweetened drinks
Spain	January 2021	Sweetened drinks
	Catalonia- May 2017	Sweetened drinks
Denmark	1930	Sweetened beverages and food
Estonia	January 2018	Sweetened beverages
Estonia	1926	Sweetened beverages and food

continued on following page

Table 2. Continued

Geographical Space	Time of implementation	Product categories
America		
Spain	January 2012	Sweetened beverages
Hungary	September 2011	Sweetened beverages, energy drinks and foods
Ireland	May 2018	Sweetened beverages
Latvia	May 2004	Sweetened beverages
Norway	1922	Sweetened beverages and foods
Poland	January 2021	Sweetened beverages and caffeinated beverages
United Kingdom	April 2018	Sweetened beverages

Source: Own elaboration based on data from Albiero et al. (2021) and UNC (2022).

In Portugal, fat tax is included in section II of the Code of Excise Duties (CIEC) - the category of drinks with added sugar or other sweeteners. Table 3 summarizes the provisions of Article 87.º-A of the CIEC, listing the products with the codes to which they are associated (Instituto Nacional de Estatísticas [INE], 2020; Official Journal of the European Union, 2010).

Table 3. Products subject to excise duty - fat tax in Portugal

Article 87.º-A CIEC	Designation	Products / Code
n.º 1, al. a)	Drinks for human consumption containing sugar or other sweeteners	- Waters, including mineral waters and aerated waters (CN 2202). - Other non-alcoholic beverages, except fruit or vegetable juices (CN 2202).
n.º 1, al. b)	Beverages with an alcohol content of more than 0.5% vol. and not more than 1.2% vol.	- Wine of fresh grapes, including fortified wines (CN 2204). - Vermouth and other wine of fresh grapes flavored with plants or aromatic substances (CN 2205). - Fermented beverages, mixtures of fermented beverages and mixtures of fermented beverages and non-alcoholic beverages (CN 2206). - Undenatured ethyl alcohol of an alcoholic strength of less than 80% vol. such as spirits, liqueurs and other spirituous beverages (CN 2208).
n.º 1, al. c)	Concentrates in liquid, powder, granular or other solid form, intended for the preparation of beverages mentioned in the previous lines, on the premises of the final consumer or retailer.	Concentrates for the preparation of beverages.
n.º 2	Products acquired in another member state are subject to tax in the national territory, unless the acquisition is made for personal use and the transportation is carried out by the person to the national territory, in accordance with article 61/2 CIEC.	

Since its implementation in 2017, the rates and the basis of incidence, for example the levels of sugar content (T.A.), have changed. To make it clearer, we have drawn up two tables (4 and 5), according to the chronological evolution of Article 87.º-C of the CIEC, which originated in Law n.º 42/2016 of December 28 of the Assembly of the Republic and the latest revision was Law n.º 82/2023 of December 29 of the Assembly of the Republic.

Table 4. Rates applied to beverages subject to fat tax in 2017 and 2018

Products	Interval	Rate from 01/2017	Rate from 01/2018	Rate change from 2017 to 2018 (%)
Beverages with added sugar or other sweeteners	T.A.< 80 g/l	8,22 €/hl	8,34 €/hl	1.46%
	T.A. ≥ 80 g/l	16,46 €/hl	16,69 €/hl	1.40%
Concentrates - Liquid form	T.A.< 80 g/l	Values applied depending on the final mixture	50,01 €/hl	not applicable
	T.A. ≥ 80 g/l		100,14 €/hl	not applicable
Concentrates - Solid form	T.A.< 80 g/l	Values applied depending on the final mixture	83,35 €/100kg de net weight	not applicable
	T.A. ≥ 80 g/l		166,90 €/100kg de net weight	not applicable

The data in table 4 shows that the rate always changed in the first two years, with the biggest change being in drinks with added sugar or other sweeteners for the first T.A. level: 1.46% [100 x (8.34 - 8.22): 8.22].

Table 5 shows the change from two to four A.T. intervals. It should be noted that the dotted line in the table indicates that there was no change in the rate applied from one year to the next.

Table 5. Rates applied to beverages subject to fat tax between 2019 and 2024

Products	Interval	Rate from 01/2019	Rate from 10/2019	Rate from 04/2020	Rate from 06/2022	Rate from 01/2023	Rate from 01/2024	Rate change from 2019 to 2024 (%)
Drinks with added sugar or other sweeteners	T.A.< 25 g/l	1 €/hl	--------	--------	1,01 €/hl	1,05 €/hl	1,16 €/hl	16%
	25 g/l ≤ T.A. <50 g/l	6 €/hl	--------	6,02 €/hl	6,08 €/hl	6,32 €/hl	6,95 €/hl	15.83%
	50 g/l ≤ T.A. <80 g/l	8 €/hl	--------	8,02 €/hl	8,10 €/hl	8,42 €/hl	9.26 €/hl	15.75%
	T.A. ≥ 80 g/l	20 €/hl	--------	20,06 €/hl	20,26 €/hl	21,07 €/hl	23.18 €/hl	15.90%
Concentrates - Liquid form	T.A.< 25 g/l	--------	6 €/hl	6,02 €/hl	6,08 €/hl	6,32 €/hl	6.95 €/hl	15.83%
	25 g/l ≤ T.A. <50 g/l	--------	36 €/hl	36,11 €/hl	36,47 €/hl	37,93 €/hl	41.72 €/hl	15.89%
	50 g/l ≤ T.A. <80 g/l	--------	48 €/hl	48,14 €/hl	48,62 €/hl	50,56 €/hl	55.62 €/hl	15.88%
	T.A. ≥ 80 g/l	--------	120 €/hl	120,36 €/hl	121,56 €/hl	126,42 €/hl	139.06 €/hl	15.88%

continued on following page

Table 5. Continued

Products	Interval	Rate from 01/2019	Rate from 10/2019	Rate from 04/2020	Rate from 06/2022	Rate from 01/2023	Rate from 01/2024	Rate change from 2019 to 2024 (%)
Concentrates - Solid form (kg in "net weight")	T.A.< 25 g/l	--------	10 € /100 kg	10,03 € /100 kg	10,13 € /100 kg	10,54 € /100 kg	11.59 €/100 kg	15.90%
	25 g/l ≤ T.A. <50 g/l	--------	60 € /100 kg	60,18 € /100 kg	60,78 € /100kg	63,21 € /100 kg	69.53 €/100 kg	15.88%
	50 g/l ≤ T.A. <80 g/l	--------	80 € /100 kg	80,24 € /100 kg	81,04 € /100 kg	84,28 € /100 kg	92.71 €/100 kg	15.89%
	T.A. ≥ 80 g/l	--------	200 € /100 kg	200,60 € /100 kg	202,61 € /100 kg	210,71 € /100 kg	231.78 €/100 kg	5,36%

For the period 2019 to 2024, the biggest variation was 16%, which corresponds to drinks with added sugar or other sweeteners with an A.T. < 25 g/l.

Graph 3 shows that consumption of these products generally fell between 2016 and 2020. However, in 2019, there was a slight increase compared to 2018. We believe that this decline may be due to the start of taxation on products subject to fat tax and the consequent dissemination of this measure. In subsequent years, 2021 to 2023, there was a rise to levels above those of 2016, the year before the measure came into force. We believe that this increase may be related to the pandemic years, i.e. confinement and social isolation leading to higher calorie consumption.

Figure 3. Consumption of products subject to fat tax in Portugal (Own elaboration based on UNESDA (2024) data)

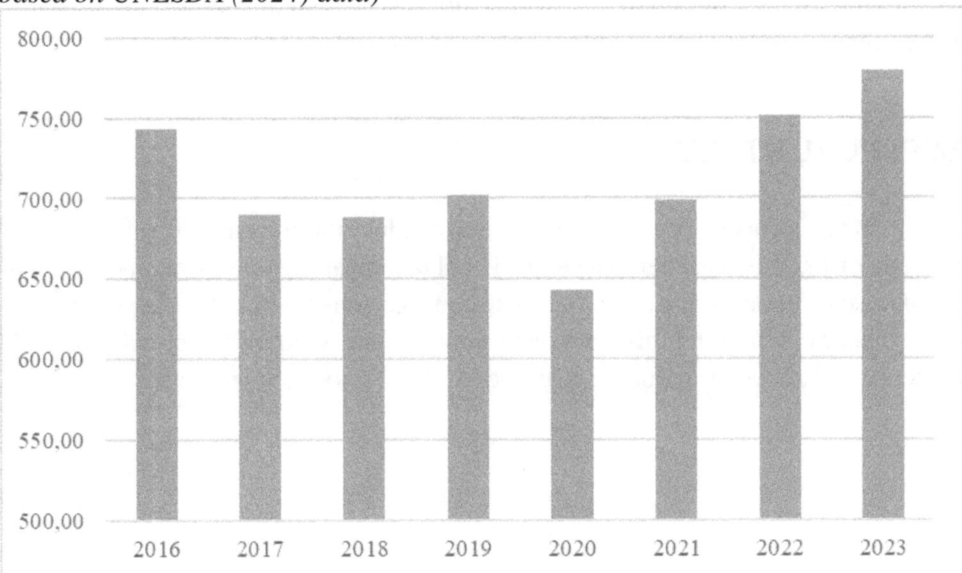

Alongside the fat tax, measures have been implemented in Portugal to complement and encourage the refusal of these foods and drinks. In June 2016, Dispatch n.º 7516-A/2016 was published, with the aim of promoting the health of the Portuguese and limiting the sale of products harmful to health in vending machines available in public health care institutions, namely hospitals and local health units. In April 2019, Law n.º 30/2019 was published, introducing restrictions on advertising with nutritionally poor foods aimed at children under 16. The restriction is aimed at products with a high energy value, salt content, saturated fats, sugar and processed fats (Law n.º 30/2019 of April 23 of the Assembly of the Republic). Subsequently, Dispatch n.º 8127/2021 of August 17 of the Office of the Assistant Secretary of State for Health was approved in August 2021, which aims to complement Dispatch n.º 7516-A/2016 of June 6 of the Office of the Assistant Secretary of State for Health, in the school context, establishing the rules for the operation of school meals and the prohibition of the sale of foods harmful to health in the machines available in the public educational environment.

Regarding school buffets, we would point out that the appropriate measure should be to teach and not to prohibit, since the ban that was carried out in schools focused on the sale of the established products and not on their consumption within school establishments (Carvalho, 2021). Such a ban can take place in the school environment, but on returning to the family environment, habits may not change. That's why we think it's important to reinforce education to change future behavior. Finally, it should be noted that at the end of 2016, the Portuguese parliament rejected restrictive measures regarding the salt content of food products (Carvalho, 2021).

In conclusion, since the fat tax was implemented, the Portuguese state has raised 432 million for the Portuguese national health service and the proportion of drinks in the highest tax bracket has fallen by 36% (Amorim, 2024).

EMPIRICAL STUDY

The fat tax is a tax whose main objective is to reduce the consumption of unhealthy food and drink. It is considered an extra-fiscal tax, meaning that its main purpose is not to raise revenue for the state, but to discourage consumption by the population. Thus, the aim of creating this tax was to improve the health of the population and, as mentioned above, to reduce consumption of the goods subject to the tax.

Data and Sample Collection Methodology

Our empirical study was based on two data collection methods: observation of consumption data provided by hypermarkets and interviews with individuals working in the health sector.

The first method made it possible to analyze real consumption data, helping to understand whether the quantities sold of products subject to the fat tax decreased after the tax was implemented.

The interviews consisted of one-to-one conversations with people specialized in the subject, so that they could provide information relevant to our research. Interviews are normally used in scientific work and follow a standardized script that must be followed rigorously. They also include open-ended questions, giving the interviewee a greater chance to freely express and justify their opinion (Oliveira & Ferreira, 2014; Sousa & Baptista, 2011; Ramos & Naranjo, 2014).

The interviews were conducted via email between January and April 2024. The interviews were all carried out during these months, online (zoom platform) according to the availability of the interviewees. The average duration of each interview was thirty minutes.

Table 6 shows the questions asked in the interview and their relation to the literature review.

Table 6. Relationship between the questions asked in the interview and the literature review

Questions	Authors
In general terms, how do you think the health of the Portuguese population has evolved over the years? Why?	IAN-AF, 2016; Portugal. Ministério da Saúde., 2022
Regarding the fat tax, are you aware of this measure in Portugal?	
What is your opinion of this type of taxation? Why?	
Do you think other foods and drinks should also be subject to this tax? If so, which ones?	Andreyeva et al., 2010; Andreyeva et al., 2011; Graça et al., 2016; Lin et al., 2011; Powell et al, 2013; Smith et al., 2010; WHO, 2015
Is taxing these foods and drinks an important way of inducing a reduction in their consumption? Why?	WHO, 2015
Do you think that users (consumers) have changed their food choices, even partially, with the introduction of this tax?	WHO, 2015

continued on following page

Table 6. Continued

Questions	Authors
What other measures can be applied to reduce consumption of products that are harmful to health?	Andreyeva et al., 2010; Andreyeva et al., 2011; Graça et al., 2016; Lin et al., 2011; Powell et al, 2013; Smith et al., 2010; WHO, 2015
In which case(s) would it be necessary to maintain this type of tax or could it no longer be in force?	Andreyeva et al., 2010; Andreyeva et al., 2011; Graça et al., 2016; Lin et al., 2011; Powell et al, 2013; Smith et al., 2010; WHO, 2016
From what you have followed since the fat tax came into force, what is your perception of the possibility of this tax inducing improvements in health?	Cutler, 1995; Albiero et al., 2021; Santos & Cordeiro, 2016; WHO, 2015

The consumption data was provided by two hypermarkets operating in Portugal. Many of the entities contacted refused to provide the data on the grounds of data protection. To ensure anonymity, each hypermarket was given a code which will be used to identify it: C1 and C2.

The group of interviewees are health professionals, particularly nutritionists and general practitioners. They provide a perspective on how the health of the Portuguese population has evolved over the years and allow us to analyze whether the interviewees see an improvement in health after the tax on unhealthy foods and drinks came into force. We therefore opted for a convenient sample, since it is difficult to collect all the perceptions indicated above. Given the anonymity we ensured, each interviewee was given a code, and they were always referred to in the masculine and singular: general practitioner (S1 to S4); nutritionist (S5 to S10).

Presentation and Discussion of Results on Consumption

Using the data provided by the hypermarkets on the consumption of goods subject to the fat tax, for the period 2016 to 2023, we calculated the variations in consumption for the eight-year interval, which are summarized in table 7.

From this observation, we can see that overall consumption by the Portuguese population has increased from 2016 to 2023. This data is in line with the literature review. The data collected by Unesda (2024) also shows that consumption has increased between 2016 and 2023, particularly of soft drinks, which include carbonated, sports, energy, and non-carbonated drinks, iced teas, iced coffee, flavored and enhanced water, as well as powdered and liquid preparations which, after dilution, produce the final product. We can therefore conclude that consumption of goods subject to the fat tax increased in Portugal during the period under review, i.e., after the tax was implemented.

Table 7. Summary of the variation in consumption of products subject to the fat tax in hypermarkets C1 and C2

Designation	Products	Variation 2016-2023 hypermarket C1	Variation 2016-2023 hypermarket C2
Drinks for human consumption containing sugar or other sweeteners	-Water, in particular mineral water, and carbonated water.	31%	344%
	Other non-alcoholic drinks, except fruit or vegetable juices.	5%	87%
Drinks with an alcohol content of more than 0.5% vol. and not more than 1.2% vol., containing sugar or other sweeteners	-Wine made from fresh grapes, including fortified wines.	-10%	67%
	-Vermouth and other wine of fresh grapes flavored with plants or aromatic substances.	—	114%
	Fermented beverages, mixtures of fermented beverages and mixtures of fermented and non-alcoholic beverages.	-59%	248%
	-Undenatured ethyl alcohol with an alcohol content of less than 80% vol. such as brandies, liqueurs, and other spirit drinks.	-7%	34%
Concentrates in liquid, powder, granular or other solid form, intended for the preparation of beverages mentioned in the previous lines, on the premises of the final consumer or retailer.	Concentrates for the preparation of beverages.	-16%	516%

Presentation and Discussion of Results on the Perception of Healthcare Professionals

In order to understand the perception of health professionals, we have summarized the answers to each question.

In general terms, how do you think the health of the Portuguese population has evolved over the years? Why?

Only three interviewees (S3, S5 and S6) indicated that health is improving, explaining this either by access to technologies that help with prevention or by a greater awareness of the importance of health. For the remaining seven interviewees, the health of the Portuguese population has been deteriorating, contributing to a reduction in lifestyle, given that this is a very old population, polymedicated and in need of complex care. They also add that there is a growing emergence of various health problems, including diabetes, high blood pressure, high cholesterol, and Alzheimer's disease. These diseases are related to sugar consumption, according to S2.

Regarding the fat tax, are you aware of this measure in Portugal?

Almost all the interviewees answered in the affirmative, while three (S1, S6 and S9) indicated that they had no knowledge of the question.

What is your opinion on this type of taxation? Why?

Seven of the interviewees (S1, S2, S5, S6, S7, S8 and S10) felt that the measure could help with food choices, emphasizing the need to pay attention to prices. However, they consider it more important to focus on food literacy. The rest said that the measure seemed to be a way for the state to raise more revenue. For S4, the tax may initially have the desired effect, but over time the consumer adapts to the price, consuming and paying more.

Do you think other foods and drinks should also be subject to this tax? If so, which ones?

Four of the interviewees (S3, S4, S5 and S9) are of the opinion that there should be no extension of the goods subject to taxation. The rest listed processed and artificial foods where sugar and fats are present.

Is taxing these foods and drinks an important way to induce a reduction in their consumption? Why?

Four of the interviewees (S3, S4, S5 and S9) believe that this type of taxation has no implications for consumption. The others considered that taxation can reduce consumption but emphasized that it all depends on consumers' monetary conditions.

Do you think that users (consumers) have changed their food choices, even partially, with the introduction of this tax?

Seven of the interviewees (S2, S3, S4, S5, S6, S8 and S9) believe that changing the price by a few cents will not have an impact on their choice. S8 indicated that literacy would be a better bet. The others (S1, S7, S10) believe that consumers have changed their food choices.

What other measures can be taken to reduce consumption of products that are harmful to health?

All the interviewees believe that "food education" would be a measure that could help reduce the consumption of unhealthy products. For S6, the price of products should be raised more, through an increase in the tax burden. Interviewees S7 and S10 suggested that advertising that increases young people's desire to consume these foods should be restricted, as should the promotion of healthy foods.

In this case(s) would it be necessary to maintain this type of taxation, or could it no longer be in force?

Nine of the ten interviewees felt that the tax should be maintained. Of these nine, three (S2, S5 and S6) stressed that there may be an increase, but the price should not escalate to unfeasible levels for the consumer.

From what you've been following since the fat tax came into force, what is your perception of the possibility of this tax inducing improvements in health?

Regarding this question, two of the interviewees (S1 and S7) indicated that they didn't have the knowledge to answer the question correctly. Seven of the ten said that they didn't think it had interfered. Finally, S10 indicated that he believes the fat tax is leading to improvements in health.

In recent years there has been a reduction in sugar consumption and an improvement in the self-perceived health of the Portuguese population (Eurostat, 2024; INE, 2024). However, the interviewees do not believe that this has happened; on the contrary, they believe that the population's health has deteriorated over the years, even though there may have been a reduction in sugar consumption. They also portray the growing increase in various diseases such as diabetes, high blood pressure, high cholesterol, and Alzheimer's, which are among the ten leading causes of death in Portugal (INE, 2023), and are related to the high consumption of unhealthy products, as also mentioned by S2.

With regard to the pricing policies mentioned by the WHO (2015), the interviewees focused on price elasticity, as they consider that: i) on the one hand, a price increase will discourage the consumption of these goods; ii) on the other hand, it can have an impact on the level of health due to economic inequalities, as they consider that this tax will have a different impact on the family budget according to the socio-economic group they belong to. This last factor is seen by the interviewees as something alarming if prices rise to unfeasible levels, thus accentuating inequalities and reinforcing the idea of regressivity associated with the fat tax (Hagenaars et al., 2017; Lin et al., 2011; Miao et al., 2011; Powell & Chaloupka, 2009; Thow, 2014).

Regarding the advantages for the consumer of taxing unhealthy products, the interviewees consider that the fat tax has not led to improvements in the health of the Portuguese population. The description presented in the literature review indicates that this taxation can increase the quality of the consumer's health and consequently promote a reduction in health expenses, namely with health insurance, medical services, hospitalizations, and medicines (Cutler, 1995; Santos & Cordeiro, 2016). However, most interviewees believe that this is not happening now.

During the interviews, health professionals presented three fundamental ideas for improving the population's health. The most cited was food education aimed at young people, because they believe that literacy in this area for this public will increase awareness and make adults more informed about the subject. In fact, the ban at school level should be accompanied by a reinforcement of education regarding health concerns, with the family, to promote an environment that changes future behaviors (Carvalho, 2021).

Another measure aims to restrict advertising that increases young people's desire to consume nutritionally poor foods. It should be noted that the weight of the soft drinks industry is an extremely important factor for the mechanism to be adopted, since the marketing strategies applied by this industry are frequent and intense, and are capable of influencing food consumption, especially among the younger and more economically disadvantaged public (Figueira et al., 2023; Graça et al., 2016; Jacobson, 2005).

Finally, the last proposal put forward by the experts involves promoting healthy foods, helping consumers to make healthier choices. According to the literature, one of the ways is to apply a subsidy to the consumer, indirectly giving a subsidy to foodstuffs with more nutrients and vitamins, leading the consumer to choose these foods over those with a worse nutritional table, improving the productivity, health, and well-being of the population (Thow, 2014; WHO, 2015).

CONCLUSION

Based on the data provided by the hypermarkets and the literature review, it was possible to understand that in the period from 2016 to 2023 consumption of goods subject to the fat tax increased in Portugal. The interviews with health professionals led to the conclusion that the health of the Portuguese population has deteriorated over the years, despite data from Eurostat (2024) and INE (2024) indicating that there has been a reduction in sugar consumption and an improvement in the population's self-perception of health. The interviewees point out that there is a growing increase in various diseases such as diabetes, high blood pressure, high cholesterol, and Alzheimer's. The experts also believe that the fat tax has not led to improvements in the health of the Portuguese population, although it could help with the food choices made by the population. They listed some processed and artificial foods, in which sugar and fats are present, as possible products that should be included in the fat tax.

To improve the population's quality of life, the interviewees put forward some proposals. The most mentioned was food literacy among the younger population, because they believe it could raise awareness among young people and develop adults who are better informed about the subject. We believe that when it comes to the choice between fat tax and food education, education should prevail, through awareness campaigns to be implemented in schools through fun activities, leading young people to learn in a didactic way. In the family environment, children's programs on the subject could be encouraged for the whole family to watch. It was also suggested that advertising that increases the desire to consume nutritionally poor foods should be restricted and that healthy foods should be promoted, helping consumers to make healthier choices.

In this way, we believe that the study carried out contributes, in the context of the Portuguese population, to a deeper understanding of the consumption of products subject to the fat tax and the perception of the quality of health after the implementation of this tax.

In this way, we believe that the study carried out contributes, in the context of the Portuguese population, to a deeper understanding of the consumption of products subject to the fat tax and to the perception of the quality of health after the implementation of this tax.

There are limitations to the study, namely the fact that the analysis of consumption data was restricted to that provided by two hypermarkets. Another limitation is the fact that the fat tax is not widely known, which means that some of the interviewees were unaware of the implementation measures.

We conclude this study by presenting some avenues for future research:

- Carrying out an international comparative study of the impact of the fat tax on consumption and health;

- Presenting and implementing a food literacy program to a young audience and following it up to see if there have been any changes in consumption;

-Study the beverage industry subject to the fat tax in Portugal, to see if there has been a decrease in the production of these goods or, on the other hand, if there has been a commitment to changing the composition.

REFERENCES

Albiero, M., Johns, P., Hassan, B., Carvalho, A., Guedes, D., Baird, M., Mattos, R., Waetge, J., & Silva, A. (2021). *Tributação de bebidas e alimentos não saudáveis no mundo- Experiências internacionais e seus impactos* [Report]. ACT Promoção da Saúde. https://evidencias.tributosaudavel.org.br/wp-content/themes/act-theme/LO_ACT_EXP-INT_Rev-03.pdf

Amorim, J. (2024, February, 22). *Em sete anos resultaram 432 milhões para o SNS e caiu em 36% a proporção de bebidas no escalão mais alto do imposto.* Jornal de Notícias. https://www.jn.pt/6804067447/acucar-nas-bebidas-diminui-devido-a-pressao-fiscal/

Andreyeva, T., Chaloupka, F. J., & Brownell, K. D. (2011). Estimating the potential of taxes on sugar-sweetened beverages to reduce consumption and generate revenue. *Preventive Medicine*, 52(6), 413–416. DOI: 10.1016/j.ypmed.2011.03.013 PMID: 21443899

Andreyeva, T., Long, M. W., & Brownell, K. D. (2010). The impact of food prices on consumption: A systematic review of research on the price elasticity of demand for food. *American Journal of Public Health*, 100(2), 216–222. DOI: 10.2105/AJPH.2008.151415 PMID: 20019319

Baptista, S., da Silva, F. G., Silva, D., Landerset, F., Simões, A. L., Gregório, M. J., Saraiva, A. I., & Belona, S. (2018, July, 30). *Impacto do Imposto Especial sobre o Consumo de Bebidas Açucaradas e Adicionadas de Edulcorantes: Relatório do Grupo de Trabalho (Despacho N.o 2774/2018).*https://repositorio-aberto.up.pt/handle/10216/118046

Carvalho, P. (2021, September 5). *Os bufetes escolares e os indignados do costume.* Público. https://www.publico.pt/2021/09/05/impar/opiniao/bufetes-escolares-indignados-costume-1976142

Cutler, D. M. (1995). Cutting costs and improving health: Making reform work. *Health Affairs (Project Hope)*, 14(1), 161–172. DOI: 10.1377/hlthaff.14.1.161 PMID: 7657201

Dispatch n.º 7516-A/2016, of June 6 from the Office of the Assistant Secretary of State for Health. Diário da República: II série, nº 108, 1º Suplemento (2016). https://diariodarepublica.pt/dr/detalhe/despacho/7516-a-2016-74604818

Dispatch n.º 8127/2021, of August 17 from the Office of the Assistant Secretary of State for Health. Diário da República: II série, nº 159 (2021) https://diariodarepublica.pt/dr/detalhe/despacho/8127-2021-169689544

Donaldson, E. A., Cohen, J. E., Rutkow, L., Villanti, A. C., Kanarek, N. F., & Barry, C. L. (2015). Public support for a sugar-sweetened beverage tax and pro-tax messages in a Mid-Atlantic US state. *Public Health Nutrition*, 18(12), 2263–2273. DOI: 10.1017/S1368980014002699 PMID: 25430945

Eurostat (2024, May 24). *Self-perceived health by sex, age and income quintile.* DOI: 10.2908/HLTH_SILC_10

Ferreira, A. (2023). *6 doenças associadas à obesidade.* Lusíadas. https://www.lusiadas.pt/blog/sintomas-tratamentos/doencas/6-doencas-associadas-obesidade

Figueira, M., Bica, M., Vicente, B., Gaspar, M., & Gregório, M. (2023). *Exposição das crianças portuguesas ao marketing digital de alimentos e bebidas: estudo piloto da ferramenta click da OMS Europa.* Direção Geral da Saúde. https://nutrimento.pt/activeapp/wp-content/uploads/2023/05/DGS_PNPAS_MarketingDigital-2.pdf

Finkelstein, E. A., Zhen, C., Bilger, M., Nonnemaker, J., Farooqui, A. M., & Todd, J. E. (2013). Implications of a sugar-sweetened beverage (SSB) tax when substitutions to non-beverage items are considered. *Journal of Health Economics*, 32(1), 219–239. DOI: 10.1016/j.jhealeco.2012.10.005 PMID: 23202266

Graça, P., Gregório, M. J., Santos, A., & Sousa, S. (2016). *Redução do consumo de açúcar em Portugal: evidência que justifica ação.* https://alimentacaosaudavel.dgs.pt/activeapp2020/wp-content/uploads/2020/01/Redução-do-Consumo-de-Açúcar-em-Portugal-Evidência-que-Justifica-Ação.pdf

Hagenaars, L. L., Jeurissen, P. P. T., & Klazinga, N. S. (2017). The taxation of unhealthy energy-dense foods (EDFs) and sugar-sweetened beverages (SSBs): An overview of patterns observed in the policy content and policy context of 13 case studies. *Health Policy (Amsterdam)*, 121(8), 887–894. DOI: 10.1016/j.healthpol.2017.06.011 PMID: 28711301

Hruby, A., & Hu, F. B. (2015). The epidemiology of obesity: A big picture. *PharmacoEconomics*, 33(7), 673–689. DOI: 10.1007/s40273-014-0243-x PMID: 25471927

Inquérito Alimentar Nacional e de Atividade Física. (2016). *O inquérito alimentar nacional e de atividade física, IAN-AF 2015-2016.* https://ian-af.up.pt/sites/default/files/IAN-AF%20Brochura%20de%20resultados.pdf

Instituto Nacional de Estatística. (2023, September 15). Óbitos (n.º) por causa de morte (lista sucinta europeia) e mês (óbito); Anual - INE, Óbitos por causas de morte. https://www.ine.pt/xportal/xmain?xpid=INE&xpgid=ine_indicadores&indOcorrCod=0010082&contexto=bd&selTab=tab2

Instituto Nacional de Estatística. (2024, February 9). Consumo humano de açúcar per capita (kg/ hab.). https://www.ine.pt/xportal/xmain?xpid=INE&xpgid=ine_indicadores&indOcorrCod=0000198&contexto=bd&selTab=tab2&xlang=pt

Jacobson, M. F. (2005). Liquid candy: how soft drinks are harming americans' health. *Center For Science in the Public Interest Washington, D.C.*https://www.cspinet.org/sites/default/files/attachment/liquid_candy_final_w_new_supplement.pdf

Jornal Oficial da União Europeia. (2010, October 29). Bebidas, líquidos alcoólicos e vinagres. https://dev.anceve.pt/wp-content/uploads/2017/12/Nomenclatura-Combinada.pdf

Law n.º 30/2019, of April 23rd of the Assembly of the Republic, Diário da República: I série, nº 79 (2019). https://diariodarepublica.pt/dr/detalhe/lei/30-2019-122151046

Law n.º 42/2016, of December 28 of the Assembly of the Republic, Diário da República: I série, nº 248 (2016). https://diariodarepublica.pt/dr/detalhe/lei/42-2016-105637672

Law n.º 82/2023, of December 29 of the Assembly of the Republic, Diário da República: I série, nº 250 (2023). https://diariodarepublica.pt/dr/detalhe/lei/82-2023-835864042

Lin, B.-H., Smith, T. A., Lee, J.-Y., & Hall, K. D. (2011). Measuring weight outcomes for obesity intervention strategies: The case of a sugar-sweetened beverage tax. *Economics and Human Biology*, 9(4), 329–341. DOI: 10.1016/j.ehb.2011.08.007 PMID: 21940223

Lopes, C., Oliveira, A., Afonso, L., Moreira, T., Durão, C., Severo, M., Vilela, S., Ramos, E., & Barros, H. (2014). *Consumo alimentar e nutricional de crianças em idade pré-escolar: resultados da coorte geração 21.* Instituto de Saúde Pública da Universidade do Porto. https://ispup.up.pt/wp-content/uploads/2023/09/2_PDFsam_RelConsG212014.pdf

Lopez, G. W., Kao, J., & Ritchie, L. (2010). To what extent have sweetened beverages contributed to the obesity epidemic? *Public Health Nutrition*, 14(3), 499–509. DOI: 10.1017/S1368980010002375 PMID: 20860886

Lusa (2016, October 11). *OMS apela à tributação de bebidas açucaradas para reduzir obesidade.* Diário de Notícias. https://www.dn.pt/sociedade/oms-apela-a-tributacao-de-bebidas-acucaradas-para-reduzir-obesidade-5435705.html

Ma, Y., He, F. J., Yin, Y., Hashem, K. M., & MacGregor, G. A. (2016). Gradual reduction of sugar in soft drinks without substitution as a strategy to reduce overweight, obesity, and type 2 diabetes: A modelling study. *The Lancet. Diabetes & Endocrinology*, 4(2), 105–114. DOI: 10.1016/S2213-8587(15)00477-5 PMID: 26777597

Meer, F. V., Laan, L., Eiben, G., Lissner, L., Wolters, M., Rach, S., Herrmann, M., Erhard, P., Molnar, D., Orsi, G., Viergever, M. A., Adan, R. A. H., Smeets, P. A. M., & Consortium, I. F. (2019). Development and body mass inversely affect children's brain activation in dorsolateral prefrontal cortex during food choice. *NeuroImage, 201*. Academic Press Inc. DOI: 10.1016/j.neuroimage.2019.116016

Miao, Z., Beghin, J. C., & Jensen, H. H. (2011). Taxing sweets: Sweetener input tax or final consumption tax? *Contemporary Economic Policy*, 30(3), 344–361. DOI: 10.1111/j.1465-7287.2011.00278.x

Mullee, A., Romaguera, D., Pearson-Stuttard, J., Viallon, V., Stepien, M., Freisling, H., Fagherazzj, G., Mancini, F., Boutron-Ruault, M., Kuhn, T., Kaaks, R., Boeing, H., Aleksandrova, K., Tionneland, A., Halkjaer, J., Overvad, K., Weiderpass, E., Skeie, G., Parr, C., & Murphy, N. (2019). Association between soft drink consumption and mortality in 10 european countries. *JAMA Internal Medicine*, 179(11), 1479–1490. DOI: 10.1001/jamainternmed.2019.2478 PMID: 31479109

Oliveira, E. R., & Ferreira, P. (2014). *Métodos de investigação: Da interrogação à descoberta científica*. Vida Económica.

Portugal. Ministério da Saúde. (2022). *Programa nacional para a promoção da alimentação saudável 2022-2030* (M. da G. Freitas & R. Mestre, Eds.). Direção-Geral da Saúde. https://nutrimento.pt/activeapp/wp-content/uploads/2022/10/PNPAS2022_2030_VF.pdf

Powell, L. M., & Chaloupka, F. J. (2009). Food prices and obesity: Evidence and policy implications for taxes and subsidies. *The Milbank Quarterly*, 87(1), 229–257. DOI: 10.1111/j.1468-0009.2009.00554.x PMID: 19298422

Powell, L. M., Chriqui, J. F., Tamkeen, K., Wada, R., & Chaloupka, F. J. (2013). Assessing the potential effectiveness of food and beverage taxes and subsidies for improving public health: A systematic review of prices, demand and body weight outcomes. *National Institutes of Health, 14*(2), 110–128. DOI: 10.1111/obr.12002

Ramos, S., & Naranjo, E. (2014). *Metodologia da investigação científica*. Escolar Editora.

Santos, M. C., & Cordeiro, F. R. (2016). *A Introdução das fat taxes em Portugal: Algumas considerações*. Observatório de Taxas e Contribuições, CEDIPRE- Centro de Estudos de Direito Público e Regulação, Faculdade de Direito da Universidade de Coimbra. https://www.fd.uc.pt/cedipre/observatorio/publicacoes/estudos_1.pdf

Saw, S. M., & Rajan, U. (1997, March). The epidemiology of obesity: A review. *Annals of the Academy of Medicine, Singapore*, 39(1), 1–7. DOI: 10.47102/annals-acadmedsg.V35N1p1 PMID: 9395816

Silva, R. (2021, February 1). *Imposto sobre bebidas açucaradas "funciona" e pode tornar Portugal um exemplo contra a obesidade.* TSF. https://www.tsf.pt/portugal/economia/imposto-sobre-bebidas-acucaradas-funciona-e-pode-tornar-portugal-um-exemplo-contra-a-obesidade-13300793.html

Smith, T. A., Lin, B., & Lee, J. (2010, July). Taxing caloric sweetened beverages: Potential effects on beverage consumption, calorie intake, and obesity. *Economic Research Service*. https://www.ers.usda.gov/webdocs/publications/44732/8311_err100_1_.pdf?v=0

Sousa, M., & Baptista, C. (2011). *Como fazer investigação, dissertação, teses e relatórios: Segundo Bolonha*. PACTOR.

Tamir, O., Cohen-Yogev, T., Furman-Assaf, S., & Endevelt, R. (2018). Taxation of sugar sweetened beverages and unhealthy foods: A qualitative study of key opinion leaders' views. *Israel Journal of Health Policy Research*, 7(1), 43. DOI: 10.1186/s13584-018-0240-1 PMID: 30064503

Thow, A. M., Downs, S. M., & Jan, S. (2014). A systematic review of the effectiveness of food taxes and subsidies to improve diets: Understanding the recent evidence. *Nutrition Reviews*, 72(9), 551–565. DOI: 10.1111/nure.12123 PMID: 25091552

Unesda (2024, abril). *Sales and consumption*.https://www.unesda.eu/sales-and-consumption/

University of North Carolina. (2022). *Sugary drink taxes around the world*.https://www.globalfoodresearchprogram.org/wp-content/uploads/2022/02/Sugary_Drink_Tax_maps_2022_02.pdf

World Health Organization. (2015). Using price policies to promote healthier diets. DOI: 10.13140/RG.2.1.4853.3923

World Health Organization. (2020, December 9). *The top 10 causes of death*.https://www.who.int/news-room/fact-sheets/detail/the-top-10-causes-of-death

World Health Organization. (2021, June 9). *Obesity and overweight.*https://www.who.int/news-room/fact-sheets/detail/obesity-and-overweight

World Health Organization. (2022). *Who european regional obesity*. https://www.who.int/europe/publications/i/item/9789289057738

KEY TERMS AND DEFINITIONS

Excise taxes: Are indirect taxes that apply to the sale or use of goods such as alcohol, tobacco and energy products.

Fat Tax: A tax whose main objective is to reduce the consumption of unhealthy foods and drinks.

Healthier Lifestyle: Incorporate a set of food policies that promote the adoption of a diet rich in healthy products. Policies can affect prices, increasing them for unhealthy foods and drinks, and adopting subsidies to support the consumption of fruits, vegetables, and others to replace harmful foods.

Nutrition Education: Food and drinks literacy allows you to increase awareness to change future behaviors.

Obesity: Is a chronic disease characterized by excess fat accumulated in the body. It results from an imbalance between the calories ingested through food and the number of calories spent through physical exercise or daily activities.

Social Function of Taxes: The social function of the taxes is to enable the provision by the government of services essential to the social well-being of the population, particularly in the health sector.

Unhealthy foods and drinks: Foods and drinks which contain ingredients harmful to human health, namely sugar, fat, artificial sweeteners, and salt.

Chapter 6
Green and Inclusive Taxation Towards a Sustainable Model That Strengthens the Colombian Economy

Franz Esteban Rodríguez Franky
https://orcid.org/0000-0002-5253-3015
Fundación Universitaria Compensar, Colombia

ABSTRACT

This chapter proposes to analyze green and inclusive taxation as a tool for the construction of a sustainable economic model in Colombia. The need for a change in the Colombian tax system is addressed, incorporating practical environmental and social criteria that are adjusted to MSMEs and SMEs, which allow promoting a fairer and more equitable economic development, in harmony with the environment. The Chapter analyzes the need for a green and inclusive tax reform, in which the economic and social impact is evaluated; issues related to the challenges for the implementation of green and inclusive taxation in Colombia are addressed, including the strategies that should be implemented and how these progressive taxes can benefit vulnerable populations and the targeting of public spending, which is key to reducing inequalities. "An equitable tax system strengthens social cohesion".

DOI: 10.4018/979-8-3693-3908-4.ch006

1. INTRODUCTION

The chapter offers a comprehensive literature review on green and inclusive taxation in Colombia, providing a solid foundation for understanding this crucial issue in the international context. The evolution of environmental fiscal policies in Colombia and Latin America is explored, contrasting them with some significant international experiences such as Germany, Sweden and Costa Rica. These case studies illustrate how the effective implementation of green taxes can reconcile environmental objectives with economic growth and social equity. The analysis covers the proposals of various authors over time, highlighting innovative business strategies that promote more efficient sustainable management systems. It examines how these initiatives can be adapted to the Colombian landscape, considering the country's unique challenges and opportunities. The chapter also assesses the potential impact of these policies on reducing greenhouse gas emissions, promoting renewable energy, and creating green jobs. In addition, mechanisms to ensure that these fiscal policies are inclusive are discussed, addressing equity concerns and exploring how the revenues generated can be reinvested in social and environmental programs. This comprehensive review not only provides a solid theoretical foundation, but also offers practical insights for policymakers, entrepreneurs, and academics interested in driving a transition to a greener and more equitable economy.

A tax reform integrating green taxation and social inclusion aligns economic, environmental and social objectives towards sustainable development. This allows us to move towards a low-carbon economy, reduce negative environmental impacts and advance in social inclusion. Among the green taxes that could be implemented are taxes on CO2 emissions, single-use plastics and bags, polluting vehicles, extractive activities or perverse subsidies for fossil fuels. This would discourage unsustainable practices, which is why the resources collected would be used for investment in environmental conservation, clean energy, sustainable transport and adaptation to climate change. This text also takes a look at how green taxes, their applicability through the generation of public policies and the impact they generate in an emerging economy such as Colombia's; It can be a political, economic, environmental and social strategy for small, medium and large companies to transform their productions into a more environmentally friendly order.

For Arguedas Alberto (2020) "The 1960s and 1970s were the scene of politicization and institutionalization of the environmental issue, in the 1990s by a paradigm that seeks to make the environmental/climate issue compatible with developmentalist and market economist thinking, which is called green capitalism." (pp.197-198). On the other hand, this chapter effectively illustrates the problems and trends related to green and inclusive taxation in the Colombian context, which is adequately aligned with the theme of the proposed book. The main strength of the chapter lies in its focus on a robust literature review, a series of strategic proposals for the implementation of green taxes, and business actions that can transform and innovate sustainable business models.

1.1 Constructive and analytical evaluation

Contextualization: The chapter succeeds in focusing specifically on the Colombian context, which allows for a deeper and more relevant understanding of the topic for readers interested in this region.

Temporal evolution: The document includes perspectives from various authors over time, offering a dynamic view of how ideas and strategies in this field have evolved.

Practical approach: The document emphasizes business actions and strategies aimed at the implementation of sustainable management systems, which suggests a balance between theory and practical application.

1.2 Chapter Scope

Case studies: The text incorporates specific case studies of Colombian companies that have implemented green and inclusive taxation strategies.

Comparative analysis: The text allows for comparison with international experiences, which could offer valuable perspectives on best practices and lessons learned.

Future projections: The chapter includes a section that explores future trends and anticipated challenges in the implementation of green taxation policies in Colombia, which increases the relevance and usefulness of the book.

Regulatory framework: The chapter analyzes the current legal and regulatory framework in Colombia, relating the different actions to green taxation, identifying possible areas for improvement or reform.

Socioeconomic impact: The document broadened the discussion on how these fiscal policies can affect different sectors of Colombian society, addressing issues of equity and sustainable development.

Stakeholder participation: The chapter includes perspectives from different stakeholders (government, business, civil society) on the implementation of these fiscal policies.

One of the strengths of this chapter lies in its contextualized approach to the Colombian reality. The synthesis of diverse academic and business positions over time which provides a theoretical, experiential and evolutionary perspective of the subject. This strength contributes significantly to the value and quality of the chapter, offering a deep and multifaceted understanding of green and inclusive taxation. These strengths can be leveraged to strengthen potential weak areas, such as practical application, by incorporating concrete examples derived from the literature reviewed. In addition, Colombian contextualization can serve as a starting point for a broader comparative analysis, thus enriching the discussion on the adaptability of global strategies to the local scenario. The document also addresses the problems and trends of green and inclusive taxation in Colombia, but there are areas that could be strengthened for a more complete and updated analysis. On the other hand, the study by Romero et al. (2022) on the political economy of environmental taxes in Latin America could provide valuable insights.

However, it is important to broaden the discussion on global trends and their applicability to the Colombian context. The work of Sterner et al. (2022) on policy design for the Anthropocene provides a useful framework for this analysis. The text benefits from a greater emphasis on the economic and social impacts of these policies. Research by Ohlendorf et al. (2021) on the distributional effects of carbon prices provides relevant insights. Baranzini et al.'s (2021) analysis of carbon pricing policies in developing countries is a valuable source for understanding and deepening sustainable and tax analyses. Another relevant author that allows us to investigate and explore the impact of green tax strategies is the study by Grubb et al. (2021) on the transformation of energy systems, which offers a useful forward-looking view.

However, a sustainable tax reform must be aligned with global commitments such as the 2030 Agenda and the Paris Agreement. But this type of practice is not so easy to implement on the planet, as it faces an unprecedented environmental crisis. Climate change, pollution and the degradation of natural resources threaten the health of the planet and the well-being of people. While the extractivist processes in production given by the increase in demand in the markets and a low change in the cultures of consumption of goods, make it almost impossible to implement this type of strategy. In this context, the search for sustainable economic models has become an imperative need. Colombia, as a country with a rich biodiversity and a growing economy, has a fundamental role to play in building a more sustainable future, which frames actions that impact not only the Latin American region but also an international trend. "The correct use of various renewable energy resources is the key to obtaining a sustainable future where greenhouse gas emissions are low." (Galarza, R. & Cuji, C. 2022. p72)

Colombia has made progress in recent years in the implementation of tax policies that promote sustainability and inclusion. However, there are still challenges to overcome to achieve a truly sustainable and inclusive tax model. In this context, green taxation refers to the imposition of taxes on activities that generate negative impacts on the environment, such as the emission of greenhouse gases or water pollution. These taxes seek to internalize the environmental costs of these activities, incentivizing companies to adopt more sustainable practices. In the case of Colombia, a green taxation approach could focus on sectors such as mining, agriculture and transport, which have a high environmental impact

2. CONTEXT OF GREEN AND INCLUSIVE TAXATION

When talking about green taxation, it is important to mention that it is part of a broad and contextualized perspective, allowing a deep understanding of how these concepts are applied and adapted to the particularities of countries. The study given in this chapter examines the evolution of academic and practical thinking in this field, presenting a synthesis of the ideas of various experts who have contributed to the debate over time. The innovative proposals and corporate strategies that these authors have developed are highlighted, all oriented towards the creation and implementation of more effective sustainable management systems adapted to the Colombian context.

Through this review, the chapter not only exposes the current state of knowledge on green and inclusive taxation in Colombia, but also illustrates how the different theoretical and practical approaches have evolved to address the country's specific challenges in terms of sustainability and fiscal equity. This exploration provides a solid basis for future analysis and for the formulation of more effective environmental fiscal policies adapted to the Colombian reality. However, there are great experiences from Germany, Sweden and Costa Rica in implementing green and inclusive tax policies, in which they offer valuable lessons for other countries seeking to adopt similar strategies. Germany, a pioneer in this field, introduced its "Green Tax Reform" in 1999, which increased taxes on energy and created a new levy on electricity. The revenue generated was used to reduce social security contributions, which boosted employment and demonstrated how green tax policies can have broader economic benefits. According to Lutz and Levell (2021), these measures have had a positive impact on reducing CO2 emissions and creating jobs in the renewable energy sector.

For its part, Sweden implemented a carbon tax in 1991, which has become one of the highest in the world, covering about 40% of the country's total greenhouse gas emissions. A World Bank report (2023) notes that this tax has been effective in reducing emissions without significantly affecting economic growth, and part of the revenue has been used to reduce other taxes, making the system more inclusive. Costa Rica, on the other hand, has adopted a comprehensive approach that combines green fiscal policies with conservation and rural development objectives. The country implemented a carbon tax in 1997 and, in 2019, launched its National Decarbonization Plan, which includes a review of its tax system to align it with climate goals. A study by ECLAC (2022) highlights how Costa Rica has used the revenues from these taxes to finance forest conservation and biodiversity programs, contributing to both climate change mitigation and sustainable development. These experiences demonstrate that green tax policies, when carefully designed and implemented, can achieve multiple objectives: reducing greenhouse gas emissions, fostering innovation in clean technologies, creating green jobs, and at the same time generating revenues that can be used to make the tax system more equitable and support other sustainable development goals. However, it is important to note that the success of these policies depends to a large extent on the specific context of each country, including its economic structure, its energy matrix and its development priorities. Therefore, while other countries can learn from these experiences, it is crucial that they tailor these lessons to their own unique circumstances and needs

Inclusive taxation is presented as a fundamental way to build a fairer and more equitable development model. This approach seeks to use the tax system as a tool to reduce social inequalities and promote the inclusion of historically marginalized groups, while combating the effect of climate change. This environmental crisis is one of the greatest challenges facing humanity in the 21st century. Its effects are already having a major impact on our societies and economies. In view of this, it is necessary to adopt urgent measures to reduce greenhouse gas emissions and move towards sustainable development models. According to the United Nations (2022) in its "Emissions Disparity Report 2021", it states that the gap on emissions of polluting gases into the atmosphere shows that new national climate commitments combined with other mitigation measures are putting the world on track for a global temperature increase of 2.7 °C by the end of the century. This is well above the goals of the Paris climate agreement and would lead to catastrophic changes in the Earth's climate (para. 1). One of the key tools to achieve this is green taxation. Green taxes seek to internalize the negative externalities of polluting activities and encourage more environmentally friendly behaviors. By taxing pollution, an economic signal is sent to producers and consumers to modify their patterns. However, the design of green taxes faces several challenges. One of the main ones is to avoid regressive effects on the most vulnerable sectors. Lower-income households tend to spend a larger proportion of their budget on goods and services taxed by green taxes, such as electricity and fuel, which can increase inequality. In several of the most developed economies, fiscal policies remain flexible and are geared towards strengthening their economies through a green transition, digital transformation and other long-term investments; However, fiscal policies in advanced economies are evolving to reflect the importance of environmental sustainability, innovation, and long-term growth. (International Monetary Fund, 2021. p.11).

This is where the concept of inclusive green taxation becomes relevant. Inclusion must be a guiding principle in the construction of sustainable tax systems. Mechanisms are needed to protect the poorest from the impact of new environmental taxes. Some options are to use the resources collected to finance targeted transfers, reduce other regressive taxes, or provide direct compensation to affected groups.

However, the productive processes of organizations must mutate to more optimized and automated processes with natural resources. According to the OECD (2020) The effectiveness of financial support measures varies depending on the context. In some cases, social spending, such as social assistance programs or cash transfers, may be more effective in providing support to households than general fiscal measures. For businesses, fiscal cash flow support through measures such as tax cuts or payment deferrals can be helpful, but it is also important to consider managing corporate debt and accessing credit. High indebtedness can limit firms' ability to invest and grow, while limited access to credit can make it difficult for firms to obtain the resources they need to operate. (p.21). Table 1 shows how green taxation is designed in order to contribute to the construction of more profitable, rational economies with a greater impact in the sustainable sphere.

Table 1. Advantages of green taxation

Advantages	Description
Reduction of polluting emissions	The increase in the cost of carbon-intensive activities encourages the transition to clean energy and more efficient processes
Revenue Generation	The resources collected can be used to finance environmental policies, social protection or to reduce other distorting taxes
Greater innovation	By penalizing negative externalities, investments in research and adoption of clean technologies are promoted
Competitiveness	Having a more demanding environmental institutional framework prepares companies for a low-carbon world
Quality of life	Cities with less air and noise pollution have positive effects on the health and well-being of the population

Source: Own elaboration

A number of countries have implemented green taxes in recent decades, mainly on carbon and energy. A prominent case is that of the Nordic countries, pioneers in the use of economic instruments for environmental management. For example, since the 1990s Sweden has imposed taxes on CO2 emissions and nuclear energy, managing to reduce its emissions while maintaining high economic growth. Another relevant case is that of Colombia, which has implemented a national carbon tax since 2016. The proceeds have made it possible to finance environmental projects and encourage forest conservation. Compensations have been incorporated to protect lower-income households from the impact of the tax. At the global level, the International Monetary Fund has called for carbon taxes of at least US$75 per ton by 2030 to meet the goals of the Paris Agreement, which estimates revenue generation of up to 4% of global GDP, creating crucial fiscal space for low-carbon investments and reducing inequalities.

For Hepburn et al (2020) "The climate emergency is like the COVID-19 emergency, only in slow motion and much more serious. Both involve market failures, externalities, international cooperation, complex science, issues of system resilience, political leadership, and actions that depend on public support." (p.360), therefore, a responsible and objective debate is needed on the best mechanisms to implement this fiscal transition, learning from international best practices.

The private sector also has a fundamental role to play, moving towards environmentally sustainable business models. With a long-term vision and understanding its multiple benefits, inclusive green taxation can become a pillar of prosperity and well-being in the 21st century. Green and inclusive taxation is a comprehensive approach to strengthening the economy in a sustainable and equitable manner. Taxing activities that generate negative impacts on the environment and promoting social inclusion through the tax system can contribute to building a more prosperous and equitable future for all. However, it is important to note that the implementation of green and inclusive tax policies must be part of a broader approach that includes regulatory measures, economic incentives, and awareness-raising programs to bring about real and lasting change towards a more sustainable economy. Table 2 provides an overview of green and inclusive tax policies in some countries, including Colombia, Sweden, Germany, and the United States.

The evolution of tax policies in Colombia has been a complex and dynamic process, shaped by economic, political, and social factors over the decades. This historical trajectory has laid the groundwork for the challenges and opportunities the country faces today in its quest for a greener and more inclusive tax system. Since the 1990s, Colombia has undergone a number of significant tax reforms. These reforms have sought to increase tax revenues, improve the efficiency of the tax system, and promote equity. Rodríguez and Ávila (2023) point out that many of these reforms have been partial and have failed to comprehensively address the structural problems of the Colombian tax system. The persistent dependence on indirect taxes, particularly VAT, has been a notable feature of tax developments in Colombia. Bonilla et al. (2022) argue that this dependence has contributed to the regressiveness of the tax system, disproportionately affecting lower-income sectors. Additionally, Cano et al. (2023) analyze how this tax structure has impacted income inequality in the country

Regarding environmental tax policies, Gómez-Sabaini and Morán (2021) argue that, despite some progress in the implementation of green taxes, Colombia still has a long way to go in aligning its tax system with environmental sustainability objectives. This observation is supported by Montes-Vergara et al. (2022), who analyze the potential of green taxes to promote the energy transition in Colombia, therefore, recent tax reforms, such as the Social Investment Law of 2021, have attempted to address some of these historical challenges. Castañeda et al. (2023) assess the impact of these reforms on the progressivity of the tax system and the fight against tax evasion. For their part, Núñez et al. (2022) examine how these reforms have affected income distribution and poverty in Colombia.

However, the COVID-19 pandemic has highlighted the need for a more resilient and equitable tax system. Lora and Mejía (2022) analyse how the crisis has exacerbated existing inequalities and underlined the importance of green fiscal policies that can respond effectively to economic and social shocks. Complementing this analysis, Gallego et al. (2021) study the impact of the pandemic on the informal economy and its implications for tax policy and how actions emphasizing sustainability are a comprehensive strategy to combat the new challenges of an emerging economy such as Colombia's. Looking ahead, the transition to a green and inclusive tax model represents both a challenge and an opportunity for Colombia. Pardo Martínez and Alfonso (2023) suggest that the implementation of well-designed environmental taxes could not only generate additional revenue, but also promote more sustainable behaviors and contribute to climate change mitigation, This perspective is complemented by the work of Romero-Jordán et al. (2022), who analyze the effectiveness of environmental taxes in reducing CO2 emissions in developing countries.

In addition, Ocampo-Rodríguez et al. (2023) explore the potential of green tax policies to foster innovation and sustainable development in Colombia. For their part, Vargas-Chaves et al. (2022) analyze the intersection between tax policies and the circular economy in the Colombian context, actions that are necessary to be able to efficiently structure sustainable economic investments. However, informality continues to be a major challenge for the Colombian tax system. Fernández and Villar (2023) examine how tax policies can influence the transition from informality to formality in the Colombian economy seen from a sustainable, profitable approach and environmentally friendly business models. In summary, in the context of regional integration, Barreix et al. (2022) analyze how Colombia's green tax policies compare with those of other Latin American countries and how fiscal harmonization could benefit the region, thus the historical evolution of tax policies in Colombia has left a mixed legacy. While past reforms have made some progress in terms of collection and efficiency, significant challenges remain in terms of equity and environmental sustainability. The path to a green and inclusive tax system will require addressing these historic challenges while seizing emerging opportunities in the global context of transition to more sustainable economies.

2.1 Implications of green tax policies in Colombia

The evolution of tax policies in Colombia towards a greener and more inclusive model is framed in a global context of growing concern for environmental sustainability and social equity. A thorough analysis of the recent literature reveals significant trends and persistent challenges in this area, which require detailed attention and a multidisciplinary approach.

Environmental taxes and emission reduction

According to a study by Romero-Jordán et al. (2022), environmental taxes have proven to be effective in reducing CO2 emissions in developing countries, with a particularly notable impact on the energy sector. The authors found that a 1% increase in environmental taxes is associated with a 0.3% decrease in CO2 emissions per capita. This finding underscores the potential of green fiscal instruments for Colombia. Montes-Vergara et al. (2022) delve into this topic, specifically analyzing the Colombian case. Their research reveals that the implementation of a carbon tax in Colombia in 2017 has contributed to an estimated 2-3% reduction in the country's CO2 emissions in the first three years of its implementation

Innovation and green tax policies

Ocampo-Rodríguez et al. (2023) analyze the interaction between environmental taxes and innovation in Colombia, finding a positive but complex relationship. Their study reveals that while environmental taxes can stimulate innovation in clean technologies, their effect varies significantly between economic sectors. In particular, they found that companies in high-tech sectors increased their investments in green R+D by 15% in response to the introduction of environmental taxes.

Fiscal Equity and Poverty Reduction

In terms of fiscal equity, Bonilla et al. (2022) provide quantitative evidence on the impact of tax reforms on reducing poverty and inequality in Colombia. Using micro simulations, which demonstrate that a combination of progressive taxes and targeted transfers could reduce the Gini coefficient by up to 3 percentage points, Núñez et al. (2022) complement these findings, estimating that a comprehensive green tax reform that includes a 10% increase in social spending financed through more progressive taxes could reduce the poverty rate in Colombia by up to 4 percentage points.

Informality and tax policy

Informality remains a crucial challenge for the Colombian tax system. Fernández and Villar (2023) analyze how tax policies can influence the transition from informality to formality. Their results suggest that a 10% reduction in the tax burden on formal work could increase formality by approximately 5 percentage points.

Circular economy and taxation

In the context of the circular economy, Vargas-Chaves et al. (2022) explore the potential of fiscal instruments to promote sustainable practices in Colombia. Their analysis reveals that tax incentives for reuse and recycling could reduce solid waste by up to 25% in five years.

Comparative regional perspective

From a regional comparative perspective, Barreix et al. (2022) analyze fiscal policies for sustainable development in Latin America and the Caribbean. They find that Colombia, like other countries in the region, could benefit significantly from greater tax harmonization, especially with regard to environmental taxes. Their study suggests that regional tax harmonization could increase tax collection by an average of 2% of GDP in participating countries.

Impact of the pandemic

It is important to note that the COVID-19 pandemic has had a significant impact on Colombia's fiscal policies. Castañeda et al. (2023) assess the effects of recent tax reforms on inequality and poverty, finding that the emergency measures implemented during the pandemic had a positive but temporary effect on poverty reduction. Specifically, they estimate that these measures prevented an increase in poverty of up to 3 percentage points during the peak of the crisis. To better illustrate these findings, Table 2 shows information associated with the progressive impact of strategies and actions associated with green taxes.

Table 2. Description of green tax actions in Colombia

Indicator	Value	Fountain
Estimated reduction in CO2 emissions due to a 1% increase in environmental taxes	0.3%	Romero-Jordán et al. (2022)
Estimated reduction of CO2 emissions from carbon tax in Colombia (2017-2020	2-3%	Montes-Vergara et al. (2022)
Increase in investment in green R+D in high-tech sectors	15%	Ocampo-Rodríguez et al. (2023)
Potential reduction of the Gini coefficient with progressive tax reform	3 percentage points	Bonilla et al. (2022)
Potential Poverty Rate Reduction with Comprehensive Tax Reform	4 percentage points	Núñez et al. (2022)
Estimated increase in labor formality due to a 10% reduction in tax burden	5 percentage points	Fernández and Villar (2023)
Potential reduction of solid waste with tax incentives (in 5 years)	25%	Vargas-Chaves et al. (2022)
Potential increase in tax collection with regional tax harmonization	2% of GDP	Barreix et al. (2022)
Impact of emergency measures on preventing increased poverty during the pandemic	3 percentage points	Castañeda et al. (2023)

Source: Own elaboration

These recent studies and statistical data underscore the complexity of implementing a green and inclusive tax system in Colombia. Evidence suggests that while there are significant opportunities to use fiscal instruments to promote sustainability and equity, a carefully calibrated approach that takes into account the particularities of the Colombian context is required. In conclusion, the transition to a greener and more inclusive tax model in Colombia requires a multifaceted approach that balances environmental, social, and economic objectives. Recent empirical evidence suggests that, with the right policies, Colombia has the potential to achieve significant improvements in sustainability and equity through innovative tax reforms. However, it is crucial that these reforms are designed and implemented in ways that simultaneously address the challenges of informality, inequality, and environmental degradation, while fostering innovation and sustainable economic growth.

Table 3. Green and inclusive tax policies in some countries

Country	Regulations or Law	Taxes on CO2 emissions	Tax benefits	Social impact	Environmental impact	Economic impact	Amounts in USD (in millions)
Colombia	Law 1819 of 2016	Yes	Yes	It allocates resources to social and health programs, which can increase the quality of life of the population and reduce social inequalities.	It reduces carbon emissions and encourages more sustainable business practices, which can improve air quality and reduce environmental impact.	It can stimulate innovation and the development of clean technologies, as well as job creation in sustainable sectors. Tax benefits for sustainable companies can improve their competitiveness and encourage investment in cleaner and more sustainable sectors.	$ 500
Sweden	Environmental Tax Act (Miljöbalken)	Yes	Yes	It allocates resources to social welfare programs, which can reduce poverty and promote social inclusion.	It reduces carbon emissions and promotes the use of renewable energy, which can decrease dependence on fossil fuels and foster the transition to a more sustainable economy.	It can improve energy efficiency and encourage innovation in green technologies, which can increase the productivity and competitiveness of Swedish companies. Tax benefits for sustainable companies can stimulate investment in cleaner and more sustainable sectors.	$ 700

continued on following page

Table 3. Continued

Country	Regulations or Law	Taxes on CO2 emissions	Tax benefits	Social impact	Environmental impact	Economic impact	Amounts in USD (in millions)
Germany	Energy and Energy Products Tax Act	Yes	Yes	It allocates resources to social and housing programs, which can improve the quality of life of the population and reduce social inequalities.	It reduces carbon emissions and encourages efficient energy use, which can decrease dependence on fossil fuels and promote the transition to a more sustainable economy.	It can stimulate investment in green technologies and job creation in sustainable sectors, which can increase the competitiveness of the German economy in the long term. Tax benefits for sustainable companies can encourage the adoption of more sustainable practices.	$ 600
United States	Varies by state	No	No	The lack of policies at the federal level can have mixed impacts on the economy, depending on individual state policies.	Without taxes at the federal level, environmental policies vary significantly between states, which can result in a lack of consistency and effectiveness in protecting the environment.	The lack of environmental taxes at the federal level may limit innovation and the development of clean technologies in the United States, which could negatively affect the competitiveness of the economy in the global market.	$ 400
Portugal	Law 82-D/2014	Yes	Yes	It allocates resources to social welfare programs, which can reduce poverty and promote social inclusion.	It reduces carbon dioxide emissions and encourages more sustainable business practices, which can improve air quality and reduce environmental impact.	It can stimulate innovation and the development of clean technologies, as well as job creation in sustainable sectors. Tax benefits for sustainable companies can improve their competitiveness and encourage investment in cleaner and more sustainable sectors.	$ 800

continued on following page

Table 3. Continued

Country	Regulations or Law	Taxes on CO2 emissions	Tax benefits	Social impact	Environmental impact	Economic impact	Amounts in USD (in millions)
Spain	Law 15/2012	Yes	Yes	It allocates resources to social and health programs, which can increase the quality of life of the population and reduce social inequalities.	It reduces emissions of fluorinated greenhouse gases and promotes energy efficiency, which can contribute to the fight against climate change and the protection of the environment.	It can stimulate innovation in green technologies and job creation in sustainable sectors. Tax benefits for sustainable companies can improve their competitiveness and encourage investment in cleaner and more sustainable sectors.	$ 900
France	Energy Transition for Green Growth Law	Yes	Yes	It allocates resources to education and training programs, which can improve employment opportunities and reduce inequality.	It reduces greenhouse gas emissions and promotes energy efficiency, which can contribute to the fight against climate change and the protection of the environment.	It can foster innovation in clean technologies and job creation in sustainable sectors. Tax benefits for sustainable companies can improve their competitiveness and encourage investment in cleaner and more sustainable sectors.	$ 300
Canada	Carbon Pricing Act	Yes	Yes	It allocates resources to nature conservation and environmental protection programs, which can improve the quality of the natural environment and promote biodiversity.	It reduces greenhouse gas emissions and encourages the transition to a low-carbon economy, which can contribute to climate change mitigation and environmental protection.	It can stimulate investment in clean technologies and job creation in sustainable sectors, which can	$ 200

Source: Prepared by the authors based on information associated with the Ministry of Finance and Public Credit of Colombia. (2016). Law 1819 of 2016, Government of Sweden. (n.d.). Environmental Tax Act (Miljöbalken), Government of Germany. (n.d.). Law on Taxes on Energy and Energy Products, Government of Portugal. (2014). Law 82-D/2014, Government of Spain. (2012). Law 15/2012, Government of France. (2015). Energy Transition for Green Growth Act, Government of Canada. (n.d.). Canada's Carbon Tax Act.

Green and inclusive tax policies have a positive impact on social welfare by allocating resources to social and health programs, which can reduce poverty and promote social inclusion in countries such as Colombia, Sweden, Germany, Portugal, and Spain. On the other hand, these types of activities allow for a positive impact on the environment by reducing carbon emissions and encouraging more sustainable business practices, which can improve air quality and reduce environmental impact. Even more so if we take into account the latest report by the Stockholm Environment Institute, Climate Analytics, E3G, the International Institute for Sustainable Development and the United Nations Environment Programme (UNEP) (2023), in which they state that governments plan to produce 110% more fossil fuels than would allow global warming to be kept to 1.5°C. This amount is 69% higher than what would be compatible with an increase of 2°C as evidenced in Figure 1. This excessive production threatens to aggravate climate change and its negative consequences for the planet and the economy.

For Escribano et al (2022)

In Europe, some Member States and their Mediterranean neighbours have renewable resources with enough potential to become competitive green hydrogen producers. However, despite the fact that almost all European energy players anticipate significant economic opportunities for hydrogen, Member States reflect divergent preferences in their technological and market integration paths. (p.86)

The need for massive investments in infrastructure and technology, along with the implementation of effective policies, are critical aspects to drive this transition. In addition, the lack of international coordination and collaboration could limit the development of this emerging industry. It is therefore crucial that actors such as companies work together to overcome these challenges and fully harness the potential of green business in building a more sustainable future.

Figure 1. Production projection by 2050 (United Nations Environment Program, 2023)

Figure 1. Production projection by 2050

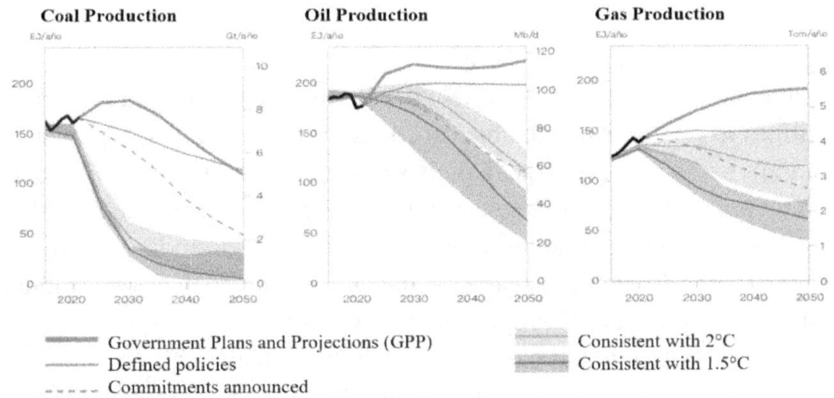

Source: United Nations Environment Programme (2023)

2.2 Benefits of inclusive green taxation

As we have seen, the climate crisis represents one of the greatest global challenges of our time. Its effects on ecosystems, biodiversity and climate patterns pose a serious threat to sustainable development. In this context, it is essential to move towards low-carbon and environmentally sustainable economic models. One of the key tools to facilitate this transition is inclusive green taxation. Well-designed environmental taxes and charges can incentivize changes in production and consumption patterns, discouraging polluting activities and accelerating the adoption of clean technologies. In addition, the revenues collected through these instruments allow financing low-carbon investments and redistributive policies, in this approach inclusive green taxation is presented as a fundamental instrument to build a fairer, more equitable and sustainable development model.

2.3 Types of benefits from green taxation

Addressing the challenges and seizing the opportunities it offers requires a joint effort between governments, businesses and civil society. Building a green and inclusive tax system is a shared responsibility that will allow us to achieve sustainable development for present and future generations. A green and inclusive tax system is characterized by progressivity, where those with more resources pay more taxes, and these funds are redistributed through social programs for the most vulnerable sectors, such as education, health, and social assistance. To protect low-income households from the impact of environmental measures, green taxation can implement tax exemptions or credits that offset the increase in the cost of living resulting from environmental policies.

Green taxation also serves to protect the environment, using tax incentives and disincentives to promote sustainable practices and discourage the production and consumption of polluting goods. This is achieved through taxes on carbon emissions, water pollution and waste generation, making polluting products and services more expensive and discouraging their consumption and production. In addition, tax incentives are offered to invest in clean technologies such as renewable energy and sustainable transport. This type of taxation not only seeks social justice and environmental protection, but can also contribute to sustainable economic growth, generating new jobs in sectors such as renewable energies and attracting national and international investment, as described in table 3. However, there are challenges such as tax evasion and avoidance, labor informality, and the need to strengthen institutional capacities. Measures such as stricter taxation, international cooperation, formalization of employment and awareness of the importance of inclusive green taxation are required. In conclusion, a sustainable tax policy that internalizes negative environmental externalities, incentivizes the adoption of clean technologies, and raises funds for a just transition, can yield enormous economic, social, and environmental benefits. Countries that manage to implement green reforms quickly and equitably will take the lead in building carbon-neutral, resilient, and prosperous societies. Moving towards inclusive, progressive and environmentally friendly tax models will be key to the well-being of future generations.

Table 4. Types of benefits of green taxation

Benefit Type	Benefit Context
Reducing pollution and greenhouse gas emissions	Taxes on carbon and other negative externalities make emissions-intensive activities more expensive, sending an economic signal to agents to modify their behaviour. This incentivizes the use of renewable energies, energy efficiency and innovation in cleaner production methods. Studies show that well-designed green taxes can be a highly effective mechanism for reducing the environmental footprint
Generating income for sustainable investments	The resources collected through environmental taxes allow for expanding fiscal space to finance expenditures and investments aimed at climate action. For example, funds can be allocated to expand renewable energy infrastructure, electrify public transportation, conserve strategic ecosystems, and adopt regenerative agricultural practices. This constant income stream also gives certainty to plan long-term policies
Boosting innovation and competitiveness	By making polluting technologies and processes more expensive, green taxes work as an incentive for the private sector to invest in research and development of low-carbon alternatives. This encourages the creation of new business models, efficient energy solutions and circular product design, which can translate into comparative advantages and greater competitiveness
Just transition and reduced inequalities	Through offsets, targeted aid and strategic use of the revenues collected, inclusive green taxation can mitigate the regressive impact on the most vulnerable households. It also allows financing labor reconversion programs and economic diversification in regions dependent on carbon-intensive industries, facilitating a socially equitable transition
Strengthening public health	The reduction in air pollution thanks to the changes incentivized by green taxes has proven positive effects on human health and quality of life in cities, preventing respiratory and cardiovascular diseases. It is estimated that air pollution causes millions of premature deaths each year
Meeting global climate commitments	Green taxes are a centerpiece of the decarbonization strategies proposed by international organizations to meet the goals of the Paris Agreement and limit global warming to 1.5°C. Institutions such as the IMF and the World Bank have called for ambitious and socially responsible carbon pricing schemes

Source: Own elaboration

2.4 Characteristics of the benefits of green taxation

Emerging economies face the challenge of implementing green fiscal reforms in contexts of high inequality, poverty, and informality. It is key that this process is carried out in a socially responsible way, protecting the most vulnerable sectors and taking advantage of the benefits of the energy transition. That is why this type of action must have a series of characteristics that allow green taxation to be successfully implemented mainly in emerging economies such as Colombia and countries in the region. Some of these characteristics are reflected in:

Increased reliance on carbon-intensive sectors: Emerging countries such as India, South Africa and Brazil still derive a high proportion of their GDP

from highly polluting activities such as coal mining or oil extraction. This makes the distributional impacts of taxing these industries a sensitive issue.
High inequality and poverty: There is a risk of regressive effects of environmental taxes on low-income households, given the higher proportion they allocate to taxed goods such as electricity. Focused trade-offs are required.
Limited institutional capacity: Emerging countries tend to have less capacity for efficient and progressive tax collection, given the high levels of informality and weakness of tax administrations.
Unequal access to clean sources: Low-carbon technologies are not yet available or are very expensive for large sections of the population in these economies. This makes the transition difficult.
High urbanization: Rapid urban growth in emerging economies demands integrated environmental planning and clean transportation strategies for cities.
High biodiversity: Many emerging countries are home to ecosystems critical to global climate regulation, where payments for environmental services can be implemented.
Growing middle class: The increase in the purchasing power of growing middle segments implies greater pressure on resources, but also greater environmental awareness.

For Celi Frugoni A. (2022) "The energy transition and social transformation of Latin America and the Caribbean requires, in our opinion, a rereading of sovereignty and the way in which it has been exercised by States, in the face of global problems". (p.503). Therefore, green taxes should come into force progressively to allow time for households and companies to adapt, along with this, some of the mechanisms such as direct cash transfers and cross-subsidies between high- and low-income sectors help mitigate regressive impacts on poverty.

Some of the integrating characteristics of green taxation, such as investment in infrastructure and clean technology, must be based on the collection in which low-carbon alternatives for an inclusive energy transition can be massively disseminated, with an emphasis on transport and efficient housing. Likewise, the fight against informality as a characteristic should improve the capacity for control and the formalization of the economy, expand the tax base and allow less dependence on indirect regressive taxes. These types of benefits must be articulated with the policies of governments. According to Wyczykier Gabriela (2023). "The socio-ecological crisis of the present is therefore linked to the climate emergency caused by the impact of activities of anthropogenic origin on a global scale (p.456). This requires multilevel coordination in which the environmental and tax policy objectives of national, subnational and municipal governments can be aligned, along with educational campaigns to raise awareness of the need for green taxation that aim to generate political and citizen support. The transition to sustainable economies is an ethical and survival imperative. Emerging countries have the opportunity to lead this process through creative, ambitious and socially inclusive green tax reforms. With differentiated policies according to national realities and learning from global best practices, green taxation can become the engine of a new paradigm of human development in harmony with the planet

3. STRATEGIES FOR THE IMPLEMENTATION OF GREEN AND INCLUSIVE TAXATION

Implementing green and inclusive taxation requires carefully designed strategies that consider both environmental and social aspects equitably and effectively. Beyond simple tax collection, green and inclusive taxation becomes a fundamental instrument for redistributing wealth, combating poverty and promoting social inclusion. Through progressive design and the implementation of tax incentives, this approach seeks to create a fairer and more equitable system, where those who have the most contribute the most to social and environmental well-being.

Since 2017, Colombia has embarked on a crucial path for the protection of its natural resources; the implementation of green taxes. These instruments, more than simple taxes, represent an effort to discourage practices that threaten the social and environmental well-being of the planet. In a modern world where needs and pressures on resource-rich countries abound, Colombia joins other nations in the region in consolidating environmental protection policies, with green taxes as a fundamental tool. The objective is clear; to combat the loss of environmental resources head-on and guarantee sustainability for present and future generations. Through these mechanisms, it seeks to penalize those who with their actions deteriorate the environment, generating a deterrent effect and motivating the adoption of more responsible practices. But beyond the simple sanction, green taxes also have a leading role in promoting sustainable development. By internalizing environmental costs in the prices of goods and services, the search for cleaner and more efficient alternatives is incentivized, driving innovation and the creation of new economic opportunities in sectors such as renewable energies and the circular economy. One of the sectors that receives the most attention in the fight against climate change is energy. For this reason, public policies are being promoted to promote a transition to more sustainable energy sources around the world. Currently, a global energy transition is underway towards a more sustainable development model. Although there is no single definition of the concept of energy transition, it mainly seeks to reduce dependence on fossil fuels and promote the use of renewable energies. (Florencia M, et al. 2023. pp.96-97)

However, the road is not without its challenges. Strengthening institutional capacities, combating tax evasion and labor informality, and generating social awareness about the importance of green taxation are some of the obstacles that must be overcome. Despite the difficulties, the commitment to environmental protection is unwavering. Colombia, along with other countries in the region, is taking firm steps towards a greener and more inclusive future. The implementation and strengthening of green taxes are key pieces in this process, an effort that will allow us to build a legacy of responsibility and sustainability for generations to come. Table 4 shows one of the states of the art on which Colombia bases its tax reforms focused on green taxation. In this context, an in-depth analysis of the current situation of green taxes in Colombia is necessary. It is essential to assess their real impact on environmental protection, identify the areas that require greater attention and propose strategies to strengthen their effectiveness. Only through a joint effort between governments, businesses and civil society will it be possible to achieve the goal of a green and prosperous future for Colombia. The responsibility lies with all of us to protect the natural resources that sustain us and ensure a healthy planet for generations to come.

Table 5. Tax reforms in Colombia in relation to the green tax

Tax Reform	Norm	Green and inclusive taxation measures
Structural Tax Reform (Law 1607 of 2012)	Law 1607 of 2012	National Carbon Tax
Structural Tax Reform (Law 1819 of 2016)	Law 1819 of 2016	Carbon tax rate increase 40% of the proceeds allocated to environmental projects
Economic Growth Law (Law 2010 of 2019)	Law 2010 of 2019	Progressive increase in the carbon tax rate VAT compensation for vulnerable households
Social Investment Law (Law 2155 of 2021)	Law 2155 of 2021	Carbon tax rate increase Tax on single-use plastics
Tax Reform for Equality and Social Justice (Law 2159 of 2021)	Law 2159 of 2021	Tax on sugary drinks and single-use plastics Tax benefits for environmental investments

Source: Authors' elaboration based on the Congress of Colombia (2021)

It is important to note that the implementation of green and inclusive taxation in Colombia has been a gradual process. The first reform to include this type of measure was Law 1819 of 2016, which created the carbon tax. Subsequently, Law 1943 of 2018 established the tax on the consumption of plastic bags. Law 2155 of 2021 marked an important milestone in the matter by introducing the consumption tax on sugary drinks. This measure has been the subject of debate, with arguments for and against its impact on public health and the economy. Law 2277 of 2022, the most recent tax reform, introduces a new consumption tax on meat and processed meat products. This measure seeks to discourage the consumption of meat, which has a significant impact on the environment.

It is important to mention that, in addition to the rules mentioned in the table, there are other legal provisions that also implement green and inclusive taxation in Colombia. Among these are:

Decree 1625 of 2016: Regulates the carbon tax.

Decree 2150 of 2018: Regulates the tax on the consumption of plastic bags.

Decree 1278 of 2021: Regulates the consumption tax on sugary drinks.

Decree 1745 of 2022: Regulates the consumption tax on meat and processed meat products.

The implementation of green and inclusive taxation in Colombia is an important step in the right direction. However, more work is needed to strengthen this approach and make a real impact on protecting the environment and promoting social equity.

3.1 Global strategies for the implementation of green taxation

Determine the degree and level of strategies that should be implemented to achieve green and inclusive taxation; It is important that these are congruent with international markets, these strategies not only pursue objectives of social equity and environmental protection but can also promote sustainable economic growth. Investment in clean technologies and the creation of green jobs can energize the economy and ensure a more resilient future for generations to come. Despite its benefits, the implementation of green taxation faces significant challenges. It is necessary to strengthen institutional capacities, combat tax evasion and labor informality, and promote social awareness of the relevance of this strategy. Although there are obstacles, green taxation is postulated as an indispensable path towards a more equitable, sustainable and fair future. Figure 2 shows some of the characteristics that green taxation implementation strategies should contain. Overcoming these challenges and seizing the opportunities it offers requires collaboration between governments, businesses and civil society. Making this commitment is essential to building a better world for current and future generations.

Figure 2. Strategies for the implementation of green taxation (Own elaboration)

Figure 2. Strategies for the implementation of green taxation

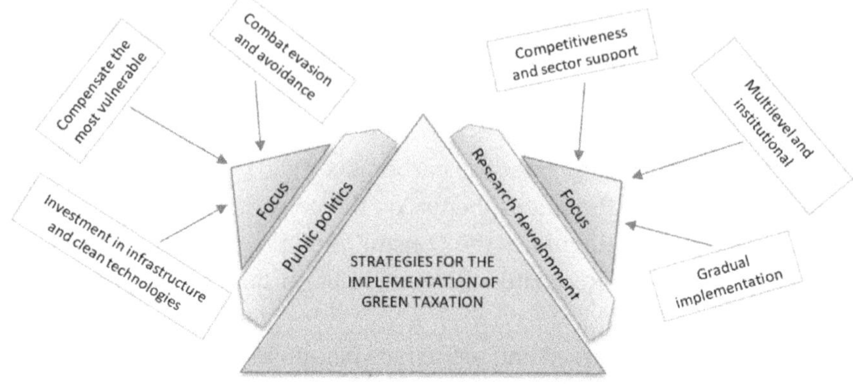

Source: Own elaboration

3.2 Gradualness in implementation

Carrying out organizational strategies that result in an effective green tax response is one of the keys to the success of SMEs, so it is important to start with low rates and increase the tax progressively over the years (Klenert et al., 2018). This gives time for companies and consumers to adapt, make clean investments and change behaviors. It also allows you to improve technical aspects of the tax based on experience. Predictability about future increases sends a powerful signal to economic agents, which permeate government policies and gives greater strength to commercial decisions on the use of materials, processes and productive methodologies in conservation with the environment.

It is important to mention that, for Colombia, particularly the gradualness of the implementation of policies and strategies depends on the legal and juridical path taken by the regulations when they are approved, which generally have to be between 2 and 3 years, a time that establishes a transition between the socialization and knowledge of the laws and the implementation by business organizations.

3.3 Compensating the most vulnerable

Mechanisms such as direct cash transfers to low-income households help mitigate the regressive impact of environmental taxes on fuels and electricity. The revenues collected can also be used to expand cross-subsidies between socioeconomic groups.

Progressivity should be a guiding principle of green taxation. According to Groote et al. (2021), "cash transfer programs have proven to be powerful tools for mitigating the negative impacts of climate and environmental policy on poor and vulnerable households" (p. 12).

Therefore, the idea is that, by providing subsidies or economic aid focused on vulnerable families, the higher cost they would have to assume due to the increase in prices derived from taxing fossil fuels and the most polluting energy sources is compensated. As Araar et al. (2022) point out, "targeted transfers emerge as a key instrument to compensate households for the regressive impact of energy taxes" (p. 21). In other words, the wealthiest segments would indirectly subsidize lower-income households through environmental revenue. This is supported by the analysis of Klenert et al. (2023), who state that "subsidies financed by carbon tax revenues can make climate policies net progressive" (p. 1185).

3.4 Investment in infrastructure and clean technologies

A substantial part of the resources should be directed towards accelerating the adoption of low-carbon alternatives, such as renewable energy, electric public transport and thermal retrofitting of homes (Hepburn et al., 2020). This is key to an inclusive energy transition that does not burden disadvantaged groups on costs. Some of the key areas where these resources should be focused, as mentioned by Hepburn et al. (2020), are:

Renewable energies: It involves allocating funds for the deployment of technologies such as solar, wind, geothermal, tidal energy, etc. This allows for the progressive replacement of conventional generation with fossil fuels. The International Renewable Energy Agency (IRENA, 2021) estimates that achieving climate goals will require annual investments of $4.4 trillion in renewables globally.

Electric public transport: It consists of investing in the electrification of mass transport systems such as trains, metros, trolleybuses, etc. As well as in the construction of charging infrastructure for electric vehicles. According to the World Bank (2022), the electrification of transport is key to decarbonising cities and improving air quality.

Energy efficiency in buildings: It involves financing programs to improve insulation, windows, heating, air conditioning, etc. to reduce the energy consumption of homes, offices and other buildings. The European Commission (2020) estimates that improving efficiency in buildings could reduce CO2 emissions by up to 60%.

These investments not only contribute to decarbonizing critical sectors such as energy, transport and buildings that represent the largest source of emissions. They also generate economic benefits by creating green jobs, saving energy consumption and improving global competitiveness in cutting-edge industries. The transition to a low-carbon economy will require a massive mobilization of private and public capital towards these clean solutions. Therefore, channeling resources from green taxes is an opportunity to catalyze that change in an environmentally responsible and socially inclusive way.

3.5 Facilitating measures and pedagogical communication

One of the important actions that allows the implementation of green tax aspects is the emphasis on environmental education, aimed at information campaigns, which helps to generate citizen support, raising the social acceptance of green taxes (Carattini et al., 2018). Articulating complementary incentives such as subsidies for clean technologies and regulatory reforms that facilitate the transition is also key. These are actions that structurally permeate society and contribute to initiatives having greater adherence due to economic results and their influence on global warming.

3.6 Multilevel and institutional coordination

Alignment between the environmental and tax policy objectives of national and subnational governments is required (OECD, 2020). This is facilitated through coordination bodies, binding commitments and technical support from international organizations. On the other hand, there needs to be harmonization and coherence between the objectives of environmental policies and the objectives of tax policies, both at the level of national governments and subnational governments (states, provinces, municipalities, etc.). Achieving this alignment and avoiding contradictions or working against the grain is essential. To facilitate this coordination between different levels of government and different areas of public policy, specific mechanisms and instances are required. Some useful tools are: the creation of joint commissions or working groups, the establishment of binding commitments and goals between different entities, and the technical support provided by international organizations that are experts in the subject. Multilateral organizations such as the United Nations, OECD, World Bank, etc. can provide valuable technical advice to countries to help them harmonize their regulatory frameworks and environmental strategies with their tax and fiscal regimes. This is so that both components of public policy work in a coordinated and complementary manner towards climate and sustainability objectives.

3.7 Combating evasion and avoidance

It is one of the vital actions for the implementation processes of sustainable tax benefits to allow for business success. The effectiveness of green taxes depends on the existence of institutional capacities for efficient collection and dissuasive sanctions for environmental tax evasion practices (United Nations, 2021). Accounting rules are also key to discourage avoidance. Without the appropriate tools and processes, the collection of these taxes can be seriously hampered. In addition, it is essential to have a dissuasive and forceful sanctioning regime that punishes illegal practices of environmental tax evasion. If there are not sufficiently severe penalties, some companies or individuals may be tempted to evade these taxes illegally. However, accounting rules and standards that discourage tax avoidance schemes in the environmental field are also critical. Avoidance, unlike evasion, involves legally permissible but unethical practices to artificially reduce the tax burden by exploiting loopholes.

3.8 Competitiveness and sectoral support

Specific measures can be applied to safeguard the international competitiveness of economic sectors that are particularly exposed to competition from countries without carbon taxes (FMF, 2019). Likewise, comprehensive plans for the reconversion and support of workers in carbon-intensive industries are required. In summary, an appropriate combination of these strategies increases the viability of implementing green taxation that discourages negative externalities while accelerating a socially inclusive and cost-efficient energy transition. Well-designed environmental taxes are a powerful lever to move towards decarbonised economies and fairer, more prosperous and sustainable societies.

4. RECOMMENDATIONS

Green and inclusive taxation represents an invaluable opportunity for Colombia to move towards a more sustainable and equitable economic model. This innovative approach seeks to harmonize environmental protection, social justice, and economic growth through comprehensive tax reform.

First, green taxation aims to internalize the environmental costs generated by polluting activities with a high impact on ecosystems. This would be achieved through the implementation of taxes or levies on greenhouse gas emissions, the unsustainable exploitation of natural resources and the excessive generation of waste.

By increasing the cost of these harmful activities, businesses and consumers are incentivized to adopt more environmentally friendly practices, thereby fostering the transition to a low-carbon and circular economy. In addition, the revenues collected through these environmental taxes can be reinvested in conservation programs, reforestation, renewable energy development, and energy efficiency. In this way, a virtuous circle is created in which the country's natural heritage is protected, the ecological footprint is reduced and innovation in clean technologies is promoted, generating new employment opportunities and sustainable economic growth. On the other hand, inclusive taxation focuses on achieving a more equitable distribution of the tax burden, ensuring that higher-income sectors and large companies contribute fairly to the financing of public spending. This means reviewing and adjusting tax rates, eliminating unjustified tax benefits, and combating tax evasion more effectively.

The resources obtained through more progressive taxation can be channeled into social investment programs, improving access to basic services such as education, health and decent housing for the most vulnerable segments of the population. In addition, tax incentives can be implemented to encourage labor formalization, entrepreneurship, and the creation of quality jobs, thus promoting inclusive economic development. Importantly, green and inclusive taxation not only benefits the environment and social equity, but can also have a positive impact on competitiveness and long-term economic growth. By promoting efficiency in the use of resources, technological innovation and business formalization, more favorable conditions are created to attract investment, increase productivity and generate quality jobs. However, the implementation of this tax model requires a gradual and balanced approach, considering the needs and capacities of the different economic sectors. Constructive dialogue with all stakeholders, including the private sector, workers, local communities and civil society, is essential to achieve broad consensus and ensure a just transition.

5. FUTURE RESEARCH DIRECTIONS

The path to a sustainable future in Colombia and/or other Latin American countries requires a profound transformation in various areas, including the tax system. The implementation of a green and inclusive tax model is presented as a fundamental tool to achieve this objective, not only by encouraging responsible environmental practices but also by promoting social equity and the strengthening of the national economy. While the benefits of effective implementation require rigorous research work in various areas. It is essential that for LATAM countries, study processes are replicated that can be an example and multiply it even for countries of the European Union, for them processes associated with:

1. Sectoral impact analyses: It is essential to carry out detailed studies on the potential impact of environmental taxation on the different economic sectors. These analyses should assess the risk exposure, transition costs and adaptability of each sector. In this way, compensatory measures and appropriate productive conversion plans can be designed to facilitate a just transition to a greener economy.
2. Economic modelling and simulations: Sophisticated economic models are required to simulate the macroeconomic impact of green and inclusive taxation. These models must consider variables such as GDP, employment, inflation and the trade balance. The resulting simulations will be critical to properly calibrate the necessary tax levels and complementary policies, ensuring a positive impact on the economy as a whole.
3. Social acceptance studies: To ensure the viability and success of green and inclusive tax reforms, it is crucial to understand the perception and level of acceptance of citizens. Research based on surveys, focus groups and participatory methodologies will make it possible to identify the concerns and expectations of the population, facilitating the design of effective communication strategies and the generation of social consensus around these policies.
4. Analysis of monitoring and compliance systems: The effectiveness of green and inclusive taxation depends to a large extent on the existence of robust monitoring, verification, and compliance systems. The use of emerging technologies, such as artificial intelligence and big data analytics, to detect and prevent tax evasion and irregular environmental practices needs to be explored. In this way, transparency and fairness in the application of these measures will be guaranteed.
5. Evaluation of incentives and subsidies: The implementation of well-designed tax incentives and subsidies can be a powerful tool to promote the adoption of clean technologies, sustainable practices, and labor formalization. These analyses should consider not only the short-term fiscal cost, but also the long-term environmental, social, and economic impact.
6. Participatory and co-creation approaches: The success of green and inclusive taxation requires the participation of the various actors involved, including the private sector, local communities, academic experts and civil society. Participatory and co-creation approaches will make it possible to design policies that are more inclusive, legitimate and adapted to local realities, ensuring greater acceptance and commitment by the population.
7. International comparative studies: Learning from the experiences of other countries that have implemented green and inclusive tax reforms can be invaluable for Colombia. Comparative research on best practices, lessons learned, and challenges faced in other contexts will provide valuable insights for the design and implementation of these policies in the country.

These priority lines of research will make it possible to move towards a green and inclusive tax model that promotes economic and social sustainability for Colombia and all of Latin America. Interdisciplinary collaboration among economists, environmentalists, sociologists, legal experts, and other professionals will be crucial to meet the new challenges that arise along the way. A fair and sustainable tax model will contribute to the construction of a more prosperous and equitable future for all Colombians.

6. CONCLUSION

As a conclusion of this research process, it is undeniable that the adoption of a green and inclusive tax model represents a transformative opportunity for Colombia and LATAM countries. This innovative approach would make it possible to make concerted progress towards meeting the Sustainable Development Goals, by harmonizing environmental protection, social equity and long-term economic growth. Green taxation, through taxes and levies on polluting activities with a high ecological impact, would generate powerful incentives to move towards a low-carbon, circular and efficient economy in the use of natural resources. Likewise, the revenues collected could be reinvested in conservation, renewable energy and technological innovation programs, promoting the creation of green jobs and Colombia's leadership in the fight against climate change.

On the other hand, inclusive taxation seeks to achieve a more equitable distribution of the tax burden, ensuring that higher-income sectors and large companies contribute fairly to the financing of public spending. This would make it possible to channel resources towards strategic social investments in education, health and decent housing, reducing inequality gaps and promoting inclusive economic development. However, the successful implementation of this tax model will require a gradual, balanced, and broadly participatory approach. Constructive dialogue with all stakeholders, including the private sector, workers, local communities and civil society, will be critical to building consensus and ensuring a just transition.

In this sense, the proposed future lines of research will be key to supporting informed decision-making and the effective implementation of green and inclusive taxation. Sectoral analyses, economic modelling, social acceptance studies, evaluation of incentives and subsidies, participatory approaches and international comparisons, among others, will provide valuable knowledge to design sound policies, adapted to local realities and aligned with global best practices. In short, green and inclusive taxation represents a bold and necessary vision for the future of Colombia. By aligning economic incentives with the objectives of environmental sustainability and social equity, the foundations are laid for a truly resilient, competitive and prosperous development model for present and future generations. With strategic implementation backed by rigorous research, Colombia can position itself as a regional leader in the transition to a sustainable and strengthened economy. Finally, in this chapter, the author thanks sustainable organizations in Colombia, their importance and the need to strengthen them, as well as the 75% of the ecological SMEs that have been participating in the research processes, the more than 50 students of the Business Administration Program of the Compensar University Foundation, colleagues, among others, for the support and participation in the academic impact that has been had by studying business variables and organizational activities that bring to analyze green taxation and its impact on the Colombian economy.

On the other hand, the references used in the chapter are appropriate and updated, covering recent studies (2021-2022) on green and inclusive taxation in the Latin American and global context. However, to further strengthen the bibliographic base and offer a more complete perspective, it is suggested to analyze these following additional references:

REFERENCES

Alberto Gutiérrez Arguedas. (2020). Green capitalism and "clean" energies: Costa Rica as a "global decarbonization laboratory". Yearbook of the Center for Research and Political Studies, ISSN: 2215-2873195-228. DOI: DOI: 10.15517/aciep.v0i11.43238

Alina Celi Frugoni. (2022). Energy transition in Latin America and the Caribbean Energy transition in latin america and the Caribbean. Revista novos estudos jurídicos - eletrônica, vol. 27- n. 3 - set-dez 2022. Doi: https//:d oi.org/10.14210/nej.v27n3 .p500-516

Araar, A., Choueiri, N., & Verme, P. (2022). The compensating differentiated cash transfers for energy pricing reform. *Energy Economics*, 105, 105718. DOI: 10.1016/j.eneco.2021.105718

Baranzini, A., Borzykowski, N., & Carattini, S. (2021). Carbon offsets out of the woods? The acceptability of domestic vs. international reforestation programmes in the lab. *Journal of Forest Economics*, 32, 1–12. DOI: 10.1016/j.jfe.2018.02.004

Barreix, A., Corrales, L. F., Díaz de Sarralde, S., & Garcimartín, C. (2022). Fiscal policy for sustainable development in Latin America and the Caribbean. *Bulletin of Latin American Research*, 41(5), 783–799. DOI: 10.1111/blar.13398

Bonilla, L., Londoño-Vélez, J., Pirttilä, J., & Rossi, M. (2022). How to reduce poverty and inequality through tax-benefit reform and transfers. *World Development*, 160, 105812. DOI: 10.1016/j.worlddev.2021.105812

Cano, L., Ordóñez-Matamoros, G., & Ramírez, J. C. (2023). Taxation and Inequality in Colombia: An Analysis for the Period 2000-2019. *Cuadernos de Economía y Dirección de la Empresa*, 26(1), 100001. DOI: 10.1016/j.cesjef.2022.100001

Castañeda, A., Díaz-Bahamonde, J., & Laajaj, R. (2023). The effects of Colombia's tax reform on inequality and poverty. *The World Bank Economic Review*, 37(2), 391–411. DOI: 10.1093/wber/lhac012

Congress of Colombia. (December 26, 2012). Law 1607 of 2012. By which rules on tax matters are issued and other provisions are issued. Official Gazette. https://www.funcionpublica.gov.co/eva/gestornormativo/norma.php?i=50323

Congress of Colombia. (December 27, 2019). Law 2010 of 2019. By means of which rules are adopted for the promotion of economic growth, employment, investment, the strengthening of public finances and the progressiveness, equity and efficiency of the tax system, in accordance with the objectives that on the matter promoted by Law 1943 of 2018 and other provisions are dictated. Official Gazette. https://dapre.presidencia.gov.co/normativa/normativa/LEY%202010%20DEL%2027%20DE%20DICIEMBRE%20DE%202019.pdf

Congress of Colombia. (December 29, 2016). Law 1819 of 2016. By means of which a structural tax reform is adopted, the mechanisms for the fight against tax evasion and avoidance are strengthened, and other provisions are issued. Official Gazette. https://www.suin-juriscol.gov.co/viewDocument.asp?id=30020048

Congress of Colombia. (June 04, 2021). Law 2155 of 2021. By means of which the Social Investment Law is issued and other provisions are issued. Official Gazette. https://www.funcionpublica.gov.co/eva/gestornormativo/norma_pdf.php?i=167156

Congress of Colombia. (September 14, 2021). Law 2159 of 2021. By means of which cross-cutting norms are adopted for the executive branch at the national and territorial level and for individuals who perform public and/or administrative functions, in relation to the rationalization of procedures and other provisions are issued. Official Gazette. https://www.funcionpublica.gov.co/eva/gestornormativo/norma_pdf.php?i=167770

ECLAC. (2022). "Fiscal Policy and Climate Change: Recent Experiences of Latin American and Caribbean Countries". Santiago: United Nations. https://repositorio.cepal.org/handle/11362/47913

Economic Commission for Latin America and the Caribbean (ECLAC). (2019). The Climate Change Emergency in Latin America and the Caribbean: Do We Still Have Time? https://repositorio.cepal.org/handle/11362/44969

Gonzalo Escribano, Lara Lázaro & Ignacio Urbasos. (2022). The development of hydrogen: strategies and policies in Europe and Spain. International review of economic policy. DOI: 10.7203/IREP.4.2.25807

European Commission. (2020). Working document: EU Building Renovation Strategy. https://ec.europa.eu/energy/sites/ener/files/eu_renovation_wave_strategy.pdf

Fernández, C., & Villar, L. (2023). Informality and labor market policies in Colombia. *Labour Economics*, 81, 102310. DOI: 10.1016/j.labeco.2022.102310

Galarza, R.; Cuji, C. (2022). "Optimal Energy Management in a Gradual and Controlled Process to Contribute to the Decarbonization of the Electricity Sector". Technical Journal "energy". No. 19, Issue I, Pp. 71-84 ISSN On-line: 2602-8492 - ISSN Print: 1390-5074. Doi:DOI: 10.37116/revistaenergia.v19.n1.2022.518

Gallego, J. A., Hoffmann, B., Ibarrarán, P., Medina, M. P., Pecha, C., Romero, O., Stampini, M., Vargas, D., & Vera-Cossio, D. A. (2021). Impacts of the Solidarity Income program in the face of the COVID-19 crisis in Colombia. *World Development*, 149, 105316. DOI: 10.1016/j.worlddev.2020.105316

Gómez-Sabaini, J. C., & Morán, D. (2021). Fiscal policy and the SDGs: From theory to practice in Latin America and the Caribbean. In *United Nations, Recover better: Economic and social challenges and opportunities* (pp. 165–184). United Nations., DOI: 10.18356/9789210054980c011

Groote, O., Valdez, R. M., & Contreras-Araneda, S. J. (2021). Cash transfers for mitigating the social costs of climate change. *Environment Systems & Decisions*, 41, 5–15. DOI: 10.1007/s10669-021-09815-7

Grubb, M., Drummond, P., Poncia, A., McDowall, W., Popp, D., Samadi, S., & Patt, A. (2021). Induced innovation in energy technologies and systems: A review of evidence and potential implications for CO2 mitigation. *Environmental Research Letters*, 16(4), 043007. DOI: 10.1088/1748-9326/abde07

Hepburn, C., O'Callaghan, B., Stern, N., Stiglitz, J., & Zenghelis, D. (2020). Will COVID-19 fiscal recovery packages confront climate change? *Oxford Review of Economic Policy*, 36(Supplement_1), S359–S381. DOI: 10.1093/oxrep/graa015

Hepburn, C., O'Callaghan, B., Stern, N., Stiglitz, J., & Zenghelis, D. (2020). Will COVID-19 fiscal recovery packages accelerate or retard progress on climate change? *Oxford Review of Economic Policy*, 36(Supplement_1), S359–S381. DOI: 10.1093/oxrep/graa015

International Energy Agency (IEA). (2021). Energy taxes for a sustainable future. https://www.iea.org/reports/taxing-energy-use-2019

International Labour Organization (ILO). (2022). Just transition to environmentally sustainable economies and resilient societies. https://www.ilo.org/global/topics/green-jobs/publications/WCMS_828094/lang--es/index.htm

International Monetary Fund. (2021). Fiscal Monitor: Strengthening the Credibility of Public Finances. https://www.imf.org/en/Publications/FM/Issues/2021/10/13/fiscal-monitor-october-2021

IRENA. (2021). World Energy Transitions Outlook 2021. International Renewable Energy Agency. https://irena.org/publications/2021/March/World-Energy-Transitions-Outlook

Klenert, D., Mattauch, L., & Narassima, V. (2023). Progressive carbon taxation. *European Economic Review*, 151, 104382. DOI: 10.1016/j.euroecorev.2023.104382

Lora, E., & Mejía, L. F. (2022). Reforming for a post-COVID world. *Bulletin of Latin American Research*, 41(1), 34–49. DOI: 10.1111/blar.13294

Lutz, B., & Levell, P. (2021). Green Taxation and Employment: Evidence from Germany's Ecological Tax Reform. *Journal of Environmental Economics and Management*, 107, 102442. DOI: 10.1016/j.jeem.2021.102442

Montes-Vergara, F. J., Arango-Miranda, R., & Rojano, R. (2022). A review of carbon pricing instruments implementation: Lessons for the Colombian case. *Energies*, 15(9), 3303. DOI: 10.3390/en15093303

Núñez, J., Olivieri, S., Parra, J., & Pico, J. (2022). The distributive impact of taxes and expenditures in Colombia. *Cuadernos de Economía y Dirección de la Empresa*, 25(1), 100005. DOI: 10.1016/j.cesjef.2021.100005

Ocampo-Rodríguez, K. V., Ávila-Díaz, A. J., & Soto-Paz, J. (2023). Effect of environmental taxes on innovation and sustainable development in Colombia. *Sustainability*, 15(3), 2054. DOI: 10.3390/su15032054

OECD. (2023). "Taxing Energy Use for Sustainable Development: Opportunities for energy tax and subsidy reform in selected developing and emerging economies". https://www.oecd.org/tax/tax-policy/taxing-energy-use-for-sustainable-development.htm

Ohlendorf, N., Jakob, M., Minx, J. C., Schröder, C., & Steckel, J. C. (2021). Distributional impacts of carbon pricing: A meta-analysis. *Environmental and Resource Economics*, 78(1), 1–42. DOI: 10.1007/s10640-020-00521-1

Organization for Economic Cooperation and Development (OECD). (2022). Environmental Taxes: A Policy Approach. https://doi.org/DOI: 10.1787/638fe8c4-es

Pardo Martínez, C. I., & Alfonso, W. H. (2023). Environmental taxes as a tool to foster sustainability in Colombia. *Sustainability*, 15(6), 5263. DOI: 10.3390/su15065263

Pigato, M. A. (Ed.). (2019). Fiscal Policies for Development and Climate Action. World Bank Publications. https://doi.org/. This book provides a comprehensive analysis of green fiscal policies in developing countries, which could offer valuable insights for the Colombian context. On the other hand, the information related toDOI: 10.1596/978-1-4648-1358-0

Rodríguez, D., & Ávila, F. (2023). Fiscal policy and income redistribution in Latin America: Challenging the conventional wisdom. *The Journal of Development Studies*, 59(5), 816–833. DOI: 10.1080/00220388.2022.2161688

Romero, G., Álvarez, F., & Caldentey, E. P. (2022). The political economy of environmental taxes in Latin America: Carbon taxes and distributional impacts. *Ecological Economics*, 193, 107318. DOI: 10.1016/j.ecolecon.2022.107318

Romero-Jordán, D., del Río, P., & Peñasco, C. (2022). An analysis of the factors influencing CO2 emissions in developing countries: The role of renewable energy and environmental taxes. *Energy Economics*, 114, 105990. DOI: 10.1016/j.eneco.2022.105990

Sterner, T., Barbier, E. B., Bateman, I., van den Bijgaart, I., Crépin, A. S., Edenhofer, O., & Robinson, A. (2022). Policy design for the Anthropocene. *Nature Sustainability*, 5(1), 5–13. DOI: 10.1038/s41893-021-00755-x

Sterner, T., Barbier, E. B., Bateman, I., van den Bijgaart, I., Crépin, A. S., Edenhofer, O., & Robinson, A. (2022). Policy design for the Anthropocene. *Nature Sustainability*, 5(1), 5–13. DOI: 10.1038/s41893-021-00755-x

Stockholm Environment Institute. Climate Analytics, E3G, the International Institute for Sustainable Development, and the United Nations Environment Programme (UNEP) (2023). The production gap. https://www.un.org/es/climatechange/reports#:~:text=El%20informe%202023%20concluye%20que,que%20ser%C3%ADa%20con%202%20%C2%BAC

UNCTAD's BioTrade Initiative. (2007). Biotrade Principles and Criteria. United Nations Conference on Trade and Development. BioTrade Initiative (pp. 6-14). Geneva, Switzerland: UNCTAD. http://www.asocam.org/sites/default/files/publicaciones/files/2807acffecd17b29a5d3ee02ca4395a5.pdf

United Nations. (2022). 2021 Emissions Disparity Report. https://www.unep.org/emissions-gap-report-2021

United Nations Development Programme (UNDP). (2018). Environmental taxation and equity in Latin America. https://www.undp.org/es/latin-america/publications/environmental-taxation-and-equity-latin-america

United Nations Environment Programme. (2023). Emissions Gap Report 2023: Broken Record – Temperatures hit new highs, yet world fails to cut emissions (again). https://wedocs.unep.org/20.500.11822/43922

Vargas-Chaves, I., Luna-Galván, M., & Franco-Gántiva, A. M. (2022). Circular economy and environmental taxation in Colombia: An analysis from sustainable development. *Sustainability*, 14(11), 6572. DOI: 10.3390/su14116572

World Bank. (2022). Electrification and Electric Mobility. https://www.worldbank.org/en/topic/transport/brief/electrification-and-electric-mobility

World Bank. (2023). "State and Trends of Carbon Pricing 2023". Washington, DC: World Bank. https://openknowledge.worldbank.org/handle/10986/39551

World Bank. (2020). Fiscal Policies for an Inclusive Green Economy

Wyczykier, G. (2023). Trails of the Energy Transition: Green Hydrogen in the Era of Climate Change. Revista temas sociológicos n°31, pp. 453-484 DOI: 10.29344/07196458.31.3164

Zabaloy, M. F., Guzowski, C., & Recalde, M. Y. (2023). Public policies for the Argentine energy transition: Past, present and future. Rev. *Est. de Políticas Públicas*, 9(1). Advance online publication. DOI: 10.5354/0719-6296.2023.69379

ADDITIONAL READING

Delsaux, V. (2022). Nudging and environmental taxation: A green perspective to correct carbon dioxide emissions. *Environmental Science & Policy*, 136, 48–56. DOI: 10.1016/j.envsci.2022.05.014

Economic Commission for Latin America and the Caribbean (ECLAC). (2022). Challenges for environmental taxation and the transition to a circular economy in Latin America and the Caribbean. https://repositorio.cepal.org/handle/11362/48163

Hansen, M. B., McGlade, C., van der Zwaan, B., & Walbeck, J. (2022). Exploring the implications of fossil fuel subsidy reform for global carbon emissions. *Energy Economics*, 113, 106236. DOI: 10.1016/j.eneco.2022.106236

Organization for Economic Cooperation and Development (OECD). (2022). Financing the Future: Tax Policy for a Transition to Cleaner Energy Sources. https://doi.org/DOI: 10.1787/9c6abbf9-es

Oueslati, W., Zgehri, Y., & Nguyen, N. (2022). Inclusive green taxation and environmental quality: An investigation among developed and developing countries. *Energy Economics*, 108, 105855. DOI: 10.1016/j.eneco.2022.105855

Semieniuk, G., Campiglio, E., Mercure, J.-F., Volz, U., & Edwards, N. R. (2021). Low-carbon transition risks for finance. *Wiley Interdisciplinary Reviews: Climate Change*, 12(5), e716. DOI: 10.1002/wcc.716

Sumaila, U. R., Skerritt, D. J., Schuhbauer, A., Villasante, S., Macho, G., Sinan, H., Vartdal Fyllingsnes, M., Saidykhan, R., Christensen, V., & Bing Camara, S. (2021). Green taxation to protect marine ecosystems. *Frontiers in Marine Science*, 8, 661186. DOI: 10.3389/fmars.2021.661186

World Bank. (2022). Rethinking the taxation of natural resources: Promoting a comprehensive approach to sustainable development. https://openknowledge.worldbank.org/handle/10986/37275

KEY TERMS AND DEFINITIONS

Circular Economy: Economic model based on the principle of "closing the life cycle" of products, encouraging the reuse, repair, refurbishment and recycling of materials and resources (Economic Commission for Latin America and the Caribbean [ECLAC], 2019).

Decarbonization: The process of reducing emissions of carbon dioxide (CO2) and other greenhouse gases, generally through the transition to renewable energy sources and the implementation of clean technologies (OECD, 2022).

Ecological Footprint: An indicator that measures the environmental impact of human activities and the consumption of natural resources compared to the regenerative capacity of ecosystems (World Bank, 2020).

Economy of the Common Good: An alternative economic model that seeks to maximize social and ecological well-being over individual profit, promoting cooperation, sustainability, and economic democracy (Sachs, 2015).

Environmental Externalities: Costs or benefits derived from an economic activity that are not reflected in market prices and that affect third parties not directly involved in said activity (Stiglitz, 2019).

Extended Producer Responsibility: Principle that assigns responsibility for waste management to producers, encouraging the design of products and packaging with a lower environmental impact (ECLAC, 2019).

Green Jobs: Employment in economic sectors that contribute to preserving or restoring the environment, whether in ecosystem protection activities or production of environmentally sustainable goods and services (International Labour Organization [ILO], 2022).

Green Taxation: Taxes, levies, or fiscal instruments designed to internalize the environmental costs of polluting activities and promote more sustainable practices (Organization for Economic Cooperation and Development [OECD], 2022).

Low-Carbon Economy: Economic model that seeks to significantly reduce greenhouse gas emissions and dependence on fossil fuels, promoting energy efficiency and renewable energy sources (International Energy Agency [IEA], 2021).

Pigouvian Taxation: Taxes applied on activities that generate negative externalities, with the aim of internalizing these social costs and correcting market failures (Piketty, 2014).

Social Equity: Principle of justice that promotes equal opportunities and the fair distribution of the benefits of economic development (International Labour Organization [ILO], 2022).

Sustainable Development: An approach that seeks to meet the needs of the present without compromising the ability of future generations to meet their own needs, integrating economic, social, and environmental aspects (United Nations Development Programme [UNDP], 2018).

Chapter 7
Green Taxation and Sustainable Tourism Destinations:
A Bibliometric Analysis

Vânia Costa
https://orcid.org/0000-0002-4202-8779
Polytechnic Institute of Cávado and Ave, Portugal

Raquel Pereira
https://orcid.org/0000-0003-4545-4754
Polytechnic Institute of Cávado and Ave, Portugal

ABSTRACT

This research aims to analyse the evolving literature of green taxation or tourist taxes and the development of sustainable tourism destinations. Using the PRISMA Method, this study is based on a bibliometric analysis of articles published in SCOPUS and Web of Science. The study analyses all publications over time, with the keywords "taxes", "tourism destinations" and "sustainability" in titles, keywords and abstracts. Tourism taxation is a public policy instrument applied to solve externalities caused by tourism and serves as a means of financing the maintenance and continuous improvement of services and infrastructures that directly and indirectly support tourism activity. The main contribution of our research is therefore to identify the evolving literature concerning tourism taxes and destinations, as well as to explore public strategies that contribute to rethinking, revitalizing and increasing the sustainability of tourism destinations through conceptual frameworks based on the integration of sustainable management practices in the planning processes of tourism destinations.

DOI: 10.4018/979-8-3693-3908-4.ch007

INTRODUCTION

Tourism is a strategic sector recognised for its economic, social, cultural, and environmental impact on the economy. Over the last few decades, it has experienced continuous growth and intense diversification, emerging as one of the world's fastest-developing sectors. Due to its multiplier effect on economic activity and employment, the sector's development is fundamental for some regional economies. In a world facing pressing environmental conservation and sustainable practice imperatives, taxation has assumed paramount importance in the drive toward a more environmentally sound future. Tourism taxes are a critical measure implemented in numerous countries to address the conflict between tourism development and sustainability. In addition to famous tourist spots, some countries have implemented tourist taxes to address the negative impacts caused by the influx of visitors. There has been ongoing debate in recent years about the effects of these taxes on the appeal and competitiveness of destinations. Opinion articles have presented various viewpoints on this issue, although it has not received much attention in academic literature. The economic and financial rationale behind local taxes is a topic that is frequently overlooked.

The world experienced an atypical situation marked by the COVID-19 pandemic. The rapid spread of the disease globally on all continents caused the World Health Organization (WHO) to consider it a pandemic, closing economies overnight. Physical distancing measures immediately impacted the demand in the tourism sector. The crisis is an opportunity to strengthen the emphasis on developing strategies and coordinated actions to promote sustainable and socially responsible tourism. It is an opportunity to accelerate the UN Sustainable Development Goals (SDGs) targets by 2030. Including these values in strategy and planning will ensure competitiveness and resilience for Tourism (UNWTO, 2021).

Implementing municipal tourist taxes in various forms (overnight stay tax, arrival tax by air or sea) is a way of financing destination investment funds and allows cities to invest in projects of interest.

This research aims to identify and analyse the evolving literature on the importance of green taxation or tourist taxes to the development of sustainable tourism destinations. This study is based on a systematic literature review and a bibliometric analysis of articles published in SCOPUS and Web of Science (WoS) between 1998 and 2024, using the PRISMA Method and the keywords “taxes”, “tourism destinations” and “sustainability” in titles, keywords and abstracts. In addition, a set of eligibility and exclusion criteria were determined to refine the articles selected for the study. We excluded book series, books, chapters in books, and conference proceedings as their contents are not available in the defined database.

The study method consists of a bibliometric analysis of the scientific production of green taxation and the sustainable development of territories. This type of analysis is motivated by the need to evaluate the results of the scientific output. It allows a compilation of the most relevant results of a set of bibliographic documents in a summarised form. In this sense, this study aims to identify new research trends and increase the possibilities of cooperation among researchers.

The study results have implications for both public and private managers of tourism destinations. Our research makes a significant contribution by identifying the evolving literature on tourism taxes and destinations and exploring public strategies that help rethink, revitalise, and enhance the sustainability of tourism destinations. These strategies are based on integrating sustainable management practices into the planning processes of tourism destinations. The study is divided into five parts: introduction, background, research methodology, literature review results, and a discussion of the main results, conclusions, and study limitations.

BACKGROUND

The COVID-19 pandemic has introduced a new perspective to the ongoing debate on tourism taxes. This has prompted crucial inquiries into their efficacy in regulating visitor behaviour and flow, their contribution to recovery and resilience, and their potential for revitalising a destination's natural, cultural, social, and economic assets.

According to Nobanee and Ullah (2023), the term green tax emerged in the context of converting the economy into a green economy. According to the authors, in 1920, the American economist Pigou proposed a tax on activities that harm the environment and society. In this sense, the green economy encourages economic activities that help reduce pollution and carbon emissions, contribute to increased energy transition efficiency and resource utilisation and reduce the destruction of the ecosystem. According to the literature, the transition to the objectives of the green economy can be achieved through different measures, such as taxes on environmentally harmful activities or incentives for activities or incentives for green initiatives.

According to the authors, the green tax is considered an emerging issue in the environmental field and can help promote environmentally sustainable behaviour by providing economic incentives to individuals and companies that reduce their environmental impact. Thus, the authors advocate that policymakers include taxes by adopting policies that promote the adoption of sustainable technologies and stimulate demand for environmentally sustainable products and services.

According to Araña & León (2016), according to the literature, tourists are used to making decisions at various stages of the consumption process, from choosing a destination to making travel plans. Many different motivations can drive these decisions, and it is recognised that tourists ultimately seek pleasure and satisfaction in their choices. However, for the authors, these decisions can lead to environmental impacts and unsustainable tourism practices. In this sense, issues such as the design and implementation of efficient destination development policies from a sustainable perspective appear to be extremely important and a challenge given the supply trends of destinations and private tourism companies and the demand and preferences of tourists.

UNWTO (2003) argues that sustainable development in tourism can be defined as meeting the needs of current tourists and host regions while protecting and promoting opportunities for the future. Sustainable tourism thus aims to manage resources from a broad perspective, including a vision of economic, social, respect for cultural identity, ecological and all aspects essential to life support systems.

According to Araújo et al. (2023), applying measures that guarantee economic sustainability through tax incentives has made obtaining financial resources from central, sub-national and municipal governments possible. However, according to the authors, other studies reinforce that these measures are means of facing adversity and meeting society's demands and future challenges by dealing with mechanisms for composing strategic decision-making plans.

According to Cárdenas-García et al. (2022), public intervention is essential since mass tourism destinations are a reality today and continue attracting millions of tourists yearly. For the authors, a preventative approach requires tourism strategies and the development of action plans that integrate the principles of sustainable development. However, these new strategies require funds, so establishing taxes and/or levies on tourism can be an economic and fiscal policy instrument contributing to generalised public revenue. This allows public policies related to sustainability and the design of a differentiated offer in a given destination.

Researching and discussing tourism taxes and related taxation is more complex and dynamic than it may seem. The tourism sector can be subject to various types of taxes and levies due to its wide range of economic activities (Destination Sustainability Movement e Group Nao (2020).

.According to Cárdenas-García et al. (2022), the UNWTO (1998) defined tourism taxes as taxes applicable to tourists and the tourism sector. On the other hand, the OECD (2014) defined tourism taxation as indirect taxes, fees and levies that mainly affect tourism-related activities, which appear as a contribution to raising tax revenue, financing environmental protection and public investment and the development of infrastructure to improve the management of tourism's impact on sensitive areas.

The resources tourists use are mostly common and consumed by local inhabitants (Durán-Román et al., 2022). In this sense, according to the authors, for tourism to deserve the label of the hospitality industry, it must look beyond its customers and carefully consider the environmental, social and cultural impacts it is creating on the host community in general. Once there is a saturation level for tourism in any locality or region, and if that level is exceeded, the costs of tourism begin to outweigh the benefits. After a certain level of tourist activity, local inhabitants compete with tourists for resources such as space, water, parking, rubbish, sewage, and transport. According to the same study, these inconveniences caused by the increase in tourist volume can be offset by some benefits for the locality.

According to the same source, the internalisation of the environmental and social costs of tourism and its production function is necessary and possible through public intervention. In particular, in some destinations, tourists pay some general indirect taxes, such as sales and consumption taxes, and the tourism industry also contributes to the government's fiscal budget through income tax. However, some authors claim that more specific taxes are needed to justify the distribution of costs associated with tourism activity, including accommodation tax. According to the authors, other methods are also used to charge tourists directly, namely fees such as visa fees, entry supplements, and car hire fees, among others. These fees are designed to transfer part of the tax burden to non-residents.

According to Durán-Román et al. (2021a), tourism taxation is an instrument for dealing with the problems arising from the development of tourism and is an activity taxed to increase revenue and, on the other hand, compensate for the costs derived from the provision of goods and services of a public nature and correct market failures or negative externalities caused by tourism activity. In addition, according to the authors, it can also be used to achieve other ends, such as creating jobs, promoting economic development, environmental protection, promoting destinations, etc.

Thus, the authors argue that tourism taxation becomes an instrument for distributing the costs associated with tourism activity by establishing specific taxes aimed directly at the activity. These taxes pursue an extra-fiscal purpose and aim to improve the product and the tourist experience.

The Destination Sustainability Movement e Group Nao (2020) highlight seven roles to be played by tourism taxes that may influence their design, those being 1. Revenue Generation: Many destinations implement tourism taxes as a source of general tax revenue to fund local development and infrastructure projects. 2. Regulation of Flows and Behavior: Taxes can be designed with parameters such as differentiated rates based on seasonality, city zones, and types of establishments to manage tourist flows and behaviours effectively. 3. Crisis Relief: During times of crisis, such as the COVID-19 pandemic, some states have suspended or reduced tourism taxes to provide financial relief to the tourism industry and support businesses. 4. Destination Promotion and Branding: Tax revenues can be allocated to promote the destination, invest in marketing efforts, and enhance the destination's branding to attract more visitors. 5. Tourism Innovation and Research: Some destinations allocate tax revenue to drive innovation in the tourism sector and fund research initiatives to enhance the overall tourist experience. 6. Resource Regeneration: Advanced destinations use tax revenues to regenerate their resources by investing in initiatives such as nature conservation, restoration of cultural heritage sites, and community development projects.7. Taxation for Resilience: While currently a theoretical concept, there is potential to build up funds through tourism taxes to meet future crises and provide insurance and cancellation guarantees for event organizers and conference planners. This approach can enhance the destination's resilience in the face of unexpected challenges (Destination Sustainability Movement & Group Nao (2020).

According to Durán-Román et al. (2021a), the maturity of tourist destinations, the growing competitiveness of the sector and the evolution of tourist habits require the implementation of a series of strategies to increase the sustainability of these destinations and simultaneously improve the tourist experience. On the other hand, Durán-Román et al. (2021), emphasise that since tourism is a demand-driven activity and the price variable is one of the main factors in the selection of a destination, due to the numerous alternatives capable of satisfying the same tourist motivations, destination managers must know the willingness of tourist demand to pay in advance, as well as the sensitivity of tourist demand in the case of the implementation of fiscal instruments linked to tourist activity.

However, the literature emphasises the complexity involved and the need to carefully analyse fiscal policy, since it has an impact on the economic system, influencing a number of other economic variables, such as employment levels, price levels, consumption, and added value, among others (Araújo et al., 2023). In this sense, it is essential to articulate various measures in order to achieve results in terms of growth and income distribution.

Tourism must encompass the components of sustainable development in all its guises. In this sense, and given the importance of this issue, it is essential to establish new business models, digital devices, user-generated content, big data and online commerce have positive effects on sustainable tourism (Scrioşteanu et al., 2022). It is essential that tourism encompasses the components of sustainable development in all its forms. In this sense, and given the importance of this issue, it is essential to establish new business models, digital devices, user-generated content, big data and online commerce that have positive effects on sustainable tourism (Scrioşteanu et al., 2022). In this sense, given the importance of this topic, this study aims to analyse the evolution of the literature on green taxation or tourist taxes and the development of sustainable tourist destinations and to contribute to the reflection on the analysis of political scenarios in tax dynamics.

METHODOLOGY

This study uses a literature review and content analysis as the research methodology. This type of study provides a comprehensive overview of the literature related to a specific topic or theory and analyses previous studies to consolidate existing knowledge under new approaches. The study took a systematic approach to map and analyse the existing literature related to taxation and tourism destinations. The literature selection followed a narrative review, with the collection of key studies being fundamental. This approach follows the logic of a narrative review, where the most critical aspect is to collect relevant information that provides context and substance to the study's general objective.

The study method is based on a protocol based on the search terms, the database used, and the selection criteria. This analysis arises from the importance of evaluating the results of scientific production and compiling the most relevant results from a set of bibliographic documents. In this sense, this study allows for identifying a historical evolution of the literature and new research trends, thus increasing the possibilities for cooperation among researchers.

The research data and bibliometric analysis in this study were obtained from the SCOPUS and Web of Science (WoS) databases. In addition, a set of eligibility and exclusion criteria was determined to refine the articles selected for the study (Table 1). Book series, books, chapters in books, and conference proceedings were excluded as their contents are not available in the defined database. The data collected in the two databases were integrated using the R program and later analysed using the VOSViewer software.

Table 1. Research selection criteria

Database	SCOPUS and WoS
Review period	from 1998 to 2024
Types of sources	Articles and review articles.
Subject area	Social Sciences; Business, Management and Accounting; Environmental Science; Energy; Economics, Econometrics and Finance; Agricultural and Biological Sciences; Earth and Planetary Sciences; Engineering; Computer Science; Multidisciplinary, Mathematics; Decision Sciences; Arts and Humanities
Language	English, Spanish and Portuguese.

Source: Own elaboration

RESULTS

There were distinct phases in the systematic review process (Figure 1). The inclusion criteria centred the search on articles whose central theme of study focused on taxation, especially green taxation, in the context of tourist destinations. Thus, in the first phase, searches were made in the SCOPUS and Web of Science (WoS) databases with the general keywords "taxes", "sustainability", and "tourism" for the titles, abstracts and/or keywords. Publications from recent years with these keywords were analysed in the database.

The search results identified 94 publications. The selection criteria for the articles in the search were then applied. 19 articles were excluded at this stage, leaving the database with 75 articles. They were then exported to an Excel file to continue the filtering process. Firstly, duplicate publications had to be eliminated, and no duplicate articles were identified. Subsequently, a filtering process was carried out in which the authors, by reading the title and abstract, analysed the content to include publications aimed at studying green taxation and sustainable destinations. After this stage, all the publications continued in the process. Thirdly, the content of the abstract was analysed to eliminate the articles that did not meet the inclusion criteria. All the articles met the inclusion criteria, so 75 publications were selected. The VOSViewer software was used to construct and visualise the bibliometric maps. The results of the analysis are presented in the following section.

Figure 1. Stages of implementation of Prisma statement

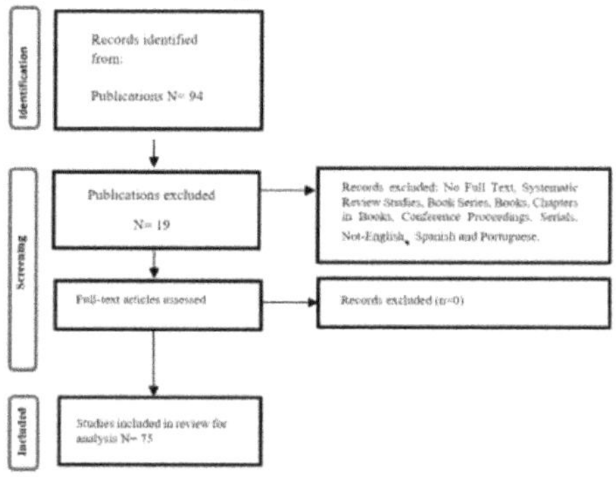

FINDINGS AND DISCUSSION

Publications' evolution and scientific area

The first article published in the SCOPUS database linking taxes, tourist destinations, and sustainability was published in June 1998 in the journal Tourism Economics (Mananyi, 1998). The number of articles published was low until 2021, but there was a sharp increase after that date (Figure 2). More than half of the articles were published in the last five years, with 2022 being the year with the highest number of publications, showing a marked increase in studies related to taxation and sustainable tourism destinations.

A trend line has been plotted, showing that annual growth is exponential. More than 8 papers are expected to be published by 2024 (Figure 2).

Figure 2. Number of publications by year

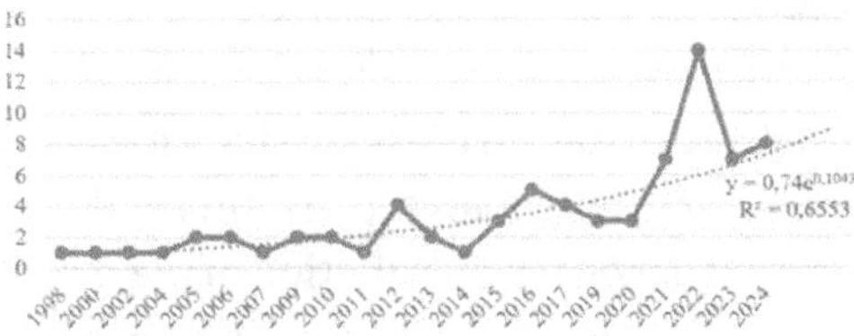

The articles selected have been published in a large number of journals in the fields of tourism, economics, management and sustainability, among others. 75 articles have been published in 58 different journals. The journals with the highest number of published articles are Sustainability Switzerland (8.0%), Tourism Economics (5.3%), Current Issues In Tourism (4.0%) and Worldwide Hospitality And Tourism Themes (2.7%), Tourism Review (2.7%), Tourism Management (2.7%), Journal Of Sustainable Tourism (2.7%), European Journal Of Tourism Research (2.7%), Advances In Science Technology And Innovation (2.7%) and other journals with only one published article (1.3%, respectively).

Table 2 shows that the study of the relationship between taxes and tourist destinations has mainly interested research in the areas of Social Sciences, Business, Management and Accounting and Environmental Sciences.

Table 2. Number of publications by research areas

Area	Quotes
Social Sciences	28.1%
Business, Management and Accounting	21.9%
Environmental Science	18.1%
Energy	8.1%
Economics, Econometrics and Finance	5.0%
Agricultural and Biological Sciences	4.4%
Earth and Planetary Sciences	3.8%
Engineering	3.8%
Computer Science	2.5%
Arts and Humanities	0.6%

Analysis of article keywords

To obtain a synthesised representation of the various ideas in a given document, the keywords used by the authors were analysed. To this end, using the VOSviewer programme, a study was carried out on the distribution of the most frequent keywords, investigated through the co-occurrence of keywords (keywords that appear together in the same document), which makes it possible to highlight the topics covered and possible future research topics. To this end, the VOS viewer software was used to understand better the hot spots in this area and their main issues, as seen in Figure 3. This figure represents the co-occurrence network of the keywords of the articles selected with the keywords "taxes", "tourism destinations", and "sustainability" in titles, keywords and abstracts in the SCOPUS and WoS databases.

Applying the search filter to the co-occurrences of the authors' keywords, 322 words were found. Figure 3 shows these occurrences, reflecting the keywords with the most frequent co-occurrences, as the size of the label and the circle indicate the frequency of occurrence of the keywords. The results show that the two labels that stand out the most are sustainability and sustainable tourism, followed by tourism and competitiveness. The lines between the articles represent the links between the keywords. The closer the keywords are to each other, the stronger their relationship. The colour of an article is determined by the group it belongs to.

In the bibliometric review of the 75 articles under study, 323 author keywords were identified, which shows that different themes and particular issues have been considered in 43 clusters (Figure 3).

Figure 3. Co-occurrence network of Author's keywords

The results identify 11 main keywords, with a minimum of three occurrences representing 3.4% of the total 323 keywords. The top keywords were sustainability (19 occurrences and 84 total link strength), sustainable tourism (8 occurrences and 38 total link strength), sustainable development (5 occurrences and 26 total link strength), tourism taxation (4 occurrences and 20 total link strength); tourism tax and willingness to pay (4 occurrences and 20 link strength, each keyword respectively), tourism (4 occurrences and 19 link strength), ecotourism (3 occurrences and 17 link strength), economic impact, environmental management and globalisation (3 occurrences and 13 link strength, each keyword respectively). On the other hand, the keywords results identify 312 keywords with fewer occurrences, with a minimum of three occurrences, representing 96.6% of the 323 keywords.

Countries, organizations' and authors' analysis

Concerning the country of origin of the study, the results indicate that the articles originate from 46 countries. Some countries with the highest number of publications stand out. The analysis of Figure 4 shows that it is in Spain that more research has been done on this topic (n = 13, 17.33%), followed by USA (n = 6, 8.0%), England (n = 5, 6.67%), Brazil (n = 4, 5.33%), Canda (n = 4, 5.33%), China (n = 4, 5.33%) and Turkey (n = 4, 5.33%).

Figure 4. Publications by the original country

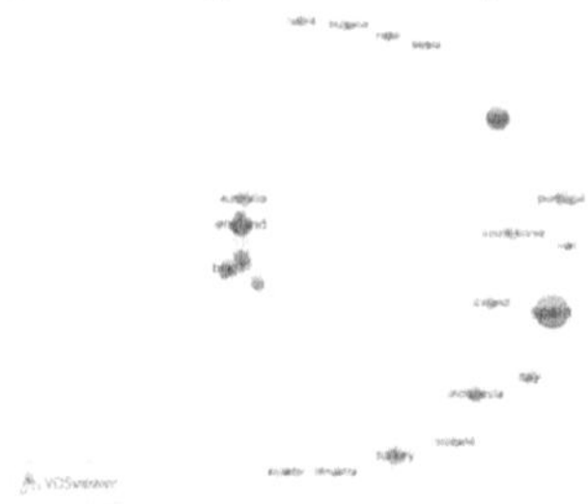

To analyse the authors' affiliation of the articles under analysis, the results indicate that the articles originate from 119 organisations. Some organisations with the highest number of publications stand out. The analysis of Figure 5 allows us to conclude that it is the University of Jaén that has a more significant number of research within the scope of the topic under study (n = 6, 50.40%), followed by Ryerson University (n = 3, 2.52%), Australian Institute Marine SCI (n = 2, 1.68%), University of Johannesburg (n = 2, 1.68%), University of Otago (n = 2, 1.68%), University of Western Australia (n = 2, 1.68%), Istanbul University (n = 2, 1.68%), University of Mid Sweden (n = 2, 1.68%), University of Bozen Bolzano (n = 2, 1.68%) and University of Iceland (n = 2, 1.68%).

Figure 5. Publications by organizations

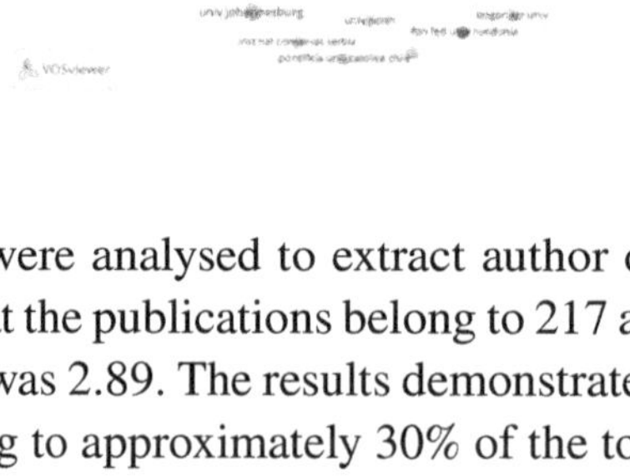

The publications were analysed to extract author data. The author analysis in Figure 6 illustrates that the publications belong to 217 authors. The average number of authors per article was 2.89. The results demonstrate that 6 authors published 22 articles, corresponding to approximately 30% of the total studies.

Figure 6. Publications by authors

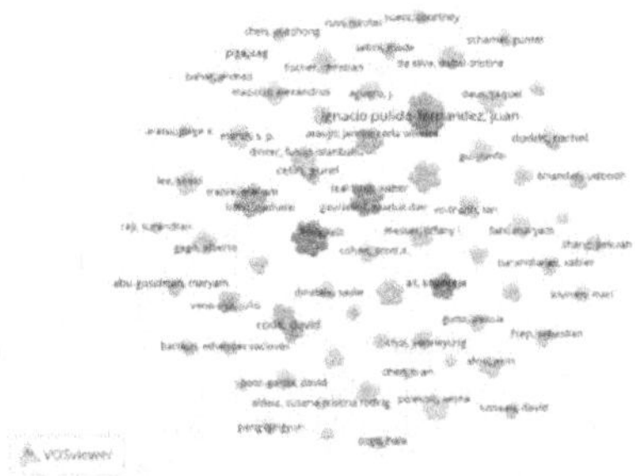

Analysis of relevant expressions in the title, abstract and citations

The results of the analysis of the expressions present in the titles of the articles under analysis reveal that the titles of the articles contained 297 terms and expressions, specifically the terms "tourism" (n=12, 16%), "sustainability" (n=11, 14.67%), "destination" (n=8, 10.67%), "sustainable tourism" (n=7, 9.3%), "evidence" (n=5, 6.7%) and "willingness" (n=4, 5.3%). The VOSViewer software was used to understand better the relationship and association between these terms in the article titles (Figure 7).

Figure 7. Terms and expressions in the titles of the articles

The results show that the terms are associated in two clusters, specifically the terms "evidence", "sustainable tourism", and "tourism" in cluster 1 and the terms "destination", sustainability", and "willingness" in cluster 2 (Table 3).

To analyse the content of the abstracts, the words and expressions present in the abstract were analysed, and 2733 terms were identified in the articles under study. The results show that the most relevant words and expressions present in the abstracts are reduced to 21 terms, which correspond to 60% of the most relevant terms mentioned in the abstracts of the articles (Figure 4).

Table 3. Cluster analysis of title expressions

Clusters	**Keywords**	**Analysis**	**References**
***Cluster* 1**	"evidence", "sustainable tourism" and "tourism"	Tourism must guarantee and evidence that its growth is based on sustainable development.	(Araújo et al., 2023; Bahar et al., 2020; Bartkus & Grunda, 2011; Camacho-Ruiz et al., 2023; Cárdenas-García et al., 2022; Cerina, 2007; Cetin et al., 2017; Dodds & Holmes, 2011; J. Durán-Román et al., 2020, 2021a, 2021b; J. L. Durán-Román et al., 2022; Fajriyati et al., 2020; Göktaş & Çetin, 2023; Jamal & Watt, 2011; Mikulic et al., 2023; Milman et al., 2010; Neher et al., 2021; Ngwu et al., 2023; Onifade & Haouas, 2023; Özgit & Uludağ, 2022; Perles-Ribes et al., 2020; Raimi & Aljadani, 2020, 2022; Ren & Hong, 2017; A.-I. S. Silva et al., 2022; Soliman K.S., 2017; Stabler, 2003; Trutescu, 2020; Zhang & Zhang, 2020)
***Cluster* 2**	"destination", "sustainability", and "willingness"	In the context of the development of tourist destinations and applying the tourist tax for sustainability, it is essential to determine the willingness to pay tourists to support the strategic decision of tourist destination planning.	(Araújo et al., 2023, 2023; Bahar et al., 2020; Bartkus & Grunda, 2011; Camacho-Ruiz et al., 2023; Cárdenas-García et al., 2022; Cerina, 2007; Cetin et al., 2017; Dodds & Holmes, 2011; J. Durán-Román et al., 2020, 2021a, 2021b; J. L. Durán-Román et al., 2022; Fajriyati et al., 2020; Göktaş & Çetin, 2023; Jamal & Watt, 2011; Mikulic et al., 2023; Milman et al., 2010; Neher et al., 2021; Ngwu et al., 2023; Onifade & Haouas, 2023; Özgit & Uludağ, 2022; Perles-Ribes et al., 2020; Raimi & Aljadani, 2020, 2022; Ren & Hong, 2017; A.-I. S. Silva et al., 2022; Soliman K.S., 2017; Stabler, 2003; Trutescu, 2020; Zhang & Zhang, 2020)

Figure 8. Terms and expressions in the abstracts of the articles

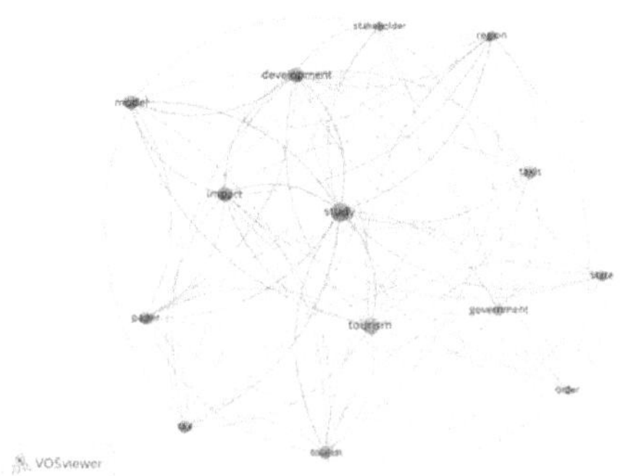

The results highlight 13 terms and expressions present in the abstracts with a minimum of 10 occurrences, including: "study" (n=48, 15.00%), "tourism" (n=41, 12.80%), "sustainability" (n=36, 11.20%), "development" (n=28, 8.70%), "model" (n=26, 8.1%), "tourist" (n=24, 7.5%), "taxis" (n=22, 6.9%), "tax" (n=22, 6.9%), "government" (n=18, 5.6%), "state" (n=17, 5.3%), "region" (n=15, 4.7%), "stake-holder" (n=12, 3.7%), "order" (n=10, 3.1%).

According to the results, the terms are associated with three clusters: in cluster 1, the terms "development," "impact," "model," "region," "stakeholder," and "study; in cluster 2, "government, """order, """state, """taxis," and "tourism; and in cluster 3, the terms "paper," "tax," and "tourist" (Table 4).

Table 4. Cluster analysis of abstract expressions

Clusters	**Keywords**	**Analysis**	**References**
***Cluster* 1**	"development", "impact", "model", "region", "stakeholder", and "study",	Within the scope of regional planning and development of sustainable tourist destinations, the study and creation of collaborative spaces between different stakeholders is essential.	(Barandiarán et al., 2019, 2019; J. L. Durán-Román et al., 2022)
***Cluster* 2**	"government", "order", "state", "taxis" and "tourism"	The analysis of state and order is essential for the continuity of destinations and support of strategic governance decisions and application of tourist taxes.	(Araújo et al., 2023, 2023; Bahar et al., 2020; Bartkus & Grunda, 2011; Camacho-Ruiz et al., 2023; Cárdenas-García et al., 2022; Cerina, 2007; Cetin et al., 2017; Dodds & Holmes, 2011; J. Durán-Román et al., 2020, 2021a, 2021b; J. L. Durán-Román et al., 2022; Fajriyati et al., 2020; Göktaş & Çetin, 2023; Jamal & Watt, 2011; Mikulic et al., 2023; Milman et al., 2010; Neher et al., 2021; Ngwu et al., 2023; Onifade & Haouas, 2023; Özgit & Uludağ, 2022; Perles-Ribes et al., 2020; Raimi & Aljadani, 2020, 2022; Ren & Hong, 2017; A.-I. S. Silva et al., 2022; Soliman K.S., 2017; Stabler, 2003; Trutescu, 2020; Zhang & Zhang, 2020)

continued on following page

Table 4. Continued

Clusters	**Keywords**	**Analysis**	**References**
Cluster 3	"study", "tax", "tourism" and "tourist"	In developing tourist destinations and applying the tourist tax for sustainability, it is essential to study the tourist's perspective.	(Abdillah et al., 2023; Afrizal et al., 2019; Aguero et al., 2006a, 2006b, 2006c, 2006d; Aires et al., 2022; Araña & León, 2016; Araújo et al., 2023; Bahar et al., 2020; Barandiarán et al., 2019; Blomberg-Nygard & Anderson, 2016; Butnaru et al., 2014; Camacho-Ruiz et al., 2023; Cantallops, 2004; Cárdenas-García et al., 2022; Cashman et al., 2012; Cepni et al., 2023; Cerina, 2007; Chang et al., 2022; Chen, 2022; Chouhan, 2022; de Lange & Dodds, 2017; Devkota et al., 2020; Diakomichalis & Diakomihalis, 2024; J. Durán-Román et al., 2020, 2021a; Edelmann et al., 2022; Fernandez Morales & Mayorga Toledano, 2018; Gago et al., 2009; Gallato et al., 2012; Gallo et al., 2021; Gössling et al., 2005; Graci, 2013; Grillini et al., 2024; Grytsevych et al., 2019; Gu et al., 2022; Hasan, 2024; Josep Pons-Vives et al., 2022; Jurigova, 2016; Karim et al., 2020; Kent et al., 2002; Khoo-Lattimore & Prideaux, 2014; Kronenberg & Fuchs, 2022; Laporte et al., 2018; Li et al., 2018; Maleki et al., 2024; Mananyi, 1998; Mazilu et al., 2014; Melo et al., 2022; Melubo et al., 2019; Muñoz Barriga, 2017; Mutanga & Gandiwa, 2024; Novovic Buric et al., 2022; Osorio-Andrade et al., 2023; Panfiluk, 2021; Pang & Zhang, 2021; Peeters et al., 2006; Piga, 2003; Pirotta & Lusseau, 2015; Porto et al., 2020; Rahman et al., 2024; Raimi & Aljadani, 2020, 2022; Ramon-Cardona et al., 2022; Ribeiro et al., 2022; Sarigiannidis et al., 2024; Schubert & Schamel, 2021; Scrioşteanu et al., 2022; Sedai & Medda, 2021; A.-I. S. Silva et al., 2022; F. B. e Silva et al., 2021; Situmorang et al., 2019; Stabler, 2003; Suess & Mody, 2016; Suhardono et al., 2024; Tang & Chen, 2017; Tjahyanto & Sisephaputra, 2017; Tovar et al., 2024; Trutescu, 2020; Ulyanchenko et al., 2020; Vail & Heldt, 2000; Valdagni et al., 2009; Vianna et al., 2012; Vujicic M.D. et al., 2022; Xu & Lv, 2022; Zemla et al., 2020; Zhang & Zhang, 2020; Zimmerhackel et al., 2019)

To identify the most relevant ideas and research trends in the field of tourist taxes and ecological and sustainable tourist destinations, the five most relevant published articles on the topic under study were analysed (Table 5).

Table 5. Top 5 articles with the most relevance

R	Journal	Title	Year	Objectives	Method	Findings
1	Sustainability	Tourist tax to improve sustainability and the experience in mass tourism destinations: The case of Andalusia (Spain)	2021	This study aims to determine the amount of taxes and/or public fees that tourists appear to be more willing to pay to improve the sustainability and experience of mature tourism destinations.	The study was carried out in Andalusia, a prominently touristic region of southern Spain, which received 32.4 million tourists in 2019. To do so, a survey was conducted on 1068 tourists at the region's main tourism arrival points.	The results identify the dimensions of taxes and/or public fees that tourists are more willing to pay, linked to environmental factors and tourism services. Second, the following factors influence the tourists' willingness to pay these taxes: the purpose of the trip, income, budget, and place of origin.
2	Sustainability	Tourist taxation as a sustainability financing mechanism for mass tourism destinations	2021	The objectives of this research are, to identify tourist preferences when offered 15 different taxes and fees, and to identify which socio-demographic factors and trip characteristics condition the tourist's willingness to pay (WTP) of the five most accepted taxes and fees.	The study was carried out in Andalusia, a mass tourism destination. A total of 1068 surveys were conducted among tourists who visited Andalusia. Logistic regression models are commonly used to build a model from a linear predictor of an event's occurrence probability.	Of the 15 taxes and fees proposed, some participants showed a greater willingness to pay. Prior to establishing taxes and/or fees linked to tourist activity, marketing strategies that shed light on why the tourist is going to pay more to enjoy the tourist destination must be addressed.

continued on following page

Table 5. Continued

R	Journal	Title	Year	Objectives	Method	Findings
3	Tourism Management	Gaming can be sustainable too! Using Social Representation Theory to examine the moderating effects of tourism diversification on residents' tax-paying behavior	2016	Higher economic dependence on tourism and higher levels of community attachment led to more favourable perceptions of tourism's economic and social impacts. The economic impacts, in turn, resulted in a willingness to pay higher taxes, irrespective of the type of tourism development proposed by the Las Vegas authorities.	The present study uses Social Representation Theory as the conceptual basis to test the moderating effects of the various types of proposed tourism development on residents' willingness to pay higher taxes to support such development.	The results suggest that rural communities reinforce a hegemonic social representation of tourism to characterise the ethos of capitalist urbanism that pervades the economic development discourse. The residents' social construction of tourism has important implications for regional tourism planners. It suggests adopting an inclusive tourism diversification strategy that leverages gaming and alternative tourism.

continued on following page

Table 5. Continued

R	Journal	Title	Year	Objectives	Method	Findings
4	Economies	Willingness to pay for tourist tax in destinations: Empirical evidence from Istanbul	2017	Therefore, this paper's objectives are to evaluate tourism taxes as a compensation tool to cover the costs of tourism and to measure tourists' willingness to pay (WTP).	A qualitative approach was used and data were collected through semi-structured in-depth interviews with international travelers to Istanbul, Turkey.	The findings suggest that tourists are more likely to pay an additional tax when this is earmarked for improving their experiences, but they are reluctant to take on liability concerning matters relating to destination sustainability.
5	Advances in Science, Technology and Innovation	Tourism Economics—Tourists' Perception of the Tourist Tax in Oporto	2024	The objective of this study was, first of all, to understand the tax's importance for the local municipality treasury and, secondly, to understand how the measure was perceived by the tourists who visited Oporto city.	The methodology used was an English survey on the Google Drive platform. The survey was conducted in Porto between 20 May and 30 July 2019; 135 responses were validated.	Preliminary research led us to conclude that this was the first such study to be carried out in the city of Porto. Furthermore, our study was the first to question tourists on this topic in Porto.

CONCLUSIONS

Tourism is universally recognised for its multiplier economic, social, cultural, and environmental impact. While tourism growth generates a set of positive externalities, it also generates negative externalities, which translate into a significant impact with transversal repercussions, including direct, indirect, and induced effects.

Similarly to tourism, sustainability takes a holistic approach that considers various environmental, social and economic, cultural, and political dimensions. It recognises that by considering these dimensions together, sustainable development can be promoted to meet the needs of present generations without compromising the possibilities of future generations. Sustainable tourism planning emerges as a critical instrument in defining and implementing strategies that enable the development of competitive destinations based on the logic of sustainability.

Sustainable tourism incorporates broad terms of sustainability and the development of territories with their peculiarities, making it one of the current paradigms in the vision of strategic planning for tourist destinations. Given the particularities of the sector and its multidimensional context, sustainability in tourism considers the balance between demand and supply, the needs of visitors and communities, and its (positive and negative) environmental, economic and social impacts now and in the future. The guiding pillars of tourism argue that the sector must appropriately use the territory and natural resources, respect the socio-cultural authenticity of communities and ensure that economic activities are viable in the medium and long term.

The COVID-19 pandemic has emerged as a perfect opportunity to switch to sustainable tourism growth, rethink the activity and make sustainable choices. The World Tourism Organisation (UNWTO, 2020) states that we must take advantage of the pandemic crisis to promote sustainable tourism and accelerate the goals of the Sustainable Development Goals (SDGs). The different literature collected makes it possible to identify a change in the discussion. Sustainability is now more critical than ever, and after the pandemic, all tourism areas must consider sustainable and long-term development. However, considering tourism's sustainability must include more than just environmental issues.

According to the literature, the revenue generated by tourist taxes is a fundamental financial resource for the fulfilment of destinations, making it possible to guarantee tourism sustainability and improve the quality of tourist experiences. The economic growth generated by the tourism sector implies an increase in production and, consequently, an increase in the consumption of natural resources. The literature, therefore, stresses the importance of defining strategies to guarantee the quality of economic development and minimise negative environmental externalities in the tourism sector.

Given the importance of these issues, this study's main objective was to analyse the literature on green taxation and sustainable tourism destinations. Thus, a systematic literature review on this topic was carried out. This study analysed publications from the last years with the general keywords “taxes”, “sustainability”, and “tourism” in titles, keywords and abstracts in SCOPUS and WoS databases. Over time the literature has analysed the link between green taxation, sustainability and tourism. The first article linking taxes, tourist destinations and sustainability was published in June 1998 in the journal Tourism Economics (Mananyi, 1998). The results show a small number of articles published until 2021, highlighting a sharp increase in studies after that date.

The results identify 11 main keywords, highlighting words and terms in the literature under study such as sustainability, sustainable tourism, sustainable development, tourism taxation, tourism tax and willingness to pay, tourism, ecotourism, economic impact, environmental management, and globalisation. These conclusions support future research on the topic under study, allow for greater research efficiency, and support new lines of investigation.

Analysing the most relevant articles allowed us to conclude which lines of investigation and objectives the studies related to tourist taxes and sustainable tourist destinations have. Its main research objectives are to analyse the tax regime in tourism, specifically, tourist taxes as a compensation instrument to cover the costs and negative externalities of tourism, measure the willingness of tourists to pay, and understand the importance of the tax for the treasury of tourism, tourists, tourist destinations, as well as determining the amounts of taxes and/or public fees that tourists seem to be more willing to pay to improve the sustainability and experience of the mature tourist destination, identify tourists' preferences regarding the tax regime, identify which sociodemographic factors and trip characteristics that condition the tourist's willingness to pay and analyse the most favourable perceptions of the economic and social impacts of tourism.

The development models of tourist destinations must be based on sustainable development models. Therefore, applied research in this area appears to be emerging and essential to support the strategic planning of destinations. Although scarce, literature on this topic is growing in number. It is essential to reflect on territorial planning and carry out case studies, with the study of perceptions at a microeconomic level. Municipalities play a key role in tourism planning and the management of public expenditure inherent to tourism activity. The results of the articles studied outline sustainable development models based on green taxation, allowing the reinvention and planning of tourism based on these values, guaranteeing the sector's competitiveness, resilience and sustainability.

The main limitation of this study is the delimitation of the work to be analysed through the selected databases, SCOPUS and WoS. Although these are the most comprehensive databases with the largest scientific and academic publications, other works not indexed in this database may have been overlooked.

The study's results have implications for the managers of tourism destinations, both public and private. This study contributes to identifying the evolution of studies and new lines of investigation in the emerging literature, which provides fundamental support for planning tourist destinations based on strategic decisions to create an efficient and fair tax system.

Future work in the area could include identifying new models for implementing a tourist tax regime as a tool for the sustainable development of tourist destinations.

REFERENCES

Abdillah, N., Thamrin, T., Nofrizal, N., & Wijayanto, G. (2023). Quantifying Ecological, Economic, Social, and Governance Attributes for Urban Forest Eco-Tourism Using MDS-RAPFISH Approach. *International Journal of Sustainable Development and Planning, 18*(8), 2369–2378. *Scopus*. Advance online publication. DOI: 10.18280/ijsdp.180807

Afrizal, A. D., Rakhmawati, N. A., & Tjahyanto, A. (2019). New Filtering Scheme Based on Term Weighting to Improve Object Based Opinion Mining on Tourism Product Reviews. In Younus, A., & Herdiyanti, A. (Eds.), *Procedia Computer Science, 161, 805-812*. Elsevier., DOI: 10.1016/j.procs.2019.11.186

Aguero, J., Conway, S., & Navis, I. (2006a). *Community monitoring in a tourism-dependent economy* (C. Brebbia & F. Pineda, Eds.; WOS:000241776000027; Vol. 97, pp. 297–309). DOI: 10.2495/ST060271

Aguero, J., Conway, S., & Navis, I. (2006b). *Community monitoring in a tourism-dependent economy* (C. Brebbia & F. Pineda, Eds.; WOS:000241776000027; Vol. 97, pp. 297–309). DOI: 10.2495/ST060271

Aguero, J., Conway, S., & Navis, I. (2006c). *Community monitoring in a tourism-dependent economy* (C. Brebbia & F. Pineda, Eds.; WOS:000241776000027; Vol. 97, pp. 297–309). DOI: 10.2495/ST060271

Aguero, J., Conway, S., & Navis, I. (2006d). Community monitoring in a tourism-dependent economy. *WIT Transactions on Ecology and the Environment, 97*, 297–309. *Scopus.*, 297–309. Advance online publication. DOI: 10.2495/ST060271

Aires, J., Costa, C., & Brandao, F. (2022). Exploring Indicators and Determinants to Evaluate Innovation in Tourism Firms-A Systematic Literature Review. *Tourism (Zagreb)*, 70(4), 656–673. DOI: 10.37741/t.70.4.8

Araña, J., & León, C. (2016). Are tourists animal spirits? Evidence from a field experiment exploring the use of non-market based interventions advocating sustainable tourism. *Journal of Sustainable Tourism*, 24(3), 430–445. DOI: 10.1080/09669582.2015.1101128

Araújo, J., de Souza, F., Robles, E., Celis, L., & Lagioia, U. (2023). Fiscal policies for economic sustainability in COVID-19: What do subnational governments in Brazil and Colombia reveal? *GeSec: Revista de Gestao e Secretariado*, 14(4), 6636–6662. DOI: 10.7769/gesec.v14i4.2070

Bahar, A., & Fauzi, A. (2020). Coral reefs ecotourism sustainability assessment based on the integration of government-private-local community in Hoga Island, Wakatobi Regency. *IOP Conference Series. Earth and Environmental Science*, 564(1), 012074. Advance online publication. DOI: 10.1088/1755-1315/564/1/012074

Barandiarán, X., Restrepo, N., & Luna, A. (2019). Collaborative governance in tourism: Lessons from Etorkizuna Eraikiz in the Basque Country, Spain. *Tourism Review*, 74(4), 902–914. DOI: 10.1108/TR-09-2018-0133

Bartkus, E., & Grunda, R. (2011). Business Sustainability Assessment: Comparing Results of Two Studies. *Inžinerinė ekonomika-. The Engineering Economist*, 22(1), 32–40.

Blomberg-Nygard, A., & Anderson, C. K. (2016). United Nations World Tourism Organization Study on Online Guest Reviews and Hotel Classification Systems: An Integrated Approach. *Service Science*, 8(2), 139–151. DOI: 10.1287/serv.2016.0139

Butnaru, G. I., Stefanica, M., & Maxim, G. M. (2014). Alternative method of quality evaluation in tourism. Case study applied in tourist accommodation units. In Stefan, D., Comes, C. A., Munteanu, A., Nistor, P., & Stefan, A. B. (Eds.), *Emerging Markets Queries in Finance Business (EMQ 2013) (15), 671–678*. Elsevier Science Bv., DOI: 10.1016/S2212-5671(14)00538-3

Camacho-Ruiz, M., Carrasco, R. A., Fernandez-Aviles, G., & Latorre, A. (2023). Tourism destination events classifier based on artificial intelligence techniques. *Applied Soft Computing*, 148, 110914. DOI: 10.1016/j.asoc.2023.110914

Cantallops, A. S. (2004). Policies supporting sustainable tourism development in the Balearic Islands: The Ecotax. *Anatolia, 15*(1), 39–56. *Scopus.* Advance online publication. DOI: 10.1080/13032917.2004.9687143

Cárdenas-García, P. J., Pulido-Fernández, J. I., Durán-Román, J. L., & Carrillo-Hidalgo, I. (2022). Tourist taxation as a sustainability financing mechanism for mass tourism destinations. *International Journal of Tourism Research*, 24(4), 577–592. DOI: 10.1002/jtr.2523

Cashman, A., Cumberbatch, J., & Moore, W. (2012). The effects of climate change on tourism in small states: Evidence from the Barbados case. *Tourism Review*, 67(3), 17–29. DOI: 10.1108/16605371211259803

Cepni, O., Dogru, T., & Ozdemir, O. (2023). The contagion effect of COVID-19-induced uncertainty on US tourism sector: Evidence from time-varying granger causality test. *Tourism Economics*, 29(4), 906–928. DOI: 10.1177/13548166221077633

Cerina, F. (2007). Tourism specialization and environmental sustainability in a dynamic economy. *Tourism Economics*, 13(4), 553–582. DOI: 10.5367/000000007782696032

Cetin, G., Alrawadieh, Z., Dincer, M., Dincer, F., & Ioannides, D. (2017). Willingness to Pay for Tourist Tax in Destinations: Empirical Evidence from Istanbul. *Economies*, 5(2), 21. Advance online publication. DOI: 10.3390/economies5020021

Chang, I.-C., Horng, J.-S., Liu, C.-H., Chou, S.-F., & Yu, T.-Y. (2022). Exploration of Topic Classification in the Tourism Field with Text Mining Technology-A Case Study of the Academic Journal Papers. *Sustainability (Basel)*, 14(7), 4053. DOI: 10.3390/su14074053

Chen, T. (2022). Business Performance Evaluation for Tourism Factory: Using DEA Approach and Delphi Method. *Sustainability (Basel)*, 14(15), 9209. Advance online publication. DOI: 10.3390/su14159209

Chouhan, V. (2022). Developing a sustainable tribal tourism model vis-a-vis the tribal region of Rajasthan. *Journal of Tourism, Heritage and Services Marketing, 8*(1), 58–63. *Scopus.* Advance online publication. DOI: 10.5281/zenodo.6594696

De Lange, D., & Dodds, R. (2017). Increasing sustainable tourism through social entrepreneurship. *International Journal of Contemporary Hospitality Management*, 29(7), 1977–2002. DOI: 10.1108/IJCHM-02-2016-0096

Destination Sustainability Movement & Group Nao. (2020). *Tourism taxes by design white paper: Destination funding and the impact of tourism taxes on European cities and urban communities* (BTRP-ID: 2701).

Devkota, N., Paudel, U. R., & Bhandari, U. (2020). Tourism entrepreneurs' expectation from the provincial government in touristic city–Pokhara, Nepal. *Journal of Hospitality and Tourism Insights*, 3(3), 329–351. DOI: 10.1108/JHTI-06-2019-0082

Diakomichalis, N.-M., & Diakomihalis, M. (2024). Sustainable Tourism Within the Boundaries of Carrying Capacity and Tourism Satellite Account. Em *Palgrave. Stud. Cross-Discip. Bus. Res. Association. EuroMed. Acad. Bus.: Vol. Part F1799* (pp. 45–72). Palgrave Macmillan. DOI: 10.1007/978-3-031-37365-7_3

Dodds, R., & Holmes, M. (2011). Sustainability in Canadian B&Bs: Comparing the East Versus West. *International Journal of Tourism Research*, 13(5), 482–495. DOI: 10.1002/jtr.822

Durán-Román, J., Cárdenas-García, P., & Pulido-Fernández, J. (2021a). Tourist Tax to Improve Sustainability and the Experience in Mass Tourism Destinations: The Case of Andalusia (Spain). *Sustainability (Basel)*, 13(1), 42. Advance online publication. DOI: 10.3390/su13010042

Durán-Román, J., Cárdenas-García, P., & Pulido-Fernández, J. (2021b). Tourists' willingness to pay to improve sustainability and experience at destination. *Journal of Destination Marketing & Management*, 19, 100540. Advance online publication. DOI: 10.1016/j.jdmm.2020.100540

Durán-Román, J. L., Pulido-Fernández, J. I., Rey-Carmona, F. J., & Núñez-Tabales, J. M. (2022). Willingness to Pay by Tourist Companies for Improving Sustainability and Competitiveness in a Mature Destination. *Leisure Sciences*, 1–22. Advance online publication. DOI: 10.1080/01490400.2022.2123072

Edelmann, N., Müller, A., Steen, T., Gerhardter, B., & Holzbauer, T. (2022). Sustainable Co-Creation in the Public Sector: A Case Study in the Lower Austrian Federal Government. Em L. Amaral, D. Soares, & L. Zheng (Eds.), *KU Leuven* (WOS:001098408200016; pp. 111–118). DOI: 10.1145/3560107.3560126

Fajriyati, I., Afiff, A. Z., Gayatri, G., & Hati, S. R. H. (2020). Generic and Islamic attributes for non-Muslim majority destinations: Application of the three-factor theory of customer satisfaction. *Heliyon*, 6(6), e04324. DOI: 10.1016/j.heliyon.2020.e04324 PMID: 32637707

Fernandez Morales, A., & Mayorga Toledano, M. C. (2018). Seasonality of cruise tourism in Spanish ports. A multivariate approach. *Pasos (El Sauzal)*, 16(1), 253–264. DOI: 10.25145/j.pasos.2018.16.016

Gago, A., Labandeira, X., Picos, F., & Rodríguez, M. (2009). Specific and general taxation of tourism activities. Evidence from Spain. *Tourism Management*, 30(3), 381–392. DOI: 10.1016/j.tourman.2008.08.004

Gallato, C. G., Gallato-Reamillo, K. A., Valdez, N. P., Warokka, A., & Hilman, H. (2012). Eco-tourism in the Philippines: Educational and recreational value of the Alayan cave systems. *Journal for Global Business Advancement, 5*(2), 169–178. *Scopus*. Advance online publication. DOI: 10.1504/JGBA.2012.049509

Gallo, P., Dobrovic, J., Cabinova, V., Partlova, P., Strakova, J., & Mihalcova, B. (2021). Increasing the Efficiency of Enterprises in Tourism Sector Using Innovative Management Methods and Tools. *Social Sciences (Basel, Switzerland)*, 10(4), 132. DOI: 10.3390/socsci10040132

Göktaş, L. S., & Çetin, G. (2023). Tourist tax for sustainability: Determining willingness to pay. *European Journal of Tourism Research, 35.European Journal of Tourism Research*, 35, 3503. Advance online publication. DOI: 10.54055/ejtr.v35i.2813

Gössling, S., Peeters, P., Ceron, J.-P., Dubois, G., Patterson, T., & Richardson, R. B. (2005). The eco-efficiency of tourism. *Ecological Economics*, 54(4), 417–434. DOI: 10.1016/j.ecolecon.2004.10.006

Graci, S. (2013). Collaboration and Partnership Development for Sustainable Tourism. *Tourism Geographies*, 15(1), 25–42. DOI: 10.1080/14616688.2012.675513

Grillini, G., Streifeneder, T., Sacchi, G., & Fischer, C. (2024). Comparative analysis of alpine agritourism in Trentino, Tyrol, and South Tyrol: Regional variations and prospects. *Open Agriculture*, 9(1), 20220281. Advance online publication. DOI: 10.1515/opag-2022-0281

Grytsevych, V. S., Podvirna, K. Y., & Senkiv, M. I. (2019). Motor transport network of western region of Ukraine as a factor of development of tourism industry. *Вісник Харківського національного університету імені ВН Каразіна.Серія: Геологія. Географія. Екологія*, 50, 91–100. DOI: 10.26565/2410-7360-2019-50-07

Gu, Y., Onggo, B., Kunc, M., & Bayer, S. (2022). Small Island Developing States (SIDS) COVID-19 post-pandemic tourism recovery: A system dynamics approach. *Current Issues in Tourism*, 25(9), 1481–1508. DOI: 10.1080/13683500.2021.1924636

Hasan, A. A.-T. (2024). Theory of sustainable consumption behavior (TSCB) to predict renewable energy consumption behavior: A case of eco-tourism visitors of Bangladesh. *Management of Environmental Quality: An International Journal, 35*(1), 101–118. *Scopus*. Advance online publication. DOI: 10.1108/MEQ-05-2023-0146

Jamal, T., & Watt, E. (2011). Climate change pedagogy and performative action: Toward community-based destination governance. *Journal of Sustainable Tourism*, 19(4–5), 571–588. DOI: 10.1080/09669582.2011.575227

Josep Pons-Vives, P., Morro-Ribot, M., Mulet-Forteza, C., & Valero, O. (2022). An Application of Ordered Weighted Averaging Operators to Customer Classification in Hotels. *Mathematics*, 10(12), 1987. DOI: 10.3390/math10121987

Jurigova, Z. (2016). Tourism industry analysis with the Czech Republic as the focal point. *Procedia Economics and Finance*, 39, 305–312. DOI: 10.1016/S2212-5671(16)30328-8

Karim, R., Muhammad, F., Serafino, L., Latip, N. A., & Marzuki, A. (2020). Integration of pro-poor tourism activities in community-based development initiatives: A case study in high mountain areas of Pakistan. *International Journal of Scientific and Technology Research*, 9(4), 848–852.

Kent, M., Newnham, R., & Essex, S. (2002). Tourism and sustainable water supply in Mallorca: A geographical analysis. *Applied Geography (Sevenoaks, England)*, 22(4), 351–374. DOI: 10.1016/S0143-6228(02)00050-4

Khoo-Lattimore, C., & Prideaux, B. (2014). ZMET: A psychological approach to understanding unsustainable tourism mobility. Em *Underst. And Gov. Sustainable Tourism Mobil.: Psychological and Behavioural Approaches* (pp. 88–103). Taylor and Francis. https://doi.org/DOI: 10.4324/9780203771501-15

Kronenberg, K., & Fuchs, M. (2022). The socio-economic impact of regional tourism: An occupation-based modelling perspective from Sweden. *Journal of Sustainable Tourism*, 30(12), 2785–2805. DOI: 10.1080/09669582.2021.1924757

Laporte, A., Vandentorren, S., Détrez, M. A., Douay, C., Le Strat, Y., Le Méner, E., & Chauvin, P.Samenta Research Group. (2018). Prevalence of mental disorders and addictions among homeless people in the greater Paris area, France. *International Journal of Environmental Research and Public Health*, 15(2), 241. DOI: 10.3390/ijerph15020241 PMID: 29385053

Li, Q., Li, S., Hu, J., Zhang, S., & Hu, J. (2018). Tourism Review Sentiment Classification Using a Bidirectional Recurrent Neural Network with an Attention Mechanism and Topic-Enriched Word Vectors. *Sustainability (Basel)*, 10(9), 3313. DOI: 10.3390/su10093313

Maleki, F., Bararzadeh Ledari, M., & Fani, M., & kamelizadeh, D. (. (2024). Sustainable hydrogen supply chain development for low-carbon transportation in a fossil-based port region: A case study in a tourism hub. *International Journal of Hydrogen Energy, 65*, 95–111. *Scopus.* Advance online publication. DOI: 10.1016/j.ijhydene.2024.03.362

Mananyi, A. (1998). Optimal management of ecotourism. *Tourism Economics*, 4(2), 147–169. DOI: 10.1177/135481669800400203

Mazilu, M., Toma, E., Lazar, I., & SGEM. (2014). The Economic Complex Tourism Relationship. *University of Craiova*, 711–718.

Melo, S., Silva, M., Melo, F., & Vo-Thanh, T. (2022). The practice of (un)sustainable tourism in a National Park: An empirical study focusing on structural elements. *Journal of Outdoor Recreation and Tourism*, 39, 100548. Advance online publication. DOI: 10.1016/j.jort.2022.100548

Melubo, K., Lovelock, B., & Filep, S. (2019). Motivations and barriers for corporate social responsibility engagement: Evidence from the Tanzanian tourism industry. *Tourism and Hospitality Research*, 19(3), 284–295. DOI: 10.1177/1467358417742685

Mikulic, J., Seric, M., & Kresic, D. (2023). Asymmetric effects of wellness destination and wellness facility attributes on tourist satisfaction. *Tourism Review*, 79(4), 969–980. Advance online publication. DOI: 10.1108/TR-12-2022-0635

Milman, A., Okumus, F., & Dickson, D. (2010). The contribution of theme parks and attractions to the social and economic sustainability of destinations. *Worldwide Hospitality and Tourism Themes*, 2(3), 338–345. DOI: 10.1108/17554211011052249

Muñoz Barriga, A. (2017). Tourism Management Perceptions in two Ecuadorian Biosphere Reserves: Galapagos and Sumaco. *Investigaciones Geográficas*, 2017(93), 110–125. DOI: 10.14350/rig.47805

Mutanga, C. N., & Gandiwa, E. (2024). Contemporary Issues Affecting Wildlife Tourism: Crises and Disasters. Em *Geogr. Tour. Glob. Chang.: Vol. Part F2881* (pp. 167–180). Springer Nature; DOI: 10.1007/978-3-031-57252-4_12

Neher, T. P., Soupir, M. L., & Kanwar, R. S. (2021). Lake atitlan: A review of the food, energy, and water sustainability of a mountain lake in guatemala. *Sustainability (Switzerland), 13*(2), 1–15. *Scopus.* Advance online publication. DOI: 10.3390/su13020515

Ngwu, R. O., Onodugo, V. A., Monyei, F. E., Ukpere, W. I., Onyekwelu, P. N., & Mmamel, U. G. (2023). The Nexus between Industrial Parks and the Sustainability of Small and Medium-Scaled Ventures. *Sustainability (Switzerland), 15*(12). *Sustainability (Basel)*, 15(12), 9529. Advance online publication. DOI: 10.3390/su15129529

Nobanee, H., & Ullah, S. (2023). Mapping green tax: A bibliometric analysis and visualization of relevant research. *Sustainable Futures : An Applied Journal of Technology, Environment and Society*, 6, 100129. DOI: 10.1016/j.sftr.2023.100129

Novovic Buric, M., Jaksic Stojanovic, A., Lalevic Filipovic, A., & Kascelan, L. (2022). Research of Attitudes toward Implementation of Green Accounting in Tourism Industry in Montenegro-Practices, and Challenges. *Sustainability (Basel)*, 14(3), 1725. DOI: 10.3390/su14031725

OECD. (2014). *OECD Tourism trends and policies 2014*. OECD Publishing., DOI: 10.1787/tour-2014-6-

Onifade, S., & Haouas, I. (2023). Assessing environmental sustainability in top Middle East travel destinations: Insights on the multifaceted roles of air transport amidst other energy indicators. *Environmental Science and Pollution Research International*, 30(45), 101911–101926. DOI: 10.1007/s11356-023-29183-4 PMID: 37653199

Osorio-Andrade, C. F., Pastrana, C. A. A., & Orejuela, A. R. (2023). Evolution of scientific research on electronic word of mouth in the tourism industry: A bibliometric analysis. *Estudios Gerenciales*, 39(166), 110–123. DOI: 10.18046/j.estger.2023.166.5415

Özgit, H., & Uludağ, O. (2022). A unique destination and transportation: Current issues and possible solutions. *Worldwide Hospitality and Tourism Themes*, 14(4), 365–373. DOI: 10.1108/WHATT-03-2022-0034

Panfiluk, E. (2021). Innovativeness of Tourism Enterprises: Example of Poland. *Sustainability (Basel)*, 13(3), 1024. DOI: 10.3390/su13031024

Pang, Q., & Zhang, M. (2021). Evolutionary game analysis of land income distribution in tourism development. *Tourism Economics*, 27(4), 670–687. DOI: 10.1177/1354816619898078

Peeters, P., Gössling, S., & Becken, S. (2006). Innovation towards tourism sustainability: Climate change and aviation. *International Journal of Innovation and Sustainable Development*, 1(3), 184–200. DOI: 10.1504/IJISD.2006.012421

Perles-Ribes, J. F., Ivars-Baidal, J. A., Ramon-Rodriguez, A. B., & Vera-Rebollo, J. F. (2020). The typological classification of tourist destinations: The region of Valencia, a case study. *Tourism Economics*, 26(5), 764–773. DOI: 10.1177/1354816619838413

Piga, C. (2003). Territorial planning and tourism development tax. *Annals of Tourism Research*, 30(4), 886–905. DOI: 10.1016/S0160-7383(03)00061-6

Pirotta, E., & Lusseau, D. (2015). Managing the wildlife tourism commons. *Ecological Applications*, 25(3), 729–741. DOI: 10.1890/14-0986.1 PMID: 26214918

Porto, N., Dowbley, V., & Ines Garcia, C. (2020). Tactics for the tourism game in groups of municipalities from Buenos Aires Province: A classification for the development of sports tourism. *Revista Brasileira de Pesquisa em Turismo*, 14(3), 134–157. DOI: 10.7784/rbtur.v14i3.1915

Rahman, M. H., Tanchangya, T., Rahman, J., Aktar, M. A., & Majumder, S. C. (2024). Corporate social responsibility and green financing behavior in Bangladesh: Towards sustainable tourism. *Innovation and Green Development*, 3(3), 100133. Advance online publication. DOI: 10.1016/j.igd.2024.100133

Raimi, L., & Aljadani, A. (2020). Sustainability of public finance of rentier states. Em *Recent Advancements in Sustainable Entrepreneurship and Corporate soc. Responsibility* (pp. 88–113). IGI Global. DOI: 10.4018/978-1-7998-2347-6.ch005

Raimi, L., & Aljadani, A. (2022). Sustainability of public finance of rentier states. Em *Res. Anthology on Macroecon. And the Achiev. Of Global Stability* (pp. 1028–1047). IGI Global. DOI: 10.4018/978-1-6684-7460-0.ch055

Ramon-Cardona, J., Dolores Sanchez-Fernandez, M., Duran-Sanchez, A., & Alvarez-Garcia, J. (2022). Music as an Element of Tourism Innovation: Types of Nightlife Premises in Ibiza (Spain). *Frontiers in Psychology*, 13, 890847. DOI: 10.3389/fpsyg.2022.890847 PMID: 35795411

Ren, G., & Hong, T. (2017). Investigating Online Destination Images Using a Topic-Based Sentiment Analysis Approach. *Sustainability (Basel)*, 9(10), 1765. DOI: 10.3390/su9101765

Ribeiro, D., Machado, L. P., & Henriques, P. (2022). Tourism Economics—Tourists' Perception of the Tourist Tax in Oporto. In Vujicic, M. D., Kasim, A., Kostopoulou, S., Chica Olmo, J., & Aslam, M. (Eds.), *Adv. Sci. Tech. Inno* (pp. 135–141). Springer Nature., DOI: 10.1007/978-3-031-07819-4_12

Román, J. L. D., Fernández, J. I. P., & García, P. J. C. (2020). Delimitación de ingresos públicos aplicables en los destinos turísticos españoles. *Investigaciones Regionales Journal of Regional Research*, 47, 179–199. DOI: 10.38191/iirr-jorr.20.016

Sarigiannidis, C., Halkiopoulos, C., & Boutsinas, B. (2024). An Environmental Management Accounting System for Sustainable Tourism Based on Business Intelligence. In Katsoni, V., & Cassar, G. (Eds.), *Springer Proc. Bus. Econ* (pp. 543–556). Springer Nature., DOI: 10.1007/978-3-031-54338-8_31

Schubert, S., & Schamel, G. (2021). Sustainable tourism development: A dynamic model incorporating resident spillovers. *Tourism Economics*, 27(7), 1561–1587. DOI: 10.1177/1354816620934552

Scrioşteanu, A., Barbu, C. M., & Criveanu, M. M. (2022). Sustainable tourism in the current European context. In *Managing risk and decision making in times of economic distress, 108* (Vol. B, pp. 17–36). Emerald Publishing Limited., DOI: 10.1108/S1569-37592022000108B031

Sedai, A., & Medda, F. (2021). Complex tourism dynamics and fiscal sustainability. Em *Handb. On Entropy, Complexity and Spatial Dynamics: A Rebirth of Theory?* (pp. 321–341). Edward Elgar Publishing Ltd. https://www.scopus.com/inward/record.uri?eid=2-s2.0-85130158234&partnerID=40&md5=804e662904ac273db777de8065189e73

Silva, A.-I. S., Alves, M.-C. G., & Estevão, C. (2022). Tourism and Sustainability in Natural Parks: A Survey. *International Journal of Social Ecology and Sustainable Development*, 13(1), 1–17. Advance online publication. DOI: 10.4018/IJSESD.287879

Silva, F. B., Barranco, R., Proietti, P., Pigaiani, C., & Lavalle, C. (2021). A new European regional tourism typology based on hotel location patterns and geographical criteria. *Annals of Tourism Research*, 89, 103077. DOI: 10.1016/j.annals.2020.103077

Situmorang, V., Elyani, T., Tambunan, R., & Gulto, Y. (2019). Applying opinion mining technique on tourism study case: Lake Toba. *Journal of Physics: Conference Series*, 1175(1), 012091. Advance online publication. DOI: 10.1088/1742-6596/1175/1/012091

Soliman, K. S. (Ed.). (2017). Proceedings of the 29th International Business Information Management Association Conference—Education Excellence and Innovation Management through Vision 2020: From Regional Development Sustainability to Global Economic Growth. Em *Proc. Int. Bus. Inf. Manag. Assoc. Conf. - Educ. Excell. Innov. Manag. Vis.: Reg. Dev. Sustain. Glob. Econ. Growth*. International Business Information Management Association, IBIMA. https://www.scopus.com/inward/record.uri?eid=2-s2.0-85029738713&partnerID=40&md5=faa8180944d03c1a87a26fb3bd3cf916

Stabler, M. (2003). THE ECONOMIC EVALUATION OF THE ROLE OF CONSERVATION AND TOURISM IN THE REGENERATION OF HISTORIC URBAN DESTINATIONS. Em *Embrac. And Managing Change in Tourism: International case studies* (pp. 239–266). Taylor and Francis. https://doi.org/DOI: 10.4324/9780203360491-25

Suess, C., & Mody, M. (2016). Gaming can be sustainable too! Using Social Representation Theory to examine the moderating effects of tourism diversification on residents' tax paying behavior. *Tourism Management*, 56, 20–39. DOI: 10.1016/j.tourman.2016.03.022

Suhardono, S., Fitria, L., Suryawan, I., Septiariva, I., Mulyana, R., Sari, M., Ulhasanah, N., & Prayogo, W. (2024). Human activities and forest fires in Indonesia: An analysis of the Bromo incident and implications for conservation tourism. *Trees, Forests and People*, 15, 100509. Advance online publication. DOI: 10.1016/j.tfp.2024.100509

Tang, Y., & Chen, Y. (2017). Protecting the Biodiversity in the Fast Urbanization Age—An Ecotourism Zone in Hainan, China. *Procedia Engineering*, 198, 419–427. DOI: 10.1016/j.proeng.2017.07.097

Tjahyanto, A., & Sisephaputra, B. (2017). The utilization of filter on object-based opinion mining in tourism product reviews. *Procedia Computer Science, 124*, 38-45. Elsevier Science Bv. DOI: 10.1016/j.procs.2017.12.127

Tovar, B., Boto-García, D., & Pino, J. (2024). Meeting externalities: The effects of educational training on support for tourism activities. *Tourism Economics*, 30(3), 785–805. DOI: 10.1177/13548166231185897

Trutescu, M.-N. (2020). Satisfaction of Generations X and Baby Boomers with tourist services in resorts from the Subcarpathians of Oltenia, in line with sustainable tourism destination development. *Balneo Research Journal*, 11(1), 64–73. DOI: 10.12680/balneo.2020.318

Ulyanchenko, O., Borysova, O., Akhmedova, O. O., Sysoieva, S., Sheludko, R. M., Stankevych, S., Kovalova, T., Khalmuradov, B. D., & Kharlamova, Y. Y. (2020). Prospective use of ecological tourism in Ukraine and integrative view of international experience. *Ukrainian Journal of Ecology*, 10(1), 49–54. DOI: 10.15421/2020_8

United Nations World Tourism Organization [UNWTO]. (1998). *Tourism taxation. Striking a fair deal.* World Tourism Organization, Madrid, Spain.

United Nations World Tourism Organization [UNWTO]. (2003). *Sustainable development of tourism: Concepts and definitions*, World Tourism Organization, Madrid, Spain.

Vail, D., & Heldt, T. (2000). Institutional factors influencing the size and structure of tourism: Comparing Dalarma (Sweden) and Maine (USA). *Current Issues in Tourism, 3(4)*, 283–324. *Scopus.* Advance online publication. DOI: 10.1080/13683500008667876

Valdagni, R., Scardino, P. T., & Denis, L. (2009). The 2008 European School of Oncology Inside Track Conference, «Predictive Modeling in Prostate Cancer». *Cancer*, 115(13), 3035–3038. DOI: 10.1002/cncr.24342 PMID: 19544554

Vianna, G., Meekan, M., Pannell, D., Marsh, S., & Meeuwig, J. (2012). Socio-economic value and community benefits from shark-diving tourism in Palau: A sustainable use of reef shark populations. *Biological Conservation*, 145(1), 267–277. DOI: 10.1016/j.biocon.2011.11.022

Vujicic, M. D., Kasim, A., Kostopoulou, S., Chica Olmo, J., & Aslam, M. (Eds.). (2022). *Cultural Sustainable Tourism, CST 2020. Advances in Science, Technology and Innovation*. Springer.

Xu, H., & Lv, Y. (2022). Mining and Application of Tourism Online Review Text Based on Natural Language Processing and Text Classification Technology. *Wireless Communications and Mobile Computing*, 2022(2), 9905114. DOI: 10.1155/2022/9905114

Zemla, S., Zemla, N., & Gelo, F. (2020). FACTORS INFLUENCING TOURISM GROWTH IN CROATIA. Em M. Benazic, S. Buric, L. Tijanic, S. Laporsek, & T. Wolowiec (Eds.), *University of Juraj Dobrila Pula* (WOS:000835726900001; pp. 5–35).

Zhang, J., & Zhang, Y. (2020). Low-carbon tourism system in an urban destination. *Current Issues in Tourism*, 23(13), 1688–1704. DOI: 10.1080/13683500.2019.1641473

Zimmerhackel, J., Kragt, M., Rogers, A., Ali, K., & Meekan, M. (2019). Evidence of increased economic benefits from shark-diving tourism in the Maldives. *Marine Policy*, 100, 21–26. DOI: 10.1016/j.marpol.2018.11.004

KEY TERMS AND DEFINITIONS

Bibliometric Analysis: Bibliometric analysis is a research method used to analyze and quantify the structure, patterns, and trends of academic literature. It involves the use of statistical and mathematical techniques to evaluate various aspects of scholarly publications, such as citation analysis, co-authorship analysis, publication trends and keyword analysis. Bibliometric analysis helps in mapping the development of research fields, evaluating the impact of research, identifying influential researchers or institutions, and guiding future research directions.

Destination Management: Destination management refers to the strategic and operational process of planning, developing, and managing a tourism destination to ensure its long-term sustainability and success. It encompasses a range of activities aimed at enhancing the attractiveness, competitiveness, and functionality of a destination.

Green taxation: Green taxation refers to tax policies designed to encourage environmentally friendly practices and reduce environmental harm. It typically involves levies or incentives related to activities, products, or services that impact the environment, aiming to promote sustainability by internalizing environmental costs.

Sustainability: Concept according to which, for the human being to lead a sustainable life, the current society should be able to satisfy its needs, without compromising the needs of future generations, through the interconnection and balance between the factors: economic, social and environmental.

Sustainable Tourism: Sustainable tourism is a form of tourism that seeks to minimize negative impacts on the environment, society, and economy while maximizing positive benefits for local communities and visitors. It is guided by principles that aim to balance the needs of current and future generations, ensuring that tourism activities are environmentally responsible, culturally respectful, and economically viable. The goal is to promote a tourism industry that preserves natural and cultural resources, supports local economies, and enhances the quality of life for residents while providing meaningful and enjoyable experiences for tourists.

Tourism Destinations: A tourism destination is a specific location or area that attracts visitors and travellers due to its appeal, including cultural, natural, historical, recreational, or leisure attractions. These destinations are often chosen for vacations, holidays, or short trips and typically offer amenities and services tailored to tourists, such as accommodations, restaurants, and entertainment options.

Tourism Taxes: Tourism taxes are levies imposed on travellers and tourists to generate revenue for local governments and support tourism-related infrastructure and services. These taxes can come in various forms, such as: Accommodation Taxes: Charges applied to hotel rooms, vacation rentals, or other lodging options; Tourist Taxes: General taxes imposed on visitors, which might include fees for entering certain attractions or destinations; Sales Taxes: Additional taxes on goods and services purchased by tourists; Excise Taxes: Specific taxes on activities or services commonly used by tourists, such as transportation or entertainment. The revenue from tourism taxes is often used to fund public services that benefit both residents and visitors, such as maintaining public spaces, improving transportation, and supporting local cultural and environmental projects.

Chapter 8
Regulatory Impact Assessment of Tax Policies in the Legislative Procedure of the State Budget:
The Case of the Tax Benefit Granted to "Non-Habitual Residents" in Portugal

Ricardo Sousa da Cunha
https://orcid.org/0000-0003-2786-8195
Polytechnic Institute of Cávado and Ave, Portugal

Sara Luís Dias
Polytechnic Institute of Cávado and Ave, Portugal

ABSTRACT

The quality of the legislation is one of the foundations of the principle of the rule of law and a condition for a more effective implementation. This is even more relevant for tax legislation, one of the birthplaces of modern Constitutions and probably the field of law most directly affecting the daily life of citizens. Assessing the regulatory impact of an important contemporary tax policy in Portugal, such as the taxation of non-habitual residents, reveals the virtues and limitations of this procedure - as recently confirmed by the creation of a governmental technical unit for the evaluation of tax policies (U-TAX) on the back of the conclusions of the Working Group on Tax

DOI: 10.4018/979-8-3693-3908-4.ch008

Benefits. This is part of a methodological exercise that demands the same degree of argumentative "justification" from the legislator as from the judge - Legisprudence. In this paper the possibilities of extending this exercise to the tax policy options that are part of the State Budget are discussed.

1. INTRODUCTION

The quality of the legislation shaped by the *tax policies* that are studied in this book is one of the foundations of the principle of the rule of law and a condition for its more effective enforcement. The implementation of tax policies and legislation is one of the most decisive for the citizens and was the cradle of modern constitutionalism affirmed since the *Boston Tea Party* consecrated the principle "*no taxation without representation*" as one of the fundamental principles of contemporary constitutional law that still grants to parliaments the monopoly over the approval of legislation on taxes in most modern constitutions.

This paper aims to confront the technical evaluation of the impacts generated by tax policies imposed for the adoption of better legislation in tax matters with the legislative procedures currently in place in the Constitution and ordinary legislation, particularly the State Budget. This exercise considers the most recent developments designed both by legal doctrine and legislation for the improvement of the legislative procedures, particularly in tax matters.

The relevance of this exercise was recently confirmed as the Government of Portugal fulfilled a long waited aspiration for the creation of a technical unit for the evaluation of tax and customs policies (U-TAX), by Decree-Law n.º 19/2024, of 2 February. This reform was promoted at the time of the intervention of the Troika (IMF/ EC and ECB) during the crisis of Portuguese sovereign debt of 2011-2014 that led to the adoption of the Report by the Working Group for the study of Tax Benefits. The creation of this administrative body was a campaign promise that found its way into the governmental programme of 2022, but the demands made by the European Commission (EC) of the EU within the framework of the Programme for Recovery and Resilience (PRR) were, certainly, the decisive driving force behind its creation in 2024. This novelty builds on previous work on the regulatory impact assessment of Tax Benefits (*Benefícios Fiscais*) by a working group created by the *Center for Tax and Customs Studies of the Costumes and Tax Authority of the Minister of Finance* (hencerforth also Working Group).

This report had already proposed a set of *guidelines* for the evaluation of Tax Benefits and conducted a particular study on a particular Tax Benefit for companies (the *Sistema de Incentivos Fiscais em Investigação e Desenvolvimento Empresarial (SIFIDE)*). These suggestions, mostly qualitative, are part of the *Regulatory Impact*

Assessment (RIA) as a phase of the legislative procedure regarding Tax Benefits, that this study argues that may be completed with the quantitative analysis allowed by confronting the information produced during the legislative procedure that leads to the approval of the State Budget with that of the Court of Auditors (CoA) in its control. This exercise will be carried out regarding one of the most relevant matters, still under discussion, in the Portuguese tax system – that of the tax benefits regarding the regime of non-habitual residents.

2. THE QUALITY OF LEGISLATION

The challenges raised by the quality of the legislation, as pursued by Legisprudence (WINTGENS, 2007), have given rise to the demand of the same level of argumentative "justification" from the legislator as from the judge, as part of a movement that has found various examples all over the world - from the work on "Better Regulation" by the Organization for the Economic Cooperation and Development (OECD) to the Mandelkern Report in the European Union (EU), where various tools have been developed to improve the exercise of the legislative function, both for States and the EU, directed at ensuring greater transparency and better evidentiary instruction of the legislative procedure, in both instances aimed at guaranteeing greater coherence in the legal system.

In Portugal, the Commission for Legislative Simplification (CSL) was created in 2001, by Resolution of the Council of Ministers no. 29/2001, of March 9, with the aim of participating in the simplification and improvement of the quality of legislation and regulation, guaranteeing the greatest possible access to legislation and deregulation, in order to improve the quality of legislation as far as possible, including alternative forms of self-regulation, in an exercise that has been passed on to the Presidency of the Council of Ministers since it was abolished in 2003. In Brazil, this exercise has even found constitutional acceptance in article 59.º of the Brazilian Federal Constitution, which guarantees the "due legislative process", from which the case law in various corners of the world has even questioned its justiciability.

The legislative procedure now appears to be a circle of legislative procedure - in which the approval of legislation must always be preceded by an *ex ante* Regulatory Impact Assessment (RIA), and its implementation must be accompanied by an *ex post* RIA, which should be considered the basis for any subsequent legislative change. The impacts assessed vary, as do the methods for their assessment. In the *ex ante* regulatory impact assessment, it is particularly important to assess the costs and benefits of the different regulatory scenarios allowed in the regulatory impact assessment phase, while in the *ex post* impact assessment (which can also be the prelude to legislative intervention), the methodologies used are more diverse. The methodologies for assessing the regulatory impact are not provided for in the law - in Portugal, Resolution of the Council of Ministers n.º 74/2018, of June 8, establishes the model for the prior assessment of regulatory impact as definitive the project "Quanto Custa?" ("How much does it cost?"), and in particular for the gender regulatory impact assessment in the legislative procedure of the Assembly of the Republic (AR), in Law n.º 4/2018, of February 9.

2.1 Taking *Legisprudence* seriously

The construction of the conditions for the legislator's deliberation has been built, by scholars as well as in legislation and jurisprudence, at national and supranational level, imposing the "serious" consideration of the legislative process in these different spaces.

"Legisprudence" has endeavoured, based on the thinking of WINTGENS, to construct a "normative theory of legislation" aimed at guaranteeing the possibility of exercising individual freedom based on the promises made by HOBBES and LOCKE's theory of the social contract. The starting point for this exercise is the legitimacy of the limitation of individual freedom, and the limitations of the rational exercise of the legislative function of the state, from which WINTGENS asks the state-legislator the same questions formulated by the science of law from the point of view of the judge: "*In what sense does the legislator have to consider the systematics of the legal order? What is a valid norm? What meanings can be created and how?*" (WINTGENS, 2012: 307). Legisprudence's contribution emphasises the importance of guaranteeing an adequate methodological link between the state's legislative function and the law, by building the conditions that allow for a more perfect fulfilment of the obligations assigned to it constitutionally and systematically in the realisation of the law as a normative order of security and freedom. Improving the quality of legislative intervention is the instrument for building a practical theory of law put at the service of increasing popular recognition of the goodness of the exercise of power, in this case legislative power. These challenges are necessarily interdisciplinary and place the legal system beyond strict positivist legalism, imposing a set of measures prior to the adoption of legislation (*ex ante*) and after its entry into force (*ex post*) to assess the impact of legislation, which extends to the assessment of its jurisprudential and even administrative application, aimed at improving its quality and the recognition of its goodness and quality, conditions for its implementation and respect.

2.2 Renewed practical legislative reasoning

The renewed attention paid to the need to improve legislative procedures in order to increase their quality and the popular recognition of the goodness of this intervention has developed a set of instruments at the service of the legislator in different regulatory spaces.

2.2.1 Supra-national Recommendations

Since the middle of the last decade of the last century, the OECD has developed recommendations and principles for member states with a view to improving the regulatory environment and has produced reports monitoring their implementation by member states. Particularly relevant are Council Recommendations on Improving the Quality of Government Regulation (1995), the OECD Guiding Principles for Regulatory Quality and Performance (2005) and the Council Recommendations on Regulatory Policy and Governance (2012), which recommended the adoption of appropriate measures to fulfil this aim, in particular by promoting Regulatory Impact Assessments (RIAs).

The European Union has also taken on board the need to defend the improvement of the quality of the legislative procedure. At the Lisbon European Council of 2000, the priority of establishing quality legislation for a competitive economy was defined and a High Level Working Group, known as the Mandelkern Group, was set up, which presented a report in 2001 outlining the fundamental principles for improving legislative quality in the European Union and in the Member States. The report announces the importance of adopting quality legislation for a competitive economy, as an end in itself directed at increasing the credibility of the exercise of power and sets out the seven basic principles of legislative intervention: *necessity, proportionality, subsidiarity, transparency, responsibility, accessibility and simplicity*. To develop these principles, the following fundamental instruments are defined: *consultation/participation; impact assessment; simplification programmes and access to legislation - periodic reviews of legislation, consolidation of legislation*. Following this report, the Commission approved the Decision of June 2005 (SEC(2005)790) with the Impact Assessment Guidelines, revised on 15 January 2009 by SEC(2009)92 . This regime was more recently revised by the Working Document "Guidelines on better regulation" (SWD(2017)350) following the Interinstitutional Agreement on Better Lawmaking, concluded between Parliament, the Commission and the Council in 2016, aimed at ensuring the most efficient possible regulation within the EU framework. To this end, since 2012, the EU has established a specific programme - REFIT - which includes a set of initiatives such as a scoreboard and an expert platform[1].

Member states have implemented the OECD and EU recommendations in very different ways. They have followed institutionalised models, creating administrative structures responsible for improving legislative procedures, or non-institutionalised models, in which the fulfilment of these objectives of improving the quality of legislative production is left to each of the ministries proposing the legislation, in particular by filling in checklists to monitor compliance with the principles of quality legislative intervention, for example according to the model set out in the Mandelkern report.

2.2.2 Regulation in Portugal

In Portugal, the Commission for Legislative Simplification (CSL) was created in 2001 by Resolution of the Council of Ministers n.° 29/2001 of 9 March, with the aim of participating in the simplification and improvement of the quality of legislation and regulation, ensuring greater accessibility as possible of the legislation and the deregulation, as far as possible, including alternative forms of self-regulation. This committee ended its mandate with the end of the respective government, and the same objectives were pursued according to the Strategic Programme for the Quality and Efficiency of Government Normative Acts, approved by *Despacho* n.° 12017/2003 of the Minister of the Presidency of the Council of Ministers, of 25 June, in line with the international and European recommendations already in force at the time. With a new change of government, the Better Lawmaking Programme was approved by Council of Ministers Resolution n.° 63/2006, of 18 May, supplemented by Council of Ministers Resolution n.° 64/2006, of 18 May, also as part of the objectives of the SIMPLEX 2006 Programme. This regulatory framework was aimed at improving the quality of the legislation produced by simplifying procedures, the most important of which was the dematerialisation of procedures using new technologies to facilitate the legislative procedure and bring citizens closer together. Some of the most emblematic measures were the dematerialisation of access to the *Diário da República* (Official Gazette), as well as the demand for greater substantiation of the legislative procedure by making it compulsory to fill in checklists, modelled on international and comparative designs, which have since been abandoned. This procedure also led to a more participatory procedure of public and private consultations prior to the government's legislative procedure, with the approval of Decree-Law n.° 274/2009, of 2 October. A new impetus for reform in this area was felt in 2010, with the entry into force of the SIMPLEGIS programme by Council of Ministers Resolution n.° 77/2010, of 11 October, which approved the Rules of Procedure of the Council of Ministers of the 18th Constitutional Government and implemented various measures of the legislative simplification programme (SIMPLEX), aimed at the same objectives of simplifying and improving legislative quality. Among other emblematic measures of this programme, Decree-Law n.º 70/2011 of 16 June, which repealed 233 pieces of legislation, stands out. The Organic Law of the XXII Constitutional Government (Decree-Law n.º 169-B/2019, of 3 December) recently established the legal rules in the Annex, with consequences that should be assessed.

Taking the Legisprudence movement seriously and the role it plays in the legislative procedure implies guaranteeing judicial control of its fulfilment. National constitutional doctrine has treated this issue as one of the Constitution's procedural requirements for the legislative process, which can thus be a source of formal unconstitutionality, reducing the legislative procedure to a matter of the internal regimental procedure of the competent sovereign bodies, which is not susceptible to enhanced legality or unconstitutionality control. The relevance of this issue has, however, been increasingly addressed by comparative doctrine and jurisprudence, and in Portugal it has recently been triggered since the provision of the rules of legistics in an Annex to the Organic Law of the Government (Decree-Law no. 169-B/2019 of 3 December) may give rise to the illegality of their violation.

2.2.3 The experience of CPLP countries

The countries that make up the *Community of Portuguese-Speaking Countries* (CPLP) have joined this global movement to improve the quality of legislation as a condition for its implementation and popular recognition of its legitimacy. The CPLP has even produced a "Manual for Making Laws" (PINHEIRO ET ALL, 2006) as part of this effort. In Cape Verde, the legal rules used in the government's legislative procedure are laid down in Decree-Law n.º 6/2005, of 24 January, while in São Tomé and Príncipe it was decided to establish the rules on the legislative procedure in a parliamentary legislative act, therefore, aiming to bind the whole legislative action of the State by way of Law n.º 9/2008, of 24 September.

This is an interesting choice of legislative policy that guarantees uniformity of state legislative action, subject to the same rules, with clear advantages in terms of uniformity and legal predictability. This is an interesting legislative policy option that guarantees the uniformity of the state's legislative action, subject to the same rules, with clear advantages in terms of uniformity and guarantees of legal predictability. In Angola, Presidential Decree n.º 251/12, of 27 December, seeks to fulfil the same objective of promoting legislative quality, but in the context of a presidential system. In Brazil, the same objective is pursued by Complementary Law n.º 95, of 26 February 1998, amended by Complementary Law n.º 107 of 26 April 2001, and by Decree n.º 4176 of 28 March 2002, which introduces the model of checklists already followed in other legal systems into the Brazilian legislative procedure. These normative instruments are detailed in the Presidency of the Republic's Drafting Manual. In Timor-Leste, this process of reforming the legislative procedure led to the approval in 2019 of Government Resolution 14/2019, of 20 March, on the Legislative Reform Policy, which includes obligations to substantiate the decision to legislate through appropriate Regulatory Impact Studies, also applicable to the economic and financial substantiation of fees, and Government Resolution 21/2019, of 26 June, specifically relating to the rules on Legislation to be carried out in Timor-Leste. This includes rules of formal lawmaking, but also of substantive lawmaking that seek to revalue the moments of normative self-control by the legislator itself in the absence of adequate procedural mechanisms for this purpose.

3. JUDICIAL GUARANTEE OF THE "DUE LEGISLATIVE PROCESS"

The possibility of judicial control of due legislative process has been discussed in different legal systems with different meanings in the development of different constitutional principles, rules and jurisprudential traditions, an expression of the (relative) novelty of this issue, as well as its growing relevance. From the national perspective, the weighting of these different (external) comparative experiences is decisive in the formulation of a "comparative law argument" in its (internal) national reconstruction.

The possibility of constructing a constitutional principle of due legislative process has been discussed in relation to the provision in Article 59 of the Brazilian Federal Constitution of 1998. This provision was put into practice by the ordinary legislator in Complementary Law n.º 95 of 26 February 1998 (LC 95/98), which also leaves it up to the states to approve their own rules. The provisions of Article 18 of this law, which states that "*any formal inaccuracies in a rule drawn up through a regular legislative process shall not constitute a valid excuse for non-compliance*", seem to empty the scope of the constitutional proposition. However, the lack of a constitutional provision on the normative hierarchy between Complementary Laws and Ordinary Laws, or formal hierarchy, considering that the provisions of this Complementary Law are not to be confused with the rules of the legislative process itself may defeat this purpose. The case-law has discussed this issue over the unconstitutionality of Decree n.º 9.759, of 11 April 2019, challenged in ADI 6.121[2], for violating the principle of legal certainty and security, noting that from the Explanatory Memorandum itself "*it was possible to see that it was issued on the basis of a generalising diagnosis, without a minimally attentive examination of the adequacy of the means and ends to be used to achieve the proclaimed rationalisation of the Public Administration*".

The importance of judicial activism is not ignored, even in the Brazilian legislative process. Brazilian constitutional litigation is quite generous in its preventive control of the constitutionality of laws, even recognising parliamentarians as having active procedural legitimacy to file a Ação Direta (equivalente to a "writ of mandamus") against unconstitutional acts of the legislative process (or constitutional amendments), although this does not extend to the substantive control of the constitutionality of these solutions, nor to the control of the violation of procedural rules with merely internal effects.

In Spain, the problem of judicial control of the legislative procedure has been raised with reference to possible unconstitutionality for violation of the principle of legal certainty, defined by STC 248/2007 as "*certainty about the applicable and legally protected legal regulations, seeking clarity and not legal clarity and not normative confusion*". However, on only one occasion, in STC 46/1990, has the Constitutional Court recognised that a defect in legislative technique is sufficient to undermine the constitutional principle of legal certainty and declared it unconstitutional. The Constitutional Court's decision was not based on considerations related to the principle of legal certainty but on other constitutional principles that we must inevitably conclude prevail in the constitutional judge's consideration. The Court has affirmed the constitutional irrelevance of defects in legislative technique, such as linguistic imprecision, omissions, wrong references or even "*cavaliers legislatifs*". In the latter case MARQUEZ speaks out against the Court's position, as well as others in which the issue of legislative technique is dealt with in relation to the principle of sanctioning legality, in budgetary matters, the restriction of Fundamental Rights and the rules of distribution of competences (MARQUEZ, 2010: 24). In a subliminal way, these considerations point to a progressive expansion of the presuppositions of the principle of responsibility in the legislating state, as stated by MARQUEZ (2010: 24) after the decision of the Supreme Court of Justice of the Canary Islands, in Judgment 78/2008 of 7 March 2008, recognised that the approval of the rules implementing the so-called tourist moratorium is a case that generates patrimonial liability insofar as it violates the principle of liability insofar as it violates the principle of legal certainty and legitimate expectations.

The different forms of traditional limitations imposed by the Constitution on the legislature have been affirmed with reference to the substantive guarantee of constitutional provisions in legislation, rather than the guarantee of a fair legislative process, as seen in previous cases. The autonomisation of judicial control of the legislative process has received increasing attention from the courts in various jurisdictions and, in particular, has been raised in the very rich regulatory experience of the European Union, as we have already seen, a forerunner in terms of Better Regulation efforts.

In the United States, since Field v. Clark, 143 U.S. 649, 672 (1892), the "enrolled bill" doctrine has been established in order to effectively isolate the legislative process from judicial control, in terms that doctrine has criticised as "the Court's persistent refusal to adopt judicial review of the legislature's deliberative process" (HAMILTON, 1994: 493). Part of the doctrine has therefore sought to develop the principle of "*due legislative procedure*", which, however, the case law of the *United States Supreme Court* (USSC) has not uniformly accepted in terms that have spread to higher courts in comparison. Despite judicial resistance, there seems to be a growing number of voices proposing to invalidate federal laws on the grounds of violations of due process of law, particularly with regard to the lack of factual justification, the lack of congressional conclusions and the absence of any rational connection between the proposed legislation and the legislative objectives. ROB VAN GESTEL & JURGEN DE POORTER (2016: 155) refer to this substantive criterion in judicial review of the legislative process (with regard to measures adopted by the EU), to the standard set in the *USSC Daubert Case* (Daubert vs. Merrell Dow Pharmaceuticals 509 US 579 (1993)), which governs the admissibility of expert evidence in US federal and state courts according to a reliability test that assesses: (a) falsifiability; (b) peer review and publication; (c) the known or potential rate of error; and (d) the degree of acceptance in the scientific community in a given field (VAN GESTEL & DE POORTER, 2016: 155 et ff.).

The North American tradition is further enriched by the Canadian experience, in which HOULE (2006, p 163-166) points out how publicising evaluation documents through the official press transforms the impact evaluation into a public document whose content serves as an extrinsic argument for the interpretation of regulations. Analysing the use of this document in the Federal Court of Canada between 1988 and 2005, the author identified 128 decisions referring to the regulatory impact analysis document, of which 92 made normative use of this historical legislative material, through which the legislator's reasons influenced decision-making in 72% of the cases. In four cases judged between 1997 and 1999, the Federal Court defined the possibility of using historical legislative material as an aid to judicial interpretation, defining as a requirement only the clarity of the material, as well as that it not be an isolated source of argumentation, that is, its use must be complementary and subsidiary to traditional legal argumentation. The relevance of access to the legislator's preparatory work is found by WALDRON (1992: 30), in the case of *Pepper v. Hart*, in which the House of Lords for the first time used a contribution to interpret the will of the legislator.

The above-mentioned Anglo-Saxon experience, naturally referring to the speciality of judicial precedent in the comparative common law legal system within the framework of the separation of powers as checks and balances, also had a relevant influence in Israel, where the Supreme Court of Justice found new grounds for invalidating a legislative act based on a violation of the rules of the legislative process. The Court ruled here that judicial review of the legislative process is not limited to cases where legislators act illegally but can also include cases of inadequate legislative process when failure constitutes a serious violation of the "fundamental principles of the legislative process".

In this area too, the European Union has been a forerunner, with the *Court of Justice of the EU* (CJEU) monitoring compliance with the provisions of the Treaties on the legislative procedure for protecting proportionality (and subsidiarity) in the cases of Vodafone and Luxembourg v European[3]. The control over proportionality opens the door to new forms of review of normative decisions, especially legislative ones, which VAN GESTEL AND DE POOTER place "*between Scylla and Charybdis*" - if judges defer too much to legislators, they run the risk of selling out or balancing fundamental rights in favour of effective laws and policy formulations, while if courts are too restrictive and refuse to allow political discretion, judges will probably be accused of nullifying democratic decision-making processes, which should be left to the legislative branch (VAN GESTEL & DE POORTER, 2016: 155).

The principle of the separation of powers determines that the legislator enjoys a wide margin of discretion, but that it must be based on objective criteria. In the Vodafone case, the CJEU found that the necessary regulatory impact study had been carried out before the Commission proposed the regulation. In these circumstances, according to the CJEU, a time-limited intervention in a market subject to competition, which makes it possible to protect consumers against excessive prices, is therefore proportionate to the objective pursued, even if it may have negative economic consequences for certain operators. As LENAERTS noted, in this case the CJEU builds a procedural dimension into the principle of proportionality, since it does not carry out a substantive control of the measure sufficing the legislator to show that he has carried out the necessary study of the social, economic and environmental regulatory impact (LENAERTS, 2012: 3 et ff).

4. THE LEGISLATIVE BUDGETARY PROCEDURE IN PORTUGAL

The budgetary process in Portugal seeks to instruct the most relevant instrument of state economic intervention in the most informed way possible. Given its relevance it is enshrined in different legislative levels, from the Constitution to different pieces of legislation – organic and ordinary. The Constitution of the Portuguese Republic (CRP) establishes the general guiding principles regarding the scope and content of the budget and the structure of the respective annual law, the organisation of the budget and the presentation of revenue and expenditure and the definition of the powers of Parliament and the Government in each of the phases of the budget cycle.

In turn, the Budgetary Framework Law (an organic law, with higher hierarchical value than ordinary legislation), in the version of Law n.º 15/2015, of 11 September, promoted a relevant budgetary reform that, among other changes, started the process of programme-based budgeting, focused on achieving results that can be assessed by indicators.

The Budgetary Framework Law approved in 2015 (*Lei de Enquadramento Orçamental*, henceforth LEO) was only fully implemented for the 2021 budget year, based on the new accounting standardisation system for public administrations (SNC-AP), which has been applicable since 1 January 2018. The SNC-AP is the new accounting framework applicable to non-business entities in the central, regional and local administrations, as well as to social security organisations, and regional public entities, covering the budgetary, financial and management accounting subsystems, allowing for the harmonised production of this information by the entire public administration. At the level of the General State Account (GSA), the planned change is profound, since the information reported until now - solely from a cash perspective for central government - will be supplemented with information on the state's assets and liabilities (*Balance Sheet and Profit and Loss Account*) (CoA – PCCE 2017). This information enriches the conduct of fiscal policy at three levels: (i) it reveals the nature and totality of the state's assets and liabilities, (ii) it improves the identification and management of risks to public finances, and (iii) it strengthens the management of fiscal policy (IMF, 2018).

The budgetary process begins with the proposal of a Law on the multi-annual framework for public spending, presented by the Government to the Parliament at the start of the parliamentary term, in accordance with the Broad Options Law (*Grandes Opções do Plano*), approved under article 34.º of the LEO, which must be presented and debated at the same time as the first proposal for the State Budget Law, under article 39.º of LEO, and, in subsequent years, presented by the government to Parliament by 15 April and to the European Commission by 30 April, in the annual review of the Stability Programme. The draft State Budget Law, presented annually to Parliament by 10 October, may include, in line with the objectives set out in the Stability Programme, an update of the MTEF for the following four years.

In the preparatory work phase, the Directorate-General for the Budget (DGO) defines the rules that guide the preparation of the draft budget by each of the entities listed in the Circular for the Preparation of the State Budget. The DGO, together with "*eSPap - Entidade de Serviços Partilhados da Administração Pública, I.P.*", prepares the information system that supports the uploading of draft budgets by Central Administration entities, building the basic structure (classifiers) that supports the uploading of budget lines. According to the approved timetable, central government entities have a period (usually two to three weeks) to submit their draft budget, as well as all the elements that must accompany it (as previously stipulated in the

Circular on the Preparation of the State Budget), to the State Budget System (SOE) or via the DGO's website. At the end of this period, the DGO draws up preliminary reports by budget programme on the entities' budget proposals, and draws up the estimated general government account for the current year and a forecast for the year to which the SB relates, both in Public Accounting (i.e. from a cash perspective, of receipts and payments) and in National Accounting (accrual accounting, according to the European System of National and Regional Accounts 2010 - ESA 2010).

Also at this stage, decisions are taken on the use of budget appropriations, which can be used during budget execution with the authorisation of the Minister of Finance.

Once approved by the Council of Ministers, the Draft State Budget Law is sent to Parliament (and to the European Commission), comprising the articles of the Draft Law, the maps that make up the Draft Law, the information and budgetary developments produced by the DGO on the basis of the records in the information system that supports the preparation of the State Budget, and specific contributions from other entities, and also, the Report that accompanies the Draft State Budget, drawn up on the basis of contributions from various entities within the Ministry of Finance, the entities that coordinate the budgetary programmes and other entities.

The discussion of the draft State Budget Law lasts a maximum of 50 days, in general and in specialised form, under the terms of the article 38.º of the LEO. In the specialised discussion, the accounting statements that make up the State Budget Law are voted on individually, as well as each of the articles in the draft law, with the parliamentary groups being able to propose amendments, which may include new expenditure appropriations or revenue forecasts or changes to them – these proposals are also subject to individualised voting. The discussion is monitored in the Portuguese Parliament (AR) by the Technical Unit for Budgetary Evaluation (UTAO), a technical unit that is part of the Parliament and it is supervised by the Public Finance Council, a technical independent body, previously, concurrently and *ex post*.

The entities involved in drafting the bill monitor the discussion and voting process, including the DGO and those in charge of Tax and Customs, in order to assess the impact of the proposals drawn up by MPs and keep the government informed. After final approval, the approved amendments are incorporated into the State Budget proposal, and the DGO updates the information system that supports the preparation of the State Budget, in order to produce the inherent quantitative elements, of which the accounting maps ('Maps of the Law') stand out, which are delivered to the Assembly of the Republic for the preparation of the final version of the State Budget Law.

Finally, the Assembly of the Republic Decree approving the State Budget is sent to the President of the Republic for (eventual) promulgation as the State Budget Law, which is also an instance of political and constitutional control over the legislative functions of the State Budget. The political veto of the President, under the number 1 of article 136.º of the Constitution, expresses the non-opposition to the measures adopted, whereas the political veto expresses its disapproval. The presidential veto is mandatory after a previous pronunciation by the constitutional court on the unconstitutionality of the Decree that approves the State Budget, under the same constitutional regime. Both the political and the constitutional veto may be overcome by the AR, under number 2 of article 136.º of the Constitution, but in the latter case a subsequent decision of the Constitutional Court in the same sense for the unconstitutionality of the State Budget would render it legally inapplicable.

The judicial control over the State Budget is ensured by the *Tribunal de Contas* (*Court of Auditors*, CoA), a judicial independent organ constitutionally part of the judiciary, and takes effect during its execucion as well as in issuing the *Opinion on the Final State Account* (Parecer à Conta Geral do Estado, PCGE), which is finally approved by Parliament.

The recent creation of the U-TAX is a relevant step in the technical evaluation of the impact of tax policies as part of the legislative procedure. Despite the fact that this is not part of the legislative process leading to the adoption of the State Budget, its intervention *ex ante*, as well as *ex post*, will generate important information for the evaluation of the legislation expression decisions on tax policies. However, this administrative unit was integrated within the Tax and Customs Administration, under the direction of the Government and the Ministry of Finances, which, on the one hand, facilitates its political and administrative control, which also means access to information, but, on the other hand, may compromise the independence of its work.

5. THE CASE OF TAXATION OF NON-HABITUAL RESIDENTS IN PORTUGAL

An exercise in assessing the regulatory impact of an important contemporary tax policy in Portugal, such as the *taxation of non-habitual residents*, reveals the virtues and limitations of this procedure.

The legal and tax regime of "non-habitual residents" was created by Decree-Law n.º 249/2009, of 23 September[4], an operates by the application of preferential rates to foreigners who choose to move their fiscal residency to Portugal. This was one of the most relevant legal regimes of the Portuguese Tax System to acquire revenues, competing with other tax systems.

It was created to attract non-resident professionals qualified in high value-added activities and beneficiaries of pensions obtained abroad to Portugal. These beneficiaries paid less taxes, but they expend their income in Portugal, stimulating the economy and investment. In the words of CASALTA NABAIS (2021: 520), attracting these non-residents "will bring significant benefits to the national economy and, consequently, important tax revenues that would otherwise be impossible to obtain".

This regime was set out in paragraphs 8 to 12 of article 16 of the CIRS, which considers non-habitual residents to be taxpayers those that, having become resident in Portugal for tax purposes in a given year, have not been resident in Portuguese territory in any of the previous five years. Under the terms of Article 16(9) of the CIRS, a non-habitual resident acquired the right to be taxed as such for a period of 10 consecutive years from and including the year of their registration as a resident in Portuguese territory. In order to benefit from this regime, the non-habitual resident must carry out a professional activity considered to have "high added value" (in accordance with Ordinance no. 12/2010, of January 7, amended by Ordinance no. 230/2019, of July 23rd) or be a pensioner.

The regime provided for taxation of income from categories A and B at a rate of 20% (Article 72(10) of the CIRS) and an exemption for income from external sources. Initially, it was stablished the total exemption from taxation of certain pensions, but it was replaced by a minimum tax of 10%, as provided for in Article 72(12) of the CIRS - an amendment introduced by Law 2/2020, of March 31, which approved the State Budget for 2020. This change followed the criticism made by the authorities of countries such as Sweden and Finland, which have already unilaterally denounced the agreements to avid double taxation - notice n.º 146/2018, of 20 December and notice n.º 2/2022, of 01 February, and France.

In 2022, this benefit was calculated based on 29426 declarations, out of a total of 33010 declarations submitted. In this year, more than 70.000,00 citizens benefited from this special regime[5].

5.1 The Opinion of the Court of Auditors (CoA)

The Court of Auditors' opinion on the execution of the State Budget of 2022 (*PCGE*, the last one available at the moment this paper is being written[6]) identified as "fiscal expenditure" the loss of tax revenue charged to "non-habitual residents". In 2022, this "fiscal expenditure" amounted to €1,360 M, an increase of 41.8% compared to the forecast of €949 M in Chart 10 of the 2022 State Budget, which constitutes 67.2% of IRS tax expenditure and the second highest in 2022 (only surpassed by VAT). Compared to the 2021 tax year, this tax expenditure increased by 401 M€ (41.8%), reflecting the increase in the number of non-habitual residents. The fiscal expenditure of this benefit has increased significantly since 2017: in 2017 it increased by 257 M€ (145.8%), in 2018, €115 million (26.6%), in 2019, €72 million

(13.1%), in 2020, €273 million (44.0%) and in 2021 there was an increase of 67 M€ (7.5%) (CoA, PCGE, 2022: 191).

The Court of Auditors refers that the fiscal revenues from the special regime of "non-habitual residents" to the concept of "fiscal expenditure", which is calculated by using the "resettlement" method (cf. point 5.3.1 of the CoA, PCGE 2018), considering the difference between the amount of taxes paid and the amount that would be paid if these taxpayers were residents without benefit from the regime - which results in the application of the methodology of calculation of fiscal expenditure applied to residents.

The high amounts of such income imply significant amounts of "fiscal expenditure", which, however, do not correspond to an actual loss of revenue for the State. Therefore, following the methodology of the Court of Auditors, the qualification of the tax revenues from "non-habitual residents" as a "fiscal expenditure" is naturally doubtful, considering that much of these is revenue that, were it not for this special legal regime, would not be at all acquired. It is not easy to assess how many of the "non-habitual residents" would establish in Portugal, were it not for this special legal regime of taxation, but the conclusion is obvious.

Since this regime implies a reduction in the tax rate for these taxpayers, the proper legal qualification of this reduced revenue is a tax benefit. According to Article 2 of the Tax Benefits Statute (EBF), the creation of these benefits is justified when the aim is to protect "extra-tax" interests that are more relevant than those of taxation itself. In this case, we can consider that the attraction of foreign investment fits in here. In accordance with Article 2(3) of EBF "tax benefits are considered tax expenditures, which may be provided for in the State Budget or in an annexed document".

The Report of the State Budget for the year 2024, of 16 October 2023[7], highlights the weight of "economic issues" in the global expenses of IRS, justifying this high percentage and the increase of it with the application of the regime for non-habitual residents (inserted here). It represents around 75% of the global expenses in IRS and it was increased between 2022 and 2024 (DGO, 2023: 136). This highlights the "preferential rates" in overall IRS tax expenditure (...) also justifying this figure with the net income earned from high value-added activities by non-habitual residents in Portuguese territory (DGO, 2023: 136).

5.2 The proposals of the Working Group on Tax Benefits

The methodology proposed by the Report of the Working Group for the study of Tax Benefits (WORKING GROUP, 2019: 33 e ff)[8] for the regulatory impact assessment of Tax Benefit also includes two moments: *ex ante*, before its adoption, and *ex post*, after its implementation, in a *cycle of evaluation*, as referred, since the latter evaluation is the condition for any policy or legal changes. This evaluation *ex post* may, therefore, also include two moments: monitoring as a permanent and systematic evaluation of certain *Key Performance Indicators* (KPIs) and the more traditional one-time ex post evaluation. The methodology proposed for the *ex ante* assessment follows the model of checklists based on scripted questions to ensure that the measure is SMART (*Specific, Measurable, Achievable, Relevant e Time-bound*) (WORKING GROUP, 2019: 37). The same methodology is proposed for the *ex post* phases of assessment, monitoring and evaluation.

Finally, the information gathered must be more relevant for Tax Benefits that are fiscally more relevant, where stricter KPIs must be defined, and measured in different years – the period measured is decisive and, depending on the purpose of the evaluation, may include periods prior and after the introduction or major changes in the tax benefits to measure its impact (WORKING GROUP, 2019: 39).

The relevance of the adequate instruction of the legislative proceedings leading up to the adoption of the State Budget has also been discussed (WORKING GROUP, 2019: 55 et ff), particularly with reference to the need to adequately meet the principle of specification (article 17.º LEO). The referred critical consideration of the Tax Benefit as a reduction of revenue has the biased effect, even political, when some, like those unsusceptible of reimbursement, are treated as expenses. Besides, the fact that the Tax Benefits are treated in terms of "cash based accounting" whereas the revenue maps use and economic global criteria that does not allow for an adequate consideration – the use of both "cash based" and economic accounting criteria for the maps referring to Tax Benefits would have an important effect on the transparency of the information used in the probatory instruction of the legislative process leading to the adoption of the State Budget. The development of the best possible solutions for the adequate reasoning behind the legal regime of Tax Benefits is one of the relevant issues of contemporary multidisciplinary studies on Public Finance, one that involves legal studies, economic and accounting, among others.

5.3 Some methodological proposals

The limitations faced in the exercise of regulatory impact assessment of the Tax Benefits is mostly felt in the lack of adequate data to fulfil the methodological proposals made here. If the economic and financial data is more easily available, namely in the reports of the Court of Auditors over the State Budget, the predictions made in the State Budget may always be biased and its correct use is always mandatory (WORKING GROUP, 2019: 60). Similar criticism regarding the lack of independence of the information generated may be extended to the organic arrangement adopted for the new U-TAX in terms that had already be announced (WORKING GROUP, 2019:47).

The use of the quantitative data of the legislative process for adopting the State Budget, as well as the Final Reports, is a more reliable tool than the qualitative methodologies proposed by the Working Group, but these also never paint the full picture. On the one hand, the methodologies followed by the Court of Auditors are also arguable, as was the case of treatment of the Tax Benefit as a tax expenditure. On the other hand, the analysis of the regime of non-habitual residents reveals the difficulties in assessing social-economic impacts, which are always more difficult to measure.

The analysis of the UTAO is mainly directed at the consequences for the overall financial sustainability of the State Budget, each year.

Besides, the use of these qualitative tools may also prove more difficult the assessment of other social-economic consequences of the creation and application of this regime, as is easily admitted by the same report (CoA, PCGE2023). The system proposed by the Working Group on Tax Benefits is methodological interesting but appears to be limited in the information gathered and outdated in the choice of *checklists* to be filled during the legislative procedure – a technique that was already abandoned in Portugal. It is noteworthy that the methodologies proposed by the Working Group to the Government were not followed in present case where a Tax Benefit was, precisely, revoked.

The fact is, in both cases, that little information is available, so it must be sought from various sources, and it is easy to see the social cost caused, for example, in the housing market, one of the reasons given publicly for the proposal to change the tax regime applicable to non-habitual residents. Particularly, it is important to detect and control cases of misuse of this regime, such as situations where taxpayers are registered in the regime, declaring that they have a tax residence in Portugal (i.e. those who, under the terms of article 16 of the Personal Tax Code, have stayed for more than 183 days, consecutive or interpolated, in any 12-month period beginning or ending in the year in question and the persons who, having stayed for less time, have a dwelling here on any day of the period referred to in the previous paragraph, in conditions that suggest a current intention to maintain and occupy it as a habitual residence) but are not actually here, indicating only an address for this purpose. This realization opens up the prospects, particularly, for academic research.

All these difficulties are compounded by various factors.

The outdated classification of tax benefits, which considers increasingly high values in a residual item of "other economic affairs" (which, according to the same report, corresponds to 82.5 per cent of total tax expenditure), reducing the usefulness of this classification.

Finally, the same report by the Court of Auditors organically points to the need to set up the Technical Unit that was planned since 2020 to carry out this evaluation, among other objectives, but which was only implemented in 2024 and, therefore has no available data yet.

The fact is that the actual assessment of the impacts is not always possible. The data may simply not be available as is the present example. In any case, the purpose of the RIA is to give the legislator more information in the moment of the decision and the identification of the impacts is, in any event, a useful tool for a better decision-making process of the legislator.

6. FURTHER RESEARCH

Despite the fact that the methodologies discussed here for the adequate instruction of State Budget in matters regrading Tax Benefits were not applied in the recent reform of the regime of "non-habitual residents", and much of the qualitative research is no longer possible, the consideration of the *quantitative* results in terms of revenues and respective loss can be measured at the end of the present fiscal exercise of 2024. For the purposes pursued by the qualitative regulatory impact assessment, the tools designed by the Working Group, that were not followed *ex ante* in the revocation of the tax benefits offered to the non-habitual residents, may be used in the *ex post* evaluation of this policy and legislative decision.

The tax regime for non-habitual residents was revoked by the Law n.º 82/2023 of 29 December, but it was replaced by the so-called "tax incentive for scientific research and innovation", which is now provided for in the Statute of Tax Benefits (EBF), in the recently added article 58.º-A. There is a transitional provision provided by Article 236(3) of the aforementioned law states that the tax regime for non-habitual residents is maintained to taxpayers who, on the date of entry into force of this law, are already registered as non-habitual residents public register of taxpayers, for as long as the period referred to in period referred to in paragraphs 9 to 12 of article 16 of the IRS Code (10 years); Taxpayers who on December 31, 2023 met the conditions for registration as non-habitual residents; Taxpayers who become resident for tax purposes by December 31, 2024 and who declare, for the purposes of their registration as a non-habitual resident, that they have specific documents provided for therein. About this new regime, the Portuguese Tax Authorities has already published the Circular n.º 90068/2024.

This new tax incentive, applicable to professors, directors, managers related with scientific investigation, technologies and innovation areas aims to attract highly qualified professionals who contribute to the development of scientific and industrial research in Portugal. Therefore, this new regime does not substitute the previous one and it aims to pursue different objectives. it is therefore important to verify, in the future, the impact of this new regime both as a mechanism to attract investment in these specific areas and to understand the financial impact on our economy, especially with regard to the loss of tax revenue with the reduction of taxes for these professionals. A comparison of the results (in terms of revenue, but also considering different socio-economic impacts) of the two different legal regimes would allow to understand the impact of the legislative change produced in 2024 – the quantitative as well as the qualitative tolls discussed here would be able to furnish further information in the assessment of the regulatory impact of the change in the legal regime presented.

Further research would also be interestingly carried out on the consequences granted for the results of the regulatory impact assessment here made. Besides the obvious academic interest here shown, the possibility of political consequences arising from this exercise is clearly present – hence the specific needs for independence referred. This discussion would also involve the possible legal consequences, namely the different types of responsibility (civil, disciplinary and even criminal) available to ensure the accountability of the competent organs. As referred, legal scholars and case-law have been discussing the possible consequences for the legal acts that result from poorly instructed proceedings in terms of regulatory impact assessment, namely the possible unconstitutionality of the legislation hence approved, which judicial control has been referred. Following the development in scholarly work as well as in the comparative case-law is an important exercise for the development of the studies in this area.

7. CONCLUDING REMARKS

The relevance of assessing the regulatory impact of legislative change over the Tax Benefits granted to *non-habitual residents*, in Portugal, reveals the growing importance of carrying to the legislative procedure as much information as possible, in order to ensure the best possible decision. The possibilities of this procedure have been explored by scholars and governments alike – in Portugal, a Working Group created by the Ministry of Finance to study the impact of Tax Benefits, more recently, led to the creation of a governmental technical unit for the evaluation of *all* tax policies (U-TAX).

This would traditionally be considered a policy issue, but as the quality of the normative production is more and more regarded as a condition for popular recognition of the legitimacy of the legislative action of any State and also a condition for a more effective implementation of the legislation approved, these obligations find legal and constitutional place, at the domestic but also supra-national level. In terms of legal methodology, it is growingly accepted the demand of a higher level of argumentative "justification" from the legislator - at least the *same* as that made to the judges - these are the challenges pursued by *Legisprudence*. This movement has been found in various examples all over the world, from the OECD's work on "Better Regulation" to the Mandelkern Report in the European Union, where various tools have been developed to improve the exercise of the legislative function, both for States and the EU, directed at ensuring greater transparency and better evidentiary instruction of the legislative procedure, aimed at guaranteeing greater coherence in the legal system.

The example of the special fiscal regime of "non-habitual residents" shows the hardships faced in the exercise of regulatory impact assessment of tax policies and legislation. Nevertheless, given its relevance, political and monetary, of the revenues of the, it is fundamental to adequately assess the impacts (economic, social and other) of such legal regime (and the underlying policy options). The Portuguese Court of Auditors, specifically, pointed out that *"it is essential that tax expenditure be fully calculated so that the timeliness and effectiveness of the benefits can be assessed, by comparing their cost with the extra-fiscal objectives they aim to achieve*" (CoA, PGCE, 2022: VI). In this exercise, the combined use of qualitative and quantitative methodologies may prove necessary, both for academic studies as for those of the U-TAX. These are the conclusions of the limitations presented by the single use of each of the methodologies, as revealed by the Report of the Working Group on the evaluation of Tax Benefits and the comparison of the predictions made in the legislative process of the State Budget and its Reports, namely those of the Court of Auditors. The lack of information to "feed" the discussion over the impact of tax policies and legislation is another of the limitations found and, for this reason, on the one hand, the need arises for the development of more information, particularly by the competent authorities, which present limitations, on the other hand, it shows that in some cases, the simple identification of possible socio-economic and financial impacts may prove an improvement in the quality of the argumentation necessary for the adequate reasoning of the legislative and policy decisions made.

Considering that many of the obligations placed on the argumentative reasoning of the legislator are now found in legal and constitutional norms, this exercise opens up legal argumentation, particularly that which is involved in the legislative procedures, to the interdisciplinary suggestions of different disciplines – here the relevance of social-economic data was found decisive for policy decisions that are part of the legislative procedure of the State Budget. Among the suggestions for further research, two issues clearly remain at hand to be discussed by scholars and jurisprudence – the improvement of the methodologies proposed, which are in most case to be applied by lawyers with little training on the matter, as do the full legal consequences of this exercise, which may determine the invalidity of certain legal acts. The opportunities for this research abound since new legal regimes are everyday open to evaluation.

REFERENCES

Alemanno, A. (2011), 'A Meeting of Minds on Impact Assessment: When Ex Ante Evaluation Meets Ex Post Judicial Control', 17 European Public Law.

da Cunha, R. S. (2018). A Legisprudência na Construção de Uma Teoria Normativa da Legislação em Timor-Leste.

DGO. (2023) Report state budget for 2024 of 16 october 2023 available at https://www.dgo.gov.pt/politicaorcamental/OrcamentodeEstado/2024/Proposta%20do%20Or%C3%A7amento/Documentos%20do%20OE/OE2024_doc16_Relatorio.pdf (05/09/2024)

Hamilton, M. A. (1994). Discussion and decisions: A proposal to replace the myth of self-rule with an attorneyship model of representation. *NYUL Rev.*, 69, 477.

Houle, F. (2006). Regulatory history material as an extrinsic aid to interpretation: An empirical study on the use of RIAs by the Federal Court of Canada. Canadian journal of administrative law and practice, 19, 151-189.

IMF (2018), 'Managing Public Wealth' Fiscal Monitor, October 2018 Mandelkern Report on the Improvement of Legislative Quality – published in Lisboa, Ministério da Reforma do Estado e da Administração Pública, volume 1, March 2002 [also in Legislação. Cadernos de Ciência de Legislação, 29, Oct.-Dez. 2000}

Lenaerts, K. (2012), 'The European Court of Justice and Process-Oriented Review', Yearbook of European Law, pages 3–16. DOI: 10.1093/yel/yes009

Nabais, J. C. (2021). *Direito Fiscal*. Almedina.PINHEIRO. Alexandre Sousa; LOURENÇO, Paula Meira (2006) Manual de Feitura das Leis, CPLP, Lisboa.

OECD Guiding Principles for Regulatory Quality and Performance. (2005), available at em https://www.oecd.org/fr/reformereg/34976533.pdf (05/09/2024)

OECD Recommendations of the Council for Regulatory Policy and Governance. (2012) available at https://www.oecd.org/gov/regulatory-policy/49990817.pdf (05/09/2024)

Pereira, E. (2024), "Incentivo Fiscal à Investigação Científica e Inovação". *In Vida Económica*, pages 21 et ff., available at https://www.occ.pt/sites/default/files/public/2024-02/109744423.pdf

REPORTS. CoA (2022) Parecer sobre a Conta Geral do Estado 2022, available at https://www.tcontas.pt/pt-pt/ProdutosTC/PareceresTribunalContas/ParecerCGE/Documents/2022/pcge2022.pdf (05/09/2024)

Van Gestel, R., & De Poorter, J. (2016). Putting evidence-based law making to the test: Judicial review of legislative rationality. *The Theory and Practice of Legislation*, 4(2), 155–185.

Vázquez, F. M. (2011). Técnica Legislativa y seguridad jurídica:¿ Hacia el control constitucional de la calidad de las Leyes? *Teoría y Realidad Constitucional*, (28), 681.

Waldron, J. (2003). *A dignidade da legislação*. Trad. Luís Carlos Borges. São Paulo: Martins Fontes, 2003.

Wintgens, L. J. (2016). Legitimacy and legitimation from the legisprudential perspective. In *Legislation in context: Essays in legisprudence* (pp. 17–68). Routledge.

Working Group. (2019) Grupo de Trabalho para o Estudo dos Benefícios Fiscais, os Benefícios Fiscais em Portugal, Available at https://www.portugal.gov.pt/pt/gc21/comunicacao/documento?i=estudo-dos-beneficios-fiscais-em-portugal (27/06/2024)

KEY TERMS AND DEFINITIONS

Legislation: The action of legislating; specifically, the exercise of the power and function of making rules (such as laws) that have the force of authority.

Legislative Procedure: Legislative procedure is usually defined as a series of actions by means of which laws are considered and adopted.

Public Policies: Public policy is the framework of laws, regulations, and actions governments implement to achieve social and economic goals.

Regulatory Impact Assessment: A regulatory impact analysis or regulatory impact assessment (RIA) is a document created before a new government regulation is introduced.

State Budget: The state budget lists the revenues and expenditures of the Government in a particular year.

Tax Policies: All the decisions and main directions that determine the characteristics of a tax system and make it possible to finance public spending and support economic activity.

Taxation: Taxation refers to the practice of a government collecting money from its citizens to pay for public services.

ENDNOTES

1 *OECD Guiding Principles for Regulatory Quality and Performance (2005)*, available at em https://www.oecd.org/fr/reformereg/34976533.pdf. *Recommendations of the Council for Regulatory Policy and Governance (2012)* available at https://www.oecd.org/gov/regulatory-policy/49990817.pdf, completed by a Toolbox available at https://ec.europa.eu/info/sites/info/files/better-regulation-toolbox_2.pdf. Decision of 2005 (SEC(2005)790) with the *Impact Assessment Guidelines*, https://ec.europa.eu/agriculture/sites/agriculture/files/sfs/documents/documents/sec2005-791_en.pdf, reviewed on 15 January 2009 by SEC(2009)92 in https://ec.europa.eu/smart-regulation/impact/commission_guidelines/docs/iag_2009_en.pdf The REFIT – which includes a set of initiatives such as a scoreboard and an expert platform. More information available at https://ec.europa.eu/info/law/law-making-process/evaluating-and-improving-existing-laws/refit-making-eu-law-simpler-and-less-costly_enhttps://observador.pt/2023/10/03/numero-de-residentes-nao-habituais-com-direito-a-beneficio-fiscal-disparou-em-2022-costa-anunciou-travao-para-2024/ (05/09/2024).

2 Available in https://portal.stf.jus.br/processos/detalhe.asp?incidente=5678906 (03/07/2024).

3 Case n.º C-58/08, Vodafone Ltd and Others v Secretary of State for Business, Enterprise and Regulatory Reform e no [2010] ECR I-4999; and Case n.º C176/09, Luxembourg v European Parliament/Commission [2011] ECR I-0000. About this consult A. ALEMANNO (2011), 'A Meeting of Minds on Impact Assessment: When Ex Ante Evaluation Meets Ex Post Judicial Control', 17 European Public Law).

4 This law was later revoked by Decree-Law no. 162/2014, of October 31, which approved a new Investment Tax Code.

5 See https://observador.pt/2023/10/03/numero-de-residentes-nao-habituais-com-direito-a-beneficio-fiscal-disparou-em-2022-costa-anunciou-travao-para-2024/ (05/09/2024).

6 Available at https://www.tcontas.pt/pt-pt/ProdutosTC/PareceresTribunalContas/ParecerCGE/Documents/2022/pcge2022.pdf (05/09/2024).

7 Available at https://www.dgo.gov.pt/politicaorcamental/OrcamentodeEstado/2024/Proposta%20do%20Or%C3%A7amento/Documentos%20do%20OE/OE2024_doc16_Relatorio.pdf (05/09/2024)

8 Available at https://www.portugal.gov.pt/pt/gc21/comunicacao/documento?i=estudo-dos-beneficios-fiscais-em-portugal

Chapter 9
Significance of Tax Reforms as a Solution of Economic Problems

Saurabh Chandra
https://orcid.org/0000-0003-4172-9968
Bennett University, India

Bhumika Muchan
https://orcid.org/0009-0003-5294-998X
Independent Researcher, India

ABSTRACT

The latest changes to India's taxes have had an impact on recent economic development and growth. To really understand what those changes meant, it's necessary to grasp a thorough understanding of them—something this qualitative study seeks to attain in order to evaluate the GST and corporate tax rate revisions comprehensively. The research investigates how the changes may affect key sectors like agriculture, industry, services, and international trade—that is, any ramifications they may have on fostered economic expansion via these sectors. Using current literature, the study considers how the changes might affect investment patterns, company performance, and income distribution; it also takes a look at the potential opportunities and challenges associated with implementing tax reform—including compliance issues and administrative capacity. It concludes that the tax system in India remains a substantial impediment to improvement, despite eight years of reforms.

DOI: 10.4018/979-8-3693-3908-4.ch009

INTRODUCTION

The primary source of funding for economic expansion is the government's take, via direct and indirect taxes. When it comes to finding ways to generate adequate funds, our federal and state governments are always looking for new and innovative ideas. Why? Because despite budget cuts and efficient management of the nations' stabilization funds, both the federal center and the states themselves are feeling the pressure of expanding demands on their fiscal resources. There are two sides to every tax issue; therefore, the government's decision to provide tax relief to the general public negatively impacted its finances (Acharya, S. 2005).

Since gaining independence, India's economy has grown at a steady rate. Tax policies have had a role in shaping this growth trajectory, since they significantly affect a country's economic development. Encouraging entrepreneurial activity, motivating people to pay their taxes on time, and attracting foreign investment all depend on having a tax policy that is open, progressive, and business-friendly. A tax-friendly environment is crucial for the creation of new employment since it encourages enterprise and entrepreneurship. For a nation like India to foster job possibilities, its economy has to grow at a certain pace. In order to achieve these growth objectives, it is crucial to enact a tax reform that is attractive and helpful. In an effort to encourage entrepreneurship on a national level, the government of India has launched a new program called Make in India (Bhalla, S. 2005).

To improve the tax code's utility and user-friendliness for taxpayers, both the federal government and state governments have started implementing changes at different stages. The reason for this is that taxes make up a large amount of the government's revenue and that taxing a variety of products and services is a divisive issue (Moore, M.,2007). For this reason, the government has formed many committees tasked with changing the current tax system. These panels considered the constantly evolving standards set by the government and by corporations. As per the study, under a federal fiscal system, the function of central and sub-central governments will need to undergo a major transition (Bagchi, A. 2003). In a period of growing globalization, a significant change in the kind and standard of government involvement is necessary to ensure market-oriented economic development.

BACKGROUND OF THE STUDY

Taxes are essential to the operation of contemporary economies as they furnish governments with the necessary funds to finance social welfare programmes, public products and services, and infrastructure projects. India's economic growth, similar to that of numerous other nations, has been substantially impacted by the progression of tax administration and policy. The complex Indian tax system that persisted following the establishment of British colonial rule was the result of numerous inequities and ineffectiveness. Over the course of history, numerous administrations have implemented diverse tax reforms in an effort to increase compliance, streamline the tax code, and broaden the revenue base. The aforementioned modifications have had an impact on both direct and indirect taxes, thereby illustrating the intricate and diverse nature of the tax system in India.

India has enacted adjustments to its direct taxation framework, encompassing corporation tax and income tax, alongside modifications to its indirect tax system, exemplified by GST. The primary objectives of these measures have been to optimize tax rates, reduce compliance burdens, and enhance revenue collection. Furthermore, endeavors have been made to transform tax administration through the implementation of technological innovations and the improvement of services provided to taxpayers (Krishnaswamy, H. 2021).

Sustained implementation of tax reforms is imperative due to the dynamic nature of India's economy and its integration into the global market. The primary objective here is to augment understanding of the Indian tax system through the analysis of trends in direct tax revenues, assessment of the efficacy of tax administration, and development of policy recommendations to facilitate future advancements. To support the nation's economic growth objectives and ensure a fair and efficient tax system for all stakeholders, the purpose hereby is to identify areas of India's tax system that require modification and to trace its historical development (Rao, M. G., & Rao, R. K. 2010).

The liberalization movement has relied heavily on indirect tax changes since 1991. In the first stage, India has achieved consistent progress towards a simple, reasonable, easy-to-manage, and plain tax structure. On a national scale, there have been initiatives to reduce taxes (including customs and excise fees), streamline the system, eliminate red tape, and cut down on interactions with the government. A substantial amount of state income comes from indirect taxes that the states are authorized to collect on top of what the federal government charges.

Given the wide variety of tax systems, our attention has been narrowed to direct taxes, particularly those pertaining to tax administration. Additionally, tax policy reforms are not the primary emphasis of the research, which is centered on direct tax administration.

LITERATURE REVIEW

Tax Structure and Economic Growth

The tax policy and tax administration of a nation are crucial for achieving social and economic goals (Vaid, 1972). In developing countries, tax administration plays a key role in shaping tax policy and can significantly impact fiscal deficits and tax burdens (Mansfield, 1987). In Asia, the shift from customs tariff revenues to value-added tax and the need for improved tax administration have been highlighted (Martínez-Vázquez, 2011). In the US, tax policy has been a tool for economic and social change, with a complex and often contentious history (Steuerle, 2004).

The Indian tax structure is a crucial tool for economic development, with income tax serving as a key revenue source and a means of reducing economic disparity (Alagappan, 2019). However, the system is complex and in need of reform to address issues such as tax evasion and the existence of a parallel economy (Das, 2020). The tax-GDP ratio is low due to the untaxed agricultural sector and the under-taxed service sector (Purohit, 2014). Despite these challenges, the Indian government has made significant strides in tax collection, particularly in direct taxes (Bholane, 2020). The introduction of the Direct Tax Code and Goods and Services Tax is expected to further improve the tax structure and administration (Purohit, 2014).

The Indian tax system has a significant impact on economic growth, with various components of direct and indirect taxes playing different roles. Poirson (2006) highlights the high dependence on indirect taxes, low average effective tax rates, and high marginal effective tax rates, which can distort investment and financing decisions. Venkataraman (2017) further dissects the impact of specific tax components, finding that corporate income tax and customs duty have a positive effect on economic growth. Neog (2020) adds to this by identifying a 'U' shape relationship between tax structure and growth performance, with property and capital transaction taxes having a positive impact. Mishra (2011) underscores the importance of a well-designed and efficient tax system in achieving higher economic growth.

The Indian tax system has undergone significant changes over the years, influenced by different governance regimes (Kapoor, 2023). While tax liberalization has been found to promote economic growth, the system still faces challenges such as inadequate tax revenues and the need for systemic improvements (Gurnak, 2018). The introduction of new forms of direct and indirect taxes has had revenue and equity implications, and the system continues to evolve to meet the requirements of international competition (Rao, 2000). Despite these challenges, the tax system has played a crucial role in India's development, and further research is needed to understand its impact on the country's economic growth.

The Indian tax system has undergone significant reforms, with a focus on improving revenue productivity and minimizing distortions (Rao, 2005). However, challenges remain, including the need to broaden the tax base and enhance efficiency (Rao, 2005). The dominance of a complex and outdated indirect taxation system is a key issue, and the introduction of a VAT structure is a notable reform (Bernardi, 2005). The unique nature of the Indian tax reform, shaped by domestic factors and international best practices, presents valuable lessons for other countries (Misra, 2011).

Tax administration in developing countries plays a crucial role in sustainable economic development and employment growth (Thaçi, 2018). However, it faces significant challenges, including administrative constraints that can weaken the tax revenue structure (Mansfield, 1987). To address these challenges, tax administrators can help implement more efficient and equitable tax systems (Mansfield, 1987). In particular, the replacement of international trade tax and VAT with domestic taxes can enhance the impact of tax effects on the economy (Thaçi, 2018). Tax administration in India plays a crucial role in the country's social and economic welfare. It is a key source of public finance, enabling the government to undertake welfare and development activities (Kumawat, 2014). The tax policy is designed to promote social justice and prevent wealth concentration (Vaid, 1972), while the tax system has evolved to mobilize resources for developmental and administrative activities (Nainwal, 2015). However, the system has been plagued by tax evasion, leading to the implementation of measures such as capital gains tax, net wealth tax, expenditure tax, and gift tax (Eigner, 1959). Recent tax reforms have focused on simplification, rationalization, and international alignment, with a shift towards lower rates and a fully integrated goods and services tax (Nainwal, 2015).

Tax Reforms in India

Tax reforms play a crucial role in addressing economic problems, particularly in the context of China's economic development (Shao-ke, 2012). These reforms can help create fiscal space and stimulate investment, as seen in the EU and Ukraine (Lunina, 2020). However, the success of these reforms depends on effective tax administration and the consideration of local features (Удк, 2017). In transition countries, the adoption of market economy taxes has been a positive step, but challenges remain in improving system functioning and reducing implementation problems (Grabowski, 2005).

Tax reforms in India have been a significant focus, with a shift towards a more efficient and broad-based system (Rao, 2005). These reforms were prompted by the fiscal and balance of payments crises of 1991, leading to a reorientation of the tax system to meet the needs of a market economy (Varghese, 2007). The government has also implemented measures to promote savings, encourage investment, and ensure a stable economic framework (Palanichamy, 2011). However, the unique history and institutional constraints in India have made comprehensive and coordinated tax reforms challenging (Misra, 2011).

The Indian taxation regime has undergone significant legislative reforms in recent years, with a focus on enhancing transparency and efficiency (Jain, 2018). Despite these improvements, challenges remain in broadening the tax base and making the system more productive and efficient (Rao, 2005). The tax system in India is still in need of significant reform, particularly in transitioning towards a VAT structure and addressing the dominance of indirect taxation (Bernardi, 2005). The need for systematic tax reforms was highlighted in the 1991 fiscal and balance of payments crises, which prompted a reorientation of the tax system to meet the requirements of a market economy (Varghese, 2007).

Tax reforms have been shown to have a significant positive impact on economic growth and stability. Multiple studies have found that tax reforms are positively related to GDP growth (Herbert et al., 2018; Ebimobowei, 2012; Ekwueme & Chikezi, 2016; Odukwu Victory Chika et al., 2022). Petroleum profit tax and company income tax are identified as key contributors to fiscal stability and economic growth (Herbert et al., 2018; Ekwueme & Chikezi, 2016). While VAT reforms have a positive relationship with economic stability, their effect is relatively small (Herbert et al., 2018). Researchers emphasize the importance of targeted and industry-focused fiscal initiatives to stimulate productivity and competitiveness (Herbert et al., 2018). Additionally, improving tax administration efficiency, reviewing obsolete tax laws, and ensuring transparency in tax revenue management are recommended to enhance the effectiveness of tax reforms (Ebimobowei, 2012; Ekwueme & Chikezi, 2016).

The Indian taxation regime faces challenges in revenue collection and administration, leading to a heavy reliance on federal transfers (Nayudu, 2019). Corruption in tax collection can be reduced through simplification of laws and procedures, and professionalized audits (Vijayakumar, 2005). The tax capacity and effort of Indian states have been affected by the limitations in expanding fiscal space and the proposed Goods and Services Tax regime (Mukherjee, 2017). However, the effectiveness of minimum tax legislation in achieving horizontal equity among taxpayers is questionable due to its administrative and compliance costs (Gujarathi, 2001).

The Indian government has made significant strides in improving tax administration and compliance, resulting in a doubling of direct tax collections as a percentage of GDP (Investigator, 2014). However, there is a need for a review of federal relations, including tax, expenditure, and transfers, to ensure stability and predictability in the country's growth (Jha, 2013). The introduction of the Goods and Service Tax (GST) has been a major reform in the Indian tax regime, addressing the issues of cascading and distorting taxes (Rupa, 2017). Furthermore, the incorporation of environmental tax reform within the GST system has been proposed to promote sustainable development (Srivastava, 2010).

The introduction of GST in India has had a significant impact on the country's tax scene. It has simplified the tax structure, improved compliance, and increased revenue collection (Chhatwani, 2023). The system has also created a unified, transparent, and efficient tax system across the country (Chhatwani, 2023). However, the impact of GST has been mixed, with both positive and negative implications on various sectors of the Indian economy (Chhatwani, 2023). Despite this, the implementation of GST has been considered a significant tax reform in the Indian tax structure (Mutkule, 2020).

A series of studies have examined the tax buoyancy of India, with varying results. Pathania (2019) found that the buoyancy of central taxes is higher for direct taxes, while Purohit (1978) focused on state taxes and their income-elasticity. Krushna (2016) observed that tax buoyancy has been consistently higher than national income, with a peak in the 1970s and 1960s, and a decline from the 1980s to 2000s. Upender (2008) further explored the impact of tax reforms, finding that the gross tax buoyancy was moderately elastic before the reforms, but became relatively inelastic after. These studies collectively highlight the complexity and variability of tax buoyancy in India.

Rao's research consistently highlights the challenges of reforming the Indian tax system, attributing them to a fragmented constitutional assignment of taxes, multiple policy objectives, and tax abuse by multinational companies (Rao, 2015, 2016). These challenges are further compounded by a poor organizational setting and low administrative capacity (Rao, 2016). Despite some progress, such as the introduction of new direct and indirect taxes, the system remains in need of improvement (Rao, 2000, 2005). The "tyranny of the status quo" is a key barrier to effective reform, as those who stand to lose from changes often resist them (Rao, 2015, 2016).

A range of studies have explored the impact of indirect tax reforms in India. Ojha (2022) found that the introduction of the Goods and Services Tax (GST) significantly boosted economic growth, with a potential increase in GDP of 1.0% to 3.0%. Srivastava (2010) and Jha (2013) both emphasized the need for environmental tax reform and the importance of fiscal federalism in the context of these reforms. Agarwal (2021) provided a comprehensive overview of the various indirect taxes implemented in India from 2000 to 2019, highlighting the complexity of the tax structure and the potential for simplification through the GST.

A series of tax reforms in India, including a reduction in corporate income tax rates and the removal of tax concessions, have been implemented to improve the investment climate (Thomas, 2017). These reforms have aimed to broaden the tax base, increase revenue productivity, and improve efficiency (Rao, 2005). However, the long-term impact of these reforms on economic growth and development is uncertain (Babar, 2020). In parallel, significant efforts have been made to overhaul corporate governance in India, with a focus on both voluntary and mandatory requirements (Afsharipour, 2011).

The impact of economic reform and globalization on India's federal system is a complex and multifaceted issue. Singh (2002) and Wallack (2006) both highlight the challenges and opportunities presented by these processes, particularly in the areas of financial sector reform, infrastructure development, and the need for more efficient intergovernmental transfer systems. Saxena (2004) and Nayar (2011) further emphasize the role of political and economic reforms in shaping India's federal system, with the former noting a shift from cooperative federalism to jurisdictional conflicts, and the latter underscoring the role of globalization in fostering domestic economic integration. These studies collectively underscore the need for a nuanced understanding of the interplay between economic reform, globalization, and India's federal system.

The period after 2020 has seen significant developments in Indian federalism, economic reform, and globalization. Arora (2020) highlights the government's efforts to attract investment and strengthen the economy, particularly in the wake of the Covid-19 pandemic. Gautam (2023) discusses the impact of economic liberalization on India's federal structure and national security, emphasizing the need for a balanced approach. Wani (2023) provides a comprehensive overview of the Indian economy's evolution, from controls to growth, and emphasizes the importance of inclusive growth, infrastructure development, and international collaborations. Hussain (2022) explores the transition of globalization and social transformation in India, underscoring the need for a more equitable distribution of the benefits of economic reform.

A series of tax reforms have been implemented in India since last two decades, with a focus on enhancing revenue collection, simplifying tax laws, and increasing the tax to GDP ratio (Kanungo, 2019). The introduction of the Goods and Services Tax (GST) in 2017 has been a significant part of these reforms, replacing a range of consumption taxes and creating a more uniform tax structure (Agarwal, 2021). However, there is a need for further reform, particularly in the areas of income and property taxes, to make the tax system more growth-friendly and redistributive (Joumard, 2017). The overall aim of these reforms is to promote inclusive growth and improve resource allocation

The research looks at how India's tax system has changed since the early 1990s and how other nations' systems have changed over the last 20 years for different reasons. The assessment methods, their effects (on income and equity), and results (or lack thereof) of their implementation are all laid forth in this chapter. It concludes that the tax system in India remains a substantial impediment to improvement, despite eight years of reform.

Challenges

The Indian taxation system faces several challenges as it evolves towards a more efficient and transparent structure. Key issues include the complexity arising from multiple taxes and fragmented constitutional assignments, which hinder comprehensive income taxation and facilitate tax avoidance (Rao, 2016). The system is burdened by numerous exemptions and preferences, leading to revenue loss and unintended distortions (Rao, 2016). Recent reforms, such as the introduction of faceless assessments and appeals, aim to reduce disputes between taxpayers and tax officers (Deb, 2024). The transition to a Goods and Services Tax (GST) is expected to remove cascading effects and provide a common nationwide market, but challenges remain in harmonizing rates and administration across states (Mukherjee, 2015). The shift from a centrally planned to a market-based economy necessitates adapting the tax system to maintain competitiveness while raising funds for infrastructure development (Das, 2022). Addressing these challenges is crucial for creating a simpler, more efficient taxation system in India.

ISSUES, CONTROVERSIES AND PROBLEMS

Current Tax System

Protecting the nation, funding social welfare programs and developmental endeavors, and meeting operational and administrative expenses all need substantial financial resources. Taxes and other non-tax revenues account for the bulk of these funds. The Indian Constitution establishes a federal framework within which the powers of the Central Government and the State Governments are vested, making India a federal state. Taxes are likewise imposed in conformity with the principles laid forth in the Constitution, which provide the Federal and State Governments the power to impose and collect various forms of taxation. Art 265, which states that "No tax shall be imposed or collected except by the authority of law," places a constraint on the government's ability to levy and collect taxes. In India, tax collection falls on both the federal and state levels of government. It is possible to classify taxes in two main ways: directly and indirectly. Factors such as an increase in taxpayers, turnover, economic development, efficient tax administration, inflation, and, most crucially, reforms to the tax system's structure and administration all have a role in determining the overall amount of tax revenue. Reforming the tax system is a major problem with far-reaching consequences for everything else (Chattopadhyay, S., & Das-Gupta, A. 2002).

GST Tax System

With the introduction of new economic policies in 1991, our economy saw profound shifts, most notably a rise in the service sector's share of GDP growth. To develop a uniform indirect tax structure and, more importantly, to include the service sector in our tax system, the GST model was put in place in 2017. As far as independent India was concerned, it represented a major shift in indirect taxes. Consistent tax rates are one of several aspects of the Goods and Services Tax (GST), an indirect tax system. France is where the Goods and Services Tax (GST) model of indirect taxes was first introduced to the world. The positive revenue effect and other advantages of GST, such as easy tax compliance and efficient tax administration, have attracted many other countries to adopt it. If you want to compare GST with the VAT system, the only real difference is that GST is essentially VAT at the national level.

Production, sale, and consumption are all subject to the GST, which is a comprehensive national tax on products and services. The merchant or supplier of the service may claim an input credit for the tax they paid when purchasing the goods or receiving the service under the Goods and Services Tax (GST). This tax is imposed at each point of sale or supply and applies to all goods and services. It is essentially a tax on the final product. This system of taxation involves levies by both the federal and state levels of government. The whole GST expense would fall on consumers. Every stage of the supply chain, from production to retail, will be responsible for collecting and remitting GST, with input tax credits being awarded at each transaction level. A 12-or 14-digit taxpayer identification number (similar to a Permanent Account Number) is assigned by the GST authorities for the purpose of filing returns and making GST payments. A shared platform will be available for the provision of three key services, namely registration, returns, and payments (Poddar,S 2009).

Under the goods and services tax, all taxable items and services are consolidated into one category and subject to a single, flat rate of taxation. The fundamental objective of this reform is to standardize the indirect system, which our country has long required. A system similar to the GST would accomplish this. Even though it will be challenging for our nation to achieve all of the objectives, the system that was put in place in 2017 is being improved upon all the time. The government hopes that by successfully implementing GST, it would boost the economy and create a favorable climate for future programmes like "Make in India." This is despite the fact that business owners and consumers are now facing certain challenges. Following the implementation of the GST, the number of income tax assesses increased, which is a well-known fact. This indicates that the GST system will not only increase direct tax revenue but also enhance indirect tax collection (Rustagi, T. R. 1998).

The Goods and Services Tax (GST) is a significant tax reform implemented in India on July 1, 2017, aimed at creating a unified national market and reducing cascading effects (Tekwani & Pabla, 2021). India's GST model follows a dual structure similar to Canada and Brazil (Tekwani & Pabla, 2021; Kir, 2021). The GST Council, a unique center-state body, operates on principles of cooperative federalism to coordinate the tax system (Kir, 2021). However, the binding nature of its decisions remains uncertain, potentially leading to constitutional challenges (Kir, 2021). India's GST rates are comparatively high, with the top slab of 28% being the second highest among 115 countries (Tekwani & Pabla, 2021; Shukla & Shukla, 2020). The new tax regime is destination-based, replacing the previous origin-based structure (Shukla & Shukla, 2020). While GST has simplified India's tax system, its complex rate structure and high rates pose challenges compared to other countries' implementations. GST was introduced in India after a struggle of more than a decade. The multiple tier indirect tax system in India had a cascading effect, to overcome which GST was introduced by 101th constitutional amendment. This has considerably simplified the tax regime in the country. GST has already been implemented in more than 160 countries around the globe, as a result of which we can take examples of its effective implementation procedure. The basic difference between the old and the new tax structure is that the new regime is destination-based charge whereas the old regime followed origin based tax structure. The rate of GST in India is extremely high as compared to that of other Countries which makes it all the more complex (Shukla & Shukla, 2020).

INDIAN TAXATION SYSTEM – EVOLUTION, CHARACTERISTICS AND REFORMS

The Indian tax system was developed as a result of British dominion. Since India's independence, numerous reforms have been implemented to better align the direct and indirect tax systems with the nation's evolving needs. However, the legacy of British laws severely impacted the systems for an extended period. Despite the progress made in tax design and administration in recent years, the system remained challenging at both the central and state levels. The tax system was intricate due to the presence of numerous exemptions, rebates, and rates. Because of this complexity, numerous legal issues and complications arise.

Furthermore, the intricate tax system impedes revenue collection. Another concern is the cascading effect of taxation. Central and state taxes have cascading effects due to their partial coverage. Certain taxes are assessed on expenses that already incorporate service tax or other taxes. As a consequence of these cascading effects, the cost of the final product increased, rendering the Indian industry less competitive in the global market. The mechanism is unable to establish a connection between the Indian economy and the global economy. The globalization of the Indian economy has resulted in the transformation of the world into a single marketplace. Consequently, it is logical that the system should be updated to reflect these changes. The confluence of tax systems has made it difficult to enact and implement comprehensive and coordinated tax reforms (Rao, M. G. 2000).

Additionally, there are concerns about the tax system's selectiveness and discretion in its design, implementation, and administration. It is challenging to expand the tax base. Because of this structural flaw, powerful interest groups emerged, and the concept of "negotiated settlement" became part of the tax code. The indirect tax system in India is only one of several problems with the country's tax system overall. For example, the ever-increasing expense of tax collection is a major drag on the economy. Changes were initiated due to the fact that indirect taxes are unjust. One example is the salt tax in India, which had a disproportionate impact on the poor. Regardless of one's socioeconomic status, the market prices goods and services at the same rate, which is unjust. The present indirect tax structure makes self-tax assessment quite difficult due to the presence of many levies (Kaldor, N. 1959).

The initiation of a rate war was precipitated by the fact that a variety of states had varying VAT rates. Fairness is a consequence of transparency, which was also absent in the previous indirect tax system. Tax evasion is a substantial concern for the Indian tax system, in addition to these. In addition to reducing government revenue, this immorality is causing a variety of economic, social, and political issues.

Tax Reforms in India

Precipitated by the fact that a variety of states had different VAT rates, the introduction of a rate war was inevitable. Several fair practices were absent in the previous system of indirect taxes, which lacked both transparency and simplicity. Of all these unfair practices, tax evasion was (and is) a substantial concern for the Indian tax system. In addition to reducing government revenue, this immorality is causing a variety of economic, social, and political issues (Matta, A. M. 1979).

There has to be a complete overhaul of the tax law and the banking system immediately. Policy, tax structure, and compliance procedures must be promptly and appropriately adjusted if the tax system is to continue to be relevant in the face of changing domestic and global economic circumstances. The implementation of the Goods and Services Tax (GST) was the most recent major change to India's indirect tax system; previous changes had started in 1953 and had generally continued until then. The main objectives of these improvements are to increase revenue, reduce complexity, eliminate negative feedback loops, and create a more efficient, open, and taxpayer-friendly tax system (Samantara, D. (2021).

The reform introduces a destination-based value-added tax levied at each stage of the supply chain, eliminating cascading effects (Gupta, 2017). Despite its benefits, the implementation faced challenges, including political issues and conflicting stakeholder interests (A. Nayyar & Inderpal Singh, 2018; Singh, 2024). The new system impacts various sectors of the economy, requiring adaptation from businesses, taxpayers, and government agencies (Singh, 2024).

The implementation of Goods and Services Tax (GST) in India has faced numerous challenges due to the country's federal structure (Sathe, 2020). Key issues include designing a suitable GST model, harmonizing rates across states, and addressing administrative concerns (Mukherjee, 2015). The dual GST model adopted by India is unique, with only Canada and Brazil having similar systems (Singh & Jaiswal, 2021). Post-implementation problems include complications for exporters, errors in archived returns, and discrepancies between expectations and reality regarding simplified tax structure and ease of doing business (Singh & Jaiswal, 2021). The evolution of GST in India has been a long process, spanning four decades of deliberations (Rao & Mukherjee, 2019). Major considerations in its development included tax inclusion and exclusion, handling inter-state transactions, ensuring revenue neutrality, providing compensation to states, and coordinating GST administration (Rao & Mukherjee, 2019). Despite challenges, the government has been proactive in addressing taxpayer concerns (Singh & Jaiswal, 2021).

Table 1. Major tax reforms

Income Tax	In 1973–1974, there were 11 income tax brackets, with rates ranging from 10% to 85%. If an additional 15% surcharge were implemented, high-income earners would be subject to an effective tax rate of 97% of their incomes. The wealth tax has exacerbated their financial circumstances. As a consequence, individuals begin to avoid paying taxes. The tax revisions of 1986–1987 resulted in a reduction of the number of tax categories from 8 to 4, as well as a reduction in the marginal tax rate from 60% to 50%. The marginal tax rate was reduced to 35% as a result of the substantial tax revisions that occurred in 1991–1992 and 1996–1997. These modifications also resulted in the elimination of the wealth tax. The government implemented the Kelkar Task Force's recommendations for simplifying the tax code in 2005–2006, with a few modifications.
Corporation Tax	The rates of taxation for different categories of corporations varied significantly until two decades ago. The effective tax rate for corporations varied from 45 to 65 percent. The marginal tax rates were reduced to 40% and subsequently to 35% as a consequence of tax reforms in 1991–1992 and 1996–1997, respectively. The current tax rate is 30%, but a plan has been established to reduce it to 25% in the years ahead. The marginal tax rates have been further reduced in subsequent budgets.
Custom Duty	An import substitution strategy was the foundation of India's economic development following its independence. This necessitates the preservation of foreign exchange reserves. As an outcome, India implemented increased customs tariffs on its imports. Throughout the 1970s and 1980s, India's custom duty system was exceedingly intricate and retrogressive. India also maintains a comprehensive negative inventory of imports in addition to quantitative limits. The Indian economy was liberalized and opened up following the 1991 Crisis. Consequently, the greatest rates of customs tax were reduced from 300% to 30% in subsequent budgets. Following the establishment of the World Trade Organization (WTO), the apex rate was further reduced, decreasing to 25%, 20%, and 12.5% in 2003–2004, 2005–2006, and 2006–2007, respectively). The current average customs duty's lower bound is 10%.
Excise Duty	Indian manufacturers are discouraged by the country's excise tax structure. Due to the absence of an input credit for the producer, the excise duty had a multiplicative impact, adding to the tax that he had previously paid on his prior purchases. The outcome was disastrous for production and industry. In an effort to reinvigorate India's industry, the GOI chose to make substantial changes to the excise charge structure. After the MODVAT was simplified and renamed CENVAT, India became the first country to take this step in 1986. A manufacturer might get a return of the duty he had previously paid under the CENVAT's input credit rules if he bought an input for which duty had already been paid.

continued on following page

Table 1. Continued

Sales Tax/ VAT	With the intention of making recommendations for reforms to India's indirect tax system, the indirect taxation investigation committee was formed in 1976. Their high income elasticity led the committee to recommend an ad valorem tax. The group also proposed doing away with sales tax and excise duty in favor of a unified commodities tax, like VAT. The authorized group of state finance ministers came to a thorough agreement in June 2004 to start implementing VAT in April 2005. Consequently, value-added tax (VAT) replaced sales tax.
Service Tax	Among its many shortcomings, India's tax system treated commodities unfairly. There are very few services in India that are handed down from the federal government to the individual states; they include entertainment and power, among others. Because goods and services are taxed differentially, the neutrality of taxes was violated. When the services in question are thought of as a progressive form of taxation and exhibit larger income elasticities, this becomes even more apparent. In an effort to level the playing field, the Government of India (GOI) introduced a service tax on three industries in 1994 and 1995: insurance, share trading, and telephone services. There has been an annual expansion of the service net beginning in 1994–1995. After starting at 10% in 2012–13, the government gradually increased it to 15% in 2017–18. Members of M. Govind Rao's Committee on Service Taxation and Raja J. Chelliah's Tax Reforms Committee of 1991 both voted in favor of the service tax. Similar recommendations have come from the Vijay Kelkar Committee on Direct and Indirect Taxes.

1. **Income Tax Reforms:**
    - **Reduction of Marginal Tax Rates:** In 1973-74, India had 11 income tax brackets with rates ranging from 10% to 85%. During fiscal year 1986-87, there was a reduction in the number of tax categories to four, accompanied by a decrease in the marginal tax rate from 60% to 50%. Further significant reductions occurred in 1991-92 and 1996-97, culminating in the marginal tax rate being reduced to 35%. These reductions were implemented with the intention of encouraging investment and labour.
    - **Abolition of Wealth Tax:** The elimination of the Wealth Tax was a component of the reforms. A progressive tax was imposed on the net worth of individuals surpassing a specified threshold. The objective of its abolition was to reduce the compliance burden and streamline the tax system.
    - **Simplification:** The ratification of the recommendations of the Kelkar Task Force was intended to streamline the tax code. Appointed in 2002, the Kelkar Task Force put forth recommendations aimed at streamlining tax regulations, overhauling tax rates, and expanding the tax base. The purpose of these reforms was to mitigate compliance expenses and enhance tax administration.
2. **Corporation Tax Reforms:**

- **Reduction in Rates:** Twenty years ago, companies were subject to effective tax rates between forty-five and sixty-five percent. The tariffs were progressively lowered to 30% with an additional promise to get them down to 25%. Improving the business climate, luring investors, and fostering economic development were the goals of these reductions.
- **Competitiveness:** It is clear that India is making an attempt to maintain its competitiveness on the world stage by pledging to significantly lower the corporate tax rate. Tax cuts encourage investment from both inside and beyond the country, which in turn boosts economic growth.

3. **Custom Duty Reforms:**
   - **Liberalization:** To safeguard its own industries, India has always levied hefty customs tariffs. The maximum customs tax rate was lowered from 300% to 30% during the liberalisation that followed the 1991 Crisis. The peak rates were further reduced to 25%, 20%, and 12.5% as a result of further decreases. Trade liberalisation, lower import prices, and increased economic efficiency were the goals of these cuts.
   - **Compliance:** The point of making customs duties simpler and lower is to get people to follow the rules. "We want to encourage compliance," says Michael Rees, a senior fellow at the nonpartisan Peterson Institute for International Economics. One way to do that is by taking away the incentives for tax evasion and contraband. If you make a duty system simple and transparent, people are more likely to play by the rules. And if playing by the rules is easy, they're more likely to do it.
4. **Excise Duty Reforms:**
   - **Input Credit:** When MODVAT was first implemented in 1986, its primary goal was to alleviate the "domino effect" of excise duty. Manufacturers paid too much in duties because they could not deduct the amount they had already paid on certain goods—particularly those that were important for investment, such as metals and equipment—that were subject to excise duty. The reform reduced the tax burden on finished goods and made investment more attractive to manufacturers.
5. **Sales Tax/VAT Reforms:**
   - **Transition to VAT:** In April 2005, the transition from sales tax to VAT commenced. The implementation of VAT sought to consolidate indirect taxation, diminish tax cascading, and enhance efficiency by substituting the conventional sales tax system. In contrast to sales tax, value-added tax (VAT) levies taxes on the value added at each stage of production and distribution, rendering it a more neutral and less distortionary tax.
6. **Service Tax Reforms:**

- **Neutrality:** The objective of broadening the service tax base was to rectify the disparity in taxation rates between commodities and services. The service tax net, which was initially imposed on three services in 1994-1995, grew annually. The objective of this expansion was to achieve tax neutrality across various economic sectors and to broaden the sources of government revenue.

INSTITUTIONAL FRAMEWORK FOR TAX ADMINISTRATION IN INDIA

The institutional framework for tax administration in India has undergone significant reforms to enhance efficiency and transparency. The implementation of GST has led to technological advancements and improved administrative structures (Bhasin, 2018). India has adopted cooperative compliance measures aligned with OECD guidelines, including faceless assessments and dispute resolution mechanisms (Martini & Tandon, 2023). Recent legislations, such as the Prevention of Money Laundering Act and the Black Money Act, have strengthened the financial and taxation regulatory framework (Jain, 2018). However, a comprehensive diagnostic approach is crucial for effective revenue administration, considering environmental factors, historical effects, and organizational strategies (Gill, 2000). While India has made progress in modernizing its tax administration system, there is still room for improvement in areas such as establishing a single point of contact in administration and implementing a structured cooperative compliance approach (Martini & Tandon, 2023).

The Indian tax system has undergone significant reforms since independence, evolving to become more comprehensive and aligned with international practices (Nainwal, 2015). The Income Tax Department administers direct taxes, with various authorities established under the Income Tax Act (Gupta, 2015). Recent initiatives have focused on digitization and the use of IT-enabled services to enhance efficiency and transparency in tax administration (Bhasin, 2022). However, challenges persist, including unreasonable delays in refunds and issues with the physical environment in tax offices (Rani & Arora, 2012). The tax system has shifted towards lower rates with fewer exemptions, aiming to expand the tax base and improve voluntary compliance (Nainwal, 2015). Ongoing reforms seek to simplify and rationalize both direct and indirect taxes, with a focus on implementing a fully integrated goods and services tax (GST) for indirect taxation (Nainwal, 2015).

The mandate of a tax administration body is to assess and collect tax according to tax laws.

Tax administration bodies have three common organizational characteristics specific to their
functions:

(i) Tax administration requires a network of offices that covers an entire country.
(ii) A large number of personnel are required.
(iii) Personnel are required to have specific technical expertise on tax laws and administration. (Asian Development Bank. 2012)

Central Board of Direct Taxes (CBDT)

The CBDT is India's top income tax authority. The organisation sets norms, standards, and oversees the Income Tax Department (ITD) nationwide, making it vital. Tax policy and its execution depend on the CBDT, highlighting its importance (Wagle,Namrata 2022).

CBDT's authority to interpret and enforce direct tax laws, particularly the Income Tax Act, 1961, is crucial. CBDT helps generate money, shape fiscal policy, and promote tax compliance. Taxpayers and businesses benefit from clear and uniform tax administration rules.

A Chairman and a team of members handle legislation, policy, administration, and investigation at the CBDT. The hierarchical structure improves coordination and specialisation, boosting organisation success.

The CBDT has successfully formulated policies, made recommendations, and supervised direct taxes, primarily income tax, in India. Tax policymaking by the organisation has increased revenue and compliance. Tax evasion, litigation, and dispute resolution delays need additional improvement. The CBDT has advanced tax administration digitization. However, efficiency, transparency, and taxpayer services may be improved.

Central Board of Indirect Taxes and Customs (CBIC)

The CBIC is essential to India's GST implementation and indirect tax administration, including customs and excise taxes. CBIC is crucial because it sets policies, makes orders, and manages indirect tax offices countrywide.

CBIC's authority to interpret and administer indirect tax laws like the Customs Act, 1962, Central Excise Act, 1944, and CGST Act, 2017 is crucial. Legislative and administrative operations of CBIC generate money, ease trade, and enforce indirect tax regulations.

CBIC, like CBDT, has a chairperson and several customs, GST, excise, and enforcement members. CBIC organises and executes its functions using this structure to provide uniform indirect tax administration nationwide.

CBIC has helped India manage indirect taxes including customs, excise, and GST. Its policies, directives, and taxes have boosted trade and income. However, technical, compliance, and administrative issues hindered GST rollout. System advancements and taxpayer outreach activities have helped CBIC address these difficulties, but further modifications are required to ensure GST system efficiency and taxpayer compliance (Menon, S. P., & KP, A. 2022).

State Tax Authorities

State tax agencies are crucial to managing VAT, sales tax, and excise levies. Their function as frontline agency for state policymaking, law enforcement, and tax collection makes them relevant.

State VAT, sales tax, and excise duty legislation empower state tax agencies. These rules allow them to tax intrastate transactions, helping state governments raise income. State tax bodies usually have a hierarchy of Commissioners to Assessing Officers. Each officer is responsible for assessment, audit, and enforcement in their area. This decentralised system allows state tax authorities to meet local needs and administer taxes effectively at the grassroots level.

VAT, sales tax, and state excise levies are administered by state tax officials, who are crucial. Some states have strong tax administration, whereas others struggle with tax evasion, corruption, and infrastructure. Capacity building, resource restrictions, and political meddling may affect performance. State tax agencies have modernised tax administration via IT and taxpayer education, but enforcement, openness, and accountability may be improved (Choudhary, M. 2023).

Judicial Perspective

Taxation is relevant to the court because of its constitutional duty to preserve the rule of law and safeguard basic rights like property and equality before the law. Tax laws, administrative actions, and enforcement tactics are reviewed by courts to ensure constitutionality and procedural fairness. Courts interpret statutes, arbitrate taxpayer-tax authority disputes, and advise on complicated tax problems, ensuring legal clarity and predictability in tax administration.

1. **UOI v. Azadi Bachao Andolan, AIR 2004 SUPREME COURT 1107.**: The facts of the case boil down to the practice of treaty shopping and tax evasion in the context of double taxation avoidance agreements (DTAAs). An NGO Azadi

Bachao Andolan challenged the tax assessment of the offer gains made by a predominantly Mauritian company on the shares of an Indian company, arguing that they are exempt from taxation in India because they are explicitly excluded by the Indo-Mauritius DTA. The Supreme Court implemented the substance over form doctrine, assuming that the true intention and purpose of tax treaties should prevail over their literal interpretation. Such a purposive construction intends to avoid the use of tax treaties for abusive tax evasion.

2. **Vodafone International Holdings BV v. UOI [2012] 1 S.C.R 579.**: In one of India's most contentious tax disputes, Vodafone International Holdings BV challenged the Indian tax authority's authority to tax the purchase of Hutchison Essar Limited's shares through a Cayman Islands-based company. Initial ruling in favour of Vodafone was that the transaction occurred outside of India and was therefore exempt from taxation. In an effort to reverse the court's decision, the Indian government amended tax legislation retroactively under the Finance Act of 2012. After this decision, retroactive taxes and taxpayer rights versus revenue interests were the subject of heated debate.
3. **GE India Technology Centre Pvt. Ltd. v. CIT [2010] 327 ITR 456/193**: The subject matter of the GE India case was transferring pricing adjustments concerning royalties compensated for the use of proprietary materials. The tax authority contended that the royalty payments made by GE India to its parent company in the United States were excessively substantial and did not comply with the arm's length principle. The Supreme Court reaffirmed the arm's length principle, which states that transactions involving related parties must be valued as if they were conducted between unrelated parties. Moreover, the court assigned considerable importance to the procedural equity of transfer pricing examinations, emphasising the critical nature of allowing taxpayers to submit arguments and evidence in support of their defence. The ruling bolstered taxpayer trust in India's transfer pricing system and reduced tax disputes by encouraging the disclosure of tax assessments and adherence to global transfer pricing norms.
4. **CIT v. B.C. Srinivasa Setty 1981 SCR (2) 938**: The current matter concerned the concept of "commercial expediency" in relation to the provisions of the Income Tax Act of 1961 concerning deductions. B.C. Srinivasa Setty, an entrepreneur, withdrew interest payments made on loans acquired for investment purposes. The Supreme Court emphasised the criticality of a direct correlation between the expenditures accrued and the taxpayer's business objectives in order to qualify for deductions. The decision established a precedent concerning the deductibility of business expenses: they must be commercially necessary and relevant to the taxpayer's trade or business. The legal principle established by the Income Tax Act provided guidance to taxpayers and tax authorities on

how to assess the legitimateness of business expenses, elucidating the scope of allowable deductions.

5. **Eicher Motors Ltd. v. UOI (1999) 2 SCC 361**: Eicher Motors Ltd. sought clarification from the Income Tax Act concerning the manner in which voluntary retirement compensation is regarded with respect to taxes. The Supreme Court's decision established that voluntary retirement compensation for employees is categorised as a revenue expenditure and is therefore eligible for tax deduction. The decision solidified a consensus concerning the tax ramifications of employee benefits by affirming that expenses committed to the welfare of personnel are eligible for tax deductions on the condition that they are used solely and completely for the benefit of the taxpayer's business. This ruling enhanced the clarity surrounding the tax implications for employers regarding voluntary retirement plans and contributed to the growth of Income Tax Act case law concerning employee compensation.
6. **CIT v. Vegetable Products Ltd. 1973 SCR (3) 448**: This major legal case examined the differentiation between revenue and capital expenditure. Vegetable Products Ltd. sought deductions on the grounds that renovation expenses for its tea estates constituted revenue expenses. The "enduring benefit test," which was established by the Supreme Court, places emphasis on the classification of expenditures that provide enduring benefits as capital and, as such, prohibits their deduction as revenue expenses. The court offered direction regarding the deductibility of costs associated with the enhancement or development of assets by elucidating the differentiation between revenue and capital expenditures. This decision contributed to the formulation of principles regulating the treatment of capital and revenue expenditures under the Income Tax Act and established a precedent for subsequent tax assessments.
8. **Navnit Lal C. Javeri v. K.K. Sen, AAC 1965 SCR (1) 909**: The taxpayer was the subject of a Supreme Court examination regarding the tax treatment of gifts in this specific case. The donations acquired by Navnit Lal C. Javeri from his father-in-law were liable to be taxed as income by the relevant tax authorities. The fundamental principle established by the court, which states that gifts received in exchange for nothing are exempt from taxation under the Income Tax Act, continues to be relevant in tax assessments pertaining to bequests and gifts. This judicial ruling upheld the principle that income must have a "quid pro quo" characteristic to qualify as taxable, thus forgoing the taxation of gratuitous transfers. The validation by the court of the tax-exempt classification of gifts provided assurance and clarity to taxpayers regarding the way in which gifts are evaluated in accordance with the Income Tax Act.

9. **S. Sundaram Pillai v. V.R. Pattabiraman (1985) 1 RENCJ 267**: When two people own property that generates rent, they are both personally responsible for the income taxes on the rent even though the assessor may assess the property as a whole and not in halves. That is because it was established in S. Sundaram Pillai v. The Assistant Commercial Tax Officer and Anr., (1962) 3 SCC 41, that each co-owner of rental real estate is liable for tax on his or her share of the rent regardless of whether he or she receives all of the rent or just a portion of it. In this case, Pattabiraman received all of the rent but still had to pay taxes on it despite only owning half of the property because he was held personally liable for half of the amount constituting "rental income."
10. **CIT v. Sun Engineering Works Pvt. Ltd. (1992) 198 ITR 297**: The Supreme Court considered a very straightforward issue in this case: how should we treat subsidies that a private firm obtains from the government? We had a taxpayer, Sun Engineering Works Pvt. Ltd., which received a subsidy from the government to help finance the construction of an industrial facility. Subsidies associated with capital assets are not treated as income for tax purposes (unlike, say, subsidies for welfare), but they may be subject to "depreciation," which is determined by the court. This ruling then becomes the precedent for how we handle investments in what is now called the "stimulus."

SOLUTIONS AND RECOMMENDATIONS

For tax reforms in India to work better, many smart and strategic changes are necessary. These are not dramatic shifts, but alterations made after much forethought. We are offering some recommendations.

To begin, the establishment of tax incentives aimed directly at certain sectors of the economy, notably for agriculture and SMEs, could lead to enhanced productivity and economic expansion.

If the tax compliance process is made simpler, especially for small businesses, it may promote not just better overall compliance but also a reduction in the amount of work that those businesses have to do to keep up with the tax end of their financial operations.

Tax authorities can become stronger and more efficient by regularly training their personnel and adopting the advanced technologies that are revolutionizing tax administration and making it possible to reshape enforcement. This is an ideal way to improve institutional knowledge and loss of institutional memory.

Moreover, for equity to be achieved, reforms must focus on the grounds of offering greater benefits of tax reductions to groups with low income and very few resources.

Emerging economies similar to that of India can yield valuable lessons when one is studying the agrarian-to-urban transition that more or less every poor society has undergone or is going through. Yet, when one is talking about the agrarian-to-urban transition in the case of India, one is talking about a long-duration process that is likely to extend well into the next century. The more time a social scientist spends on this process, the more he/she is likely to conclude that with numerous lessons and narratives arrayed on either side of the developmental path, it is truly dangerous to oversimplify.

In the end, carrying out studies that take place over an extended period can examine the effects of the kinds of major policy shifts represented here.

The proposals in this report strive to create a tax system that works better in fundamental ways. They are the outcome of a vision shared with stakeholders around the world—a vision of a tax system flexible enough to weather the broad range of unanticipated threats we know, historically, economies and societies must face.

FUTURE RESEARCH AND DIRECTIONS

Future research on the significance of tax reforms in India should focus on the different impacts they have, especially on agriculture, industry, services, and international trade. It is also crucial to understand how they influence investment and business sentiment more broadly. We need to look at how the reforms affect income distribution and economic inequality. Because compliance is such a big issue in taxation, we must also address the administrative problems of the tax authorities and find ways to remedy them. Another important area for future research is on the long-term effectiveness of these reforms in generating resources for public purposes and enabling inclusive growth. Comparison with experiences in other emerging economies can help us identify best practices. Overall, we must use better methods and an enlarged body of evidence to inform our understanding of what these reforms have accomplished thus far and where they might be going in terms of their impact on both fiscal health and private sector performance.

CONCLUSION

The tax policy and tax administration of a nation have a significant impact on its overall ability to collect taxes. The legislative and procedural framework for potential tax collection is established by tax policy, while tax administration is dedicated to the efficient and effective realization of potential tax revenues in consideration of economic growth, tax bases, and tax structures. Tax policy initially establishes the legislative and procedural framework, despite the fact that both objectives are significant. The administration of a tax system has an impact on both its efficiency and yield. It is not advisable to neglect the administrative aspect of tax reform, as experience has shown that any administrative issues that may arise cannot be assumed to be resolved quickly and easily. It is also imprudent to assume that any administrative complications that may arise can be resolved quickly and effortlessly. Contrary to the substantial volume of research that has been conducted on the topic of tax policy reform, it is clear that tax administration, a subject of comparable significance, has not garnered nearly the same level of attention.

Despite the fact that paying taxes is a moral and legal obligation and that tax payers are aware that the money they contribute to the government is used to enhance society, the taxation system is so complex that they still encounter some difficulty in making their contributions. Regardless of whether they are caused by the inefficiency of tax administration or the complex nature of tax legislation, high compliance expenses continue to be a significant source of frustration. Another prevalent misconception among taxpayers is that the government may not effectively utilize the funds it collects through taxation and may be exploited by dishonest individuals. This perspective cultivates resentment toward the taxation process and frequently leads to taxpayers making futile attempts to conceal their income and evade paying taxes, which severely impedes the nation's economic development. Therefore, it is essential to improve the current tax system by first enacting legislation that is beneficial to taxpayers and subsequently modifying the tax collection process to ensure that all individuals who are responsible for paying taxes do so voluntarily and with respect.

As a result, the Tax Administration's primary objective is to facilitate the tax payment process and provide assistance to individuals in fulfilling their tax obligations. The second most critical responsibility of the tax administration is to offer guidance and assistance to taxpayers throughout the entire process, and to treat them with the same level of respect as they would customers. Nevertheless, the most critical measure that can be implemented is to inculcate in them a sense of assurance that the funds they contribute in the form of taxation are allocated to the country's advancement. The implementation of programs for tax awareness, education, and outreach will facilitate substantial progress in the cause. Individuals will continue to engage in illicit tax evasion strategies if this issue is not resolved, which could potentially impede the nation's growth trajectory.

The Indian taxation system faces numerous challenges and controversies. Despite fiscal reforms, public finances remain problematic, with distortionary and fragmented taxation, inefficient government expenditures, and fiscal imbalances (Srivastava,

2005). Key issues include the need for comprehensive tax reforms, broadening the tax base, and improving revenue collection through direct and indirect taxes (Jain, 2016). The fragmented constitutional assignment of taxes on agricultural and non-agricultural income hinders the implementation of a comprehensive income tax and facilitates tax avoidance and evasion (Rao, 2016). Multiple objectives imposed on the tax system result in numerous exemptions and preferences, causing revenue loss and unintended distortions (Rao, 2016). The difficulty in taxing unorganized sector incomes further narrows the tax base (Rao, 2016). Poor organizational settings, low administrative capacity, and resistance to change due to vested interests contribute to the slow pace of effective tax reforms in India (Rao, 2016).

REFERENCES

Acharya, S. (2005). Thirty years of tax reform in India. *Economic and Political Weekly*,, 2061–2070.

Afsharipour, A. (2011). A Brief Overview of Corporate Governance Reforms in India. *Corporate Law: Corporate Governance Law eJournal*.

Ahmad, E., & Stern, N. (1984). The theory of reform and Indian indirect taxes. *Journal of Public Economics*, 25(3), 259–298. DOI: 10.1016/0047-2727(84)90057-4

Alagappan, S. (2019). Indian Tax Structure – An Analytical Perspective. *IRPN: Other Innovation & Management Science* .

Aslam, A., & Shah, M. A. (2017). *Taxation and the peer-to-peer economy*. International Monetary Fund. DOI: 10.5089/9781484313763.001

Athira, A., & Lukose, P. J. (2024). The Increasing Trend in Effective Tax Rates in India: Role of Macroeconomic Factors, Tax Policy Changes and Firm Characteristics. *Journal of Emerging Market Finance*, 09726527231214075.

Babar, D. (2020). A Macro analysis of Corporate Tax Cuts: A Strategy to improve India's Competitiveness. *Political Economy: Taxation*.

Bagchi, A. (2003). *Fifty years of fiscal federalism in India: An appraisal*. National Institute of Public Finance and Policy.

Bernardi, L., & Fraschini, A. (2005). Tax system and tax reforms in India. *Department of Public Policy and Public Choice-POLIS, Working Paper*, (51).

Bhalla, S. (2005). *Tax Rates*. Tax Compliance and Tax Revenues.

Bhasin, R. (2018). Technological Infrastructure and Institutional Set-up for Effective Implementation of GST. *VISION: Journal of Indian Taxation*, 5(1), 104–109.

Chattopadhyay, S., & Das-Gupta, A. (2002). *The compliance cost of the personal income tax and its determinants*. National Institute of Public Finance and Policy.

Chika, O. V., Oshiogwemoh, D., & Promise, E. (2022). Impact of tax reforms on economic growth of Nigeria (2000-2021). *Goodwood Akuntansi dan Auditing Reviu, 1*(1), 79-95.

Choudhary, M. (2023). Legacy Issues & Emerging Challenges in Indian Customs from the Standpoint of Valuation & Assessment. *Issue 1 Indian JL & Legal Rsch., 5*, 1.

Das, P. (2022). India's evolving tax system: Its successes and challenges. *RESEARCH REVIEW International Journal of Multidisciplinary*, 7(7), 118–124. DOI: 10.31305/rrijm.2022.v07.i07.016

Deb, R. (2018). Tax Reforms and GST: A Systematic Literature Review. *Journal of Commerce and Accounting Research*, 7(1), 40.

Deb, R. (2024). Tax Administration Reform: End of Tax Disputes in India?. *MDIM Journal of Management Review*, 46.

Deshmukh, A. K., Mohan, A., & Mohan, I. (2022). Goods and services tax (GST) implementation in India: A SAP–LAP–Twitter analytic perspective. *Global Journal of Flexible Systems Managment*, 23(2), 165–183. DOI: 10.1007/s40171-021-00297-3 PMID: 37522093

Gautam, M. (2023). Federalism and National Security in India After Liberalisation. *Global Journal for Research Analysis*.

Ghuge, N. R., & Katdare, V. V. (2015). Indian tax structure-An analytical perspective. *International Journal of Management and Social Sciences*, 3(9), 242–252.

Goel, M. (2022). Evolution of Indian Tax System-Tax Policy, e-initiatives and administrative reforms. *Special Education*, 2(43).

Grabowski, M. (2005). Reforms of Tax Systems in Transition Countries. *Transition Studies Review*, 12(2), 293–312. DOI: 10.1007/s11300-005-0063-y

Gurnak, A.V. (2018). Problems and prospects of Indian tax system development: industrial context Section: Macroeconomic and regional problems of industrial development.

Herbert, W. E., Nwarogu, I. A., & Nwabueze, C. C. (2018). Tax reforms and Nigeria's economic stability. *International Journal of Applied Economics. Finance and Accounting*, 3(2), 74–87.

Jacob, R., Binu, K., & Anjana, P. B. (2024). A Comprehensive Study on Goods and Services Tax in India. *International Journal of Engineering and Management Research*, 14(1), 58–64.

Jain, S. (2018). Strengthening Financial and Taxation Regulatory Framework in India: A Review of Recent Legislations. *VISION: Journal of Indian Taxation*.

Jha, R. (2013). Indirect Tax Reform and Fiscal Federalism in India. *Public Economics: National Government Expenditures & Related Policies eJournal*.

Joumard, I., Thomas, A., & Morgavi, H. (2017). *Making Income and Property Taxes More Growth-Friendly and Redistributive in India*. OECD Publications.

Kapoor, S., & Singh, A. (2023). *Development of Indian Tax System: Pre and Post-Colonial Influences*. FIIB Business Review.

Krishnaswamy, H. (2021). Do The Indian Tax Enactments & Fiscal Policies? Incentivise & Facilitate Tax Evasion?-A Critical Study.

Krushna, A. V. (2015). Tax buoyancy of India: An empirical analysis. *International Journal of Research in Management. Economics & Commerce*, 5(12), 46–55.

Lunina, I., Bilousova, O., & Frolova, N. (2020). Tax Reforms for the Development of Fiscal Space. *Baltic Journal of Economic Studies*, 6(3), 48–58. DOI: 10.30525/2256-0742/2020-6-3-48-58

Mansfield, C.Y. (1987). Tax Administration in Developing Countries: An Economic Perspective. *Political Economy (Topic)*.

Martini, M. H., & Tandon, S. (2023). A review of India approaches to Cooperative Compliance in light of the International Tax Practice and the OECD Framework. *Intertax*, 51(10).

Matta, A. M. (1979). Search and Seizure Under Income-Tax Law. *Journal of the Indian Law Institute*, 21(4), 575–591.

Menon, S. P., & KP, A. (2022). An Analytical Perspective of the Indian Tax Structure. *Issue 6 Indian JL & Legal Rsch., 4*, 1.

Monika chhatwani, D., & Asthana, P.K. (2023). A Study Of Impact Of GST On Indian Economy.

Mukherjee, S. (2017). Changing Tax Capacity and Tax Effort of Indian States in the Era of High Economic Growth, 2001-2014.

Nayudu, A. (2019). Tax Revenue Efficiency in India States: The case of Stamp Duty and Registration Fees.

Neog, Y., & Gaur, A. K. (2020). Tax structure and economic growth: A study of selected Indian states. *Journal of Economic Structures*, 9(1), 9. DOI: 10.1186/s40008-020-00215-3

Ojha, A., Chouriya, I., & Anute, N. (2022). Impact of Indirect Tax Reforms in India. *Journal of Accounting Research, Business and Finance Management*.

Palanichamy, A. P. (2011). Fiscal policy reforms in India â€“ Overviews. *International Multidisciplinary Research Journal*,, 1.

Pathania, R. (2019). Estimation of Central Tax Buoyancy in India. *Journal of Global Economics*, 15, 158–166.

Poddar, S., & Ahmad, E. (2009). GST reforms and intergovernmental considerations in India. *Government of India, Ministry of Finance, Department of Economic Affairs. Working Paper*, 1, 2009.

Poirson, H. (2006). The Tax System in India: Could Reform Spur Growth? *Corporate Finance: Valuation*.

Rani, V. (2014). Tax reforms in India since 1991: An overview. *VISION: Journal of Indian Taxation*, 1(1), 36–54.

Rao, M. G. (2000). Tax reform in India: Achievements and challenges. *Asia-Pacific Development Journal*, 7(2), 59–74.

Rao, M. G. (2005). Tax system reform in India: Achievements and challenges ahead §. *Journal of Asian Economics*, 16(6), 993–1011. DOI: 10.1016/j.asieco.2005.10.003

Rao, M. G. (2016). Tyranny of the status quo: The challenges of reforming the Indian tax system. In *Indian Policy Forum 2015* (Vol. 16, No. 12, pp. 47-101).

Rao, M. G., & Rao, R. K. (2010Tax System Reform in India. In *Taxation in Developing Countries: Six Case Studies and Policy Implications* (pp. 109-152). Columbia University Press.

Rupa, R. (2017). GST in India: An Overview. *International Education and Research Journal*,, 3.

SAMANTARA. D. (2021). Tax reforms in India: A critical analysis. *Journal Homepage:*http://ijmr. net. *in, 9*(1).

Shao-ke, C. (2012). On the Reform Approach of China's Tax System under the Circumstances of the Transformation of the Pattern of Economy Development.

Singh, A., & Jaiswal, K. S. (2021). Post Implementation Issues of Goods and Services Tax in India. *Management Insight*, 17(02), 81–87. DOI: 10.21844/mijia.17.2.9

Singh, N., Srinivasan, T.N., Aziz, J., Cashin, P., Chaudhuri, S., Nair, M.R., Govinda Rao, M., Reddy, Y.V., Sahay, R., Towe, C.M., & Bhandari, L., Aarti, & Federalism, I. (2002). Indian Federalism, Economic Reform and Globalization. *The Developing Economies*.

Srivastava, S., Sultan, A., & Chashti, N. (2017). Influence of innovation competence on firm level competitiveness: An exploratory study. *Asia Pacific Journal of Innovation and Entrepreneurship*, 11(1), 63–75. DOI: 10.1108/APJIE-04-2017-021

Tekwani, K., & Pabla, C. K. (2021). Goods and Services Tax in India and Other Countries: A Comparative Study. *The Management Accountant Journal*, 56(7), 40–44. DOI: 10.33516/maj.v56i7.40-44p

Thaçi, L., & Gërxhaliu, A. (2018). Tax Structure and Developing Countries. *European Journal of Economics and Business Studies*, 4(1), 213–220. DOI: 10.26417/ejes.v10i1.p220-227

Vaid, B. (1972). Tax Policy and Tax Administration in India. *The Indian Journal of Public Administration*, 18(3), 426–435. DOI: 10.1177/0019556119720308

Venkataraman, S., & Urmi, A. (2017). The impact of taxation on economic growth in India: A disaggregated approach using the ARDL bounds test to co-integration. *International Journal of Accounting and Economics Studies*, 5(1), 19–21. DOI: 10.14419/ijaes.v5i1.7040

Vijayakumar, J., Rasheed, A. A., & Krishnan, V. (2005). Corruption and taxation: Lessons from the indian experience. *Journal of Public Budgeting, Accounting & Financial Management*, 17(3), 398–419. DOI: 10.1108/JPBAFM-17-03-2005-B007

KEY TERMS AND DEFINITIONS

Direct Tax: A direct tax is a tax that is paid directly to the entity that imposed it by an individual or organization.

Excise Tax: A statutory charge on certain products or services at the moment of purchase is known as an excise tax. Instead of being international taxes levied across national boundaries, they are intranational taxes levied inside a government infrastructure.

GST: The Goods and Services Tax is abbreviated as GST. In India, this indirect tax has taken the place of several other indirect taxes.

Indirect Tax: An indirect tax is one that is charged to the customer in addition to the cost of the commodity or service.

Tax: A charge, typically in the form of money, that is imposed by a governing body on individuals or property to fund public purposes.

Tax Administrator: Authority responsible for implementing tax laws and reforms.

Value Added Tax (VAT): The Central Government of India imposes Value Added Tax (VAT) as a kind of tax on the sale of goods and services to consumers. It is eventually imposed on the consumers who buy the products and services when they tend to buy and pay for them, even if it is meant to be paid by the producers of goods and services.

Chapter 10
Sustainable Economies:
Government Measures for Integrating Green Taxation in Higher Education Curricula

Sílvia Coutinho Santos
https://orcid.org/0009-0006-1123-658X
SDRI, Technological University of the Shannon, Ireland & CICF, Polytechnic University of Cávado and Ave, Portugal

Ana Arromba Dinis
https://orcid.org/0000-0003-3945-5726
Research Centre on Accounting and Taxation, Polytechnic University of Cávado and Ave, Portugal

Liliana Pereira
https://orcid.org/0000-0002-0211-6205
Research Centre on Accounting and Taxation, Polytechnic University of Cávado and Ave, Portugal

Shane O'Sullivan
Sustainable Development Research Institute, Technological University of the Shannon, Ireland

ABSTRACT

The protection of the environment is a matter of global concern that effects the population and endangers future generations. Consequently, the implementation of measures such as green taxation (also referred to in the international literature as environmental taxation and environmental law) is significant to effect behavioural change. In this context, the role of Higher Education Institutions (HEIs) is utmost importance in terms of sustainability and economic growth. This study aims to

DOI: 10.4018/979-8-3693-3908-4.ch010

critically analyse the courses offered in the field of green taxation at the top 100 universities in the Shanghai Ranking, 2023. This analysis will contribute to the body of knowledge about the progress made in teaching green taxation and the measures that have been put in place by governments to this end. The study revealed that in European Union and China, the teaching of science and technology continues to be a dominant force.

INTRODUCTION

The term globally accepted "sustainable development" was first introduced in 1987 by the United Nations World Commission on Environment and Development in their "Our Common Future" report, also known as the Brundtland Report. The concept refers to development that meets the needs of the present without compromising the ability of future generations to meet their own needs. It outlines long-term actions to ensure access to basic resources like water, food and energy, to preserve biodiversity and ecosystems, to manage urbanisation, and to meet basic social needs such as health, education and housing. Internationally, the report has helped to raise global awareness of this important environmental issue and aims to harmonise the existing growth/environment dilemma by prioritising the three pillars common to several international instruments: environment, economy and social equity (Hariram *et al.*, 2024; Lobo, 2019).

The United Nations Conference on Environment and Development, also known as the "Earth Summit", was held in June 1992, and resulted in Agenda 21, a global agreement on several aspects of sustainable development, as well as the adoption of the Convention on Climate Change, the Convention on Biological Diversity (Rio Declaration) and the Declaration of principles on Forests. Although Agenda 21 is not legally binding, it is a comprehensive document that sets out methods of action for implementation and forms of funding for sustainable development (Moallemi *et al.*, 2020).

Though efforts made, urgent measures are still needed to achieve sustainable development and fight climate change. Several authors such as Farooq *et al.* (2023) and Ozel (2022),have noted that, because of economic development since the Industrial Revolution, CO_2 emissions have increased in parallel with fast climate change due to its adverse effects. There was consensus on the need to reduce CO_2 emissions and stimulate economic growth through low-carbon policies (Farooq *et al.*, 2023). Thus, in December 1997, the 3rd United Nations Climate Change Conference adopted the Kyoto Protocol, which aims to reduce emissions below 1990 levels, and it has made the reduction of greenhouse gas emissions an urgent political goal. Despite criticism on ethical, moral and economic grounds, the Kyoto Protocol formalised the international community's commitment to tackling excessive CO_2 emissions by setting emissions reduction targets through a flexible mechanism that allows countries to increase and decrease emissions through the sale of credits, known as tradable emissions rights.

Acknowledging progress made since the Earth Summit, cost-benefit issues have become more prominent and asymmetry in development has led to an understanding that costs and benefits are not shared fairly and equitably. Therefore, governments have adopted measures to facilitate the transition to lower-carbon economies (Franky, 2023).

In September 2015, the international community adopted the 2030 Agenda for Sustainable Development (SD), which includes 17 Sustainable Development Goals (SDGs). These goals aim to achieve a broad range of targets, such as ending poverty and hunger, promoting quality education, decent work and economic growth, promoting equality, protecting the environment, and promoting peace and justice, among others. The concept of sustainable development and environmental protection is a top priority.

As the literature highlights, economists tend to favour command and control measures or market-based instruments such as taxes or licences to address environmental issues (Kühnhenrich, 2023). Hence, taxes are an essential means of achieving the 17 SDGs set out in the 2030 Agenda and financing defence, security and healthcare (Monteiro *et al.*, 2023). Green taxation has been advocated by several authors as a solution to climate change (Dinis *et al.*, 2023; Saraiva & Nylander, 2023).Furthermore, promoting and achieving the SDGs requires changes in procedures at several levels and sectors, which can create socio-economic, political, and financial pressures, despite the country's level of development (Raji & Demehin, 2023).

Education, and in particular HEIs, whose primary function is to disseminate knowledge, is considered the main strategy for raising awareness among young people and future professionals (Monteiro *et al.*, 2023). Hence, HEIs become a factor in changing attitudes and behaviour, playing a fundamental role in sustainable development and in changing the behaviour of society in general (Kougias & Efstathopoulos, 2020). The literature suggests that sustainability issues, in particular green taxation, should be included and improved in current curricula. This can be achieved by improving lecturer training on these issues and by introducing the available educational tools. Not necessarily create new subjects, but rather to improve the educational offer (Olcina & Morote, 2023).

As previously mentioned, market-based economic instruments are used to change public behaviour and encourage technological innovation to protect and rehabilitate the environment. These instruments include taxation, fees/charges, subsidies and allow trading, and are designed to internalise environmental externalities under Pigou's Theorem (also known as the "Polluter Pays Principle") established in 1920

(Tan *et al.*, 2022). Under this Theorem, Arthur C. Pigou argues that governments have a responsibility to use tax policy instruments, such as green taxation (also known as Pigouvian taxes), as the most effective means of reducing environmental degradation (Manta *et al.*, 2023).

In line with social and economic development, a governance model for the implementation of green taxation for environmental prevention is emerging at several levels. For instance, in the United States of America (USA), Nixon promulgated regulations and laws to protect the environment, such as the Gaz-Guzzler tax, introduced in 1978 by the Energy Tax Act. The United Kingdom (UK), where the Industrial Revolution began and where the environment has undergone significant changes, was one of the first countries to introduce legislation to fight climate change, and it is now considered to have one of the most comprehensive systems (Bell *et al.*, 2017). Furthermore, studies suggest that achieving environmental quality requires a balance between accountability and taxation and that promoting high standards of accountability can help reduce the need for taxation and contribute to environmental quality (Andıç, 2023; Tan *et al.*, 2022). In this vein, HEIs have a fundamental role in the teaching of sustainable development. This is widely recognised, and as a result, subjects such as green taxation have been introduced into their curricula (Rosário & Raimundo, 2024).

In this scope, with this study, the authors aim to evaluate the government measures and initiatives for the implementation of green taxation in the curricula of HEIs. It also aims to identify strategies, challenges and barriers in teaching these topics. Therefore, the authors will analyse the management, taxation, law and accounting courses of the top 100 universities from the Shanghai Ranking to analyse the inclusion of green taxation and research the measures adopted for its implementation. Finally, the authors aim to identify the causes of success or failure in the teaching of sustainable development in HEIs and provide recommendations for incorporating green taxation into their curricula. Following this introduction, section two is dedicated to a literature review. Section three describes the research methodology, section four presents and discuss the results. Finally, in the fifth section, the main conclusions of the study are presented.

BACKGROUND

Green Taxation and Higher Education Institutions

As argued by Adhikari & Shrestha (2024), the concept of implementation and research for sustainable higher education in universities was formed in the mid-1990s. This transition concept gained further solidity with the target 4.7 of SDG 4, established by the Global Action Programme (GAP, 2015-2019), approved by the United Nations Educational, Scientific and Cultural Organization (UNESCO) General Conference at its 40th Session and accepted by the United Nations (UN) General Assembly at its 74th Session in 2019. In this regard, the authors posit that HEIs have a fundamental responsibility to achieve and promote the UN 2030 Agenda. Similarly, McCowan (2023) postulates that higher education is of critical importance in the attainment of the SDGs. This assertion is predicated upon the premise that HEIs provide training in disciplines and specialties that are of paramount significance to the achievement of the 17 SDGs.

In this scope, as emphasised by Lima *et al.* (2024), the SDGs serve as a framework for the development of medium- and long-term planning, thereby providing the alignment of social, environmental, and economic policies. Sustainability is not solely concerned with environmental issues, but also encompasses cultural and societal considerations. In addition to the more general issues that are of concern to the global community, such as the pandemic, the challenges of poverty, terrorism, and war, as well as the phenomenon of mass migration, the issue of global warming is a matter of urgent concern to both the public and private sectors alike (Olcina & Morote, 2023). Thus, education plays a crucial role in the process of increasing awareness and encouraging critical thinking regarding the development of solutions to fight climate change.

In relation to the issue of climate change, the actions proposed for the implementation of strategies to mitigate its effects include: firstly, decarbonisation, which is the reduction of carbon emissions from human activity; secondly, the circular economy, which is based on the principle of recycling; thirdly, biodiversity, which is the maintenance of ecosystems and the protection of wildlife; fourthly, the reduction of pollution in the environment, specifically in air, water and soil; and fifthly, the development of sustainable food systems and rural areas (Ceko & Cakrani, 2023). Hence, the implementation of green taxation is regarded as a key instrument for the dual purpose of tackling environmental issues and economic development. In alignment with the European Green Deal, it can be argued that green taxation plays an instrumental role in facilitating a greener and more sustainable economy (Gore *et al.*, 2022).

Initially, the prevailing perception of green taxation was that it represented a less costly approach to addressing environmental issues than through the imposition of regulations. This concept was based on the British political agenda, through the "Pearce Repot" for the Department of the Environment in 1989 (Ceko & Cakrani, 2023). However, considering the alarming scale of environmental crisis and the realisation of the necessity for urgent environmental protection measures, the primary rationale for green taxation has shifted towards the "polluter pays principle", i.e., this principle was designed with the objective of reducing activities that are detrimental to the environment.

Furthermore, Dias & Ribeiro (2023) emphasised the interrelationship between tax law and green taxation and underscores the necessity to use economic mechanisms in the fight of climate change. Nevertheless, since the primary function of taxation is to collect funds for States to fulfil the needs of their citizens and when they adopt a function other than this core purpose, the result is corrective taxation, which are regarded as an effective instrument in the suppression of socially undesirable activities, such as pollution, CO_2 emissions, among others. It is also the case that such taxes can be viewed as an additional revenue-raising measure for governments. In this sense, green taxation is not widely accepted or understood, but is perceived as another tax burden (Ewald *et al.*, 2022).

The carbon tax is the principal tax policy within the scope of green taxation in several countries. However, as the literature asserts, this green tax is challenging to design (Uddin *et al.*, 2023). To achieve the necessary acceptance of taxes, for example on energy, and understanding of green taxation, and to change society's behaviours, the green tax must be collected, and the tax revenue must be distributed through appropriate mechanisms. Thus, in order to facilitate the adoption of renewable energies and encourage compliance with the SDGs, instruments such as government subsidies are essential (Yan *et al.*, 2024). Academics and professionals have advocated for education as a pivotal instrument in the fight to climate change, as evidenced by references to SDG targets 4.7, 13.3 and 12.8 in the Agenda 2030. Education plays a fundamental role in achieving SDG 4, particularly regarding environmental protection and the social consequences of climate change (Ilgov *et al.*, 2021). Furthermore, it is posited that education can be used as a tool by governments, institutions, communities, and organisations to implement measures to disseminate knowledge, as understanding about green taxes policies to citizens and encourage them to fight climate change. Also, as states McKenzie *et al.* (2024), it is not currently possible to measures progress on the indicators corresponding to climate change education, in particular on green taxation, due to the lack of appropriate and consistent indicators. Hence, as stated by Ilgov *et al.* (2021), it is imperative that government and civil society collaborate to integrate the SDGs, in addition to green taxation and green tax incentives, into the educational curricula of HEIs, irrespective of their geographical location.

Likewise, several authors reiterate the fundamental role of green taxation in fighting climate change. They propose it as a mean of changing behaviour and to charge the social costs associated with pollution and ecological devastation on the costs of the polluting activities (Ali *et al.*, 2023; Hua, 2024). For the authors, teaching, in common with learning and sustainability, is a tool design to alter entrenched consumption patterns. It is therefore of the utmost importance to integrate values inherent to SD at all levels and in all aspects of learning, adopting a holistic and multidisciplinary approach to sustainability and its impact on SD. Such an approach should facilitate the understanding, application of critical thinking, problem-solving and action to meet the challenges to fighting the climate change (Ilgov *et al.*, 2021). Thus, with this study the authors intend to contribute to a better understanding of the teaching of green taxation, in particularly in HEIs, as well as the government measures implemented to achieve this goal.

Government Initiatives and Green Tax Policies

Education, in general, and universities in particular, are crucial for developing national identities. They have a special role in educating state bureaucrats, civil servants, lecturers and leaders, known as the social elite, who defend, govern and develop Nation States. In this sense, as Uljens & Elo (2024) argues, universities adopt a conservative and reproductive stance in society, generally framed in this concept from a financial, legal and political point of view. Conversely, the notion that universities are responsible for disseminating knowledge and educating individuals is increasingly being reinforced. This entails accessibility to all, with local and global connections. Additionally, universities have assumed a third mission: to assist regions and national needs. Higher education is an asset for economic and labour market policies worldwide, as the knowledge imparted is expected to be useful for regional economic purposes. Hence, the role of education is to facilitate the participation of young people in and the transformation of several social domains, including politics, economics, and culture (Uljens & Elo, 2024).

It is widely acknowledged by Feigin *et al.* (2023) that to ensure the continued viability of future living conditions, urgent measures must be taken at all social levels in relation to climate change. Sustainability issues have been a concern since 1960s, and there has been a growing focus on sustainability and sustainable development since the 1990s. In the context of UNESCO, sustainability is defined as a long-term objective, whereas sustainable development is the process leading to that objective. Thus, the concept of sustainability emerged in the 1960s, and it was in the 1980s that sustainable development became a political agenda. This culminated in the year 2015 and the 2030 Agenda, which includes 17 SDGs and 169 targets. These aim to fight climate change, harmonise humanity's relationship with nature and develop a more equal world, with the goal of ending poverty and hunger (Wolff *et al.*, 2024).

Nevertheless, the outcome of the 28th Annual Conference of the Parties (COP) of the United Nations Framework Convention on Climate Change (UNFCCC), held in Dubai from November 30th to December 13th 2023, revealed a discrepancy between climate change regulations and the standards established by scientific consensus and actual state-level practices. Consequently, there is an urgent need for these states to rethink and improve their regulatory mechanisms to guarantee the proposed targets (Desai & Desai, 2024). The solution that several states have identified as a mean of fighting climate change is green taxation. This involves the use of taxes to internalise the external costs of environmental degradation, as well as the implementation of green tax incentives with the aim of promoting sustainable and environmentally "friendly" practices and choices. The results of several studies have reiterated the effectiveness of green taxation in protecting the environment, particularly in reducing CO_2 emissions, through the implementation of carbon taxes and waste disposal taxes, among others (Levaggi & Panteghini, 2023; Soku *et al.*, 2023). Regarding green tax incentives, it is important to note that these are forms of governmental intervention in order to protect non-tax public interest. Such green tax incentives can be presented in the form of deductions and reductions, which are designed to influence environmentally responsible consumer behaviour. Reference can be made to the U.S. Code and the Inflation Reduction Act (IRA) of 2022, Section 13301, which provides a consumer tax credit for energy-efficiency improvements of residential homes, rate of 30 per cent of the cost, with limits for each type of improvement and total per year (Revenue Service, 2023). Also, the Portuguese Law and the Tax Benefits Statute (EBF)[1], articles 44º-A and 44º-B, which provide reduction in the Municipal Property Tax (IMI) rate of 25 and 50 per cent for buildings and properties designed to produce energy from renewable and energy-efficient sources[2].

It is evident that governments have a pivotal role in environmental policies, encourage responsible consumerism and serve as a mechanism for the implementation and development of environmentally sustainable policies that are economically viable, without jeopardizing the environment (Cheng *et al.*, 2024). In this regard, it is also the responsibility of governments to establish guidelines for the dissemination of knowledge to achieve this objective, particularly through higher education.

Integration of Green Taxation in Higher Education Curricula

It is irrefutable that environmental issues have been intensifying globally, with the primary driver being the unsustainable exploitation of natural resources driven by human desires, which is further compounded by population growth. Therefore, it is evident that a multitude if environmental issues have arisen because of industrialisation, including pollution, global warming, acid rain, the destruction of the ozone layer, the generation of toxic waste, the loss of biodiversity, and the depletion of natural resources (Siddiqua *et al.*, 2022).

The prevailing opinion in the academic literature asserts that the failure of governments to adopt sufficient measures to regulate industrial activity has a detrimental effect not only on the environment itself, but also on human health and safety, and the occurrence and intensity of natural disasters, such as earthquakes and floods (Patel & Jhalani, 2024).

It can generally be observed that, in the business world, profit remains the principal objective of organisations, with the environment and its environmental impact taking a secondary position, despite the implementation of regulations and guidelines aimed at prompting organisations to devise strategies for minimising their environmental impact. This approach serves to reinforce the role of education, particularly higher education, as a mean of equipping future professionals with the knowledge and skills required to make decisions in line with the principles of sustainable development.

There are several economic instruments that can be employed to achieve sustainability, which include green taxation, economic compensation, investment in infrastructure construction, and so forth. Of these, green taxation is regarded as one of the most important instruments, being described by Hua (2024) as a mandatory levy imposed on activities that have a significant adverse impact on the environment, such as the discharge of sewage, waste gas, noise and waste. For the author, this is done in order to maintain the ecological environment.

The utilisation of green taxes and tax incentives has emerged as a favoured instrument in the pursuit of sustainable development, with studies indicating that their effectiveness can be enhanced by further action despite potential political implications (European Commission, 2020). The conclusion of Green Keynesianism is that a green tax policy will be an effective means of mitigating the deterioration of the environment. Furthermore, it will act as an instrument associated with economic growth, influencing production levels, energy use and the environment (Ya *et al.*, 2024).

As previously stated, the acquisition of knowledge and development of skills in these subjects is of the utmost importance and is subject to the content, programme and curricula for environmental protection (Thanh & Van Toan, 2023). Consequently, a comprehensive and coherent approach to the core subjects will be essential, encompassing a multidisciplinary approach with the objective of equipping students with the skills they will require in the future. It can be argued that the contemporary understanding of education should encompass a global perspective. Therefore, those in charge of educational institutions must collaborate with several actors within and outside the institution to create curricula with environmental protection as their overarching objective.

Challenges to the inclusion of Green Taxation in the Higher Education Curricula

On 18 September 1988, the *Magna Charta Universitatum* was signed by several European University Rectors in Bologna, Italy. This document reaffirmed the vital role of universities in lifelong learning in a fast-evolving global society, where the autonomy of educational institutions is a fundamental principle. This autonomy is manifested in the research and teaching activities that facilitate the development and dissemination of scientific knowledge.

According to the Lisbon Declaration, which resulted from the Fourth Convention of HEI in the European Union (EU) under the theme: "Universities of Europe beyond 2010: Diversity with a common goal" in March 2005 and formally adopted by the Council of the European University Association (EUA) in April 2007, academic autonomy has four dimensions. These include: (i) academic autonomy, this is, the provision of diplomas, curriculum, teaching methods, areas of study, scope, objectives and research methods; (ii) financial autonomy, which pertains to the acquisition and allocation of funds, the determination of tuition fees, and the accumulation of surpluses; (iii) organisational autonomy, which concerns the establishment of university structures and statutes, contracts, as well as the election of decision-making bodies and personnel; and (iv) staffing autonomy, which encompasses matters related to the recruitment, wage allocation, and promotion of the personnel. It is therefore acknowledged that, as in the past, institutional autonomy and academic freedom are essential characteristics of a democratic society. Nevertheless, as the literature reiterates, these fundamental principles are jeopardised in situations of political crisis, thereby presenting a challenge for higher education institutions (Qorraj *et al.*, 2022).

In view of the growing globalisation of higher education, curricula have become a pivotal factor in determining the role and status of HEIs. This is particularly relevant in relation to academic autonomy in designing teaching and research objectives and content.

Conversely, a consideration of the financial aspects of higher education reveals that universities are reliant on several external sources of funding, including government subsidies, charitable donations, and grants from private organisations. These financial resources can present a challenge to the principles of academic freedom and institutional autonomy that are fundamental to the mission of HEIs. According to (Mundy, 2023), when it comes to the allocation of funds for the education sector and global partnerships for their financing, it can be observed that this point is not yet optimally efficient due to the lack of a more autonomous financing system capable of effectively addressing the need for progress in the field of education. Furthermore, as the authors argue in the present research, to integrate subjects aimed to achieving sustainability into university curricula, it will be necessary to integrate means to provide teaches with training and skills in teaching these subjects.

This should not be limited to topics directly related to environmental protection, namely green taxation, but should be also target other areas to make students aware of the problems and instil in them critical thinking to solve them. In this context, Moreno-Pino *et al.* (2022) proposes in his study the integration of mathematics lecturer training for the inclusion of sustainability domains in the curricula of that subject, with the support of the Network of Green Curricula of Curricular Environmentalization in Higher Education (ACES), created in 2000 in accordance with the European Union's Alpha programme, which aimed to establish criteria for the development of a sustainable curriculum.

While there have been some advances in monitoring the advancement of the 2030 Agenda development, more specifically SDG 4, these have not yet reached the desired level of effectiveness. The UNESCO World Education Monitoring Report team and the UNESCO Institute for Statistics have made notable contributions, but their efforts are still not deemed sufficient. It is acknowledged that monitoring and accountability for learning outcomes in education are of great importance, yet there is no common, independent body for this monitoring and evaluation (Mundy, 2023).

METHODOLOGY

This study employs an exploratory and descriptive qualitative design, with the collection of data on the websites of the top 100 universities from the Shanghai Ranking, also known as the Academic Ranking of World Universities (ARWU), which is widely regarded as one of the most respected universities ranking systems (Luque-Martínez, 2023). Hence, the analysis focused on courses in management, taxation, accounting, and law, to determine whether sustainable development and green taxation were included in their curricula. In addition, it was analysed related research articles and collected data from institutional and governmental websites to evaluate the management and implementation measures of green taxation in the curricula of the universities under study. The collected data was compiled in a Microsoft Excel database for accumulation, sorting, visualisation, and processing. Ethical issues will be handled confidentially to ensure the study's ethical integrity. No human participants were involved in this research.

In view of these considerations, it appears pertinent to carry out a study on government measures to integrate the teaching of green taxation into HEIs curricula in the USA, China and the EU, since in these matters the UK follows the EU guidelines, and given that these countries and regions account for the highest number of universities in the top 100 universities in the Shanghai Ranking, as illustrated in

Figure 1. The countries and regions analysed collectively represents 74 per cent of the 100 HEIs under study.

Figure 1. The Top 100 universities from the Shanghai Ranking 2023 by countries/ regions (Shanghai Ranking, 2023)

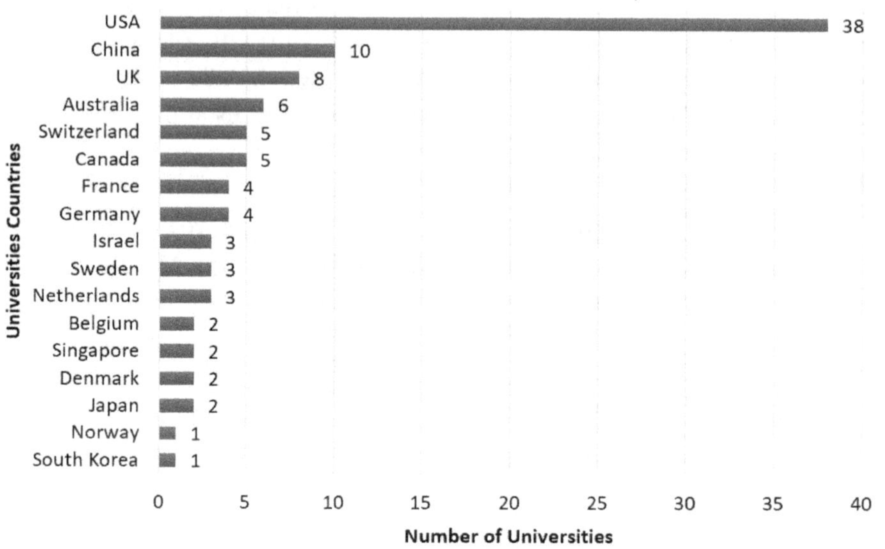

Following the adoption of the UN's 2030 Agenda and its SDGs in 2015, there was a collective concern among Member States and the international community to ensure that governments aided in the advancement of capabilities, knowledge dissemination and student engagement in sustainable development. In fact, guidelines were issued for HEIs, but they are not compulsory, and HEIs are free to adopt them. Indeed, several have chosen to do so, such as USA, France and the UK. In this scope, several universities in the USA signed the United States Department of Education's Climate Action Plan, which the main objective is achieve the climate neutrality in campus operations and academic programs (Ilgov *et al.*, 2021). In the National Environmental Policy Act of 1969 is referred to the federal government's policy of cooperation with state and local governments and other public and private organisations. This is with a view to providing technical and financial assistance for the promotion of well-being and harmony between humans and nature. The aim is to fulfil the social and economic requirements of the present and future generations ('National Environmental Policy Act of 1969', 2023). Thus, the US Congress authorises and orders that policies and regulations be interpreted and administrated in accordance with the policies set out therein, namely regarding the use of systematic and interdisciplinary approach, through the natural and social sciences, for the design, planning and decision-making with an impact on the environment. This is to the extent possible, which could suggest that the sense of obligation may be perceived in a rather subtle manner.

However, it is through the National Environmental Education Act that environmental education is promoted, reinforcing this need due to a several threats to human health, global warming, and the pollution of the oceans, among others. The Act emphasises the importance of a considered approach, informed by an understanding of the environment and the origins of environmental issues, to implement measures and programmes to train and educate capable professionals. This includes the introduction of subjects in the curricula of HEIs, such as those related to environmental engineering. It is evident from this analysis that the Federal Government, through the Environmental Protection Agency, is proposing to provide financial support for these measures, although their implementation is not mandatory.

It is assumed that the programme will support the development and dissemination of curriculum models, environmental education seminars, and other forms of educational outreach. Additionally, it implemented programmes to train lecturers to teach environmental education, environmental sciences, and other related subjects. Finally, the National Environment Education Advisory Council and a Federal Task Force on Environmental Education were established to provide counsel and recommendations regarding the activities and polices within the scope of the document ('National Environmental Education Act 1', 2022).

As an example of some government measures, in 2022, the National Science Foundation (NSF), an independent federal agency that supports science and engineering, awarded Ohio State University, through its Division of Graduate Education, a pilot programme for multidisciplinary graduate research fellowships to study climate change and socioeconomic inequality. The NSF Innovations of Graduate Education (IGE) programme, called "Wicked Problems", aims to train young researchers in multidisciplinary skills and then validate innovative approaches in higher education in those fields (DGE Division of Graduate Education, 2022).

China, is a country widely associated with the environmental damage, and thus it is not surprising that the literature reinforces the use of green taxation to control consumption and production and improve the environment, achieve innovation and sustainability (Ya *et al.*, 2024). Indeed, China has undergone several changes in higher education, including the management of HEIs, which has been entrusted to partnerships between the central and provincial governments and is undergoing a gradual process of decentralisation (Baocun & Yalun, 2020).

As part of this restructuring process, the main projects are: (i) Project 211, implemented in 1995, aimed at measures to strengthen the quality of higher education and new technologies; (ii) Project 985, implemented in 1998, whose main objective is to promote the internalisation of higher education; and (iii) Plan 2011, i.e., the 'National Medium-Long Term Plan for the Development of Science and Technology (2006-2020)', which remains in effect and aims to improve science and technology by encouraging the creation of research departments associated with HEIs, until the year of 2020 (Oliveira & Poiatti, 2022), as reflected in the predominant curricula of HEIs, e.g., Fundan University.

In this regard, despite the intended internationalisation, the supposed autonomy of HEIs in their management and the influence of the SDGs adopted by the international community, higher education in China still must overcome some challenges, namely the lack of complete clarity about the responsibilities and duties in the management of HEIS due to insufficient decentralisation on the part of the government, which undermines their autonomy and power. Finally, as (Sun & Sun, 2022) emphasises, there still a lack of lecturer training in subjects such as green taxation and of initiative to include it in the curricula. Meanwhile, the gap between rural and urban areas in terms of education is still not resolved, and opportunities for rural youth are fewer and unequal, which affects their access to higher education (Guo & Li, 2024).

In the EU, the fundamental role of HEIs in education, research and innovation in addressing societal challenges and economic growth is increasingly recognised, with particular focus on sharing knowledge and resources, and creating opportunities through alliances between countries, in line with EU interests and values. A case in point is the European University initiative, which forms part of the creation of a European Higher Education Area (EHEA). This includes European Education Area (EEA) and the European Research Area (ERA) (Council Resolution on a Strategic Framework for European Cooperation in Education and Training towards the European Education Area and beyond (2021-2030), 2021).

Considering the necessity for students and the general population to be adequately prepared with the requisite skills for a sustainable development, recommendations are put forth and a framework is proposed to guide Member States in the formulation of national education and training policies, with the objective of achieving the EES by 2025, implementing initiatives such as the European Student Card, joint European degree, among others. Regarding monetary support measures, the EU provides a multiannual financial framework to support HEIs, between the 2021/2027 period, coming from programmes such as Erasmus+, Horizon Europe, Recovery and Resilience Facility, Digital Europe, etc., and each has a specific objective (Communication from the Commission to the European Parliament, The Council, The European Economic and Social Committee and the Committee of the Regions: On a European Strategy for Universities, 2022).

In point, the EU presents measures to be applied in higher education of its Member States. However, it will be up to each of them to make use of these instruments, to follow the guidelines given, with a view to achieving the goal of sustainable development. Nevertheless, as is the case in Germany, achieving sustainability mainly involves engineering and science.

Figure 2. The Top 100 universities from the Shanghai Ranking 2023 by universities/ courses (Shanghai Ranking, 2023)

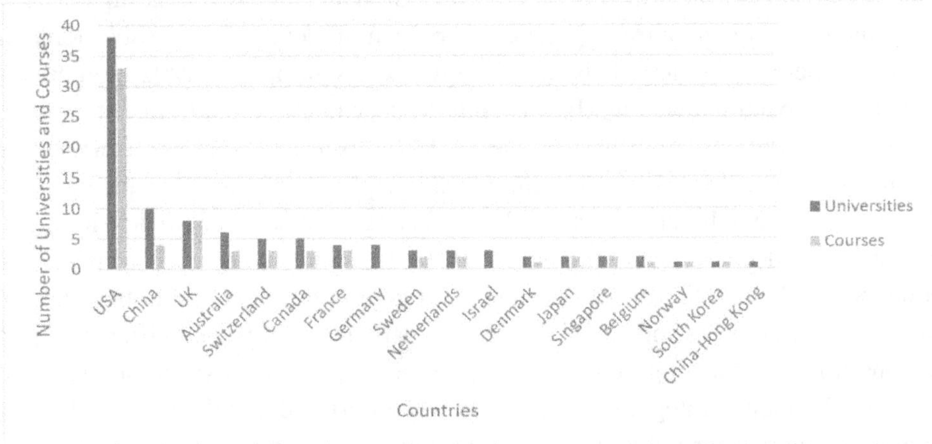

Figure 2 illustrates the number of universities per country, as well as the total number of courses in the field of green taxation. In the USA, our findings indicate that approximately 70 percent of HEIs offer courses in this area. It is noteworthy that four universities only offer courses in the field of medicine, biomedicine and health sciences. Regarding China, it was not possible to verify the curricula at five HEIs due to language barriers. The course programmes were not in English, and it was not possible to use a translator for the analysis. Additionally, two universities offer courses in the fields of medicine and technology sciences. Thus, 20 per cent of the courses offered in the field under study were identified. Finally, in the EU, which includes the UK, approximately 31 per cent of HEIs offer training exclusively in the fields of medicine, life sciences, and engineering. Conversely, 65 per cent of HEIs offer courses in green taxation.

SOLUTIONS AND RECOMMENDATIONS

It can be argued that education should not be solely regarded as a conduit for disseminating knowledge. Rather, it should be conceptualized as a multifaceted undertaking. For example, according to (Moreno-Pino *et al.*, 2022), mathematics and mathematics education should be developed from a critical perspective and with a view to finding solutions to the problems facing society today, such as climate change.

It is therefore of paramount importance to emphasise the necessity of restructuring higher education, adopting an integral vision and an understanding between traditional teaching and a more practical approach, to develop viable solutions for the environment and society. This is, as Kougias & Efstathopoulos (2020) reiterates, a holistic approach to teaching. In this vein, as previously stated in this study, it is crucial to implement training programmes for lecturers in areas such as green taxation and sustainability, this will enable the multidisciplinary nature of teaching, with subjects that have a direct impact on climate change and sustainable development.

Considering the constraints, namely the HEIs financial resources, it is imperative to underscore the pivotal role of the state in spearheading initiatives to this end. To illustrate, the Recovery and Resilience Plan (PRR) represents a significant step in this direction. A financing and loan programme, aligned with six pillars relevant to the development strategy, was signed between Portugal and the EU in 2021. Of note is the support for political reforms, in particular improvements to access to higher education, quality and inclusiveness. This is but one example of a measure that HEIs could employ to implement lecturer training for the delivery of quality education and sustainable development.

FUTURE RESEARCH DIRECTIONS

Although the study is of great significance and could be considered a starting point for the research of government measures, particularly with respect to the integration of green taxation and sustainability in higher education, there is an opportunity to extend it further, with emphasis on the implementation of internal multidisciplinary training for lecturers to the teaching of these subjects, the link between them, students and society, etc. The results will provide a foundation for the implementation of good practices in HEIs.

Finally, it is important to emphasise the role of HEIs in achieving the SDGs and ensuring the future of future generations. This is achieved through the transmission of knowledge and examples of good practice. Therefore, it is pertinent to conduct in-depth studies related to education in HEIs.

CONCLUSION

Regarding the fundamental principles of autonomy and academic freedom of HEIs, it can be argued that these should be considered inviolable. However, it is possible for these principles become fragile due to political influence, particularly in countries where higher education is under the control of governments with low levels of popularity and a history of repression, commonly referred to as countries in transition, such as China (Feng *et al.*, 2022). In such contexts, the principles of autonomy and academic freedom are likely to be weaker than in countries that enjoy greater levels of political stability. Therefore, one of the key challenges in introducing the teaching of green taxation into HEI curricula emerges.

On the other hand, it is indisputable that lecturers occupy a pivotal position within the field of education, which means that they should be equipped with exemplary skills and motivation, as multidisciplinary learning and the well-being of those responsible for teaching are of paramount importance. To achieve this, it is recommended that states incorporate tools into their education systems with the objective of fostering and supporting innovation and quality in teaching. This is in line with the understanding of EU (Council Resolution on a Strategic Framework for European Cooperation in Education and Training towards the European Education Area and beyond: 2021-2030, 2021).

Thus, it is important to transfer knowledge and awareness to people in general, and young people in particular, to promote understanding of environmental risks, as well as tools to protect the environment, which means an investment in both the short-term and long-term impact they can have on climate change. As it is supported by literature, environmental education is an important tool for achieving sustainable development (Thanh & Van Toan, 2023; Uljens & Elo, 2024).

In the context of higher education and teaching of green taxation, it is evident that, in view of the challenges young people will face, it is of the utmost importance to incorporate this subject into the curriculum, along with other related subjects, from an innovative perspective. This should be achieved by promoting multidisciplinary and interactive curricula, to stimulate critical thinking and encourage innovative and alternative solutions (Gomes *et al.*, 2023; Lafuente-Lechuga *et al.*, 2024).

ACKNOWLEDGMENT

This research was supported by national funds through the FCT – Foundation for Science and Technology, I.P., under the project PRT/BD/154681/2023, UIDB/04043/2020 and UIDP/04043/2020. We acknowledge the anonymous reviewers for their valuable feedback and contributions in refining this article to its present form.

REFERENCES

Adhikari, D. R., & Shrestha, P. (2024). The context and concept of higher education for sustainable development: The case of Nepal. *International Journal of Sustainability in Higher Education*, 25(2), 238–264. DOI: 10.1108/IJSHE-12-2021-0521

Ali, K., Jianguo, D., Kirikkaleli, D., Oláh, J., & Bakhsh, S. (2023). Do environmental taxes, environmental innovation, and energy resources matter for environmental sustainability: Evidence of five sustainable economies. *Heliyon*, 9(11), e21577. DOI: 10.1016/j.heliyon.2023.e21577 PMID: 38034728

Andıç, N. Ö. (2023). Green Taxes in the Solution of Environmental Problems and the Case of Türkiye. In *Taking on Climate Change Through Green Taxation* (pp. 198–217). DOI: 10.4018/978-1-6684-8592-7.ch008

Baocun, L., & Yalun, A. (2020). Educational Administration and Leadership in China. In *Oxford Research Encyclopedia of Education*. Oxford University Press., DOI: 10.1093/acrefore/9780190264093.013.629

Bell, S., McGillivray, D., Pedersen, O. W., Lees, E., & Stokes, E. (2017). *Environmental law* (9th ed.). Oxford University Press. DOI: 10.1093/he/9780198748328.001.0001

Ceko, E., & Cakrani, E. (2023). Environmental Tax Reform in Western Balkan Countries. In *Taking on Climate Change Through Green Taxation* (pp. 101–153). DOI: 10.4018/978-1-6684-8592-7.ch005

Cheng, Y., Zhao, G., Meng, W., & Wang, Q. (2024). Resources utilization, taxation and green education: A path to sustainable power generation. *Resources Policy*, 88, 104389. Advance online publication. DOI: 10.1016/j.resourpol.2023.104389

Communication from the Commission to the European Parliament. The Council, The European Economic and Social Committee and the Committee of the Regions: On a European Strategy for Universities, European Commission (2022). https://europa.eu/eurobarometer/surveys/detail/2186

Council Resolution on a Strategic Framework for European Cooperation in Education and Training towards the European Education Area and beyond (2021-2030), Official Journal of the European Union (2021).

Desai, B. H., & Desai, J. B. (2024). The Climate Change Conundrum: A Case for Course Correction in the Global Regulatory Approach. *Environmental Policy and Law*, 54(1), 3–14. DOI: 10.3233/EPL-239028

DGE Division of Graduate Education. (2022). *NSF Award Search Award # 2224769 - Training Scientists to Tackle Grand Challenge Societal Problems through Convergent Action in Transdisciplinary Teams*. https://www.nsf.gov/awardsearch/showAward?AWD_ID=2224769

Dias, S. L., & Ribeiro, J. S. (2023). Taxation Policies as an Environmental Protection Instrument: The Portuguese Case. In A. A. Dinis, F. David, L. Pereira, & S. L. Dias (Eds.), *Taking on Climate Change Through Green Taxation* (pp. 265–281). IGI Global. DOI: 10.4018/978-1-6684-8592-7.ch011

Dinis, A. A., Carvalho, A., & Dias, S. L. (2023). Sustainable Taxi Fleet: An Approach to the Contribution of Green Taxation. In *Taking on Climate Change Through Green Taxation* (pp. 241–264). IGI Global. DOI: 10.4018/978-1-6684-8592-7.ch010

European Commission. (2020). *Taxation in support of green transition: an overview and assessment of existing tax practices to reduce greenhouse gas emissions Final Report*. DOI: 10.2778/343194

Ewald, J., Sterner, T., & Sterner, E. (2022). Understanding the resistance to carbon taxes: Drivers and barriers among the general public and fuel-tax protesters. *Resource and Energy Economics*, 70, 101331. Advance online publication. DOI: 10.1016/j.reseneeco.2022.101331

Farooq, U., Haider Subhani, B., Nouman Shafiq, M., & Gillani, S. (2023). Assessing the environmental impacts of environmental tax rate and corporate statutory tax rate: Empirical evidence from industry-intensive economies. *Energy Reports*, 9, 6241–6250. DOI: 10.1016/j.egyr.2023.05.254

Feigin, S. V., Wiebers, D. O., Lueddeke, G., Morand, S., Lee, K., Knight, A., Brainin, M., Feigin, V. L., Whitfort, A., Marcum, J., Shackelford, T. K., Skerratt, L. F., & Winkler, A. S. (2023). Proposed solutions to anthropogenic climate change: A systematic literature review and a new way forward. *Heliyon*, 9(10), e20544. Advance online publication. DOI: 10.1016/j.heliyon.2023.e20544 PMID: 37867892

Feng, Y., Tan, X., & Wang, R. (2022). The value of higher education to entrepreneurial performance: Evidence from higher education expansion in China. *China Economic Review*, 73, 101789. Advance online publication. DOI: 10.1016/j.chieco.2022.101789

Franky, F. E. R. (2023). Analysis of financial and tax support for green businesses in Colombia. In *Taking on Climate Change Through Green Taxation* (pp. 1–25). IGI Global., DOI: 10.4018/978-1-6684-8592-7.ch001

Gomes, P., Teixeira, C., & Azevedo, G. (2023). Debate: Integrating new perspectives in public sector accounting education (PSAE). *Public Money & Management*, 43(7), 727–728. DOI: 10.1080/09540962.2023.2248409

Gore, T., Urios, J., & Karamperi, M. (2022). Green and fair taxation in the EU - Green EU tax systems tend to also be more progressive. *Institute for European Environmental Policy*. https://ieep.eu/publications/green-and-fair-taxation-in-the-eu/

Guo, Y., & Li, X. (2024). Regional inequality in China's educational development: An urban-rural comparison. *Heliyon*, 10(4), e26249. Advance online publication. DOI: 10.1016/j.heliyon.2024.e26249 PMID: 38379968

Hariram, N. P., Mekha, K. B., Suganthan, V., & Sudhakar, K. (2024). Decoding the epics of sustainable world: Sustainalism. *Social Sciences & Humanities Open*, 10, 100958. Advance online publication. DOI: 10.1016/j.ssaho.2024.100958

Hua, L. (2024). The impact of environmental taxation on the structure and performance of industrial symbiosis networks: An agent-based simulation study. *Heliyon*, 10(3), e25675. Advance online publication. DOI: 10.1016/j.heliyon.2024.e25675 PMID: 38356598

Ilgov, V., Gardanova, Z., & Nikitina, N. (2021). Sustainable development of the universities in the 21stcentury. *E3S Web of Conferences, 250*. DOI: 10.1051/e3sconf/202125004010

Kougias, K., & Efstathopoulos, J. (2020). The Operational Framework of the Greek Educational System as an Obstacle to the Implementation of Sustainable School. *Frontiers in Education*, 5, 142. Advance online publication. DOI: 10.3389/feduc.2020.00142

Kühnhenrich, D. (2023). The German Environmental Tax Reform: A difference-in-differences analysis of its impacts in European comparison. *Environmental Economics and Policy Studies*. Advance online publication. DOI: 10.1007/s10018-023-00375-z

Lafuente-Lechuga, M., Cifuentes-Faura, J., & Faura-Martínez, Ú. (2024). Teaching sustainability in higher education by integrating mathematical concepts. *International Journal of Sustainability in Higher Education*, 25(1), 62–77. DOI: 10.1108/IJSHE-07-2022-0221

Levaggi, R., & Panteghini, P. M. (2023). Environmental taxation and profit-shifting activities. In *Ecological Economics* (Vol. 214). Elsevier B.V., DOI: 10.1016/j.ecolecon.2023.107972

Lima, J. M., Borsatto, S., Marcolin, C. B., Cardoso Abdalla, E., & Dutra Amaral, F. (2024). Aligning community outreach initiatives with SDGs in a higher education institution with artificial intelligence. *Cleaner and Responsible Consumption*, 12, 100160. DOI: 10.1016/j.clrc.2023.100160

Lobo, C. B. (2019). *Finanças e Fiscalidade do Ambiente e da Energia* (S. A. Edições Almedina, Ed.; Vol. 1).

Luque-Martínez, T. (2023). Sensibilidad y elasticidad de las universidades españolas a los indicadores del Ranking de Shanghái (ARWU) Enhanced Reader. *Revista Española de Documentación Cientifica*, 45(1), e350. Advance online publication. DOI: 10.3989/redc.2023.1.1947

Manta, A. G., Doran, N. M., Bădîrcea, R. M., Badareu, G., & ăran, A. M. (2023). Does the implementation of a Pigouvian tax be considered an effective approach to address climate change mitigation? *Economic Analysis and Policy*, 80, 1719–1731. DOI: 10.1016/j.eap.2023.11.002

McCowan, T. (2023). The crosscutting impact of higher education on the Sustainable Development Goals. *International Journal of Educational Development*, 103, 102945. Advance online publication. DOI: 10.1016/j.ijedudev.2023.102945

McKenzie, M., Benavot, A., & Redman, A. (2024). Global indicators of progress on climate change education: Non-state actor data collaboration for SDG 4. *International Journal of Educational Development*, 104, 102968. Advance online publication. DOI: 10.1016/j.ijedudev.2023.102968

Moallemi, E. A., Malekpour, S., Hadjikakou, M., Raven, R., Szetey, K., Ningrum, D., Dhiaulhaq, A., & Bryan, B. A. (2020). Achieving the Sustainable Development Goals Requires Transdisciplinary Innovation at the Local Scale. In *One Earth* (Vol. 3, Issue 3, pp. 300–313). Cell Press. DOI: 10.1016/j.oneear.2020.08.006

Monteiro, S., Guzmán, B. A., & García Sánchez, I. M. (2023). The role of sustainability reporting in corporate tax transparency. In *Taking on Climate Change Through Green Taxation* (pp. 318–334). IGI Global., DOI: 10.4018/978-1-6684-8592-7.ch014

Moreno-Pino, F. M., Jiménez-fontana, R., Domingo, J. M. C., & Goded, P. A. (2022). Training in Mathematics Education from a Sustainability Perspective: A Case Study of University Teachers' Views. *Education Sciences*, 12(3), 199. Advance online publication. DOI: 10.3390/educsci12030199

Mundy, K. (2023). SDG4 and state capacity: The missing link. *International Journal of Educational Development*, 103, 102937. Advance online publication. DOI: 10.1016/j.ijedudev.2023.102937

National Environmental Education Act 1. (2022). In *Public Law 101–619*.

National Environmental Policy Act of 1969. (2023). In *Public Law 91–190*.

Olcina, J., & Morote, Á. F. (2023). Climate Change and Sustainable Development Goals (SDG): Adaptation and Education as main Challenges in the Mediterranean Area. *Finisterra*, 58(122), 39–61. DOI: 10.18055/Finis28898

Oliveira, I. T., & Poiatti, N. D. (2022). The importance of Higher Education for Innovation: the Chinese Example. *Educacao e Sociedade, 43*. https://doi.org/DOI: 10.1590/ES.234975

Ozel, M. (2022). Corporate Sustainability Practices of the European Commission in Higher Education. *Professional Studies: Theory and Practice*, 25(1), 66–75. DOI: 10.56131/pstp.2022.25.1

Patel, S. K., & Jhalani, P. (2024). Formulation of variables of environmental taxation: A bibliometric analysis of Scopus database (2001–2022). *Environment, Development and Sustainability*, 26(3), 7687–7714. DOI: 10.1007/s10668-023-03027-0

Qorraj, G., Krasniqi, B., & Jusufi, G. (2022). Academic freedom and higher education governance in the Western Balkans: The case of Kosovo. *Issues in Educational Research*, 32(3), 1092–1110.

Raji, S. A., & Demehin, M. O. (2023). "Long walk to 2030": A bibliometric and systematic review of research trends on the UN sustainable development goal 3. *Dialogues in Health*, 2, 100132. Advance online publication. DOI: 10.1016/j.dialog.2023.100132 PMID: 38515499

Revenue Service, I. (2023). *Guidance on Requirements for Home Energy Audits for Purposes of the Energy Efficient Home Improvement Credit under Section 25C.*

Rosário, A. T., & Raimundo, R. (2024). Sustainable Entrepreneurship Education: A Systematic Bibliometric Literature Review. *Sustainability (Basel)*, 16(2), 784. Advance online publication. DOI: 10.3390/su16020784

Saraiva, R. N. C. e G., & Nylander, V. G. R. (2023). Ways of Using the Tribute for Environmental Protection. *Taking on Climate Change Through Green Taxation*, 16, 350–371. DOI: 10.4018/978-1-6684-8592-7.ch016

Siddiqua, A., Hahladakis, J. N., & Al-Attiya, W. A. K. A. (2022). An overview of the environmental pollution and health effects associated with waste landfilling and open dumping. In *Environmental Science and Pollution Research* (Vol. 29, Issue 39, pp. 58514–58536). Springer Science and Business Media Deutschland GmbH. DOI: 10.1007/s11356-022-21578-z

Soku, M. G., Amidu, M., & William, C. (2023). Environmental tax, carbon emmission and female economic inclusion. *Cogent Business and Management*, 10(2), 2210355. Advance online publication. DOI: 10.1080/23311975.2023.2210355

Sun, M., & Sun, W. (2022). A Study to Explore Environmental Education in the Curriculum Development in China. *International Journal for Cross-Disciplinary Subjects in Education*, 13(2), 4685–4691. DOI: 10.20533/ijcdse.2042.6364.2022.0576

Tan, Z., Wu, Y., Gu, Y., Liu, T., Wang, W., & Liu, X. (2022). An overview on implementation of environmental tax and related economic instruments in typical countries. In *Journal of Cleaner Production* (Vol. 330). Elsevier Ltd., DOI: 10.1016/j.jclepro.2021.129688

Thanh, N. V., & Van Toan, N. (2023). Building awareness of environmental protection among university students in Vietnam. *Perspektivy Nauki i Obrazovania*, 63(3), 160–174. DOI: 10.32744/pse.2023.3.10

Uddin, K. M. K., Rahman, M. M., & Saha, S. (2023). The impact of green tax and energy efficiency on sustainability: Evidence from Bangladesh. *Energy Reports*, 10, 2306–2318. DOI: 10.1016/j.egyr.2023.09.050

Uljens, M., & Elo, J. (2024). Grounding Higher Education Leadership Research in Non-affirmative Education Theory. In *Educational Governance Research* (Vol. 25, pp. 1–44). Springer Science and Business Media B.V., DOI: 10.1007/978-3-031-55116-1_1

Wolff, L. A., Elo, J., & Uljens, M. (2024). Higher Education Curriculum Leadership in the Anthropocene. In *Educational Governance Research* (Vol. 25, pp. 65–96). Springer Science and Business Media B.V., DOI: 10.1007/978-3-031-55116-1_3

Ya, D., Quddus, A., Feng, M., Ullah, E., & Ameer, W. (2024). Assessing the impact of fiscal policy and natural resources on environmental degradation in BRICS countries: A resource management perspective. *Resources Policy*, 90, 104792. Advance online publication. DOI: 10.1016/j.resourpol.2024.104792

Yan, S., Lv, C., & Yao, L. (2024). Social welfare and equality equilibrium based carbon tax subsidy incentive approach for biomass-coal co-firing towards carbon emissions. *Energy*, 291, 130282. Advance online publication. DOI: 10.1016/j.energy.2024.130282

ADDITIONAL READING

Aibar-Guzmán, B., Monteiro, S., David, F., & Somohano-Rodríguez, F. M. (2023). The Waste Hierarchy at the Business Level: An International Outlook. *Mathematics*, 11(22), 4574. DOI: 10.3390/math11224574

Dlouhá, J., White, R. M., Petry, R., Reeves, A., & Lozano, R. (2023). Editorial: The role of the human dimension in promoting education for sustainable development at the regional level. *Frontiers in Sustainability* (Vol. 4). Frontiers Media SA.

Girón, A., & Ivanova, A. (2023). Climate Action, Institutional Investors, and Just Transition. *Journal of Economic Issues*, 57(2), 575–585. DOI: 10.1080/00213624.2023.2202142

Kozera, A., Satoła, Ł., & Standar, A. (2024). European Union co-funded investments in low-emission and green energy in urban public transport in Poland. *Renewable & Sustainable Energy Reviews*, 200, 200. DOI: 10.1016/j.rser.2024.114530

Lv, X., & Wu, Z. (2024). The green effect of digital transformation: The impact of digital transformation in fiscal and taxation on regional green development. *Economic Analysis and Policy*, 81, 787–800. DOI: 10.1016/j.eap.2023.12.025

Monteiro, S., Ribeiro, V., Vilhena, E., Lemos, K., & Molho, C. (2024). Determinants of online-reporting on sustainable development goals: The case of Portuguese Higher Education Institutions. *Social Responsibility Journal*, 20(3), 462–484. DOI: 10.1108/SRJ-01-2023-0044

Norris, L., Bristow, G., Cotterill, E., Healy, A., & Marshall, A. P. (2024). Decarbonisation, place attachment and agency: Just transition in old industrial regions. *Contemporary Social Science*, 19(1-3), 283–302. DOI: 10.1080/21582041.2024.2323106

Novoselova, L. V. (2022). MODERN CHINA: CHANGING ECONOMIC PARADIGM. *World Economy and International Relations*, 66(10), 24–33. DOI: 10.20542/0131-2227-2022-66-10-24-33

KEY TERMS AND DEFINITIONS

European Student Card: serves to establish a common European identity for students engaged in higher education. It facilitates the verification of student status across Europe, allowing students to present their European Student Card as proof of their status.

Government Measures: in the scope of this study, government measures are defined as policies, regulations, funding initiatives, and programs established by government organisations with guidelines for enhancing the effectiveness and quality of higher education. Currently, the overarching goal of these measures is to integrate subjects and initiatives that contribute to excellence in research, innovation, social equity, and sustainable development.

Green Taxation: it is widely acknowledged that there is an urgent need to drastically reduce CO_2 emissions to mitigate the adverse effects of climate change. To achieve this goal, several states have implemented a range of measures, including the introduction of taxes and tax incentives, known as green taxation (also referred to in the international literature as environmental taxation, environmental law and environmental fiscal policies). Such taxes are applied to activities that are harmful to the environment, i.e., those that generate pollution. In contrast, green tax incentives are designed to encourage environmentally beneficial behaviours and practices, such as tax incentives for the generation of renewable energy.

Higher Education Curricula: the curricula of higher education are designed in accordance with specific academic standards and accreditation requirements to ensure that graduates receive an education that will facilitate their success in the professional world. Consequently, such curricula are developed in the form of structured courses with diverse educational content, the objective of which is to facilitate the imparting of knowledge and skills to students enrolled at HEIs. The curriculum may comprise core courses, optional courses, specialised courses and among others.

Higher Education Institutions (HEIs): primarily, these institutions are designed to disseminate knowledge in a variety of academic disciplines to young people, with the objective of equipping them with the necessary skills to navigate their future lives. Considering the current situation, it is evident that HEIs have an indispensable role to play in the promotion of a sustainable society and the achievement of the SGDs, i.e., equipping young students with the requisite knowledge and critical thinking abilities regarding environmental, social, and economic issues, with a view to ensuring the long-term sustainability of the planet.

Joint European degree: certify that the student has achieved the learning outcomes as part of a joint programme among several institutions across Europe. The degree could be offered by alliances of HEIs, for example the European Universities, based on a common set of European criteria.

Network of Green Curricula of Curricular Environmentalization in Higher Education (ACES): is an international network of Higher Education Institutions committed to integrating environmental considerations into their curricula.

Pigouvian Taxes: in 1920, Arthur C. Pigou developed the concept of Pigouvian Taxes, which is based on the "Polluter Pays Principle" (PPP). This principle states that taxes are used to "correct" harmful externalities, such as pollution, when a good is produced or consumed. The "polluter" is the entity thar causes damage in to third parties and the environment and is therefore responsible for paying the tax. These taxes, which are regarded as corrective, have been implemented in several legal systems as a mean of environmental protection, prevention and remediation. For instance, Germany introduced the PPP in 1984, France formally introduced with the Barnier Law in 1995 and the EU, through Directive 200/35/CE of 12 April 2004, introduced this principle into environmental policy.

Sustainable Development (SD): conservative approach to the management of materials from renewable and non-renewable resources, with the goal of ensuring their natural return and preventing the suppression of biodiversity. This is, to preserve the world's natural resources and safeguard biodiversity, to achieve a balance between meeting the current needs of the global population and safeguarding human life, while also protecting the environment for future generations.

Sustainable Development Goals (SDGs): to guarantee a sustainable future to the next generations, the international community adopted the 2030 Agenda, in 2015, which comprises 17 SDGs and 169 targets across the socio-cultural. Economic and environmental spheres. The SDGs encompass a range of guidelines pertaining to climate change, economic inequality, innovation, sustainability, consumption, peace and justice.

ENDNOTES

1 Approved by Decree Law No. 215/89, 1st July, 149 *Republic Diary* Série I 2578 (1989), in its current version.

2 Decree Law No. 108/2008, 26th June, 122 *Republic Diary* Série I 3929 (2008).

Chapter 11
Tax on Urban Property and Land (IPTU) and Tax Benefits in the Municipality of Salvador/Bahia, Brazil

Tânia Cristina Azevedo
https://orcid.org/0000-0003-4242-4576
State University of Feira de Santana, Brazil & Federal University of Bahia, Brazil

José Renato Sena Oliveira
State University of Feira de Santana, Brazil

Mirian Gomes Conceição
https://orcid.org/0009-0005-1250-1042
State University of Feira de Santana, Brazil

ABSTRACT

This chapter aims to explore in detail the Tax on Urban Property and Land (IPTU, in portuguese), a Brazilian tax of municipal jurisdiction, specifically the tax benefits. For this purpose, the panorama of this tax, its context, and characteristics were approached and possibilities of tax benefits and incentives that have been used in the city of Salvador, capital of the state of Bahia, Brazil, were presented. This study brings the discussion of possible ecological and sustainable tax incentives in the city from the perspective of an urban development that contributes to the environmental, social, economic, cultural, and educational dimensions, and to the integration into the commitments of the 2030 Agenda of Sustainable Development Goals (SDGs). As

DOI: 10.4018/979-8-3693-3908-4.ch011

for the methodological procedures, this is a case study, supported by bibliographical and documentary research. The research results bring possibilities of urban policy tax instruments in the matter of the IPTU, that can be associated with incentives aimed at the sustainable development.

INTRODUCTION

In Brazil, the Tax on Urban Property and Land (IPTU) is a municipal tax that reaches the properties of urban real estate, potential in the fulfilling of the social function of the property and important in financing local infrastructure. It refers to a typically local tax, which burdens the owners of urban real estate and acts as an instrument of enabling the social function of the city, mainly through regulation that deals with the artificial environment, having a strong link to urban policy, to the extent that it can promote the rational use of land and discourage real estate speculation (Afonso et al., 2013; Azevedo, 2017; De Cesare et al., 2015; Fiorillo & Ferreira, 2010).

The Property Tax is one of the oldest in Brazil: created in the colonial period, it began to be charged in the year 1799. It focused on the ownership of edified properties and received the name "eleventh tax" in 1834, with the implementation of the Provincial Assemblies, when its jurisdiction was passed to the Municipalities (Fiorillo & Ferreira, 2010).

Currently, the IPTU is provided for in the Brazilian Constitution as an exclusive competence of the municipalities. It is an unbound tax, because its revenue is unbound from any exchange or utility to be provided by the State, that is, its collection is intended for general expenses. Oliveira (2014, p. 164) clarifies that this tax is a non-earmarked levy, basically due to the mismatch between the value of the collection and the respective application of resources.

In turn, through Article 4th, Title IV, subsection "a", the City Statute (Law No 10.257, by July 10, 2001), establishes that the property tax integrates one of the instruments of urban policy, as a tax and financial instrument that can act as a disciplinarian of urban policy for the collective good. Also, according to the Statute, the property tax is configured as an important instrument for tax policy that, linked to the correct use of urban land, helps in the development of the artificial environment and the implementation of public policies to improve the population's quality of life.

In this context, the Property Tax (IPTU) is an instrument for promoting urban development, is important in the construction of sustainable cities and the promotion of urban policy. And, although it has a fiscal purpose, this tax may advance to an extra fiscal perspective (De Cesare et al., 2015).

In Brazil, Azevedo & Portella (2020) recalled that IPTU is a municipal competence, typically local, reaching urban real estate, being fundamental in fulfilling the social function of the property and important in the financing of local infrastructure. That is, this tax has the function of acting as an instrument of the viability of the social function of the city.

In the city of Salvador, the capital of the state of Bahia, the Organic Law of the Municipality (LOM) provides, in Article 153, that this tax is a responsibility of the municipality, which is also expressed in the Tax and Income Code of the Municipality of Salvador (CTRMS), Law No 7.186/2006. Thus, the Tax System of the Municipality (STM) of Salvador foresees the IPTU in Article 2 of its CTRMS, which is characterized as a tax on assets that has as a generator fact the property, useful domain or ownership of the urban real estate (Azevedo, 2017).

It is noteworthy that the CTRMS brings the predictability of tax benefits in the forms of exemption, amnesty and remission of taxes, which should meet the general character, with a defined duration and be aimed at the public interest. It is observed that, in Salvador, as indicated, the Organic Law of the Citizen (Organic Law of the Municipality of Salvador/BA, 2024) establishes that tax benefits may not have a duration longer than 10 years. The same legislation states that, for these situations, the budget proposal must demonstrate the impact on the revenues and expenses of the possible tax benefits to be granted.

Given the above, the present chapter aims to detail the Tax on Urban Property and Land. To do so, the panorama of this tax, its context, elements and characteristics will be addressed, and the possibilities of ecological and sustainable tax benefits and incentives in the city of Salvador/ Bahia will be detailed, that has inserted in the perspective of an urban development that contributes to the environmental, social, economic, cultural and educational dimensions, in integration with the commitments of the 2030 Agenda of Sustainable Development Goals (SDGs).

By discussing the legal provisions regarding tax benefits for the IPTU in the municipality of Salvador, the study contributes to the dissemination of possible urban policy tax instruments, which can be associated with incentives oriented towards sustainable development.

This is applied research, which aims to acquire knowledge for application in a specific situation (Gil, 2019) since the work presupposes the generation of knowledge for practical effect as a subsidy for the conduction of governmental strategies regarding benefits and tax incentives in terms of the IPTU in the city of Salvador/ BA. As a research strategy, the case study was adopted, supported by a base of references on IPTU and the tax benefits and incentives in the local context. It is noteworthy that the option for the city of Salvador was because the study of Azevedo & Portella (2020) analyzed the tax benefits in the property tax of Salvador, specifically in its ecological perspective, not advancing to other dimensions, which justifies this methodological cut.

Regarding the form of approach, this research can be classified as qualitative, obtained from the interpretation of an inductive analysis by the researcher to verify the benefits and tax incentives in relation to property taxes in the municipality of Salvador/ BA. The study reflected whether the tax incentives adopted in the capital of Bahia are in accordance with the commitments foreseen in the 2030 Agenda SDG.

The study was carried out in three stages, in which different technical procedures were adopted. The **first stage** consisted of constructing the research theoretical framework, through bibliographical research that allowed the foundation of the subject. The bibliographical research was supported by books, articles published in scientific journals, theses and dissertations to identify the main theoretical contributions on the subject. This is reconciled with the present work, since it uses a set of knowledge available in the literature, with emphasis on the discussion of the concepts and characteristics of IPTU and the tax benefits attributed to it. Tthe articles used in this stage of the study were obtained through consultation in the CAPES Journals portal.

The **second stage** consisted of verifying how the city of Salvador has adopted tax benefits and incentives in terms of the IPTU. Therefore, in addition to the bibliographical research, the technique of documentary research was adopted to obtain norms, regulations, legislation and other legal provisions in electronic pages related to the theme, whose data were collected on government websites, the city's Transparency Portal and other legal databases published until December/2023, with content analysis as a research technique (Bardin, 2016). At the end of this stage, we obtained the municipal panorama of the tax benefits that come from IPTU.

In the **third stage**, we sought to verify whether the tax benefits in terms of property taxes adopted by the city of Salvador are in accordance with the commitments provided for in the 2030 Agenda of the SDGs. At this stage, the sources verified were government websites and specific databases, such as Sustainable Cities Program, United Nations (UN), regulatory documents and other information that integrate the SDGs with local taxation.

Finally, the chapter is structured in five parts: the introduction of the study; the theoretical foundation, which discusses the concepts and previous studies of the subject; the methodological detail of the research; the presentation and discussion of the results; and the conclusion.

TAX ON URBAN PROPERTY AND LAND (IPTU) - CONTEXT, CONCEPTS AND CHARACTERISTICS

The Tax on Urban Property and Land (IPTU) is a tax of municipal jurisdiction that reaches the properties of urban real estate, potential to fulfill the social function of property and important in financing local infrastructure that burdens the owners of urban real estate (Afonso et al., 2013; Azevedo, 2017).

It is important to highlight that the property tax acts as an instrument to enable the social function of the city, mainly through the regulation that deals with the artificial environment. This tax has a strong link with urban policy, as it can promote the rational use of land and discourage real estate speculation (De Cesare et al., 2015; Fiorillo & Ferreira, 2010). In addition, it has the potential to act in the social function of property and building sustainable cities.

It is important to highlight that the IPTU acts as an instrument to make the social function of the city viable, mainly through the regulation that deals with the artificial environment, this tax has a strong link to urban policy, insofar as it can promote the rational use of land and discourage real estate speculation (De Cesare et al., 2015; Fiorillo & Ferreira, 2010). In addition, it has the potential to act in the social function of owning and building sustainable cities

It can be said that in Brazil, the Property Tax is one of the oldest, having been instituted in 1799, with state scope. Still in the colonial period, it began to be charged when it focused on the ownership of edified buildings. At the time it was named "eleventh" (Fiorillo & Ferreira, 2010, pp. 88–91). Over the years, this tax has been under the responsibility of several federal entities, as shown in Table 1 below:

Table 1. Federal scope of property tax in Brazil

Period	Federal Scope
1799	State Scope of the colony, focused on the ownership of edified buildings, called the tax of the "eleventh".
1834 to1890	Implementation of Provincial Assemblies - jurisdiction passed to municipalities.
1891 to 1933	Constitution of the Republic, returned to be of exclusive jurisdiction of the States, with the denomination of territorial and building tax.
1946	Constitution of this period kept the jurisdiction exclusive to the States
1988	With the reformulation of the Brazilian Constitution, it was expressed in Article 156, item I, of the Magna Carta, that the property tax is a tax of exclusive jurisdiction of the municipalities.
Constitutional Amendment No. 132/123	Exclusive jurisdiction of the municipalities. Executive power will establish, in complementary law, the criteria to be adopted in municipal laws to update the IPTU calculation basis.

Source: Elaborated by the authors based on Azevedo (2017) and Fiorillo & Ferreira (2010).

Table 1 summarizes how the federative reorganization of the property tax in its more than 200 years of existence occurred.

It is worth mentioning that it was in the National Tax Code (CTN), established by Law No. 5.172/1966, in Article 32, that the guidelines for the conditions in the establishment of the IPTU generator fact were laid out, which, according to the device, must have the property, useful domain or possession of real estate by nature (land) or by physical access (building) and is located in the urban area, defined by local legislation (Lei No. 5.172, de 25 de Outubro de 1966, 1966).

The IPTU is one of the most important sources of municipal revenue for the provision of urban infrastructure, it is a non-earmaked tax, basically due to the mismatch between the amount of revenue collected and the respective application of resources, this revenue does not have a predefined destination, and the local Public Administration is responsible for the allocation of resources from the tax (Taranu, V., & Verbeeck, G., 2022; Merlin, L. V. D. C. T., & Vasconcelos, J. A. S., 2020 & Oliveira, 2014). Thus, by focusing on urban property, the collection of property tax is essential to enable municipalities to meet urban demands, such as providing "quality of life" - which, in a broad sense, means respect for public spaces, access to housing, conditions to the coming and going of people and a harmonized environment.

As for the characteristics of the property tax, it is emphasized that it refers to a tax that achieves property, ownership, or entitlement of the useful domain of urban real estate and focuses on a real right. Its base of calculation is the real estate value; its rate is a percentage defined by specific local law, charged directly from the taxpayer, and has predictability of tax benefits, for example, exemptions and immunity.

The revenue from the collection of this tax can be allocated to urban public services in cities and contribute to guiding behavior in sustainable land use (Taranu, V., & Verbeeck, G., 2022; Azevedo, 2017; De Cesare et al., 2015; Oliveira, 2014). De Cesare et al, (2015, p. 17) indicated that the IPTU is an adequate instrument for the sustainable financing of cities with regard to continuous public spending, such as: maintenance of pavement, cleaning of roads and preservation of squares and parks. Revenue stability is related to the tax periodicity, its low sensitivity to cyclical economic fluctuations and the reduced mobility of the tax base.

Regarding the tax criteria for the definition of tax incidence of IPTU, studies such as those of Fiorillo & Ferreira (2010), Passos & Pozzetti (2012) and De Cesare et al (2015) brought criteria of the matrix rule of this tax, as presented in Table 2.

Table 2. Elements or tax criteria from the IPTU matrix rule

Elements / Criteria	Perspective
Material	Be the owner of urban property or in an area of urban expansion under the terms of the National Tax Code, Article 32, § § 1 and 2. Be the owner of your useful domain or be the possessor or holder of it. Property observing the social function.
Spatial	Municipality Territory place of verification of the IPTU generator fact.
Temporal	In general, January 1st of each year. Annual incidence.
Personal	Passive subject, according to Article 34 of the NTC, is the owner of the property, the entitled of its useful domain, or its owner in any way, being called taxpayer. The active subject is the Municipality (Article 34, caput of the NTC).
Quantitative	basis of calculation: the market value of the property (determined through the generic blueprint of values contained in the real estate register). The rates: proportional, differentiated, or selective and progressive. The provision of differentiated rates is presented in Article 156, § 1 and Article 182, § 4, II, as redacted by Constitutional Amendment No. 29/2000 and Article 47 of the City Statute. Tax incentives and benefits in the form of immunity, exemption, rebates, rate reduction and discounts previously defined in specific municipal law (emphasis added by the author).

Source: Azevedo (2017).

Given the presented in Table 2, it is possible to infer that the elements that integrate the matrix rule of tax incidence of IPTU represent the basis of architecture to the definition of this tax. Its five elements indicated are equally relevant in its construction and should be supported by the national constitutional and tax assumptions, which will be the subject of specific law in the municipal tax codes.

In the quantitative aspect, to define rates, the municipalities have greater autonomy, since they may practice different rates, such as, by type of real estate (residential, commercial, industrial, land plot) according to the demands of each location (Azevedo, 2017). However, this autonomy was subject to modification provided for in the Constitutional Amendment No. 132/2023, which indicates that there will be a complementary law containing the criteria that will be adopted in municipal legislation to update the IPTU calculation basis.

It can be inferred that the IPTU is a relevant tax as an alternative source of financing for cities, important for local infrastructure and urban public services and as a driver for sustainable behaviors. However, it is up to municipal administrations to adopt tax governance mechanisms to strengthen this source of revenue.

The property tax may act as a relevant instrument in urban policies, given that the resources generated allow the municipality public funding, which means investments in infrastructure of the city, such as expansion and access to public spaces, arborization of streets and avenues, promotion of decent housing, improvements in public roads, action in improving urban sanitation and waste management, among other actions. Undoubtedly, it is a tax that contributes to an environmental public policy and can guide behaviors, with a view of achieving sustainable development in cities.

Regarding the extra tax dimension of IPTU, in a broad sense, the Constitutional Amendment No 29/2000 (Constitutional Amendment No. 29, from September 13th, 2000) allowed Brazilian municipalities to apply progressive tax rates due to the value of the property and with different rates, according to their location and use. The property tax progressive by time is one of the tax instruments of urban policy that enables "extra fiscality". It is provided for in Article 182, § 4th, subsection II of the Federal Constitution, and regulated by the City Statute, which assigns powers to the municipalities for its imposition when the unappropriated use of urban land occurs.

The progressive rate applied to property tax is one of the urban policy instruments provided for in the City Statute, Article 7, item 1, which establishes that properties that fail to comply with the social function of property will have their IPTU rate increased for five consecutive years, with a maximum rate of up to 15%. It will be applied when there is a need for public power intervention in the regulation of the disorderly use of urban land, and is characterized as a particular form of penalty for lack of use or improper use of the property, intending to ensure concrete actions aimed at fulfilling the social function of urban property (Azevedo, 2017; De Cesare et al., 2015). This mechanism represents a vital instrument for urban policy, in the sense of fulfilling the effective social function of property, as well as the proper use of urban land.

The second way to highlight the extra tax dimension of the property tax occurs when the local government adopts practices to encourage actions that are beneficial to the city. This situation is verified when taxpayers are encouraged to adopt such conduct, whose model is called tax induction and usually occurs in the form of immunity, tax benefit or incentive, total or partial tax exemption, in addition to discounts, rebates, reduction of aliquots and others. Environmental protection actions that encourage the sustainable development of the city are examples of urban policy in environmental matters (Azevedo, 2017).

It is important to remember that the granting of tax benefits and incentives from the property tax covers wide situations, from those foreseen by the Federal Constitution and National Tax Code, to those that the municipalities started to establish. This is because they have autonomy and flexibility to institute in local laws exemptions, discounts, reduction of rate or even establish the non-imposition of this tax, as well as the time and periodicity of effect.

However, it is not possible to lose sight of the conditions legally provided for this, especially regarding active taxation and revenue renunciation, given the principles and rules of the National Tax System for its constitutional validity (Azevedo, 2017; Passos & Pozzetti, 2012). Table 3 shows some possibilities that reach the tax benefits/incentives of the property tax.

Table 3. Possibilities of tax benefits/incentives in the matter of IPTU

Type	Description and Reach	Normative source
Immunity	Real estate belonging to the Union, States, Federal District and Municipalities, local authorities and public foundations. Properties of political parties, workers' unions, educational institutions and non-profit social assistance, used to carry out the activities purposed. Properties of religious temples of any cult.	Article 150, Title VI of the Federal Constitution and Article 14 of the NTC
Exemptions	Granted in based on social, sectorial or economic interests. Can be conditional or unconditional	Municipal law
Exemption due to low contributive capacity	Refers to the possibility of guaranteeing to individuals living in situations of poverty. This situation meets criteria, such as: a) low value real estate; b) absence of income or low family income; owning a single property; c) widows, pensioners or orphans.	Municipal law
Incentives that aim the preservation of historical, cultural and environmental patrimony	Occur through the concession of discounts for situations where there are sustainable practices developed by real estate projects and real estate located in areas of environmental preservation. In properties of historical and cultural value, discounts or exemption from property tax.	Municipal law
Incentive based on the reduction of the value-to-pay from other local taxes	Reduction of the IPTU value, through the discount of value paid in other taxes. For example, incentives for individuals to adopt electronic invoicing and the possibility of reducing the value of the property tax.	Municipal law
Granting of credits to the IPTU payment	Exemptions to educational, hotel service, assistance, cultural, recreative and sports institutions; reduction of the tax value to recreative clubs.	Municipal law
Remission and Amnesty	Forgiveness of tax credit	NTC (Article 156, Title IV, and Articles 180 and 182), combined with municipal legislation

Source: De Cesare et al. (2015, pp. 41–46), FC and NTC, with adaptations of Azevedo (2017).

Table 3 displayed the main forms adopted to give tax benefits and incentives in the IPTU, which mostly confirmed the autonomy of local government (municipal) for its institution.

It is important to draw attention to some forms of tax benefits attributed to the property tax that may cause the weakening of this tax, for example: exemptions granted to companies to increase economic activity without effective compensation, which may impact the tax rate increase for urban property owners. Another situation refers to the tax benefit that consists of the granting of credits from other municipal taxes to reduce the amount of IPTU to be paid.

As for the benefits and incentives aimed at the conservation and preservation of the environment, it is considered possible that local laws will stipulate less expensive rates for real estate located in places considered historic or where natural resources are being preserved. It is a way for the public power to stimulate conducts that propitiate an ecologically balanced environment, through the insertion of urban policy instruments that enable benefits to those who develop actions with a view to sustainable development (Amaral, 2013; Azevedo, 2017; Passos & Pozzetti, 2012).

The perspective that attributes the "extra fiscality" dimension of the property tax as a form of protection the environment has been contemplated in the form of revenue renunciation, through the granting of exemptions, discounts, rebates and reduction of the tax rate.

However, it should not be forgotten that, for the public entity to stop collecting by stimulus or even reward certain behaviors, aiming at the institution of this systematic, the municipality must observe the provisions of Article 14 of the Fiscal Responsibility Law (Complementary Law No 101/2000, 2000) which specifies the conditions for the application of any and all revenue renunciation.

ECOLOGICAL AND SUSTAINABLE INCENTIVES OF IPTU AND 2030 AGENDA

Ecological and sustainable tax incentives in terms of property taxes represent an important instrument of urban policy and contribute to environmental public policies aimed at sustainable management of cities. In this sense, Leal et al. (2022), understand that public environmental policy is materialized through governmental and non-governmental actions and aims to preserve the environment and promote sustainability. Rangel, Aranha & Silva (2015), in turn, argue that it is possible to classify this type of policy as regulatory, structuring and inducing. The regulatory way is responsible for drafting specific legislation to regulate rules and standards for the use and access to the environment. The structuring policy is the one that intervenes directly, through the public power or non-governmental organizations, in the protection of the environment. Finally, there is also the inducing policy, which aims to influence the behavior of society and its groups, being identified with the notion of sustainable development.

Therefore, sustainable management of the cities integrated with environmental public policies can be associated with the commitments of the SDGs. It should be noted that these refer to an unfolding of the Millennium Development Goals (MDGs), which guided global actions to eradicate the basic needs of poor countries between 2000 and 2015.

According to Sachs (2015), Sustainable Development (SD) has moved towards a more practical and less focused approach, and a normative analytical approach, which includes four complex integrated systems: (1) A global economy that now encompasses all parts of the world; (2) Focuses on social interactions of trust, ethics, inequality and social support networks in communities (including new global online communities made possible by revolutions in information and communication technologies); (3) Analyzes changes in complex land systems such as climate and ecosystems; (4) Studies governance problems, including the performance of governments and businesses. Based on this understanding, putting the SD into practice represents an ambitious challenge and is met with wide obstacles for governments, companies and society, which have important participation in trying to meet commitments.

Hence, the SDGs have instruments that can act as guidelines for the future development of the planet and contribute to local public policies (Azevedo, 2017). Somohano-Rodríguez et al. (2023) recall that the United Nations General Assembly, in 2015, together with countries around the world, signed the document called "Transforming our World: The 2030 Agenda for Sustainable Development" (Transforming Our World: The 2030 Agenda for Sustainable Development, 70/1, 2015). This is a global agreement on human rights and climate change to achieve sustainable development, which includes 169 specific targets on the eradication of inequalities, poverty and other social problems, the fight against climate change and the protection of the environment, with a commitment that they will be achieved by 2030.

Azevedo (2017) recalls that, in the context of cities, the 2030 Agenda highlighted goal "eleven": "*Make cities and human settlements inclusive, safe, resilient and sustainable" (Transforming Our World: The 2030Agendafor Sustainable Development, 70/1, 2015, p. 21)*, which prioritizes efforts to make cities and human settlements inclusive, safe and resilient by 2030. It is understood that this commitment aims to touch the city lifestyle and proposes ten commitments for a city to achieve sustainable urban development, which will require changes in the forms of consumption and production; efficient low-carbon energy system; competence in water management; preservation of natural resources and protection of ecosystem and biodiversity; development of clean technologies for local waste management; monitoring and controlling the effects of climate change; improvements in housing conditions and universal access to green areas, allowing a design and construction of cities that promote inclusive human and economic development (Azevedo, 2017).

Based on the above, it appears that SDG 11 can relate to urban policy, to guide the sustainable management of cities, integrated with environmental public policies, for example, by adopting through the adoption of ecological and sustainable taxation in terms of IPTU. This perspective is in line with the studies of Azevedo &

Portella (2020) and Silva, Azevedo & Oliveira (2022), as well as Paz et al. (2022) and Ortiz, A. C. T. D. T et al. (2022) in emphasizing that, for the scope of the SDGs, especially in the municipal spheres, a tax restructuring that includes ecological taxes are demanded to enable the reordering of the tax system, in order to integrate urban environmental sustainability in the purpose of local taxation.

Discussions on environmental preservation go beyond the provisions provided for in Chapter VI of the Federal Constitution (Constitution of the Federative Republic of Brazil, 1988), intended for the environment (Sustainable Development - Article 225). The collaboration between the state and society becomes an essential element in the debate, since this relationship shares the responsibilities and benefits of preserving the environment.

In this sense, ecological and sustainable taxation is an instrument used to reconcile the strategies of economic consumption of the society with the preservation of natural resources, which will be able to be supported by green tax incentives, helping in the improvement of the quality of life in cities. Azevedo & Portella (2019) corroborate this understanding by arguing that it is an important tool for sustainable development and the preservation of natural resources, with the attraction for the population not only the tax benefits but the maintaining of life quality conditions as well.

In the international scenario, studies portrayed that in local taxation there are records of tax benefits in the form of deductions and bonuses for certain economic sectors or activities that impact the environment. For example, in Spain, there is a reduction in the Real Estate Tax (IBI) for properties that invest in solar energy and an exemption from the IBI for properties that preserve and conserve reforested mountains and regeneration of afforestation. (Maillo, 2016; Ventosa et al., 2015; Amorim, 2018).

The research by Taranu, V., & Verbeeck, G. (2022), investigated whether property taxation could effectively guide sustainable development patterns in the residential building sector. There has been limited literature on the subject, and existing reviews are generally supported by empirical findings of the actual behavior of landowners. The work pointed out that property taxes can influence landowners' decisions about what, how and when to build. Evidence was found that in practice, property taxation is not an effective policy to encourage sustainable land use. The study also revealed that property tax can be an effective tool to reduce urban sprawl and different tax regimes can affect the building activity.

In Portugal, there is a tax benefit that encourages environmental sustainability practices, with the promotion of urban regeneration. The study by Dinis (2024) brought an approach to environmental taxation as an extra-fiscal policy that influences the behavior of taxpayers when adopting urban regeneration habits. His research showed a picture of how Portuguese municipalities advanced in tax incentives linked to urban regeneration (Dinis, 2024).

In Brazil, since the 1980s, ways to reduce property tax were sought as a stimulus to environmental sustainability practices, when proven. Aiming to encourage citizens to adopt ecological practices in their homes, there is a tax incentive called "IPTU Verde" (Green IPTU), with the aim of promoting green infrastructure in the municipalities, through tax discounts on property taxes. Azevedo (2017) clarified that it constitutes one of the instruments of urban policy, in the form of a tax benefit.

The implementation of the "Green IPTU" in Brazil began to be adopted in the late 1980s. Azevedo and Dantas (2023) confirmed that it was the municipality of Jales (Jales, 2003), located in the State of São Paulo, in 2003, the first to draft legislation that would provide for the reduction of IPTU for owners who put into practice protection, preservation and recovery of the environment measures. Among the measures adopted, there is the water reuse system, construction using sustainable materials, energy efficiency with photovoltaic panels, among others.

Thus, it is noted that the application of IPTU as an ecological incentive contributes to environmental sustainability practices and is configured as an extra-fiscality mechanism, with possible consequences the development of sustainable cities and aligning with the SDGs set out in the United Nations 2030 Agenda (Transforming Our World: The 2030 Agenda for Sustainable Development, 70/1, 2015). The program seeks to improve the quality of life of residents, in line with the minimization of impacts on the environment.

The benefits from ecological taxation are in the form of discounts based on the actions of each taxpayer. Among the actions considered for tax discounts, it can be mentioned: separation of solid waste; water abstraction system; water reuse system; waterproof areas; solar hydraulic heating system, afforestation, among others. Gonçalves et al. (2019) emphasize that the actions foreseen in ecological taxation can mean improvements in the air, flora, fauna, and decentralize the green areas of the municipalities that have the Green IPTU implemented.

Previous studies point to surveys of cities in different regions or individual city studies. It is observed that, in both modalities, there is a similarity between the Green IPTU programs spread throughout the country, such as the actions established for the tax incentive (Azevedo, 2017; Souza & Oliveira, 2017; Azevedo & Portella, 2020; Gonçalves et al., 2019; Accioly et al., 2021; Ortiz et al, 2022).

As a practical effect of the IPTU tax policy with the granting of ecological tax incentives, the increase in taxpayers benefiting from a tax discount stands out, In Salvador this amount increased from 672 to 2,252 between 2023 and 2024, the deduction increased from R$ 396.000,00 to R$ 773.000,00 in the same period (Sedur, 2024).

In the regulatory dimension, Brazil began to strive to establish legislation of national scope through the Proposed Amendment to the Constitution No. 13/2019, authored by Senator Plínio Valério (Brazil, 2019), called "PEC do IPTU Verde", which proposes to change Art. 156 of the Federal Constitution. The goal of the proposal is to establish environmental criteria for the collection of property tax through differentiated rates due to the adoption of environmental sustainability practices.

In view of the above, the concession of the tax incentive, called "*IPTU VERDE*" is a form of waiver of a portion of future revenue, used by the local public management as an instrument of urban policy to encourage sustainable practices and conducts. It is an action of the State to offer differentiated conditions for taxpayers, in such a way that the reduction in the amounts collected encourages good practices in accordance with the interests of that incentive (Gonçalves et al, 2019 and Azevedo & Portella, 2020).

THE MUNICIPALITY OF SALVADOR AND PROPERTY TAXATION

According to census data from the Brazilian Institute of Geography and Statistics (IBGE, 2023), the municipality of Salvador, capital of the State of Bahia, in 2022, had 2,417,678 inhabitants, which represented a population increase of 140%, compared to the population of the 1970s. Salvador was susceptible to intense land occupation, arising from the impacts of economic growth, which contributed to triggering a demographic expansion in the city: its urbanization rate is approximately 99%. The intense use and occupation of the soil reflected in the quality of life of its inhabitants, with interferences in their spaces, which cause environmental impacts. It is in this context that real estate taxation has relevance in the capital of Bahia. The appendix of this chapter presents occupied areas in Salvador, the image shows the points representing 200 people residing in a certain locality of the city. In the municipality, the largest population concentrations occur in the coastal strip, suburb and core of the peninsula.

In Salvador, the Organic Law of the Municipality (OLM) provides, in Article 153, the taxes under the jurisdiction of the municipality (Organic Law of the Municipality of Salvador/BA, 2024), which is also expressed in the Tax and Income Code of the Municipality of Salvador (CTRMS) established by Law No. 7.186/2006 (Law No. 7.186, of December 27th, 2006). Thus, the Municipal Tax System (MTS) of Salvador provides in Article 2 of its CTRMS that the Tax on Urban Property and Land (IPTU) and the Real Estate Transmission Tax (ITIV) are classified as property and property transfer taxes, being directly associated with real estate taxation.

Specifically, about the property tax of the municipality of Salvador, Article 60, § 1, of the CTRMS indicates that it has as a taxable event the ownership, useful domain or possession of urban real estate. To define the spatial criterion, the CTRMS was based on the provisions of Article 32, § 1 and 2 of the National Tax Code for this purpose. In addition, recreation and leisure areas are also considered as conditioning of improvements for its establishment. Thus, the incidence of property taxes in Salvador reaches residential and commercial properties, edified or not, and land plots, as defined in Article 61 of CTRMS.

The matrix rule of the property tax of Salvador defines, in Article 62 of the CTRMS, that the incidence occurs on January 1st of each civil year. The taxpayer is the owner of the property, the owner of its useful domain or its owner under any title, which may be a physical person or legal entity under public or private law, in addition to the estate and the bankrupt estate (CTRMS, Law 7,186/ 2006, Article 63).

As for the IPTU calculation basis, Article 64 of the Municipal Tax Code indicates it to be raised from the "real estate value". This measure is used by the municipality to calculate the tax, considering the current conditions of the real estate market, as provided for in Article 65 of the CTRMS. Its determination will occur upon evaluation made by the tax area of the municipality, based on Standard Unit Values (SUV) contained in the Generic Blueprint of Real Estate Values.

In addition, other factors, according to local legislation, can be determinants in assessing the market value of a property and consequently, the definition of the calculation basis for IPTU purposes, such as the characteristics of the region, patio, infrastructure, building potential, enhancement of the street and guidelines that may be defined in the Urban Development Master Plan (PDDU) (Law No. 9.069, of June 30th, 2016).

The property tax rates of Salvador are progressive for residential, non-residential and land plot properties. These rates are established annually by the local government through the disclosure of Normative Instruction, which establishes a table of revenues covering the range and parameters of the property's market value, percentages of the rates, possible amounts to be deducted and the number of real estates registered in the real estate register of the city until November 30th of each year. These aspects are regulated in Article 73 of the CTRMS.

The revenues of the IPTU, in Salvador, according to the Manual of Programming and Budget (MPO), are classified as Current Tax, and represent income from resources in the public coffers to enable the financing of the objectives defined in the budgetary programs and actions, to satisfy public purposes of the municipality. They should be accounted for and demonstrated in accordance with Resolution No. 1.268/2008 of the Court of Auditors of the Municipalities in the State of Bahia (TCM).

In 2016, the capital of Bahia reorganized the local Urban Policy to establish: guidelines, actions, plans, projects and instruments for territorial planning and environmental management; urban management planning and municipal financing funds, improvement of precarious settlements, occupations and housing conditions; public services provided in health, education, social assistance, public security, mobility, public lighting, cleaning and solid waste management, rain drainage, water supply, sanitation, leisure, recreation, sport and citizen service (Law No. 9.069, of June 30th, 2016).

Given the above, the tax legislation of the Municipality of Salvador established tax benefits from the IPTU: a) concession of discount in the value of the tax when a real estate enterprise adopts environmental sustainability practices; b) predictability of the establishment of fiscal incentives as a means of maintaining, conserving and repairing listed public and private properties of artistic or cultural historical value; c) tax benefits in the form of a tax rate reduction for areas that integrate the Environmental and Cultural Value Areas System (SAVAM) (Law No. 9.069, of June 30th, 2016).

The next session of this chapter unfolds the ecological and sustainable tax incentives in the capital of Bahia in line with the dimensions that the municipality of Salvador has adopted.

TAX BENEFITS IN THE MATTER OF IPTU IN THE CITY OF SALVADOR

The benefits and tax incentives attributed to the IPTU are indicated in the CTRMS, which includes a special chapter on exemptions. In addition, the municipality has established supplementary legislation that regulates discounts, rate reductions and other tax benefits attributed to that tax and are classified as: a) scope of the contributory capacity and value of the real estate; b) properties of public institutions; and c) of local urban policy.

The categories of contributory capacity, market value and the properties of public institutions may be exempt from IPTU. Table 4 highlights the tax benefits attributed.

Table 4. Main tax benefits in the matter of IPTU in the city of Salvador

Category	Reference local legislation	Tax Incentive Description
Exemptions to the military	Article 83 of CTRMS, item I	Exclusive property for residence of the military and Navy members who actively participated in war operations in the last world conflict.
Exemptions on real estate of public companies	Article 83 do CTRMS, item III	Real estate of public enterprises of the municipality for the carrying out its activities, transferred free of charge to bodies of the direct administration of the Union, the State and the Municipality, local authorities and foundations, property of an entity of external public law, diplomatic representations.
Exemptions to public servants with low contributive capacity; Excmption by market value	Article 83 of CTRMS, items II and IX	Municipal server, admittedly poor. Market value of up to R$ 131,917.16 (Salvador, SEFAZ, 2023). Updated annually by an act of the local executive power.

Source: Elaborated by the authors based on Azevedo (2017); CTRMS, 2016 and updates of complementary legislations.

Regarding tax incentives that integrate the local urban policy, the municipality of Salvador adopts dimensions unfolding the tax incentives of the property tax in the following axes: a) Environmental Development; b) Cultural and Educational Development; c) Economic Development; d) Social Development; and e) Urban Development. It is emphasized that this perspective can contribute to the integration of urban environmental sustainability in the purpose of local taxation and serve as a direction to integrate real estate taxation into the SDGs. Tables 5 to 9 portray the tax incentives grouped according to their respective dimensions.

Table 5. Environmental dimension of the tax incentives in the matter of IPTU

Category/Type	Local Reference Legislation	Tax Incentive Description
Land on Environmental Protection Areas (EPA) and Permanent Protection Areas (PPA)	Law No. 8.723/2014 and Decree No. 29.100/2017, changed by the Decrees No. 30.094/2018 and No. 36.288/2022. Atlantic Forest included in Law No. 9.548/2020	Reduction of 80% in the market value of land, or parts of land inserted in EPA, PPA, Areas with Atlantic Forest coverage and servitudes of public service passages with the sealing of edifications.
Photovoltaic Solar Energy Installation Incentive Program	Law No. 8.474/2013 and Decree No. 30.738/2018; Law No. 9.620/2022	SOLAR SALVADOR – "IPTU Amarelo". Establishes tax benefits to program participants through a discount to encourage sustainable actions and practices that include the adoption of a distributed generation system of photovoltaic solar energy in residential properties and non-residential in the City of Salvador. 5%, 7% and 10% tax discount
Sustainable Certification Program IPTU VERDE in edifications	Article 5 of Law No. 8.474/2013, 8.723/2014; and Decree No. 29.100/2017, changed by the Decrees No. 30.094/2018 and 36.288/2022	Establishes tax benefits for program participants. Tax discount of 5%, 7% and 10% for property owners who adopt measures that encourage the protection, preservation and recovery of the environment, sustainable actions and practices
Area System of Environmental and Cultural Value (SAVAM)	Article 391, subsection I, item "b", Law No. 9.069/2016	Reduction of rates applicable to the areas of private property included in SAVAM, as a way to stimulate their conservation

Source: Elaborated by the authors based on Azevedo (2017) & Salvador (2024)

The possibility of reducing the property tax with a view to sustainable development in Salvador occurred with Law No. 8,474/ 2013, which established the predictability of the tax benefit in the form of discount for property owners who adopted sustainability practices. Since 2014, the Environmental Protection Areas (EPA) were contemplated with tax benefit prediction. The regulation of these two possibilities of tax benefit occurred in 2015, amended by Decrees No. 29,100/2017 and No. 36,288/2022. This device established the conditions of the Sustainable Certification Program "IPTU VERDE" for the participants of this program to obtain benefits in buildings in the Municipality of Salvador and incorporated the EPA as the second category of tax benefit.

As for the tax benefits that have actions aimed at conservation and environmental preservation as axis, there are highlighted the discount in the tax collection when carrying out sustainability practices and the reduction in the market value of land located in Environmental Protection Areas (APA) stands out when sustainability practices are implemented.

Table 6. Cultural and educational development dimensions of tax incentives in the matter of IPTU

Category/Type	Local Reference Legislation	Tax Incentive Description
People and communities of religious character (Terreiros)	Law No. 8,930/2015 and Decree No. 27,014/2016.	Tax relief, remission of the IPTU incident on real estate used by people and communities of Terreiros recognized and registered in the database of the Municipality of Salvador.
Social and recreative clubs, regattas, associations and clubs of a sporting and football character	Law 8.953/2015, changed by Law 9.304/2017, and Decree No. 27.157/2016.	Reduction of 85% of the tax value-to-pay.

Source: Elaborated by the authors based on Azevedo (2017) & Salvador (2024).

It is noteworthy the reduction of the property tax value in Salvador in the form of tax benefit for social and recreational clubs, regattas and associations and clubs of a sports and football character, if they have no lucrative purpose. It was instituted in 2015, by Law No. 8.953/2015 (Salvador, 2015) and regulated by Municipal Decree No. 25.157/2016 (Salvador, 2016), which grants a reduction in the value of this tax by 70%.

Table 7. Economic development dimension of the tax incentives in the matter of IPTU

Category/Type	Local Reference Legislation	Tax Incentive Description
IPTU/TRSD Deferral Program of real estate sold by the municipality	Law No. 9.233/2017 and Decree No. 29.525/2018	The winning bidder will have the IPTU and the TRSD (Tax on Solid Waste) deferred for a period of 3 (three) years, or until the permit to dwell.
Private Investiment Program- Salvador 360°	Law No. 9,285/2017 (amended by Laws No. 9,434/2018, 9,519/2020, 9,548/2020 and 9,552/2020) and Decree No. 29.547/2018 (amended by Decrees No. 30,755/2019 and 31,229/2019).	Reduction of IPTU by 50% for requalified properties that generate and maintain jobs in the city of Salvador for the teleservice, billing and textile sectors.
Program of Stimulus to the implementation of industries in social projects	Law No. 9.548/2020 and Decree No. 32.925/2020	Discount of 50% in IPTU and TRSD incidents on real estate that shelter industries that are part of social projects, located in public areas.
Program of stimulus to the implantation of distribution center.	Law No. 9.548/2020 and Decree No. 32.925/2020	Discount of 40% in IPTU and TRSD incidents on properties that shelter or come to house distribution center in Salvador.

continued on following page

Table 7. Continued

Category/Type	Local Reference Legislation	Tax Incentive Description
Modernization and improvement of quality of the hotel sector – Proturismo	Law No. 9.504/2019 (changed by Law No.9.548/2020) and Decree No. 32.088/2019 (changed by Decree No. 33.784/2021).	Reduction of up to 40% in the annual property tax in the fiscal years from 2020 to 2023, related to real estate units where the activity of hotels, inns or motels are carried out.
Inova Salvador Program – Municipal Innovation Policy	Law No. 9.534/2020 and Decree No. 33.405/2020	50% reduction in IPTU on the property where the company develops or will develop activities that are part of the Municipal Innovation Ecosystem, within five years.
Program of Incentive to Sustainable Development and Innovation (PIDI)	Law No. 8.962/2015 (changed by Law 9.581/2021) and Decree No. 36.006/2022	Public Policy of Tax Incentives, granting credit to pay IPTU and ISS (Tax on Services), for activities that generate employment, use sustainable policies to requalify properties.

Source: Elaborated by the authors based on Azevedo (2017) & Salvador (2024).

Table 8. Social development dimension of the tax incentives in the matter of IPTU

Category/Type	Local Reference Legislation	Tax Incentive Description
Tax exemption program for housing projects of social interest	Law No. 8.930/2015 and Decree No. 27.014/2016	IPTU exemption for real estate used in the construction of endeavors linked to housing programs of social interest, intended for families with a monthly income of up to 3 (three) minimum wages and developed by public agencies or entities during the construction period.
Program to support the popular housing offer "Minha Casa Minha Vida"	Law No. 7.719/2009 (amended by Laws No 8.421/2013 and No. 9.562/2021)	Exemption from property tax on the real estate unit for the "Minha Casa Minha Vida" Program.
Program for Cooperatives of Recyclable Materials	Law No. 9.767, de 11/30/2023	IPTU exemption, since properly registered with the Urban Cleaning Company of Salvador - LIMPURB

Source: Elaborated by the authors based on Azevedo (2017) & Salvador (2024).

Table 9. Urban development dimension of the tax incentives in the matter of IPTU

Category/Type	Local Reference Legislation	Tax Incentive Description
Program of incentive to the edification in non-edified land	Law No. 8.474/2013, with changes by Laws No. 8.621/2014 and 8.723/2014 and Decrees No. 25.899/2015, 29.100/2017 and 30.738/2018	Reduction of up to 30% of the property tax of real estate units consisting of land in which construction is underway, up to the limit of 04 (four) years, from the date of the initial issue of the license for construction.
Revitalizar Program	Law No. 9.215/2017 Decree No. 28.775/2017	Encourages the restoration and recovery of real estate and activities located in the Cultural and Landscape Protection Area of the Old Center of Salvador, through the remission of tax credit related to the property tax constituted until 12.31.2020, incident on properties intended for buildings and restorations completed within 03 (three) years, recovery or renovation completed in 24 (twenty-fourth) months.

Source: Elaborated by the authors based on Azevedo (2017) & Salvador (2024).

Based on the presented, in 2013, the local government of Salvador promoted the restructuration of CTRMS through Law No. 8.474/2013 (Law No. 8.474, of October 2nd, 2013), and, in that document, redefined a series of tax benefits in terms of IPTU. For example: it expanded the universe of total exemptions for this tax; brought tax reduction for specific segments, and the possibility of discounts in the value of the tax due to the adoption of environmental sustainability practices. As for the connection of the tax incentives of the municipality of Salvador to the commitments of the 2030 Agenda that make up the SDGs, from the verified, there is an integration, even if partial.

It is possible to infer that the dimension of "Environmental Development" is integrated with commitment No. 07, by encouraging the taxpayers to adopt renewable energy and, with that, contribute to mitigating the effects of climate change; and with commitment No. 11, due to tax incentives giving preference to the adoption of environmental sustainability practices. Regarding the dimension of "Cultural and Educational Development", it also connects with Goal 11 as an incentive for the protection and safeguarding of Salvador's cultural heritage.

On the other hand, the ecological and sustainable tax incentives, and the connection with the commitments of the 2030 Agenda, in the "Economic Development" category, stimulate practices for the generation and maintenance of jobs, increasing the activities of the productive sector such as hotel services, tourism sector, innovation activities, industries participating of social projects located in public areas, adoption of sustainable policies, and the requalification of real estate. This axis is in line with commitment No. 08, for encouraging productive activity and the generation of businesses that prioritize the maintenance of jobs, promote culture and local products, as well as increase sustainable tourism in the capital of Bahia.

The "Social Development" dimension brings ecological and sustainable tax incentives in the matter of property taxes focused primarily on safe, adequate and affordable housing for those living in the capital of Bahia: for these cases, the total exemption of property tax occurs. This action integrates directly with SDG No. 11, which prioritizes the management of settlements that provide inclusive and sustainable urbanization. This axis also brings the possibility of exempting from IPTU the recycling cooperatives, as a way to encourage the reduction of negative environmental impact by the municipal waste generation, being also aligned with SDG 11.

As to the "Urban Development" dimension, the local management started to stimulate, through the adoption of ecological and sustainable tax incentives, the projects and programs that contemplate the areas of Cultural and Landscape Protection of the historic and old centre of Salvador and promote the preservation of non-buildable land. Commitment 11 of the SDGs integrates with this dimension by supporting the protection and safeguarding of historical and cultural heritage.

CONCLUSION AND FUTURE RESEARCH DIRECTIONS

Brazilian cities have instituted tax benefits from the IPTU in the form of discounts to encourage sustainability practices. In the city of Salvador, since 2015, local tax legislation provides this possibility through the Sustainable Certification Program, with the insertion of the stimulus to environmental sustainability practices.

This chapter achieved its objective by discussing the tax benefits of the property tax in the city of Salvador from an ecological and sustainable perspective and connected them with the approach to urban development that contributes to the environmental, social, economic, cultural and educational dimensions. In addition, it integrated them into the commitments of the 2030 Agenda of the Sustainable Development Goals (SDG).

The institution of tax incentives, such as the "IPTU *Verde*" and the "IPTU *Amarelo*" (Green and Yellow IPTU, respectively), in the municipality of Salvador, is a valid attempt to stimulate actions that induce sustainable development, under the environmental aspect, covering the improvement of life quality. Through it, a potential to be in line with premise No. 11 of the 2030 SDG Agenda is glimpsed.

The adoption of tax benefits in the matter of property tax is valid and important for the urban management of the city; however, this revenue is fundamental for urban infrastructure, that is, municipal financial sustainability needs to be considered in this decision. For that reason, it is necessary to establish consistent criteria for revenue renunciation, to avoid a weakening of local revenue.

It is emphasized that the study under consideration is part of an ongoing research project that investigates urban environmental governance as an instrument of ecological and sustainable taxation in Brazilian cities, and for this reason, this discussion does not end with this research.

Studies that analyze how the adoption of government strategies of tax policies can contribute to the advancement and solution of gaps related to "greening" of taxation are suggested so that the states act as inducers of public policies aligned with the commitments of the SDGs. In addition, research that expands the spatial cut to detail the situation of ecological and sustainable taxation of real estate in other cities. There should also emerge studies that include local tax incentives for women, as well as research that culminates in proposals to public management to institute sustainable gender taxation, which promotes tax equality between men and women in the city.

Future studies are recommended that compare the implementation and adoption of ecological tax incentives in Brazilian municipalities, Latin American cities or capitals of countries that are part of economic blocs, for example OECD. Research is suggested to analyze the impact of the granting of municipal tax incentives on municipal revenue and urban infrastructure.

Finally, studies should be conducted that suggest indication of tax incentives in the form of exemption or reduction of the rate in the new taxes and contributions provided for in CA No. 132/2023 for the adoption by companies in the sector of specific services for the female public.

ACKNOWLEDGMENT

National Council for Scientific and Technological Development – CNPq and Financial Aid Program for Research (No. 14/2023) and Innovation Projects – Notice No. 01/2021 of the State University of Feira de Santana (UEFS).

REFERENCES

Accioly, S. M. D. L., & Brito, L. L. A. D. (2021). Análise comparativa de programas municipais de IPTU Verde. *Engenharia Urbana em Debate*, 2(1), 215–229. DOI: 10.59550/engurbdebate.v2i1.58

Afonso, J. R. R., Araujo, E. A., & da Nóbrega, M. A. R. (2013). *IPTU no Brasil: Um diagnóstico abrangente*. FGV Projetos.

Amaral, M. D. (2013). A tributação como mecanismo de estímulo à proteção e à preservação do meio ambiente. Revista da Faculdade de Direito da Universidade Federal de Minas Gerais, 2013(62). DOI: 10.12818/0304-2340.2013v62p405

Amorim, J. de C. (2018). Os incentivos fiscais em matéria de Fiscalidade verde. Revista de Ciências Empresariais e Jurídicas / Review of Business and Legal Sciences, 303-318 Pages. DOI: 10.26537/REBULES.VI30.3165

Azevedo, T. C. (2017). Tributação municipal como incentivo ao desenvolvimento sustentável nas cidades: O caso do "IPTU VERDE" de Salvador [Doctorate, Chatolic University of Salvador]. http://ri.ucsal.br:8080/jspui/handle/prefix/367

Azevedo, T. C., & Dantas, I. G. (July 31st, 2023). Análise das publicações sobre o IPTU Verde no Brasil: Revisão sistemática da produção dos programas de pós-graduação. *XXIII USP International Conference in Accounting*. São Paulo

Azevedo, T. C., & Portella, A. A. (2020). Sustainable certification program of the city of Salvador: Analysis of the green IPTU criteria and benefits on its ecological perspective. *Revista de Direito da Cidade*, 12(3), 64–93. DOI: 10.12957/rdc.2020.46762

Bardin, L. (2016). *Análise de conteúdo* (1st ed). 70 Editions

Complementary Law No. 101/2000, 101/2000 (2000). https://www.planalto.gov.br/ccivil_03/leis/lcp/lcp101.htm

Constitution Amendment Proposal No. 13, of 2019 (2019). https://www.camara.leg.br/proposicoesWeb/fichadetramitacao?idProposicao=2344523

Constitution of the Federative Republic of Brazil. (1988). http://www.planalto.gov.br/ccivil_03/Constituicao/Constituicao.htm

Constitutional Amendment No. 29, of September 13th, 2000 (2000) https://www.planalto.gov.br/ccivil_03/constituicao/emendas/emc/emc29.htm

De Cesare, C. M., Fernandes, C. E., & Cavalcanti, C. B. (2015). Imposto sobre a Propriedade Predial e Territorial Urbana (Vol. 3). Ministério das Cidades https://www.caubr.gov.br/wp-content/uploads/2017/10/CAPACIDADES3.pdf

de Oliveira, D. B. (2014). "IPTU Verde": Uma perspectiva legislativa no município de Pelotas. *Revista da Faculdade de Direito de Pelotas*, 1(1), 159–182.

Dinis, A. A. (2024, March). Promoting Fiscal Incentives for Urban Regeneration: Local Government Digital Presence. In World Conference on Information Systems and Technologies (pp. 335-343). . Cham: Springer Nature SwitzerlandDOI: 10.1007/978-3-031-60328-0_34

Fiorillo, C. A. P., & Ferreira, R. M. (2010). Direito ambiental tributário (3o ed). Saraiva Publisher

Gil, A. C. (2019). *Métodos e técnicas de pesquisa social.* Atlas Ltda Publisher.

Gonçalves, R. da R., Oliveira, C. de R. de, Carvalho, A. B., & Santos, R. Á. (2019). O impacto da política pública de IPTU Verde no município de Curitiba. Revibec. *Revista de la Red Iberoamericana de Economia Ecológica*, 30(1), 120–137.

Junior, P. C., & De Cesare, C. (2022). Who pays the property tax? Evidence from Brazil. *Land Use Policy*, 120, 106235. DOI: 10.1016/j.landusepol.2022.106235

Law, No. 5.172, of October 25th, 1966 (1966). https://www.planalto.gov.br/ccivil_03/leis/l5172compilado.htm

Law, No. 10.257, of July 10th, 2001, 10,257 (2001). http://www.planalto.gov.br/ccivil_03/leis/LEIS_2001/L10257.htm

Law, No. 3.686, of November 11th, 2003, 3.686 (2003). https://jales.siscam.com.br/arquivo?id=24777

Law, No. 7.186, of December 27th, 2006, 7.186 (2006). http://leismunicipa.is/ekbmt

Law, No. 8.474, of October 2nd, 2013 (2013). http://leismunicipa.is/mktgd

Law, No. 8.953, of December 25th, 2015, 8.953 (2015). http://leismunicipa.is/qgoul

Law, No. 9.069, of June 30th, 2016 (2016). http://leismunicipa.is/cjuot Organic Law of the Municipality of Salvador/BA (2024).https://www.cms.ba.gov.br/lei-organica

Leal, M. V. O., Oliveira, J. R. S., Azevedo, T. C., & Conceição, M. G. (November 1st, 2022). Características dos programas de IPTU Verde em municípios baianos. Anais do XXIV ENGEMA 2022. Encontro Internacional sobre Gestão Empresarial e Meio Ambiente (ENGEMA), São Paulo https://engemausp.submissao.com.br/24/anais/arquivos/319.pdf?v=1716844002

Maillo, M. Á. G. (2016). Usos y abusos en la fiscalidad ambiental. Congreso Salamanca/FMU: Derecho Ambiental Contemporâneo España/Brasil, Salamanca (España).

Merlin, L. V. D. C. T., & Vasconcelos, J. A. S. (2020). Tributação predial e territorial urbana no município de Afuá. Revista Científica do UniRios, 282

Municipal Decree No. 25.157, of April 18th, 2016 (2016). http://leismunicipa.is/noaru

Ortiz, A. C. T. D. T., Brandao, L. P., Rabelo, J. S., Gama, L. U., & Malvestio, A. C. (2022). Tax incentives as an instrument of environmental policy: An analysis of the green IPTU on municipalities of Minas Gerais. *Urbe. Revista Brasileira de Gestão Urbana*, 14, e20210181. DOI: 10.1590/2175-3369.014.e20210181

Passos, A. B. da M., & Pozzetti, V. C. (2012). IPTU VERDE: Extrafiscalidade aplicada a proteção ambiental do cenário urbano brasileiro. Hiléia: Revista do Direito Ambiental da Amazônia, 18(jan-jun/2012) http://periodicos.uea.edu.br/index.php/Hileia/article/view/151

Paz, M. S., Azevedo, T. C., Conceição, M. G., & Oliveira, J. R. S. (2023). Práticas e medidas sustentáveis como instrumento de política pública local ambiental e os ODS para as cidades: um estudo das estratégias adotadas nos municípios baianos. Revista de Administração e Contabilidade da FAT, 14(3).

Rangel, A. C. L. D. C., Aranha, K. C., & Da Silva, M. C. B. C. (2015). Os telhados verdes nas políticas ambientais como medida indutora para a sustentabilidade. *Desenvolvimento e Meio Ambiente*, 35. Advance online publication. DOI: 10.5380/dma.v35i0.39177

Sachs, J. (2015). *The age of sustainable development*. Columbia University Press. DOI: 10.7312/sach17314

Salvador, (Municipality). (2024). Incentivos tributários. https://www2.sefaz.salvador.ba.gov.br/transparencia/incentivos-tributarios

Sedur, Secretaria de Desenvolvimento Urbano do Munícipio de Salvador. (Mucniciplaity). IPTU Verde: número de beneficiados pelo incentivo tributário cresce 235% em 2024. https://sedur.salvador.ba.gov.br/noticias/852-iptu-verde-numero-de-beneficiados-pelo-incentivo-tributario-cresce-235-em-2024

Silva, L. F. D., Azevedo, T. C., & Oliveira, J. R. S. (2022). Panorama da legislação sobre tributação ecológica em países Latino-Americanos. Research. *Social Development*, 11(7), e3711729566. DOI: 10.33448/rsd-v11i7.29566

Somohano-Rodríguez, F. M., David, F., & Azevedo, T. C. (2023). Spanish business commitment to the 2030 Agenda in uncertain times. *AIMS Environmental Science*, 10(2), 246–266. DOI: 10.3934/environsci.2023015

Taranu, V., & Verbeeck, G. (2022). Property tax as a policy against urban sprawl. *Land Use Policy*, 122, 106335. DOI: 10.1016/j.landusepol.2022.106335

United Nations. (2015). Transforming our world: The 2030 Agenda for Sustainable Development, 70/1. https://documents.un.org/doc/undoc/gen/n15/291/89/pdf/n1529189.pdf?token=TtFoPNjXD5KjtHiSdb&fe=true

Ventosa, I. P., Forn, M. C., Sora, M. J., & Sanz, E. S. (2015). Estado actual de la fiscalidad ambiental en España y perspectivas de futuro. In *F. A. Martínez (Org.), Fiscalidad ambiental en España: Situación actual y perspectivas de futuro*. Arazandi.

ADDITIONAL READING

Azevedo, T. C., & Portella, A. A. (2019). Incentivos fiscales verdes como instrumento de apoyo a la política urbana: Un estúdio sobre el IPTU VERDE en municipios brasileños. *HOLOS*, 1, 1–18. DOI: 10.15628/holos.2019.7913

De Mello, K., Tavares, P. A., Von Glehn, H. Q. C., Nalon, M. A., & Sparovek, G. (2023). The são paulo state (Brazil) ecological fiscal transfer: Distributive and environmental effects. *Perspectives in Ecology and Conservation*, 21(4), 318–325. DOI: 10.1016/j.pecon.2023.11.001

Liberalesso, T., Cruz, C. O., Silva, C. M., & Manso, M. (2020). Green infrastructure and public policies: An international review of green roofs and green walls incentives. *Land Use Policy*, 96, 104693. Advance online publication. DOI: 10.1016/j.landusepol.2020.104693

Mpofu, F. Y. (2022). Green taxes in africa: Opportunities and challenges for environmental protection, sustainability, and the attainment of sustainable development goals. *Sustainability (Basel)*, 14(16), 10239. Advance online publication. DOI: 10.3390/su141610239

Rana, A., Sadiq, R., Alam, M. S., Karunathilake, H., & Hewage, K. (2021). Evaluation of financial incentives for green buildings in canadian landscape. *Renewable & Sustainable Energy Reviews*, 135, 110199. DOI: 10.1016/j.rser.2020.110199 PMID: 34234620

Silva, L. F., & da, .; Silva K. O. S.; Azevedo, T. C. (2022). Tributação ecológica municipal: Um estudo em cidades portuguesas e espanholas. [RBDU]. *Revista Brasileira de Direito Urbanístico*, 8(14), 125–146.

KEY TERMS AND DEFINITIONS

Green IPTU: Tax benefit in the form of deductions, discounts, or reductions in the tax amount when the taxpayer engages in practices that encourage sustainable development in the environmental dimension.

Sustainable Development Goals: Global commitments that aim to guide countries to make efforts between the years 2016-2030 towards adopting sustainability practices.

Extra fiscality: Inducing behaviors where the central element of taxation is not revenue generation, but rather the guiding and encouraging nature of actions in favor of a sustainable environment.

Tax Immunity: Constitutional assumption that prohibits federative entities from instituting and collecting taxes.

Tax Incentives Ecological and Sustainable: Exemption, discount, or reduction of taxes as a way to encourage urban environmental sustainability practices that promote the conservation and preservation of the environment, fight the effects of climate change, socioeconomic inequalities, and foster the sustainable development of cities.

Tax on Urban Property and Land (IPTU): A municipal tax that property and urban landowners pay annually to the municipality where the property is located.

Urban Policy Environmental and Sustainability: Actions and instruments that prioritize ensuring the conservation and preservation of natural resources, promoting renewable production sources, reducing waste volume, utilizing low CO2 emission equipment, and encouraging constructions that use sustainable technologies for the well-being and improvement of the quality and living conditions of city inhabitants.

APPENDIX I

Figure 1. Population concentration of the Municipality of Salvador/BA-2010 (Prepared by Luis Henrique C. Paixão, 2017)

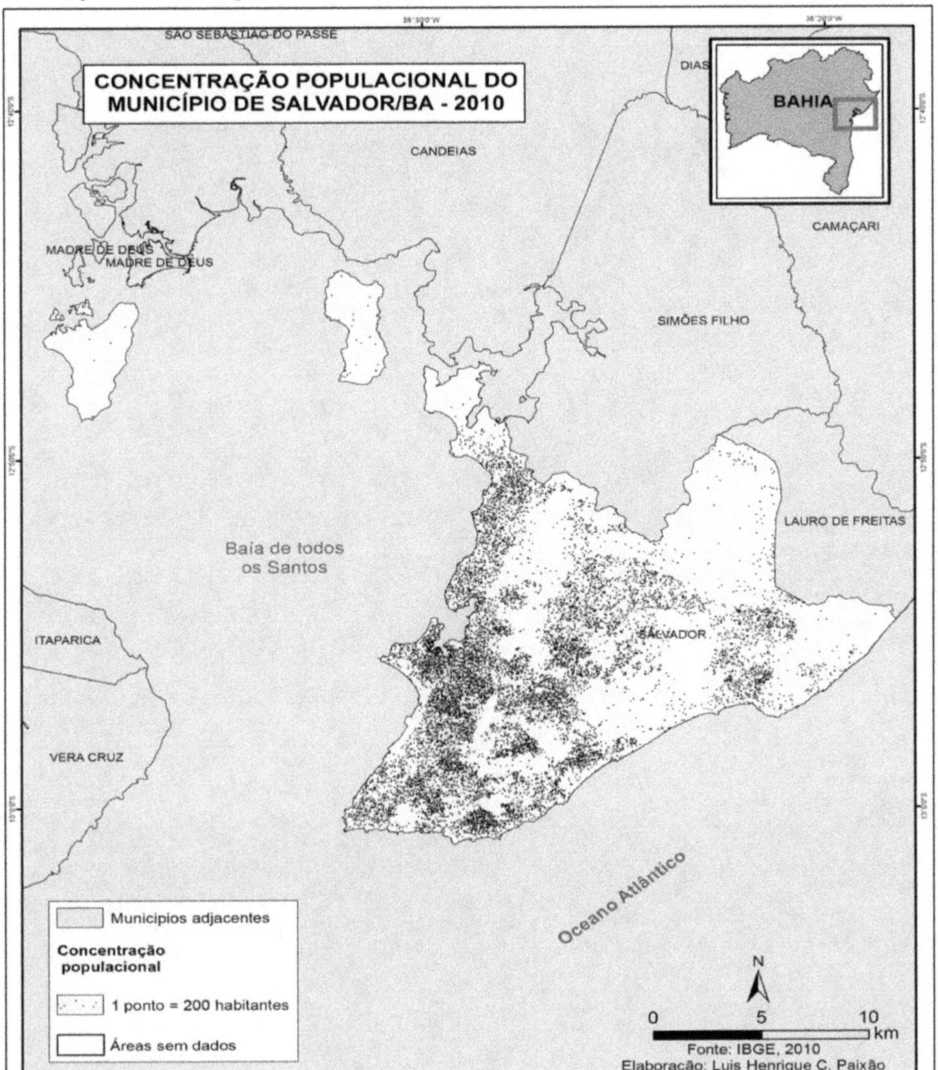

Chapter 12
Tax Policy Responses to Economic Crises:
The Case of Post-COVID-19 Reform in Morocco (2023-2026)

Rida Belahouaoui
https://orcid.org/0000-0003-1625-6732
Cadi Ayyad University, Marrakesh, Morocco

El Houssain Attak
Cadi Ayyad University, Marrakesh, Morocco

ABSTRACT

This chapter explores Morocco's tax policy responses to the economic crises induced by the COVID-19 pandemic, focusing on the comprehensive tax reform initiatives implemented between 2023 and 2026. It examines how these reforms aim to balance the need for increased fiscal revenue with the principles of tax equity and efficiency amidst the economic disruptions caused by the pandemic. The chapter discusses the background of Morocco's tax system, the objectives and strategies of the reforms, and their implementation and outcomes. It also addresses the challenges faced and lessons learned during the reform process. The chapter concludes by reflecting on the significance of Morocco's tax policy response in enhancing fiscal sustainability and economic resilience, while suggesting areas for future research and policy development.

DOI: 10.4018/979-8-3693-3908-4.ch012

1 INTRODUCTION

The general context is established around the Finance Laws of 2023 and 2024, marking the beginning of a four-year tax reform spanning from 2023 to 2026. This fiscal transformation is primarily based on the recommendations from the Third National Tax Conference (Ministry of Economy and Finance, 2019) and the provisions of Framework Law 69-19 (2021), which has been guiding tax reform since 2021. The implementation of an effective, fair, equitable, and balanced tax system is at the heart of this reform. Designed as a major lever for financing the national economy, this system aims to mobilize fiscal potential to fund public policies fully. Consequently, it contributes to economic development and strengthens social inclusion and cohesion, in line with Framework Law 69-19 (2021).

One of the key objectives of this reform is the intensification of the fight against tax fraud and evasion. According to the Taxe Justice Network (2023), these issues cost Morocco over \$982.5 million annually, compared to \$876.6 million in 2022. Of this 2023 amount, \$919.5 million is due to corporate tax abuse, given that 76% of companies report zero or negative results. The remaining \$63.1 million is attributable to international tax evasion and offshore wealth, with an additional annual tax loss of \$61.5 million, as reported by Taxe Justice Network (TJN) (2023).

Despite the efforts made, as praised by the IMF in its January 2023 report, there is still progress to be made (IMF, 2023). The report particularly highlights the need to mobilize more tax revenues. Indeed, Morocco does not fully exploit its fiscal capacity, showing a gap of more than 10% between actual and potential tax revenues. Therefore, to mitigate this differential, Morocco needs to further optimize its tax system. This necessity aligns with the ambition of the 2023 Finance Law, demonstrating the relevance of the ongoing reform.

In addressing the issue of tax equity, it is notable that only 140 companies contribute 50% of the revenues from three major components of Moroccan taxation: Corporate Income Tax (CIT), Personal Income Tax (PIT), and Value Added Tax (VAT). Among these elements, VAT emerges as the central pillar of the kingdom's fiscal revenues, representing 34% of the total, or 95 billion dirhams (Finance Law, 2024). This predominance underscores the crucial importance of its reform, initiated by the 2024 Finance Law (Finance Law, 2024). CIT, constituting only 22% of tax revenues, or 61 billion Dhs, faces a structural equity problem, with less than 1% of companies generating more than 80% of their revenues (Belahouaoui & Attak, 2023). Regarding PIT, which accounts for 19% of revenues, or 52.8 billion Dhs, it is also marked by a notable structural imbalance. Indeed, 73% of its revenues come from a single category of income (salaries and similar) among the five taxable categories of PIT contributors (Court of Audit, 2019).

The progressive tax reform plan in Morocco envisions several key measures, which include:

- Standardization of corporate income tax: By 2026, a major revision of the corporate income tax is planned. The tax rate will be standardized at 20%, with exceptions for companies with a net profit exceeding 100 million dirhams and financial institutions, which will be subject to a tax rate of 35% and 40%, respectively (Finance Law, 2023).
- Exemption of certain essential goods and introduction of VAT withholding: The 2024 Finance Law provides for the exemption of certain essential goods and the application of a VAT withholding regime (Finance Law, 2024).
- Modification of personal income taxation: There will be a reduction in income tax for employees and civil servants through a revision of deductions and exemptions, thereby reducing their taxable income. This decrease in revenue will be offset by including all individual incomes in the tax base and introducing withholding at the source for certain types of income.

These changes within the Moroccan tax system aim to enhance its efficiency and progressivity while broadening the tax base. By adopting a prudent approach, these reforms could potentially increase tax revenues, especially in a post-COVID-19 context marked by significant revenue mobilization, in accordance with the triennial budget plan. It is thus anticipated that tax revenues will reach 375 billion dirhams by 2027, marking a 50% increase compared to the 251 billion dirhams collected at the end of 2022 (IMF, 2023).

This chapter delves into Morocco's tax policy responses to the economic crises induced by the COVID-19 pandemic, focusing on the comprehensive tax reform initiatives implemented between 2023 and 2026. It examines how these reforms aim to balance the need for increased fiscal revenue with the principles of tax equity and efficiency, in the wake of the economic disruptions caused by the pandemic.

The rest of this chapter is structured as follows: it begins with a discussion on the institutional and theoretical framework, providing the necessary context for understanding the tax reforms. Next, the methodology section outlines the approach used to evaluate the fiscal policies and reforms implemented in Morocco between 2023 and 2026. Following this, the results and discussion section presents the findings and analyzes the impact of the reforms. Finally, the conclusion summarizes the key insights and implications of the study. Theoretical

2 THEORETICAL BACKGROUND

2.1 The international tax reform journey

The international tax reform journey reflects the story of how and why countries collaborate on tax matters. National sovereignty guards the right to tax, but countries choose to collaborate on international tax rules and standards when collective action is necessary to secure or facilitate domestic policy objectives, or when the lack of coordination hinders these objectives (OECD, 2024).

2.1.1 Past:

For over 100 years, governments have collaborated on international taxation, developing rules that promote stability and growth by removing barriers to cross-border investment while protecting domestic tax bases. However, the global financial crisis revealed that these rules, developed in a "brick and mortar" economy, were inadequate for a digitalized and globalized world (OECD, 2024). Tax transparency initiatives, like the OECD-hosted global forum on transparency and exchange of information for tax purposes, have significantly combated offshore tax evasion, generating USD 126 billion in additional revenues. The Base Erosion and Profit Shifting (BEPS) project, initiated by the OECD/G20 Inclusive Framework, has also played a crucial role in reducing tax avoidance by multinational enterprises (MNEs).

2.1.2 Present:

Today, the international tax reform journey aims to modernize the tax system and make it fairer. The Global Forum has expanded to 170 jurisdictions, with a majority being developing countries. The Inclusive Framework on BEPS has grown to 145 members, prioritizing inclusivity (OECD, 2024). Key developments include the implementation of automatic exchange of information and the introduction of the Crypto-Asset Reporting Framework (CARF) to address risks posed by crypto-assets. The landmark international tax agreement of October 2021, known as the Two-Pillar Solution, reallocates taxing rights on profits of large MNEs and introduces a global minimum corporate tax rate of 15%. Additionally, the International VAT/GST Guidelines have helped countries like Thailand, South Africa, and Chile achieve significant revenue gains (OECD, 2024).

2.1.3 Future:

The future of international tax reform will build on past successes while ensuring greater inclusivity and capacity building. The OECD is preparing a comprehensive action plan to support the implementation of the Two-Pillar Solution, including bilateral and multilateral training, peer reviews, and stakeholder dialogues. The joint OECD-UNDP tax inspectors without borders initiative will continue to assist jurisdictions in implementing global minimum tax rules. The future agenda, set through a bottom-up process, will address emerging issues like the impact of mobile workers on tax systems, simplification of corporate tax systems, and new frontiers in tax transparency (OECD, 2023).

The OECD remains committed to collaborating with countries, international and regional organizations, the business community, civil society, and other stakeholders to shape the future of international tax reform, focusing on supporting domestic resource mobilization to further sustainable development goals (OECD, 2024).

2.2 Tax reform in the post COVID-19 context:

The global economic crisis triggered by the COVID-19 pandemic disproportionately impacted developing countries, exacerbating poverty, food insecurity, and income inequality. Van der Hoeven & Vos (2022) noted that richer nations mitigated the worst impacts through massive fiscal and financial support programs, whereas developing countries lacked this capacity and received limited multilateral contingency financing. They argued for four key reforms to make the International Financial and Fiscal System (IFFS) more suitable for sustainable development: equitable international tax coordination, a sovereign debt workout mechanism, overhauling policy conditionality, and increasing Special Drawing Rights.

Popescu & Šebestová (2022) highlighted the pandemic as a catalyst for advancing global tax initiatives. They focused on the OECD's efforts to address BEPS, promoting responsible tax principles and ending corporate tax evasion and the use of tax havens. The study emphasized the need for fiscally responsible businesses to regain control of national tax systems and ensure adherence to tax principles. Kobbi-Fakhfakh & Bougacha (2023) examined the impact of COVID-19 on US publicly listed firms, noting a reduction in tax avoidance activities due to decreased profits. They argued that fiscal policies should stimulate growth to help firms tackle post-pandemic challenges while addressing public finance deterioration and rising inequalities. They advocated for reviewing public fiscal policies to achieve equity, growth, and sustainability, suggesting that progressive tax reform could mitigate the negative economic effects of the pandemic.

Makin & Layton (2021) provided a critical evaluation of global fiscal responses to the pandemic. They argued that while fiscal intervention was necessary, the nature of responses varied significantly across countries, with some being overly expansive and poorly targeted. They highlighted the future macroeconomic risks associated with elevated public debt levels and emphasized the need for fiscal consolidation to address the crisis's fiscal legacy. Sainsbury & Breunig (2020) focused on the weaknesses exposed in Australia's tax system by the COVID-19 crisis. They argued for comprehensive reform to reduce reliance on income taxes, particularly labor taxes, and to apply more equal tax treatment to different income sources. They believed this approach would support well-being and labor market activity, helping to restore a sound structural budget position. Khan & Khan (2022) discussed India's Goods and Services Tax (GST) as a significant tax reform aimed at consolidating various indirect taxes into a single structure, enhancing transparency, and reducing tax evasion and corruption. They highlighted GST's features and its positive impact on the Indian economy.

Overall, the literature highlights the necessity for both national and international tax reforms to address the challenges posed by the COVID-19 pandemic. It underscores the importance of equitable and responsible tax policies, global cooperation, and targeted fiscal measures to support sustainable development and economic recovery.

2.3 International tax policy responses

The COVID-19 pandemic has had a profound impact on tax systems around the world, prompting countries to reconsider and reform their fiscal policies to address the unprecedented economic challenges. While many governments have implemented tax measures aimed at stimulating economic recovery and supporting vulnerable sectors, the nature and effectiveness of these reforms have varied widely. To gain a comprehensive understanding of how different nations have responded to the fiscal pressures induced by the pandemic, it is crucial to examine the specific tax policy responses adopted by various countries. This section provides an overview of key international tax policy responses to the COVID-19 pandemic, highlighting how different countries have navigated the crisis through targeted tax reforms. These examples will offer insights into the strategies employed globally and underscore the diversity of approaches taken to manage the fiscal fallout of the pandemic.

Table 1. Examples of tax policy responses to the COVID-19 pandemic in various countries

Country	Tax policy response	Objective	Key outcomes	Source
Indonesia	The government implemented tax incentives and relief, including reductions in tax payments, to support economic recovery.	To stimulate economic growth and recovery post-COVID-19 by alleviating financial burdens on businesses and individuals.	While the tax incentives improved local sales, exports, turnover, and imports, they also led to a decline in state tax revenue.	Ispriyarso & Wibawa (2023)
Australia	Green Tax Reform (GTR) with energy tax and different tax revenue recycling methods: reduction of payroll tax, GST, and a mixed approach.	To achieve a triple dividend of lower emissions, higher GDP, and higher employment, while promoting sustainability in post-COVID-19 recovery.	Productivity gains in GTR improve GDP and employment outcomes, with GST reduction showing the highest potential for achieving the triple dividend.	Maxim & Zander (2020)
International	Proposed reforms to the International Financial and Fiscal System (IFFS): equitable international tax coordination, sovereign debt workout mechanism, policy conditionality overhaul, and increased Special Drawing Rights.	To enhance the IFFS's ability to support sustainable development and better respond to global crises like COVID-19.	The proposed reforms aim to reduce the disparity in crisis response capacity between developed and developing countries, improving resilience and equity in the global economy.	Van der Hoeven & Vos (2022)
45 Developing Countries	Implementation of tax reforms in response to pandemics, focusing on corporate income taxes, excises, and property taxation.	To strengthen fiscal capacity and revenue generation in response to the fiscal challenges posed by pandemics.	Past pandemics have driven tax reforms in developing countries, particularly in areas like corporate income taxes, excises, and property taxation, though they have not led to significant changes in revenue administration.	Gupta & Jalles (2022)
Morocco	Digitalization of tax administration as part of tax reform efforts.	To reduce tax avoidance and increase compliance through improved transparency and service facilitation.	Digitalization has promoted compliance, but challenges remain, particularly in building trust and transparency to effectively reduce tax avoidance.	(Belahouaoui & Attak, 2024)

continued on following page

Table 1. Continued

Country	Tax policy response	Objective	Key outcomes	Source
OECD Countries	Introduction of a minimum effective tax rate on global profits of multinational firms.	To address issues of corporate tax avoidance and ensure fair contributions to national budgets, especially in the context of underfunded public services highlighted by COVID-19.	A minimum tax on global profits is proposed to curb corporate tax avoidance and improve funding for essential public services, reducing the sense of unfairness.	(Laffitte et al., 2020)
Sierra Leone	Analysis of taxpayer attitudes towards taxation during the COVID-19 pandemic, with a focus on support for taxation, progressive taxation, and tax compliance linked to government service delivery.	To understand how the pandemic has influenced taxpayer attitudes and the implications for future tax reforms and revenue generation.	Initial support for taxation increased, particularly in Freetown, but over time, there was a decline in willingness to pay more taxes, especially if government services were not perceived as adequate.	Orgeira Pillai et al. (2024)

Source: Created by authors

The section on international tax policy responses highlights how countries have adapted their tax systems in response to the COVID-19 pandemic. These responses include a range of strategies, from tax incentives in Indonesia to green tax reforms in Australia and the digitalization of tax administration in Morocco. Additionally, international efforts, such as the OECD's initiatives, emphasize the importance of global coordination to address tax challenges. The analysis also notes the specific impact on developing countries and the varied success of these reforms in fostering economic recovery, tax compliance, and equitable growth. This overview underscores the critical role of tax policy in navigating the fiscal challenges posed by the pandemic.

3 METHODOLOGY

3.1 Approach and method

This study adopts a descriptive approach based on a documentary analysis of the framework laws related to the progressive tax reform launched in Morocco. This methodology is chosen due to its effectiveness in contexts where interviews or ethnographies may be inappropriate or impractical (Gorsky & Mold, 2020). They discuss the utility of documentary approaches in qualitative research, noting that documents can serve as primary sources of data, particularly in policy analysis.

The adoption of documentary analysis allows for an in-depth examination of the legal texts, official reports, and policy documents that underpin the tax reforms. Bowen (2009) emphasized that document analysis is a systematic procedure for reviewing or evaluating documents—both printed and electronic (computer-based and Internet-transmitted) material. This approach involves skimming (superficial examination), reading (thorough examination), and interpretation. It is especially useful for obtaining unobtrusive data, providing background and historical context, and corroborating or augmenting evidence from other sources.

Furthermore, Bailey (2008) pointed out that documents are stable, unobtrusive, and exact sources of data, providing detailed and comprehensive evidence that may be difficult to obtain through other methods. The use of official documents, such as government reports and legislative texts, ensures that the data is both reliable and valid, supporting a rigorous analysis of the tax reform process.

3.2 Data collection and analysis

The data collection and analysis for this study was based on a thorough examination of key legislative documents, including the Organic Law on Finance Laws (LOF) of 2015, Framework Law no. 69-19 on tax reform of 2021, and the Finance Laws of 2023 and 2024. A descriptive analysis of these framework laws was conducted to evaluate their impact on the post-COVID-19 response and the mobilization of tax revenues for financing the Sustainable Development Goals (SDGs). The method involved several steps:

Figure 1. Data collection and descriptive analysis method (Created by authors)

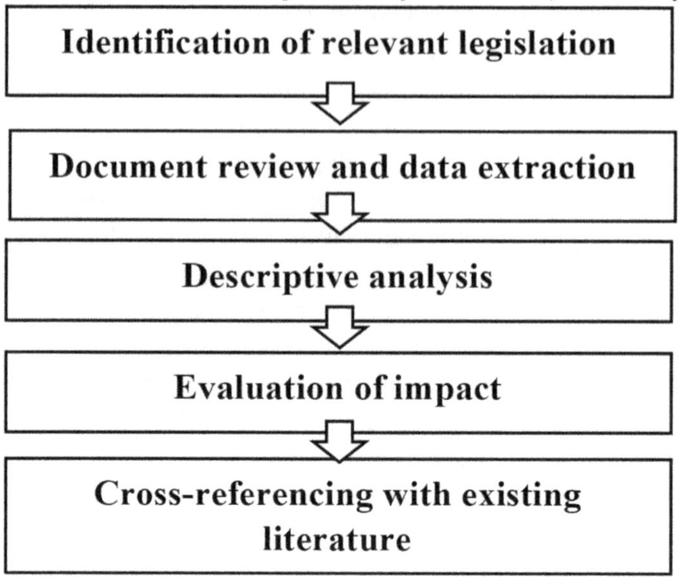

The method involved several steps: Initially, relevant legislative documents, including the LOF of 2015, Framework Law no. 69-19 of 2021, and the Finance Laws for 2023 and 2024, were identified and gathered. Each document was systematically reviewed to extract pertinent information related to tax policy changes, fiscal measures, and anticipated outcomes. A descriptive analysis was conducted to identify trends and understand how the reforms address COVID-19 challenges, enhance tax system efficiency and equity, and contribute to sustainable development revenue mobilization. The impact of these reforms was evaluated based on their support for economic recovery and financing critical sectors like health and education. Finally, the findings were cross-referenced with existing literature and reports from organizations such as the IMF and OECD to validate the results and provide comprehensive context.

This methodological approach allowed for a detailed and nuanced understanding of the legislative framework governing Morocco's tax reforms and their implications for economic recovery and sustainable development post-COVID-19. Future empirical research, including qualitative interviews and quantitative impact assessments, will build on this foundation to provide deeper insights into the effectiveness and broader implications of these reforms.

4 RESULTS AND DISCUSSION

4.1 Moroccan tax reform law

In accordance with the provisions of the second paragraph of Article 71 of the Constitution, this Framework Law outlines the fundamental objectives of the State's fiscal policy, the modalities for their implementation, and the principles of good governance that should guide the State's actions in this area. It also establishes the necessary conditions for the State to implement a tax policy that is fair, equitable, coherent, effective, and transparent. To implement its tax policy, the State must take into account the following priorities:

- Encouraging productive investment that creates added value and quality employment;
- Efficient redistribution and reduction of inequalities to enhance social justice and cohesion;
- Territorial development and the strengthening of spatial justice;
- Improving the efficiency and effectiveness of tax administration and building mutual trust with users;
- Embracing international best practices in the field of taxation.

4.1.1 Key objectives of tax reform framework

According to Chapter II, the fundamental objectives of the Framework Law on tax reform, as outlined in Article 3, are multifaceted. It includes strengthening the contribution of state and local government taxation for the financing of economic and social development policies and reducing the tax burden on taxpayers as the tax base expands. The reform aims to uphold the principle of tax neutrality concerning value-added tax (VAT) and align tax provisions with general legal rules and current accounting standards. It also seeks to harmonize preferential tax regimes with international standards and best practices, encouraging enterprises to enhance their competitiveness both nationally and internationally.

Additionally, the objectives focus on mobilizing savings and directing them towards productive sectors, gradually implementing the principle of comprehensive income taxation for individuals, and rationalizing tax incentives based on their socio-economic impact. Simplifying and streamlining local government taxes, aligning local government tax rules with state tax regulations, and consolidating taxes on economic activities and real estate assets are also key goals. The framework aims to simplify and adapt the tax regime for local income-generating activities with modest returns, integrate the informal sector into the structured economy, and strengthen measures to combat tax fraud and evasion.

4.1.2 Implementation mechanisms and procedures of tax reform framework

To implement the aforementioned fundamental objectives, the priority measures that will be enacted, in accordance with paragraph a) of Article 19 of this Framework Law, mainly focus on upholding the principle of VAT neutrality while maintaining the exemption for basic products. This will be achieved by expanding its scope and reducing the number of rates, and generalizing the right to reimbursement. There is also a goal of gradually converging towards a unified corporate tax rate, particularly for industrial activities, and aligning the rates provided by preferential regimes, applicable to industrial and service acceleration zones, towards a unified rate.

The reform aims to enhance the contribution of corporate tax from public institutions and enterprises, as well as companies operating in regulated activities or monopoly or oligopoly situations. Another objective is to gradually reduce the rates of the minimum contribution and implement incentives to promote the development of innovative businesses, particularly young "start-up" companies in the fields of new technologies, research and development, and social enterprises. Support structures known as incubators and accelerators, which provide entrepreneurs with business creation services, and companies that aim to group self-employed individuals into structures providing services, known as "Self-employed Aggregators," will also be promoted.

The progressive income tax rates applicable to individuals will be revised and the tax base broadened. The single professional contribution regime will be adapted and improved to accelerate the integration of the informal sector. Ensuring compliance with good governance rules in international taxation in accordance with the agreements and conventions concluded for this purpose is also a priority. Lastly, guaranteeing the rights of taxpayers and the administration is an essential part of the reform framework.

4.2 Deployment of the tax reform

4.2.1 Case of 2023 Finance Law

The "flat tax", or uniform tax rate, is a fiscal system characterized by applying the same tax rate to all taxpayers, regardless of their income or profits. According to various definitions, the flat tax is seen as a means to simplify the current complex tax system and streamline the declaration procedures (Belahouaoui, 2023). Hall

& Rabushka (2013) argued that the flat tax involves shared responsibility among all taxpayers, with contributions proportional to their income. They believe this approach is logical, as public services' benefits are proportional to income. Hall & Rabushka (2013) also linked the flat tax to eliminating tax advantages, reductions, and exemptions, making the system more transparent and efficient. They suggest maintaining a non-taxable threshold to preserve some progressivity. However, the flat tax is criticized for its lack of progressivity and potential inequity towards low-income individuals, as it does not consider the relative contributive capacity of taxpayers.

Keen et al. (2008) associated the flat tax with Hall & Rabushka (2013) proposal, which recommends a well-defined tax structure combining a tax on business income and a tax on employment income, both levied at the same rate, with a personal allowance against the wage tax. They describe the flat tax as essentially a consumption-type VAT collected by the subtraction method, supplemented by a non-refundable tax credit on labor income. In summary, the flat tax proposes a simplification of the tax system but raises debates about its ability to ensure fiscal equity, particularly for lower-income earners.

Over the past decade, corporate tax has undergone more than seven continuous reforms, regularly adjusting between proportional and progressive rates, tax advantages for companies, and moving towards uniform rates by 2026.

The 2023 Finance Law has instituted a comprehensive reform of corporate tax rates through a progressive methodology towards unified rates over four years. Article 19 of the CGI has set the target corporate tax rates as follows:

- 20% as the unified standard rate applicable to all companies;
- 35% for companies with a net profit equal to or exceeding 100 million dirhams;
- 40% for credit institutions and similar organizations, Bank Al-Maghrib, the Deposit and Management Fund, and insurance and reinsurance companies.

Continuing the progressive reduction of minimum contribution rates initiated by the 2022 Finance Law, the 2023 Finance Law has introduced the following measures:

- Reduction of the standard minimum contribution rate to 0.25% for all companies, regardless of the declared current result excluding depreciation;
- Reduction of the minimum contribution rate from 0.25% to 0.15% for commercial companies' transactions on certain basic products.

Additional measures were introduced by the 2023 Finance Law, particularly for companies with the Casa Finance City status, limiting the five-year corporate tax exemption to the first sixty months following their establishment. Another measure rationalizes the tax advantages for financial companies in industrial acceleration zones (formerly free zones). To ensure fiscal equity, the 2023 Finance Law excluded financial companies from benefiting from these zones' tax advantages, in line with the 2021 Finance Law for companies with Casa Finance City status. This includes:

- credit institutions, as defined by current legislation;
- insurance and reinsurance companies, as defined by current legislation.

Companies with Casa Finance City status and those located in industrial acceleration zones have benefited from either permanent or temporary exemptions followed by reduced tax rates of 8.75% and 15%. These companies will gradually transition to a corporate tax rate of 20% by 2026.

The reform is expected to increase revenues by 0.1% of GDP, or approximately USD 9 million by 2026. IMF projections estimate that tax revenues could reach 375 billion dirhams by 2027, a significant increase from previous years (IMF, 2023). This reform should also encourage more companies, particularly SMEs, whose tax rate will gradually rise from 10% to 20% by 2026, to contribute to corporate tax. It also aims to reduce common tax evasion practices among these companies. In summary, Morocco's ongoing corporate tax reform seeks to simplify the tax system, increase revenues, and promote fiscal equity, aligning with international tax standards, notably BEPS measures and those recommended by the Financial Action Task Force (FATF).

While effective in increasing tax revenues and combating fraud, Morocco's corporate tax reform raises equity concerns, particularly due to regulatory instability and the increase in the corporate tax rate for SMEs, which will rise from 10% to 20% by 2026. This situation could affect investor confidence in the tax system. It is essential for companies, especially SMEs, to comply with their tax obligations responsibly and ethically, contributing to the national budget, which relies on 64% of tax revenues.

For a comprehensive tax reform, several measures are suggested: ensuring fiscal equity, especially for SMEs, reducing the tax burden on new businesses, strengthening the relationship between the tax administration and taxpayers through digitization and service simplification, and providing practical support to startups and SMEs. Additionally, developing strategies against fraud and tax evasion, improving tax administration performance in revenue collection and mobilization, and implementing research programs to analyze fiscal behaviors and develop more effective strategies are recommended. These measures aim to reinforce trust and fiscal responsibility, which are crucial for Morocco's economic and fiscal stability (Belahouaoui, 2023).

4.2.2 Case of 2024 finances law

The central role of VAT in fiscal revenue highlights the importance of its reform, as proposed by the 2024 Finance Law. This reform becomes particularly crucial in light of the distribution of contributions: according to the 2019 National Tax Conference statistics, 7.4% of taxpayers finance 90% of VAT revenue. Additionally, 86% of VAT-subject companies submitted null or credit declarations, and 80% of VAT revenue is generated by the standard rate of 20%. These figures indicate a significant concentration of contributions and a potential for fraud or tax avoidance. Therefore, the VAT reform aims not only to improve collection efficiency but also to address these anomalies, ensuring a more balanced and fair fiscal contribution.

One of the key provisions of the 2024 Finance Law is the introduction of a new VAT withholding regime under Article 117. To promote fiscal transparency and effectively counter the use of false invoices, two new VAT withholding mechanisms are proposed: if suppliers of goods and works do not present a recent (less than 3 months old) tax compliance certificate to their VAT-subject clients, the due tax is withheld at the source by these clients (Article 117 of the CGI, 2024). However, the state, local authorities, and certain public entities subject to public procurement regulations are not required to perform this withholding.

Withholding on transactions by service providers subject to VAT: for certain specified services under Article 89-I (5°, 10°, and 12°), 75% of the VAT amount is withheld at the source when paid by:

a) public entities such as the state, local authorities, and public establishments, to their VAT-subject providers;
b) private entities and certain taxable individuals, when they pay remuneration to individual service providers who have provided the aforementioned certificate. Without this certificate, the withholding is 100% of the tax.

However, several operations and services are excluded from this withholding, including electricity and water sales to public networks, certain sanitation services, telecom operators' services, insurance brokers' services, and any operation below 5,000 dirhams, within a monthly limit of 50,000 dirhams per supplier. The amount withheld at the source, as mentioned in paragraphs IV and V, must be remitted to the tax administration the month following each payment, accompanied by a form provided by the administration. Withholdings by administrations and public accountants are directly transmitted to the Treasury General of the Kingdom.

The introduction of a new VAT withholding regime represents a significant step in combating tax fraud. As an indirect tax, VAT presents particular challenges in collection and compliance. Its mechanism, based on collecting during sales and deducting on purchases, unfortunately opens the door to fraudulent manipulations. The phenomenon of false invoices is especially concerning, as these fictitious or manipulated documents allow companies to artificially inflate their purchases to claim undue VAT deductions. Consequently, instead of remitting the collected VAT to the state, these companies claim a VAT credit. The alarming figure of 86% of companies submitting null or credit declarations is a clear indicator of the problem's magnitude.

The implementation of withholding aims to reduce these fraudulent behaviors by introducing additional control during the transaction itself. By withholding directly at the source, it limits opportunities for companies to manipulate their VAT declarations. This provides the tax administration with a more direct and immediate means of ensuring VAT collection while actively discouraging the production of false invoices. Furthermore, this system could also encourage a culture of compliance among businesses. Knowing that each transaction is potentially subject to closer scrutiny, companies might be more inclined to adhere strictly to tax rules. Ultimately, this measure could not only increase tax revenues but also restore confidence in the tax system by demonstrating that the state is proactive in combating fraud.

On the other hand, the introduction of this new VAT withholding regime could increase complexity for taxpayers. They would face the dual challenge of managing their tax obligations while ensuring withholdings for others. This layering of responsibilities could lead to inadvertent errors or even discourage some businesses, especially smaller ones or those with limited administrative resources.

To counter fraudulent behaviors, the implementation of withholding introduces stricter control during the transaction itself. This measure limits opportunities for companies to manipulate their VAT declarations. Additionally, sanctions are in place to ensure compliance. According to Article 117 of the CGI 2024, a 30% surcharge rate is applies to taxpayers subject to VAT and withholding obligations. Moreover, a 20% penalty is imposed for non-payment or late payment of the due VAT or withheld amounts. However, taxpayers can regularize their situation by submitting a corrective declaration to the tax administration, as per Article 232-III. This regularization allows taxpayers to correct errors and fulfil their tax obligations appropriately while avoiding potential non-compliance penalties.

It is imperative for the tax administration to simplify the procedures associated with this regime. A proactive approach to clarifying new obligations, coupled with an education program targeting taxpayer categories less familiar with fiscal complexities, is essential. The success of this reform largely depends on the administration's ability to facilitate the transition and ensure taxpayers have the necessary resources and knowledge to comply with the new requirements without unduly increasing their administrative burden.

4.2.3 The case of income tax reform: A much-awaited necessity

Despite the progressive tax reform, the 2024 Finance Law does not propose any measures for restructuring the progressive income tax rates, as envisioned by the Framework Law. Additionally, there is no defined implementation schedule for the 2023-2026 period, unlike the corporate tax, which has such visibility. As a result, labor remains more heavily taxed than capital in Morocco, with a marginal tax rate of 38% for income tax, while capital (notably financial, such as income from financial investments) is taxed at only 15% and will see this rate reduced to 10% by 2026 (according to Article 19-IV of the General Tax Code, 2023).

A comprehensive reform of the income tax is necessary to achieve several objectives, including creating an efficient and effective tax system to improve revenue collection, enhance the equity and transparency of the tax system, promote taxpayer compliance, combat tax evasion and fraud, and integrate the informal sector into the formal economy through fiscal incentives, particularly during business creation and early stages of operation. These incentives could include reduced tax rates or tax exemption periods for new businesses. Simplifying tax declaration and payment processes for small businesses is also crucial. Other measures could involve tax credits, training on tax obligations, and awareness campaigns about fiscal responsibility. These strategies aim to encourage the formalization of informal sector activities, improving tax compliance and broadening the tax base, thereby mobilizing more fiscal revenues, particularly from indirect taxes. Income tax revenues represented only 17% of total tax revenues at the end of 2022. The proposed reform should focus on three main axes:

- Revising the progressive income tax rate structure:

the progressive income tax rate structure has long been expected to be revised. However, no measures have been taken to address this situation. It is essential to review the current marginal tax rate of 38% to relieve the tax burden on the middle class, which, according to Bank Al-Maghrib, finances more than 73% of income tax revenues. The tax system also includes four other categories of taxable income and profits: professional income, agricultural operations, rental income, and investment income. It is also important to continue revising the taxation of wages and similar income by modifying deductions and exemptions to lower taxable income and reduce tax levels for employees and retirees. This loss of tax revenue should be offset by fairly taxing all income subject to income tax.

- Aligning income tax establishment and payment modalities:

this alignment aims to uphold the principle of equity among all categories of income and profits subject to income revenue by rationalizing the tax establishment and payment rules. Currently, some categories benefit from a declarative system and/or reduced rates, while others are taxable at general rate scales or through withholding, creating discrimination and a lack of equity among taxpayers. Therefore, it is necessary to reform these rules in favor of categories currently subject to less favorable tax treatment.

- Building a trustful relationship between tax administration and taxpayers:

to achieve this, three complementary approaches can be employed (see Table 1):

Table 2. Complementary approaches of building a trustful relationship between tax administration and taxpayers

Approach	Description
Traditional approach	Focuses on improving the detection of fraudulent behaviors and imposing strict penalties for non-compliance with tax obligations. This includes strengthening tax audits and controls, using advanced data analysis techniques to identify irregularities, and conducting thorough inspections. Taxpayers found in violation of tax laws may face financial penalties, interest on overdue taxes, and in some cases, legal prosecution. While important for deterring fraud, this approach can sometimes create a climate of distrust between the tax administration and taxpayers.
Service approach	Aims to improve the quality of tax administration services by making them more accessible, digital, and user-friendly. This approach seeks to simplify tax procedures and facilitate taxpayers' lives. By developing innovative digital tools and improving taxpayer support, the tax administration can help build trust between citizens and the state.
Trust approach	Seeks to encourage a cultural shift in taxpayers' attitudes towards paying taxes by promoting voluntary compliance. This strategy relies on transparent communication and raising awareness of the importance of taxes for funding public services. It aims to build a trustful relationship between the tax administration and taxpayers by highlighting the crucial role of tax contributions in collective well-being and simplifying tax processes to facilitate compliance.

Source: (Alm, 2019)

4.3 Moroccan tax reform: response to post COVID-19 context

4.3.1 Tax revenues mobilization

The comprehensive corporate tax reform in Morocco is projected to generate additional revenues of approximately 0.1% of GDP, which translates to about 9 million USD by 2026. The IMF has welcomed these changes to the tax system, noting that they should enhance its overall efficiency and progressivity while broadening the tax base. The IMF also expressed confidence that the measures introduced in the 2023 Finance Law could prudently generate more revenue as outlined in the triennial budget plan. According to the IMF, tax revenues are expected to reach 375 billion dirhams by 2027, a significant increase from 232.1 billion dirhams in 2017.

Tax revenues have seen a notable increase over recent years. In 2022, tax revenues amounted to 251.9 billion dirhams, with a forecasted rise to 263.24 billion dirhams by the end of 2023, and further to 280.4 billion dirhams by the end of 2024. The year 2024 has been particularly marked by a 10% increase in tax revenues by the end of May, reaching 135.3 billion dirhams. This growth is reflected in a 12.2% increase in direct tax revenues, primarily driven by a 16.3% rise in corporate tax revenues. Additionally, personal income tax revenues grew by 7.8%.

Indirect tax revenues also saw significant growth, increasing by 15.3%. This includes a substantial 17.3% rise in VAT revenues. These figures highlight the success of Morocco's tax reforms in boosting revenue mobilization and strengthening the fiscal framework in response to the economic challenges posed by the COVID-19 pandemic.

4.3.2 Sustainable Development Goals (SDGs) financing

Tax revenues in Morocco constitute the primary source of financing for the country's general budget, accounting for 90% of ordinary revenues in 2024 (Finance Law, 2024). This substantial increase in tax revenues is crucial for funding major development projects aligned with the SDGs. These projects primarily target the health and education sectors, aiming to enhance the quality and accessibility of essential services for all citizens.

In the health sector, increased tax revenues support the expansion and improvement of healthcare infrastructure, ensuring better access to medical services, and enhancing the overall public health system (Doghmi, 2020). This includes building new hospitals, upgrading existing facilities, and investing in advanced medical technologies to provide high-quality care. In education, the additional funds are directed towards building and renovating schools, improving educational resources, and training teachers. These efforts aim to provide a better learning environment, reduce dropout rates, and ensure that all children have access to quality education, which is fundamental for the country's long-term development (Belahouaoui & Attak, 2023).

Moreover, the boost in tax revenues facilitates the universalization of social protection programs, particularly targeting vulnerable families. This includes expanding social safety nets, providing financial assistance, and ensuring access to essential services for those most in need. By supporting these families, the government aims to reduce poverty and inequality, promoting social cohesion and stability (Belahouaoui & Attak, 2024). Overall, the increase in tax revenues not only strengthens Morocco's fiscal framework but also plays a pivotal role in achieving sustainable and inclusive growth by funding key initiatives in health, education, and social protection.

4.3.3 Socio-economic impacts of the tax reforms in Morocco

The reform of the tax system is a national priority for all stakeholders, given the critical role that taxation plays in financing public policies, maintaining financial and macroeconomic stability, and serving as a key lever for economic, social, and environmental development. These tax reforms are strategically aimed at establishing an efficient, just, equitable, and balanced fiscal system that serves as a fundamental tool for financing the national economy. By mobilizing the full fiscal potential, these reforms are expected to support both economic growth and social inclusion and cohesion. One of the significant socio-economic impacts of these reforms is the increased capacity to mobilize tax revenues, which will be instrumental in financing major initiatives such as the strategy for the universalization of social coverage. The state's fiscal policy will be designed to ensure effective redistribution and reduce inequalities, thereby reinforcing social justice and cohesion. Additionally, tailored fiscal measures will be implemented to promote the social economy, further contributing to the broader goals of economic development and social equity in Morocco.

The Moroccan state is committed to achieving a fundamental fiscal objective: mobilizing savings and directing them towards productive sectors while integrating the informal sector into the structured economy. To facilitate the inclusion of production, commerce, and service units operating in the informal sector into the formal economic fabric, the state will implement a simplified and accessible tax regime. Additionally, a national awareness and support program will be developed and implemented in close collaboration with relevant stakeholders.

These reforms also aim to improve the single professional contribution regime to accelerate the integration of informal sector participants into the formal economy. Tailored fiscal measures will be introduced to promote the cultural sector, recognizing its importance in the socio-economic landscape. Moreover, the state emphasizes the need for a comprehensive reform of the public sector to address structural inefficiencies in public institutions and enterprises. This reform seeks to ensure optimal complementarity and coherence between their respective missions, thereby enhancing their economic and social efficiency. These measures will have significant impacts across various demographic groups and regions in Morocco, fostering greater economic inclusion and regional development.

4.3.4 Challenges and solutions in implementing post-Covid-19 tax reform in Morocco

Implementing post-COVID-19 tax reforms in Morocco presents several challenges, particularly in balancing economic recovery with fiscal sustainability and ensuring equitable outcomes across different sectors and populations. To address these challenges, a strategic approach is necessary, focusing on tailored solutions that can effectively overcome potential obstacles.

Table 3. Challenges and solutions in implementing post-COVID-19 tax reform in Morocco

Challenges	Proposed solutions and perspectives
Resistance from the informal sector	Implement a simplified tax regime and conduct a comprehensive awareness campaign to encourage formalization. Provide incentives and support programs to ease the transition into the formal economy.
Complexity of integrating the informal sector	Develop targeted support mechanisms, such as financial and technical assistance, to facilitate the integration of informal businesses into the structured economy.
Balancing tax collection with economic stimulation	Design tax policies that stimulate economic activity while ensuring fair and efficient tax collection, including temporary tax relief for sectors hardest hit by the pandemic.
Ensuring equity across different demographic groups	Tailor tax measures to address the specific needs of vulnerable populations and regions, ensuring equitable distribution of tax burdens and benefits.
Administrative capacity and efficiency	Invest in digitalization and training for tax administration to improve efficiency and reduce compliance costs for taxpayers.
Public sector structural inefficiencies	Launch comprehensive public sector reform to address structural dysfunctions and enhance the coherence and efficiency of public institutions.
Ensuring compliance with international standards	Align tax reforms with international best practices and standards, while maintaining flexibility to address local socio-economic conditions.
Monitoring and evaluation of reform impacts	Establish robust monitoring and evaluation mechanisms to assess the impact of reforms and make necessary adjustments to ensure their effectiveness.

Source: Created by authors

This table outlines the key challenges that may arise during the implementation of post-COVID-19 tax reforms in Morocco and proposes potential solutions and strategies to address these challenges effectively.

5 CONCLUSION

In conclusion, creating an equitable tax system requires combining traditional approaches, improved services, and a culture of trust. By doing so, we can create an environment where taxpayers understand their obligations, see the value of their contributions, and are encouraged to comply with tax rules.

Income tax reform could significantly impact the perception of fiscal equity among taxpayers. If seen as fair and balanced, it could strengthen taxpayer confidence in the tax system and increase their willingness to pay taxes. Conversely, if perceived as unjust, it could negatively affect tax compliance, leading to increased tax evasion and avoidance. In some cases, this could even drive taxpayers towards the informal sector, where they would no longer be subject to income tax. This sector, representing up to 30% of Morocco's GDP and about 77% of total employment, poses a significant challenge to the country's tax system. Its high prevalence limits the government's ability to collect tax revenues and creates unfair competition for formal businesses. Addressing this issue in tax reforms is crucial, with a focus on simplifying tax processes, reducing burdens on small businesses, and promoting the transition to the formal sector. It is essential that tax reforms be perceived as equitable by the majority of taxpayers to ensure their compliance and maintain a stable and effective tax system.

Tax revenues in Morocco constitute the primary source of financing for the country's general budget, accounting for 90% of ordinary revenues in 2024. This significant increase in tax revenues enables the financing of major projects aligned with the SDGs, particularly in the sectors of health and education. It also supports the universalization of social protection for Moroccan citizens, with a special focus on vulnerable families.

Implications of the study

This study provides critical insights into the effectiveness and impact of Morocco's tax policy responses to the economic challenges posed by the COVID-19 pandemic. By examining the reforms implemented between 2023 and 2026, the study highlights how strategic tax policy adjustments can enhance fiscal revenue mobilization, support economic recovery, and promote social equity. The findings underscore the importance of comprehensive tax reforms that balance efficiency, equity, and sustainability. The study also reveals the significant role of tax revenues in financing essential public services and development projects, particularly in health, education, and social protection. Furthermore, the analysis of Morocco's experience offers valuable lessons for other developing countries facing similar economic crises, emphasizing the need for robust tax systems, international cooperation, and targeted fiscal policies to build resilient economies and achieve sustainable development goals.

Limits and future research directions

The main limitation of this study is its reliance on a descriptive approach based on document analysis of the framework laws related to the progressive tax reform launched in Morocco. Future studies will employ empirical analyses and qualitative methods, such as semi-structured interviews with tax experts in the Moroccan context, to explore the relationship between tax reform, the response to the COVID-19 crisis, and the achievement of sustainable development goals. Additionally, further quantitative analysis should be conducted to assess the impact of tax reform on the mobilization of increased tax revenues. These future research directions will provide a more comprehensive understanding of the effectiveness and broader implications of Morocco's tax policy responses to economic crises.

REFERENCES

Alm, J. (2019). Tax compliance and administration. In *Handbook on taxation* (pp. 741–768). Routledge. DOI: 10.4324/9781315093161-30

Bailey, K. D. (2008). *Methods of social research*. Simon and Schuster.

Belahouaoui, R. (2023). *La réforme de l'IS:" FLAT TAX" entre consécration de l'équité et lutte contre la fraude fiscale*.

Belahouaoui, R., & Attak, E. H. (2023). The importance of perceived fairness regarding tax burden in compliance behavior: a qualitative study using the Delphi method in Morocco. *Journal of Financial Reporting and Accounting*.

Belahouaoui, R., & Attak, E. H. (2024). Digitalization of Tax Administration and Tax Avoidance: Evidence on Tax Reform Dynamics in Morocco. In *Impact of Digitalization on Reporting, Tax Avoidance, Accounting, and Green Finance* (pp. 200–225). IGI Global.

Bowen, G. A. (2009). Document analysis as a qualitative research method. *Qualitative Research Journal*, 9(2), 27–40. DOI: 10.3316/QRJ0902027

Court of Audit. (2019). *Report on the execution of budget 2019 Morocco*. https://www.courdescomptes.ma/en/publication/report-on-the-execution-of-the-finance-law-for-the-year-2019/

Doghmi, H. (2020). *The capacity to mobilize tax revenue in Morocco*.

Finance Law for the 2024 Financial Year (2024).

Gorsky, M., & Mold, A. (2020). Documentary analysis. *Qualitative Research in Health Care*, 83–96.

Gupta, S., & Jalles, J. T. (2022). Can COVID-19 induce governments to implement tax reforms in developing countries? *Applied Economics*, 54(20), 2288–2301. DOI: 10.1080/00036846.2021.1987380

Hall, R. E., & Rabushka, A. (2013). *The flat tax*. Hoover Press.

IMF. (2023). *Morocco: 2022 Article IV Consultation-Press Release and Staff Report; IMF Country Report No. 23/42; December 16, 2022*. http://www.imf.org

Ispriyarso, B., & Wibawa, K. C. S. (2023). Reconstruction of the national economy post-covid-19 pandemic: Critical study of tax reforms in Indonesia. *Cogent Social Sciences*, 9(1), 2174517. DOI: 10.1080/23311886.2023.2174517

Keen, M., Kim, Y., & Varsano, R. (2008). The "flat tax (es)": Principles and experience. *International Tax and Public Finance*, 15(6), 712–751. DOI: 10.1007/s10797-007-9050-z

Khan, R., & Khan, S. (2022). Reform of Indirect Taxes in India through the Plexus of Goods and Services Tax (GST); A post-COVID 19 Fiscal Stimulus. *International Journal of Multidisciplinary: Applied Business and Education Research*, 3(6), 1011–1016. DOI: 10.11594/ijmaber.03.06.06

Kingdom of Morocco. (2021). *Framework Law 69-19 on Tax Reform.*

Kingdom of Morocco. (2023). *Finance Law.*

Kingdom of Morocco (2024).

Kobbi-Fakhfakh, S., & Bougacha, F. (2023). The impact of the COVID-19 pandemic on corporate tax avoidance: Evidence from S&P 500 firms. *Journal of Financial Reporting and Accounting*, 21(4), 847–866. DOI: 10.1108/JFRA-06-2022-0216

Laffitte, S., Martin, J., Parenti, M., Souillard, B., & Toubal, F. (2020). International corporate taxation after COVID-19: Minimum taxation as the new normal. *CEPII Policy Briefs*, 30, 1–6.

Makin, A. J., & Layton, A. (2021). The global fiscal response to COVID-19: Risks and repercussions. *Economic Analysis and Policy*, 69, 340–349. DOI: 10.1016/j.eap.2020.12.016

Maxim, M. R., & Zander, K. K. (2020). Green tax reform in Australia in the presence of improved environment-induced productivity gain: Does it offer sustainable recovery from a post-COVID-19 recession? *Sustainability (Basel)*, 12(16), 6514. DOI: 10.3390/su12166514

Ministry of Economy and Finance. (2019). *National Tax Forum*. https://www.finances.gov.ma/fr/Pages/detail-actualite.aspx?fiche=4431

OECD. (2023). *Tax Administration 2023: Comparative Information on OECD and Other Advanced and Emerging Economies.*

OECD. (2024). *The International Tax Reform Journey: Past — Present — Future.*

Orgeira Pillai, N., Van den Boogaard, V., & Prichard, W. (2024). The politics of taxation and tax reform in times of crisis: Covid-19 and attitudes towards taxation in Sierra Leone. *The Journal of Development Studies*, 60(2), 196–216. DOI: 10.1080/00220388.2023.2255717

Popescu, C. R. G., & Šebestová, J. D. (2022). Fiscally Responsible Businesses as a Result of COVID-19 Pandemic Shock: Taking Control of Countries' Tax Systems by Putting an End to Corporate Tax Evasion and Tax Havens. In *Handbook of Research on Changing Dynamics in Responsible and Sustainable Business in the Post-COVID-19 Era* (pp. 161–192). IGI Global.

Sainsbury, T., & Breunig, R. (2020). The urgent need for Tax Reform in Australia in the COVID-19 World. *Australian Journal of Labour Economics*, 23(2), 211–230.

Taxe Justice Network (TJN). (2023). *State of Tax Justice 2023*. https://taxjustice.net/reports/the-state-of-tax-justice-2023/

van der Hoeven, R., & Vos, R. (2022). Reforming the international financial and fiscal system for better COVID-19 and post-pandemic crisis responsiveness. In *Covid-19 and international development* (pp. 9–27). Springer. DOI: 10.1007/978-3-030-82339-9_2

KEY TERMS AND DEFINITIONS

Tax reform: tax reform refers to the process of changing the way taxes are collected or managed by the government. It usually involves modifications to the tax structure, rates, and administration to achieve objectives such as increased efficiency, equity, revenue generation, or economic growth.

Tax policy: tax policy is the use of government spending and taxation to influence the economy. It includes decisions on the level and composition of government expenditures and tax policies to manage economic cycles, stimulate economic growth, and achieve macroeconomic stability.

Tax compliance: tax compliance refers to the degree to which taxpayers meet their tax obligations as required by law. It includes timely filing of tax returns, accurate reporting of income, and payment of taxes owed. High levels of tax compliance are crucial for the effective functioning of a tax system.

Tax Avoidance: tax avoidance involves legally exploiting the tax system to reduce the amount of tax that is payable by means of loopholes, deductions, exemptions, or allowances. While legal, it is often viewed as unethical and can undermine the tax base.

Digitalization of tax administration: digitalization of tax administration refers to the use of digital technologies, such as online filing systems, electronic invoicing, and data analytics, to improve the efficiency and effectiveness of tax collection and compliance monitoring.

Base Erosion and Profit Shifting (BEPS): BEPS refers to tax planning strategies that exploit gaps and mismatches in tax rules to artificially shift profits to low or no-tax locations where there is little or no economic activity, eroding the tax base of higher-tax jurisdictions.

Progressive taxation: progressive taxation is a tax system in which the tax rate increases as the taxable amount increases. It is based on the principle that those with higher incomes or wealth should pay a higher percentage of their income in taxes, contributing to greater income redistribution and equity.

Flat Tax: A flat tax is a tax system that applies a single, uniform tax rate to all levels of income or profits, regardless of the taxpayer's earnings. Unlike progressive tax systems, where tax rates increase with higher income brackets, a flat tax imposes the same rate on all taxpayers, simplifying the tax structure but often raising concerns about its impact on equity, as it does not account for the varying ability of individuals to pay.

Chapter 13
Taxation of the Non-Profit Sector in Portugal:
In the Light of the Recent Developments in the European Union

Ana Paula Rocha
https://orcid.org/0000-0003-3259-9436
ISCAP, Instituto Politécnico do Porto, Portugal

ABSTRACT

The encouragement and development of the social economy sector are recognized as values of general interest in Portugal. Therefore, the promotion of the social economy by the Portuguese public authorities is legally foreseen, namely through the provision of a more favorable tax status for the non-profit entities. However, the need to rethink and (perhaps) update the Portuguese tax legislation applicable to the social economy sector has often been discussed, namely, to guarantee that the tax benefits in force truly respect the most important tax principles. Moreover, the need to rethink the tax legislation applicable to the social economy sector have also been recognized at the European Union' level. Accordingly, and with the use of the legal methodology, the objective of our work is to identify and analyze the major opinions and recommendations that have been issued in this context by several European' organisms, in order to understand whether the Portuguese tax system is already upon those recommendations or, on the contrary, needs to be amended to keep up with them.

DOI: 10.4018/979-8-3693-3908-4.ch013

INTRODUCTION

The encouragement and development of the social economy sector (also known as non-profit sector) are recognized as values of general interest in Portugal. Therefore, the promotion of the social economy by the Portuguese public authorities is a legal obligation, namely in the provision of a more favorable tax status for the non-profit entities. This tax regime reflects a clear method of the State's intervention in the economy and in the society; also, it stands as a public instrument for promoting and protecting the non-profit organizations that develop social and economic activities of general interest, such as the protection of citizens in sickness, disability, old age and invalidity, the development of medical and scientific knowledge, the resolution of the population's housing, environmental, educational or consumer problems, among many other situations of social and economic intervention carried out by these entities (Amorim, 2011).

In a nutshell, through the legal provision of specific tax benefits, the tax regime for the non-profit sector is currently positioned in the context of a clear adoption of policies aimed at pursuing economic and social objectives through taxation – commonly referred to as tax policies or measures of an extra-tax nature. However, the legal provision of these measures must always respect the boundaries imposed by the major tax principles (such as the ability-to-pay principle) which means, among other aspects, that the establishment of tax benefits to the non-profit sector must take into account the substrate and nature of each beneficiary entity, in order to measure the degree of intensity with which such entity effectively pursuits objectives of general, public or mutual interest.

Bearing this in mind, it shall be stressed that the need to rethink and (perhaps) update the Portuguese tax legislation applicable to the social economy sector has often been discussed. And this is considered not only to guarantee that the tax benefits in force truly respect the most important tax principles (such as the ability-to-pay principle referred above) but, also, to solve some significant problems identified by a part of the doctrine and several law enforcers, such as the legislative dispersion of the rules throughout the most varied tax laws currently in force in Portugal.

Moreover, the need to rethink the tax legislation applicable to the social economy sector has also been recognized by the European Union. Accordingly, the objective of our work is to identify and analyze the major opinions and recommendations that have been issued in this context by several European institutions, in order to understand whether the Portuguese tax system already meets those recommendations or, on the contrary, needs to be amended. In fact, although those opinions and recommendations are not binding, they were issued following an in-depth study and an extensive reflection by experts in taxation and in the social economy sector, which is why we believe there is a significant interest to look into the Portuguese tax legislation in the light of those recommendations (without forgetting that those organisms occasionally refer to the advantages of a future harmonization of all the Member States' tax legislations in this context).

To do so, we will begin to understand the most recent chronology of the key developments regarding the social economy among several institutions of the European Union, naturally focusing our attention on the advances concerned with the taxation of that economy sector. Once the substantial and chronological link between those developments is understood, we intend to specifically analyze, using the legal methodology as a doctrine that enables the practical application of the Law, the most important European recommendations regarding taxation, comparing them with the current Portuguese tax legislation.

The topic that we set out to work on is broad and is difficult, which is due to the breadth and difficulty of the subjects it covers. In fact, our attention will be focused on a topic that intertwines the already well-known vastness and complexity of the Portuguese tax system with the diversity and heterogeneity of the social economy organizations', which naturally poses significant difficulties not only for the tax legislator but also for the interpreters and enforcers of the law text. Therefore, it would be impossible to analyze, in this single study, the Portuguese tax regime applicable to the non-profit entities in general and global terms, once that the vast number of subjects related to these topics would not suit the concrete purpose of our work.

Bearing this in mind, and knowing that there are still few scientific studies regarding the Portuguese tax regime applicable to the non-profit sector (Fernandes, 2022), we hope to make a serious and objective contribution to assess policy landscapes in taxation dynamics in this context, through the evaluation of the European trends in what concerns the taxation of the non-profit sector and, to that extent, the perspectives that may be considered by (or may be *imposed* to) the Portuguese tax legislator in the near future.

BACKGROUND

Already in 2009, the European Parliament adopted the Resolution 2008/2250/INI, which recognized the social economy as a key operator for fulfilling the Lisbon Strategy objectives, as set out in the Treaty of Lisbon (OJ C 306, 17.12.2007), which amended the Treaty on European Union and the Treaty that established the European Community. On this basis, several institutions of the European Union have dedicated their attention to the non-profit sector in the most recent years.

On December 7th, 2015, the Council of the European Union issued the document *Promotion of the social economy as a key driver of economic and social development in Europe – Council Conclusions* (ST 15071/15). In this Conclusions, and following to the recognition of the social economy as an important player "in the transformation and evolution of contemporary societies, welfare systems and economies" as well as in the "social and human development across and beyond Europe", the Council invited the Member States and the Commission to "establish, implement and further develop, as appropriate, European, national, regional and/or local strategies and programs for enhancing the social economy, social entrepreneurship and social innovation".

Aligned with these Conclusions, the European Commission adopted, on 9th December, 2021, the document *Building an economy that works for people: an action plan for the social economy* (COM(2021) 778 final), which was welcomed by the European Parliament in its Resolution of 6th July 2022 (2021/2179/INI – *Resolution on the EU action plan for the social economy*). In this action plan, the Commission put forward concrete measures to be implemented both at Union and national level, aimed to boost social innovation, to support the development of the social economy and to unlock its social and economic transformative power, therefore contributing to the Commission's priority of building an economy that works for the people. In particular, the Commission recognized taxation policies as an important tool to develop coherent frameworks for the social economy, although noticing that in Member States that do have specific tax measures in this field, the access to the "incentives can be complex, and the different actions do not always benefit from appropriate coordination".

Therefore, the Commission established the compromise to encourage mutual learning through the publication of guidance on *1)* "relevant taxation frameworks for social economy entities, based on available analysis and input provided by Member States' authorities and social economy stakeholders" and *2)* on the clarification of "the existing rules on the tax treatment of cross-border public benefit donations affecting foundations and associations and the implementation of the principle of non-discrimination with Member States". In this context, the Commission proposed "a Council Recommendation on developing social economy framework conditions in 2023", namely in what concerns to taxation and to financial and non-financial support tailored to all stages of the business lifecycle.

In order to fulfill this objective, the Comission issued, in 2023, two extensive studies regarding the taxation of the social economy sector, as follows:

– The Commission Staff Working Document on the *Relevant taxation frameworks for Social Economy Entities* (SWD(2023) 211 final) that provides a comparative overview of the key aspects of the tax framework in which social economy entities operate in each Member State, as well as an overview of the tax framework applicable to public benefit organizations in many Member States; and

– The Commission Staff Working Document on the *Non-discriminatory taxation of charitable organizations and their donors: principles drawn from EU case-law* (SWD(2023) 212 final) regarding the principles drawn from case-law of the Court of Justice of the European Union on cross-border donations to charitable organizations.

These two working documents were essencial to the adoption, on 27th November 2023, of the *Council Recommendation on developing social economy framework conditions* (C/2023/1344 – that will be referred to as Council Recommendation C/2023/1344). Among other considerations, the European Council recognized that social economy entities "can stimulate sustainable economic and industrial development and promote the active participation of citizens in society", also "complementing public services" and creating "economic opportunities that promote social inclusion and the integration of disadvantaged groups". In this recommendation, and "without prejudice to State aid rules"[1], the Council particularly advised the Member States to:

– Ensure "that taxation systems do not hinder the development of the social economy and assess whether tax systems sufficiently encourage its development" (which was already recognized in the *Liège Roadmap for Social Economy in the European Union*, a document issued on the margins of the Conference of European ministers responsible for the social economy hosted on February 12th, 2024 in Liège);

– "Develop tax incentives for the social economy, if not already granted, in line with their social policy objectives and the current practices across Member States and in accordance with Union law, which may include" corporate tax exemptions on profits retained by social economy entities and "income tax incentives in the form of deductions or tax credits granted to private or institutional donors or a designation scheme according to which taxpayers can indicate to their tax authority the set percentage of their income tax liability to be allocated to public-benefit entities"; and

– Make sure that "social economy entities are not used for tax evasion, tax avoidance, aggressive tax planning or money laundering purposes, while ensuring the related administrative procedures are effective and proportionate".

Ultimately, the European Economic and Social Committee (EESC) – Section for Economic and Monetary Union and Economic and Social Cohesion issued, on June 27th, 2024, the opinion on *Taxation framework for social economy entities* (ECO/641, that will be referred to as Taxation Framework ECO/641). In this Opinion, the EESC expressed some conclusions and recommendations regarding the taxation of the social economy entities throughout the European Union, with a view to empower the several tax systems of the Member States with the "conditions for social economy entities to further develop in Europe, making their own distinctive contribution to achieving a competitive social market economy, as laid down in the founding Treaties".

Although the institutions of the European Union are expected to continue, in the near future, to issue their opinions and recommendations (and, perhaps, legal standards) regarding this subject, we understand that the importance of the developments already known are worthy of a thoughtful analysis, bridging and comparing those opinions and recommendations with the current situation of the Portuguese tax legislation.

THE PORTUGUESE TAX SYSTEM IN THE LIGHT OF THE RECENT DEVELOPMENTS IN THE EUROPEAN UNION

Legislative Provision of a Tax Framework For The Social Economy

According to the Council Recommendation C/2023/1344, taxation policy can "have a significant role in fostering the social economy and ensuring that social economy entities can afford to operate alongside mainstream businesses, creating a more equitable business environment while contributing to social inclusion and improved access to employment". This consideration led the European Council to advise the Member States to reflect on the revision of "the tax compliance burden for social economy entities and where possible reduce it". Alongside with this recommendation, the EESC recognized, in the Taxation Framework ECO/641, that the development of tax incentives for the social economy is essential, although it should always be implemented in line with the "social policy objectives and the current practices across Member States", "in accordance with Union law", and always with a particular attention to the potential use of the social economy entities "for tax evasion, tax avoidance, aggressive tax planning or money laundering purposes".

At the same time, the European Commission stressed in its Action Plan that "few countries have developed a specific and consistent taxation framework for social enterprises. Many provide incentives ranging from corporate tax exemptions on retained profits to VAT exemptions or reduced rates, social insurance costs reduced/covered by subsidies, or tax reductions for private and institutional donors". Alongside, the European Council and the EESC acknowledge the complexity of the generality of those social economy's tax regimes already in force. Therefore, the European Council stressed that "the wide range of frameworks and tools available can be a challenge, particularly for entities with fewer resources", while the EESC highlighted that this complexity partly results from the "coexistence of different contexts in which taxation affects social economy entities".

Carrying out an analysis on the current status of the Portuguese regime, it is noticeable that the Portuguese legislator does not have a legal tax diploma specifically and solely applicable to the Social Economy Sector. In fact, and contrary to what happens, for example, in Spain (in the *Ley 49/2002, de 23 de diciembre, de régimen fiscal de las entidades sin fines lucrativos y de los incentivos fiscales al mecenazgo*, which last update was published on 20.12.2023), the Portuguese tax regime applicable to the organizations of the social economy is dispersed throughout the legislation, a circumstance that accentuates the difficulties regarding the interpretation, integration and application of the tax law on this subject (precisely, as identified by the institutions of the European Union).

Notwithstanding, we do understand that given the heterogeneity of the entities that are included in the social economy sector, the tax regime shall be differentiated among them, considering the degree to which they pursue general interest objectives (Meira, 2013), in the context of a selective evaluation according to the substrate and nature of each entity (Aguiar, 2016). Therefore, we believe that it is neither possible, desirable nor advisable to approve a single tax statute applicable *as a block* to the social economy sector, since it is necessary to take into account the special features of each non-profit entity in what concerns their organic, legal and accounting regime – and not only in what concerns to the application of the tax benefits, but also regarding the obligation to pay taxes and its determination (Fernandes, 2022).

However, this circumstance does not justify, in our opinion, the current legislative dispersion that is noticeable in this area in Portugal. In fact, the tax and contributory regime applicable to social economy organizations is scattered across the most varied tax legal diplomas, which clearly hinders the overall knowledge and understanding of the tax regime applicable to those entities. Moreover, we are also concerned about the existence of several exceptions to the “basic” tax regime built by the Portuguese tax legislator for the social economy sector, including the wide scope of the real estate exemption applicable to specific entities (as it is the case of the “Santas Casas da Misericórdia”) or the value added tax exemptions provided in *ad hoc* legislation (as it happens with the transfers of goods and the provision of services made by youth associations registered in the National Register of Youth Associations – in Portuguese, “Registo Nacional do Associativismo Jovem”).

Therefore, and as it follows from the European Union’s recommendations, it is strongly advisable to efficiently systematize the legal rules applicable to the social economy in Portugal in order to guarantee the unity and rationality of the tax system, the general respect for the fundamental tax principles and the update of the legal rules to the current times. At the same time, it is important to rethink the existence and the extent of these exceptions, considering that their legal provision, combined with the current legislative dispersion amongst the tax legislation applicable to the social economy in Portugal, naturally harms the unity of the legal system, the purposes for which the benefits are granted and the observance of the fundamental principles of taxation (Rocha, 2024).

Despite this criticism, we understand that the Portuguese legislation currently in force is adequate when it prioritizes the attribution of tax benefits to the non-profit entities that do have a qualified legal status, such as the status of the Private Institutions of Social Solidarity (in Portuguese, "Instituições Particulares de Solidariedade Social": IPSS) or the status of public utility persons (in Portuguese, "Estatuto de Utilidade Pública") that pursue, exclusively or predominantly, scientific, cultural, charity, assistance, beneficence, social solidarity, defense of the environment or agro-food interprofessionalism purposes (although the use of tax benefits by other types of non-profit entities is not completely prohibited). Since the administrative attribution of such status depends on the effective pursuit of purposes of public or general interest by the beneficiary entities, this circumstance seems to be adequate to observe the degree to which the organizations pursue general interest objectives (as predictably defined in their bylaws) and to reveal that the corresponding attribution of tax advantages to those entities is effectively aimed to protect and promote relevant public interests, in compliance with the essential principles of justice and equality in taxation (Rocha, 2024).

In fact, a tax benefit constitutes a derogation from the general rules of taxation, as tax advantages with an exceptional nature. As determined by article 2 of the Portuguese Statute of Tax Benefits (in Portuguese, *Estatuto dos Benefícios Fiscais*), tax benefits are measures of an exceptional nature, such as total or partial tax exemptions, instituted to protect relevant extra-fiscal public interests that are greater than those of the actual taxation that they prohibit. Without underlying objectives, such advantages could not truly be called tax benefits, rather constituting "a privilege that, given the principle of equality, have no reason to exist", which is why it is not possible to conceive "a tax benefit that do not constitute a mean to achieve a hierarchically higher value purpose than" the tax justice and the equality of all the taxpayers (Pereira, 2014). This happens because the principle of fiscal equality is embedded in the idea of generality and universality, according to which all the citizens and legal persons are bound to the duty to pay taxes, and uniformity, requiring that this duty shall be measured by the same criteria – the ability to pay' criteria (Nabais, 2021).

Therefore, and as foreseen in the article 11 of the Portuguese Law on the Social Economy (in Portuguese, "Lei de Bases da Economia Social" – LBES), the establishment of a more favourable tax status can only be interpreted as a path to encourage and promote the activities that are developed by the social economy entities and that do benefit, directly or diffusely, all the members of society. To this extent, it is important to ensure that the granting of tax benefits is in line with the fundamental principles of justice and equality in taxation, in order to *i)* ensure that such concession is effectively aimed at encouraging the performance of activities of true public and general interest by social economy entities and to, at the same time, *ii)* overcome the tight scrutiny of the European Union state aid regime and to *iii)* ensure that the granting of the tax benefits will not be used as a vehicle towards abusive tax planning (Aguiar, 2016), as warned by the EESC.

VALUE ADDED TAX ("VAT")

In the Recommendation C/2023/1344, the Council recalled that certain goods and services, often supplied by social economy entities, can benefit from a reduced VAT rate in compliance with the Article 98 and the Annex III of the Council Directive 2006/112/EC, of November 28th, 2006, on the common system of value added tax (OJ L 347, 11.12.2006).

Bearing this is mind in the Taxation Framework ECO/641, the EESC welcomed "the fact that in certain Member States, social economy entities are subject to specific VAT rates (5% and 10%), which are compatible with the existing EU framework on VAT", and encouraged "the European Commission and the Member States to also consider particular VAT rates for public benefit activities carried out by social economy entities and for social services, particularly for the sector of health and social care for older people, as well as the personal services, long-term care and education sectors". In this context, the EESC explained that "solutions that provide for reduced VAT or preferential VAT arrangements are always preferable to exemptions, especially where entities operate in economically significant contexts. Situations that penalise social economy entities may indeed be created, given that VAT exemptions, when applied to activities carried out by ordinary businesses, end up giving such businesses a competitive advantage over social economy entities that carry out all their activities outside the scope of VAT and find themselves in a 'final consumer's position".

In Portugal, the VAT rates applicable to the activities carried out by social economy entities are the general rates provided in the article 18 of the Portuguese VAT' Code. Thus, for all economic operations subject to tax and not exempt from it, social economy entities must settle VAT and use, in principle, the standard rate applicable in the national territory: 23%.

However, it is possible to apply the reduced VAT rate (6%) to some operations currently carried out by social economy entities, such as the provision of home care services to children, elderly, drug addicts, ill or disabled persons (item 2.28 of the List I annexed to the VAT Code), the provision of singing, dancing, music, theatre or cinema shows (item 2.32 of the List I annexed to the VAT Code) and, for housing and construction cooperatives, the provision of works specifically provided in items 2.25 and 2.26 of the List I annexed to the VAT' Code. Notwithstanding, these reduced rates result from the nature of the operation carried out and not from the nature of the organization, which is why they may be applicable to any type of entity (regardless of whether it is a social economy organization or not).

If the association charges VAT on its active operations, it will be able to deduct the tax supported upstream, e.g., the VAT paid on eventual purchases of goods and services. In fact, and once it is harmonized at the European level, VAT is configured as a multi-phase tax based on the indirect subtractive method, which is the technique of *settlement and deduction of the tax* in each of the economic circuit's phases (Palma, 2015), as imposed by the principle of neutrality. This principle enforces "that the tax burden must be exclusively and effectively borne by the final consumers", being fundamental to guarantee the correct functioning of the *settlement and deduction' technique* (Palma, 2016). Which is not the case of the VAT exemptions in *domestic operations*.

In fact, and despite the broad scope of VAT incidence (and, consequently, the vast number of operations that are subject to taxation), the non-profit entities may benefit from VAT exemptions in the *domestic or internal operations* in the Portuguese territory and in their international and intra-European Union transactions (in this case, as it happens with the generality of the economic operators under the destination principle). In this context, please note that the Sixth VAT Directive (Council Directive 77/388/EEC of May 17th, 1977) harmonized exemptions for domestic transactions and that the current VAT Directive (Council Directive 2006/112/EC of November 28th, 2006) set them up as exhaustive exemptions, thus preventing the Member States to grant additional exemptions or alter the content of the exemptions provided for in European legislation (Laires, 2012).

Focusing on the tax exemptions on the domestic operations in the Portuguese territory (which are provided in Article 9 of the VAT' Code), they are subject to legal conditions regarding the nature of the entity and the nature of the economic operation in question. Therefore, not only is it mandatory that the specific goods sold or the services delivered by the organization are in the list provided by the Article 9 of the VAT Code, but it is also necessary that the entity is qualified as an *IPSS* or as a *non-profit organization* as a result of the compliance with the cumulative requirements of the article 10 of the VAT Code (Ribeiro & Santos, 2013), which were built on the basis of the densification carried out by the European legislator in the Article 133 of the Directive 2006/112/EC of the European Council (Silva & Soares, 2015).

Considering that we are dealing with incomplete exemptions, the organizations will not charge VAT on their transfer of goods and provision of services but are, however, forbidden to deduct the VAT supported upstream (Tracana & Dias, 2020), which constitutes "a significant obstacle to the neutral functioning of the tax" (Silva

& Soares, 2015). As such, Palma (2016) states that the application of incomplete exemptions without the possibility of deduction represents, in certain cases, a real *poisoned gift*, considering that, although the exemption may represent an advantage in the price charged, this advantage may be nullified by the impossibility to apply the deduction technique.

However, it is important to note that there is an exception for IPSS. In accordance with the specific requirements and limits set out in the Decree-Law 84/2017, of July 21st, and on the Official Letter 90025/2017, of August 14th, IPSS can request a full or partial refund of the tax incurred on: the construction, maintenance and upkeep of real estate used wholly or predominantly in the pursuit of their statutory purposes; tangible fixed assets subject to depreciation and used solely and exclusively for statutory purposes (with the exception of vehicles and their repairs); and with the acquisition of food and beverage goods and services as part of their social activities. Although we understand the impossibility of extending this mechanism to all social economy entities – especially given the concerns associated with the possible abusive and unfounded use of this measure –, we believe that it would be relevant to consider its application to the non-profit organizations that also benefit from a qualified legal status (such as the public utility entities), even if the access to reimbursement in this case would also depend on a prior recognition by the Portuguese Tax Authority (Rocha, 2024).

In fact, we do believe that, in what concerns to the Portuguese tax system, it would be more appropriate to extend the possibility of refunding the VAT under the terms mentioned above than to introduce a general reduction of the VAT rates *solely* for the social economy entities once that, as we had the opportunity to mention above, VAT rates are essentially applied according to the nature of the transaction performed and not according to the nature of the entity that carried it out. In our opinion, this measure would mitigate the negative consequences associated with the granting of incomplete tax exemptions without having an adverse impact on the final price of the products and services supplied by the social economy entities, thus respecting free market competition in transactions that the European legislator deemed as not eligible for exemption.

TAXATION OF THE PROFITS REINVESTED IN THE PURSUIT OF STATUTORY OBJECTIVES

In the Taxation Framework ECO/641, the EESC supported "national tax measures aimed at offering differentiated tax treatment to profits that are reinvested either in pursuit of statutory objectives or allocated to the social economy entity's indivisible reserves, noting that these reserves often cannot be distributed among stakeholders either while the company is in operation or even after its dissolution. These profits that are reinvested or allocated to indivisible reserves are fundamental for fostering the capitalisation of social economy entities" (specifying the EESC that we are facing "entities that experience similar difficulties to those faced by SMEs in accessing credit, and that cannot always access financial markets because of their specific organisational form").

The Portuguese tax regime is already in line with this recommendation, namely in what concerns the Corporate Income Tax (in Portuguese, "*Imposto sobre o Rendimento das Pessoas Coletivas*" – IRC). In fact, the exemption of *IPSS* or *public utility persons* is conditioned on the continued compliance of the following requirements:

– Effective exercise, in an exclusively or predominantly manner, of activities associated to the statutory object of the organization;
– Imputation, to the purposes referred in the previous paragraph, of at least 50% of the overall net income that would be subject to taxation under general terms, until the end of the 4th tax period subsequent to the one in which the income was obtained (except in the event of a fair impediment to meet the assignment deadline, that should be notified to the Portuguese General-Director of the Tax Authority, duly accompanied by a written justification, until the last working day of the 1st month following the deadline);
– Absence of any direct or indirect interest of the members of the statutory bodies, by themselves or through an intermediary, in the results of the exploitation of the economic activities pursued by the non-profit organization.

Nevertheless, we understand that the Portuguese tax legislation currently in force regarding cooperatives must be revised, as in this context (and particularly in what concerns to the income taxation) there is a mismatch between the tax regime and the aim to protect the cooperative's mutuality zone, which calls for the introduction of legislative changes.

The legal concept of a cooperative is currently laid down in the article 2(1) of the Cooperative Code (Law no. 119/2015, of August 31st), according to which cooperatives are autonomous legal persons, freely constituted, with variable capital and composition, which, through the cooperation and mutual help of their members, and in compliance with cooperative principles, aim, on a non-profit basis, to satisfy their economic, social or cultural needs and aspirations. Therefore, the scope of the cooperatives must be mutualist, which means that their activity must be geared towards their members, who are the main beneficiaries of the social and economic activities that cooperatives develop and in which they must actively participate, under the provisions of Article 22 of the Cooperative Code (Bandeira, Meira & Alves, 2017; Tracana & Dias, 2020; Rocha, 2024).

However, and highlighting some of the most significant aspects, the obligation to globally subject cooperative surpluses to taxation, i.e., without any measurement regarding their effective return to cooperators (or to the constitution of reserves), is not in line with the mutualistic and non-profit purpose pursued by those entities. Likewise, the tax regime provided in the article 66.º-A of the Portuguese Statute of Tax Benefits not only does not promote the protection of the cooperative's mutuality zone, as it introduces legal uncertainty in what concerns the interpretation of the types of cooperative gains or results that shall be considered as included within the scope of the tax benefit (being even possible to verify that this regime ends up promoting the "demutualization" of certain types of cooperatives, such as worker production, handicraft, fishing, education, services, trade and credit cooperatives) (Rocha, 2024).

Consequently, it is important to consider the introduction of legislative amendments that extinguish the imbalances mentioned above (Meira, Aguiar & Raquel, 2016; Silva & Soares, 2015) and that, by clarifying the types of results that should be considered as included in the tax exemption, will encourage the respect for the cooperative mutuality zone, as the only way to guarantee the fulfillment of the purposes for which the tax benefits for the cooperative sector are established.

DONATIONS

In the Council Recommendation C/2023/1344, the European Council encouraged the Member States to consider the implementation of "income tax incentives in the form of deductions or tax credits granted to private or institutional donors or a designation scheme according to which taxpayers can indicate to their tax authority the set percentage of their income tax liability to be allocated to public-benefit entities".

Although in line with the importance of the donations as a way to increase the access to financial resources for social economy entities, the EESC pointed, in the Taxation Framework ECO/641, to the importance to "avoid distortions and opportunistic or evasive behaviour", mainly by "checking that these donations and related incentives are actually going to social economy entities that are operational and genuinely engaged in activities of general interest". Therefore, the EESC considers that it is important that "all Member States have public, accessible and transparent registers in which social economy entities that receive donations are registered. These registers should be set up to allow for the submission of financial statements and mission statements, clearly identifying the activities of general interest that are carried out by the entities thanks to donations, subsidies and public contributions or private donations".

The Portuguese tax legislation encompasses specific provisions to encourage corporate patronage, i.e., the distribution of donations with the nature of a liberality by legal persons and individual entrepreneurs to the social economy organizations (Ribeiro & Santos, 2013). For tax purposes, and in accordance with the article 61 of the Portuguese Statute of Tax Benefits, these donations constitute deliveries in cash or in kind that, without counter obligations of pecuniary or commercial nature, are granted to public or private entities which activity consists predominantly of carrying out initiatives in the social, cultural, environmental, sports or educational areas, as precisely foreseen in the Portuguese Statute of Tax Benefits (Amorim, 2011).

Focusing specifically on the Corporate Income Taxation rules, it is possible to verify that corporate patronage constitutes a true tax benefit once that *i)* regarding the social economy entities, the donations are tax exempt if they are used for the direct and immediate fulfillment of the statutory purposes of the organization (article 54 of the IRC' Code), and *ii)* regarding the patrons, it is possible not only to accept the expense for tax purposes but also, in some situations, theoretically increase it for the same purposes, in an operation called as *majoração* (Rocha, 2024).

Among other limitations, please note that the tax regime regarding the corporate patronage can only be applicable if the beneficiary complies with the several obligations listed in the article 66 of the Portuguese Statute of Tax Benefits, namely:

– Issue a document proving the amount received in each donation, which must include:
  - The legal status of the beneficiary entity and the corresponding legal provisions;
  - The framework of the donation within the scope of the Portuguese Statute of Tax Benefits;
  - The amount of cash or, alternatively, the identification of the goods received; and
  - The mention that the donation is granted without counter obligations of pecuniary or commercial' nature.

– Have a complete and up-to-date record of its patrons with the identification of their name or designation, the tax identification number and the date and value of each donation awarded, among other additional references that are deemed as necessary; and

– Submit the so-called "Model 25 Declaration" by the end of February of each year, declaring all the donations with tax relevance that were received in the previous year.

In our opinion (and as referred in Rocha, 2024), these obligations are fundamental to allow a greater control over the use of the tax benefits under consideration, to ensure that such benefits are not subject to abusive tax planning and that they are *effectively* a path to encourage and promote the activities solely developed by the non-profit organizations in benefit of all the society, precisely in harmony with the understanding expressed by the institutions of the European Union.

This is exactly one of the reasons why we understand that it could be difficult to implement one of the European recommendations regarding cross-border donations.

In the 2021 Action Plan, the European Commission expressed its concerns on the administrative barriers that remain in several Member States concerning the tax treatment of public-benefit donations across borders, despite the Treaty's principle of non-discrimination. The European Commission noticed that "the procedures applied by Member States increase compliance and administrative costs and create uncertainty for both philanthropic entities and donors", stressing that the "European Commission can open infringement procedures in cases where barriers to cross-border activities result from non-transposition, violation or wrongful implementation of EU law". In this regard, the European Council, in the Council Recommendation C/2023/1344, had sugested, as a possible measure to operationalize the international donations, the issuing of "a standardised form of the recipient entity established in another Member State on the amount of the donation, identifying both the recipient and the donor".

However, we understand that the implementation of this measure may face several obstacles, namely with regard to the proof of the legal status of the beneficiary entity and the corresponding legal provisions, to the framework of the donation within the statutory objectives provided in the Portuguese Statute of Tax Benefits and to the confirmation that the amounts transferred to another jurisdiction do not consist of a disguised form of taxable profit shifting.

In a final note, the EESC showed, in the Taxation Framework ECO/641, that it is aware "that some Member States allow citizens the possibility to allocate a pre-defined share of their taxes to projects and initiatives carried out by social economy entities or other non-profit actors, such as Italy with its 'five per thousand' measure, allowing citizens to direct resources towards a social objective. These measures have the advantage of not only enhancing taxpayers' choices and freedom, but also encouraging social economy entities to develop transparent and effective reporting systems".

This measure is already in place in Portugal, being recognized as one of the financing instruments of the non-profit sector. In fact, every individual who is a taxpayer of Personal Income Tax (in Portuguese, *Imposto sobre o Rendimento das Pessoas Singulates – IRS*) can assign a quota equivalent to 0,5% of the tax settled on their annual income tax return (referred, in Portugal, as *Declaração Modelo 3*) to a duly registered religious organization or to a non-profit entity, indicating in the referred tax return the specific beneficiary entity to whom they want to allocate the assigned amounts (Ribeiro & Santos, 2013).

SOLUTIONS AND RECOMMENDATIONS

Regarding the issues previously identified, and considering the most significant developments at the European' level regarding the taxation of social economy entities in the most recent years, we objectively understand and recommend:

- To efficiently systematize the legal rules applicable to the social economy in Portugal in order to guarantee the unity and rationality of the tax system, the general respect for the fundamental tax principles and the need to update some of the legal rules to the current times. At the same time, it is important to rethink the existence and the extent of some legislative exceptions, considering that their legal provision, combined with the legislative dispersion that currently is verified amongst the tax legislation applicable to the social economy in Portugal, naturally harms the unity of the legal system, the purpose for which the benefits are granted and the observance of the fundamental principles of taxation;
- To continue to prioritize the attribution of tax benefits to the non-profit entities that do have a qualified legal status, such as IPSS or public utility persons. Since the administrative attribution of such status depends on the effective pursuit of purposes of public or general interest by the beneficiary entities, this circumstance seems to be adequate to observe the degree to which the organizations pursue general interest objectives and to reveal that the corresponding attribution of tax advantages to those entities is effectively aimed to protect and promote relevant public interests, in compliance with the essential principles of justice and equality in taxation;
- To reflect on the possibility to extend the mechanism that allows IPSS to request a full or partial refund of the VAT incurred on the purchases of goods and services to the non-profit organizations that also benefit from a qualified legal status (such as the public utility entities), even if the access to reimbursement in this case would also depend on a prior recognition by the Portuguese Tax Authority;
- To consider the introduction of legislative amendments that, by clarifying the types of results that should be considered as included in the tax exemption applicable to cooperatives, encourage the respect for the cooperative mutuality

zone, as the only way to guarantee the fulfillment of the purpose for which the tax benefits for the cooperative sector are established;
– Finally, and in what concerns to the tax benefits created by the Portuguese tax legislator in order to promote the corporate patronage, we believe that it is important to keep this system immune from abusive tax planning. Therefore, the provision of a closed list of beneficiary entities in the Portuguese Statute of Tax Benefits and the requirement to comply with several declarative obligations shall be maintained in the future.

FUTURE RESEARCH DIRECTIONS

In the near future, we believe that it will be important to:

– Continue to monitor the opinions and recommendations (and, perhaps, legal standards) on the subject under analysis that will potentially be published by different institutions of the European Union over the next few years; and
– Further deepen the analysis on the Portuguese tax legislation in order to understand the eventual aspects that shall be subject to amendments – beyond (or in addition to) the recommendations of the European Union.

We believe these studies may have a relevant impact on the global comprehension and evolution of the Portuguese tax policies regarding the non-profit organizations.

CONCLUSION

The encouragement and development of the social economy sector are recognized as values of general interest not only in Portugal, but also at the European Union's level.

Bearing this is mind, this work was aimed to identify and analyze the major opinions and recommendations that have been issued by several institutions of the European Union organisms concerning the taxation of the non-profit sector, in order to understand whether the Portuguese tax system already meets those recommendations or, on the contrary, needs to be amended. In fact, although those opinions and recommendations are not binding, they were issued following an in-depth study and an extensive reflection by experts in taxation and in the social economy sector, which increases the significative interest to look into the Portuguese tax legislation in the light of those recommendations (without forgetting that those organisms occasionally refer to the advantages of a future harmonization of all the Member States' tax legislations in this context).

In the course of our analysis, and referring to the most important conclusions, we have found that the Portuguese tax legislation currently in force is sufficiently developed and adequate in what concerns the prioritization of the attribution of tax benefits to the non-profit entities that do have a qualified legal status (such as IPSS or public utility persons) and in what regards the imposition of several declarative obligations and the provision of a closed list of beneficiary entities in order to profit from the corporate patronage' tax regime.

However, it shall be taken into consideration the importance to efficiently systematize the legal rules applicable to the social economy in Portugal, aiming to guarantee the unity and rationality of the tax system, the general respect for the fundamental tax principles and the need to update of the legal rules to the current times. In addition, the Portuguese legislator shall consider the introduction of legislative amendments regarding the tax exemption applicable to cooperatives (in order to encourage the respect for the cooperative mutuality zone) and the extension of the mechanism that allows IPSS to request a full or partial refund of the VAT incurred in by their purchases of goods and services to the non-profit organizations that also benefit from a qualified legal status (such as the public utility entities), even if the access to the reimbursement in this case would also depend on a prior recognition by the Portuguese Tax Authority.

REFERENCES

Aguiar, N. (2016). O Problema da Tributação do Rendimento das Cooperativas – reflexão a partir do direito português. *Revista Cooperativismo e Economía Social, n.º 28*. Pp. 163-190.

Amorim, J. C. (2011). Regime fiscal aplicável às Entidades sem Fins Lucrativos em Portugal e em Espanha. *Journal of Business and Legal Sciences / Revista De Ciências Empresariais e Jurídicas, n.º 20*. Pp. 179-202.

Bandeira, A. M., Meira, D., & Alves, V. (2017). Los diferentes tipos de resultados en las cooperativas portuguesas. Un estudio de caso múltiple. *REVESCO, n.º 123 – Primer Cuatrimestre*. Pp. 37-63.

Fernandes, F. V. (2022). *Direito Fiscal do Terceiro Setor*. AAFDL Editora.

Laires, R. (2012). *O IVA nas actividades culturais, educativas, recreativas, desportivas e de assistência médica ou social – Cadernos IDEFF N.º 14*. Almedina.

Meira, D. (2013). A Lei de Bases da Economia Social Portuguesa: do projeto ao texto final. *CIRIEC-España, Revista jurídica de economía social y cooperativa (number 24/2013)*. Pp. 21-52.

Meira, D., Aguiar, N., & Raquel, S. (2016). Estudio sobre la eficácia del régimen fiscal cooperativo português. *REVESCO, n.º 121*. Pp. 7-32.

Nabais, J. C. (2021). *Direito Fiscal* (11th ed.). Almedina.

Palma, C. C. (2015). *Introdução ao Imposto Sobre o Valor Acrescentado* (6th ed.). Almedina.

Palma, C. C. (2016). *A interpretação das normas de isenção de IVA pelo Tribunal de Justiça da União Europeia – Algumas notas. Temas de Direito Tributário – IRC*. IVA e IRS, Centro de Estudos Judiciários.

Pereira, M. F. (2014). *Fiscalidade* (5th ed.). Almedina.

Ribeiro, F. M., & Santos, S. F. (2013). *A Fiscalidade e as Organizações de Economia Social*. Vida Económica.

Rocha, A. P. (2023). The Portuguese Tax Regime applicable to the Environmental Non-Governmental Organizations. In *Dinis, Ana et al (Coord.): Taking on Climate Change Through Green Taxation* (pp. 82–100). IGI Global. DOI: 10.4018/978-1-6684-8592-7.ch004

Rocha, A. P. (2024). A tributação da Economia Social em Portugal. *CIRIEC-España. Revista Jurídica de Economía Social y Cooperativa*, (44), 349–386.

Silva, S. T., & Soares, C. D. (2015). *Regime Fiscal das Entidades da Economia Social e Civil*. Vida Económica.

Tracana, D., & Dias, C. C. (2020). Tributação do Setor Cooperativista em Portugal: Análise dos principais aspetos e questões em aberto. *Revista Eletrónica de Fiscalidade da Associação Fiscal Portuguesa*, II, 2.

ADDITIONAL READING

Santos, L. M. (2022). *Donations and Tax: The Corporate Conundrum*. IBFD Doctoral Series. DOI: 10.59403/2rng413

KEY TERMS AND DEFINITIONS

Corporate Patronage: Donations granted, with a liberality' character, by legal persons and individual entrepreneurs to the Social Economy Organizations

IPSS: As determined by the *Estatuto Jurídico das IPSS* (Decree-Law number 172-A/2014, of 14th November), the IPSS are Portuguese legal persons, constituted exclusively on the initiative of individuals, with a non-profit purpose in order to contribute to the fulfillment of the social rights of citizens, namely in what concerns to the support of children and youth, of the family, the elderly and the people with disabilities, among other social responses.

IRS allocation: Assignment made by individual taxpayers, equal to a quota of 0,5% of the tax settled on their annual income tax return, in favor of a duly registered religious organization or a non-profit entity

Lei de Bases da Economia Social **(LBES):** Law that establishes the fundamental political options of the Portuguese legal regime applicable to the social economy, that should be implemented by the Portuguese government through development decrees

Public utility status: Status foreseen in the *Lei-quadro do Estatuto de Utilidade Pública* (Law number 36/2021, 14th June) assigned to legal persons that pursue diffuse and generalized goals, act in accordance with the guiding principles provided by the Portuguese LBES and cooperate, to that extent, with the public administration of the Portuguese State

Portuguese Social Economy Sector: Although it is an open concept under permanent construction (Meira, 2013), the social economy sector integrates the organizations that, endowed with legal personality, pursue purposes that benefit the community at large and which, to that extent, are deemed as altruistic or disinterested purposes with social relevance. They also comply with the guiding principles provided in the article 5 of the LBES and appear in the Portuguese database regarding the Social Economy Sector

State aid rules: According with the European Commission, a company that receives government support gains an advantage over its competitors. Therefore, the European Treaty generally prohibits State (article 107 TFUE) aid unless it is justified by reasons of general economic development. To ensure that this prohibition is respected, and exemptions are applied equally across the European Union, the European Commission ensures that State aid complies with European Union rules

Tax benefits: Measures of an exceptional nature that are established to protect relevant and public interests that are greater than the receipt of taxes

Tax justice or tax equality: Tax principles embedded by the idea of generality or universality, according to which all citizens (and legal persons) are bound by the duty to pay taxes, and the idea of uniformity, which requires that this duty shall be measured by one only criterion – the ability to pay criteria

ENDNOTES

1 Although this is an issue that goes beyond the analysis of the Portuguese legislation in the terms of this investigation, it is important to note that in the Taxation Framework ECO/641, the EESC highlighted that it would be important to consider the introduction of a definition for 'social economy entity' in the General Block Exemption Regulation on State aid, while at the same time developing appropriate mechanisms to exempt the financing of social economy entities from State aid rules in terms of tax (in this context, the EESC pointed out that "in its judgment of 8 September 2011, joined cases C-78/08 to C80/08 – Paint Graphos and others, the Court of Justice of the EU ruled on the Italian corporation tax exemption for cooperatives, arguing that precisely because of their characteristics, cooperatives are not in a comparable situation to that of commercial companies, and that therefore the tax treatment accorded to such entities by Italian law could not be automatically considered selective State aid").

Chapter 14
Taxation on Online Gaming Industry and Allied Stakeholders: An Elusive Policy?

Siddharth Kanojia
https://orcid.org/0000-0002-1479-5292
O.P. Jindal Global University, India

ABSTRACT

The online gaming industry in India has undergone remarkable growth in the recent years. According to few reports, the industry envisaged to reach a market size of INR 290 billion by end of the year 2025 i.e., approximately USD 4 billion, growing at a CAGR of 21.4% from 2020 to 2025. Wherein, the mobile gaming segment is the prodigious and burgeoning segment in Indian online gaming market, accounting for nearly 85% of the market share. Whereas, e-sports market is expected to grow rapidly in the coming years, with the potential to reach a market size of INR 11 billion (approximately USD 150 million) by 2025 (Arora 2019). Accordingly, In light of the ever increasing popularity of online gaming, the government of Indian government has proposed to include specific clauses pertaining the taxability of online games in the Finance Bill of year 2023. Hence, this chapter shall explore the connotation of imposing taxes on online gaming industry in India.

DOI: 10.4018/979-8-3693-3908-4.ch014

INTRODUCTION

The term 'online games' are referred to the simulated video games that are played over the internet or through a network connection, typically on a computer, gaming consoles, smart phones or tablets (Gainsbury et al, 2014). These games can be played solo or in collaboration with other players from around the world and range from simple games like puzzles and card games to complex multiplayer games like massively multiplayer online role-playing games (MMORPGs) & first person shooter games. Many of these online interactive games offers features such as chat rooms, forums, and in-game messaging, allowing players to interact and collaborate with one another. Some online games also include microtransactions, allowing players to purchase virtual goods or currency within the game. The online gaming industry have lately became increasingly popular in recent years, with the advent growth of mobile gaming and the rise of e-sports across the nations. In India, the inevitable growth of online games was driven by varied factors such as increasing internet penetration, the proliferation of smartphones, and the rise in the popularity of e-sports. There are various subsectors of the gaming business, including the PC and console games that dominated the market in the early 2000s (Guruswamy & Singh, 2008). Millions of individuals have been drawn online by the internet revolution as casual players who play short-duration, easy-to-learn games. Therein, the casual games are available for free to play and mostly rely on advertising income, whereas Real Money Games (RMG) are those that require an entrance fee from players and provide them the possibility to win prizes in excess of the money they have invested. Meanwhile, major e-sports competitions are anticipated to be held on a worldwide scale as esports tournaments have been increasing popularity. Teams, sponsors, and notable players frequently compete in these intense competitions in an effort to win. There are currently 0.1 million e-sports teams and 0.6 million e-sports participants in India. Similarly, fantasy sports is another sub-segment of the sports industry. In this sub-segment, users or "managers" create a virtual cadre of real-life players who lately receives fantasy points through their real-life performance metrics in offline games and competitions. Hence, it can construed that the usage of Virtual Reality (VR) and Augmented Reality (AR) technologies to immerse players in the game environment and improve the overall gaming experience for consumers is another example of how technology has advanced. According to a recently published report by KPMG, this industry is expected to reach a market size of almost INR 290 billion (approximately USD 4 billion) by the end of year 2025, growing massively at a CAGR of 21.4% from 2020 to 2025 (Moinuddin, 2021). The renowned mobile games in India include PUBG Mobile, Call of Duty: Mobile, and Free Fire. While, e-sports has gained popularity through the several major sports tournaments and leagues, including the Indian Premier League (IPL) and the India Gaming Championship (IGC). Given that India has evidenced the appearance of more than 100 unicorns in the past half-decade, the size of the online gaming sector in that country may be estimated by the fact that, although being in its infancy, it has already created three unicorns i.e., Games 24X7, Dream11, and Mobile Premier League (MPL). The finance and M&A sectors have both contributed considerable sums to the gaming industry. The industry garnered more than $1.6 billion in investments during the first 9 months of year 2021, with Real Money Games (RMG) bringing in $700 million from investors.

Therefore, considering the expeditious growth of this industry, Imposition of taxes on online games, like any other economic activity, was inevitable in India as it would lead to generation of revenue for governments, which can be used to fund public services and infrastructure development. Additionally, imposition of taxes would have ensured that the online gaming industry contributes its fair share to the economy and reduces the risk of tax evasion and fraud. Consequently, on February 01, 2023, Mrs. Nirmala Sitharaman has announced the imposition of 30% tax on the net winning from online games which shall be effective from April 01, 2023. The concerned Finance Bill 2023 has proposed to bring in the distinct provisions pertaining to deduction of tax under Section 194BA and Thereon, promulgating taxability of online games under Section - 115BBJ of Income Tax Act of 1961. As a matter of fact, Section 194BA specifies TDS on the net winnings in the respective user accounts at the conclusion of the fiscal year (the "FY"). While, Section 115BBJ provides for the levying of income tax at a fixed rate of 30% on the net winnings from any online game where the assessee's total income from the profits earned from any online game.

History and Legislative Overview

India essentially saw the development of online gaming from the early years of the 2000s onward, meant for reaching internet cafes or simple multiplayer games like Counter-Strike and Age of Empires, also able to garner a niche community of gamers (Mukherjee 2022). But really speaking, the gaming ecosystem began with the advent of affordable smartphones, high-speed internet, and a proliferation of mobile gaming apps. The introduction of 4G networks in 2016 marked a turning point that really drove up the numbers of mobile internet users, thereby exploding the mobile gaming market (Patro and Simon 2016). Online games such as PUBG Mobile and Clash of Clans reached household names; other platforms such as Dream11 tapped into the fantasy sports segment. Casual gamers and professional esports players alike came into recognition with this boom. The Indian online gaming industry turned into a multi-billion-dollar industry and today comprises everything from real-money gaming, fantasy sports, and online rummy to massively multiplayer online role-playing games (Zhouxiang 2022). Buoyed by innovations in AR, VR, and AI across gaming, India's gamer base is set to reach around 500 million by 2025 (Recanati 2023).

Online Gaming was formerly considered to be in a regulatory grey area because of the lack of existing comprehensive regulation. The Constitution of India has stipulated the legislative authority over "*betting and gambling*" in its 7th schedule through entry 34 of List-II, yet there are no equivalent item in the concerned list for "online gaming" (Kamath et al., 2021). Subsequently, as per entry 97, the Centre has the default authority to govern in this manner. As a result, it has been emphasised in the Parliament that online gaming platforms are intermediaries & they should fall within the ambit of substance & rules of Income Tax Act. Thereon, the former Public Gambling Act of 1867 and the contemporary legislation of Information Technology Act of 2000 are two pieces of legislations that are frequently mentioned in regulatory discussions pertaining to the online gaming. Therein, the Public Gambling Act of 1867 deals with outlawing gambling and betting, while exempting games that need "mere skill" from its restrictions (Sayta 2012). The relevancy of this act is apparently did not encompass the technological advancements of this era. On the contrary stance, the Information Technology Act, 2000 intends to governs online activity and lays out the consequences for specific online offences. In this area as well, the legislation was not recently sufficiently developed to deal with the developments occurring in the online gaming industry (Kunar 2010). Hence, The Ministry of Electronics and Information Technology (MeitY) will soon have control over the online gaming business, according to a recent announcement by the central government. In addition to this, government has also suggested changes to the existing Information Technology Rules (Intermediary Guidelines and Digital Media Ethics Code), 2021, as an continuing attempt to administer this sector in India (Vijayanand 2022).

Concerning the application of Income Tax Act of 1961, Section 2(24)(ix) has ensured that profits or winnings from speculative games such as lotteries, puzzles, blackjack and other forms of gambling of any kind whatsoever are included in the definition of "income" for the purposes of computing the cumulative taxable income of the concerned assessee. Meanwhile, As per Section 56(2)(ib), all the enlisted 'income' referred to in Section 2(24)(ix) shall be taxed under the 5th head of income i.e., "Income from Other Sources". As a result, it can be construed that winning from online games would likewise fall within this head of income. Considering the scenario before April 01, 2023, Section 115BB levied taxes on the winning from games at a fixed rate of 30%. Yet, taking into consideration the unique characteristics of online gaming, the amended provision aim to impose tax online game earnings individually under proposed Section 115BBJ. Nonetheless, the tax rate, which is 30%, stays the same. While, the exclusion of earnings from online gaming from the scope of Section 115BB has also been proposed as a consequential modification. Furthermore, the threshold limit of INR. 10K for computing TDS on the winning from online gaming has been repealed, more information on the computation method is still awaited. In essence, this means that TDS will no longer be applied to any winnings except from those that are net at the moment of withdrawal from the game wallet or at the conclusion of the fiscal year. Besides, the contemplated amendment is set up to impose tax on online game "net winnings". Therefore, the definition of certain allied terms has been expanded to tackle the ambiguities in interpretations. Accordingly, a game that is offered online and can be accessed by a user through the usage of a computer device, including a telecommunication device, is what is meant by the phrase "online game," . Subsequently, this definition is likely to include any online game as one that falls under its purview. While, any online account of a user which is registered with an online gaming application, platform or intermediary is referred as a "*user account*". Whereas, the crucial term 'Net winnings' is not yet defined.

The proposed changes are meant to protect online players from precariousness and attain control over several facets of online gaming. The suggested changes, however, provide a unique set of difficulties. The mandate for online gambling organisations to employ a Chief Compliance Officer and a nodal contact officer for managing consumer complaints is considered to be one of the biggest challenge related to compliance as small and medium-sized businesses & start-ups may lack the sufficient monetary & non-monetary resources to meet the requisites of proposed regulations. Thus, it can be claimed that the proposed revisions to the IT Rules 2021 are generally a positive step, and it is foreseen that over the upcoming years, the Indian online gaming sector will expand significantly. Despite being exemplary in its efforts to simply the tax regime, the recent proposal also has the possibility to deter stakeholders such as player from taking active participation. The crucial step of eliminating of the TDS threshold limit will affect people who don't spend enough money or win loads of money since even minor gains would be liable to tax. Consequentially, this may impact the development and involvement of casual participants, which would be despairing for an online gaming industry that is presently well-liked, prosperous, and has the capacity to expand rapidly in the future.

Impact on Consumer Behaviour

Taxation of online games, specifically RMG-based games, has an impact on consumers' behavior. On one hand, high rates of taxation will discourage casual gamers from participating in online game services, hence fewer users. On the other side are low tax rates, which could encourage participation en masse and thus reduce overall revenues to the government. A delicate balance thus has to be struck between encouraging growth in the online gaming industry and capturing tax revenue. Studies indicate that a reasonable tax levy on gaming, such as levied in the UK, is normally associated with better compliance and long-term growth of the industry, while nations applying heavy taxation policies generally result in lower compliance and slower growth.

The main challenge in the field of taxation is balancing this against the fact that this is one of the best-developing sectors: online gaming (Runge 2014). The high taxation of RMG is only going to prompt players and operators to run away into the unregulated or offshore sites to continue the play, which generally need not be as fettered by regular supervision and checking on compliance (Aulbur and Kapoor 2016). This will give an impetus toward more illegal gambling and consequently serious revenue losses for the state. Moreover, such heavy taxation often depresses innovation in the industry because developers and startups cannot be competitive in such a highly taxed environment. All this ultimately dampens the overall growth of the sector and lowers the competitive edge of the domestic platforms. On the contrary, a more balanced and properly structured tax regime as in the UK helps an industry in achieving sustainable growth while at the same time securing for the government a long flow of revenues (Stahel 2013). Thus, by allowing the taxing of only net profits and not gross turnovers, this regime has a general effect of encouraging the operator to innovate and provide increased value to players, without an unduly heavy burden upon profitability. In turn, this will help to retain the attractiveness of the licensed platform, to which players go because they feel more secure, and where the leakage from the tax regime is reduced.

In addition, balanced taxation can also favor the drive toward responsible gambling. A lower level of taxation gives operators a wider scope for investment in responsible gaming initiatives, including player education, means to self-exclude, and support for problem gamers. Such a holistic approach, in turn, may establish a better public perception for the online gaming industry, leading to reduced social taboo underlined with gaming and becoming both legitimate and sustainable in the longer run. In the Indian context, policymakers have to ensure the rate of tax reform in the online gaming space is gradual. This would encompass continuous judgment on how tax policies impact revenue growth with industry growth and, therefore, afford adjustments that take into consideration changeable market dynamics. If India fosters an incentivizing tax environment that balances growth with regulation, it would itself be a global leader in the online gaming sector, attracting investment and safeguarding the interests of the public and the economy.

Tax Regimes – Global Scenario

The taxing of online gaming has, on the global landscape, been one area that has received increased attention as governments come to the realization of how this particular industry is growing very fast and its grand potential of being a source of revenue. Other countries, like the And the tax treatment of online gaming in the European Union is still inconsistent among its various states, with some imposing a value-added tax on purchases made for and within games, while others levy specific taxes only on real money earned through gaming platforms (Keune et al., 2018). In certain significant markets of Asia, such as China and South Korea, there is a general trend toward more stringent laws regarding loot boxes, with similar governmental viewpoints about them as gambling, therefore having higher taxes imposed (Ang 2020). Moreover, many countries are struggling to distinguish between categorizing various games into either games of skills or games of chance since this will determine the basis on which they will be taxed. Generally speaking, the heightened interest in finding a balance between consumer protection and its taxation so that consumers are protected from being exploited and, at the same time, governments benefit from this form of industry.

The imposition of Tax regimes on online gaming platforms vary depending on the jurisdiction and the specific laws and regulations in place. In general, online gaming platforms may be subject to various taxes such as income tax, value-added tax (VAT), GST and gaming taxes. In India, Goods and Services Tax (GST) is applicable to online gaming platforms. The GST rate on online gaming services is 18%, which is the same rate as for other digital services. As per the concerned provisions, any company or individual who provides online gaming services in India is required to register for GST if their annual turnover exceeds a certain threshold. Once registered, they must collect and remit GST on the gaming services provided. It's worth noting that there has been some debate around the classification of online gaming under GST, with some arguing that it should be taxed as a form of entertainment rather than a digital service. Whereas, there are various other nations, who have adopted the mixed approach in imposing the taxes on online gaming. Few of such noteworthy models are Gross Gaming Revenue Tax Model (Hereinafter 'GGR') and Turnover Tax Model (hereinafter 'TTM').

The GGR is a tax system commonly used in the gambling industry to generate revenue for the government. Under this model, the tax is based on the total amount of money that is wagered by customers minus the amount that is paid out in winnings. In most jurisdictions, the GGR tax rate varies depending on the type of gambling activity, the location of the casino, and the amount of revenue generated (Philander 2013). The tax rate can be a fixed percentage of the GGR or a tiered system with different rates for different levels of revenue. The core advantage of the this model is that it is relatively simple to administer and enforce. It also encourages casinos to maximize their revenue by offering attractive games and promotions to customers. However, some critics argue that the GGR tax model can be regressive, as it places a greater burden on low-income individuals who are more likely to gamble (Webster & Webster 2004). In contrary context, the TTM is another tax system that can be used in the gambling industry. Under this model, the tax is based on the total amount of money wagered by customers (i.e., the turnover) rather than the gross gaming revenue. This model can provide a more stable source of revenue for governments compared to the GGR tax model. This is because the tax is based on the total amount of money wagered, rather than the amount of revenue generated after pay-outs to winners. Whereas, the potential disadvantage of the TTM is that it can be more complex to administer and enforce, as it requires more data collection and reporting from the gambling operators. Additionally, the model may not incentivize casinos to maximize their revenue in the same way that the GGR tax model does.

Accordingly, In order to find an appropriate balance between establishing a vigorous taxing regime for an industry given its popularity and addressing the need for social control, nations throughout the world have implemented a variety of tax rates and approaches. At present, the majority of the developed nations rely on the GGR tax model for ensuring comprehensive taxability on the online gaming industry. In this model, the platform fee sum is subject to GST. While, few nations also use the model of the TTM, wherein the GST is applied to the entry fee of the contest rather than the platform fee. For instance, France adopted the GGR tax model as a result of operators resorted to the techniques of black marketing, which cost the government money and resulted in non-compliance with the licencing and regulating system. The GGR tax scheme is adopted in Sweden and the United Kingdom as well. Both of these nations experienced substantial surge in tax collection due to higher rate of compliance among the stakeholders of this industry. Contrariwise, Austria has attempted to distinguish between games which require skill and games which do not require skill i.e., merely based on luck or chance, and it levies varied taxes on each. Herein, the skill-based games are taxed at a lower rate than betting or gambling as lotteries are taxed at 18% & winnings from skill-based games are taxed at 5%. The GGR tax approach apparently assisted the business to stay viable, according to evidence from nations where the sector has evolved effectively. Contrarily, the TTM model gradually pushes the sector out of existence, eventually results in causing a loss to the exchequer due to the much larger tax effect & efflux in tax revenues caused by the movement of business from legal platforms to illicit offshore operators.

These regimes can be compared with a hypothetical example to establish better interpretation of their applicability (See – Table 1). It is evident that the application of turnover tax model significantly raises the tax impact which effectively reduce the prize pool by 38%, which may deter people from playing online games and lead to impacting the profitability of the section while simultaneously lowering the government's overall tax collection. On the other hand, the GGR tax model has increased the tax revenue by almost 55% i.e., from 18% to 28% & in return, causing the 1% reduction in the prize pool. Hence, this regime seems more viable as it ensures higher revenues for government while maintaining the substantiality of the prize pool.

Table 1. Application & effect of different tax regime on prize pool

Tax Regimes	Particulars	Rate of Taxation	Entry Fee (A)	Platform Fee (B)	Imposed GST (C)	Prize Pool A-B-C	% reduction in prize pool
Applicable Regime		18% GST on platform fee	1000	100	18 (B*18%)	882	11.8%
GGR Tax Model		28% GST on platform fee	1000	100	28 (B*28%)	872	12.8%
Turnover Tax Model		28% GST on Entry Fee	1000	100	280 (A*28%)	620	38%

Grey Areas

Section 58 of the Income Tax Act specifies the amount that can be deducted while determining the cumulative income which is subject to taxation under the head "IFOS." Whereas, according to sub-section (4) of this section, an assessee who has won the prize from lotteries, puzzles, races, card games like blackjack and other forms of gambling or betting of any kind shall not be able to claim any deduction for any expense or allowance in connection with such income. Thus, it can be construed that the player winning an online game may not be able to claim deduction of any expenditures due to the precise bar imposed by this provision. Nevertheless, it can be countered that the proposed Section 115BBJ begins with a non-obstante clause. Hence, the restrictive covenant set out in Section 58(4) might not be prevalent in this context. Therefore, In the absence of relevant rules related to imposition of taxes, It would be important to determine now if any costs or expenses associated with the online games are eligible for a deduction or not.

Similarly, the ability to offset a loss from one game's revenue against gains from another game is still another imperative area which requires clarification. The fact that there is no specific which prohibits or restrict the assessee to set-off of his/her losses in computing the net gains. Yet, there are Certain limitations which only apply to the carrying over of losses to succeeding years. Therefore, it must be possible to include intra and inter-source set-off of current year's losses when calculating net winnings from online games.

Simultaneously, there is lack of clarity related to the following aspects or situations in the present status of proposed amendment.

(i) How can it be assured that tax is eventually imposed on the net gains from playing online games if an assessee has acquired unified wallet for both general and gaming purposes?
(ii) What method the gaming intermediaries would use to confirm that tax has been paid if an assessee has received a perquisite such as automobile, vacation, mobile devices as the winning prize?
(iii) How the tax administrative bodies will ensure the applicability of taxes on foreign gaming platforms or on non-resident Indian playing games on Indian gaming platforms?
(iv) How the taxing authorities will collate the relevant information of the TDS for non-PAN holders?
(v) In absence of the concrete distinction between online gaming, betting & gambling, whether the online gaming intermediaries must abide by the current betting and gaming regulations of each state.

Way Forward

To ensure the progenitive growth of Indian online gaming industry, the government must provide full & unambiguous assistance by implementing specific measures, both at the level of the federal and the state. One of such way is to draft a simple, clear & defined rules and procedures of imposition of taxes on the platforms & the players as the presence of ambiguities in the system of taxation may cause the deterrence among the stakeholder of the stakeholder for taking an active participation. Moreover, it has been observed that the over-taxation would eventually drive reputable gamers away in favour of illicit offshore gambling applications. Thus, leading to lower the revenues for reputable gaming businesses, and ultimately result in a loss to the exchequer through lower direct and indirect taxes. In this regard, the GGR tax approach proved to be a competent tax regime which led to the increase in tax revenues for nations while ensuring the sustenance & survival of online gaming industries.

REFERENCES

Ang, Y. Y. (2020). *China's gilded age: The paradox of economic boom and vast corruption*. Cambridge University Press. DOI: 10.1017/9781108778350

Arora, P. (2019). *The next billion users: Digital life beyond the West*. Harvard University Press. DOI: 10.4159/9780674238879

Aulbur, W., & Kapoor, A. (2016). *Riding the Tiger: How to Execute Business Strategy in India*. Random House India.

de Prato, G., & Simon, J. P. (2016). Global trends in mobile: A new global landscape for supply and demand. In *Emerging perspectives on the mobile content evolution* (pp. 1–31). IGI Global. DOI: 10.4018/978-1-4666-8838-4.ch001

Gainsbury, M., S., Hing, N., Delfabbro, P. H., & King, D. L. (. (2014). A taxonomy of gambling and casino games via social media and online technologies. *International Gambling Studies*, 14(2), 196–213. DOI: 10.1080/14459795.2014.890634

Guruswamy, M., & Singh, Z. D. (2008). *Chasing the dragon: Will India catch up with China?* Pearson Education India.

Kamath, N., Shrivastava, A., & Shekar, R. S. (2021). Emerging from the shadows: The evolving legal treatment of fantasy sports in India. *The International Sports Law Journal*, 21(3), 188–202. DOI: 10.1007/s40318-021-00190-2

Keune, M., Payton, N., Been, W., Green, A., Mathieu, C., Postels, D., ... & Wright, S. (2018). –Innovation and Job Quality in the Games Industry in Germany, the Netherlands, Sweden and the UK. *Virtuous circles between innovations, job quality and employment in Europe? Case study evidence from the manufacturing sector, private and public service sector*, 234.

Kuner, C. (2010). Data protection law and international jurisdiction on the Internet (part 1). *International Journal of Law and Information Technology*, 18(2), 176–193. DOI: 10.1093/ijlit/eaq002

Moinuddin, S., & Moinuddin, S. (2021). Mapping digital political economy in India. *Digital Shutdowns and Social Media: Spatiality, Political Economy and Internet Shutdowns in India*, 1-34.

Mukherjee, S. (2022). *Videogames in the Indian Subcontinent: Development, culture (s) and Representations*. Bloomsbury Publishing. DOI: 10.5040/9789354359637

Philander, K. S. (2013). A normative analysis of gambling tax policy. *UNLV Gaming Research & Review Journal*, 17(2), 2.

Recanati, A. M. (2023). *AI Battle Royale: How to Protect Your Job from Disruption in the 4th Industrial Revolution*. Springer Nature. DOI: 10.1007/978-3-031-19278-4

Runge, W. (2014). *Gameforge AG. Technology entrepreneurship: A treatise on entrepreneurs and entrepreneurship for and in technology ventures*. KIT Scientific Publishing.

Sayta, J. (2012). Legality of Poker and Other Games of Skill: A Critical Analysis of India's Gaming Laws. *NUJS L. Rev.*, 5, 93.

Stahel, W. R. (2013). Policy for material efficiency—sustainable taxation as a departure from the throwaway society. *Philosophical Transactions of the Royal Society A: Mathematical, Physical and Engineering Sciences, 371*(1986), 20110567.

Vijayanand, K. (2022). Regulation of E-Sports in India: Can Online Gaming Be Brought under the Purview of Cyber Laws in India? *Jus Corpus LJ*, 3, 1050.

Webster, G. R., & Webster, R. H. (2004). Taxing issues: Geography, politics and the 2003 tax reform referendum in Alabama. *Southeastern Geographer*, 44(2), 190–215. DOI: 10.1353/sgo.2004.0031

Zhouxiang, L. (2022). *A history of competitive gaming*. Routledge. DOI: 10.4324/9781003095859

ADDITIONAL READING

Camp, B. T. (2020). Taxation of electronic gaming. *Wash & Lee Law Review, 77*, 661. Available at *SSRN*: https://ssrn.com/abstract=3585945

Garrett, T. A., Paton, D., & Williams, L. V. (2020). Taxing gambling machines to enhance public and private revenue. *Kyklos*, 73(4), 500–523. DOI: 10.1111/kykl.12247

Günay, H. (2023). Taxation as a policy instrument for social and economic effects of gambling. *Journal of Gambling Issues*. Advance online publication. DOI: 10.4309/MKME8615

Hybka, M. (2015). Casino taxation in a normative and economic context: The case of Poland. *Przedsiebiorczosc i Zarzadzanie*, 16(1), 23–37. DOI: 10.1515/eam-2015-0002

Sung, M. H., & Umar, W. (2020). "Virtual" v.s. "Reality"—On taxing e-sports virtual goods transaction in Indonesia. *Indonesian Comparative Law Review*, 3(1), 45–62. DOI: 10.18196/iclr.v3i1.11159

Vidal-Puga, J. (2017). On the effect of taxation in the online sports betting market. *SERIEs*, 8(2), 145–175. DOI: 10.1007/s13209-017-0156-y

Vvedenskaya, A. (2022). Taxes in video games: Overview, purposes, relevance. *Interactive Entertainment Law Review*, 5(1), 46–55. DOI: 10.4337/ielr.2022.01.04

KEY TERMS AND DEFINITIONS

Elusive Policy: Policy that is difficult to understand or enforce clearly, being ambiguous or hard to pin down in practice.

e-Sports: Short for electronic sports, is a form of competition using video games. Esports often takes the form of organized, multiplayer video game competitions, particularly between professional players, played individually or as teams.

Fantasy Sports: Games often played using the Internet, where participants assemble imaginary or virtual teams composed of proxies of real players of a professional sport.

Online Games: Online games refer to games that are played over some form of computer network, most often the Internet.

Online Gaming Industry: The video game industry is the tertiary and quaternary sectors of the entertainment industry that specialize in the development, marketing, distribution, monetization and consumer feedback of video games.

Online Gaming Taxes: Any gaming duties, taxes, levies, imports or other similar charges.

Taxation: Refers to the practice of a government collecting money from its citizens to pay for public services

Chapter 15
Transfer Pricing for Baseline Distribution Structures:
Assessing the Simplified and Streamlined Approach of Pillar One - Amount B

Pascal René Marcel Kubin
https://orcid.org/0000-0002-1133-7157
University of Speyer, Germany

ABSTRACT

Baseline distribution transactions are relatively simple yet frequently occurring transactions within multinational enterprises. However, from a transfer pricing perspective, they are often associated with high compliance costs and substantial uncertainties for taxpayers. Against this background, the OECD/G20 Inclusive Framework on BEPS has introduced the Simplified and Streamlined Approach (SSA) under Pillar One - Amount B. By providing standardized, arm's length return on sales margins for the wholesale distribution of goods, the SSA intends to reduce compliance costs and increase tax certainty. This chapter initially presents the key aspects of the approach, before critically assessing their implications. The analysis particularly indicates that an incongruent implementation of the SSA across jurisdictions may undermine the intention of simplifying transfer pricing. Moreover, the narrow price range of the SSA could increase the importance of software solutions for controlling transfer prices.

DOI: 10.4018/979-8-3693-3908-4.ch015

INTRODUCTION

In a globalized world, a local distribution presence is of enormous strategic importance for multinational enterprises in order to be able to assert themselves in increasingly diversified and dynamic markets. However, such a local market presence is associated with substantial efforts to comply with transfer pricing rules and regulations. "Transfer pricing (TP) refers to the practice of pricing transactions between and within enterprises under common ownership and control" (Kumar et al., 2021, p. 275). Regarding this, it is generally expected that the transfer prices within multinational groups comply with the arm's length principle. The arm's length principle determines "the price that would be used if the same transaction[s] were undertaken by unrelated third parties" (Rogers & Oats, 2022, p. 83). Against this background, transfer prices "impact the allocation of profits and tax liabilities across different jurisdictions" (Kalra & Afzal, 2023, p. 172). As many instances of double taxation have their origins in transfer pricing, it is not surprising that transfer pricing represents one of the most pressing tax topics for many managers of multinational enterprises (Chan et al., 2015; Kumar et al., 2021). Given the vague and sometimes contradictory rules in relation to the interpretation of the arm's length principle, there is considerable uncertainty and complexity for multinational enterprises with regard to transfer pricing. Moreover, the arm's length nature of transfer prices must generally be proven by means of costly and complex benchmark analysis. In addition, affected multinational enterprises can never be sure whether the results of their benchmark studies will be accepted by the respective tax authorities for verifying the arm's length nature of their transfer prices.

Especially small and medium-sized enterprises often suffer from the costs and complexities that arise when proving the arm's length nature of their transfer prices. This often concerns the aforementioned distribution structures on foreign markets, which many small and medium-sized enterprises establish as part of their internationalization strategy. Even though these are often so-called baseline distribution activities with rather limited functions and risks, they still cause considerable compliance costs and may even trigger lengthy international tax conflicts (OECD, 2024). As the transfer pricing-related compliance costs of small and medium-sized enterprises are in some countries already twice as high as the costs for traditional corporate tax compliance (Solilová et al., 2017), a selective simplification in relation to these baseline distribution activities would certainly be desirable. In addition, tax jurisdictions with limited resources (low-capacity jurisdictions) often tend to experience difficulties when engaging in protracted international tax disputes. Accordingly, transfer pricing for baseline distribution activities is often associated with considerable costs and complexities for both taxpayers and tax authorities.

Against this background, the OECD/G20 Inclusive Framework on BEPS has introduced the so-called Simplified and Streamlined Approach (SSA) under Pillar One - Amount B (OECD, 2024). The final report on the SSA has been published on February 19, 2024 and has been preceded by two controversially discussed public consultation papers (OECD, 2022b, 2023). The SSA provides a set of rules designed to simplify and streamline transfer pricing for baseline distribution structures. Drawing upon a global benchmark analysis, the SSA offers standardized, arm's length return on sales margins structured in the form of a two-dimensional pricing matrix. This means that taxpayers can or even must apply the reference margins of the pricing matrix if their distribution transactions fall within the scope of the SSA. By providing a common frame of reference for these activities, the SSA intends to "alleviate administrative burden, cut compliance costs, and enhance tax certainty for tax administrations and taxpayers alike" (OECD, 2024, p. 3). The SSA is integrated as an appendix into the OECD Transfer Pricing Guidelines for Multinational Enterprises and Tax Administrations. In jurisdictions that decide to implement the SSA, it will effectively apply from January 1, 2025.

As part of Pillar One of the Two-Pillar Solution by the OECD/G20 Inclusive Framework on BEPS, the SSA represents a very important policy in the context of international business taxation. Given the cross-border nature of transfer pricing, the associated taxation dynamics largely take place at the intergovernmental level (particularly at the level of the OECD). The aim of such intergovernmental efforts is to achieve a certain degree of uniformity, coherence, and consistency with regard to transfer pricing and especially in relation to the interpretation of the arm's length principle. Even though these intergovernmental policies such as the SSA and the OECD Transfer Pricing Guidelines only become a direct element of national law in specific jurisdictions (e.g., Great Britain), they are generally regarded as the consensus of the OECD member states, thereby representing 'highly influential soft law'. This means that tax authorities often use them as a reference for interpreting their own transfer pricing rules and regulations. Accordingly, this chapter assesses an important taxation dynamic in the area of transfer pricing at the intergovernmental level. Regarding this, it aims to present and critically assess the key aspects of the SSA.

BACKGROUND

The following section lays the foundations for analyzing the SSA. For this purpose, it begins by briefly discussing the Two-Pillar Solution proposed by the OECD/G20 Inclusive Framework on BEPS before outlining the fundamental principles of transfer pricing.

The Two-Pillar Solution

As already mentioned, the SSA is part of Pillar One of the Two-Pillar Solution proposed by the OECD/G20 Inclusive Framework on BEPS. The Two-Pillar Solution aims to address the challenges posed by the digitalization of the economy and the shifting nature of global business activities (OECD, 2021). Amount A of Pillar One focuses on reallocating taxing rights to countries where multinational enterprises have significant consumer markets, regardless of whether they have a physical presence in these countries (OECD, 2021). In contrast, Pillar Two introduces a global minimum tax to prevent multinational enterprises from shifting profits to low-tax jurisdictions and to ensure that they pay a minimum level of tax regardless of where they operate (OECD, 2021).

So far, Pillar One - Amount B has been somewhat overshadowed by Pillar One - Amount A and the global minimum tax of Pillar Two in the public debate. One of the reasons for this is probably that both Amount A and the global minimum tax focus on the taxation of large companies with very successful (digital) business models. However, the impact of Amount B and the SSA is probably underestimated, as the reduction of transfer pricing compliance costs and the improvement of tax certainty could be of considerable practical benefit to many companies with cross-border baseline distribution transactions.

The Fundamental Principles of Transfer Pricing

Transfer pricing rules dictate how arm's length prices can be set for transactions of goods, services, intellectual property, or financial arrangements between different divisions of the same organization in different countries. Even though transfer pricing remains an important element of international corporate tax planning (Cooper & Nguyen, 2020), the possibilities of shifting profits to low-taxed jurisdictions by using transfer pricing structures have become more difficult. Especially since transfer pricing has been addressed in the Action Plan on Base Erosion and Profit Shifting (BEPS) by OECD/G20 countries, national tax authorities are paying greater attention to the arm's length principle. In this regard, particularly the Action Points 8 to 10 of the 15-point action plan are dedicated to the challenges around transfer pricing (OECD, 2015). These Action Points emphasize the need to ensure that profits are taxed where the economic activities generating them are performed and where value is created, thereby addressing the misallocation of profits through transfer pricing (OECD, 2015). This requires a comprehensive analysis of the actual conduct of the parties, including the functions, risks, and assets associated with the respective transaction (OECD, 2015). Based on this analysis, an appropriate transfer pricing method can be identified in order to determine a transfer price that reflects economic reality and the actual value creation along the value chain (Treidler, 2020).

These Action Points were integrated into the OECD Transfer Pricing Guidelines, which provide a comprehensive framework for tax authorities and businesses to assess and adjust transfer prices consistently and in accordance with the arm's length principle (OECD, 2015, 2022a). The guidelines outline various methods for establishing arm's length pricing. They also contain directives for ensuring proper documentation of transactions and provide mechanisms for resolving disputes between tax authorities and multinational enterprises.

Despite these comprehensive guidelines, it remains difficult to determine arm's length transfer prices, as there is substantial room for interpretation and an inherent risk for double taxation. In addition, taxpayers must generally resort to complex and expensive benchmark studies in order to substantiate the appropriateness of their transfer prices. This indicates the substantial value of a simplifying framework, as provided by the SSA.

Baseline Distribution Transactions within Multinational Enterprises

The SSA refers to typical baseline distribution transactions in multinational enterprises. These transactions typically consist of basic distribution entities with limited functional and risk profiles alongside a principal (or strategic) entity with a broad and complex functional and risk profile. The basic distribution entities primarily execute the local operational marketing and distribution tasks with limited autonomy, while all strategic decisions, core intangible assets, and significant risks are owned, managed, and controlled by the principal entity. From a business perspective, this set-up ensures that the principal entity retains control over the critical aspects while minimizing the financial and operational risks associated with foreign markets. Given their limited functional and risk profiles, basic distribution entities should typically generate stable yet modest profits from a transfer pricing perspective. As they represent the least complex party within the respective transaction, they are considered to be the tested parties for which it is generally easier to identify reliable comparables. Whenever baseline distribution activities are mentioned in the following, this also encompasses very basic marketing activities as envisaged by the SSA.

THE PRICING MECHANISM OF THE SIMPLIFIED AND STREAMLINED APPROACH

For the purpose of assessing the main principles of the SSA, I start by elucidating its standardized pricing mechanism before addressing its implementation options and its application requirements. As analyzing the application requirements presupposes an initial understanding of the systematology of the SSA, its core logic is examined before the requirements for its application are discussed. Otherwise, it is difficult to understand the purpose and the intention of the application requirements of the SSA. Accordingly, the following section presents and critically evaluates the pricing mechanism of the SSA.

Transfer Pricing Method

Given the limited functions, risks, and assets associated with baseline distribution activities, the arm's length nature of the corresponding transfer prices is typically tested by applying the transactional net margin method (TNMM) (OECD, 2024, p. 25). The TNMM is a transfer pricing method widely used to assess whether the pricing of transactions between associated enterprises falls within the arm's length range. By focusing on the net profit relative to an appropriate base (such as sales, assets, or costs), the TNMM seeks to ensure that intercompany transactions are priced in a manner consistent with what would be expected between unrelated parties. The pricing matrix of the SSA draws upon the TNMM by providing arm's length return on sales margins, which can be compared with the actual margins of the associated distribution entities (tested parties). Hence, insofar as the SSA is applicable, it eliminates the need for taxpayers to prepare costly and sometimes ambiguously interpretable benchmark studies for their baseline distribution transactions. Instead, they can refer to the standardized pricing matrix of the SSA, which has been compiled based on a global benchmark study.

Notwithstanding this, the final report on the SSA also includes the reference to apply the internal comparable uncontrolled price (CUP) method if it is more appropriate under the given conditions (OECD, 2024, p. 25). By comparing the prices of transactions between related parties with those of similar transactions with unrelated parties, the internal CUP method offers a straightforward means of assessing the arm's length nature of transfer prices. The SSA allows to use the internal CUP method if its application is in line with the respective provisions of the OECD Transfer Pricing Guidelines and if internal comparables as well as other relevant information are available to assess its appropriateness (OECD, 2024, p. 25).

Pricing Scheme

However, the standard case, for which the SSA has been created, is the verification of transfer prices based on the TNMM using the standardized pricing matrix. The pricing matrix represents a comprehensive pricing framework, which encompasses a range of 15 target return on sales margins spanning from 1.5% to 5.5% (OECD, 2024, pp. 26–27). These margins are deemed to reflect the entire spectrum of baseline distribution activities that are covered by the SSA. Hence, the primary objective of the pricing matrix is to establish arm's length return on sales margins that account for the diverse array of baseline distribution transactions within multinational groups. Regarding this, two dimensions, namely the industry affiliation as well as the factor intensity determine which one of the 15 margins is applicable for the pricing of the respective transaction.

In terms of industry affiliation, the SSA distinguishes between three industry groups, each of which is associated with different profit expectations (OECD, 2024, p. 27). If the sales activity relates to several industry groups, an industry-specific sales allocation is necessary. If at least 80% of sales are attributable to a single industry group, then the selection of the corresponding margin from the pricing matrix is exclusively based on this dominant group (OECD, 2024, p. 27).

In addition, taxpayers must also determine the factor intensity by calculating the ratio of net operating assets to net revenue (net operating asset intensity) as well as the ratio of operating expenses to net revenue (operating expense intensity) of the tested party (OECD, 2023, p. 5, 2024, p. 12). Operating expenses encompass "total costs excluding cost[s] of goods sold, pass-through costs appropriately excluded under the accurate delineation of the transaction and costs related to financing, investment activities or income taxes" (OECD, 2024, p. 12). The classification of the factor intensity depends on the values of these two metrics, ultimately dictating the appropriate return on sales margin together with the relevant industry group (OECD, 2024, p. 27). Thus, in order to determine the appropriate pricing range for their baseline distribution transactions, taxpayers must determine the industry group and calculate the factor intensity of their distribution entity. As already mentioned, the return on sales margins are between 1.5% and 5.5%, whereby a deviation of 0.5% is permissible (OECD, 2024, pp. 27–28). The pertinent return on sales margin of the pricing matrix then serves as a standardized reference for verifying the arm's length nature of the transfer prices for the baseline distribution transactions of the taxpayer (OECD, 2024, p. 28).

Operating Expense Cap-and-Collar Range

Furthermore, the SSA has a mechanism to prevent the target return on sales margins from being too high or too low (operating expense cap-and-collar range) (OECD, 2024, pp. 28–29). This mechanism is based on the return on operating expense ratio. In order to determine the return on operating expense ratio, the first step is to derive the target return on sales margin for the tested party from the pricing matrix (by calculating the factor intensity and by identifying the industry affiliation of the tested party; as already described above). In a second step, the identified target margin from the pricing matrix can be used to determine the target return (EBIT) by multiplying it with the actual sales of the tested party. The target return (EBIT) can then be divided by the operating expenses of the tested party in order to determine the return on operating expense ratio.

If this calculated return on operating expense ratio is outside the cap-and-collar range, an adjustment is required (OECD, 2024, p. 29). Depending on the factor intensity of the tested party, the cap rates in relation to the return on operating expense ratio range between 40% and 70% or between 45% and 80% in case of qualifying jurisdictions. The requirements for being a qualifying jurisdiction within the meaning of section 5.2 of the SSA will be published at a later stage and updated every five years (OECD, 2024, p. 13). In contrast, the collar rate is consistently set at 10% regardless of whether it is a qualifying jurisdiction (OECD, 2024, p. 29).

If this calculated return on operating expense ratio of the tested party falls within the previously described range, no adjustment is required. If, however, the return on operating expense ratio is higher than the respective cap rate, the return on sales margin must be readjusted downwards until the return on operating expense ratio corresponds to the cap rate (upper limit) (OECD, 2024, p. 29). If the return on operating expense ratio is below the specified collar rate of 10%, the return on sales margin must be raised until the return on operating expense ratio corresponds to the collar rate (lower limit) (OECD, 2024, p. 29).

Data Availability Mechanism

In addition to the operating expense cap-and-collar range, the SSA contains a so-called data availability mechanism for qualifying jurisdictions. This mechanism leads to an adjustment of the relevant arm's length margin from the pricing matrix if the tested party is located in a country that is underrepresented in the global data set and constitutes a qualifying jurisdiction within the meaning of section 5.3 of the SSA (OECD, 2024, pp. 29–30). In such constellations, the previously determined return on sales margin from the pricing matrix is increased by the product of the net operating asset intensity percentage of the tested party and a net risk adjustment percentage of the respective qualifying jurisdiction (limited to a maximum of 85%) (OECD, 2024, p. 30). The net risk adjustment percentage depends on the credit rating category of the respective jurisdiction and can range from 0% for a rating of BBB or better to 8.6% for a rating of CCC- or worse (OECD, 2024, p. 31).

Updates and Supplementary Provisions

The analysis behind the pricing matrix and the "operating expense cap-and-collar rates" are updated every five years, provided there have been no significant changes in the market structure in the meantime (OECD, 2024, p. 31). The data in relation to the pricing matrix and the data availability mechanism for qualifying jurisdictions are reviewed annually and updated if necessary (OECD, 2024, p. 31). Figure 1 shows the core logic of the pricing mechanism of the SSA. Hence, the figure not only depicts the pricing matrix, but also illustrates its interplay with the operating expense cap-and-collar range as well as with the data availability mechanism.

Figure 1. The core logic of the pricing mechanism of the SSA (Own Illustration)

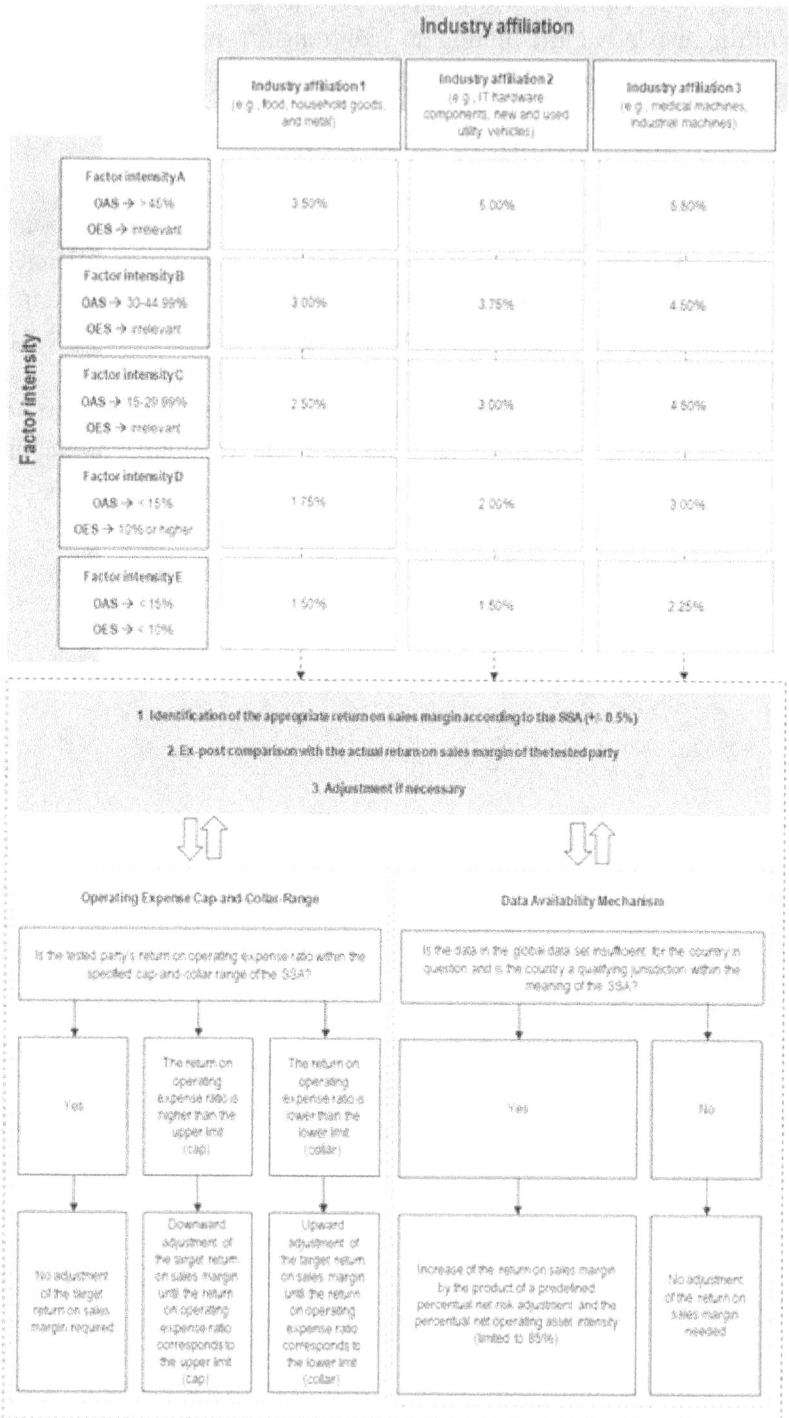

Critical Assessment

With regard to the pricing mechanism of the SSA, it becomes apparent that the pricing matrix requires a high degree of data availability and data quality. The provision and processing of this data can lead to considerable additional administrative work and will pose major challenges, especially for small and medium-sized enterprises with baseline cross-border distribution transactions. For example, in order to derive the appropriate return on sales margin from the pricing matrix, it is necessary to prepare and process data for calculating the net operating asset intensity and the operating expense intensity of the tested party. This may not be a substantial problem for multinational enterprises with only a few distribution entities on foreign markets or for multinationals with a high degree of system integration across the entire group. However, it might pose a substantial problem for companies with many baseline distribution entities across the globe and with a highly fragmented system landscape, because adequate data availability cannot be ensured in these constellations. In addition, the SSA only allows a minor deviation from the target return on sales margin of +/-0.5%.

These two aspects will generate additional costs for the respective companies. Thus, with regard to the application of the pricing matrix, the SSA counteracts its actual objective of simplifying transfer pricing.

Furthermore, the SSA neglects exceptional economic situations. For instance, the initial set-up of distribution structures on foreign markets is most likely associated with additional start-up costs. In this regard, the question arises whether such costs must be entirely borne by the principal entity or whether they can be at least partially attributed to the basic distribution entity. In the latter case, the basic distribution entity would temporarily deviate from the target margins of the SSA. Given the limited functional and risk profile, this would undermine the nature of a basic distribution entity, which should typically generate a stable yet modest profit from a transfer pricing perspective. Similar scenarios could be adverse economic developments on a global scale such as during the COVID-19 pandemic. However, the SSA does not contain provisions on the allocation of costs under these exceptional economic conditions. Thus, in order to cover economic situations beyond the standard scenario, it would have been desirable to add more specific provisions in this regard.

Practical Implications

Given the aforementioned narrow price range of only +/-0.5%, the operational management of transfer prices must be as accurate as possible throughout the year in order to avoid retrospective year-end adjustments and their associated risks in relation to indirect taxes. For instance, if transfer prices are adjusted retroactively, it can affect the customs value of goods declared at the time of import. A correction of the customs value is typically complex and involves additional efforts. Moreover, in some jurisdictions, such as Austria, year-end adjustments may not be accepted by the tax authorities unless the taxpayer can provide evidence of intra-year monitoring (Ditz & Nowotny, 2022).

Regarding this, affected multinational enterprises can ideally implement a technology-based solution to facilitate the ongoing calculation of transfer prices for their baseline distribution transactions throughout the year. In this way, it can be ensured that the return on sales margins at the end of the year correspond to the applicable target margins provided by the pricing matrix of the SSA. Hence, by using software solutions, year-end adjustments can be reduced or even completely avoided. For this purpose, adaptable pre-built software solutions are particularly suitable, as they already provide predefined operational functionalities and can therefore be quickly implemented in accordance with the requirements of the SSA (Paczkowski & Totzek, 2024). Alternatively, companies can use general data analytics tools that enable the creation of standardized data workflows for the continuous and automated calculation of transfer prices in accordance with the SSA.

Exemplary Case Study

A multinational enterprise distributes its self-manufactured consumer electronics across multiple countries. One of its subsidiaries is located in Country X and handles the distribution of these consumer electronics. The subsidiary is classified under Industry Grouping 2 (Consumer Electronics) of the SSA. When calculating the factor intensity, the subsidiary shows a net operating asset intensity (OAS) of 20% and an operating expense intensity (OES) of 12%. This places the subsidiary in Category C of the factor intensity classification (OAS of 15% to 29.99%, at any OES level). According to the pricing matrix, this results in a return on sales margin of 3.0% (+/-0.5%). An operating expense cross-check is performed to ensure that the calculated return falls within the specified cap-and-collar range for operating expenses (cap at 60%, collar at 10% for Category C and non-qualifying jurisdictions). Therefore, the subsidiary in Country X can achieve a return on sales margin between 2.5% and 3.5% in order to fall within the arm's length range provided by the SSA.

NATIONAL IMPLEMENTATION OF THE SIMPLIFIED AND STREAMLINED APPROACH

The implementation of the SSA is not mandatory, as the OECD/G20 Inclusive Framework on BEPS lacks the authority to enact binding laws given its voluntary nature and the sovereign independence of its member states. Instead, it operates on the basis of consensus-building (and peer pressure), relying on the commitment of participating jurisdictions to implement the agreed-upon standards and recommendations. Against this background, the following section addresses and critically assesses the key aspects in relation to the implementation of the SSA.

Implementation Options

Given the aforementioned optionality of the SSA, multinational enterprises only benefit from the simplified pricing mechanism of the SSA if their baseline distribution transactions involve countries that effectively implement the SSA at the national level (OECD, 2024, p. 15). Hence, the applicability of the SSA in one jurisdiction does not automatically lead to the recognition of the outcomes of the SSA in another jurisdiction. For countries that opt for the implementation at the national level, the SSA framework provides two options. While the first option gives taxpayers the right to choose whether to apply the SSA, the second option involves its mandatory application (OECD, 2024, p. 15). If taxpayers decide to opt for the SSA under the first option, they are expected to commit to the framework for three years (OECD, 2024, p. 33). However, if the respective country makes the SSA mandatory, taxpayers are forced to apply the SSA as soon as their distribution transactions fall within its scope. At the same time, the tax authorities of the respective countries are also obliged to recognize the outcomes of the SSA, provided that the underlying transaction meets its application criteria (OECD, 2024, p. 15).

This illustrates that the national implementation of the SSA depends on two consecutive aspects. First, the question arises as to whether the relevant jurisdiction effectively decides to implement the SSA. Second, the subsequent question arises as to which of the two proposed implementation options will be chosen by the jurisdictions that are relevant to the taxpayers (optional versus mandatory implementation). Figure 2 shows the different constellations that can occur with regard to the national implementation of the SSA.

Figure 2. The different implementation constellations of the SSA (Own Illustration)

Critical Assessment

As jurisdictions are neither obliged to implement the SSA nor to respect its application in other states, there is always the possibility of a unilateral or asymmetrical application of the SSA. For the taxpayers, this can be highly problematic, as it entails the risk of double taxation. For instance, if one jurisdiction mandatorily applies the SSA while the other does not consider it and instead requests a benchmark study, then there will almost certainly be different, non-compatible transfer prices. More specifically, it is possible that the jurisdiction of the principal entity demands the application of the SSA, while the country in which the baseline distribution activities take place does not acknowledge the outcomes. This can result in a situation, where the taxable income in the country of the baseline distribution activities is higher than the amount that can be deducted in the counterparty jurisdiction (i.e., the jurisdiction that mandatorily applies the SSA and where the principal entity is located). This asymmetrical application of the SSA may lead to a potential overlapping taxation on the same income.

Thus, as soon as there are significant incongruities between the relevant jurisdictions with regard to the actual implementation of the SSA, its intended simplification and harmonization is superseded by additional uncertainty and complexity. This illustrates yet again that it is difficult to design a panacea for harmonizing transfer pricing regulation at the supranational level without having the competency to translate it into a uniform and legally binding form. Accordingly, taxpayers can only rely on a consistent application of the SSA if the approach is effectively implemented in both jurisdictions that are relevant for the underlying baseline distribution transaction. Thus, the respective countries ultimately decide whether the SSA culminates in a coherent taxation system for baseline distribution activities or whether it withers away as a fragmented framework with inherent double taxation risks. The OECD/G20 Inclusive Framework on BEPS tries to avoid the latter by urging their member states to acknowledge the application of the SSA by other countries (OECD, 2024, p. 6). Furthermore, it implicitly expects that the respective jurisdictions exhaust all plausible avenues to circumvent the possibility of double taxation in constellations with low-capacity jurisdictions, where a double tax treaty is in place (OECD, 2024, p. 6). Low-capacity jurisdictions are countries with limited resources, infrastructure, and institutional capabilities to effectively implement and enforce policies and (transfer pricing) regulations.

Despite these attempts to ensure a reasonably consistent application of the SSA, certain jurisdictions have already expressed a negative stance towards the SSA. India, for example, has already articulated its skepticism in the final report on the SSA by adding a whole series of critical aspects that may stand in the way of implementing the SSA in India (OECD, 2024). Furthermore, Australia has advocated for optionality as there are already simplification rules in place, which would presumably collide with the SSA (Stewart & Soong, 2024). Therefore, it can be assumed that Australia will also opt against implementing the approach. Moreover, New Zealand has already stated that it will not implement the SSA (Roper, 2024; Stewart & Soong, 2024).

In contrast, the United States are actively advocating for the mandatory implementation of the approach. Regarding this, they are already in the process of developing a ‘phase 2’ of the SSA, which will turn the approach into a mandatory format (Stewart & Soong, 2024). Moreover, low-capacity jurisdictions probably also embrace the SSA, as they hope for fewer resource-intensive international tax disputes (Roper, 2024). Notwithstanding this, these initial reactions to the SSA underline the unlikeliness of a uniform implementation of the approach. The resulting asymmetric application can lead to additional uncertainty for taxpayers.

Practical Implications

Given this uncertainty and complexity, taxpayers may need to take into account both the SSA and the relevant national transfer pricing regulations including the regular OECD Transfer Pricing Guidelines. For example, multinational enterprises should closely monitor how relevant jurisdictions position themselves with regard to the SSA. In particular, if jurisdictions decide to implement the SSA as a mandatory regime, companies should prepare themselves as early as possible. Regarding this, they can either prepare for the application of the SSA in these countries or avoid its applicability by restructuring their foreign distribution entities. However, they should always be aware of potentially detrimental tax consequences in relation to such restructurings.

Moreover, with regard to jurisdictions that optionally implement the SSA, it is worth assessing whether the application of the SSA provides actual benefits to the respective multinational enterprise. For instance, it may be reasonable to prepare a benchmark study instead of applying the SSA if the multinational enterprise may find it difficult to operationally manage the narrow price range of +/-0.5% as defined by the SSA.

REQUIREMENTS FOR THE APPLICATION OF THE SIMPLIFIED AND STREAMLINED APPROACH

As the benchmark study, which has served as the basis for deriving the pricing matrix, only included very specific companies (OECD, 2024, pp. 38–39), it takes relatively strict application requirements to ensure that the arm's length principle is adequately reflected when applying the SSA. For a distribution transaction to fall within the scope of the SSA, it must fulfill five requirements. Only if these five requirements are met cumulatively, the SSA is effectively applicable.

Transaction Type

The first requirement is that one of the two predefined transaction types must be present. On the one hand, these are transactions in which the distributor acquires goods from one or more affiliated companies in order to resell them to independent third parties as part of a wholesale transaction (buy/sell transactions) (OECD, 2024, p. 17). On the other hand, these can be transactions in which a sales or commission agent facilitates the wholesale distribution of goods from one or more affiliated companies to independent customers (OECD, 2024, p. 17). Moreover, distributors whose transactions fall within the scope of the SSA must assume so-called core distribution functions (OECD, 2024, p. 17). This includes, for example, "buying goods for resale", identifying "new customers" or managing "customers' relationships" (OECD, 2024, p. 11).

Economic Profile of the Transaction

The second requirement for the applicability of the SSA relates to the economic profile of the underlying transaction. From an economic point of view, the SSA requires a transaction characteristic that permits a price determination that is based on a one-sided transfer price method (e.g., TNMM) and attributes the position of the tested party to the distributor (OECD, 2024, p. 18). For example, as the deployment of unique intangible assets or a high degree of horizontal or vertical value chain integration would prevent the application of a one-sided transfer pricing method, the respective intercompany distribution transactions would be outside the scope of the SSA.

Operating Expenses of the Tested Party

Moreover, the third requirement is that the annual operating expenses of the tested party cannot be lower than 3% of the annual net revenues (OECD, 2024, p. 18). Alongside this lower limit, there is also an upper limit, according to which annual operating expenses cannot exceed between 20% and 30% of annual net revenues (depending on the country-specific implementation of the SSA) (OECD, 2024, p. 18). Regarding this, the upper limit of this quantitative criterion serves as an indicator whether the tested party has a functional profile that includes additional functions alongside baseline distribution activities. As an extended functional profile typically reduces the reliability of a one-sided transfer pricing method, the transactions in question are excluded from the scope of the SSA.

Exclusion of Intangible Goods, Services, Raw Materials, and Commodities

According to the fourth requirement, only transactions in relation to the distribution of tangible goods fall within the scope of the SSA, whereas intangible goods (in particular digital goods), services, raw materials and commodities are not covered by the SSA (OECD, 2024, p. 18). As the distribution of tangible goods typically follows a similar logic of value creation, this restriction ensures a minimum degree of structural consistency and comparability with regard to the distribution activities that are covered by the SSA.

Purity of the Underlying Transaction

The fifth requirement refers to the purity of the underlying distribution transaction. This purity is only given if the transaction does not additionally involve (supportive) non-distribution activities that are inseparable from the core distribution functions (OECD, 2024, p. 18). Therefore, a high level of integration between the respective distribution activities and non-distribution functions such as research and development or manufacturing typically undermines the purity of the respective distribution transaction. This lack of purity would prevent the transaction from being within the scope of the SSA. Furthermore, a disproportionate share of retail distribution as compared to wholesale distribution can also jeopardize the purity of the transaction. While a share of retail distribution within the 'de minimis' threshold of 20% is not detrimental to the application of the SSA in relation to the respective transaction, a share of retail distribution above the de minimis threshold of 20% would convert the entire retail share into a non-distribution activity (OECD, 2024, pp. 10–11). This means that the remaining share of wholesale distribution is only covered by the scope of the SSA if the wholesale distribution can be clearly distinguished from the retail distribution. Otherwise, the purity of the transaction would be undermined, which would prevent the SSA from being applicable. All things considered, if a distribution transaction meets all the aforementioned requirements, it is either optional or mandatory to apply the SSA, depending on the respective national implementation.

Critical Assessment

The scope of the SSA covers both buy/sell distributors as well as sales or commission agents. However, the risk profiles of buy/sell distributors on the one hand and sales or commission agents on the other hand are very different. The latter do not become the owner of the goods and therefore assume a significantly lower risk as compared to buy/sell distributors that are stuck with the goods if they are not sold on the market. This indicates that the requirements for applying the SSA may not align with the degree of differentiation of the pricing matrix. Against this background, it seems questionable to what extent the pricing matrix is differentiated enough to provide arm's length margins for all in-scope transactions. A more granular pricing matrix with margins that are not only based on the industry group and the factor intensity, but also directly consider the risk profiles of the different forms of distribution, would probably better reflect the arm's length principle. However, such a granular differentiation might have further complicated the application of the SSA.

Moreover, there probably exist distributors that not only carry out wholesale distribution but also engage in retail distribution that exceed the de minimis limit of the SSA. Such 'hybrid' distributors would be excluded from the scope of the SSA, unless the retail share can be separated from the wholesale distribution. This would probably limit the reach of the SSA in practice. However, as already mentioned above, the inclusion of further transactions may have required a more differentiated pricing matrix, which would have increased the complexity of applying the SSA.

Alongside the five requirements outlined above, the final report of the OECD/G20 Inclusive Framework on BEPS envisages the creation of an additional qualitative criterion, which can be optionally introduced by jurisdictions that implement the SSA (OECD, 2024, p. 6). This additional qualitative requirement serves as a complementary filter to exclude cross-border activities that reach beyond the narrow functional and risk profile of baseline distribution activities. In fact, taxpayers may exploit the standardized pricing matrix of the SSA by synthetically adjusting their distribution activities to the five existing requirements. An additional qualitative criterion could, at least theoretically, prevent such tax-driven, synthetic adjustments. However, a qualitative criterion always involves a higher degree of subjectivity. This inherent subjectivity could eventually lead to an arbitrary, inconsistent application of the SSA. This risk of inconsistency across different jurisdictions is further amplified by the optional nature of the qualitative criterion. Accordingly, some jurisdictions will adopt the additional qualitative criterion, while others will only apply the five requirements that are already in place.

Overall, both the subjectivity and the optionality of a potential qualitative criterion can lead to a constellation, where the same transaction falls within the scope of the SSA in one jurisdiction while it is beyond the scope in the counterparty jurisdiction. As already mentioned, this can lead to an inconsistent application and interpretation of the SSA across jurisdictions, which can result in a significant risk of double taxation. Thus, there can be incongruent developments both in terms of national implementation and in relation to the application requirements of the SSA.

In addition, the final report on the SSA excludes digital goods from the scope of the SSA, even though this has been left open in the previous consultation paper (OECD, 2023, p. 3). Given the ubiquitous presence of information technology and the widespread digitalization of different business models across industries, this narrowing of the scope seems unreasonable. Instead, the question arises as to why the distribution of digital goods should not benefit from a simplification of transfer pricing. For instance, it would have been conceivable to expand the pricing matrix in order to additionally cover the distribution of digital goods. However, similar to the previously discussed extensions of the scope, this may have further increased the complexity of the SSA.

Practical Implications

If multinational enterprises come to the conclusion that the SSA would simplify their transfer pricing practices, despite the fact that the functional and risk profile of their distribution entity exceeds the scope of the SSA, then it may be reasonable to undertake certain measures. For example, a foreign distribution entity that provides small-scale engineering services alongside its baseline distribution activities would generally be excluded from the scope of the SSA unless the engineering functions can be adequately separated from the distribution functions. This could either be achieved by calculating the margins based on separate income statements for each function or by dividing them into two separate legal entities.

Under the first option, it may again be useful to implement an adaptable pre-built operational transfer pricing tool (Paczkowski & Totzek, 2024) in order to prepare separate profit and loss statements for each functional area of the respective entity. With regard to the second option, one entity would exclusively manage the baseline distribution, while the other would solely focus on the complementary engineering function. The distribution entity could then be remunerated based on the SSA, whereas the engineering entity would be compensated according to an alternative transfer pricing model. However, it must be taken into account that an additional legal entity is always associated with additional costs. Hence, the preparation of separate profit and loss statements for each functional area would certainly be more cost-effective.

ADDITIONAL ASPECTS OF THE SIMPLIFIED AND STREAMLINED APPROACH

Besides the aforementioned aspects that directly concern the key principles of the SSA, the final report also contains recommendations on the documentation of the respective transactions as well as suggestions for increasing tax certainty and preventing potential double taxation resulting from an inconsistent application of the SSA. With regard to the documentation of the baseline distribution transaction, the final report on the SSA particularly points to the need of precisely describing the respective transaction (OECD, 2024, p. 32). This encompasses a thorough characterization of the context and the parties that are affected by the underlying transaction. Furthermore, the documentation should include any existing written contracts with regard to the respective transaction along with other important information that reflects the main characteristics of the transaction. The documentation should also contain the key figures, which have been used for determining the applicability of the SSA as well as a reference on how they relate to the financial statements. Overall, the documentation requirements in relation to the SSA are similar to what is already required by the OECD Transfer Pricing Guidelines. Accordingly, the SSA does not provide a simplification of the documentation requirements (cf. Roper, 2024).

With regard to tax certainty and the elimination of double taxation, the final report on the SSA contains recommendations on how potentially negative consequences of an incongruent application of the SSA can be remedied. As already mentioned, no country is obliged to accept the outcomes of the SSA in another jurisdiction. Accordingly, it is possible that a country rejects the application of the SSA in another jurisdiction and instead makes an adjustment of the transfer prices based on the regular OECD Transfer Pricing Guidelines (OECD, 2024, p. 36). This potentially leads to double taxation, as a different transfer price is applicable in each of the jurisdictions concerned.

For such constellations, the final report recommends the use of the remaining OECD Transfer Pricing Guidelines as a common basis. For example, the tax jurisdiction that applies the SSA should make a corresponding adjustment if the primary adjustment of the counterparty jurisdiction can be justified based on the regular OECD Transfer Pricing Guidelines (OECD, 2024, p. 36). This indicates that the SSA is retreating behind the regular OECD Transfer Pricing Guidelines as soon as there are contrary opinions or outcomes in order to protect the position of the OECD Transfer Pricing Guidelines as a largely recognized frame of reference for determining transfer prices.

CRITICAL COMPARISON BETWEEN THE FINAL REPORT ON THE SSA AND PRECEDING PUBLICATIONS

The final report on the SSA has been preceded by consultation papers and other official publications in relation to Pillar One – Amount B. Thus, even before the final report on the SSA has been published, some authors have already expressed concerns about certain aspects that were included in these previous publications. In the following, the major points raised by these authors are critically compared to the final report on the SSA.

The paper by Higinbotham et al. (2021) analyze the status quo of Amount B at a very early stage. The authors express concerns that the concept might oversimplify complex transfer pricing scenarios, potentially undermining the arm's length principle. Regarding this, Higinbotham et al. (2021) argue that a standardized pricing mechanism may not sufficiently address variability in industry practices. Traditional benchmark studies may better reflect this heterogeneity and variability than a standardized pricing mechanism. Even though the pricing matrix of the final version of the SSA attempts to bring about a certain degree of differentiation by referring to industry groups and the factor intensity, it is still too undifferentiated to entirely satisfy the high requirements of the arm's length principle. Accordingly, it can be stated that although the pricing matrix of the SSA has become more differentiated as compared to its preceding versions, it still does not adequately reflect the heterogeneous margins that can be achieved across various industries. Furthermore, the aforementioned varying functional and risk profiles of buy/sell distributors on the one hand, and sales as well as commission agents on the other hand are also not adequately reflected in the final version of the SSA.

In contrast to Higinbotham et al. (2021), van der Ham (2023) analyzes the latest consultation paper from 2023 that has been published by the OECD before the most recent final report on the SSA. She also takes a rather critical stance by arguing that the exclusion of certain retail activities and the inconsistent treatment of digital goods could introduce significant ambiguity and conflict in practice. Moreover, van der Ham (2023) highlights that the increased documentation requirements under the SSA contradict the original goal of simplification, adding complexity rather than reducing it. However, none of these points raised by van der Ham (2023) has been sufficiently addressed in the final report on the SSA. It neither reflects the increasing importance of digital business nor does it bring any noticeable relief for taxpayers in relation to transfer pricing documentation requirements.

Identical to van der Ham (2023), Bußmann et al. (2023) have also examined the latest consultation paper on the SSA from 2023. They express concerns that the simplified approach may not be consistently recognized or applied in tax audits, potentially leading to new disputes rather than reducing them. This is indeed a major practical problem that will and cannot be solved by the final report on the SSA. In principle, the field of transfer pricing is very vague and leaves substantial room for interpretation. Even with the regular transfer pricing guidelines and regulations, a certain arbitrariness can be observed when they are applied by tax authorities. Accordingly, it is nearly impossible to prevent this in relation to the SSA.

Furthermore, Bußmann et al. (2023) are concerned that the principles and thresholds established by the SSA could start to affect other, more complex business activities. This means that activities which typically involve higher risks or more value-added functions might also be assessed using the SSA. In particular, jurisdictions where the principal entity of a multinational enterprise is located may be inclined to apply the SSA to more sophisticated distribution structures abroad. In this way, the margins of the foreign sales companies can be reduced, which increases the tax base of the domestic principal entity. Obviously, such an approach is inappropriate and would undermine the arm's length principle. However, as this can also be attributed to a certain arbitrariness by local tax authorities, this cannot be prevented by adjusting the SSA.

In addition, Eden (2023) argues that setting a standardized profitability rate across diverse economic contexts could lead to inefficient allocation of resources, where businesses might either over- or under-invest in certain countries. This misallocation could distort markets and hinder economic growth, particularly in industries or regions where the fixed rate does not align with the actual economic conditions. Hence, with regard to the final report, Eden (2023) provides a strong argument for exclusively implementing the SSA as an optional 'safe harbor' framework. In contrast, as a mandatory framework, the SSA might undermine the principles of tax neutrality in relation to investments in local distribution entities on foreign markets. In summary, it can be stated that the research on the previous consultation papers and other official publications relating to Pillar One – Amount B has raised some critical aspects that have barely been improved in the final report on the SSA.

ECONOMIC ANALYSIS

From an economic point of view, it is highly questionable whether the SSA effectively provides cost savings for taxpayers. Under the assumption that the SSA is at least implemented as an optional safe harbor rule in all relevant jurisdictions, the SSA would save the respective multinational enterprise the costs of preparing a pan-European database analysis for its baseline distribution entities. For instance, consulting firms in Western Europe charge between ten to twenty thousand Euros for the preparation of a pan-European benchmark study. However, as already mentioned, there is no certainty that the SSA will be implemented by the jurisdictions relevant to the respective enterprise. In addition, even if the SSA is applicable, companies are still subject to relatively extensive documentation requirements. For example, the SSA requires a compilation of the required financial metrics as well as a comprehensive functional and risk analysis in order to determine whether it is actually applicable to the respective transaction. Accordingly, the documentation requirements under the SSA might even be more extensive than under a scenario where the remaining OECD Transfer Pricing Guidelines are applicable. Moreover, due to technological progress throughout the digital transformation, benchmark studies will be available at significantly lower cost in the future. For instance, there are already providers that offer benchmark studies created by generative artificial intelligence (AI). These AI-generated benchmark studies are far more cost-effective as compared to human-generated benchmark studies. This might further diminish the economic benefits of the SSA for multinational enterprises.

In contrast, tax authorities would probably derive greater benefit from the standardization provided by the SSA. However, the SSA is actually supposed to be geared towards the needs of the taxpayers. After all, taxpayers are the ones who are confronted with considerable costs when they are required to prepare benchmark studies in order to substantiate the appropriateness of their transfer prices.

CONCLUSION

This chapter initially presents the key aspects of the SSA, before critically assessing their implications. In general, the analysis shows that the SSA certainly has the potential to bring about substantial simplification for taxpayers and tax authorities. In particular, it would eliminate the need for taxpayers to conduct costly benchmark analysis. However, the analysis also indicates that the SSA rather adds additional complexity and uncertainty than representing actual simplification.

The main reason for this is the optionality of implementation. It is possible that jurisdictions do not implement the SSA at all, implement it on a mandatory basis or allow the taxpayer to choose whether or not to apply the SSA. Thus, there is always uncertainty for taxpayers as to how the jurisdictions that are involved in the transaction will apply the SSA. In particular, if the SSA becomes mandatory in one jurisdiction while the other does not apply it, there is substantial uncertainty, which can potentially culminate in double taxation.

Another critical aspect is the scope of the SSA. Given the varying risk profiles of the covered distribution structures, the SSA's current pricing matrix may not be differentiated enough to provide arm's length margins for all in-scope transactions. Unlike sales or commission agencies, buy/sell distributors face higher risks as they are typically stuck with unsold goods. Hence, a more granular pricing matrix that considers these differing risk profiles could better reflect the arm's length principle.

Given these drawbacks, there is a substantial need for future research to empirically explore the introduction of the SSA in different jurisdictions. It might be especially useful to conduct qualitative interviews with industry practitioners who have gained experience in relation to the SSA as soon as it is introduced in 2025. Regarding this, it can be scientifically explored whether and how the theoretical drawbacks of the SSA may manifest themselves in business practice. Furthermore, these qualitative interviews could serve as an opportunity to explore best practices for complying with the SSA.

Apart from that, the chapter also points out that the introduction of the SSA further increases the demand for transfer pricing technologies within multinational enterprises. In fact, the strict margin requirements of +/-0.5% necessitate precise operational transfer pricing management to avoid complex year-end adjustments that may affect customs values. Implementing technology-based solutions can automate and standardize workflows, ensuring continuous compliance and reducing administrative burdens and financial risks. Hence, multinational enterprises with advanced digital transfer pricing systems may be better equipped to meet these demands of the SSA. However, in many multinational enterprises the adoption of transfer pricing technologies is still in its infancy (Hemling et al., 2022). Accordingly, the SSA implicitly points to the need for research that supports multinational enterprises with the effective use of transfer pricing technologies. Moreover, this chapter serves as an indicative reminder that taxpayers need to familiarize themselves with the SSA and anticipate its impact on their intercompany transactions in view of its upcoming implementation in 2025.

REFERENCES

Bußmann, F., Majewski, I., & Buschmann, D. (2023). Fremdvergleichsgrundsatz 2.0 – die Neudefinition der Routinevertriebsvergütung im Großhandel gemäß Amount B. *Betriebs-Berater*, (36), 2007–2012.

Chan, K. H., Lo, A. W., & Mo, P. L. (2015). An empirical analysis of the changes in tax audit focus on international transfer pricing. *Journal of International Accounting, Auditing & Taxation*, 24, 94–104. DOI: 10.1016/j.intaccaudtax.2014.12.001

Cooper, M., & Nguyen, Q. T. (2020). Multinational enterprises and corporate tax planning: A review of literature and suggestions for a future research agenda. *International Business Review*, 29(3), 101692. DOI: 10.1016/j.ibusrev.2020.101692

Ditz, X., & Nowotny, C. (2022). Internationale Verrechnungspreise – Vergleich der deutschen VWG Verrechnungspreise mit den österreichischen Verrechnungspreis-Richtlinien. *IStR Internationales Steuerrecht*, (18), 669–678.

Eden, L. (2023). Pillar One Amount B: Simplifying the Arm's Length Principle for Baseline Distribution Activities (Submission to the OECD/Inclusive Framework on 1 September 2023 in Response to the 12 July 2023 Public Consultation Document on Pillar One Amount B). SSRN *Electronic Journal*, 1–11. DOI: 10.2139/ssrn.4560131

Hemling, L., Plesner Rossing, J. C., & Hoffjan, A. (2022). The use of information technology for international transfer pricing in multinational enterprises. *International Journal of Accounting Information Systems*, 44, 100546. DOI: 10.1016/j.accinf.2021.100546

Higinbotham, H., Srinivasan, N., Starkov, V., Mert-Beydilli, N., & Eden, L. (2021). Amount B: Facts and Circumstances Matter – Even for Routine Distributors. *Tax Management International Journal, 50*(2), 90–97. https://ssrn.com/abstract=3780374

Kalra, A., & Afzal, M. N. I. (2023). Transfer pricing practices in multinational corporations and their effects on developing countries' tax revenue: A systematic literature review. *International Trade. Politics and Development*, 7(3), 172–190. DOI: 10.1108/ITPD-04-2023-0011

Kumar, S., Pandey, N., Lim, W. M., Chatterjee, A. N., & Pandey, N. (2021). What do we know about transfer pricing? Insights from bibliometric analysis. *Journal of Business Research*, 134, 275–287. DOI: 10.1016/j.jbusres.2021.05.041

OECD. (2015). *Aligning Transfer Pricing Outcomes with Value Creation, Actions 8-10 - 2015 Final Reports*. OECD Publishing., DOI: 10.1787/9789264241244-

OECD. (2021). *OECD/G20 Base Erosion and Profit Shifting Project: Two-Pillar Solution to Address the Tax Challenges Arising from the Digitalisation of the Economy.* https://www.oecd.org/tax/beps/brochure-two-pillar-solution-to-address-the-tax-challenges-arising-from-the-digitalisation-of-the-economy-october-2021.pdf

OECD. (2022a). *OECD Transfer Pricing Guidelines for Multinational Enterprises and Tax Administrations 2022.* OECD Publishing., DOI: 10.1787/0e655865-

OECD. (2022b). *Public Consultation Document: Pillar One - Amount B: 8 December 2022 - 25 January 2023.* https://web-archive.oecd.org/2022-12-08/645900-public-consultation-document-pillar-one-amount-b-2022.pdf

OECD. (2023). *Public Consultation Document: Pillar One – Amount B: 17 July 2023 - 1 September 2023.* https://www.oecd.org/tax/beps/public-consultation-document-pillar-one-amount-b-2023.pdf

OECD. (2024). *Pillar One - Amount B: Inclusive Framework on BEPS, OECD/G20 Base Erosion and Profit Shifting Project.* OECD Publishing., DOI: 10.1787/21ea168b-

Paczkowski, K., & Totzek, A. (2024). Kapitel 6: Operationalisierung von Verrechnungspreisen: a) Konzeptionelle Produktgestaltung. In Vögele, A., Borstell, T., & van der Ham, S. (Eds.), *Verrechnungspreise. C. H. Beck* (subsec. 163–167). Subsec.

Rogers, H., & Oats, L. (2022). Transfer pricing: Changing views in changing times. *Accounting Forum*, 46(1), 83–107. DOI: 10.1080/01559982.2021.1926778

Roper, P. (2024). *Amount B: more sticky situation than honey sweet: Amount B of Pillar One: game changing for low-capacity jurisdictions but no buzz from multinational enterprises.* https://kpmg.com/uk/en/home/insights/2024/02/tmd-amount-b-more-sticky-situation-than-honey-sweet.html

Solilová, V., Nerudová, D., Bohušová, H., & Svoboda, P. (2017). Compliance Costs of Transfer Pricing in Case of SMEs: Czech Case. *European Financial and Accounting Journal*, 12(1), 35–50. DOI: 10.18267/j.efaj.176

Stewart, D. D., & Soong, S. (2024). *An Update on Pillar 1 Amount B.*https://www.taxnotes.com/tax-notes-live/tax-notes-talk/update-pillar-1-amount-b/7j9r1?s=03

Treidler, O. (2020). *Transfer Pricing in One Lesson.* Springer International Publishing., DOI: 10.1007/978-3-030-25085-0

van der Ham, S. (2023). Das neue OECD-Konsultationspapier zu Amount B – Verrechnungspreise einfach gemacht? *IStR Internationales Steuerrecht*, (21), 785–792.

ADDITIONAL READING

Eden, L. (2023). Pillar One Amount B: Simplifying the Arm's Length Principle for Baseline Distribution Activities (Submission to the OECD/Inclusive Framework on 1 September 2023 in Response to the 12 July 2023 Public Consultation Document on Pillar One Amount B). SSRN *Electronic Journal*, 1–11. DOI: 10.2139/ssrn.4560131

Hemling, L., Plesner Rossing, J. C., & Hoffjan, A. (2022). The use of information technology for international transfer pricing in multinational enterprises. *International Journal of Accounting Information Systems*, 44, 100546. DOI: 10.1016/j.accinf.2021.100546

Higinbotham, H., Srinivasan, N., Starkov, V., Mert-Beydilli, N., & Eden, L. Amount B: Facts and Circumstances Matter – Even for Routine Distributors. *Tax Management International Journal, 50*(2), 90–97. https://ssrn.com/abstract=3780374

Holtzman, Y., & Nagel, P. (2014). An introduction to transfer pricing. *Journal of Management Development*, 33(1), 57–61. DOI: 10.1108/JMD-11-2013-0139

Kalra, A., & Afzal, M. N. I. (2023). Transfer pricing practices in multinational corporations and their effects on developing countries' tax revenue: A systematic literature review. *International Trade. Politics and Development*, 7(3), 172–190. DOI: 10.1108/ITPD-04-2023-0011

Kumar, S., Pandey, N., Lim, W. M., Chatterjee, A. N., & Pandey, N. (2021). What do we know about transfer pricing? Insights from bibliometric analysis. *Journal of Business Research*, 134, 275–287. DOI: 10.1016/j.jbusres.2021.05.041

Rogers, H., & Oats, L. (2022). Transfer pricing: Changing views in changing times. *Accounting Forum*, 46(1), 83–107. DOI: 10.1080/01559982.2021.1926778

Treidler, O. (2020). *Transfer Pricing in One Lesson*. Springer International Publishing., DOI: 10.1007/978-3-030-25085-0

KEY TERMS AND DEFINITIONS

Arm's Lenth Principle: This concept is central to transfer pricing and requires that transactions between related entities within multinational enterprises are conducted as if these transactions would exist between unrelated parties.

Multinational Enterprise: Large corporations that operate across different jurisdictions.

Tested Party: The entity in an intercompany transaction that is considered the least complex and for which reliable comparables can be found.

Principal Entity / Strategic Entity / Entrepreneur: The entity that has the broader functional and risk profile as compared to a basic distribution entity. In typical distribution transactions, this is typically where the crucial intangible assets are located, where the main strategic decisions are made, and where the significant risks are borne and controlled.

The Simplified and Streamlined Approach of Pillar One – Amount B (SSA): A transfer pricing framework, which provides a set of rules, designed to simplify and streamline transfer pricing for baseline distribution structures.

Transactional Net Margin Method (TNMM): A transfer pricing method, which seeks to ensure that intercompany transactions are priced in a manner consistent with what would be expected between unrelated parties by focusing on the net profit relative to a suitable base (such as sales, assets, or costs).

Two-Pillar Solution: An intergovernmental approach, which aims to address the challenges posed by the digitalization of the economy and the shifting nature of global business activities.

Chapter 16
A Measure to Prevent Tax Evasion

Susana Cristina Rodrigues Aldeia
https://orcid.org/0000-0002-2611-7683
Independent Researcher, Portugal

Anna Białek-Jaworska
https://orcid.org/0000-0003-4520-8916
University of Warsaw, Poland

ABSTRACT

This research project is focused on examining the impact of transfer pricing regulations on preventing tax evasion, specifically within the context of Portuguese jurisdiction. To accomplish this, the study utilizes a legal research methodology. Extensive examination of both national and international data sources was conducted, with particular attention given to scrutinizing the corporate income tax law and related tax documents at the national level. Additionally, thorough analysis of the OECD guidelines and reports on transfer pricing was undertaken at the international level.

1. INTRODUCTION

Jurisdictions seek to attract foreign investment by creating tax mechanisms that appeal to international companies to invest in their countries (Esteller-Moré et al., 2021). However, they face significant challenges in safeguarding tax revenues and preventing tax evasion (Muller & Kolk, 2015). Additionally, countries face significant challenges due to the growth in international trade (Dias, 2024). The increasingly frequent emergence of international groups require greater attention from the tax

DOI: 10.4018/979-8-3693-3908-4.ch016

authorities and international institutions (Demko-Rihter et al., 2023), particularly the Organization for Economic Co-operation and Development (OECD) (OECD, 2022).

Economic groups engage in transactions that could provide an economic advantage for the companies involved; this is where the concept of transfer pricing (TP) comes into play (Duho et al., 2024). TP in essence, is about the conditions set in commercial and financial transactions between related entities (Mijoc et al., 2024). These related entities typically belong to the same economic group, with the arm's length principle serving as the cornerstone of their relationship (Choi et al., 2024).

This study aims to research the extent to which the transfer pricing regime is a measure to prevent tax evasion. The analysis also explains its framework in the Portuguese legal context and to what extent Portuguese domestic law has integrated international guidelines in the TP topic in the jurisdiction. For this purpose, the research applies the legal research method. Various national and international data sources were analysed, in particular, the corporate income tax law and complementary tax documents were scrutinized at the national level. The OECD guidelines and reports on transfer pricing were analysed at the international level.

The results indicate that TP practices have implications for various taxes, including income tax (Teixeira, 2023), value-added tax (Ferreira, 2020), and customs duties (Vaz, 2013). Tax revenue from these different taxes can be reduced through tax evasion or transferred through the relocation of profits (Ogunoye et al., 2023). This is due to non-compliance with the arm's length principle, which leads to an undue distribution of taxable profits.

Therefore, the transfer pricing regime is intended to ensure that the conditions applied in transactions between related entities are identical to those used between independent entities in similar transactions. In this way, it is understood that adopting the arm's length principle makes it possible to achieve parity in tax treatment between integrated companies (possibly in international groups) and independent companies. In addition, the transfer pricing regime seeks to neutralize certain potential tax evasion practices and protect states' tax bases.

Moreover, an analysis of legislative developments shows that the TF regime has been amended several times. Specifically, by Law no. 2/2014, of January 16 and Law no. 119/2019, of September 18. More recently, Ministerial Order 268/2021 was approved. This measure follows the changes already made to Article 63 of the Corporate Income Tax Law (CIT Law) and takes on board the developments resulting from the OECD's work in the various areas of this subject. Therefore, several articles, ordinances, and other documents guide transfer pricing treatment in Portugal.

Hence, the Portuguese legislator has been keeping up with international changes, bringing the OECD guidelines into domestic law (Dias, 2024). However, national legislation still needs to clarify the transfer pricing issue in intangible transactions, which needs to be fixed in the tax system (Martins, 2022). Eliminating the problem of transfer pricing as a tax evasion mechanism will only be possible by changing the paradigm on which the taxation of multinational companies is based.

The OECD has been diligently working through its guidelines and directives to establish tax uniformity in this domain. However, the issue of transfer pricing still requires attention. Profit shifting and the reduction of taxable bases remain potential concerns due to varying tax systems in different jurisdictions.

The remainder of this paper is divided as follows: The second chapter introduces transfer pricing and the profit-shifting phenomenon. The third chapter explains the TF regime as a special anti-abuse tax measure. The fourth section gives evidence from the current regulation of TF in Portugal. Thereafter, the study presents solutions and recommendations, suggestions for future research direction and conclusions.

2. TRANSFER PRICING AND TAX EVASION

a. Transfer pricing

The business world has adapted and the formation of large economic groups is a reality in the global market (Alsultan, 2021). This economic reorganization poses challenges in terms of taxation, considering the increase in transactions between entities in the same group (Catarino & Diogo, 2024). The companies that make up these international groups may be subject to double taxation of income (Lupu, 2023). The management of these entities is done using global logic, in which the decision centres define the policies aimed at the return on invested capital and the optimization of cash flows (Correia & Martins, 2018).

Globalization has, therefore, boosted operations between companies, particularly between companies of the same group. The internationalization of the production process has fostered this problem because each stage is often carried out in a different country (Grinenko et al., 2021). This dynamic makes it possible to take advantage of the differences in production costs and taxation levels. The phenomenon of globalization has been accompanied by a proliferation of territories with more favourable tax regimes, introducing new possibilities for managing the tax process (Lu & Landry, 2014).

Independent entities or companies can carry out these companies' economic transactions whithin the same group. Price determination is sometimes complex since the businesses do not operate in a free market context but between related parties (Andrade, 2023). For this reason, several transactions occur within a business group, including the sale of products (finished or semi-finished) and the provision of services. There may also be transactions involving the transfer of trademarks or patents (Martins, 2022) and the provision of technical assistance services. These transactions are not subject to the same logic as those carried out on the open market between independent companies. These transactions are assimilated into internal transfers within the same company (Pereira, 2023).

It is in the group's interest to maximize its overall result, which derives from the prices established in relations with external entities and not from the prices agreed in intra-group operations. However, operations between related entities are essential in determining the profit or loss of each group member, as they act as a distribution of this overall result to each of the group's entities (Pereira, 2023). When taxation is carried out in each entity and is not done in the same way, the tax variable must be considered (Pereira, 2023). The total taxation of the group depends on how the overall result is distributed among the members.

This is why intra-group transactions raise the transfer pricing (Nofita et al., 2021). The prices charged between companies in the same group, which means between companies with special relationships, are known as transfer prices (Istok et al., 2022). Intra-group transactions can have one of two functions: value transactions and serve as a tax avoidance mechanism (Sebele-Mpofu et al., 2021). Taxes can be essential in setting transfer prices, as these prices can be determined for tax reasons. Tax authorities face challenges in correctly determining the expenses, income and taxable profits of the entities that make up economic groups (Kuropka, 2020).

b. Transfer pricing as an instrument of tax evasion

Tax evasion can occur if transactions are used to shift profits to low-tax jurisdictions, reducing the tax burden of the group of companies (Correia & Martins, 2018). Companies operating in several countries can undervalue the prices of goods and services originating in high-tax jurisdictions (Pereira, 2023). They can also overvalue the prices of goods originating in low-tax territories and destined for high-tax countries (Pereira, 2023). Internationally, this phenomenon is known as profit shifting (Fehling, 2022; Krautheim & Schmidt-Eisenlohr, 2011).

Transfer pricing is an essential economic instrument that allows tax evasion strategies to be devised, and as a result, states have been reacting to this problem (Bormotova et al., 2021). New rules have been introduced, considering the arm's length principle (Peters, 2022). Under this principle, intra-group transactions are expected to be valued at prices shared between unrelated entities in comparable situations (Greil, 2021).

However, the comparability of economic operations is complex. Operations between group companies often have their characteristics, and it is not easy to find operations with the same specificities in the market. The complexity inherent in these operations justifies the level of litigation that has been seen between the tax authorities and companies. According to Correia and Martins (2018) in this regard, tax litigation is particularly relevant regarding issues such as the principle of comparability, the valuation of intangibles, financial operations and the methods used.

According to Teixeira (2021), tax abuse is any act that aims to (1) delay compliance with the tax obligation and (2) reduce the payment of the tax that is due by using illicit means or means that are not covered by the tax law (criminal or administrative offence). The use of this instrument is generally triggered by multinational companies or integrated economic groups. The TP regime may have to be complied with, even if the concept of "related entities" is not adhered to, it is sufficient to verify a common economic interest.

3. THE TRANSFER PRICING REGIME AS A SPECIAL ANTI-ABUSE MEASURE

a. The OECD guidelines on transfer pricing

Considering the complexity of the TP topic, several studies have analysed it, both domestically and internationally. The European Union seeks to promote social development, a well-functioning internal market, the creation of unemployment and investment (Martins & Duarte, 2024). In this context, the OECD and the European Union have made joint efforts to significantly reduce issues related to the topic. This effort has been made through the adoption of instruments that guide action and are characterized by being non-binding and by not providing sanctions for non-compliant action, i.e. through *soft* law instruments (do Amaral, 2017).

In this context, the OECD has developed several studies, in particular *Guidelines*, with the aim of combating the erosion of the tax base, the determination of actual profit and the allocation or equitable distribution of tax revenues between states (Cugova & Cug, 2019). This document, although *soft law in* nature, plays a vital role in interpreting and resolving issues arising from the application of transfer pricing.

The first attempt was made in 1979, when the first TP guidelines appeared, but the guidelines did not produce the expected results. In 1995, the first version of the *Transfer Pricing Guidelines for Multinational Enterprises and Tax Administrations was published*, bringing together guidelines from previous reports. The full version of the document was completed in 2010 (OECD, 2022).

Jurisdictions have taken these guidelines into account when regulating transfer pricing domestically. In particular, tax administrations have taken the OECD principles as a guide. Taxpayers can also use these guidelines to assert their rights when taxes are audited in the context of transfer pricing.

The Guidelines include topics such as (1) the arm's length principle, (2) the methods that can be used in determining prices, (3) analysis of the comparability of transactions, (4) administrative due diligence, (5) documentation, (6) intangible assets, (7) intra-group services, and (8) cost contribution agreements, and (9) corporate restructurings (OECD, 2022). The OECD orientations are essential because of their content and the consensus between states (Morais, 2009). These guidelines bring together the international consensus on transfer pricing, providing relevant guidance on how to ensure that the pricing methodology is in line with market conditions (Dourado, 2018).

This document contributes to increasing uniformity in international tax legislation, specifically regarding the right to tax between the various jurisdictions. The arm's length principle is the basis of these guidelines, i.e. the *guidelines state* that, in intra-group transactions, multinational companies should act as if they were transactions between independent companies (Martins, 2022). In this context, the *guidelines* provide tax administrations and multinational companies with guidance on the application of this principle. This principle seeks to promote comparability between intra-group operations and transactions between independent entities in similar circumstances (Oguttu, 2020).

b. The role of the BEPS project in the transfer pricing regime

Abusive tax planning is a worldwide problem that urgently needs to be addressed (Blank, 2009; Laddha, 2017). It represents a substantial loss of tax revenue due to the transfer of profits to jurisdictions with a more advantageous tax burden (Catarino & Diogo, 2024). In this context, it is seen as an essential promoter of tax base erosion and profit shifting (Ignat & Tache, 2023).

International tax disharmonisation allows multinational companies to take advantage of tax differences between different jurisdictions. It allows the relocation of profits to a legal system other than the jurisdiction of the effective source of the profits (OECD, 2013).

Transfer pricing can be used by economic groups as an instrument to erode the tax base. Base erosion results from the transfer of profits to territories with more favourable tax regimes. In this context, in 2013, the OECD published the report Combating Base Erosion and Profit Shifting (OECD, 2013), which aims to determine the principles that should underpin the taxation of transnational activities. The BEPS project highlights the problem of tax base erosion and presents a set of studies and information in the public domain on the subject (da Silva, 2024). In this sense, it promoted the prevention of tax evasion through tax schemes in multinational companies. In addition, it sought to reduce international tax loopholes and tax arbitration mechanisms at global level. Like the Guidelines, the BEPS project is an essential guideline in regulatory activity, with the aim of reducing the erosion of tax bases. It seeks to promote the taxation of income in jurisdictions where operations generate added value (OECD, 2022). The project has had an influence on the activity of multinational companies and tax administrations, since, on the one hand, it is an essential strategic planning tool for companies, and, on the other, it allows for the introduction of new mechanisms and changes to tax laws.

As a result of the report's analysis and recommendations, the G20 leaders asked the OECD to develop a global action plan to address critical issues identified in the BEPS project. The OECD prepared the Action Plan to combat tax base erosion and profit shifting (OECD, 2014). The 2014 report outlines the actions needed to combat tax erosion and identifies actions, resources, methods and deadlines for implementing these actions. The aim of this plan was to contribute to the reform of the international tax system by implementing measures leading to the establishment of transparent and uniform global standards. It, therefore, requires the adoption of standards and concepts in national tax systems, as well as promoting the automatic exchange of information between tax administrations.

This action plan includes actions 8, 9, 10 and 13. The first three actions concern ensuring that results are aligned with value creation. Action 13 deals with re-examining transfer pricing documentation. Action 8 deals with transfers of intangible assets between entities in the same group, namely describing new rules for the treatment of operations related to the holding, exploitation and disposal of these assets. Action 9 seeks to develop regulations that prevent tax evasion through the transfer of risks or the excessive allocation of capital between related entities. Action 10 covers the development of rules that control the erosion of tax bases through excessive transactions.

As a result of the OECD's action plan, precisely *Action* 13, a new report has emerged called *Transfer Pricing Documentation and Country-by-Country Reporting, Action 13 - 2015 Final* Report (OECD, 2015).

c. European Union Directive

Despite Member States' own national transfer pricing regulations, which are modelled on the OECD guidelines, from an EU-wide market perspective, these rules are not uniform, which creates tax uncertainty, increases tax compliance costs, increases the risk of double or excessive taxation and can lead to lengthy and costly tax disputes between jurisdictions that are keen to attract more tax from an intra-group transaction. However, at the EU level, this leads to a less efficient and competitive EU market as a single, common market competing globally for the location of new ventures of multinational corporations precisely in EU countries. Therefore, the Business in Europe: Framework for Income Taxation (BEFIT) initiative was introduced to harmonise income tax rules for entities operating in the common European market. One of its actions is the draft Directive (that is expected to apply from 2025 instead of 2026) on harmonising transfer pricing rules targeting to introduce the arm's length principle into EU legislation, harmonise key transfer pricing rules at the EU level, regulate the role and status of the OECD guidelines, open up the possibility for further transfer pricing legislation at EU level, aligning with the OECD guidelines. It aims to be consistent with MDR and other anti-dual nontaxation provisions and effectively harmonise transfer pricing rules at the EU level, reducing compliance costs and the risk of potential disputes between countries. Care is taken to ensure that the new regulations accurately address the risk of double nontaxation or double taxation, i.e., they are transparent to taxpayers and tax administrations in the various jurisdictions. This new EU Directive on harmonising transfer pricing rules proposes a consistent application of the arm's length principle, among other things, by harmonising the definition of related parties (connection through management, voting rights, capital or a share in profits - min 25%). The Directive indicates that family-related persons will be considered one person (so two companies controlled by spouses are related parties). To ensure that the arm's length principle is applied consistently and does not lead to double taxation in the case of income adjustments in one country, the Directive proposes to harmonise the rules for making corresponding adjustments and introduce a fast-track procedure to recognise the adjustment in a shorter time than through the mutual agreement procedure, which does not exclude this procedure itself. The Directive allows compensating adjustments in the form of final-year corrections under certain conditions and using five transfer pricing methods or alternatives if needed. The EU Directive proposes a rather restrictive approach towards the market range, where any point within that interval is appropriate. However, if the transfer price falls outside the market interval, the authorities have the right to adjust the price to the median and re-pricing on that basis. This Directive indicates that no revenue thresholds should exclude the TP documentation obligation. Finally, the OECD guidelines should be binding on Member States (in their latest EU-approved version).

d. The arm's length principle

The arm's length principle, or the principle of independent entities, is the basis of the transfer pricing regime (Dourado, 2019). According to this principle, intra-group transactions must be recorded and quantified according to the conditions that would be applied under identical conditions to those practised by independent entities.

Respect for the principle arises not only in relation to business groups or multinational companies but also in the case of linked transactions, particularly transactions between entities between which there are unique relationships (Pereira, 2023).

This principle derives from Article 9(1) of the OECD Model Convention, which is the basis on which bilateral conventions have been concluded. Therefore, it is widely accepted internationally, which is why it was adopted in the first OECD reports and guidelines on transfer pricing (Pereira, 2023). Hence, equal treatment between related companies and independent companies underpins this principle (OECD, 2022).

Pereira (2023) highlights problems arising from the application of the principle. In particular, the author highlights as a challenge the lack of comparative elements on the conditions practiced between independent companies. Independent companies often do not carry out specific operations, which are carried out between related companies. The author also argues that the effect of economies of scale and synergies created between associated entities is not considered. In addition, the search for an arm's length price imposes additional administrative costs on the parties involved.

e. Advance pricing agreements

The application of the transfer pricing regime reveals some subjectivity, leading to a situation of double taxation (Ramos, 2024). It is often time-consuming to resolve these cases. The uncertainty inherent in the process can be reduced by using Advancing Pricing Agreements (APAs). APAs are agreements between taxpayers and one or more tax administrations (OECD, 2022). The purpose of these agreements is to value the operations that companies will carry out in the future. These agreements make it possible to define a set of criteria for determining transfer prices over a specific period of time.

Therefore, APAs are an additional administrative tool for resolving transfer pricing issues. They establish in advance the method by which TP will be determined, in compliance with the arm's length principle, for a specific period. This mechanism can take two types, in particular, bilateral/multilateral agreements or unilateral agreements can be established, considering the number of Tax Administrations involved (Ramos, 2024).

These agreements should be implemented with caution because they do not constitute mechanisms capable of eliminating the possibility of double taxation. In addition, they do not make it possible to resolve conflicts between tax administrations when determining transfer prices. Unilateral agreements allow companies or other tax authorities to use the amicable procedure to resolve any transfer pricing disputes. In this sense, APAs aim to provide companies with a basis of legal certainty and certainty (Ramos, 2024).

The conclusion process comprises two phases: the conclusion phase and the contract validity phase. The preliminary assessment and the presentation of the proposal comprise the conclusion phase. A request for an initial evaluation must first be made, in which the feasibility of concluding the APA is evaluated, taking into account the circumstances of the operations involved. The proposal must then be submitted, evaluated and negotiated, and the process ends with the conclusion of the APA.

The prevention of transfer pricing disputes and the resulting double taxation has led to the adoption of guidelines on advance pricing agreements in the EU. These Guidelines seek to promote best practices by being a tool for conflict prevention, with advantages for both tax administrations and taxpayers.

4. TRANSFER PRICING REGULATION IN PORTUGAL

a. Framework

Transfer pricing is a rule that guides companies in their obligations to quantify and report intra-group transactions (Dourado, 2019). In this context, it applies to all transactions that take place between associated companies, in particular comprising internal and interstate transactions.

Portugal is a member of the OECD and the European Union, so it has been following the TP guidelines of both organizations. The Portuguese legislator has passed legislation seeking to respond to the challenges inherent in this issue.

Domestically, the body of legislation is based on the arm's length principle, in line with international guidelines. The first reference to this principle was made in 1964, in article 51-A of the Industrial Contribution Code. This provided for the possibility of corrections to taxable profit when there was a departure from average market prices (Barreiros et al., 1984). With the entry into force of the current corporate income tax law, this reference was included in article 57 of the CIT Law. This wording promoted an evolution in the framework of the issue, but only to a limited extent, considering the lack of clarification of the concept of unique relationships and the methodologies to be used in the context of transfer pricing. In 1996, the OECD report considered the tax measures adopted by Portugal in this area to be insufficient, prompting new changes to the framework. For this reason, the publication of Law 30-G/2000 amended article 57 and gave it a wording close to that currently in force. This change brings it closer to the OECD guidelines.

Article 63 of the CIT Law is currently responsible for regulating the transfer pricing regime. This regime falls within the scope of the special anti-abuse measures (Teixeira, 2023). The legislator seeks to prevent abuse through the manipulation of prices in commercial transactions between entities that are in a situation of unique relations (Teixeira, 2023).

According to Teixeira (2021) tax abuse is any act that seeks to postpone tax compliance or reduce tax payments. In this sense, the penalty established for non-compliance with the regime is defined in Chapter III, Section VI, in particular in Subsection I of the CIT Law, under the heading of "corrections for the purposes of determining the tax base". In situations of non-compliance with the regime, corrections may be made to the tax base, and the missing tax, interest and related fines will be due.

In Portugal, this regime covers residents (individuals or legal persons) and non-residents in Portuguese territory. The transfer pricing regime seeks to prevent manipulation of the tax base by adjusting prices in transactions between related parties. These practices are often carried out by multinationals or integrated economic groups. However, this regime is not restricted to transactions between related parties but is also applicable in situations of complete independence. In this context, the transfer pricing regime may cover operations in which there is a common economic interest between unrelated parties. In 2021 the TP regime was significantly altered by the publication of Ordinances 268/2021 and 267/2021, both of November 26.

The transfer pricing regime falls within the scope of special anti-abuse measures (Teixeira, 2023), and Articles 63 and 64 of the CIT Law regulate this system. It aims to prevent the manipulation of the tax base, through adjustments to the prices charged between intra-group entities, with the aim of saving the tax burden. The TP regime applies to resident and non-resident entities, individuals and companies.

Failure to comply with the regime gives rise to the application of a sanction. In particular, the legislator determines the correction of the tax base determination. This means that non-compliance with the regime could result in the correction of the tax base, payment of the missing tax, interest, and any associated fines.

b. The concept of special relationships

Article 9 of the OECD Model Tax Convention on Income and on Capital clarifies that two companies are associates if one of them participates in the management, control or capital of the other (OECD, 2019). The same convention also clarifies that companies fulfil the requirements of associates if the same entities participate directly or indirectly in the management, control or capital of both companies (OECD, 2019). However, the Portuguese legislator opted not for the concept of associated companies, as provided for in the OECD Convention, but for a broader concept, which is the concept of "special relationships between two entities".

This concept significantly changed with Law 30-G/2000 of 29 December. Before this change, the existence of special relationships was a matter for discussion between the tax authorities and the taxpayer (Ramos, 2024).

Currently, article 63 of the Portuguese CIT law states that the application of the transfer pricing regime depends on the fulfilment of specific conditions. In particular, (1) the existence of special relationships between the parties, (2) as a result of these relationships, conditions are established that are different from those that would be established between independent parties, and (3) that lead to the calculation of a tax result that differs from what would be calculated if these relationships did not exist (Correia & Martins, 2018). Thus, the existence of special relationships is a determining factor in the application of the TP regime.

Therefore, the concept of special relationships plays a crucial role in the application of the transfer pricing regime. In this sense, Article 63 (paragraph 4) clarifies in what terms special relationships exist. They occur between two entities when one party has the power to exercise, directly or indirectly, significant influence over the management decisions of the other. Therefore, one party can interfere in the transfer pricing policy. Although the Portuguese legislator has not defined the concept of significant influence, it presents a set of indicators in which this influence is considered to be verified. These assumptions refer to situations of interference in management, corporate links, community of interest and intervention by corporate bodies (Ramos, 2024). In this sense, this standard lists examples of situations in which there is a relationship of influence (Correia & Martins, 2018).

Special relationships are when the parties are: (i) an entity and the owners of the capital (or their family members) hold, directly or indirectly, a stake equal to or greater than 20 per cent of the capital; (ii) entities owned by the same owners of the capital; (iii) an entity and the members of its governing bodies; and (iv) companies that are in a control relationship; (v) entities in a situation of dependence in the exercise of activity; and (vi) relationships between a resident entity (or permanent establishment) and an entity subject to a privileged tax regime.

The Portuguese domestic law considers a wider range of situations than those in the OECD Model Convention. It is because the legal system admits that there may be other realities in which there are special relations between companies. In this context, the term "tied transactions" stands out. This concept is defined in Ministerial Order 268/2021 of 26 November. In addition, Article 63 (paragraphs 9 and 10) provides for additional situations that are also covered by the transfer pricing regime.

For the purposes of transparency, the law requires taxpayers to identify the entities with which they have special relationships. This information is provided each year in the annual accounting and tax statement for the period to which the return relates. In addition, it is required to provide detailed information on these operations.

Proof of the existence of these relationships is essential for the purposes of applying the transfer pricing rules. The Tax Authority will be able to apply corrections to the tax result once the special relationships have been proven and it has been shown that the conditions applied have led to a different tax result than would have been the case if the transactions had taken place between independent parties (Pires, 2006).

c. Transfer Pricing Methods

Ordinance 268/2021 (article 6) identifies the methods to be adopted by the taxpayer. There are six methods set out in the ordinance, specifically: a) the comparable market price method, b) the reduced resale price method, c) the increased cost method, d) the profit split method, e) the net margin method, and f) other methods (if the methods identified in a) to e) cannot be used).

The Portuguese legislator does not determine a hierarchy in the application of the methods. However, it clarifies that the most appropriate method will be the one that provides a reliable estimate under the terms and conditions that would normally be practised in a competitive situation (Teixeira, 2023).

The comparable uncontrolled price (CUP) Method compares the price of a good (or service), within the scope of a tied transaction, with the price practiced on the free market, in a comparable situation (Carlos et al., 2024). The resale price method takes the resale price practiced in a transaction between independent entities as a starting point. It then deducts an appropriate gross margin, i.e. the amount needed to cover selling costs and other operating expenses.

The cost plus method applies the sum of the amount of costs borne by the supplier and the gross profit margin practiced in a transaction between independent entities. The profit split method uses the overall profit obtained by the parties involved. Subsequently, the profit is split between the parties, taking into account the relative value of each party's contribution to the transaction. Finally, the transactional net margin method is based on calculating the net profit margin obtained in a transaction (or in a series of linked transactions). It is based on the profit margin obtained in a comparable transaction between unrelated entities.

Nevertheless, there is currently an alignment between Ministerial Order 268/2021 and the European Commission's Transfer Pricing Directive. The Portuguese Tax Authority has adopted the correction methodology for the median, which was legally determined in Ordinance no. 268/2021 of November 26.

This Ordinance states that "any positive correction made by the Tax Authority must, as a rule, refer to the value corresponding to the median of the range". This is in line with the proposal for a Transfer Pricing Directive presented by the European Commission (European Commission, 2023). As already mentioned, the PT Directive aims to standardize procedures to be incorporated into the legislation of each Member State. The alignment of the Directive with Ordinance no. 268/2021 of November 26 is evident in the provision for correction to the median, if the positioning of the margin/price is not between the interquartile range.

d. Advance pricing agreements

In Portugal, prior agreements on transfer pricing are provided for in Article 138 of the CIT law, and this possibility was allowed by the 2008 State Budget Law - LOE/2008 (Nabais, 2019). However, Ministerial Order 267/2021 of November 26 regulates the procedures for entering into APAs. APAs can be unilateral when the parties to the agreement are the Tax Authority and the taxpayer, who can be an individual (taxed under the personal income tax) or a legal person (taxed under the corporate income tax).

These agreements can be valid for up to 4 years and can be renewed. In this case, the taxpayer submits a written request and must comply with the stages of the initial process, although the preliminary assessment stage is waived[1]. The application for renewal must be submitted no later than 6 months before the expiry date.

The preliminary phase follows the submission of the initial assessment request. This request must be made no later than 9 months before the start of the first tax period to which the agreement is intended to apply. The proposal must be submitted no later than 6 months before the start of the first tax year. The tax authority then accepts the proposal or not; if it is received, evaluation and negotiation follow.

Article 63 of the CIT Law states that the taxpayer is obliged to follow the arm's length principle. This means that, in connected transactions, the price that would be charged in a comparable transaction between unrelated entities must be charged (Pereira, 2023).

Ministerial Order 1446-C/2001 of December 21 explains that each operation must be analysed individually. If the operations are interconnected, they must be assessed together. In this context, Ministerial Order 1446-C/2001 of December 21 requires the principle to be applied to the operations listed in paragraph 2.

5. SOLUTIONS AND RECOMMENDATIONS

Even though the OECD has worked hard to achieve tax uniformity in this area through its guidelines and directives, the issue of transfer pricing has not been resolved. Changing the paradigm on which the taxation of multinational companies is based is the only way to eliminate transfer pricing as a tax evasion mechanism. Profit shifting and the erosion of taxable bases are still possible due to different tax systems in other jurisdictions.

Many countries have flaws in their transfer pricing legislation, which makes it difficult to solve the problem. In this context, it is essential to evolve (1) the paradigm, (2) international trade and (3) the way companies operate. This evolution must take place through changes in international and national legislation, which will allow changes to the current paradigm.

6. FUTURE RESEARCH DIRECTIONS

Despite the relevance of this research, there are still many issues that have not been properly developed. The transfer pricing regime is a tax measure that seeks to promote tax compliance on the part of taxpayers. At a time when there is so much talk about sustainability issues, it would be important to analyse the relationship between transfer pricing and environmental issues. In particular, to research the role of phenomena such as the erosion of the tax base and profit shifting with the issue of the sustainability of public accounts in different jurisdictions.

7. CONCLUSION

Transfer pricing practices can affect various types of taxes, such as income tax, value-added tax, and customs duties. Non-compliance with the arm's length principle can result in reduced tax revenue from these taxes due to tax evasion or profit shifting. This non-compliance leads to an improper allocation of taxable profits.

The transfer pricing regime aims to ensure that transactions between related entities are conducted under the same conditions as those between independent entities in similar transactions. By adhering to the arm's length principle, the goal is to establish equitable tax treatment for both integrated companies (such as those in international groups) and independent companies. Additionally, the regime serves to counter potential tax evasion practices and safeguard the tax bases of states.

Portuguese legislation still requires further clarification regarding the transfer pricing matter in intangible transactions, necessitating adjustments in the tax system. Addressing the challenge of transfer pricing as a means of tax evasion will require a fundamental shift in the approach to taxing multinational corporations. The OECD has been steadfast in its efforts to promote tax consistency in this field through its guidelines and directives. However, the challenge of transfer pricing still demands attention, as profit shifting and the erosion of taxable bases continue to be potential concerns arising from differing tax systems across jurisdictions.

REFERENCES

Alsultan, S. K. (2021, Apr). The Gulf Cooperation Council (GCC) States: New Players in the International Tax Competition Game [Article]. *Intertax, 49*(4), 361-377. <Go to ISI>://WOS:000637826200007

Andrade, T. (2023, Nov). Transfer Pricing and Customs Valuation Rules in Brazil: A Challenging Reconciliation [Article]. *Global Trade and Customs Journal, 18*(11-12), 461-468. <Go to ISI>://WOS:001107742400007

Barreiros, J. A. R. M., Teixeira, M. A. C., & Ferreira, H. Q. (1984). *Código da contribuição industrial: anotado e comentado [Industrial Contribution Code: annotated and commented]*. Rei dos Livros. http://books.google.pt/books?id=P24pHQAACAAJ

Blank, J. D. (2009, Aug). OVERCOMING OVERDISCLOSURE: TOWARD TAX SHELTER DETECTION [Article]. *Ucla Law Review, 56*(6), 1629-1690. <Go to ISI>://WOS:000269944800001

Bormotova, A., Glubokova, N., Agapova, A., Alyshev, I., Larkova, E., & Lomakina, D. (2021). ASPECTS OF APPLICATION OF TAX CONTROL BY COUNTRIES FOR CROSS-BORDER OPERATIONS [Review]. *International Review (Steubenville, Ohio)*, (3-4), 173–184. DOI: 10.5937/intrev2103186B

Carlos, A. B., Abreu, I. A., Durão, J. R., & Pimenta, M. E. (2024). *Guia dos impostos em Portugal* [Guide to taxes in Portugal]. Quid Juris.

Catarino, J. R., & Diogo, S. (2024). BEPS, Boa Governança, Concorrência, e Competitividade Fiscal. [BEPS, Good Governance, Competition and Fiscal Competitiveness] In Catarino, J. R., & Pereira, P. R. (Eds.), *Fiscalidade Internacional. Questões Atuais*. Almedina.

Choi, J. P., Ishikawa, J., & Okoshi, H. (2024, April). Tax havens and cross-border licensing with transfer pricing regulation [Article]. *International Tax and Public Finance*, 31(2), 333–366. DOI: 10.1007/s10797-022-09770-w PMID: 36532959

Correia, S., & Martins, A. (2018). *Preços de Transferência, Litigância e Arbitragem Fiscal* [Transfer Pricing, Litigation and Tax Arbitration]. Petrony.

Cugova, A., & Cug, J. (2019, Apr 10-11). News and Changes in Slovak Transfer Pricing Rules. [Education excellence and innovation management through vision 2020]. 33rd International-Business-Information-Management-Association (IBIMA) Conference, Granada, SPAIN.

da Silva, B. A. (2024). BEPS 2.0: Os Pilares Um e Dois e a Tributação da Economia Digital. [BEPS 2.0: Pillars One and Two and the Taxation of the Digital Economy] In Catarino, J. R., & Pereira, P. R. (Eds.), *Fiscalidade Internacional. Questões Atuais*. Almedina.

Dias, A. C. G. (2024). *Preços de Transferência [Transfer Pricing]*. Ordem dos Contabilistas Certificados.

do Amaral, D. F. (2017). *Manual de Introdução ao Direito* [Handbook of Introduction to Law]. Vol. I). Almedina.

Dourado, A. P. (2018). *Governação Fiscal Global* [Global Tax Governance]. 2nd ed.). Almedina.

Dourado, A. P. (2019). *Direito fiscal* [Tax Law]. 4th ed.). Almedina.

Esteller-Moré, A., Rizzo, L., & Secomandi, R. (2021). The role of tax system complexity on foreign direct investment [Article]. *Applied Economics*, 53(45), 5208–5220. DOI: 10.1080/00036846.2021.1922587

European Commission. (2023). *Proposal for a Council Directive on transfer pricing*

Fehling, D. (2022). Addressing Base Erosion and Profit Shifting: The Implementation of the ATAD in Germany [Article]. *Intertax*, 50(10), 721–729. https://www.scopus.com/inward/record.uri?eid=2-s2.0-85138153176&partnerID=40&md5=7b9a5267579ff94eff9bd99ccbbf8237. DOI: 10.54648/TAXI2022076

Ferreira, A. (2020). IVA e Preços de Transferência [VAT and Transfer Pricing]. *Revista Electrónica de Fiscalidade da AFP, 2*(II).

Greil, S. (2021). The arm's length principle in the 21st century - a literature overview. *Journal of Tax Administration*, 6(2), 148–198.

Grinenko, J., Melnychuk, D., Mykhalchyshyna, L., Belei, S., & Yevtushenko, N. (2021, May). IMPROVING TRANSFER PRICING IN UKRAINE USING AMERICAN EXPERIENCE [Article]. *Independent Journal of Management & Production*, 12(3), S205–S231. DOI: 10.14807/ijmp.v12i3.1524

Ignat, L., & Tache, M. (2023, October). Transfer Pricing System of EU Countries: An Analysis in the Context of SDGS [Article]. *Transylvanian Review of Administrative Sciences*, (70E), 45–66. DOI: 10.24193/tras.70E.3

Istok, M., Solilová, V., & Brychta, K. (2022, December). Challenges in transfer pricing: A concept of safe harbours for financial transactions [Article]. *Financial Internet Quarterly*, 18(4), 23–34. DOI: 10.2478/fiqf-2022-0025

Krautheim, S., & Schmidt-Eisenlohr, T. (2011). 2011-01-01). Heterogeneous firms, 'profit shifting' FDI and international tax competition. *Journal of Public Economics*, 95(1), 122–133. DOI: 10.1016/j.jpubeco.2010.10.008

Kuropka, K. (2020). Advance Pricing Arrangements as a Tax Strategy Tool for Related Entities. *European Financial and Accounting Journal*, 15(2), 31–44. DOI: 10.18267/j.efaj.240

Laddha, H. (2017). Is India Ready for BEPS?: Foreseeable Problems and Suggestions [Article]. *Intertax, 45*(12), 828-840. <Go to ISI>://WOS:000426266600008

Lu, X. B., & Landry, P. F. (2014, August). Show Me the Money: Interjurisdiction Political Competition and Fiscal Extraction in China [Article]. *The American Political Science Review*, 108(3), 706–722. DOI: 10.1017/S0003055414000252

Lupu, M. (2023, Mar 23-25 Jul 1). International Cooperation and Solving Transfer Pricing Disputes: A Discussion about Mutual Agreement Procedures. [Proceedings of the international conference on business excellence]. 17th Edition of the International Conference on Business Excellence (ICBE), Romania.

Martins, A. (2022). *Valorização de intangíveis e preços de transferência* [Valuation of Intangibles and Transfer Pricing]. Almedina.

Martins, A., & Duarte, F. (2024). *Acordos Prévios sobre Preços de Transferência* [Advance Pricing Agreement]. Petrony.

Morais, R. (2009). Preços de Transferência - "O Sistema Fiscal no Fio da Navalha [Transfer Pricing - "The Tax System on the Razor's Edge]. *Revista de Finanças Públicas e Direito Fiscal, 2*(1).

Muller, A., & Kolk, A. (2015). Responsible Tax as Corporate Social Responsibility: The Case of Multinational Enterprises and Effective Tax in India [Article]. *Business & Society*, 54(4), 435–463. DOI: 10.1177/0007650312449989

Nabais, J. C. (2019). *Direito Fiscal [Tax Law]* (Reimpressão 2023 - 11ª ed.). Almedina.

Nofita, E., Nuryanah, S., Mulyono, K. B., Rahman, Y. A., & Astuti, D. P. (2021, Jul 27-28). Benefit Test Analysis on Intra-Group Services Transactions in Indonesia. *EAI Computing and Communication in Emerging Regions* [Ice-bees 2021]. 4th International Conference on Economics, Business and Economic Education Science (ICE-BEES), Semarang, INDONESIA.

OECD. (2013). *Addressing Base Erosion and Profit Shifting [Combate à Erosão da Base Tributária e à Transferência de Lucros].*

OECD. (2014). *Action Plan on Base Erosion and Profit Shifting [Plano de ação para o combate à erosão da base tributária e à transferência de lucros].*

OECD. (2015). *Transfer Pricing Documentation and Country-by-Country Reporting, Action 13 - 2015 Final Report.*

OECD. (2019). *Model Tax Convention on Income and on Capital 2017 (Full Version).* OECD Publishing.

OECD. (2022). *OECD Transfer Pricing Guidelines for Multinational Enterprises and Tax Administrations 2022.*

Ogunoye, A. A., Ibitoye, O. J., & Kleynhans, E. P. J. (2023, Mar). Manipulation of transfer prices by multi-national companies in Nigeria [Article]. *South African Journal of Economic and Management Sciences, 26*(1), 7, Article a4657. https://doi.org/DOI: 10.4102/sajems.v26i1.4657

Oguttu, A. W. (2020). Challenges of Applying the Comparability Analysis in Curtailing Transfer Pricing: Evaluating the Suitability of Some Alternative Approaches in Africa [Article]. *Intertax, 48*(1), 74-102. <Go to ISI>://WOS:000584419900006

Pereira, M. H. F. (2023). *Fiscalidade* [Taxation]. 7th ed.). Almedina.

Peters, C. (2022, Jan). Critical Analysis of the General Court's 'EU Arm's Length Tool': Beware of the Reflexivity of Transfer Pricing Law! [Review]. *Ec Tax Review, 31*(1), 30-49. <Go to ISI>://WOS:000754866100004

Pires, J. A. R. (2006). *Os Preços de Transferência* [Transfer Pricing]. Grupo Editorial Vida Económica.

Ramos, L. P. (2024). Preços de Transferência. [Transfer Pricing] In Catarino, J. R., & Pereira, P. R. (Eds.), *Fiscalidade Internacional. Questões Atuais*. Almedina.

Sebele-Mpofu, F., Mashiri, E., & Schwartz, S. C. (2021, Jan). An exposition of transfer pricing motives, strategies and their implementation in tax avoidance by MNEs in developing countries [Article]. *Cogent Business & Management, 8*(1), 25, Article 1944007. https://doi.org/DOI: 10.1080/23311975.2021.1944007

Teixeira, G. (2021). *Glossário Fiscal* [Tax Glossary]. Almedina.

Teixeira, G. (2023). *Preços de Transferência [Transfer Pricing].* Editora D'Ideias.

Vaz, P. F. A. C. (2013). *O Contributo do Código Aduaneiro Comunitário nos Preços de Transferência* [The Contribution of the Community Customs Code to Transfer Pricing]. Universidade do Porto.

KEY TERMS AND DEFINITIONS

Transfer Pricing: Economic groups engage in transactions that could provide an economic advantage for the companies involved.

Arm's length principle: This principle determines that in intra-group transactions, multinational companies should act as if they were transactions between independent companies.

Transfer Pricing Regime: Ensures that the conditions applied in transactions between related entities are identical to those used between independent entities in similar transactions.

BEPS: Report Combating Base Erosion and Profit Shifting published by OCDE.

Direct Taxation: Composed by taxes that are levied on direct manifestations of the ability to pay, in particular personal and corporate income taxes.

Advance pricing agreements (APAs): APAs are agreements between taxpayers and one or more tax administrations.

Related Entities: Whether the same entities participate directly or indirectly in the management, control or capital of both companies.

ENDNOTES

1 Article 14 of Ordinance no. 627/2021.

Chapter 17
Trends and Perspectives on Tax Benefits Research:
A Bibliometric Analysis

Carlos Lucas
https://orcid.org/0000-0003-1973-7718
University of Aveiro, Portugal

Sérgio Ravara Cruz
https://orcid.org/0000-0002-4454-2800
University of Aveiro, Portugal

Cecília Rendeiro Carmo
https://orcid.org/0000-0002-1883-5490
University of Aveiro, Portugal

ABSTRACT

Reducing taxation is a relevant and cross-cutting issue in society, at the level of governments, companies and citizens. There are currently a large number of scientific publications on this subject. The aim of this study is to present a mapping of scientific production on the subject of tax benefits, which will make it possible to understand the evolution and trends of research in this area. A bibliometric analysis was carried out using the Bibliometrix tool, based on the documents available on the Scopus and Web of Science platforms. The results show that the greatest growth in research on this topic has occurred from the beginning of this century to the present day. The use of dominant expressions is also observed, resulting in two clusters that separate research into tax benefits at a company level from those at an individual level. This result suggests the need for future studies to deal separately with corporate and personal tax benefits.

DOI: 10.4018/979-8-3693-3908-4.ch017

INTRODUCTION

In a letter addressed to Jean Baptiste Le Roy on November 13, 1789, Benjamin Franklin wrote "In this world nothing can be said to be certain, except death and taxes".[1] After more than two centuries, it is clear that this phrase is full of meaning. Taxes are part of the society in which we live on a permanent basis, because they are a way for states to obtain revenues, which serve for the redistribution of income, and thus guarantee to the citizens who live in them a set of common goods and services that make it possible to satisfy collective needs (Santos, 1989). This is the scenario of a Fiscal State – in which taxes are the main source of revenue – to achieve a Social State – tax revenues to be channeled to the satisfaction of the collective needs of citizens, thus performing the social function of taxes.

The tax burden has a transversal impact on the life of society, both at the private and business level. Every act we do is affected in some way by taxes. In this way, this theme presents itself as a current and relevant subject that arouses interest when related to other areas. Given that taxation, directly or indirectly, causes a decrease in acquired wealth, there is a natural tendency for society to seek to minimize its impact through tax planning. Given the several ways that may exist for tax optimization, the use of tax benefits becomes vitally important.

As a result of the above, in the academic field, research in the field of taxation has also taken on greater importance over the years and its growth is notorious. From the end of the twentieth century and in the 2000s onwards, the study of taxation, and in particular tax benefits, has grown very markedly and is expected to continue to develop. The research carried out has been addressing several aspects of taxation, namely the issues related to the taxation options of the states (Shaw, 2021) and the forms of taxation (Cnossen, 1998; Prophet & Scabrosetti, 2017).

Tax benefits are incentives promoted by states, which allow companies and citizens to reduce the tax impact on their lives and operations. These are created by governments within the framework of defined policy guidelines and with the purpose of achieving certain objectives. Tax benefits work as tools that aim to encourage or guide management options of companies and people in a certain direction. Depending on the political orientations of the states and the needs of the society it is intended to supply, the reduction in taxation can have different targets (Angelopoulos et al., 2009). Research has been studying the several issues that arise around this topic, such as the strengthening of capital versus debt structures in companies (Cruz & Soares, 2022; Fonseca et al., 2020), or support for development in current contexts such as measures to promote sustainability (Kolesnikov, 2023), or even reductions in household income taxation (Schanzenbach & Strain, 2021).

Researchers have been studying these different aspects and the scientific production on this topic is already very extensive, making it necessary to map publications in this area. In this context, the objective of this study is to present a mapping of scientific research in the field of tax benefits and for that carry out a bibliometric analysis of publications on this domain, based on documents available on the Scopus and Web of Science platforms between 1997 and 2024, seeking to answer the following research questions:

RQ1. How has the number of publications evolved over time?

RQ2. What are the most relevant sources in this area?

RQ3. Who are the most influential authors on this topic?

RQ4. What are the most cited publications on this topic?

RQ5. How have keywords evolved over time?

RQ6: What relationships are established between different approaches to the subject of tax benefits, through the analysis of co-citations?

To this end, in a first phase, several research and readings were carried out with the aim of identifying in the literature all the terms and expressions used to designate tax benefits, seeking to understand their particularities. Once these terms and expressions were identified, they were considered as equivalent expressions and synonyms of tax benefits, being used in the research strategy aimed at selecting the documents to be analyzed in the bibliometric study. The bibliometric analysis was carried out using the R software, more specifically the Bibliometrix package and the Biblioshiny tool, from which the outputs presented were obtained. The results show that the approach to the issue of tax benefits is carried out from the perspective of taxes on individual citizens and on the other hand from a corporate perspective, namely to companies. It is found that most of the studies originate in the Western world and that it is a growing area of study since the beginning of the century. It was possible to structure a list of terms/expressions that define the tax benefits and the different perspectives of analysis, so it is interesting to study each of the specific areas in the future.

After this Introduction, the document is structured as follows. In the following section, the background is presented where the concepts that support the study are introduced. The methodology used is described below, and then the results obtained. In the final part, the discussion of results and their conclusions.

BACKGROUND

Research into the subject of taxation has been increasing over time. The different aspects of this topic and the existence of several taxes, with different impacts and influences on society, lead research to seek answers to some of the questions that arise. Due to the importance of the topic, there are already studies that present a review of tax research (Graham et al., 2012; Hanlon & Heitzman, 2010; Maydew, 2001; Shackelford & Shevlin, 2001).

The subject of taxation is broadly covered. From the point of view of taxation on individuals and families, research has focused on the relationship between the taxes on income and taxes on consumption, as well as the impact on society of the policies regarding these taxes (Correia, 2005; D' et al., 2021; Lu et al., 2022). In this research we find the motivations and consequences of welfare policy choices, for example, John and Ii, (2000) finds that there are more implications for social welfare when there are changes in consumption taxes than in income taxes. In this respect Auerbach (2006) finds that different economic behaviors can be related to different applications of consumption or income tax rates. Regarding the social and employment angle, research seeks empirical evidence on the effects of tax policies implemented (Milligan & Stabile, 2011; Schanzenbach & Strain, 2021).

From the perspective of companies, taxes are an influential factor of economic performance and return on equity, since the net (and distributable) income depends on income taxes. This means that taxation influences management and/or shareholders decision-making. The literature focuses on the use of tax benefits as a tax relief tool and on earnings management to minimize income taxes. Some authors endeavors to establish this relationship and prove that earnings management influences companies board in their decisions, so that lower tax rates or tax benefits contribute positively to these decisions (Gregova et al., 2021; Tachinakis, 2022), including resorting to countries with more flexible tax regimes. Other authors have tried to establish a relationship between the use of tax benefits and capital structure choices. Since debt contracting allows a reduction in the tax burden through the deduction of financing costs, allowing for a greater return on the investments, income taxes may influence the financing options of the company managers. The tax effect on earnings influences the payment of dividends, therefore those options are also of the interest of the company owners (Faccio & Xu, 2015; Krämer, 2015). Research on capital structures and the choices made in the light of the tax impact show that taxation is important when deciding capital structures (Czerwonka & Jaworski, 2017; Hernádi & Ormos, 2012; Mishra, 2011).

Taxation assumes a determining role in society and influences the behavior and decisions of those who make it up, citizens and companies alike, who rationally seek tax optimization or reduction.

Tax benefits represent a tax relief and can take several forms and designations, all having in common the fact that they imply a lower amount of tax that a person or company must pay, compared to what it would pay if such a benefit did not exist. Tax relief can be achieved in a several ways, including deductions from the tax base or reductions in the tax payable. The reduction in taxation that tax benefits provide can also be seen as a tool that governments use to encourage behaviors, in people or companies, that are in line with certain political strategies.

Depending on their specific characteristics and applications, the tax relief measures that we refer here generically as tax benefits, can have several designations in the literature. Table 1 describes these designations and indicates examples of studies in which they were used.

Table 1. Tax benefit designations

Term / Expression	Description	Citations
Tax benefit	Measures promoted by the government that may lead to reductions in the level of the rates to be applied, tax base, or exemptions. These measures are taken on the assumption that the decrease in state revenue will be outweighed by the underlying public benefit.	(Graham, 2000; Milligan & Stabile, 2011; Wu et al., 2012)
Tax credit	It is a form of tax benefit, in which the reduction of taxation occurs through a direct reduction on the tax payable.	(Bloom et al., 2002a; Dahl & Lochner, 2012; Meyer & Rosenbaum, 2001)
Tax deduction	It comprises a tax reduction through the use of deductions from the amount that will serve as the basis for the application of tax rates.	(Leuven & Oosterbeek, 2004; Parry & Bento, 2000; Wang et al., 2021)
Tax incentive	It aims to promote choices in a certain direction through the use of a tax advantage. It is used by governments to steer economies in a certain direction.	(Graham & Rogers, 2002; Pence, 2006; Song et al., 2020)
Tax relief	It refers to decisions taken by governments to promote tax relief, i.e. a reduction in the tax burden that already exists and is considered high.	(Eom et al., 2014; Gale & Potter, 2002; Scharf & Smith, 2015)
Tax shield	It consists of rules that allow to avoid taxation in some way and thus reduce the tax impact on a given act.	(Fernandez, 2004; Kemsley & Nissim, 2002; Y. C. Liu, 2009)
Tax holidays	This is a temporary reduction consisting on measures taken for a certain period of time to meet the objectives assumed by the states in the short term and for specific topics.	(Albring et al., 2011; Chan & Mo, 2000; Lin, 2006)

METHODOLOGY

Bibliometrics/bibliometric analysis

The dissemination of scientific knowledge is the culmination of research and the final contribution to the overall enrichment of knowledge at a global level. With the current volume of scientific dissemination, to be able to analyze what is published by the scientific community, it will be necessary to use current digital tools, so it can be able to structure data that help to have a perception of the state of the art (Aria & Cuccurullo, 2017; Donthu et al., 2021; Jones et al., 2011). From authors, journals and themes of the documents, it is relevant to develop analyses that allow to guide the work, making it more efficient, namely for the direction of future research, through the discovery of possible research gaps.

Interest in the statistics of scientific publications comes from back the 20s of the twentieth century, when Lotka (1926) published an innovative statistical study on scientific production, which gave rise to Lotka's Law, in which the frequency of publication of authors in each period of time is described. Quoting Lotka (1926, p. 317) "It would be of interest to determine, if possible, the part which men of different caliber contribute to the progress of science". With the evolution of the dissemination of scientific knowledge, already in the 60's Derek John de Solla Price published the books called "Science since Babylon" (Price, 1961) and "Little Science - Big Science" (Price, 1963) which at that time revolutionized the interest in quantitative aspects related to the dimension of scientific dissemination and the use of measurement indicators such as the "Science Citation Index (SCI)" introduced by Garfield (1955).

Technological evolution has allowed for a high level of data processing and bibliographic metrics have developed significantly, also with the collaboration of databases that have been structured over time. Bibliometrics is no longer a "hobby" of some interested in scientific dissemination and has become a specific science that allows the collection and processing of data to facilitate subsequent analysis.

Currently, databases for scientific research such as "Scopus" or "Web of Science" have their own statistical tools with several metrics that allow users to build bibliometric studies. These tools apply several metrics to documents, authors, journals, connections between documents and subjects covered, or even the most commonly words or topics. Together with the databases, tools have also been developed for the analysis and treatment of the collected information, which enables the synthesis of large volumes of information and their grouping by pre-established indicators, as is the case of "Bibliometrix". These applications are developed specifically for the treatment of scientific publications and as such have parameterizations that allow in a simple way to analyze the data collected and present in a structured way the set of information contained in these documents, namely and similarly to Scopus and the Web of Science, these applications also use metrics that allow measuring and evaluating the scientific production carried out over time.

In this study, bibliometric analysis is used, which is considered by the scientific community as the most rigorous method for the statistical analysis of a higher number of scientific publications and which has proved to be fundamental in research in the accounting and financial area (Donthu et al., 2021; Moreira et al., 2020). This is also the best way to answer to a research question from the available studies, as it is a rigorous process of collecting and analyzing the several existing studies (Ellegaard & Wallin, 2015; Glänzel & Leuven, 2003).

The methodology used in this research followed the guidelines defined as the best bibliometric analysis technique (Donthu et al., 2021; Mukherjee et al., 2022). The steps followed to construct this analysis were as follows.

1. The process began by defining the scope of the study, which is the mapping of trends and perspectives around tax benefits, to organize the research and subsequent collection of information.
2. Next, the ways of searching and the information to be obtained were defined, particularly in relation to the countries and authors with the greatest influence in this field of research and the specific topics most studied, in an attempt to find research trends. At this stage, we defined the terms that would allow us to obtain the best results.
3. Once the data had been collected and structured, the information was prepared to present the results and conclusions. The Bibliometrix tool was used to process the data.
4. Finally, we move forward to summarize and describe the results obtained, ending with a presentation of the conclusions we reached.

The following section describes in detail how the analysis process was carried out.

Research Strategy and Sample Selection

This research is based on the research and analysis of documents available on the Scopus and Web of Science platforms, as they are considered the best and most comprehensive sources of scientific information (Pranckutė, 2021). Given the diversity of terms and expressions that can be used to designate tax benefits at the international level, a preliminary phase of the bibliometric study consisted of conducting research and reading to identify all the terms and expressions used in the literature to designate tax benefits. Their selection was defined on the basis of the perception gained in the process of researching the subject (Ensslin et al., 2015). These terms and expressions were presented in detail in the Background section of the present work (Table 1) and are now used as keywords in the research strategy of the bibliometric study, as shown in Table 2.

Table 2. Keywords used to designate tax benefits

Keywords List
Tax Benefit*
Tax Credit*
Tax Deduction*
Tax Incentive*
Tax Relief*
Tax Shield*
Tax Holidays*
Note: (*) applied to the length of words in the search

Subsequently, and using the same platforms, a first search strategy was carried out, looking for documents that contained the keywords selected in the title of the document, without imposing any filter or limitation, in order to have contact with all the published content. The aim was to obtain a total collection to assess the size and characteristics of the sample of documents that returned from this research. This first search strategy returned 2747 documents in Scopus and 2869 documents in the Web of Science.

The analysis of the documents returned by this research strategy allowed us to conclude that they covered several areas of study, namely in the areas of medicine, chemistry or arts and humanities. These studies address tax benefits in an indirect way, and this is not what is intended in this work. On the other hand, different types of documents can also be found in the collected publications, such as editorials, news, letters or conference summaries. For these reasons, it was decided to refine the search strategy, applying filters in the "Subject/Research area" and in the "Document type" as described in table 3.

Table 3. Search refine applied

Scopus – Research Refine	WoS - Research Refine
Subject area:	**Research area:**
Economics, Econometrics and Finance	Business Economics
Social Sciences	
Business, Management and Accounting	
Document type:	**Document type:**
Article	Article
Book chapter	

With the application of the above filters, the results returned are from 1645 documents in Scopus and 1241 documents in Web of Science.

The files were then uploaded to the Bibliometrix platform. This platform is used to work the information gathered and assist in the construction of the bibliometric study (Aria & Cuccurullo, 2017). Through this application, the information is re-exported in Excel format, where it will be managed to identify potential export errors, elimination of duplications, as well as other misrepresentations that may influence the final treatment of the data.

In the work of preparing the data obtained for the study, information gaps were observed at the level of the bibliometric analysis items. It was sought, through the cross-referencing of research in different sources, to collect as much data as possible to complete the relevant fields for the bibliometric analysis. Using the title of the publication, information was cross-referenced in Scopus, Web of Science, Research-Gate, Google Scholar and the Google search engine itself. This procedure made it possible to reach other sources of information, such as publishers, universities or other academic information database platforms. In this way, it was possible to obtain missing information in the initial collections and thus ensure a more rigorous study with a greater number of documents containing complete information for treatment.

In the next phase, the two collections were unified into a single file. To this end, the columns were standardized with bibliometric information so that the correspondence would be accurate. Once the unified file was obtained, progress was made to the elimination of duplicate publications, which in a first phase was carried out by automatic correspondence of the title. Subsequently, all the information was revised to detect duplicates where there could be small differences in writing that did not have an automatic correspondence and thus ensure the total absence of duplicate publications.

After all the procedures, the final sample consisted of 1555 documents. The sample selection process is summarized in Table 4:

Table 4. Stages of the research strategy

Stages	Source	Query	Results
1	Scopus	(TITLE("tax benefit*" OR "tax credit*" OR "tax deduction*" OR "tax relief*" OR "tax incentive*" OR "tax shield*" OR "tax holiday*"))	2747
	Web of Science	(TITLE("tax benefit*" OR "tax credit*" OR "tax deduction*" OR "tax relief*" OR "tax incentive*" OR "tax shield*" OR "tax holiday*"))	2869
2	Scopus	Limitations (Subject/Research area and Document type)	1645
	Web of Science	Limitations (Subject/Research area and Document type)	1241

continued on following page

Table 4. Continued

Stages	Source	Query	Results
3	Scopus + WoS	Final sample after elimination of duplicated documents	1555

Subsequently, the keywords were analyzed and some terms, acronyms and expressions that had the same meaning were standardized. Distortions resulting from file exports, such as unreadable characters, have also been corrected. Finally, it was decided to combine the author keywords with the keywords plus, eliminating duplicates, to obtain a more complete analysis.

As the objective of this study is to carry out a mapping trends of tax benefits topic, keywords were replaced according to the keywords used in the searches carried out. The selection of converted keywords is available in Appendix I. Finally, some keywords were eliminated, namely acronyms out of context, which biased the study and did not allow a relationship with the others.

RESULTS

Type of documents and evolution through time

The 1555 documents that make up the sample were published during the timespan defined between 1997 and 2024 (until the month of April). As can be seen from Table 5, from the total documents, 1401 are articles and 154 are book chapters. These publications are distributed in 758 journals and books (sources), encompassing 2823 authors and involving 3945 keywords and 49771 bibliographic references.

Table 5. General information

Description	Results
Documents	
Article	1401
Book Chapter	154
Total Documents	1555
Timespan	1997 to 2024 (Till April)
Sources (Journals, Books, etc)	758
Authors	2823

continued on following page

Table 5. Continued

Description	Results
Keywords	3945
References	49771

As can be confirmed by Figure 1, and in response to the first research question (RQ1), there has been an increase in the number of studies about tax benefits since the beginning of this century, with a consistent increase in the number of publications. In 1997, there were 14 documents; in 2000, 24; in 2010, 67; in 2020, 103; and, in 2023, 143 publications. In the year 2024, at the time of data collection (April), 46 documents had been published.

Figure 1. Number of documents per year (Output obtained from Bibliometrix)

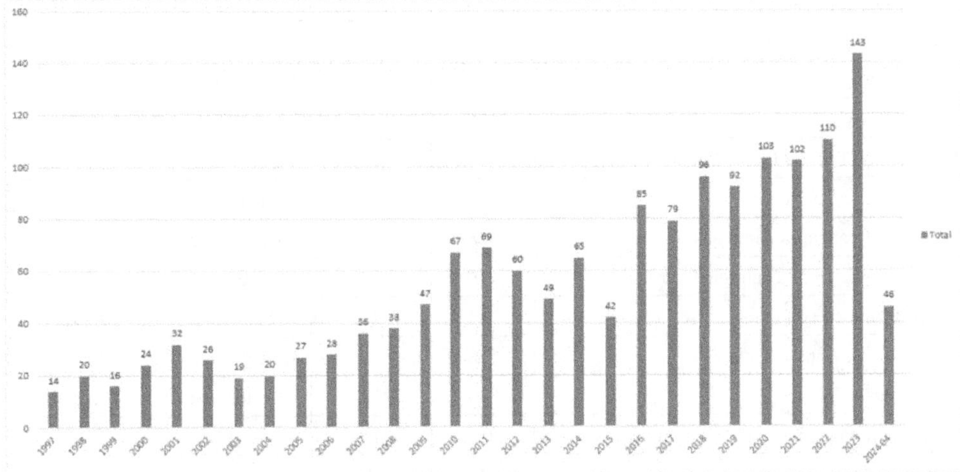

The oldest publication found in the collected results corresponds to the work that Averett et al. (1997) aimed to study the impact of tax credits granted to support related to childcare, such as children's daycare, which aimed to promote the search for employment by women with children. This study concluded that there was a positive relationship between this type of tax support and the increase in the number of women with children looking for work.

Sources

Regarding the relevance of the sources, and to be able to answer the second research question (RQ2), the 20 sources with the highest number of citations were identified, which are presented in Table 6.

Table 6. The 20 sources with the highest number of citations

Journal	Total Citations	Number of Papers	Country	Source Type
Journal of Public Economics	1511	30	Netherlands	Journal
Journal of Finance	1421	6	United Kingdom	Journal
American Economic Journal: Economic Policy	998	13	United States	Journal
Research Policy	926	11	Netherlands	Journal
National Tax Journal	870	56	United States	Journal
American Economic Review	769	6	United States	Journal
Quarterly Journal of Economics	561	2	United Kingdom	Journal
Energy Policy	506	14	United Kingdom	Journal
International Tax and Public Finance	481	25	United States	Journal
Housing Policy Debate	460	24	United Kingdom	Journal
Review of Economics and Statistics	428	4	United States	Journal
Journal of Accounting and Public Policy	410	4	United States	Journal
Small Business Economics	384	8	Netherlands	Journal
Journal of Cleaner Production	378	7	United Kingdom	Journal
Fiscal Studies	319	12	United States	Journal
Review of Economics of the Household	317	11	Netherlands	Journal
Journal of Financial Economics	314	4	Netherlands	Journal
B.E. Journal of Economic Analysis and Policy	303	7	Germany	Journal
American Sociological Review	296	2	United States	Journal
Regional Science and Urban Economics	256	10	Netherlands	Journal

The journals with the greatest relevance in the field of tax benefits and in the period analyzed are the Journal of Public Economics (1,511 citations), followed by the Journal of Finance (1,421 citations) and the American Economic Journal: Economic Policy (998 citations). These three journals originate from the Netherlands, the United Kingdom and the United States, respectively, the latter being the country with the highest number of journals, with a total of 8 out of the 20 most cited, followed by the Netherlands with 6 and the United Kingdom with 5. Germany also appears with 1 source. It turns out that the sources from western economies countries have the highest number of citations. When weighted with the number of publications on the subject under study, the National Tax Journal is the source with the highest number of publications (56 publications), followed by the Journal of Public Economics with 30 publications and International Tax and Public Finance with 25 publications. It should be noted that a source with the highest number of publications is the Journal of Taxation, with 30 publications, but it has little relevance in the number of citations, with a very small number (13 citations) when compared to those in the table above. From the above results it can also be seen that the sources with the highest number of citations are journals and there is no reference to books.

There are currently several metrics to help us to understand the importance of sources and their relevance. In this study, to consolidate the answer to the second research question (RQ2), it was decided to present the CiteScore and the Journal Impact Information of the 20 most cited sources. The choice of these two metrics is related to the fact that both have in consideration the number of citations, which is the basis of evaluation used in this study. Also, because these are metrics used to evaluate the quality, importance and influence of sources (Roldan-Valadez, Salazar-Ruiz, et al., 2019). Table 7 contains these indicators for the 20 most cited sources.

Table 7. CiteScore and JIF indicators of the 20 most cited sources

Journal	Total Citations	Number of Papers	CiteScore (Scopus)	JIF (WoS)
Journal of Public Economics	1511	30	14,1	4,8
Journal of Finance	1421	6	12,9	7,6
American Economic Journal: Economic Policy	998	13	8,2	5,6
Research Policy	926	11	12,8	7,5
National Tax Journal	870	56	3,4	1,8
American Economic Review	769	6	18,6	10,5
Quarterly Journal of Economics	561	2	24,2	11,1
Energy Policy	506	14	17,3	9,3
International Tax and Public Finance	481	25	2,4	1
Housing Policy Debate	460	24	5,4	2,8
Review of Economics and Statistics	428	4	8,5	7,6
Journal of Accounting and Public Policy	410	4	4,8	3,3
Small Business Economics	384	8	14,1	6,5
Journal of Cleaner Production	378	7	20,4	9,7
Fiscal Studies	319	12	13,5	2,2
Review of Economics of the Household	317	11	9,3	4,1
Journal of Financial Economics	314	4	15,8	10,4
B.E. Journal of Economic Analysis and Policy	303	7	1,5	1,1

continued on following page

Table 7. Continued

Journal	Total Citations	Number of Papers	CiteScore (Scopus)	JIF (WoS)
American Sociological Review	296	2	13,3	7,1
Regional Science and Urban Economics	256	10	5,3	3,5

From the data presented, the source with the highest number of citations, the Journal of Public Economics, does not have the best indicators (CS of 14.1 and JIF of 4.8), when compared to the others. The source with the highest indicators is the Quarterly Journal of Economics (CS of 24.2 and JIF of 11.1), but in the subject under study it has only two publications and occupies the seventh position in the number of citations. On the other hand, the source with the highest number of publications (56 publications) has low indicators (CS of 3.4 and JIF of 1.8). As the study has its basis of relevance the number of citations, in answer to question RQ2 we find that the most influential source is the Journal of Public Economics.

Authors

Moving on to the study of the authors, and to answer the third research question (RQ3), the number of citations and the h-index were analyzed. According to Hirsch and Cardona (2007; Roldan-Valadez, Yoselin Salazar-Ruiz, et al., 2019) the h-index, it is a very useful indicator to understand the quality of the authors' scientific production, as well as a prediction of the course of the research in a certain direction. This indicator, initially proposed by Hirsch (2005), establishes a relationship between the number of publications and the number of citations and defines this indicator as a tool to measure the scientific production of researchers. Since then, this indicator has been heavily used, despite the advantages and disadvantages identified by Mingers and Leydesdorff (2015), it continues to be a reference point in the evaluation of researchers and justifies the choice. Table 8 summarizes the information collected on the authors.

Table 8. The 20 authors with the highest number of citations

Author	Total Citations	Country Affiliation	Papers	h-Index
Graham, J. R.	1318	United States	3	3
Lochner, L.	547	United States	3	3
Dahl, G. B.	541	United States	2	2
Meyer, B. D.	526	United States	4	3

continued on following page

Table 8. Continued

Author	Total Citations	Country Affiliation	Papers	h-Index
Rosenbaum, D.	452	United States	1	1
Rogers, D. A.	431	United States	1	1
Milligan, K.	420	Canada	3	3
Van Reenen, J.	392	United Kingdom	3	2
Wu, J.	384	China	2	2
Wu, W.	375	China/United States	3	2
Hoynes, H. W.	369	United States	3	3
Bloom, N.	368	United States	1	1
Griffith, R.	368	United Kingdom	1	1
Wu, C.	359	China/United States	1	1
Zhou, C.	359	China	1	1
Hoynes, H.	353	United States	4	4
Duncan, A.	324	United States	2	2
Zhang, H.	303	China/Canada	3	1
Song, M.	302	China	1	1
Wang, S.	302	China	1	1

Graham, J. R., is the most cited author with 1,318 citations, Lochner, L., com 547 citations and Dahl, G. B., with 541 citations. In a weighting with the number of papers and the h-index indicator, we can see Hoynes, H., has the highest h-index (4) and, together with Meyer, B. D., the highest number of published papers (4), however both have the lowest number of citations in these publications (353 and 526 citations each, respectively). Graham, J. R., holds the article with the highest number of citations (685 citations) called "How big are the tax benefits of debt?", published in the year 2000. Regarding to the country of affiliation of the authors, the United States appears as the country with the largest number (10 authors), followed by China (4 authors), in addition to the fact that these two countries have two more authors who share the affiliation between China and the United States.

Still regarding the authors and the number of articles they publish, the LotkaLaw was applied, which is described as the definition of the frequency of publication of authors in a given period of time (Lotka, 1926), it shows that in the extremes, 2 433 authors have only one paper published on the subject in the selected period and on the other hand 1 author has eleven papers published. Below is the table with the description of all the data in this analysis. Table 9 shows the results obtained

Table 9. LotkaLaw data

Documents written	N. of Authors	Proportion of Authors
1	2433	86,18%
2	274	9,71%
3	78	2,76%
4	22	0,78%
5	8	0,28%
6	4	0,14%
8	2	0,07%
10	1	0,04%
11	1	0,04%

From another perspective and by assessing the origin of the corresponding authors, it was possible to ascertain that the scientific production has its origin diversified by several countries in the world, however, as seen above, the one that stands out the most is the United States of America with 404 papers, followed by China with 94, and the United Kingdom with 53. The journals with the highest number of publications are the National Tax Journal with 56 publications, the Journal of Public Economics with 30, and the Journal of Taxation with 30, as well. The authors with the highest number of publications are Michelmor, K., with 11 publications, Crandall-Hollick, M.L., with 10 and Bargain, O., with 8. Figure 2 presents a three-field analysis between authors, journals, and the author's country of origin to better demonstrate the weight of each of these elements and the relationship between them.

In view of the results presented to the authors and taking in consideration the greater number of citations and the corresponding h-index, it was assessed that the most influential authors have their origin in the United States and the majority of authors have only 1 paper published. The author with the highest h-index is Hoynes, H., and the most cited is Graham, J. R..

Figure 2. Three-field plot (Authors/Sources/Countries) (Output obtained from Bibliometrix)

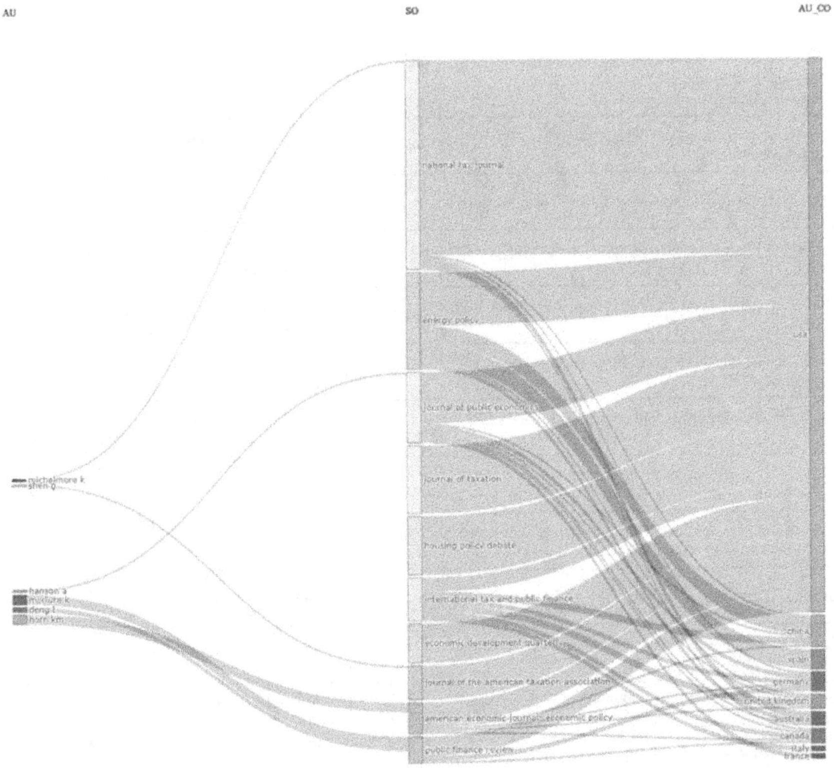

Papers citations

It is also intended to determine which publications are most relevant through the number of citations and thus answer the fourth research question (RQ4).

Of the publications collected, we present in Table 10 the 20 papers with the highest number of citations and, for this reason, the most relevant will be considered. Table 10 also shows the source, year of publication, and country of origin of the research.

Table 10. The 20 most cited papers

Title / Author	Total	Source	Pub. Year	Country
How big are the tax benefits of debt? (Graham, 2000)	685	Journal of Finance	2000	United States
The impact of family income on child achievement: Evidence from the earned income tax credit (Dahl & Lochner, 2012)	526	American Economic Review	2012	United States
Welfare, the earned income tax credit, and the labor supply of single mothers (Meyer & Rosenbaum, 2001)	452	Quarterly Journal of Economics	2001	United Kingdom
Do firms hedge in response to tax incentives? (Graham & Rogers, 2002)	431	Journal of Finance	2002	United States
Do r&d tax credits work? Evidence from a panel of countries 1979-1997 (Bloom et al., 2002b)	368	Journal of Public Economics	2002	United King-dom
Political connections, tax benefits and firm performance: Evidence from china (Wu et al., 2012)	359	Journal of Accounting and Public Policy	2012	China
Could environmental regulation and r&d tax incentives affect green product innovation? (Song et al., 2020)	302	Journal of Cleaner Production	2020	China
Income, the earned income tax credit, and infant health (Hoynes et al., 2015)	288	American Economic Journal: Economic Policy	2015	United States
Evaluating the impact of r&d tax credits on innovation: A microeconometric study on canadian firms (Czarnitzki et al., 2011)	283	Research Policy	2011	Canada
Taxes and the labor market participation of married couples: The earned income tax credit (Eissa & Hoynes, 2004)	259	Journal of Public Economics	2004	United States
Tax incentives to hedge (Graham & Smith, 1999)	202	Journal of Finance	1999	United States
The labour market impact of the working families' tax credit (Blundell et al., 2000)	202	Fiscal Studies	2000	United King-dom
Do child tax benefits affect the well-being of children? Evidence from canadian child benefit expansions (Milligan & Stabile, 2011)	194	American Economic Journal: Economic Policy	2011	Canada
Effects of prenatal poverty on infant health: State earned income tax credits and birth weight (Strully et al., 2010)	186	American Sociological Review	2010	United States
The role of wealth transformations: An application to estimating the effect of tax incentives on saving (Pence, 2006)	185	B.E. Journal of Economic Analysis and Policy	2006	United States
How do tax incentives affect investment and productivity? Firm-level evidence from china (Liu & Mao, 2019)	181	American Economic Journal: Economic Policy	2019	China
Subsidizing the stork: New evidence on tax incentives and fertility (Milligan, 2005)	175	Review of Economics and Statistics	2005	Canada
The impact of the earned income tax credit and social policy reforms on work, marriage, and living arrangements (Ellwood, 2000)	171	National Tax Journal	2000	United States
Beggar thy neighbor? The in-state, out-of-state, and aggregate effects of r&d tax credits (Wilson, 2009)	160	Review of Economics and Statistics	2009	United States
Temporary investment tax incentives: Theory with evidence from bonus depreciation (House & Shapiro, 2008)	158	American Economic Review	2008	United States

It turns out that the study by Graham, J. R., published in 2000 with the title "How Big are the Tax Benefits of Debt?" has the highest number of citations (685 citations). This research work is currently the most cited and studies the impact that tax benefits may have on the debt structure of companies. The author studies the extent to which the use of tax benefits related to the increase in debt can influence its value. In the remaining studies, in addition to focusing on the influence of tax benefits on corporate debt, there is also an approach to tax incentives for research and development, support for households, as well as a reduction of income taxes as support measures. On Table 11 we present the methodologies and main conclusions from the 20 most cited research documents.

Table 11. Methodology and main conclusions of the 20 most cited papers

Title / Author	Methodology	Conclusions
How Big Are the Tax Benefits of Debt? (Graham, 2000)	To study the tax benefit of the use of indebtedness by companies, a simulation of marginal tax rates is designed based on the deduction of the cost of interest on indebtedness in the decrease of taxable income. To carry out the analysis, the information was collected from COMPUSTAT data center in United States and the period studied was from 1973 till 1994.	In general, companies have a conservative behavior regarding the use of debt. They do not take the best advantage of the tax benefit they can have with debt costs. If the debt were used up to the limit of the effect of the marginal tax rate, the tax benefit could increase by 50%. Questions about the reasons why companies are underleveraged and the non-tax benefits associated with financing are topics for future investigations.
The Impact of Family Income on Child Achievement: Evidence From The Earned Income Tax Credit (Dahl & Lochner, 2012)	It is intended to obtain results on the impact that family income may have on decisions that influence children's development. A model is built with instrumental variables that can influence children's development and the relationship with the effect that tax credits can have on the increase in family income. Data from the National Longitudinal Surveys of Youth (NLSY) from 1986 to 2000 were analyzed.	Family income has a relative effect for children from more modest families. The results obtained indicate that scores in math and reading tests improved. It is also concluded that the greatest effect is seen in the most disadvantaged families, in younger children and boys. For future research it will be interesting to study why there is a modest immediate effect, but greater in the long term.
Welfare, The Earned Income Tax Credit, And the Labor Supply of Single Mothers (Meyer & Rosenbaum, 2001)	Through a quasi-experimental model with the use of variables that influence the decision to go to work by single mothers, it seeks to demonstrate the influence of tax credits on income in contrast to the decrease in social benefits or other social support measures for mothers or children. The analysis was carried out using data from the Current Population Survey (CPS) from 1984 to 1996.	The results obtained demonstrate that financial incentives have a positive influence on the decision to go to work by single mothers. It is concluded that tax effects have a greater influence than measures of well-being on the employment decisions of single mothers. Income tax credits played a key role in increasing the employment of single mothers between 1984 and 1996.

continued on following page

Table 11. Continued

Title / Author	Methodology	Conclusions
Do Firms Hedge in Response to Tax Incentives? (Graham & Rogers, 2002)	An empirical study is carried out using multiple regression to study the indebtedness of companies and the risk coverage policies. The information for the analysis was collected from the SEC's Electronic Data Gathering and Retrieval (EDGAR) database, for the year 1994, or tax year 1995.	The relationship between the capital structure and the risk coverage policies is proven. Evidence was also found that companies hedge to increase borrowing capacity and interest deductions. The results obtained do not prove that companies hedge for tax reasons when their tax function is convex, because the tax incentive is small.
Do R&D Tax Credits Work? Evidence From a Panel of Countries 1979-1997 (Bloom et al., 2002b)	In order to study the impact of tax incentives on the level of investments in research and development, an econometric model is used to study the sensitivity of investments in R&D, with data on tax changes and spending on R&D in 9 OECD countries (Australia, Canada, France, Germany, Italy, Japan, Spain, United Kingdom and United States), in the period from 1979 to 1997.	The analysis suggests that tax changes significantly influence the level of R&D, with a greater impact in the long term. It is not possible to conclude that tax incentives in R&D are desirable, because there are other factors to take into account in the cost-benefit analysis, which may even influence the government's policy strategies, making this an endogenous factor that should be studied in future research.
Political Connections, Tax Benefits and Firm Performance: Evidence From China (Wu et al., 2012)	Using regression models, this study aims to investigate the effects of political connections of members of private companies when related to public companies. A sample of Chinese listed companies in the period 1999 to 2007 is used.	It is verified that private companies that have managers with political connections perform better than public companies without managers with political connections. The results obtained also demonstrate that private companies that have managers with political connections can influence the optimization of tax benefits, unlike public companies. On the other hand, it appears that local public companies have greater investment. The study demonstrates that corporate ownership and political relationships are relevant to the performance of companies, whether public or private. Finally, it was found that overinvestment by public enterprises helps the performance of the economy, but negatively influences the performance of companies.

continued on following page

Table 11. Continued

Title / Author	Methodology	Conclusions
Could Environmental Regulation And R&D Tax Incentives Affect Green Product Innovation? (Song et al., 2020)	An empirical study is carried out on the effects of environmental regulations and R&D incentives for sustainable product innovation. Regression models were used to analyze data from 30 provinces in China in the period between 2009 and 2017.	The results confirm that there is no linear relationship between environmental regulations and sustainable product development. The study also shows that tax incentives in R&D are a motivation for investing in sustainable products, because it decreases the risk of that investment. As a result of the various factors that can influence investment in sustainable products, further research is suggested aimed at sectors of activity or certain characteristics of companies.
Income, The Earned Income Tax Credit, And Infant Health (Hoynes et al., 2015)	In this research, a quasi-experimental inductive variation is used to study the effect of income tax credits on child health. Information on children is collected from US databases for the period 1983 to 1999.	Higher income tax credits have been shown to influence children's birth weight, with weight increasing with increasing income. However, overall, the results show an impactful relationship between health and income tax credits.
Evaluating The Impact Of R&D Tax Credits on Innovation: A Microeconometric Study on Canadian Firms (Czarnitzki et al., 2011)	An analytical study is carried out on the data collected in a survey carried out in Canada in 1999, to measure the level of innovation in that country. It aims to study the effects of R&D tax credits on Canadian industries.	It is concluded that the R&D tax credits contributed to the increase in the levels of innovation of the companies that received them. Despite the increase in innovation and the creation of new products, there is no relationship with the performance indicators of the companies considered in the survey.
Taxes And the Labor Market Participation Of Married Couples: The Earned Income Tax Credit (Eissa & Hoynes, 2004)	To evaluate the labor supply for married couples, a survey conducted in the United States with data from 1984 to 1996 and empirical approaches is carried out through the application of the basic experimental and quasi-experimental method, to draw similar qualitative conclusions from both. This study underlies a tax incentive program to promote the incentive of couples to work.	The results suggest that the increase in income tax credits reduces the supply of family labor force. It is a contrast with the labor supply of single mothers that reacts in the opposite direction. The results also indicate that income tax credits are encouraging married mothers not to go to work, with implications for what they had been created.

continued on following page

Table 11. Continued

Title / Author	Methodology	Conclusions
Tax Incentives to Hedge (Graham & Smith, 1999)	For the study of the fiscal convexity of companies as a function of hedging instruments, simulations were used to estimate the potential tax savings with hedging. More than 80 000 observations of annual business information were carried out using the COMPUSTAT database.	The analysis suggests that there is a tax saving in using hedging to stabilize taxable income. This savings can be higher or lower, depending on the tax framework of each company, and on average the volatility of taxable income can be reduced between 1% and 5%. Five points are identified that can influence the impact of these measures, the combination of different hedging instruments, their use in various periods, tax differences that may exist derived from different jurisdictions, the weighting of tax savings with hedge costs and the possibility of tax savings being obtained by means other than hedging.
The Labor Market Impact Of The Working Families' Tax Credit (Blundell et al., 2000)	Based on the beginning of a new regulation in the United Kingdom of tax credits to encourage families to look for work, a model for the study of the labor offer for married couples and single-parent families was estimated. Data were collected from the Family Resources Survey from 1994 to 1996.	The combined results of the study show that there is a small increase in the demand for work by men and women whose partners do not work. It is also concluded that there is a reduction in the cost of the new tax credit program.
Do Child Tax Benefits Affect the Well-Being Of Children? Evidence From Canadian Child Benefit Expansions (Milligan & Stabile, 2011)	With an empirical approach, the study of the impact of tax benefits linked to children on their school development, health status and well-being is carried out. To carry out simulations, data were collected from the National Longitudinal Study of Children and Youth of Canada, with periods between 1994-95 and 2004-05, which resulted in about 56 000 observations.	Indicators were obtained that the increase in child benefits leads to better school results and increases well-being indexes, namely in terms of depression and negative emotional behaviors. The results also show a difference in the improvements seen as a function of the children's sex. In boys, physical and school health indicators stand out, and in girls, mental health stands out. It is concluded that more parameters should be included in the evaluation of the implementation of benefits for families with children.

continued on following page

Table 11. Continued

Title / Author	Methodology	Conclusions
Effects Of Prenatal Poverty on Infant Health: State Earned Income Tax Credits And Birth Weight (Strully et al., 2010)	This research uses an experimental model to analyze the relationship between prenatal poverty and the well-being of newborn children. A relationship is made between prenatal poverty through birth weight, with changes in income tax credits. Data from the period from 1980 to 2002 from the U.S. Natality Detail File are analyzed.	Results have been found that income tax credits increase maternal employment and income. They also indicate a reduction in smoking during maternity, although in this case the study has some limitations that do not give total robustness to the results. The results show that increasing income and decreasing harmful practices for health can be important. There is a greater benefit in younger women (19-35). The conclusions correspond to average data that can be altered by the influence of other factors on the variables used.
The Role of Wealth Transformations: An Application To Estimating The Effect Of Tax Incentives On Saving (Pence, 2006)	In the context of the study on the impact of tax benefits on savings, this work presents an alternative calculation method, using a transformation of the inverse hyperbolic sine model that allows the realization of estimates with changes in the variables to be measured.	This transformation becomes useful for researchers studying data that report negative values with significance. The inverse hyperbolic sine allows you to make estimates with data that include non-positive values.
How Do Tax Incentives Affect Investment and Productivity? Firm-Level Evidence from China (Liu & Mao, 2019)	Based on a tax reform that took place in China, this research performs a quasi-experimental model to analyze the impact that VAT tax credits have had on the levels of investment and productivity of companies. The period between 2005 and 2012 was analyzed.	The results obtained confirm an increase in investment and productivity of companies in the post-VAT reform period. It was also found that these tax credits benefited companies facing financing problems. The findings of this study are important in terms of policy guidance to encourage the growth of new and small businesses, especially in emerging economies.
Subsidizing The Stork: New Evidence on Tax Incentives and Fertility (Milligan, 2005)	To explore the effects of fiscal policies on fertility in Quebec, Canada, a quasi-experimental model was applied using control groups such as time, family type, and jurisdiction, to obtain a triple estimate. The data was collected from the Canadian Census and refer to the period from 1980 to 2000.	It was found that subsidies are a strong stimulus to fertility, however, due to evidence of heterogeneity, it is not possible to generalize the conclusion to all women. Evidence indicates that values are important for family decisions about fertility, but must be weighed against other factors, such as social groups and that it is difficult to define the ideal tax model.

continued on following page

Table 11. Continued

Title / Author	Methodology	Conclusions
The Impact of The Earned Income Tax Credit and Social Policy Reforms on Work, Marriage, And Living Arrangements (Ellwood, 2000)	A quasi-experimental model is used to extend and explore the difference in difference method and determine what impacts policy changes may have on single and married mothers, but with different abilities or wage levels. Information from the 1999 US Current Population Survey was used.	Tax credits, with pension reforms and economic robustness, have resulted in increased employment by single-parent families with low incomes. Changes in income tax credits appear to be the cause of the change in employment for low-wage married mothers compared to other married mothers. It is not apparent that reductions in tax credits, or social benefits on income have caused increases in the level of marriages or decrease in cohabitation of single mothers with lower qualifications, and there may be some changes in this pattern at the level of older women.
Beggar Thy Neighbor? The In-State, Out-Of-State, And Aggregate Effects Of R&D Tax Credits (Wilson, 2009)	In this work, two questions related to tax incentives in the US are raised. The study aims to ascertain the effects of in-state and out-of-state incentives. To this end, a model of estimation of R&D data in the period from 1981 to 2002 is used.	It is found that tax credits contribute to the increase in R&D in the State in which it is applied, but this increase occurs with the reduction in other States. It is concluded that the effective increases in R&D caused by tax credits in the states in contrast to the reduction in expenditure in others result in a null effect at the national level.
Temporary Investment Tax Incentives: Theory with Evidence from Bonus Depreciation (House & Shapiro, 2008)	This research analyzes temporary subsidies for investments, using an econometric model to estimate the structural parameters that guide the effects of fiscal policy on investment. The data was collected from the Bureau of Economic Analysis of the United States, analyzing the period from 2001 to 2006.	The work highlights an implication to the neoclassical theory of investment, which consists of the effect that temporary fiscal policies have on investment and that, if in the right measure, can cause an infinite investment duration. This is a contribution to the relationship of fiscal policies as a contribution to investment in key points of the economy.

In the papers identified in the Table 11, there is an approach to tax benefits from an individual, social and corporate perspective. It is noteworthy that of the 20 papers, 7 present research in which tax benefits are related to family income and its relationship with social issues, such as fertility incentives or households with children. On the other hand, and from a corporate perspective, in the most cited papers, the relationship between tax benefits and research and development (R&D), investment or company performance appears with the greatest relevance. The most recent paper with higher citations was published in 2020, under the title "Could environmental regulation and R&D tax incentives affect green product innovation?", with 302 citations.

Keywords

In this work, we tried to assess the evolution and trend of the keywords. In response to the research question (RQ5), the study reveals, as shown in Table 12, that two expressions stand out and define terminologies for the theme of tax benefits. These expressions are "Tax Incentives" and "Tax Credits". The first has 352 references and the second 238. The other relevant keywords are "Taxation", "Policy", "Incentives", "United States", "Taxes" and "Research and Development".

Table 12. Most relevant keywords

Words	Occurrences
Tax Credits	352
Tax Incentives	238
Taxation	93
Policy	90
Incentives	79
United States	79
Taxes	58
Research and Development	57
Investment	54
System	54

From the analysis carried out, we find some stability in the use of keywords and that the most used ones currently had a marked growth over the years, being at this moment the most frequent with a clear difference in relation to the others. While, in 1997, the year of the beginning of this study, the keyword "Tax Credits" only appears 2 times, in 2023 (the last full year) the keyword appears 339 times and in 2024, with the year not yet completed at the time of collection, this keyword appears 352 times. In the same sense, the keyword "Tax Incentives", which is not mentioned in 1997, in 2023 is used in 226 references as well as in 2024 it presents the same behavior as the previous keyword and already has 238 references. Due to the evolution described, these terms are a trend and are considered as Trend Topics, that are currently much discussed. Figure 3 shows the evolution of keywords over the period of this study.

Figure 3. Evolution of keywords over time (Output obtained from Bibliometrix)

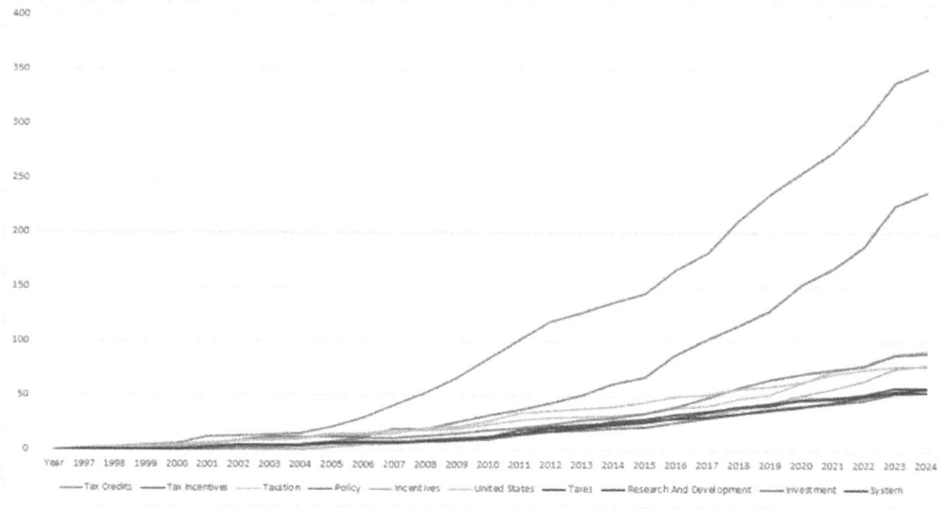

From a cluster by coupling perspective, it is noticeable that the two most relevant keywords define two clusters of agglomeration with other words, as can be seen in Figure 4. Each of the most relevant expressions tends to be related to others. These clusters allow us to understand that the two most used keywords are associated with different approaches to tax benefits. On the one hand, "Tax Credits" has a greater connection to studies related to society and individuals. Hence its greater connection with words such as "Income", "Employment", "Welfare" or "Poverty". In the other cluster, we have "Tax Incentives", which has a greater connection with business and structural themes. Here the link is made with the words "Investment", "Innovation", "Policy" or "Research and Development". Also in this cluster, two of the terms used in the research of this work appear, "Tax Benefits" and "Tax Deductions", but in connection with "Tax Incentives". In a separate cluster, but with a small dimension, is the keyword "Tax Shields". The other keywords used in the research of this study are "Tax Holidays" and "Tax Relief", but as keywords they are little used and do not reach the size to form a cluster.

Figure 4. Keywords (Clustering by Coupling) (Output obtained from Bibliometrix)

Co-citation analysis

The analysis of co-citations is a way of establishing the relationship between authors or documents that establish connections between them. These links lead to the formation of research clusters (Aria & Cuccurullo, 2017). From the information obtained, we sought to assess the relationships that are established between different approaches to the subject of tax benefits (RQ6). Using the Bibliometrix tool, the relationships between papers were obtained with the Walktrap algorithm. Figure 5 shows the existence of 5 clusters with connection between them and 2 isolates. It is possible to observe that there is a predominance of 2 clusters that concentrate most of the connections and then another 3 smaller ones that derive from the larger ones. In the 2 with the highest concentration of connections, we find that are split by an approach to corporate tax benefits and the other to those of an individual nature. Corporate tax benefits, with emphasis on the impact they have on companies in terms of sub-themes such as research, development and innovation, where the authors Lokshin, B., Czarnitzki, D., and Rao, N., stand out as the most referenced. On the other hand, tax benefits on individual income, support for families, improving social and living conditions. In this cluster, the authors Meyer, B.D., Eissa, N., and Hoynes, H., are also the ones who have the greatest influence because they are the most referenced. The 3 clusters that are linked to the two main one's present contributions that, despite being related to the major areas identified (corporate and individual), drift to other topics such as tax benefits from the perspective of sustainability, investment or the fight against poverty. Finally, we have 2 autonomous clusters that, although they also fit into the major areas (corporate and individual), present approaches to independent themes, such as tax support for housing and the use of tax benefits such as shield.

Figure 5. Co-citation network (Output obtained from Bibliometrix)

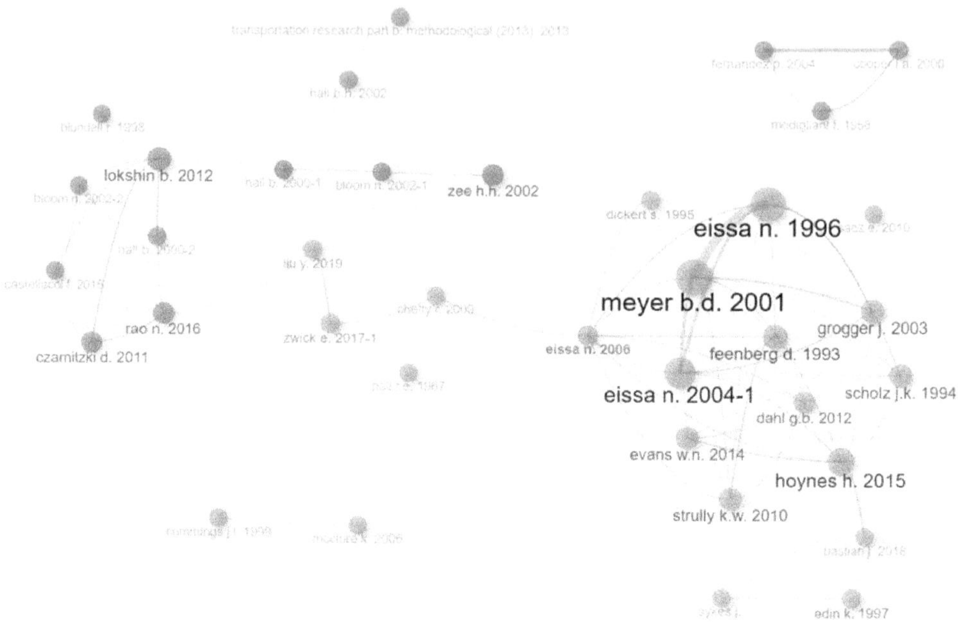

RESULTS DISCUSSION

After the presentation of the results obtained, we now move on to the discussion of the information collected and what we are able to ascertain regarding the scientific dissemination of tax benefits.

A total of 1,555 documents published in the period between 1997 and 2024 were collected. This time limit was chosen because we find in the research carried out that the greatest development and dissemination of studies in the field of tax benefits began in the year 2000 and in the following years until the present day there is an exponential growth. Behind this period, the theme was less current and discussed. Throughout the period analyzed there is an increase in the number of studies. The last full year, year 2023, reaches the maximum number of published works (143).

Data collection was restricted to the research areas of accounting, economics and management. The main sources of information are specialized journals in taxation and economics. The "Journal of Public Economics", "Journal of Finance" and "American Economic Journal: Economic Policy" stand out as the most relevant sources considering the number of citations. There is a higher incidence of North American sources, which is in line with the origin of greater scientific dissemination. The United States of America is responsible for 41% of the work collected, not considering those whose origin has not been identified. Europe comes in at 25% and China at 9%. The rest are distributed dispersed throughout the rest of the world. It is in the westernmost regions of the world that we find the most discussion on the subject, which extends to different approaches and perspectives. This trend may be justified by greater access to data available for research.

The studies on this subject are dispersed among different authors, with the highest number of publications being Michelmore, K., with 11 publications and an h-index of 8. This author has her affiliation with the University of Michigan, which is the institution with the highest number of contributions on this topic, totaling 26 articles. However, the most relevant authors according to the criterion of the highest number of citations are Graham, J. R. (1,318 citations and h-index of 3), Lochner, L. (547 citations and h-index of 3) and Dahl, G. B. (541 citations and h-index of 2). These three authors have affiliations in the United States. The multiplicity of authors is linked with the different approaches to the theme that is explored from different perspectives. The results shows that the research is essentially divided into two large clusters, one related to the connection of tax benefits to companies and the other linked to the support that tax benefits can give to families and social components. In these two large groups, it is possible to establish a link between tax incentives for corporate purposes, and in this context we find papers in the R&D, or innovation fields, as well as on foreign investment, or even attracting investment. From another perspective, there is another large group that addresses the tax benefits of individual support and here the studies are related to the reduction of income taxation or tax incentives to families, through tax benefits in the education area, housing and protection of larger households. There are also studies carried out on fiscal stimulus for the use of renewable energies or sustainability measures. These last themes, which are present in more current works, focus on the contribution of tax benefits to increasing sustainability in small companies, or circular economy.

CONCLUSION

The aim of this study was to map the scientific dissemination about the subject of tax benefits over time. To fulfil this objective and answer the research questions posed, a bibliometric analysis was carried out using the Bibliometrix tool. In the first phase, data collection was carried out on the Scopus and Web of Science platforms. In this collection, previously defined keywords were used to obtain the largest number of results. Subsequently, the information was prepared to fill as many content gaps as possible and were submitted to the tool for a bibliometric analysis. The return of results allows us to conclude that the theme has a greater development after the year 2000, with annual growth of published studies. Throughout the period under analysis, there is a diversification of approaches and the specificity of the theme. It is also concluded that the studies originate mostly in the United States of America, followed by China and United Kingdom. The results show a high diversification of dissemination by journals and authors. At the level of keywords, it is possible to identify the definition of two clear clusters that divide the theme into two approaches with greater impact. On the one hand, the study of tax benefits from the structural perspective of society (economic and social well-being) and from the corporate perspective, analyzing the impacts and effects of tax reductions in these areas. On the other hand, research on tax reductions in terms of individual income or support for families or social conditions of support for housing and education. This conclusion is also supported by analyzing the 20 most cited papers, whose topics are divided equally between the corporate field and the individual or family field. It is also concluded that the trends of the studies have changed over this period of analysis. The topics have remained the same for some time, an average of ten years, but there has been an evolution towards current issues, such as innovation, development, sustainability and better social conditions, which are the topics of the most recent research. From the keywords used for the research, it is possible to conclude that "Tax Incentive" and "Tax Credit" are the most used and those that return the largest number of results, being related to the other topics of subjects studied within the scope of tax benefits. To carry out this study there were some limitations, the most important of which was the fact that not all the documents were in open access, which made it difficult to interpret their content. As this work focused on mapping tax benefits in a global way, by the two clusters identified, tax benefits with a corporate scope and those with an individual scope, it is considered pertinent in the future to carry out a mapping study on the detail of these issues individually.

REFERENCES

Albring, S. M., Mills, L. F., & Newberry, K. J. (2011). Do debt constraints influence firms' sensitivity to a temporary tax holiday on repatriations? *The Journal of the American Taxation Association*, 33(2), 1–27. DOI: 10.2308/atax-10057

Aria, M., & Cuccurullo, C. (2017). bibliometrix: An R-tool for comprehensive science mapping analysis. *Journal of Informetrics*, 11(4), 959–975. DOI: 10.1016/j.joi.2017.08.007

Auerbach, A. J. (2006). The Choice between Income and Consumption Taxes. *PRiMER: Peer-Reviewed Reports in Medical Education Research.*

Averett, S. L., Peters, H. E., & Waldman, D. M. (1997). Tax credits, labor supply, and child care. *The Review of Economics and Statistics*, 79(1), 125–135. DOI: 10.1162/003465397556467

Bloom, N., Griffith, R., & Van Reenen, J. (2002a). Do R & D tax credits work? Evidence from a panel of countries 1979-1997. *Journal of Public Economics*, 85(1), 1–31. DOI: 10.1016/S0047-2727(01)00086-X

Bloom, N., Griffith, R., & Van Reenen, J. (2002b). Do R&D tax credits work? Evidence from a panel of countries 1979–1997. *Journal of Public Economics*, 85(1), 1–31. https://doi.org/https://doi.org/10.1016/S0047-2727(01)00086-X. DOI: 10.1016/S0047-2727(01)00086-X

Blundell, R., Duncan, A., Mccrae, J., & Meghir, C. (2000). The Labour Market Impact of the Working Families' Tax Credit. *Fiscal Studies*, 21(1), 75–104. DOI: 10.1111/j.1475-5890.2000.tb00581.x

Chan, K. H., & Mo, P. L. L. (2000). Tax holidays and tax noncompliance: An empirical study of corporate tax audits in china's developing economy. *The Accounting Review*, 75(4), 469–484. DOI: 10.2308/accr.2000.75.4.469

Correia, I. (2005). *BANCO DE PORTUGAL Economic Research Department CONSUMPTION TAXES AND REDISTRIBUTION Consumption Taxes and Redistribution*.

Cruz, S. R., & Soares, C. (2022). Use of the tax benefit of conventional remuneration of share capital by Portuguese companies. *Revista Contabilidade & Finanças*, 33(90), e1587. Advance online publication. DOI: 10.1590/1808-057x20221587.en

Czarnitzki, D., Hanel, P., & Rosa, J. M. (2011). Evaluating the impact of R&D tax credits on innovation: A microeconometric study on Canadian firms. *Research Policy*, 40(2), 217–229. DOI: 10.1016/j.respol.2010.09.017

Czerwonka, L., & Jaworski, J. (2017). Capital Structure Determinants of Industrial: Companies Listed on the Warsaw Stock Exchange. *11th International Scientific Conference on Financial Management of Firms and Financial Institutions*, 157–164.

d'Andria, D., DeBacker, J., Evans, R. W., Pycroft, J., & Zachlod-Jelec, M. (2021). Taxing income or consumption: macroeconomic and distributional effects for Italy (No. 13/2021). JRC Working Papers on Taxation and Structural Reforms.

da Fonseca, P. V., Jucá, M. N., & Nakamura, W. T. (2020). Debt Tax Benefits in a High Tax Emerging Market: Evidence from Brazil. In *International Journal of Economics and Business Administration: Vol. VIII* (Issue 2).

Dahl, G. B., & Lochner, L. (2012). The impact of family income on child achievement: Evidence from the earned income tax credit. *The American Economic Review*, 102(5), 1927–1956. DOI: 10.1257/aer.102.5.1927

Donthu, N., Kumar, S., Mukherjee, D., Pandey, N., & Lim, W. M. (2021). How to conduct a bibliometric analysis: An overview and guidelines. *Journal of Business Research*, 133, 285–296. DOI: 10.1016/j.jbusres.2021.04.070

Eissa, N., & Hoynes, H. W. (2004). Taxes and the labor market participation of married couples: The earned income tax credit. *Journal of Public Economics*, 88(9–10), 1931–1958. DOI: 10.1016/j.jpubeco.2003.09.005

Ellegaard, O., & Wallin, J. A. (2015). The bibliometric analysis of scholarly production: How great is the impact? *Scientometrics*, 105(3), 1809–1831. DOI: 10.1007/s11192-015-1645-z PMID: 26594073

Ellwood, D. T. (2000). The Impact of the Earned Income Tax Credit and Social Policy Reforms on Work, Marriage, and Living Arrangements. Https://Doi.Org/10.17310/Ntj.2000.4S1.03, *53*(4 PART 2), 1063–1103. DOI: 10.17310/ntj.2000.4S1.03

Ensslin, L., Dutra, A., Ensslin, S. R., Chaves, L. C., Dezem, V., Ensslin, L., Dutra, A., Ensslin, S. R., Chaves, L. C., & Dezem, V. (2015). Research Process for Selecting a Theoretical Framework and Bibliometric Analysis of a Theme: Illustration for the Management of Customer Service in a Bank. *Modern Economy*, 6(6), 782–796. DOI: 10.4236/me.2015.66074

Eom, T. H., Duncombe, W., Nguyen-Hoang, P., & Yinger, J. (2014). The unintended consequences of property tax relief: New york's star program. *Education Finance and Policy*, 9(4), 446–480. DOI: 10.1162/EDFP_a_00143

Faccio, M., & Xu, J. (2015). Taxes and Capital Structure. *Journal of Financial and Quantitative Analysis*, 50(3), 277–300. DOI: 10.1017/S0022109015000174

Fernandez, P. (2004). The value of tax shields is NOT equal to the present value of tax shields. *Journal of Financial Economics*, 73(1), 145–165. DOI: 10.1016/j.jfineco.2002.10.001

Gale, W. G., & Potter, S. R. (2002). An economic evaluation of the Economic Growth and Tax Relief Reconciliation Act of 2001. *National Tax Journal*, 55(1), 133–177. DOI: 10.17310/ntj.2002.1.08

Garfield, E. (1955). Citation indexes for science. *Science*, 122(3159), 108–111. DOI: 10.1126/science.122.3159.108 PMID: 14385826

Glänzel, W., & Leuven, K. U. (2003). *Bibliometrics as a research field: A course on theory and application of bibliometric indicators Topic identification challenge View project*. https://www.researchgate.net/publication/242406991

Graham, J. R. (2000). How big are the tax benefits of debt? *The Journal of Finance*, 55(5), 1901–1941. DOI: 10.1111/0022-1082.00277

Graham, J. R., Raedy, J. S., & Shackelford, D. A. (2012). Research in accounting for income taxes. *Journal of Accounting and Economics*, 53(1–2), 412–434. DOI: 10.1016/j.jacceco.2011.11.006

Graham, J. R., & Rogers, D. A. (2002). Do firms hedge in response to tax incentives? *The Journal of Finance*, 57(2), 815–839. DOI: 10.1111/1540-6261.00443

Graham, J. R., & Smith, C. W. (1999). Tax Incentives to Hedge. *The Journal of Finance*, 54(6), 2241–2262. DOI: 10.1111/0022-1082.00187

Gregova, E., Smrcka, L., Michalkova, L., & Svabova, L. (2021). Impact of tax benefits and earnings management on capital structures across V4 countries. *Acta Polytechnica Hungarica*, 18(3), 221–244. DOI: 10.12700/APH.18.3.2021.3.12

Hanlon, M., & Heitzman, S. (2010). A review of tax research. In *Journal of Accounting and Economics* (Vol. 50, Issues 2–3, pp. 127–178). DOI: 10.1016/j.jacceco.2010.09.002

Hernádi, P., & Ormos, M. (2012). Capital structure and its choice in Central and Eastern Europe. *Acta Oeconomica*, 62(2), 229–263. DOI: 10.1556/aoecon.62.2012.2.5

Hirsch, J. E. (2005). *An index to quantify an individual's scientific research output*. www.pnas.orgcgidoi10.1073pnas.0507655102

Hirsch, J. E., & Cardona, M. (2007). Does the h index have predictive power? In *PNAS December* (Vol. 4). www.pnas.orgcgidoi10.1073pnas.0707962104

House, C. L., & Shapiro, M. D. (2008). Temporary Investment Tax Incentives: Theory with Evidence from Bonus Depreciation. *The American Economic Review*, 98(3), 737–768. DOI: 10.1257/aer.98.3.737

Hoynes, H., Miller, D., & Simon, D. (2015). Income, the Earned Income Tax Credit, and Infant Health. *American Economic Journal. Economic Policy*, 7(1), 172–211. DOI: 10.1257/pol.20120179

John, W., & Ii, C. (2000). Welfare and optimum dynamic taxation of consumption and income. [). www.elsevier.nl/locate/econbase]. *Journal of Public Economics*, 76, •••.

Jones, T., Huggett, S., & Kamalski, J. (2011). Finding a Way Through the Scientific Literature: Indexes and Measures. *World Neurosurgery*, 76(1–2), 36–38. DOI: 10.1016/j.wneu.2011.01.015 PMID: 21839937

Kemsley, D., & Nissim, D. (2002). Valuation of the debt tax shield. *The Journal of Finance*, 57(5), 2045–2073. DOI: 10.1111/0022-1082.00488

Krämer, R. (2015). Taxation and Capital Structure Choice: The Role of Ownership. *The Scandinavian Journal of Economics*, 117(3), 957–982. DOI: 10.1111/sjoe.12107

Leland, H. E., & Toft, K. B. (1996). Optimal capital structure, endogenous bankruptcy, and the term structure of credit spreads. *The Journal of Finance*, 51(3), 987–1019. DOI: 10.1111/j.1540-6261.1996.tb02714.x

Leuven, E., & Oosterbeek, H. (2004). Evaluating the effect of tax deductions on training. *Journal of Labor Economics*, 22(2), 461–488. DOI: 10.1086/381257

Lin, K. Z. (2006). The impact of tax holidays on earnings management: An empirical study of corporate reporting behavior in a developing-economy framework. *The International Journal of Accounting*, 41(2), 163–175. DOI: 10.1016/j.intacc.2006.04.006

Liu, Y., & Mao, J. (2019). How Do Tax Incentives Affect Investment and Productivity? Firm-Level Evidence from China. *American Economic Journal. Economic Policy*, 11(3), 261–291. DOI: 10.1257/pol.20170478

Liu, Y. C. (2009). The slicing approach to valuing tax shields. *Journal of Banking & Finance*, 33(6), 1069–1078. DOI: 10.1016/j.jbankfin.2008.12.002

Lotka, A. J. (1926). The frequency distribution of scientific productivity. In *Source. Journal of the Washington Academy of Sciences*, 16(12), •••.

Lu, C. H., Ueng, K. L. G., & Chang, J. J. (2022). Consumption indivisibility and the optimal tax mix. *Economic Modelling*, 112, 105845. Advance online publication. DOI: 10.1016/j.econmod.2022.105845

Maydew, E. L. (2001). Empirical tax research in accounting: A discussion $. In *Journal of Accounting and Economics* (Vol. 31).

Meyer, B. D., & Rosenbaum, D. T. (2001). Welfare, the earned income tax credit, and the labor supply of single mothers. *The Quarterly Journal of Economics*, 116(3), 1063–1114. DOI: 10.1162/00335530152466313

Milligan, K. (2005). Subsidizing the Stork: New Evidence on Tax Incentives and Fertility. *The Review of Economics and Statistics*, 87(3), 539–555. DOI: 10.1162/0034653054638382

Milligan, K., & Stabile, M. (2011). Do child tax benefits affect the well-being of children? Evidence from Canadian child benefit expansions. *American Economic Journal. Economic Policy*, 3(3), 175–205. DOI: 10.1257/pol.3.3.175

Mingers, J., & Leydesdorff, L. (2015). A review of theory and practice in scientometrics. In *European Journal of Operational Research* (Vol. 246, Issue 1, pp. 1–19). Elsevier B.V. DOI: 10.1016/j.ejor.2015.04.002

Mishra, C. (2011). Determinants of Capital Structure-A Study of Manufacturing Sector PSUs in India. *2011 International Conference on Financial Management and Economics*.

Mukherjee, D., Lim, W. M., Kumar, S., & Donthu, N. (2022). Guidelines for advancing theory and practice through bibliometric research. *Journal of Business Research*, 148, 101–115. DOI: 10.1016/j.jbusres.2022.04.042

Parry, I. W. H., & Bento, A. M. (2000). Tax deductions, environmental policy, and the "double dividend" hypothesis. *Journal of Environmental Economics and Management*, 39(1), 67–96. DOI: 10.1006/jeem.1999.1093

Pence, K. M. (2006). The Role of Wealth Transformations: An Application to Estimating the Effect of Tax Incentives on Saving. *The B.E. Journal of Economic Analysis & Policy*, 5(1), 0000101515153806451430. Advance online publication. DOI: 10.1515/1538-0645.1430

Price, D. J. D. S. (1963). *Little Science, Big Science*. Columbia University Press., https://doi.org/doi:10.7312/pric91844 DOI: 10.7312/pric91844

Price, D. J. de S. (1961). *Science Since Babylon* (Vol. 67). Yale University Press.

Roldan-Valadez, E., Salazar-Ruiz, S. Y., Ibarra-Contreras, R., & Rios, C. (2019). Current concepts on bibliometrics: A brief review about impact factor, Eigenfactor score, CiteScore, SCImago Journal Rank, Source-Normalised Impact per Paper, H-index, and alternative metrics. *Irish Journal of Medical Science*, 188(3), 939–951. DOI: 10.1007/s11845-018-1936-5 PMID: 30511320

Roldan-Valadez, E., Yoselin Salazar-Ruiz, S., Ibarra-Contreras, R., & Rios, C. (2019). Current concepts on bibliometrics: A brief review about impact factor, Eigenfactor score, CiteScore, SCImago Journal Rank, Source-Normalised Impact per Paper, H-index, and alternative metrics. *Irish Journal of Medical Science*, 188(3), 939–951. Advance online publication. DOI: 10.1007/s11845-018-1936-5 PMID: 30511320

Santos, J. A. (1989). A Fiscalidade: Medição e Limites. *Estudes de Economia, IX, n.º4*, 393–426. http://hdl.handle.net/10400.5/9582

Schanzenbach, D. W., & Strain, M. R. (2021). Employment effects of the earned income tax credit: Taking the long view. In *Tax Policy and the Economy* (Vol. 35, Issue 1, pp. 87–129). University of Chicago Press. DOI: 10.1086/713494

Scharf, K., & Smith, S. (2015). The price elasticity of charitable giving: Does the form of tax relief matter? *International Tax and Public Finance*, 22(2), 330–352. DOI: 10.1007/s10797-014-9306-3

Shackelford, D. A., & Shevlin, T. (2001). Empirical tax research in accounting $. In *Journal of Accounting and Economics* (Vol. 31). DOI: 10.1016/S0165-4101(01)00022-2

Song, M., Wang, S., & Zhang, H. (2020). Could environmental regulation and R&D tax incentives affect green product innovation? *Journal of Cleaner Production*, 258, 120849. DOI: 10.1016/j.jclepro.2020.120849

Strully, K. W., Rehkopf, D. H., & Xuan, Z. (2010). Effects of Prenatal Poverty on Infant Health: State Earned Income Tax Credits and Birth Weight. *American Sociological Review*, 75(4), 534–562. DOI: 10.1177/0003122410374086 PMID: 21643514

Tachinakis, P. (2022). Tax benefits determinants and earnings management: Results from the eurozone countries. *International Journal of Computational Economics and Econometrics*, 12(3), 263–274. DOI: 10.1504/IJCEE.2022.122831

Wang, J., Shen, G., & Tang, D. (2021). Does tax deduction relax financing constraints? Evidence from China's value-added tax reform. *China Economic Review*, 67, 101619. DOI: 10.1016/j.chieco.2021.101619

Wilson, D. J. (2009). Beggar Thy Neighbor? The In-State, Out-of-State, and Aggregate Effects of R&D Tax Credits. *The Review of Economics and Statistics*, 91(2), 431–436. DOI: 10.1162/rest.91.2.431

Wu, W., Wu, C., Zhou, C., & Wu, J. (2012). Political connections, tax benefits and firm performance: Evidence from China. *Journal of Accounting and Public Policy*, 31(3), 277–300. DOI: 10.1016/j.jaccpubpol.2011.10.005

ADDITIONAL READING

Cruz, S. R., & Soares, C. (2022). Use of the tax benefit of conventional remuneration of share capital by Portuguese companies. *Revista Contabilidade & Finanças*, 33(90), e1587. Advance online publication. DOI: 10.1590/1808-057x20221587.en

Czarnitzki, D., Hanel, P., & Rosa, J. M. (2011). Evaluating the impact of R&D tax credits on innovation: A microeconometric study on Canadian firms. *Research Policy*, 40(2), 217–229. DOI: 10.1016/j.respol.2010.09.017

Eichfelder, S., Jacob, M., & Schneider, K. (2023). Do tax incentives affect investment quality? *Journal of Corporate Finance*, 80, 102403. Advance online publication. DOI: 10.1016/j.jcorpfin.2023.102403

Fialho, A., Moya, M. D. M. S., López, J. F. S., & Azevedo, P. A. (2021). Tax Benefits as a Tool for the Promotion of the Sustainable Development Goals: The Case of the Iberian Foundations. CIRIEC-Espana. *Revista Juridica de Economia Social y Cooperativa*, 2021(39), 241–277. DOI: 10.7203/CIRIEC-JUR.39.20932

Hanlon, M., & Heitzman, S. (2010). A review of tax research. In Journal of Accounting and Economics (Vol. 50, Issues 2–3, pp. 127–178). DOI: 10.1016/j.jacceco.2010.09.002

Kolesnikov, Y. A. (2023). Tax Incentives for Sustainable Development in the Context of Digitalization. In A. D. and R. B. A. and O. V. N. Lazareva Elena I. and Murzin (Ed.), Innovative Trends in International Business and Sustainable Management (pp. 115–121). Springer Nature Singapore. DOI: 10.1007/978-981-19-4005-7_13

Schanzenbach, D. W., & Strain, M. R. (2021). Employment effects of the earned income tax credit: Taking the long view. In Tax Policy and the Economy (Vol. 35, Issue 1, pp. 87–129). University of Chicago Press. DOI: 10.1086/713494

Song, M., Wang, S., & Zhang, H. (2020). Could environmental regulation and R&D tax incentives affect green product innovation? *Journal of Cleaner Production*, 258, 120849. DOI: 10.1016/j.jclepro.2020.120849

Tachinakis, P. (2022). Tax benefits determinants and earnings management: Results from the eurozone countries. *International Journal of Computational Economics and Econometrics*, 12(3), 263–274. DOI: 10.1504/IJCEE.2022.122831

KEY TERMS AND DEFINITIONS

Bibliometric analysis: a scientific computer-assisted review methodology that can identify core research or authors, as well as their relationship, by covering all the publications related to a given topic or field.

Cluster analysis: the task of grouping a set of objects in such a way that objects in the same group are more similar to each other than to those in other groups.

Tax benefits: incentives promoted by states, which allow to reduce the fiscal impact for the taxpayers. In the literature there are other terms that express the same meaning, as tax incentives, tax credits, tax deductions, tax reliefs, tax shields and tax holidays.

Tax burden: corresponds to the percentage relation between the total amount of tax revenue and actual social contributions and a country's gross domestic product.

Tax planning: the taxpayer resorts to the different instruments that the legislator makes available to him and whose use allows him to not pay or pay less tax. Thus, the taxpayer can choose the legal formula that leads to a minimization of the tax payment.

Taxes: source of revenue for a State, which serve to redistribute income, and guarantee the citizens who live there a set of common goods and services, and which enable the satisfaction of collective needs

Social function of taxes: The social function of the tribute expands to the environmental area, so the tax can also be used as an indirect form of environmental protection, to avoid economic, social, environmental risks and meet resources for several generations.

ENDNOTES

1 https://www.oxfordreference.com/display/10.1093/acref/9780191826719.001.0001/q-oro-ed4-00004582 retrieved 2024-06-10.

APPENDIX I

Table 13. Summary tables with converted keywords

Tax Incentives	
Corporate Income Tax Incentives (CITI)	Organizational Tax Incentives
Corporate Tax Incentives	R&D Tax Incentives
developing expenditure-based tax incentives	Regional Tax Incentives
Development Tax Incentives	Renewable Solar Tax Incentives
Development Tax Incentives Programs	Research and Development Tax Incentives
Direct Tax Incentives	Research and Development Tax Incentives Multiplier
effectiveness of tax incentives	State Tax Incentives
Employment Tax Incentives	Strategic Tax Incentives
energy-saving tax incentives	Tax Incentives
First-time Homebuyer Tax Incentives	Tax Incentives for
Fiscal Incentives	Tax incentives for innovation
Foreign Direct Tax Incentives	Tax incentives for low-carbon
Government Tax Incentives	Tax Incentives Mechanisms
Income Tax Incentives	Tax Incentives Policy
Internal Tax Incentives	Tax Incentives Practices
Investment Tax Incentives	Tax Incentives Promoting Migration of Skilled Labour
IP-Conditioned Tax Incentives	Tax Incentives Schemes
Multinational Tax Incentives	value-added tax incentives
non-tax incentives	
Tax Credits	
2021 Child Tax Credits	low income tax credits
45q tax credits provisions	low-income housing tax credits
Adoption Tax Credits	Low-Income Housing Tax Credits (LIHTC)
Automation Tax Credits	low-income tax credits
blender's tax credits	low-income tax credits program
child and dependent care tax credits	New Market Tax Credits
Child Tax Credits	New Markets Tax Credits
Contribution Tax Credits	Nonrefundable tax credits
Cultural Tax Credits	Ohio Historic Preservation Tax Credits
Development Tax Credits	Optimal Earned Income Tax Credits
Earned Income Tax Credit	Premium Tax Credits

continued on following page

Table 13. Continued

Tax Incentives	
Earned Income Tax Credits	Production Tax Credits
Earned Income Tax Credits (Earned Credits)	Production Tax Credits (PTC)
Earned Income Tax Credits-Recipient Families	public tax credits
Earned Tax Credits	R&E Tax Credits
Energy Tax Credits	Rehabilitation Tax Credits
Experimentation Tax Credits	Rental Tax Credits
Fair Low Income Housing Tax Credits	Research & Experimentation Tax Credits
Federal Production Tax Credits	Research and Development Tax Credits
Tax Credits	
Federal Tax Credits	State Earned Income Tax Credits
Foreign Tax Credits	State Tax Credits
Green Tax Credits	Tax Credits
halved imputation tax credits	tax credits and subsidies
health-related tax credits	Tax Credits Investigation
Housing Tax Credits	Tax Credits Rating
Income Tax Credits	Tax Credits Scheme
Income Tax Credits (ITC)	the earned income tax credits (earned credits)
Investment Tax Credits	value-added tax credits refund
Investor Tax Credits	vat tax credits
Job Creation Tax Credits	Work Opportunity Tax Credits (WOTC)
Job Tax Credits	Working Families' Tax Credits
Landfill Tax Credits Scheme	Working Families' Tax Credits
Low Income Housing Tax Credits	Working Tax Credits
Tax Benefits	
Education Tax Benefits	tax benefits of incomes
Incomes Tax Benefits	Tax Benefits System
Tax Benefits	Tax Benefits Systems
Tax Benefits Models	uncertain tax benefits
Tax Benefits of Debt	
Tax Shield	
Debt Tax Shields	present value of tax shields
discount rate for tax shields	required rate of tax shields
Dividend Tax Shields	Tax Shields
Gordon Growth Interest Tax Shields	Tax Shields Valuation

continued on following page

Table 13. Continued

Tax Incentives	
Interest Expense Tax Shields	unlevered value of tax shields
Interest Tax Shields	value of tax shields
non-debt tax shields	Value Tax Shields
Tax Deduction	
Income Tax Deduction	personal tax deductions for share purchase
Income Tax Deductions	Pre-Tax Deduction
Income tax deductions for losses	Tax Deduction
Interest Tax Deductions	tax deduction policy
investment tax deduction	Tax Deduction Ratio
Local Income Tax Deduction	Tax Deductions
monthly tax deduction	
Tax Relief	
Jobs and Growth Tax Relief Reconciliation Act	property tax relief policy
pension tax relief	Structural Tax Relief
Profit Tax Relief	Tax Relief
property tax relief	
Tax Holidays	
Foreign Tax Holidays	Tax Holiday
State Sales Tax Holidays	Tax holidays

Chapter 18
What We Can Learn From Flat Tax Research

Paulo Jorge Dias
https://orcid.org/0000-0002-0351-9751
Instituto Universitário de Lisboa, Portugal

Miguel Tavares
ISCTE, Portugal

ABSTRACT

This chapter explores the increasing academic and political interest in the "Flat Tax" system, particularly inspired by the outcomes observed in countries with proportional taxation. By analyzing a sample of 109 scientific articles from the Scopus platform using bibliometric indicators, the chapter provides a comprehensive overview of the research trends and key findings in this area. The study reveals a significant rise in publications and citations over the last few decades, with a strong focus from European researchers, though the USA shows the highest interest. The findings indicate that the topic spans various disciplines, resulting in diverse and sometimes conflicting conclusions. This chapter underscores the importance of continued investigation into the flat tax to better understand its broader implications.

INTRODUCTION

The relationship between accounting and taxation is investigated in a multi-disciplinary manner in the literature, leading to a diversity of studies on this topic (Dacian, 2010). With the increasing number of scientific articles related to taxation

DOI: 10.4018/979-8-3693-3908-4.ch018

published in specialized journals, continuous investigation of various themes related to this area is necessary to achieve a deep understanding of the subject.

Taxation is crucial for the functioning of countries as it generates fiscal revenue, the primary source of state income. It enables governments to provide essential public goods and services, ensuring the proper functioning of societies and achieving an adequate level of economic stability (Whait et al., 2018; Arab & Basariya, 2020). Additionally, taxation is used to encourage or discourage certain behaviors or consumption patterns, correct market imperfections, and redistribute wealth to make society more equitable (Amirthalingam, 2013; Arab & Basariya, 2020).

To collect these revenues, various tax systems exist, some emphasizing direct taxes, others indirect taxes, and some balancing both. There are systems with more progressive rates, others with proportional rates, and some that balance both. The construction of a tax system is crucial, as it significantly determines macroeconomic indices such as economic growth, fiscal deficit, and public debt (Amirthalingam, 2013). Each tax system has advantages and disadvantages, and the way each country structures its system and defines its rates varies not only by the country's development status but also by the political and economic views of its government and its priorities. Some governments prioritize equity, while others emphasize efficiency, the two fundamental principles in tax system construction (Dagan et al., 1999).

Regarding personal income taxation, most countries have established progressive tax systems to address societal inequalities (Popescu et al., 2019; Sabitova & Dyudina, 2015). However, global economic crises have led to economic stagnation in many countries, resulting in public discontent and increased criticism of progressive tax systems, particularly regarding the compromise of efficiency for equity. Inspired by Eastern European countries, which adopted proportional systems primarily to achieve economic growth, political parties in various countries have discussed tax reform to introduce a flat tax, meaning a single rate for taxing personal income. Proponents argue that a flat tax would offer various advantages, including improvements in macroeconomic indices, such as national economic growth, similar to the experiences of Eastern European countries.

However, opinions on the flat tax are not unanimous, with significant disagreement and debate among parties about the country's future direction. Therefore, an investigation that consolidates the main conclusions of key studies on the topic is relevant, as it allows for observing multiple viewpoints and their justifications.

Despite the political debate, the flat tax topic is not extensively studied academically, though the number of articles on it has increased over the years, indicating growing academic interest. Consequently, there is a need for a study that encompasses various investigations on the flat tax, providing a general understanding of the current state of research on this topic.

This research aims to characterize the existing research on the "Flat Tax" topic by analyzing the trends in scientific articles published on the Scopus platform. The specific objectives are (i) to analyze a set of bibliometric indicators related to the characteristics of the published articles, (ii) to analyze a set of bibliometric indicators related to the characteristics of the researchers, and (iii) to construct a summary table/chart with the objectives and conclusions of the main articles included in the research sample.

Therefore, the research questions guiding this study are (i) What are the trends in the publication of scientific articles? and (ii) What are the main conclusions of the key studies on the topic? These questions aim to understand whether the topic has gained importance in academia as it has in the political sphere and to identify the reasons for the lack of consensus in the debate on this topic.

To answer the research questions, a characterization study was developed. Characterization studies are considered highly relevant as they allow for conclusions about the trends of scientific articles over the years, as well as a set of inherent characteristics. Additionally, this research consolidates the conclusions of key articles on the Scopus platform regarding the "Flat Tax," which is also considered highly relevant in academia, as aggregating existing literature information allows other authors to identify the most relevant publications and thus have a foundation to guide their research.

This investigation followed a PRISMA methodology, developed specifically for systematic reviews and meta-analyses, to assist in reporting the rationale behind the research, what was done by the authors, and their conclusions.

Initially, a literature review was conducted based on scientific articles from prestigious databases such as Scopus or journals listed in quality research rankings like the Academic Journal Quality Guide 2018, ensuring the quality of information. The literature review focused on the flat tax topic but also covered broader themes like the importance of taxation and fiscal revenues to facilitate understanding the conceptual foundations of the flat tax.

Next, data collection for this research was conducted. The search was performed using the Scopus platform, chosen for its high-quality content and global database coverage, ensuring relevant scientific information is not overlooked. The sample definition and data collection process will be further detailed in the methodology chapter.

Subsequently, to evaluate scientific production and characterize research on the flat tax, bibliometric indicators were used to analyze the selected articles for the study sample. Bibliometric indicators were chosen because bibliometrics is a quantitative and statistical technique used to determine knowledge production and dissemination indices (Costa et al., 2012). The analyzed indicators included scientific activity, scientific impact, and thematic associations.

To simplify data visualization and analysis, Excel and VOSviewer software were used, along with metrics provided by the Scopus platform. These tools enabled the development of a set of graphs, tables, and maps, facilitating better analysis of the collected data and characterizing research on the "Flat Tax.

LITERATURE REVIEW

2.1. Taxation

Taxation is fundamental for the functioning of the State, the economy, and society, as fiscal revenue represents the primary source of income for the State (Gribnau, 2015). Consequently, the survival of a government partly depends on its ability to levy taxes since it needs to raise funds to provide not only infrastructure but also public goods and services that cannot be adequately produced by the competitive market, such as schools, roads, and national defense (Whait et al., 2018; Arab & Basariya, 2020).

Thus, increasing the amount of tax revenue is crucial for a country's development (Arab & Basariya, 2020). However, it is relevant to highlight that increasing taxation can negatively affect the incentive for investment in various sectors of the economy, which can impact its long-term growth rate. Additionally, motivation for work and saving may be negatively affected (Popescu et al., 2019; de Hek, 2006).

The stance of each country's government on whether tax revenues should be higher or lower depends on the country's exact position on the Laffer curve (Evans & Aligica, 2008). According to this curve, neither a 100% tax rate nor a 0% tax rate would generate revenue for the State. With a 100% tax rate, people would not work, resulting in no revenue. On the other hand, with a 0% tax rate, although many individuals would work, revenues would still be nonexistent. Thus, what is obtained is a curve in which the aim is to maximize tax revenues (Laffer, 2019).

In addition to providing public goods and services and financing government expenditures, another essential function of taxation, as clarified in the Constitution of the Portuguese Republic, is to ensure a "fair distribution of income and wealth" (Article 103, nr.1), as social welfare is maximized when resources are distributed more equitably (Pántya et al., 2016; Popescu et al., 2019). For this reason, ensuring a fair distribution of the tax burden among individuals has been a central concern in policy-making over time (Popescu et al., 2019).

In summary, the effective use of tax revenues is at the center of a long-standing economic debate aimed at finding the best way to optimize tax revenues while maintaining a balance between equity and efficiency (Arab & Basariya, 2020; Laffer, 2019). It is important to emphasize that all systems have advantages and disadvantages and that the balance between equity and effectiveness can only be achieved through a fiscal policy adapted to each economy (Popescu et al., 2019; Sabitova & Dyudina, 2015).

2.2. Tax Structures

To obtain tax revenues, there are various forms of taxation, both for corporations and individuals, with the quest for the perfect tax structure being the goal of many politicians and economists (Gouveia & Oliver, 1995; Arab & Basariya, 2020). The choice of tax structure should consider various factors, such as its effects on economic incentives, its fairness among individuals with similar taxable capacity, its effects on distribution between high-income and low-income individuals, whether it is compatible with desirable international economic relations, and also based on its simplicity, ease of understanding, and absence of excessive administrative costs (Popescu et al., 2019).

2.2.1. Direct and Indirect Taxes

Taxes can be classified in multiple ways. One distinction that can be made is between direct taxes, which are levied on income, and indirect taxes, which are levied on consumption. There are various arguments in favor of an indirect tax, such as its lesser negative effects on labor supply and less interference in the choice between present and future consumption (Musgrave & Musgrave, 1989). However, consumption taxes cause distortion in optimal consumption (Watrin & Ullmann, 2008). The main argument in favor of a direct tax is that it is generally the most suitable for income redistribution among income groups (Watrin & Ullmann, 2008). Additionally, in many countries, the largest budget revenues come from income tax returns, with only about 15 out of approximately 200 countries not applying it (Sabitova & Dyudina, 2015). Within income taxes, one of the sources that allows the State to address various economic and social problems in society is the personal income tax (Ibragimov et al., 2014).

2.2.2. Regressive, Progressive, and Proportional Taxes

In addition to being classified as direct or indirect, taxes can also be distinguished as progressive, proportional, or regressive. Regressive taxation, usually a fixed amount tax, imposes a higher percentage of tax burden on low-income workers, decreasing with increasing income. Although regressive taxation demonstrates extreme simplicity in terms of administrative efficiency, lower administrative costs, and reduces the possibilities of tax evasion, it is rarely considered because it fails to generate high tax revenues and has negative effects on wealth distribution (Dabrowski & Tomczynska, 2001). One potential way to ensure a fair redistribution of wealth is through the establishment of a progressive tax system, in which average and marginal tax rates increase with income (Pántya et al., 2016). Ensuring a fair redistribution of wealth is one of the main arguments in favor of this form of taxation and results from the opinion, advocated by authors such as Marx and Engels (1848), that economic differences among citizens should be corrected. Therefore, citizens with higher incomes should be taxed at higher marginal rates, and these tax revenues should be redistributed to lower-income citizens through state expenditures (Bonga-Bonga & Perold, 2014). Another advantage advocated by proponents of a progressive system is that it acts as an automatic stabilizer against economic cycles of countries, as there is a possibility of taxpayers moving from one bracket to another, minimizing the effects of economic shocks, offering greater stability to the economy (Popescu et al., 2019; Bonga-Bonga & Perold, 2014). In practice, in case of a recession, if workers' salaries are reduced, they will be taxed at a lower marginal rate, thus retaining a higher percentage of their income, which reduces the impact of the recession on their incomes. In the case of an economic expansion, the opposite would occur. Thus, despite macroeconomic shocks, due to the stabilizing effect provided by progressive taxation, aggregate consumption would remain relatively constant at any phase of economic cycles (Bonga-Bonga & Perold, 2014). However, critics of the progressive system argue that the State can stabilize the economy through more effective means and that the benefits of stabilizing the economy are only realized if governments behave responsibly and do not incur additional expenses during periods of economic expansion; otherwise, the desired countercyclical function is not fulfilled (Popescu et al., 2019; Bonga-Bonga & Perold, 2014).

Despite the identified advantages, the progressive tax system also faces criticism. Some authors argue that there is injustice in the progressive system as it penalizes individuals who work and save more, and removes incentives for labor supply and savings decisions, both for families and private companies. By withdrawing income from those who earn more, the incentive to produce is removed, and by providing another source of income to those who earn less, the incentive to produce is similarly diminished (Laffer, 2019). Consequently, economic agents may choose to work less, allocating more time to leisure and engaging in simpler tasks, thereby hampering economic growth (Conesa & Krueger, 2006; Bonga-Bonga & Perold, 2014). Another critique relates to the fact that this is the most complex tax system, which can trigger a feeling of increased tax pressure, one of the most relevant factors regarding tax non-compliance and the growth of the shadow economy (Pántya et al., 2016; Bonga-Bonga & Perold, 2014).

Due to these criticisms, many countries have been discussing tax reform, with the proportional tax system, in which there is only one tax rate on income, gaining emphasis (Ventura, 1999).

2.3. Flat Tax

2.3.1. History

The flat tax, or proportional tax, is not a recent idea, having been discussed and utilized throughout history up to the present day (Evans & Aligica, 2008). During the medieval period in feudal Europe, taxation was carried out through a system similar to what is now considered a proportional system, in which landowners received a fixed proportion of agricultural production (Fischer & Ferraro, 2019). Following the medieval period, Adam Smith (1776), one of the most recognized economists of his time, although stating that "it is not unreasonable that the rich should contribute to the public expense not only in proportion to their revenue but something more than in proportion," also advocated for proportional rates, stating that "the subjects of every state ought to contribute to the support of the government, as nearly as possible, in proportion to their respective abilities, that is, in proportion to the revenue which they respectively enjoy under the protection of the state" (Fischer & Ferraro, 2019). Additionally, according to the same author, a country's tax system should be simple, efficient, transparent, and fair. Although no tax system is perfect, a proportional system is the one that comes closest to these criteria (Heath, 2006). Also, in the Classical school, taxation was a constant focus of attention for economists. Authors such as Ricardo (1817) and Mill (1848) concluded that reasonable tax systems should be based on two fundamental principles: efficiency and equity. Consequently, two theories of taxation were developed, each emphasizing one of the two principles. The proportional tax was designed primarily to satisfy the principle of efficiency, while the progressive tax addressed the principle of equity (Dagan et al., 1999). Most countries, in an attempt to address some income inequalities in their societies, have opted to establish progressive tax systems (Popescu et al., 2019; Sabitova & Dyudina, 2015). In the 20th century, authors of economic liberalism revived the idea that a proportional system could be a viable alternative to a progressive system. Hayek (1960) developed arguments against the idea that ensuring a fair income redistribution required progressive income taxation. Friedman (1962) complemented the idea, arguing that the best way to alleviate poverty would be through a flat tax on income (Evans & Aligica, 2008; Fischer & Ferraro, 2019). In 1983, economists Robert E. Hall and Alvin Rabushka first developed and formalized academic work on the existence of a single tax rate on income, applied to both personal and business income, combined with a deduction or base subsidy (Heath, 2006; Fischer & Ferraro, 2019). In the system proposed by Hall and Rabushka, all salaries, wages, and pensions above the exemption threshold would be subject to a single marginal tax rate, resulting in an increase in average tax rates as labor income increased (Ventura, 1999). Thus, in practice, this combination of a flat income tax rate with a base deduction leads to a progressive regime, albeit different from the notion of progressivity in which both marginal and average rates increase with income (Ventura, 1999; Fossen, 2009). Until around the end of the 20th century, fixed income taxes could only be found in tax havens such as Hong Kong or the Channel Islands, such as Guernsey and Jersey (Fuest et al., 2008). However, in the last decade of the 20th century, the poor countries of Eastern Europe, which were under the communist regime of the Soviet Union, began to adopt proportional systems for income tax as they regained independence and aimed primarily for economic growth. The first wave of these tax reforms began in 1994 in Estonia, followed by Lithuania and Latvia in the following years, characterized by relatively high tax rates, close to the highest marginal rate before the reform (Barrios et al., 2020). Starting in 2001, the second wave began with tax reform in Russia, continuing in countries such as Serbia (2003), Romania (2005), and Hungary (2011), characterized by reduced tax rates, close to the lowest marginal rate before the reform (Barrios et al., 2020). In less than fifteen years, the flat tax ceased to be considered an inconceivable alternative, as although these reforms were implemented only in the former socialist economies of Eastern Europe, the economic growth observed in these countries has generated the opinion that this concept could also be adopted by Western European countries (Evans & Aligica, 2008; Peichl, 2009). For this reason, along with the other advantages provided by a proportional tax system, an increasing number of European countries, especially those facing financial difficulties and stagnant economies, have been considering the possibility of adopting this fiscal policy (Evans & Aligica, 2008).

2.3.2. Advantages

When discussing a personal income tax reform, one of the objectives is its simplification. Simplicity is understood as an important characteristic of tax systems, as system complexity is often considered a barrier to equity and efficiency because it can allow high-income taxpayers to exploit tax loopholes to reduce their tax burden (Fuest et al., 2008). One of the advantages of adopting a proportional tax system is precisely its administrative simplicity (Evans & Aligica, 2008). A simple system combined with low tax rates brings benefits in terms of reducing compliance costs, reducing the need for expensive accountants and consultants, understanding, and minimizing collection costs by facilitating the work of tax authorities (Fuest et al., 2008; Heath, 2006). This cost reduction could potentially reduce tax evasion and underreporting of income, thus widening the tax base (Duncan & Peter, 2010). However, critics of the flat tax argue that a change in the tax system is not necessary to observe a decline in tax evasion and income underreporting, as this could be achieved through investment and improvement of tax authorities (Popescu et al., 2019). It is also important to note that the effect of reducing tax evasion, which is usually a central point in tax reforms in countries with developing economies, may have less impact in countries with more developed economies since these countries usually have a lower percentage of informal economy and tax evasion (Paulus & Peichl, 2009).

In addition to the advantages outlined regarding the administrative simplicity of the flat tax, its adoption, if implemented with low tax rates, is also associated with a potential significant increase in efficiency, employment, and economic growth through improved incentives (Fischer & Ferraro, 2019; Peichl, 2009; Benczúr et al., 2018). A reduction in tax rates would incentivize work by making it more rewarding, especially for households in higher tax brackets, and discourage leisure time by increasing its opportunity cost (Heath, 2006; Ventura, 1999; Bonga-Bonga & Perold, 2014; Conesa & Krueger, 2006). It is noteworthy that lower marginal rates not only lead to an increase in labor supply but also alter the way income is compensated, allowing workers to retain more of their income and companies to reduce costs (Feldstein, 1995; Ventura, 1999). Thus, the reduction in tax rates should result in increased savings and investment, facilitating entrepreneurship and the creation of small businesses, which, coupled with greater work motivation, attraction of foreign investment, and qualified immigrants, would stimulate the economy (Duncan & Peter, 2010; Skipper & Burton, 2008; Bonga-Bonga & Perold, 2014). This economic stimulus would provide more jobs and consequently more work opportunities for all citizens, potentially leading to greater social mobility (Heath, 2006). However, there are also those who argue that reducing tax rates would not lead to substantial economic growth (Skipper & Burton, 2008). These authors argue that a more egalitarian society would have higher long-term economic growth since investment in human capital increases efficiency and, the better the wealth redistribution, the more opportunities low-income citizens will have due to access to public goods, better education, and healthcare (Aghion et al., 1999; Osberg, 1995). Furthermore, individuals with lower incomes tend to demonstrate higher performance compared to those with higher incomes under a progressive tax system (Pántya et al., 2016). Finally, it is also observed that in countries where there is already a lot of private initiative and a large part of the active population is employed, a proportional tax system without being accompanied by profound reforms in the education, labor, and health systems of the state will not result in substantive differences (Pogátsa, 2009).

2.3.3. Disadvantages

Despite the specified advantages of adopting a proportional system, it also contains disadvantages, which from the perspective of the International Monetary Fund and some European Union officials, outweigh the benefits derived from it, which is why they have strongly criticized it, vehemently opposing the idea of this method of taxation (Voinea, 2013). A negative consideration is the decrease in state revenues. However, proponents of the flat tax cite the advantage of broadening the tax base due to the decline in tax evasion and income underreporting to demonstrate that the decrease would be less than expected. Additionally, although it is expected that revenues will be lower in the short term, in the long term, the dynamic effect on growth should result in an increase in tax revenues (Heath, 2006). Another disadvantage presented regarding proportional taxation, and considered by many as the main disadvantage of this system, is that it shows a negative impact on wealth distribution, since the tax burden is mostly borne by low-income individuals (Ventura, 1999; Barrios et al., 2020; Popescu et al., 2019; Benczúr et al., 2018). Unlike the middle and upper class who benefit from this fiscal policy in the long run, the lower class experiences a significant loss as the decline in tax progressivity cannot be compensated for by economic growth (Altig et al., 2001). In this way, an exacerbation of inequalities is expected, which is why the spread of flat tax to developed countries is limited (Paulus & Peichl, 2009; Popescu et al., 2019; Peichl, 2009). However, its proponents argue that the redistributive effect depends on the tax rate and deductions applied and suggest that specific combinations can lead to highly redistributive personal income tax systems. Still, if considerable tax deductions or low tax rates are not established, the flat tax indeed provides little redistribution in society (Domonkos, 2016; Paulus & Peichl, 2009). It is practically consensual among authors that progressive taxation is the best way to achieve equality. However, some authors like Rawls (1971) argue that a certain level of inequality is acceptable if with these inequalities society as a whole is better off than it would be without them. Aaberge et al. (2004) in their study draw an analogy between wealth redistribution and dividing a cake, suggesting that the progressive system would result in a more equitable distribution of slices, but a proportional system would result in a larger cake.

METHODOLOGY

To construct a scientific investigation, which is an organized and methodical process, one or more research questions must be established (Merriam, 2009). The declarative research questions of this study are to determine the publication trends of scientific articles and to understand the main conclusions of the major studies conducted on the subject. To answer these questions, a characterization of the research will be performed through bibliometric analysis, which allows drawing conclusions about the characteristics and trends of scientific articles over the years.

In this bibliometric analysis, the PRISMA methodology (Preferred Reporting Items for Systematic Reviews and Meta-Analyses) will be utilized, specifically developed for application in systematic reviews and meta-analyses (Liberati et al., 2009). The PRISMA methodology serves as guidance to help authors prepare protocols aimed at providing the foundation for the review and the methodological and analytical approach, providing a minimum set of items to be included in systematic reviews and meta-analyses (Moher et al., 2015). In this research, some items of the PRISMA methodology were used, including the title, abstract, introduction, objectives, the adopted methodology, and the results.

Additionally, to conduct any research, a solid knowledge base is necessary in the initial phase. Thus, the literature review was conducted through a search of academic journals present in prestigious databases such as Scopus or in rankings based on research quality, such as the Academic Journal Quality Guide 2018, ensuring the quality of the information source. The focus of the literature review was on flat tax; however, it also included a broader explanation of related topics, such as tax systems and progressive taxes, resulting in a better understanding of the conceptual basis of the flat tax.

With the theoretical framework finalized, data collection and analysis were carried out in three distinct phases: data collection, identification of bibliometric indicators, and data analysis.

3.1 Data Collection

The initial phase of the analysis focused on a search on the Scopus platform. Scopus was chosen because it provides high-quality information, such as metadata for all indexed content, allowing for a more precise search and data collection of scientific articles, and its database has global coverage to ensure that relevant scientific information is not omitted (Scopus - Content Coverage Guide, n.d.; Why choose Scopus, n.d.; High-Quality Data, n.d.). The search was filtered so that publications had to present the term "flat tax" in their keywords or have the term "flat tax" present in their title. It is important to note that the last data collection was carried out at the end of October, in order to include the largest possible number of publications in 2021 in the sample. Thus, with the search with the mentioned filters, 134 results were obtained. Subsequently, the sample was limited to only scientific articles since these are published in peer-reviewed scientific journals, thus ensuring the quality of the publication. With this limitation, the sample became 113 scientific articles. Finally, due to the impossibility of determining the author of 4 articles, these were removed, resulting in a final sample of 109 articles. The relevant information for this research was then collected through the export of a document from the Scopus platform containing citation information, bibliographical information, abstract & keywords, funding details, and other information. The process of the imposed limitations and the subsequent definition of the sample are shown in Figure 1, and the titles, authors, and publication years of the 109 articles included are represented in Table 1.

Figure 1. Sample definition process used (Own elaboration)

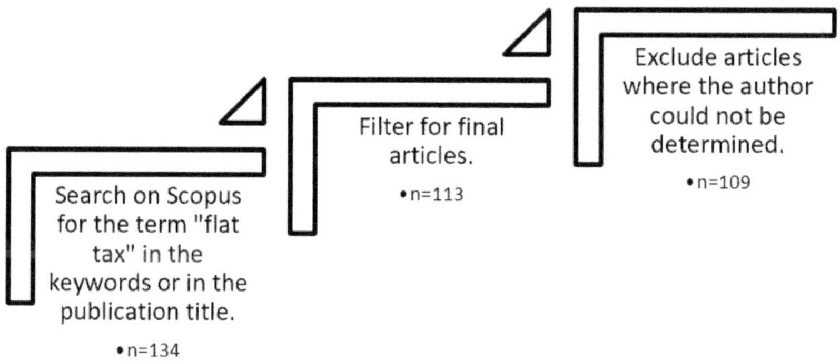

Figure 1 - Sample Definition Process Used (Source: Own elaboration)

Table 1. Articles comprising the utilized sample (title, authors, and publication year)

Title	Authors	Publication Year
Flat tax? Maybe not a bad idea after all	Castelluccio, M.	2021
Flat tax: European experiences and Italian Proposals	Baldini, M.; Rizzo, L.	2021
Flat-rate personal income tax in Lithuania, Romania and Hungary: A revolutionary policy	Kovács, B.	2021
Recent research on labor supply: Implications for tax and transfer policy	Kean, M.P.	2021
Taxes and the incentive to work under flat and progressive tax systems in Slovakia	Nadirov, O.; Dehning, B.; Pavelkova, D.	2021
Flat tax system and heterogeneity of self-employment	Safarov, S.; Abdurazzakova, D.	2021

continued on following page

Table 1. Continued

Title	Authors	Publication Year
Does the Personal Income Flat Tax fit with Economic Growth and Inequality in Italy?	Socci, C.; D'Andrea, S.; Pretaroli, R.; Severini, F.	2021
The politics of flat taxes	Carroll, D. R.; Dolmas, J.; Young, E. R.	2021
Progressive Tax Reforms in Flat Tax Countries	Barrios, S.; Ivaškaitė-Tamošiūnė, V.; Maftei, A.; Narazani, E.; Varga, J.	2020
Universal basic income with flat tax reform in France	Magnani, R.; Piccoli, L.	2020
Reflections on economic policy	Laffer, A.B.	2020
How Much Does Basic Income Cost? Modelling Basic Income as Universal Life Annuity	Gan, W. C.	2019
Investment expensing and progressivity in flat-tax reforms	Díaz-Giménez, J.; Pijoan-Mas, J.	2019
The end of the flat tax experiment in Slovakia: An evaluation using behavioural microsimulation in a dynamic macroeconomic framework	Horváth, M.; Senaj, M., Siebertová, Z.; Švarda, N.; Valachyová, J.	2019
A proposal for a simple average-based progressive taxation system	Fischer, D.-H.; Ferraro, S.	2019
A briefing for a tax system reform	Visco, V.	2019
Why post-communist countries choose the flat tax: A comparative welfare approach	Ganchev, G.; Tanchev, S.	2019
Flat tax - Could it be really flat?	Ondrejovič, S.	2019
On Italy's flat tax needs and sustainability of the public budget	Mele, M.	2019
The flat tax in the Italian reform policy	Romagnoli, G. C.	2019
The flat tax as a fiscal detoxification therapy. Proposals for its introduction in stages in a rough situation	Forte, F.; Guardabascio, D.	2019
Envelope wages, hidden production and labor productivity	Di Nola, A.; Kocharkov, G.; Vasilev, A.	2019
'Flattening' tax evasion?: Evidence from the post-communist natural experiment	Filer, R. K.; Hanousek, J.; Lichard, T.; Torosyan, K.	2019
Minimum Income and Flat Tax Revisited: A Combined CGE-Microsimulation Analysis for Germany	Schubert, S.	2018
Assessing the economic and social impact of tax and benefit reforms: A general-equilibrium microsimulation approach applied to Hungary	Benczúr, P.; Kátay, G.; Kiss, Á.	2018
How Neoliberal Reforms Lose Their Partisan Identity: Flat Tax Diffusion in Eastern Europe and Post-Soviet Eurasia	Appel, H.	2018
Bifurcation Mechanism Design—From Optimal Flat Taxes to Better Cancer Treatments	Yang, G.; Basanta, D.; Pilouras, G.	2018

continued on following page

Table 1. Continued

Title	Authors	Publication Year
Basic income and flat tax: The Italian Scenario	Colombino, U.; Islam, N.	2018
Corporate flat tax reforms and businesses' investment decisions: evidence from Switzerland	Galletta, S.; Redonda, A.	2017
Higher Tax for Top Earners	FitzRoy, F.; Jin, J.	2017
Does a Progressive PIT Stabilize the Economy? A Comparison of Progressive and Flat Taxes	Krajewski, P.; Pilat, K.	2017
Getting the poor to work: Three welfare-increasing reforms for a busy Germany	Jessen, R.; Rostam-Afschar, D.; Steiner, V.	2017
Weak differential monotonicity, flat tax, and basic income	Yokote, K.; Casajus, A.	2017
Labour force participation elasticities and the move away from a flat tax: the case of Slovakia	Senaj, M.; Siebertova, Z.; Svarda, N.; Valachyova, J	2016
Evaluating the economic effects of flat tax reforms using synthetic control methods	Adhikari, B.; Alm, J.	2016
Work performance and tax compliance in flat and progressive tax systems	Pántya, J.; Kovács, J.; Kogler, C.; Kirchler, E.	2016
Who Wants a Progressive Income Tax?: Determinants of Tax Policy Preferences in Post-socialist Eastern Europe	Domonkos, S.	2016
Differentially monotonic redistribution of income	Casajus, A.	2016
Welfare gains from the adoption of proportional taxation in a general-equilibrium model with a grey economy: the case of Bulgaria's 2008 flat tax reform	Vasilev, A.	2015
Russia's flat tax reform: redefining its effects on employment	Kryvoruchko, I.	2015
Equal taxation as a basis for classifying financial instruments as debt or equity-a Swedish case study	Hilling, A.; Vilhelmsson, A.	2015
Income taxation as a tool of income redistribution	Sabitova, N.M.; Dyudina, M.P.	2015
Reporting import tariffs (and other taxes)	Tonin, M.	2014
Why is "new" europe more neoliberal?: Pension privatization and flat tax in the postcommunist eu member states	Beblavý, M.	2014
A cge simulation of a flat tax as a possibility for tax reform in South Africa	Bonga-Bonga, L.; Perold, M.	2014
Behavioral responses and the distributional effects of the Russian 'flat' tax	Duncan, D.	2014
Revisiting crisis generators in Romania and other new EU member states	Voinea, L.	2013
Ideas Versus Resources: Explaining the Flat Tax and Pension Privatization Revolutions in Eastern Europe and the Former Soviet Union	Appel, H.; Orenstein, M. A.	2013

continued on following page

Table 1. Continued

Title	Authors	Publication Year
A "modest" proposal to balance the federal budget	Matthews, R.B	2013
Progressive or "flat" tax -economic and political dilemma	Blechová, B.	2012
The Effect of Taxation on Informal Employment: Evidence from the Russian Flat Tax Reform	Slonimczyk, F.	2012
Tax evasion, minimum wage noncompliance, and informality	Basu, A.K.; Chau, N.H.; Siddique, Z.	2012
A Flat Tax Reform in an Economy with Occupational Choice and Financial Frictions	Boháček, R.; Zubrický, J.	2012
Expected future earnings, taxation, and university enrollment	Fossen, F.M.; Glocker, D.	2011
On the use of some optimal strategies of fiscal administration during economic crisis	Brojba, L.C.; Dumitru, C.G.; Belciug, A.V.	2010
Income tax reform in France: A case study	Cremer, H.; Gahvari, F.; Ladoux, N.	2010
Flat tax reform: The Baltics 2000-2007	Azacis, H.; Gillman, M.	2010
Does labour supply respond to a flat tax?	Duncan, D.; Peter, K.S.	2010
Flat tax and labour taxation - The Czech and Slovak experience	Beblavý, M.	2010
The impact of the flat tax reform on inequality - The case of Romania	Voinea, L.; Mih escu, F.	2009
Tatra Tig er growth miracle or belated recovery?	Pogátsa, Z.	2009
Effects of flat tax reforms in Western Europe	Paulus, A.; Peichl, A.	2009
Would a flat-rate tax stimulate entrepreneurship in germany? a behavioural microsimulation analysis allowing for risk	Fossen, F. M.	2009
Myth and reality of flat tax reform Micro estimates of tax evasion response and welfare effects in Russia	Gorodnichenko, Y.; Martínez-Vázquez, J.; Peter, K. S.	2009
Independence between the efficient tax rate and tax progressiveness in the Czech Republic during 1993-2007	Široký, J.; Maková, K.	2009
The benefits and problems of linking micro and macro models - Evidence from a flat tax analysis	Peichl, A.	2009
Flatliners Ideology and rational learning in the adoption of the flat tax	Baturo, A.; Gray, J.	2009
Does a simpler income tax yield more equity and efficiency?	Fuest, C.; Peichl, A.; Schaefer, T.	2008
The "flat tax(es)": Principles and experience	Keen, M.; Kim, Y.; Varsano, R.	2008

continued on following page

Table 1. Continued

Title	Authors	Publication Year
Is a flat tax reform feasible in a grown-up democracy of Western Europe? A simulation study for Germany	Fuest, C.; Peichl, A.; Schaefer, T.	2008
Ramifications of a flat tax - Shifting the burden to the middle class	Skipper, D.W.; Burton, H.A.	2008
The ups and downs of flatter taxes	Owens, J.	2007
Flat tax experiments	Osterkamp, R.	2007
Non-manipulable division rules in claim problems and generalizations	Ju, B.G.; Miyagawa, E.; Sakai, T.	2007
On the optimal progressivity of the income tax code	Conesa, J.C.; Krueger, D.	2006
Flat tax reforms: A general equilibrium evaluation for Spain	González-Torrabadella, M.; Pijoan-Mas, J.	2006
Russia's flat tax: Myths and facts	Gaddy, C. G.; Gale, W. G.	2006
Une flat tax en Belgique Quelques éclairages sur les principes et les conséquences d'une telle réforme	Valenduc, C.	2006
Quelques éléments d'analyse de la flat tax	Maggiulli, C.; Mors, M.	2006
Taxation: Circling the flat tax	Matlack, C.; Ewing, J.; Bush, J.; Granitsas, A.; Vitzhum, C.	2005
The Russian 'flat tax' reform	Ivanova, A.; Keen, M. J.; Klemm, A.	2005
Growth effects of shifting from a graduated-rate tax system to a flat tax	Cassou, S. P.; Lansing, K. J.	2004
The welfare of investment deductibility under a flat tax	Cugno, F.; Zanola, R.	2002
Can anyone beat the flat tax?	Epstein, R. A.	2002
Financial repression and optimal taxation	Bai, C.E.; Li, D.D.; Qian, Y.; Wang, Y.	2001
The effect of policy objectives, complexity, and self-interest on individuals' comparative fairness judgments of a flat tax	Bobek, D. D.; Hatfield, R. C.	2001
Flat tax proposals: A current review, with a history of the arguments pro and com	Kyj, L. S.; Romeo, G. C.; Marshall, P. S.	2001
The uneasy case for the flat tax	Buckley, F. H.; Rasmusen, E. B.	2000
Ironing Out the Flat Tax	Weisbach, D. A.	2000
Labor supply responses and welfare effects from replacing current tax rules by a flat tax: Empirical evidence from Italy, Norway and Sweden	Aaberge, R.; Colombino, U.; Ström, S.	2000
Feasible implementation of taxation methods	Dagan, N.; Serrano, R.; Volji, O.	1999
Flat tax reform: A quantitative exploration	Ventura, G.	1999

continued on following page

Table 1. Continued

Title	Authors	Publication Year
Flat taxes and effective tax planning	Calegari, M. J.	1998
Estimating flat tax incidence and yield: A sensitivity analysis	Dunbar, A.; Pogue, T. F.	1998
Flat taxes and distributional justice	FougÈre, M.; Ruggeri, G.C.	1998
Revenue, progressivity, and the flat tax	Ho, M. S.; Stiroh, K. J.	1998
The Complexity of Tax Structure in Competitive Political Systems	Warskett, G.; Winer, S.L.; Hettich, W.	1998
A flat tax without bumpy philanthropy: Decreasing the impact of a "low, single rate" on individual charitable contributions	Davies, R. P.	1997
Flat tax intriguing, but will it fly?	Ichniowski, T.; Schriener, J.	1996
Origins of a flat tax	Bank, S. A.	1996
Is there a simpler, flatter tax in our future?	Penner, R. G.	1996
Presidential hopefuls pump up flat-tax debate.	Weissenstein, E.	1996
A snag in Forbes's flat tax?	Shear, J.	1996
The forbes flat tax	Veramallay, A. I.	1996
An analysis of the distributional effects of replacing the progressive income tax with a flat tax	Iyer, G. S.; Seetharaman, A.; Englebrecht, T. D.	1996
Voting over flat taxes in an endowment economy	Gouveia, M.; Oliver, D.	1996
Flat tax' raises interesting questions.	Pallarito, K.	1995
Treasury's modified flat tax proposal could adversely affect tax-exempt hospitals.	Kapp, R. H.; Sterling, M. A.	1984
Examining flat tax rate proposals The equity issues	Beardsley, G. L.	1984

(Source: Own elaboration)

3.2. Bibliometric Indicators

After the data has been collected, it is necessary to evaluate scientific production through bibliometric indicators. Bibliometrics is a quantitative and statistical technique used to assess indices of knowledge production and dissemination, as well as to examine the evolution of various scientific areas and authorship and publication trends (Costa et al., 2012). The assessment of scientific production is carried out using various bibliometric indicators, including indicators of scientific quality, indicators of scientific activity, indicators of scientific impact, and indicators of thematic associations (Costa et al., 2012).

Indicators of scientific quality are based on peer review evaluations of publications for their scientific content and are not quantifiable, and therefore were not analyzed in this investigation (Costa et al., 2012).

Indicators of scientific activity allow the assessment of the level of activity in terms of scientific articles published over time. For this purpose, the following indicators were analyzed: number and distribution of published works, author productivity, collaboration in work authorship, and the distribution and geographical collaboration of articles.

Indicators of scientific impact allow the assessment of the impact of works and sources. The indicator addressed in this study that helps measure the impact of works was the number of citations to the articles in the sample under study. To measure the impact of sources, the influence of scientific journals and their impact factor was evaluated using the CiteScore metric.

Indicators of thematic associations allow the evaluation of article characteristics. In this case, an analysis of the keywords of the scientific articles under study was conducted.

3.3. Data Analysis

To process and analyze the collected data, two software tools were used: Excel and VOSviewer, along with metrics provided by the Scopus platform. Through Excel, a set of tables and graphs was developed to organize a large amount of data and simplify its interpretation. VOSviewer enabled the production of network maps that facilitate the visualization and analysis of relationships between authors, their countries of affiliation, as well as keywords. Finally, through Scopus, metrics such as H-Index and CiteScore were analyzed to complete the characterization of flat tax research.

RESULTS

In this chapter, the results of the characterization study of research on "Flat Tax" will be presented, considering bibliometric indicators of scientific activity, scientific impact, and thematic associations, as well as a summary table with the main conclusions of the primary investigations from the study sample.

4.1. Indicators of Scientific Activity

Indicators of scientific activity allow the assessment of the level of activity in terms of scientific articles published over time. Indicators such as the distribution of published articles, author productivity, collaboration in article authorship, and the geographical distribution of articles will be analyzed in the following subsections.

4.1.1. Number and distribution of articles published per year

Through Figure 2, it is possible to observe that the scientific articles observed in this study were published between 1984 and 2021, spanning a temporal horizon of 37 years. However, it was observed that in the period between 1985 and 1994, as well as in the year 2003, no articles meeting the search criteria mentioned in the Methodology chapter were published on the Scopus platform, reducing the number of years under analysis to 27 years. In this period, a total of 109 articles were published, reflecting an average of 4.04 articles published per year.

Additionally, it can be observed from the same figure that in 2019, 12 articles were published, which corresponds to the maximum number of articles published in the analyzed period. On the contrary, the years 1995, 1997, 2004, and 2011 were the ones with the fewest articles published, with only one article published in each of these four years. Another conclusion that can be drawn is that the most frequent number of articles published in a year is 5, which occurred in 6 years.

Regarding the evolution over time, there is an increase in the number of articles published over the decades, with 2 in the 1980s, 17 in the 1990s, 31 in the 2000s, and 48 in the 2010s, demonstrating that interest in the topic has been gradually increasing. At the beginning of the current decade, 11 articles have already been published in two years, compared to the beginning of the previous two decades when only 6 articles had been published in the first two years, indicating an expectation of an increase in the number of articles published.

Figure 2. Evolution of the number of published articles (Own elaboration)

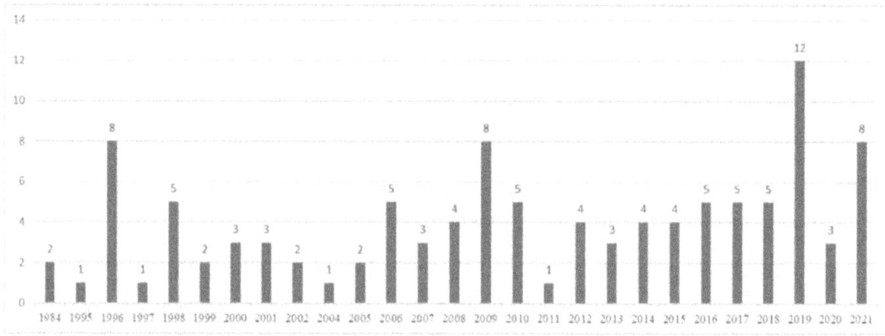

Figure 2 - Evolution of the number of published articles

(Source: Own elaboration)

4.1.2. Author Productivity

Analyzing the productivity of authors allows us to conclude which authors produce the most knowledge regarding a specific subject, in this case, which authors have published the most scientific articles on "Flat Tax".

As previously mentioned, the sample of this study includes 109 scientific articles. A total of 201 authors contributed to these publications. Of these, 93% contributed only one article, while 7% published two or more articles. Figure 3 graphically presents this information in absolute values.

Figure 3. Author productivity (Own elaboration)

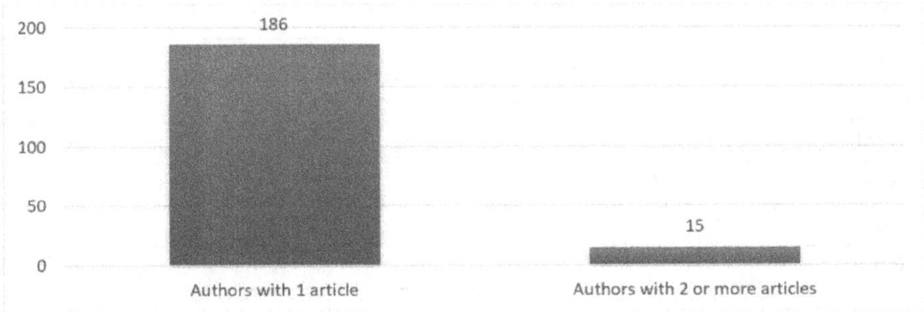

Figure 3 - Author Productivity

(Source: Own elaboration)

Following Figure 3, Table 2 was prepared to detail the most productive authors, i.e., those who published at least two scientific articles. As can be seen from the figure, the author who published the most articles was Peichl with 4 articles, followed by 14 different authors with 2 articles each, and the remaining 186 authors with only 1 article each. It is therefore possible to conclude that, concerning articles published in scientific journals available on the Scopus platform, there is no author who stands out with many articles written on the topic. Instead, the topic in question is one where attention is divided among many authors. This fact leads to various types of studies with different origins, methodologies, and assumptions, which can result in very divergent conclusions.

Table 2. Number of articles published per author

Author	Number of Articles	%
Peichl, A.	4	1,83%
Fuest, C:	2	0,92%
Schaefer, T.	2	0,92%
Duncan, D.	2	0,92%
Senaj, M.	2	0,92%
Peter, K.S.	2	0,92%
Keen, M.	2	0,92%
Pijoan-mas, J.	2	0,92%

continued on following page

Table 2. Continued

Author	Number of Articles	%
Fossen, F.M.	2	0,92%
Voinea, I.	2	0,92%
Appel, H.	2	0,92%
Beblavy, M.	2	0,92%
Casajus, A.	2	0,92%
Colombino, U.	2	0,92%
Vasilev, A.	2	0,92%
remaining 186 authors	1	85,32%
Total	**218**	**100%**

4.1.3 Collaboration in Article Authorship

The preparation of an article can be done individually, involving only one author, or collectively, involving two or more authors. Figure 4 shows a pie chart illustrating the percentage of articles written individually and collectively. It is evident that the majority of the published articles were written collectively. Out of the 109 articles included in this study sample, 68 were co-authored, representing 62% of the total published articles. The articles written by a single author were 41, which accounted for 38% of the total published articles.

Figure 4. Type of authorship (Own Elaboration)

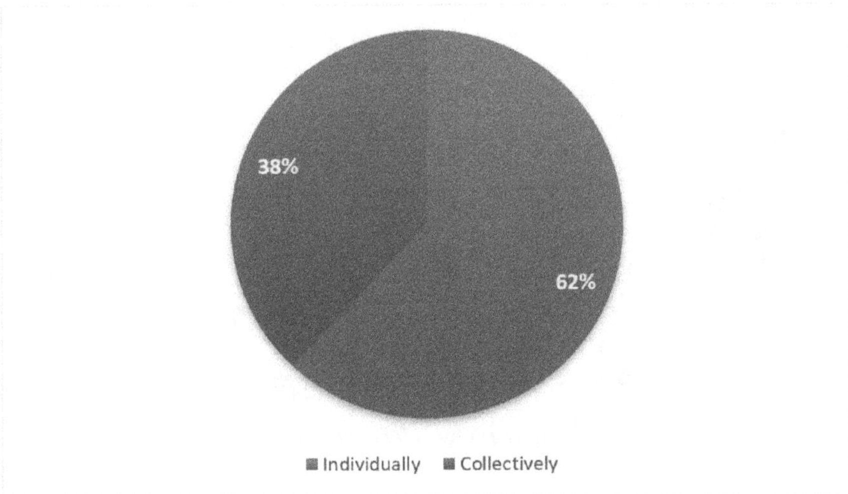

Figure 4 - Type of Authorship

(Source: Own Elaboration)

Following this, Figure 5 presents the number of articles written according to the number of contributing authors. In addition to individually authored articles, the distribution of co-authored articles among those with two, three, four, or five authors is depicted. Articles written by two authors are the most prevalent, with 40 articles, followed by those written by three authors, totaling 20 articles. The least common are articles written by four and five authors, with only 5 and 3 articles respectively.

Figure 5. Number of authors per article (Own elaboration)

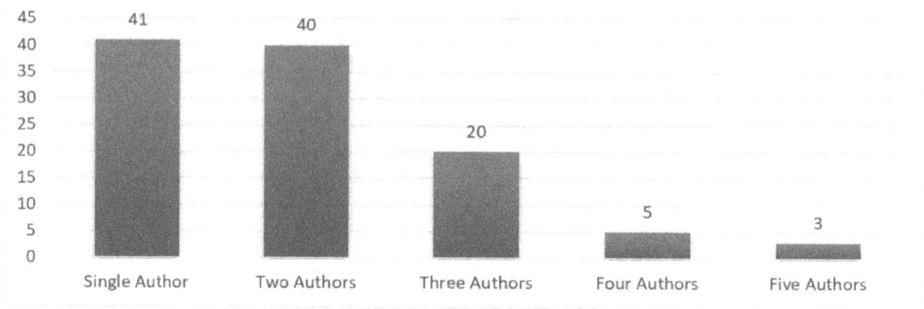

Figure 5 - Number of Authors per Article

(Source: Own elaboration)

To analyze the level of collaboration among the most prolific authors, a co-authorship network map was created using VOSviewer software. In this map, authors are represented by circles, which are larger for authors who have published more articles. The connections between authors are represented by lines, which are thicker for stronger collaboration links.

Figure 6 displays the connections among the most productive authors, specifically those who contributed to 2 or more articles, grouped into clusters. As previously mentioned, 15 authors contributed at least 2 articles, and of these, 10 have no connections with other authors, meaning they published articles individually. The remaining 5 authors are divided into 2 clusters. One cluster, represented in green, consists of 2 authors (Peter, K.S. and Duncan, D.), and the other cluster, represented in red, consists of 3 authors (Schaefer, T.; Peichl, A.; and Fuest, C.). In the latter cluster, each author has a connection strength of 2 with the others, as they co-authored two articles together, namely "Does a simpler income tax yield more equity and efficiency?" and "Is a flat tax reform feasible in a grown-up democracy of Western Europe? A simulation study for Germany," both published in 2008.

Figure 6. Co-authorship associations of the most productive authors (Own Elaboration using VOSviewer)

Figure 6 - Co-authorship Associations of the Most Productive Authors

(Source: Own Elaboration using VOSviewer)

4.1.4 Geographic Distribution and Collaboration

Another significant indicator of the study is the geographic distribution of the published articles. For this analysis, each author was assigned to the country where they are affiliated with a university or another institution.

It is important to note that the number of affiliated authors is not equal to the number of authors who published the articles analyzed in this study, as some authors are affiliated with more than one country, and some are not affiliated with any. Therefore, although there are 201 contributing authors to this study, the number of affiliated authors is considered to be 208. In total, the authors of the articles in this study sample are affiliated with 35 countries. The United States is the country with the highest number of published articles, specifically 42, followed by Germany with 17, the United Kingdom with 14, and Italy with 10. On the other hand, there are 12 countries with only one published article each. It is also important to highlight that the European Commission and the International Monetary Fund were added as “Others” in the table, as authors were affiliated with these organizations, which cannot be associated with any specific country.

In order to understand the level of communication among the most influential countries in this research, a network map was constructed using VOSviewer software, illustrating the geographic collaborations among countries with at least two published scientific articles. It is worth noting that in Figure 7, there is a green circle representing Hungary, which is not labeled due to its proximity to a larger circle representing the United Kingdom.

Thus, Figure 7 demonstrates the connections among 12 countries to which authors affiliated with at least two scientific articles belong. These 12 countries are grouped into 4 clusters, with a total of 20 connections among them. Germany stands out with the highest number of geographic associations, with 8 connections to other countries (USA, Japan, France, Spain, Italy, Czech Republic, UK, and Hungary). The strongest relationships are with the UK and the USA, with connection strengths of 4 and 2 respectively. Subsequently, the United States of America has 6 connections (Canada, Japan, France, Spain, Germany, and Czech Republic), followed by the United Kingdom with 5 connections (Germany, Czech Republic, Spain, Hungary, and Slovakia).

Figure 7. Geographic associations (Own Elaboration using VOSviewer)

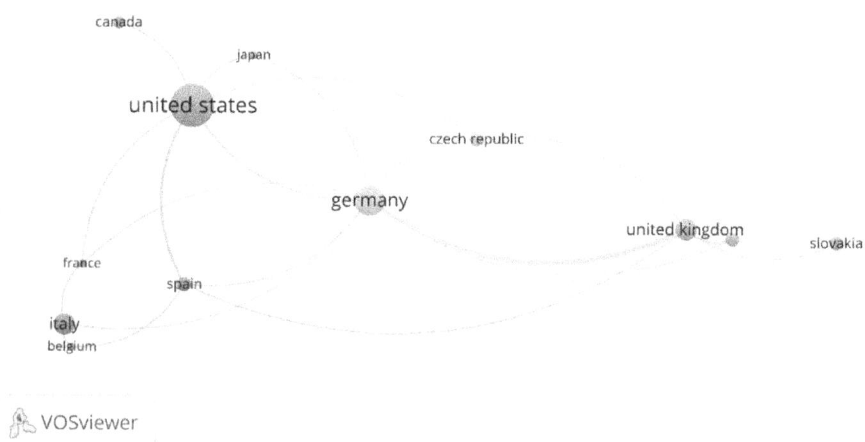

Figure 7 - Geographic Associations

(Source: Own Elaboration using VOSviewer)

4.2. Scientific Impact Indicators

Scientific impact indicators allow for the evaluation of the degree of impact that articles have at the scientific level. These can be divided into indicators of the impact of the works, such as the number of times the articles have been cited, and indicators of the impact of the sources, such as the distribution of articles by scientific journal or research area, which will be analyzed in the following subsections.

4.2.1. Indicators of Work Impact

The number of times articles have been cited is one of the indicators that should be analyzed regarding the impact of the works, as it allows understanding whether the articles in the research sample are being used by other researchers and how relevant they are to science. A scientific article is considered more relevant the more times it is cited, as this indicates that it is serving as a source of knowledge for new scientific articles.

The analysis of this indicator was performed on October 24, 2021, using information from the csv file extracted from the Scopus database. This information is relevant because it is expected that the number of citations will increase as new articles are published. Thus, Figure 4.8 was constructed with the most cited articles, with a minimum of 10 citations, through which it can be observed that, within this sample, the most cited articles are "On the optimal progressivity of the income tax code" published by Conesa, J.C. and Krueger, D. (2006), and "Myth and reality of flat tax reform Micro estimates of tax evasion response and welfare effects in Russia" published by Gorodnichenko, Y.; Martínez-Vázquez, J. and Peter, K. S. (2009) with 98 and 85 citations respectively, which together account for more than 20% of the total citations. Another important fact is that 78.14% of the total citations are concentrated in 21 articles and that there are 34 articles that have not received any citations.

Figure 8. Most cited articles (Own Elaboration)

Title	Citations	%
On the optimal progressivity of the income tax code	98	10,88%
Myth and reality of flat tax reform Micro estimates of tax evasion response and welfare effects in Russia	85	9,43%
Flat tax reform: A quantitative exploration	68	7,55%
Non-manipulable division rules in claim problems and generalizations	53	5,88%
Ideas Versus Resources: Explaining the Flat Tax and Pension Privatization Revolutions in Eastern Europe and the Former Soviet Union	45	4,99%
The Russian 'flat tax' reform	41	4,55%
The "flat tax(es)": Principles and experience	38	4,22%
Labor supply responses and welfare effects from replacing current tax rules by a flat tax: Empirical evidence from Italy, Norway and Sweden	35	3,88%
Is a flat tax reform feasible in a grown-up democracy of Western Europe? A simulation study for Germany	28	3,11%
Effects of flat tax reforms in Western Europe	27	3,00%
Evaluating the economic effects of flat tax reforms using synthetic control methods	25	2,77%
The benefits and problems of linking micro and macro models - Evidence from a flat tax analysis	25	2,77%
Flatliners: Ideology and rational learning in the adoption of the flat tax	23	2,55%
The Complexity of Tax Structure in Competitive Political Systems	22	2,44%
Growth effects of shifting from a graduated-rate tax system to a flat tax	21	2,33%
Can anyone beat the flat tax?	14	1,55%
Ironing Out the Flat Tax	14	1,55%
The Effect of Taxation on Informal Employment: Evidence from the Russian Flat Tax Reform	11	1,22%
The impact of the flat tax reform on inequality - The case of Romania	11	1,22%
Would a flat-rate tax stimulate entrepreneurship in germany? a behavioural microsimulation analysis allowing for risk	10	1,11%
Feasible implementation of taxation methods	10	1,11%
Subtotal	**704**	**78,14%**
Others	197	21,86%
TOTAL	**901**	**100,00%**

Additionally, through Figure 8, it is possible to observe the number of citations per year of publication of the articles. The years 1984 and 1995 do not present any cited articles, thus they are not included in the figure. It can be observed that 2009 was the year of publication with the highest number of citations, with 187 citations from 8 scientific articles.

Figure 9. Number of citations to articles published each year (Own Elaboration)

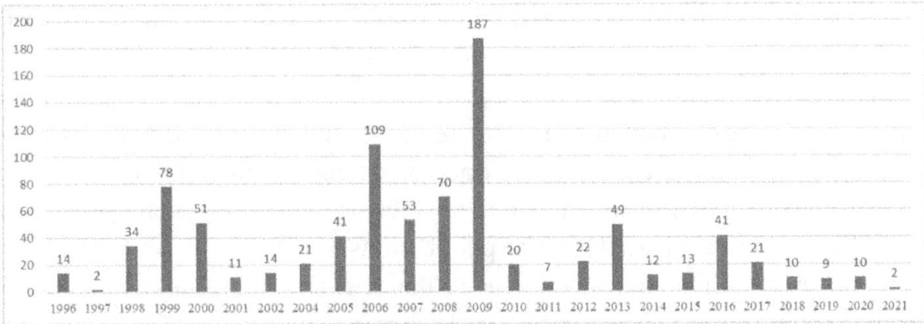

Figure 8 - Number of citations to articles published each year

(Source: Own Elaboration)

Furthermore, an analysis of the annual evolution of the number of article citations was conducted. As can be seen in Figure 10, the first year in which one of the sample articles was cited was in 1998. From then until the present year, only in 1999 and 2000 were there no citations to any of the articles. A positive trend in article citations can be noted since 1998, with 2019, 2020, and 2021 being the years in which they were most cited, with 73, 90, and 102 citations respectively. It is worth noting that the year 2021 has not yet ended, so the number of citations is likely to increase, further contributing to the idea that interest in the "Flat Tax" topic has been increasing.

Figure 10. Number of citations per year (Own Elaboration)

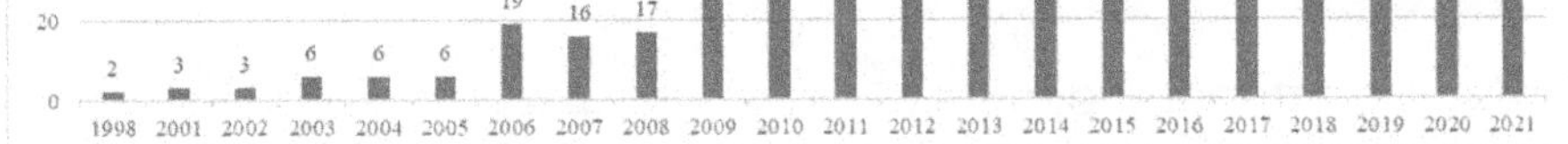

Figure 9 - Number of citations per year

(Source: Own Elaboration)

Finally, using the Scopus platform, an analysis of the H-Index was also conducted, a metric that considers the number of published articles and citations to those articles in a balanced way, thus being useful for indicating the impact of a researcher on the development of their scientific field and for making comparisons between researchers (Hirsch & Buela-Casal, 2014). It is important to mention that for this analysis to be conducted, the metric requires the time horizon to be restricted to 15 years and that the analysis can be done on a single publication or on a set of publications. Thus, the choice was made to select the most recent 15 years, from 2006 to 2021, and to analyze the set of publications.

Through Figure 11, it can be concluded that this study has an H-Index of 16, meaning that out of the 109 scientific articles composing the sample of this study, 16 have been cited at least 16 times.

Figure 11. H-Index of the scientific articles composing the research sample (Scopus)

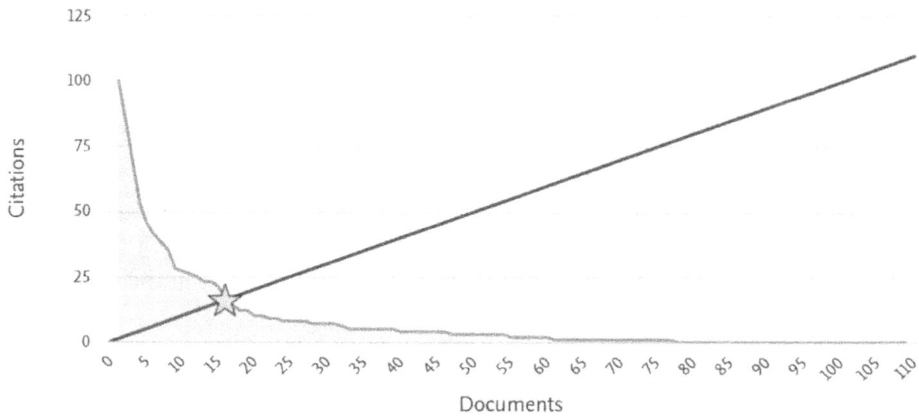

Figure 10 - H-Index of the scientific articles composing the research sample

Source: Scopus

4.2.2. Source Impact Indicators

To gauge the impact of the sources, it is important to conduct an analysis of the scientific journals in which the articles are published. For this purpose, the number of articles published in each journal was determined. The 109 articles under analysis were published in a total of 85 scientific journals. It can be observed in Table 3 that there is no standout journal with many published articles. The vast majority, identified in the figure as "Other 68 journals," have only one article published. Nonetheless, the scientific journal with the most published articles is the International Tax and Public Finance with 6 articles, followed by Economics Letters with 4, and the Journal of Policy Modeling with 3 published articles.

Table 3. Distribution of articles published by scientific journal

Journal	Number of published articles	%
International Tax and Public Finance	6	5,50%
Economics Letters	4	3,67%
Journal of Policy Modeling	3	2,75%
Acta Oeconomica	2	1,83%
Atlantic Economic Journal	2	1,83%
CESifo DICE Report	2	1,83%
Economic Modellng	2	1,83%
Eastern European Economics	2	1,83%
Ekonomicky casopis	2	1,83%
FinanzArchiv	2	1,83%
Journal of Applied Business Research	2	1,83%
Modern healthcare	2	1,83%
National Tax Journal	2	1,83%
Notizie di Politeia	2	1,83%
Reflets et Perspectives de la Vie Economique	2	1,83%
Research in Labor Economics	2	1,83%
Romanian Journal of Economic Forecasting	2	1,83%
Others	1	62,39%
TOTAL	109	100,00%

(Own Elaboration)

Another metric that can be analyzed to understand the relevance and importance of scientific journals is the CiteScore. CiteScore is a metric for evaluating the impact of scientific journals, calculated by dividing the number of citations over a 3-year period by the number of documents published in the same period. The published documents include scientific articles, conference papers, book chapters, reviews, and data papers. Thus, the CiteScore indicates the average number of citations per document published over a three-year period, reflecting whether the documents produced by a scientific journal are more or less cited, which aids in its evaluation since the greater the impact of a journal, the better the perception of its quality.

In Figure 12, the five scientific journals with the highest CiteScore values can be observed, as well as the three journals that contributed the most articles to the sample of this study. The Journal of Political Economy and Economic Policy are the journals with the highest CiteScore, 10.9, meaning that on average, each document they published was cited 10.9 times. The journals that contributed the most articles to the sample of this investigation, such as the Journal of Policy Modeling, Economic Letters, which is the journal with the most documents produced between 2017 and 2019, and International Tax and Public Finance, have a lower CiteScore, suggesting that they have a lesser impact compared to the others.

Figure 12. Top 5 journals with the highest citescore impact factor and top 3 journals with the highest number of published articles (Own elaboration with data extracted from Scopus)

Journal	Published Articles	*CiteScore*	Percentil	Citations	Documents	%
Journal of Political Economy	1	10.9	97%	3023	277	86%
Economic Policy	1	10.9	97%	459	42	81%
European Journal of Political Research	1	6.4	96%	1237	193	88%
Comparative Political Studies	1	6.3	96%	1626	259	84%
Economic Journal	1	5.9	90%	2486	424	80%
Journal of Policy Modeling	3	3.5	78%	1013	291	70%
Economics Letters	4	2.7	70%	4483	1640	50%
International Tax and Public Finance	6	1.7	51%	326	195	60%

Finally, it is also important to conduct an analysis of the study areas in which the scientific articles are categorized. The scientific articles present in this investigation are inserted into various study areas. It is worth mentioning that some articles fall into more than one of these areas, so the number of articles considered is 162 and not 109. Thus, as seen in Figure 13, there are three main areas of focus: "Social Sciences" and "Business, Management and Accounting" with 29 articles each, and especially "Economics, Econometrics and Finance" with 87 articles. The remaining areas with less representation are "Arts and Humanities," "Medicine," "Mathematics," "Decision Sciences," "Engineering," "Environmental Science," and "Psychology," as can be observed in the figure below.

Figure 13. Distribution of articles by study area (Own elaboration)

Study Area	Published Articles	% Published Articles
Economics, Econometrics and Finance	86	53,09%
Business, Management and Accounting	29	17,90%
Social Sciences	29	17,90%
Arts and Humanities	7	4,32%
Medicine	5	3,09%
Mathematics	2	1,23%
Decision Sciences	1	0,62%
Engineering	1	0,62%
Environmental Science	1	0,62%
Psychology	1	0,62%
Total	**162**	**100%**

4.3. Indicators of thematic associations

The analysis of keywords is one of the main indicators of thematic associations. Keywords require careful analysis to understand which themes related to "Flat Tax" are most researched by the authors of scientific articles. Once again, using the VOSviewer software, a network map was created with the main keywords used by the authors to help understand the interconnection between them. As in the previous network maps, the keywords are represented by circles, which are larger the more times that keyword has been used in published scientific articles, and the connection between them is represented by lines that unite them, which are thicker the stronger the connection. It is also important to note that the closer the circles are, the stronger their relationship. The keywords that appear in 3 or more scientific articles were selected for this map. Of the 322 keywords present in the articles, only 38 meet this requirement.

Through Figure 14, it is possible to observe that, naturally, the keyword that appears in the most articles is "flat tax." Following this, "tax reform" and "tax system" are the terms that most frequently appear as keywords in the articles, 14 and 12 times respectively, suggesting that the main topics under analysis concerning articles related to the flat tax are the analysis of tax systems, as well as reforms and possible tax reforms.

Figure 14. Association of keywords used in the articles (Own elaboration using VOSviewer)

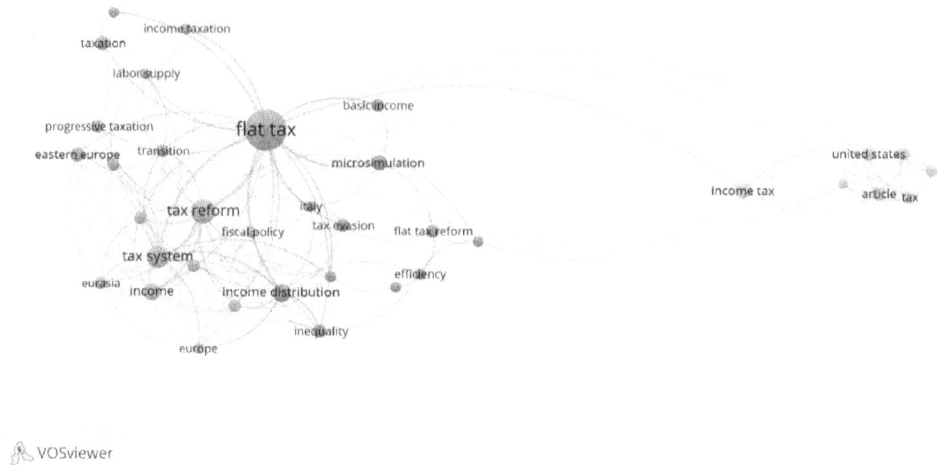

Figure 11 - Association of Keywords Used in the Articles

(Source: Own elaboration using VOSviewer)

4.4. Table with the conclusions of the main articles

Finally, a summary table/chart was developed to group the main conclusions of the main articles with more than 5 citations that are part of the sample of this study, aiming to facilitate the study of the topic and serve as a basis for future research.

Table 4. Objectives and conclusions of the main articles in the sample

Article Title	Study Objectives	Conclusions
On the Optimal Progressivity of the Income Tax Code	Calculate the optimal progressivity of the US income tax code.	The optimal US income tax would be a flat tax of 17.2% with a fixed deduction of about $9,400.
Myth and Reality of Flat Tax Reform: Micro Estimates of Tax Evasion Response and Welfare Effects in Russia	Examine the effects of the 2001 Russian tax reform, which introduced a flat income tax, on consumption, income, and tax evasion.	Significant changes in tax evasion are associated with changes in voluntary compliance; the productivity response to the tax reform is small compared to the evasion response.
Flat Tax Reform: A Quantitative Exploration	Explore a revenue-neutral tax reform where the current US income and capital income tax structure is replaced with a flat tax.	The elimination of effective capital income taxation has a significant positive effect on capital accumulation; profit, income, and especially wealth distributions become more concentrated.
Ideas Versus Resources: Explaining the Flat Tax and Pension Privatization Revolutions in Eastern Europe and the Former Soviet Union	Examine the rapid spread of pension privatization and the flat tax in former communist countries to understand the role of material resources in the diffusion of new political ideas.	Material resources can accelerate the diffusion of political ideas and encourage adoption in larger states, but are not necessary; political networks with ideas can rapidly spread reforms in competitive environments even without significant financial resources.
The Russian 'Flat Tax' Reform	Determine if the substantial increase in income tax revenue was a direct consequence of the flat tax reform in Russia.	There is no strong evidence of a supply-side effect of the reform; however, tax compliance improved significantly, accounting for about a third of the increase in revenue, though it remains unclear if this was due to the tax reform or changes in law enforcement.
The "Flat Tax(es)": Principles and Experience	Review the experience with flat taxes that have been adopted in many countries in recent years.	There is no evidence that behavioral responses of the Laffer type generate revenue increases from the tax-cutting elements of these reforms; their impact on tax compliance is theoretically ambiguous, but evidence suggests improved compliance; the distributive effects may have increased progressivity; the adoption of flat taxes has not solved the challenges of taxing capital income.
Labor Supply Responses and Welfare Effects from Replacing Current Tax Rules by a Flat Tax: Empirical Evidence from Italy, Norway, and Sweden	Examine labor supply responses and welfare effects of replacing the current tax systems in Italy, Norway, and Sweden with a flat income tax.	Efficiency costs of the current tax relative to a flat tax can be quite high in Norway and much lower, but positive, in Italy and Sweden; in all three countries, "rich" families - defined by pre-reform income - tend to benefit more than "poor" families; in Italy and Sweden, a majority would lose from a switch to a flat tax, while in Norway a majority would benefit from the switch.

continued on following page

Table 4. Continued

Article Title	Study Objectives	Conclusions
Is a Flat Tax Reform Feasible in a Grown-up Democracy of Western Europe? A Simulation Study for Germany	Analyze the equity and efficiency effects of revenue-neutral flat tax reforms for Germany.	Due to its limited efficiency effects and problematic distributive impact, it is unlikely that these tax reforms will be implemented in mature Western European democracies.
Effects of Flat Tax Reforms in Western Europe	Determine if there is room for a political reform toward a flat tax in Western Europe.	Under specific circumstances, these tax reforms can increase income equality and improve work incentives; however, in most cases, there is a trade-off between efficiency and equity.
Evaluating the Economic Effects of Flat Tax Reforms Using Synthetic Control Methods	Analyze the impact of flat income tax reform in eight Eastern and Central European countries that adopted it between 1994 and 2005.	Positive economic impacts are found in all eight countries, in variables such as per capita GDP and employment; however, impacts differ between countries that adopted the flat tax in an initial wave of reforms and those that adopted it in a second wave, with higher impacts in the former.
The Benefits and Problems of Linking Micro and Macro Models - Evidence from a Flat Tax Analysis	Describe the latest generation of simulation analyses and illustrate the benefits and problems of linking micro and macro models through the analysis of tax reform proposals to introduce a flat tax in Germany.	A flat tax on personal income can indeed overcome the fundamental equity-efficiency trade-off while simultaneously increasing tax revenue; however, this conclusion does not hold for a flat tax that combines a flat tax on personal income with a flat tax on corporate cash flow.
Flatliners: Ideology and Rational Learning in the Adoption of the Flat Tax	Understand what factors explain the wave of flat tax adoption in Eastern Europe.	The wave of flat tax adoption stems from rational learning, where economically right-leaning governments evaluated the reform's success (measured by its ability to attract foreign investment) over the medium term; rational emulation in a shorter period also contributes to the likelihood of adoption, as does a shift toward economically liberal ideology.
The Complexity of Tax Structure in Competitive Political Systems	Explore the nature of tax complexity in competitive political systems.	Simple tax systems (such as a flat tax) are not compatible with vigorous political competition.
Growth Effects of Shifting from a Graduated-rate Tax System to a Flat Tax	Assess the growth effects of shifting from a graduated-rate tax system to a flat tax.	Empirical evidence regarding the links between tax policy and long-term growth is somewhat inconclusive; the growth effects of taxes are sensitive to the choice of parameter values, particularly the elasticity of labor supply, which has a substantial impact on the growth implications of the reform.

continued on following page

Table 4. Continued

Article Title	Study Objectives	Conclusions
Can Anyone Beat the Flat Tax?	Assess whether proportional taxes are fair and determine if a superior alternative exists.	The flat tax may be inferior to the ideal progressive tax system, if it could be determined what the ideal system is; since it cannot, the flat tax offers a robust second-best choice for public finance, which, in an imperfect world, counts as the best choice.
Ironing Out the Flat Tax	Address the lack of detail on how to implement a flat tax, considering design issues.	The scheme would be complex and difficult to implement, though still somewhat simpler than the current system.
The Effect of Taxation on Informal Employment: Evidence from the Russian Flat Tax Reform	Study the effect of the Russian tax reform on informal employment.	The tax reform led to a significant reduction in the share of informal workers; the reform seems to have had the strongest effect on the prevalence of informal irregular activities; stronger effects were also documented for individuals who benefited from the largest tax rate reductions. The strong response to the tax reform supports the hypothesis that informal and formal labor markets are well integrated.
The Impact of the Flat Tax Reform on Inequality: The Case of Romania	Determine the impact of the flat tax on inequality in Romania.	Inequality indicators show an increase in inequality caused by the flat tax.
Would a Flat-Rate Tax Stimulate Entrepreneurship in Germany? A Behavioral Microsimulation Analysis Allowing for Risk	Estimate the ex-ante effects of the 2000 German tax reform and two hypothetical flat tax scenarios on entries and exits of self-employment based on a structural microsimulation model with transition rates under risk estimated econometrically.	Flatter tax systems do not encourage people to choose self-employment; on the contrary, they discourage it.
Welfare Gains from the Adoption of Proportional Taxation in a General-Equilibrium Model with a Grey Economy: The Case of Bulgaria's 2008 Flat Tax Reform	Provide a quantitative assessment of the welfare effect resulting from the introduction of proportional taxation in Bulgaria in 2008, an effect that works through the grey economy channel.	The lower effective tax in the new tax regime induces a relocation of people to the official sector, stimulates investment, and increases output and consumption; under a flat tax, the size of the informal sector is smaller.
Flat Tax Reform: The Baltics 2000-2007	Understand how a balanced flat tax system, or a move towards it, can be optimal, as applied to the tax reform in the Baltic economies from 2000 to 2007.	Equal flat taxes on personal and business income would have increased welfare more in all three countries than the current reforms; a move towards balance between labor and capital tax rates, through adjusting just one rate, achieves utility gains as high or higher than the current reforms.

continued on following page

Table 4. Continued

Article Title	Study Objectives	Conclusions
Getting the Poor to Work: Three Welfare-Increasing Reforms for a Busy Germany	Study three budget-neutral reforms of the German tax and transfer system designed to improve work incentives for low-income people.	The three reforms reduce labor supply in the first decile of the income distribution; the flat tax scenario reduces overall labor supply by about 5%; the reform designed to increase participation reduces labor supply by 1%; the reform that provides incentives to work full-time has negligible effects on overall labor supply.
Does Labour Supply Respond to a Flat Tax?	Identify the effect of taxes on the labor supply of men and women.	The tax reform led to a statistically significant increase in men's working hours but had no effect on women's working hours; the reform increased the likelihood of finding a job for both men and women.

Estimating flat tax incidence and yield: A sensitivity analysis	**To estimate the distributive effects of replacing existing federal income taxes with a flat tax as proposed by Representative Richard Armey and Senator Richard Shelby.**	**The proposed flat tax would increase the tax burden for most taxpayers and significantly redistribute the tax burden, primarily from the top decile to other taxpayers. If the flat tax were modified to become more progressive, although the gains for the top decile would be reduced, this pattern of redistribution persists.**
Assessing the economic and social impact of tax and benefit reforms: A general-equilibrium microsimulation approach applied to Hungary	To evaluate the long-term macroeconomic, fiscal, and distributive consequences of tax and benefit reforms in Hungary.	The Hungarian tax reform may have boosted production by improving work incentives for high-wage workers (along the intensive margin), but reduced work incentives and employment levels for low-wage workers. The policy measures introduced since 2008 have substantially increased income inequality.
Behavioral responses and the distributional effects of the Russian 'flat' tax	To simulate the distributive impact of the Russian personal income tax following the 2001 tax reform that introduced a flat tax, using data from the Russian Longitudinal Monitoring Survey.	The direct tax effects increased net income inequality. However, the changes in pre-tax distribution (indirect effect) had a significant negative impact on inequality, leading to an overall decline in net income inequality. Regarding the non-tax factor, the reform had little overall effect on income inequality, suggesting that objections based on income inequality to flat tax structures are largely unfounded, especially in transition countries with high levels of tax evasion.
Expected future earnings, taxation, and university enrollment	To estimate the impact of taxes on the university enrollment process.	A revenue-neutral flat tax scenario with an unchanged base deduction would significantly increase the cumulative probability of university enrollment for male high school graduates by 1.8 percentage points (5 years after high school graduation), corresponding to a relative increase of 3.1%.
Flat tax reforms: A general equilibrium evaluation for Spain	To quantify the aggregate and distributive implications of a series of tax reforms aimed at introducing a revenue-neutral flat tax in Spain.	A flat tax with a marginal rate of 23.11% and a fixed deduction equal to 30% of per capita income would result in increases in aggregate output, aggregate consumption, and labor productivity by 5.1%, 4.8%, and 2.8%, respectively. These reforms also generate increases in the Gini indices of post-tax income and consumption. The proposed reform reduces the tax burden for those in the bottom 60% of the income distribution. However, the consumption level for those in the bottom 20% decreases by 1.6%.
Progressive Tax Reforms in Flat Tax Countries	To analyze the effects of shifting from a proportional tax system to a progressive tax system.	A reduction in income inequality can be achieved with a positive, albeit negligible, impact on employment and growth.

continued on following page

Table 4. Continued

Estimating flat tax incidence and yield: A sensitivity analysis	**To estimate the distributive effects of replacing existing federal income taxes with a flat tax as proposed by Representative Richard Armey and Senator Richard Shelby.**	**The proposed flat tax would increase the tax burden for most taxpayers and significantly redistribute the tax burden, primarily from the top decile to other taxpayers. If the flat tax were modified to become more progressive, although the gains for the top decile would be reduced, this pattern of redistribution persists.**
Universal basic income with flat tax reform in France	To assess the effects of a revenue-neutral tax reform introducing a universal basic income regime combined with a flat income tax that replaces the current minimum income subsidy, several other conditional benefits, and the current progressive income tax.	The reform induces not only a significant reduction in income inequality and poverty but also a slightly positive macroeconomic effect.
Does a Progressive PIT Stabilize the Economy? A Comparison of Progressive and Flat Taxes	To examine the impact of progressive personal income tax rates and their effectiveness as an automatic economic stabilizer.	The analyzed tax acts relatively efficiently as an automatic stabilizer. However, it was also observed that the progressivity of the tax is not the primary reason for the effectiveness of a progressive personal income tax as an automatic stabilizer. Personal income tax acts as an automatic stabilizer mainly due to employment sensitivity to GDP fluctuations.
Who Wants a Progressive Income Tax?: Determinants of Tax Policy Preferences in Post-socialist Eastern Europe	To investigate the determinants of public opinion on personal income taxation in Central and Eastern European countries.	Socioeconomic and demographic variables, such as household income, occupational social class, and age, are important in determining preferences for personal income tax. Beliefs about fairness and perceptions of corruption also play a significant role.
The effect of policy objectives, complexity, and self-interest on individuals' comparative fairness judgments of a flat tax	To identify how individuals form impartial judgments about a tax system and the factors they rely on when comparing the fairness of a flat tax system with the current tax system.	Individuals were influenced by their ideas about the economic objectives achieved by each tax system, unwarranted complexity, and especially self-interest.

(Source: Own elaboration based on the scientific articles under analysis)

CONCLUSION

5.1. Conclusion of Results

The main objective of this research was to characterize existing studies on the topic of "Flat Tax" to analyze trends in scientific articles published on the Scopus platform. Information was gathered and processed from Scopus and subsequently analyzed using Excel and VOSviewer software, applying bibliometric indicators to evaluate the level of activity in published scientific articles, the impact of these works and sources, and the characteristics of the articles.

In this investigation, 109 scientific articles published over 27 distinct years were analyzed. It was observed that, on average, 4 articles were published per year, with a positive trend in the number of articles published over the decades. The most productive year to date was 2019, with 12 articles published. This increase in the number of published articles over the years was also accompanied by an increase in the number of citations. From 1998 to 2021, a substantially positive trend in citations was noted, with only two citations in 1998 and 73, 90, and 102 citations in 2019, 2020, and 2021 respectively. This indicates that academic interest in the topic has been increasing in recent decades.

Regarding author productivity, it was found that 201 authors contributed to the 109 scientific articles. Of these, 186 contributed only one article, while 15 published two or more articles, corresponding to 93% and 7%, respectively. Of the authors who published two or more articles, 14 published two articles, and only one author, Peichl, A., published more than two, with four articles. This suggests that the topic "flat tax" attracts the attention of many authors.

Concerning collaboration in authorship, it was observed that the majority of published articles (62%) were written collectively, meaning by more than one author, while 38% were written individually. Among the collaboratively authored articles, those with two authors were most common, with 40 articles published. A network map revealed that among the 15 authors who published more than one article, only Peter K.S., Duncan D., Schaefer T., Peichl A., and Fuest C. have connections with each other, indicating that most of the most productive authors on the topic do not have relationships with each other.

Analyzing geographical distribution and collaboration, authors contributing to the analyzed articles were affiliated with institutions in 35 countries across all continents except Antarctica. More than half were affiliated with countries in Europe, the continent with the most countries investigating the topic, spanning 24 countries. Nevertheless, the USA had the most authors interested in the topic, with 64 affiliated authors publishing scientific articles. A network map showed that Germany, the

USA, and the UK had the most connections with other countries, indicating higher communication levels with other countries.

Regarding the impact of sources, it was observed that the 109 articles were published in 85 scientific journals. Of these, 68 published only one article. The journals with the most articles were International Tax and Public Finance, Economics Letters, and Journal of Policy Modeling, with 6, 4, and 3 articles respectively. This indicates a wide dispersion across journals, with no single journal specializing in the "flat tax" topic.

The study also categorized the articles into 10 different fields, indicating that various types of topics can be studied through the research theme. The predominant fields were "Economics, Econometrics and Finance" with 87 articles, and "Social Sciences" and "Business, Management and Accounting" with 29 articles each.

An analysis of keywords showed that 322 different keywords were used by the authors, indicating that a multitude of topics can be investigated in relation to the flat tax. However, the most frequently used keywords were "tax reform" and "tax system," suggesting that the main themes of analysis in flat tax-related articles are taxation systems and fiscal reforms.

Finally, a summary table was developed to group the conclusions of the main articles in the sample. The table indicates that, as mentioned previously, the scientific articles analyzed were written over several years by many authors. Influenced by the time period in which they conducted their research and their diverse origins, these authors performed different types of studies on a wide range of topics with distinct objectives, methodologies, and assumptions, resulting in diverse and sometimes divergent conclusions, making comparisons difficult.

5.2. Limitations

One limitation of this research was the difficulty in comparing articles, as they addressed different themes related to the flat tax. Another limitation arose from the restrictions imposed on the sample selection. The scientific articles were sourced exclusively from the Scopus platform, and only articles with the keyword or title "flat tax" were included, potentially excluding relevant articles from the analysis. The existence of articles with unidentified authors, which had to be excluded, also reduced the sample size, posing a limitation. Finally, the inability to compare the research results with other studies that might have used a different sample of scientific articles was considered a limitation, as no other characterization of research on the "flat tax" was found.

5.3. Suggestions

Given the limitations imposed on the sample definition in this study, it would be interesting to reduce these restrictions by including articles published in other databases similar to Scopus or by not limiting the sample to articles with the keyword or title "flat tax." This would provide a broader and more comprehensive investigation of the flat tax. Another suggestion is for future research to focus on more specific topics within the flat tax, such as comparing articles that analyze only the effect of the flat tax on economic growth, inequality, or any other relevant study topic.

REFERENCES

Aaberge, R., Colombino, U., & Storm, S. (2004). Do more equal slices shrink the cake? An empirical investigation of tax-transfer reform proposals in italy. *Journal of Population Economics*, 17(4), 767–785. DOI: 10.1007/s00148-004-0193-2

Aghion, P., Caroli, E., & Garcia-Penalosa, C. (1999). Inequality and economic growth: The perspective of the new growth theories. *Journal of Economic Literature*, 37(4), 1615–1660. https://www.jstor.org/stable/2565487. DOI: 10.1257/jel.37.4.1615

Altig, D., Auerbach, A. J., Kotlikoff, L. J., Smetters, K. A., & Walliser, J. (2001). Simulating fundamental tax reform in the united states. *The American Economic Review*, 91(3), 574–595. https://search.proquest.com/scholarly-journals/simulating-fundamental-tax-reform-united-states/docview/233038607/se-2?accountid=38384. DOI: 10.1257/aer.91.3.574

Amirthalingam, K. (2013). The importance of taxation and the role of indirect taxes in developing countries: A survey of literature. *Colombo Business Journal*, 4(1), 43–52.

Arab, H. R., & Basariya, S. R. (2020). A study on the uses of taxation in developing countries. *Journal of Critical Reviews*, 7(1), 457–463. DOI: 10.31838/jcr.07.01.90

Barrios, S., Ivaškaitė-Tamošiūnė, V., Maftei, A., Narazani, E., & Varga, J. (2020). Progressive tax reforms in flat tax countries. *Eastern European Economics*, 58(2), 83–107. DOI: 10.1080/00128775.2019.1671201

Benczúr, P., Kátay, G., & Kiss, Á. (2018). Assessing the economic and social impact of tax and benefit reforms: A general-equilibrium microsimulation approach applied to Hungary. *Economic Modelling*, 75, 441–457. DOI: 10.1016/j.econmod.2018.06.016

Bonga-Bonga, L., & Perold, M. (2014). A CGE simulation of a flat tax as a possibility for tax reform in South Africa. *Journal of Applied Business Research*, 30(6), 1693–1708. DOI: 10.19030/jabr.v30i6.8883

Conesa, J. C., & Krueger, D. (2006). On the optimal progressivity of the income tax code. *Journal of Monetary Economics*, 53(7), 1425–1450. DOI: 10.1016/j.jmoneco.2005.03.016

Costa, T., Lopes, S., Fernández-Llimós, F., Amante, M. J., & Lopes, P. F. (2012). A bibliometria e a avaliação da produção científica. ACTAS – Congresso Nacional de Bibliotecários. *Arquivistas e Documentalistas*, 11, 1–7.

Dabrowski, M., & Tomczynska, M. (2001). Tax reforms in transition economies - A mixed record and a complex future agenda. *SSRN*, (231). Advance online publication. DOI: 10.2139/ssrn.1440219

Dacian, C. D. (2010). The relationship between accounting and taxation: A brief international literature review. *Faculty of Economics and Business Administration*, 1(1), 496–502.

Dagan, N., Serrano, R., & Volij, O. (1999). Feasible implementation of taxation methods. *Review of Economic Design*, 4(1), 57–72. DOI: 10.1007/s100580050026

de Hek, P. A. (2006). On taxation in a two-sector endogenous growth model with endogenous labour supply. *Journal of Economic Dynamics & Control*, 30(4), 655–685. DOI: 10.1016/j.jedc.2005.02.006

Domonkos, S. (2016). Who wants a progressive income tax? Determinants of tax policy preferences in post-socialist Eastern Europe. *Eastern European Politics and Societies*, 30(2), 423–448. DOI: 10.1177/0888325415602055

Duncan, D., & Peter, K. S. (2010). Does labour supply respond to a flat tax? *Economics of Transition*, 18(2), 365–404. DOI: 10.1111/j.1468-0351.2009.00383.x

Evans, A. J., & Aligica, P. D. (2008). The spread of the flat tax in eastern europe: A comparative study. *Eastern European Economics*, 46(3), 49–67. DOI: 10.2753/EEE0012-8775460303

Feldstein, M. (1995). Behavioral responses to tax rates: Evidence from the tax reform act of 1986. *The American Economic Review*, 85(2), 170–174. https://search.proquest.com/scholarly-journals/behavioral-responses-tax-rates-evidence-reform/docview/233022407/se-2?accountid=38384 PMID: 10160509

Fischer, D.-H., & Ferraro, S. (2019). A proposal for a simple average-based progressive taxation system. *Public Sector Economics*, 43(2), 141–165. DOI: 10.3326/pse.43.2.2

Fossen, F. M. (2009). Would a flat-rate tax stimulate entrepreneurship in Germany? A behavioural microsimulation analysis allowing for risk. *Fiscal Studies*, 30(2), 179–218. DOI: 10.1111/j.1475-5890.2009.00093.x

Friedman, M. (1962). *Capitalism and Freedom*. University of Chicago Press.

Fuest, C., Peichl, A., & Schaefer, T. (2008). Does a simpler income tax yield more equity and efficiency? *CESifo Economic Studies*, 54(1), 73–97. DOI: 10.1093/cesifo/ifn003

Fuest, C., Peichl, A., & Schaefer, T. (2008). Is a flat tax reform feasible in a grown-up democracy of Western Europe? A simulation study for Germany. *International Tax and Public Finance*, 15(5), 620–636. DOI: 10.1007/s10797-008-9071-2

Gouveia, M., & Oliver, D. (1995). Voting over flat taxes in an endowment economy. *Economics Letters*, 50(2), 251–258. DOI: 10.1016/0165-1765(95)00749-0

Gribnau, H. (2015). Corporate social responsibility and tax planning: Not by rules alone. *Social & Legal Studies*, 24(2), 225–250. DOI: 10.1177/0964663915575053

Hall, R. E., & Rabushka, A. (1983). *Low tax, simple tax, flat tax*. McGraw-Hill Companies.

Hayek, F. (1960). *The constitution of liberty*. University of Chicago Press.

Heath, A. (2006). *Flat tax: Towards a british model*. Stockholm Network.

High-Quality Data. (n.d.). Retrieved from Elsevier: https://www.elsevier.com/solutions/scopus/how-scopus-works/high-quality-data

Hirsch, J., & Buela-Casal, G. (2014). The meaning of the h-index. *International Journal of Clinical and Health Psychology*, 14(2), 161–164. DOI: 10.1016/S1697-2600(14)70050-X

Ibragimov, M. Y., Ibragimov, R. M., Sinnikova, Y. M., & Tufetulov, A. M. (2014). About progressive tax systems of labor remuneration in Russia. *Asian Social Science*, 10(23), 28–35. DOI: 10.5539/ass.v10n23p28

Laffer, A. B. (2019). Reflections on economic policy. *Business Economics (Cleveland, Ohio)*, 55(1), 41–44. DOI: 10.1057/s11369-019-00150-7

Liberati, A., Altman, D. G., Tetzlaff, J., Mulrow, C., Gøtzsche, P. C., Ioannidis, J. P., Clarke, M., Devereaux, P. J., Kleijnen, J., & Moher, D. (2009). The PRISMA statement for reporting systematic reviews and meta-analyses of studies that evaluate healthcare interventions: Explanation and elaboration. *Journal of Clinical Epidemiology*, 62(10), 1–34. DOI: 10.1016/j.jclinepi.2009.06.006 PMID: 19631507

Marx, K., & Engels, F. (1848). The communist manifesto.

Merriam, S. B. (2009). *Qualitative research: A guide to design and implementation* (3rd ed.). Jossey-Bass.

Mill, J. S. (1848). Principles of political economy.

Moher, D., Shamseer, L., Clarke, M., Ghersi, D., Liberati, A., Petticrew, M., Shekelle, P., & Stewart, L. A. (2015). Preferred reporting items for systematic review and meta-analysis protocols (PRISMA-P) 2015 statement. *Systematic Reviews*, 4(1), 1. Advance online publication. DOI: 10.1186/2046-4053-4-1 PMID: 25554246

Musgrave, R. A., & Musgrave, P. B. (1989). *Public finance in theory and practice* (International Editions). McGraw-Hill.

Osberg, L. (1995). The equity/efficiency trade-off in retrospect. Canadian Business Economics, 3, 5-19. Retrieved from http://hdl.handle.net/10222/34134

Pántya, J., Kovács, J., Kogler, C., & Kirchler, E. (2016). Work performance and tax compliance in flat and progressive tax systems. *Journal of Economic Psychology*, 56, 262–273. DOI: 10.1016/j.joep.2016.08.002

Paulus, A., & Peichl, A. (2009). Effects of flat tax reforms in Western Europe. *Journal of Policy Modeling*, 31(5), 620–636. DOI: 10.1016/j.jpolmod.2009.06.001

Peichl, A. (2009). The benefits and problems of linking micro and macro models - Evidence from a flat tax analysis. *Journal of Applied Econometrics*, 12(2), 301–329. DOI: 10.1016/S1514-0326(09)60017-9

Pogátsa, Z. (2009). Tatra tiger: Growth miracle or belated recovery? *Acta Oeconomica*, 59(4), 377–390. DOI: 10.1556/aoecon.59.2009.4.1

Popescu, M. E., Militaru, E., Stanila, L., Vasilescu, M. D., & Cristescu, A. (2019). Flat-rate versus progressive taxation? An impact evaluation study for the case of Romania. *Sustainability (Basel)*, 11(22), 6405–6421. DOI: 10.3390/su11226405

Rawls, J. (1971). *A theory of justice*. Belknap Press/ Harvard University Press. DOI: 10.4159/9780674042605

Ricardo, D. (1817). *Principles of political economy and taxation.*

Sabitova, N. M., & Dyudina, M. P. (2015). Income taxation as a took of income redistribution. Mediterranean Journal of Social Sciences, 6(1 S3), 174-178. DOI: 10.5901/mjss.2015.v6n1s3p174

Scopus - Content Coverage Guide. (n.d.). Retrieved from Elsevier: https://www.elsevier.com/?a=69451&fbclid=IwAR2WBehEx2U6n9VoMkyyVzm00gWEFD1RtsvgjXpKtdew4_pLVcbhbUsZtMo

Skipper, D. W., & Burton, H. A. (2008). Ramifications of a flat tax - Shifting the burden to the middle class. *International Advances in Economic Research*, 14(4), 460–471. DOI: 10.1007/s11294-008-9168-5

Smith, A. (1776). *The wealth of nations.*

Ventura, G. (1999). Flat tax reform: A quantitative exploration. *Journal of Economic Dynamics & Control*, 23(9-10), 1425–1458. DOI: 10.1016/S0165-1889(98)00079-7

Voinea, L. (2013). Revisiting crisis generators in romania and other new EU member states. *Review of International Political Economy*, 20(4), 979–1008. DOI: 10.1080/09692290.2012.733315

Watrin, C., & Ullmann, R. (2008). Comparing direct and indirect taxation: The influence of framing on tax compliance. *The European Journal of Comparative Economics*, 5(1), 33–56.

Whait, R. B., Christ, K. L., Ortas, E. B., & Burritt, R. L. (2018). What do we know about tax agressiveness and corporate social responsability? An integrative review. *Journal of Cleaner Production*, 204, 542–522. DOI: 10.1016/j.jclepro.2018.08.334

Why choose Scopus. (n.d.). Retrieved from Elsevier: https://www.elsevier.com/solutions/scopus/why-choose-scopus?fbclid=IwAR3h_5tDC9qSJL3jcHIX2EE6N1fNos4Nd-zxiuxULoaGAxsD3pGFqf7Auhc

KEY TERMS AND DEFINITIONS

Taxation: The process by which a government collects revenue from individuals and businesses to finance public goods, services, and infrastructure, and to redistribute wealth. It serves as the state's primary source of income and influences economic behavior, investment, and growth.

Tax System: A structured framework through which taxes are imposed on income, consumption, property, or other financial transactions. Tax systems can vary between progressive, regressive, and proportional forms, each affecting income distribution and economic efficiency differently.

Flat Tax: A type of tax system where a single constant tax rate is applied to all levels of income, without progressive brackets. It simplifies taxation by removing graduated rates but can have implications for income inequality and fiscal policy.

Progressive Tax: A tax structure where the tax rate increases as the taxable amount increases. It aims to ensure wealth redistribution by placing a heavier tax burden on higher-income individuals, often used to reduce economic inequality.

Tax Reform: Legislative changes to a tax system aimed at improving efficiency, fairness, or revenue generation. Tax reforms may involve simplifying tax structures, adjusting tax rates, or changing the tax base to better meet the economic and social objectives of a country.

Direct Taxes: Taxes that are directly levied on individuals or corporations, such as income or property taxes. They are paid directly to the government and are often used for wealth redistribution and revenue generation.

Indirect Taxes: Taxes imposed on goods and services rather than on income or profits. Examples include Value Added Tax (VAT) and sales taxes. These taxes are generally passed on to consumers and are less progressive than direct taxes.

Compilation of References

Aaberge, R., Colombino, U., & Storm, S. (2004). Do more equal slices shrink the cake? An empirical investigation of tax-transfer reform proposals in italy. *Journal of Population Economics*, 17(4), 767–785. DOI: 10.1007/s00148-004-0193-2

Abdillah, N., Thamrin, T., Nofrizal, N., & Wijayanto, G. (2023). Quantifying Ecological, Economic, Social, and Governance Attributes for Urban Forest Eco-Tourism Using MDS-RAPFISH Approach. *International Journal of Sustainable Development and Planning, 18*(8), 2369–2378. *Scopus*. Advance online publication. DOI: 10.18280/ijsdp.180807

Abdullah, S., & Morley, B. (2014). Environmental taxes and economic growth: Evidence from panel causality tests. *Energy Economics*, 42, 27–33. DOI: 10.1016/j.eneco.2013.11.013

Accioly, S. M. D. L., & Brito, L. L. A. D. (2021). Análise comparativa de programas municipais de IPTU Verde. *Engenharia Urbana em Debate*, 2(1), 215–229. DOI: 10.59550/engurbdebate.v2i1.58

Acharya, S. (2005). Thirty years of tax reform in India. *Economic and Political Weekly*,, 2061–2070.

Adame Martínez, F. (2015). La compatiblidad de diversas medidas adoptadas por las Comunidades Autónomas con el Derecho europeo. In *Patón García, G. (dir.), Libertades comunitarias, autonomía tributaria y medio ambiente* (pp. 83–109). CEF.

Adamou, A., Clerides, S., & Zachariadis, T. (2012). Trade-offs in CO2-oriented vehicle tax reforms: A case study of Greece. *Transportation Research Part D, Transport and Environment*, 17(6), 451–456. DOI: 10.1016/j.trd.2012.05.005

Adhikari, D. R., & Shrestha, P. (2024). The context and concept of higher education for sustainable development: The case of Nepal. *International Journal of Sustainability in Higher Education*, 25(2), 238–264. DOI: 10.1108/IJSHE-12-2021-0521

Afonso, J. R. R., Araujo, E. A., & da Nóbrega, M. A. R. (2013). *IPTU no Brasil: Um diagnóstico abrangente*. FGV Projetos.

Afrizal, A. D., Rakhmawati, N. A., & Tjahyanto, A. (2019). New Filtering Scheme Based on Term Weighting to Improve Object Based Opinion Mining on Tourism Product Reviews. In Younus, A., & Herdiyanti, A. (Eds.), *Procedia Computer Science, 161, 805-812*. Elsevier., DOI: 10.1016/j.procs.2019.11.186

Afsharipour, A. (2011). A Brief Overview of Corporate Governance Reforms in India. *Corporate Law: Corporate Governance Law eJournal*.

Aghion, P., Caroli, E., & Garcia-Penalosa, C. (1999). Inequality and economic growth: The perspective of the new growth theories. *Journal of Economic Literature*, 37(4), 1615–1660. https://www.jstor.org/stable/2565487. DOI: 10.1257/jel.37.4.1615

Aguero, J., Conway, S., & Navis, I. (2006a). *Community monitoring in a tourism-dependent economy* (C. Brebbia & F. Pineda, Eds.; WOS:000241776000027; Vol. 97, pp. 297–309). DOI: 10.2495/ST060271

Aguiar, N. (2016). O Problema da Tributação do Rendimento das Cooperativas – reflexão a partir do direito português. *Revista Cooperativismo e Economía Social, n.º 28*. Pp. 163-190.

Ahmad, E., & Stern, N. (1984). The theory of reform and Indian indirect taxes. *Journal of Public Economics*, 25(3), 259–298. DOI: 10.1016/0047-2727(84)90057-4

Aires, J., Costa, C., & Brandao, F. (2022). Exploring Indicators and Determinants to Evaluate Innovation in Tourism Firms-A Systematic Literature Review. *Tourism (Zagreb)*, 70(4), 656–673. DOI: 10.37741/t.70.4.8

Akdag, S., & Yıldırım, H. (2020). Toward a sustainable mitigation approach of energy efficiency to greenhouse gas emissions in the European countries. *Heliyon*, 6(3), e03396. DOI: 10.1016/j.heliyon.2020.e03396 PMID: 32154402

Alagappan, S. (2019). Indian Tax Structure – An Analytical Perspective. *IRPN: Other Innovation & Management Science* .

Alberto Gutiérrez Arguedas. (2020). Green capitalism and "clean" energies: Costa Rica as a "global decarbonization laboratory". Yearbook of the Center for Research and Political Studies, ISSN: 2215-2873195-228. DOI: DOI: 10.15517/aciep.v0i11.43238

Albiero, M., Johns, P., Hassan, B., Carvalho, A., Guedes, D., Baird, M., Mattos, R., Waetge, J., & Silva, A. (2021). *Tributação de bebidas e alimentos não saudáveis no mundo- Experiências internacionais e seus impactos* [Report]. ACT Promoção da Saúde. https://evidencias.tributosaudavel.org.br/wp-content/themes/act-theme/LO_ACT_EXP-INT_Rev-03.pdf

Albrecht, J. (2006). The use of consumption taxes to re-launch green tax reforms. *International Review of Law and Economics*, 26(1), 88–103. DOI: 10.1016/j.irle.2006.05.007

Albring, S. M., Mills, L. F., & Newberry, K. J. (2011). Do debt constraints influence firms' sensitivity to a temporary tax holiday on repatriations? *The Journal of the American Taxation Association*, 33(2), 1–27. DOI: 10.2308/atax-10057

Alemanno, A. (2011), 'A Meeting of Minds on Impact Assessment: When Ex Ante Evaluation Meets Ex Post Judicial Control', 17 European Public Law.

Ali, K., Jianguo, D., Kirikkaleli, D., Oláh, J., & Bakhsh, S. (2023). Do environmental taxes, environmental innovation, and energy resources matter for environmental sustainability: Evidence of five sustainable economies. *Heliyon*, 9(11), e21577. DOI: 10.1016/j.heliyon.2023.e21577 PMID: 38034728

Alina Celi Frugoni. (2022). Energy transition in Latin America and the Caribbean Energy transition in latin america and the Caribbean. Revista novos estudos jurídicos - eletrônica, vol. 27- n. 3 - set-dez 2022. Doi: https//:d oi.org/10.14210/nej.v27n3 .p500-516

Allan, G. J., Lecca, P., McGregor, P. G., McIntyre, S. G., & Kim Swales, J. (2017). Computable General Equilibrium Modelling in Regional Science. In R. Jackson & P. Schaeffer (Eds.), *Regional Research Frontiers—Vol. 2* (pp. 59–78). Springer International Publishing. DOI: 10.1007/978-3-319-50590-9_4

Allen, D. W., Berg, C., & Novak, M. (2018). Blockchain: An entangled political economy approach. *Journal of Public Finance and Public Choice*, 33(2), 105–125. DOI: 10.1332/251569118X15282111163993

Alm, J. (2019). Tax compliance and administration. In *Handbook on taxation* (pp. 741–768). Routledge. DOI: 10.4324/9781315093161-30

Alsultan, S. K. (2021, Apr). The Gulf Cooperation Council (GCC) States: New Players in the International Tax Competition Game [Article]. *Intertax, 49*(4), 361-377. <Go to ISI>://WOS:000637826200007

Altenburger, O. A. (2022). Applying VAT to financial services: Is the new mobile-ratio method adequate for insurance?. *Zeitschrift für die gesamte Versicherungswissenschaft*, 111(3), 353-360.

Altig, D., Auerbach, A. J., Kotlikoff, L. J., Smetters, K. A., & Walliser, J. (2001). Simulating fundamental tax reform in the united states. *The American Economic Review*, 91(3), 574–595. https://search.proquest.com/scholarly-journals/simulating-fundamental-tax-reform-united-states/docview/233038607/se-2?accountid=38384. DOI: 10.1257/aer.91.3.574

Amaral, M. D. (2013). A tributação como mecanismo de estímulo à proteção e à preservação do meio ambiente. Revista da Faculdade de Direito da Universidade Federal de Minas Gerais, 2013(62). DOI: 10.12818/0304-2340.2013v62p405

Amirthalingam, K. (2013). The importance of taxation and the role of indirect taxes in developing countries: A survey of literature. *Colombo Business Journal*, 4(1), 43–52.

Amorim, J. (2024, February, 22). *Em sete anos resultaram 432 milhões para o SNS e caiu em 36% a proporção de bebidas no escalão mais alto do imposto.* Jornal de Notícias. https://www.jn.pt/6804067447/acucar-nas-bebidas-diminui-devido-a-pressao-fiscal/

Amorim, J. C. (2011). Regime fiscal aplicável às Entidades sem Fins Lucrativos em Portugal e em Espanha. *Journal of Business and Legal Sciences / Revista De Ciências Empresariais e Jurídicas, n.º 20.* Pp. 179-202.

Amorim, J. de C. (2018). Os incentivos fiscais em matéria de Fiscalidade verde. Revista de Ciências Empresariais e Jurídicas / Review of Business and Legal Sciences, 303-318 Pages. DOI: 10.26537/REBULES.VI30.3165

Andıç, N. Ö. (2023). Green Taxes in the Solution of Environmental Problems and the Case of Türkiye. In *Taking on Climate Change Through Green Taxation* (pp. 198–217). DOI: 10.4018/978-1-6684-8592-7.ch008

Andrade, T. (2023, Nov). Transfer Pricing and Customs Valuation Rules in Brazil: A Challenging Reconciliation [Article]. *Global Trade and Customs Journal, 18*(11-12), 461-468. <Go to ISI>://WOS:001107742400007

Andreyeva, T., Chaloupka, F. J., & Brownell, K. D. (2011). Estimating the potential of taxes on sugar-sweetened beverages to reduce consumption and generate revenue. *Preventive Medicine*, 52(6), 413–416. DOI: 10.1016/j.ypmed.2011.03.013 PMID: 21443899

Andreyeva, T., Long, M. W., & Brownell, K. D. (2010). The impact of food prices on consumption: A systematic review of research on the price elasticity of demand for food. *American Journal of Public Health*, 100(2), 216–222. DOI: 10.2105/AJPH.2008.151415 PMID: 20019319

Ang, Y. Y. (2020). *China's gilded age: The paradox of economic boom and vast corruption*. Cambridge University Press. DOI: 10.1017/9781108778350

AR - Assembleia da República. (2001). *Lei n.º 16/2001, 22.06.2001 - Lei da Liberdade Religiosa*. Available in: https://diariodarepublica.pt/dr/legislacao-consolidada/lei/2001-34483475 [Accessed in January 2024].

AR - Assembleia da República. (2005). *Lei Constitucional nº 1/2005, 12.08.2005 - Sétima da Constituição da República Portuguesa*. Available in: https://files.dre.pt/1s/2005/08/155a00/46424686.pdf [Accessed in January 2024].

AR - Assembleia da República. (2009). *Acordo com o Imamat Ismaili*. Available in: https://files.dre.pt/1s/2010/09/18700/0427104275.pdf [Accessed in January 2024].

AR - Assembleia da República. (2015). *Acordo com o Imamat Ismaili com vista ao estabelecimento da sua Sede em Portugal*. Available in: https://files.diariodarepublica.pt/1s/2015/10/21000/0924609253.pdf [Accessed in January 2024].

Araar, A., Choueiri, N., & Verme, P. (2022). The compensating differentiated cash transfers for energy pricing reform. *Energy Economics*, 105, 105718. DOI: 10.1016/j.eneco.2021.105718

Arab, H. R., & Basariya, S. R. (2020). A study on the uses of taxation in developing countries. *Journal of Critical Reviews*, 7(1), 457–463. DOI: 10.31838/jcr.07.01.90

Araña, J., & León, C. (2016). Are tourists animal spirits? Evidence from a field experiment exploring the use of non-market based interventions advocating sustainable tourism. *Journal of Sustainable Tourism*, 24(3), 430–445. DOI: 10.1080/09669582.2015.1101128

Araújo, J., de Souza, F., Robles, E., Celis, L., & Lagioia, U. (2023). Fiscal policies for economic sustainability in COVID-19: What do subnational governments in Brazil and Colombia reveal? *GeSec: Revista de Gestao e Secretariado*, 14(4), 6636–6662. DOI: 10.7769/gesec.v14i4.2070

Arellano, M., & Bond, S. (1991). Some tests of specification for panel data: Monte Carlo evidence and an application to employment equations. *The Review of Economic Studies*, 58(2), 277–297. DOI: 10.2307/2297968

Arellano, M., & Bover, O. (1995). Another look at the instrumental variable estimation of error-components models. *Journal of Econometrics*, 68(1), 29–51. DOI: 10.1016/0304-4076(94)01642-D

Aria, M., & Cuccurullo, C. (2017). bibliometrix: An R-tool for comprehensive science mapping analysis. *Journal of Informetrics*, 11(4), 959–975. DOI: 10.1016/j.joi.2017.08.007

Arora, P. (2019). *The next billion users: Digital life beyond the West*. Harvard University Press. DOI: 10.4159/9780674238879

Aslam, A., & Shah, M. A. (2017). *Taxation and the peer-to-peer economy*. International Monetary Fund. DOI: 10.5089/9781484313763.001

AT - Autoridade Tributária e Aduaneira. (2024a). *Lei Geral Tributária*. Available in: https://info.portaldasfinancas.gov.pt/pt/informacao_fiscal/codigos_tributarios/lgt/Pages/lei-geral-tributaria-indice.aspx [Accessed in January 2024].

AT – Autoridade Tributária e Aduaneira. (2024b). *Estatuto dos Benefícios Fiscais*. Available in: https://info.portaldasfinancas.gov.pt/pt/informacao_fiscal/codigos_tributarios/bf_rep/Pages/estatuto-dos-beneficios-fiscais-indice.aspx [Accessed in January 2024].

Athira, A., & Lukose, P. J. (2024). The Increasing Trend in Effective Tax Rates in India: Role of Macroeconomic Factors, Tax Policy Changes and Firm Characteristics. *Journal of Emerging Market Finance*, 09726527231214075.

Auerbach, A. J. (2006). The Choice between Income and Consumption Taxes. *PRiMER: Peer-Reviewed Reports in Medical Education Research*.

Auerbach, A. J., & Gordon, R. H. (2002). Taxation of Financial Services under a VAT. *The American Economic Review*, 92(2), 411–416. DOI: 10.1257/000282802320191714

Aulbur, W., & Kapoor, A. (2016). *Riding the Tiger: How to Execute Business Strategy in India*. Random House India.

Averett, S. L., Peters, H. E., & Waldman, D. M. (1997). Tax credits, labor supply, and child care. *The Review of Economics and Statistics*, 79(1), 125–135. DOI: 10.1162/003465397556467

Azevedo, T. C. (2017). Tributação municipal como incentivo ao desenvolvimento sustentável nas cidades: O caso do "IPTU VERDE" de Salvador [Doctorate, Chatolic University of Salvador]. http://ri.ucsal.br:8080/jspui/handle/prefix/367

Azevedo, T. C., & Dantas, I. G. (July 31st, 2023). Análise das publicações sobre o IPTU Verde no Brasil: Revisão sistemática da produção dos programas de pós-graduação. *XXIII USP International Conference in Accounting*. São Paulo

Azevedo, T. C., & Portella, A. A. (2020). Sustainable certification program of the city of Salvador: Analysis of the green IPTU criteria and benefits on its ecological perspective. *Revista de Direito da Cidade*, 12(3), 64–93. DOI: 10.12957/rdc.2020.46762

Aziz, S., Rahman, M., Hussain, D., & Nguyen, D. K. (2021). Does corporate environmentalism affect corporate insolvency risk? The role of market power and competitive intensity. *Ecological Economics*, 189, 107182. DOI: 10.1016/j.ecolecon.2021.107182

Babar, D. (2020). A Macro analysis of Corporate Tax Cuts: A Strategy to improve India's Competitiveness. *Political Economy: Taxation*.

Bagchi, A. (2003). *Fifty years of fiscal federalism in India: An appraisal*. National Institute of Public Finance and Policy.

Bahar, A., & Fauzi, A. (2020). Coral reefs ecotourism sustainability assessment based on the integration of government-private-local community in Hoga Island, Wakatobi Regency. *IOP Conference Series. Earth and Environmental Science*, 564(1), 012074. Advance online publication. DOI: 10.1088/1755-1315/564/1/012074

Bailey, K. D. (2008). *Methods of social research*. Simon and Schuster.

Bandeira, A. M., Meira, D., & Alves, V. (2017). Los diferentes tipos de resultados en las cooperativas portuguesas. Un estudio de caso múltiple. *REVESCO, n.º 123 – Primer Cuatrimestre*. Pp. 37-63.

Baocun, L., & Yalun, A. (2020). Educational Administration and Leadership in China. In *Oxford Research Encyclopedia of Education*. Oxford University Press., DOI: 10.1093/acrefore/9780190264093.013.629

Baptista, S., da Silva, F. G., Silva, D., Landerset, F., Simões, A. L., Gregório, M. J., Saraiva, A. I., & Belona, S. (2018, July, 30). *Impacto do Imposto Especial sobre o Consumo de Bebidas Açucaradas e Adicionadas de Edulcorantes: Relatório do Grupo de Trabalho (Despacho N.o 2774/2018).*https://repositorio-aberto.up.pt/handle/10216/118046

Barandiarán, X., Restrepo, N., & Luna, A. (2019). Collaborative governance in tourism: Lessons from Etorkizuna Eraikiz in the Basque Country, Spain. *Tourism Review*, 74(4), 902–914. DOI: 10.1108/TR-09-2018-0133

Baranzini, A., Borzykowski, N., & Carattini, S. (2021). Carbon offsets out of the woods? The acceptability of domestic vs. international reforestation programmes in the lab. *Journal of Forest Economics*, 32, 1–12. DOI: 10.1016/j.jfe.2018.02.004

Bardin, L. (2016). *Análise de conteúdo* (1st ed). 70 Editions

Barreiros, J. A. R. M., Teixeira, M. A. C., & Ferreira, H. Q. (1984). *Código da contribuição industrial: anotado e comentado [Industrial Contribution Code: annotated and commented]*. Rei dos Livros. http://books.google.pt/books?id=P24pHQAACAAJ

Barreix, A., Corrales, L. F., Díaz de Sarralde, S., & Garcimartín, C. (2022). Fiscal policy for sustainable development in Latin America and the Caribbean. *Bulletin of Latin American Research*, 41(5), 783–799. DOI: 10.1111/blar.13398

Barrios, S., Ivaškaitė-Tamošiūnė, V., Maftei, A., Narazani, E., & Varga, J. (2020). Progressive tax reforms in flat tax countries. *Eastern European Economics*, 58(2), 83–107. DOI: 10.1080/00128775.2019.1671201

Bartkus, E., & Grunda, R. (2011). Business Sustainability Assessment: Comparing Results of Two Studies. *Inžinerinė ekonomika-. The Engineering Economist*, 22(1), 32–40.

Baydur, I., & Yilmaz, F. (2021). VAT Treatment of the Financial Services: Implications for the Real Economy. *Journal of Money, Credit and Banking*, 53(8), 2167–2200. DOI: 10.1111/jmcb.12780

Belahouaoui, R. (2023). *La réforme de l'IS:" FLAT TAX" entre consécration de l'équité et lutte contre la fraude fiscale.*

Belahouaoui, R., & Attak, E. H. (2023). The importance of perceived fairness regarding tax burden in compliance behavior: a qualitative study using the Delphi method in Morocco. *Journal of Financial Reporting and Accounting*.

Belahouaoui, R., & Attak, E. H. (2024). Digitalization of Tax Administration and Tax Avoidance: Evidence on Tax Reform Dynamics in Morocco. In *Impact of Digitalization on Reporting, Tax Avoidance, Accounting, and Green Finance* (pp. 200–225). IGI Global.

Bell, S., McGillivray, D., Pedersen, O. W., Lees, E., & Stokes, E. (2017). *Environmental law* (9th ed.). Oxford University Press. DOI: 10.1093/he/9780198748328.001.0001

Benczúr, P., Kátay, G., & Kiss, Á. (2018). Assessing the economic and social impact of tax and benefit reforms: A general-equilibrium microsimulation approach applied to Hungary. *Economic Modelling*, 75, 441–457. DOI: 10.1016/j.econmod.2018.06.016

Berg, F., & Donarelli, A. (2019). Energy Performance Certificates and Historic Apartment Buildings: A Method to Encourage User Participation and Sustainability in the Refurbishment Process. *The Historic Environment*, 10(2), 224–240. DOI: 10.1080/17567505.2019.1592836

Bernardi, L., & Fraschini, A. (2005). Tax system and tax reforms in India. *Department of Public Policy and Public Choice-POLIS, Working Paper*, (51).

Bhalla, S. (2005). *Tax Rates*. Tax Compliance and Tax Revenues.

Bhasin, R. (2018). Technological Infrastructure and Institutional Set-up for Effective Implementation of GST. *VISION: Journal of Indian Taxation*, 5(1), 104–109.

Blank, J. D. (2009, Aug). OVERCOMING OVERDISCLOSURE: TOWARD TAX SHELTER DETECTION [Article]. *Ucla Law Review, 56*(6), 1629-1690. <Go to ISI>://WOS:000269944800001

Blasco Delgado, C. (1996). La financiación de las Comunidades Autónomas y la corresponsabilidad fiscal. In Sánchez Domingo, R. (Coord.), *Estudios sobre el ordenamiento jurídico español: libro conmemorativo del X aniversario de la Facultad de Derecho, Universidad de Burgos* (255-272). Universidad de Burgos, Facultad de Derecho: Caja de Burgos.

Blomberg-Nygard, A., & Anderson, C. K. (2016). United Nations World Tourism Organization Study on Online Guest Reviews and Hotel Classification Systems: An Integrated Approach. *Service Science*, 8(2), 139–151. DOI: 10.1287/serv.2016.0139

Bloom, N., Griffith, R., & Van Reenen, J. (2002a). Do R & D tax credits work? Evidence from a panel of countries 1979-1997. *Journal of Public Economics*, 85(1), 1–31. DOI: 10.1016/S0047-2727(01)00086-X

Blundell, R., & Bond, S. (1998). Initial conditions and moment restrictions in dynamic panel data models. *Journal of Econometrics*, 87(1), 115–143. DOI: 10.1016/S0304-4076(98)00009-8

Blundell, R., Duncan, A., Mccrae, J., & Meghir, C. (2000). The Labour Market Impact of the Working Families' Tax Credit. *Fiscal Studies*, 21(1), 75–104. DOI: 10.1111/j.1475-5890.2000.tb00581.x

Boadway, R., & Gahvari, F. (2006). Optimal taxation with consumption time as a leisure or labor substitute. *Journal of Public Economics*, 90(10-11), 1851–1878. DOI: 10.1016/j.jpubeco.2006.05.002

Boadway, R., & Keen, M. (2003). Theoretical perspectives on the taxation of capital income and financial services: a survey. In Honohan, P. (Ed.), *Taxation of Financial Intermediation: Theory and Practice for Emerging Economies* (Vol. 27). World Bank and Oxford University Press.

Bonga-Bonga, L., & Perold, M. (2014). A CGE simulation of a flat tax as a possibility for tax reform in South Africa. *Journal of Applied Business Research*, 30(6), 1693–1708. DOI: 10.19030/jabr.v30i6.8883

Bonilla, L., Londoño-Vélez, J., Pirttilä, J., & Rossi, M. (2022). How to reduce poverty and inequality through tax-benefit reform and transfers. *World Development*, 160, 105812. DOI: 10.1016/j.worlddev.2021.105812

Bormotova, A., Glubokova, N., Agapova, A., Alyshev, I., Larkova, E., & Lomakina, D. (2021). ASPECTS OF APPLICATION OF TAX CONTROL BY COUNTRIES FOR CROSS-BORDER OPERATIONS [Review]. *International Review (Steubenville, Ohio)*, (3-4), 173–184. DOI: 10.5937/intrev2103186B

Bowen, G. A. (2009). Document analysis as a qualitative research method. *Qualitative Research Journal*, 9(2), 27–40. DOI: 10.3316/QRJ0902027

Bußmann, F., Majewski, I., & Buschmann, D. (2023). Fremdvergleichsgrundsatz 2.0 – die Neudefinition der Routinevertriebsvergütung im Großhandel gemäß Amount B. *Betriebs-Berater*, (36), 2007–2012.

Butnaru, G. I., Stefanica, M., & Maxim, G. M. (2014). Alternative method of quality evaluation in tourism. Case study applied in tourist accommodation units. In Stefan, D., Comes, C. A., Munteanu, A., Nistor, P., & Stefan, A. B. (Eds.), *Emerging Markets Queries in Finance Business (EMQ 2013) (15), 671–678*. Elsevier Science Bv., DOI: 10.1016/S2212-5671(14)00538-3

Cai, K., Wang, H., Wang, J., Bai, J., Zuo, J., Chan, K., Lai, K., & Song, Q. (2023). Mitigating lifecycle GHG emissions of building sector through prefabricated light-steel buildings in comparison with traditional cast-in-place buildings. *Resources, Conservation and Recycling*, 194, 107007. DOI: 10.1016/j.resconrec.2023.107007

Calderón Carrero, J. M., & Ruíz Almendral, V. (2006). Autonomía financiera de las CC.AA. *vs*. Derecho Comunitario (la doctrina del TJCE en el caso Azores). *Jurisprudencia Tributaria Aranzadi*, 24, 21261–21269.

Calvo Ortega, R. (2008). Financiación de las Comunidades Autónomas y Constitución. *Nueva Fiscalidad*, 1, 9–24.

Camacho-Ruiz, M., Carrasco, R. A., Fernandez-Aviles, G., & Latorre, A. (2023). Tourism destination events classifier based on artificial intelligence techniques. *Applied Soft Computing*, 148, 110914. DOI: 10.1016/j.asoc.2023.110914

Cano, L., Ordóñez-Matamoros, G., & Ramírez, J. C. (2023). Taxation and Inequality in Colombia: An Analysis for the Period 2000-2019. *Cuadernos de Economía y Dirección de la Empresa*, 26(1), 100001. DOI: 10.1016/j.cesjef.2022.100001

Cantallops, A. S. (2004). Policies supporting sustainable tourism development in the Balearic Islands: The Ecotax. *Anatolia, 15*(1), 39–56. *Scopus.* Advance online publication. DOI: 10.1080/13032917.2004.9687143

Cárdenas-García, P. J., Pulido-Fernández, J. I., Durán-Román, J. L., & Carrillo-Hidalgo, I. (2022). Tourist taxation as a sustainability financing mechanism for mass tourism destinations. *International Journal of Tourism Research*, 24(4), 577–592. DOI: 10.1002/jtr.2523

Carlos, A. B., Abreu, I. A., Durão, J. R., & Pimenta, M. E. (2024). *Guia dos impostos em Portugal* [Guide to taxes in Portugal]. Quid Juris.

Carvalho, P. (2021, September 5). *Os bufetes escolares e os indignados do costume.* Público. https://www.publico.pt/2021/09/05/impar/opiniao/bufetes-escolares-indignados-costume-1976142

Carvalho, A., Dinis, A., & Pereira, L. (2024). Enhancing urban regeneration through digital transparency and open government. *19th Iberian Conference on Information Systems and Technologies (CISTI)*, Salamanca, Spain.

Cashman, A., Cumberbatch, J., & Moore, W. (2012). The effects of climate change on tourism in small states: Evidence from the Barbados case. *Tourism Review*, 67(3), 17–29. DOI: 10.1108/16605371211259803

Castañeda, A., Díaz-Bahamonde, J., & Laajaj, R. (2023). The effects of Colombia's tax reform on inequality and poverty. *The World Bank Economic Review*, 37(2), 391–411. DOI: 10.1093/wber/lhac012

Catarino, J. R., & Diogo, S. (2024). BEPS, Boa Governança, Concorrência, e Competitividade Fiscal. [BEPS, Good Governance, Competition and Fiscal Competitiveness] In Catarino, J. R., & Pereira, P. R. (Eds.), *Fiscalidade Internacional. Questões Atuais*. Almedina.

Ceko, E., & Cakrani, E. (2023). Environmental Tax Reform in Western Balkan Countries. In *Taking on Climate Change Through Green Taxation* (pp. 101–153). IGI Global., DOI: 10.4018/978-1-6684-8592-7.ch005

Cepni, O., Dogru, T., & Ozdemir, O. (2023). The contagion effect of COVID-19-induced uncertainty on US tourism sector: Evidence from time-varying granger causality test. *Tourism Economics*, 29(4), 906–928. DOI: 10.1177/13548166221077633

Cerina, F. (2007). Tourism specialization and environmental sustainability in a dynamic economy. *Tourism Economics*, 13(4), 553–582. DOI: 10.5367/000000007782696032

Cetin, G., Alrawadieh, Z., Dincer, M., Dincer, F., & Ioannides, D. (2017). Willingness to Pay for Tourist Tax in Destinations: Empirical Evidence from Istanbul. *Economies*, 5(2), 21. Advance online publication. DOI: 10.3390/economies5020021

Chang, I.-C., Horng, J.-S., Liu, C.-H., Chou, S.-F., & Yu, T.-Y. (2022). Exploration of Topic Classification in the Tourism Field with Text Mining Technology-A Case Study of the Academic Journal Papers. *Sustainability (Basel)*, 14(7), 4053. DOI: 10.3390/su14074053

Chan, K. H., Lo, A. W., & Mo, P. L. (2015). An empirical analysis of the changes in tax audit focus on international transfer pricing. *Journal of International Accounting, Auditing & Taxation*, 24, 94–104. DOI: 10.1016/j.intaccaudtax.2014.12.001

Chan, K. H., & Mo, P. L. L. (2000). Tax holidays and tax noncompliance: An empirical study of corporate tax audits in china's developing economy. *The Accounting Review*, 75(4), 469–484. DOI: 10.2308/accr.2000.75.4.469

Chattopadhyay, S., & Das-Gupta, A. (2002). *The compliance cost of the personal income tax and its determinants*. National Institute of Public Finance and Policy.

Cheng, Y., Zhao, G., Meng, W., & Wang, Q. (2024). Resources utilization, taxation and green education: A path to sustainable power generation. *Resources Policy*, 88, 104389. Advance online publication. DOI: 10.1016/j.resourpol.2023.104389

Chen, T. (2022). Business Performance Evaluation for Tourism Factory: Using DEA Approach and Delphi Method. *Sustainability (Basel)*, 14(15), 9209. Advance online publication. DOI: 10.3390/su14159209

Chen, X., & Duan, J. (2022). What they talk about when they talk about urban regeneration: Understanding the concept 'urban regeneration' in PRD, China. *Cities (London, England)*, 130, 103880. DOI: 10.1016/j.cities.2022.103880

Chika, O. V., Oshiogwemoh, D., & Promise, E. (2022). Impact of tax reforms on economic growth of Nigeria (2000-2021). *Goodwood Akuntansi dan Auditing Reviu, 1*(1), 79-95.

Choi, J. P., Ishikawa, J., & Okoshi, H. (2024, April). Tax havens and cross-border licensing with transfer pricing regulation [Article]. *International Tax and Public Finance*, 31(2), 333–366. DOI: 10.1007/s10797-022-09770-w PMID: 36532959

Choudhary, M. (2023). Legacy Issues & Emerging Challenges in Indian Customs from the Standpoint of Valuation & Assessment. *Issue 1 Indian JL & Legal Rsch., 5*, 1.

Chouhan, V. (2022). Developing a sustainable tribal tourism model vis-a-vis the tribal region of Rajasthan. *Journal of Tourism, Heritage and Services Marketing, 8*(1), 58–63. *Scopus.* Advance online publication. DOI: 10.5281/zenodo.6594696

Christiansen, V. (2017). Indirect Taxation of Financial Services, Working paper. CESifo area conferences on Public Sector Economics. Munich, April 27-29 2017.

Christiansen, V., & Smith, S. (2021). *Economic Principles of Commodity Taxation (Elements in Public Economics).* Cambridge University Press., DOI: 10.1017/9781009004497

Chung, J., & Yoon, S. (2023). Effects of Tax Incentive Policies for Land Use on Local Socioeconomic Conditions: A Case of Tax Policies for Urban Regeneration Projects in Republic of Korea. *Land (Basel)*, 12(9), 1801. DOI: 10.3390/land12091801

Communication from the Commission to the European Parliament. The Council, The European Economic and Social Committee and the Committee of the Regions: On a European Strategy for Universities, European Commission (2022). https://europa.eu/eurobarometer/surveys/detail/2186

Complementary Law No. 101/2000, 101/2000 (2000). https://www.planalto.gov.br/ccivil_03/leis/lcp/lcp101.htm

Conesa, J. C., & Krueger, D. (2006). On the optimal progressivity of the income tax code. *Journal of Monetary Economics*, 53(7), 1425–1450. DOI: 10.1016/j.jmoneco.2005.03.016

Congress of Colombia. (December 26, 2012). Law 1607 of 2012. By which rules on tax matters are issued and other provisions are issued. Official Gazette. https://www.funcionpublica.gov.co/eva/gestornormativo/norma.php?i=50323

Congress of Colombia. (December 27, 2019). Law 2010 of 2019. By means of which rules are adopted for the promotion of economic growth, employment, investment, the strengthening of public finances and the progressiveness, equity and efficiency of the tax system, in accordance with the objectives that on the matter promoted by Law 1943 of 2018 and other provisions are dictated. Official Gazette. https://dapre.presidencia.gov.co/normativa/normativa/LEY%202010%20DEL%2027%20DE%20DICIEMBRE%20DE%202019.pdf

Congress of Colombia. (December 29, 2016). Law 1819 of 2016. By means of which a structural tax reform is adopted, the mechanisms for the fight against tax evasion and avoidance are strengthened, and other provisions are issued. Official Gazette. https://www.suin-juriscol.gov.co/viewDocument.asp?id=30020048

Congress of Colombia. (June 04, 2021). Law 2155 of 2021. By means of which the Social Investment Law is issued and other provisions are issued. Official Gazette. https://www.funcionpublica.gov.co/eva/gestornormativo/norma_pdf.php?i=167156

Congress of Colombia. (September 14, 2021). Law 2159 of 2021. By means of which cross-cutting norms are adopted for the executive branch at the national and territorial level and for individuals who perform public and/or administrative functions, in relation to the rationalization of procedures and other provisions are issued. Official Gazette. https://www.funcionpublica.gov.co/eva/gestornormativo/norma_pdf.php?i=167770

Constitution Amendment Proposal No. 13, of 2019 (2019). https://www.camara.leg.br/proposicoesWeb/fichadetramitacao?idProposicao=2344523

Constitution of the Federative Republic of Brazil. (1988). http://www.planalto.gov.br/ccivil_03/Constituicao/Constituicao.htm

Constitutional Amendment No. 29, of September 13th, 2000 (2000) https://www.planalto.gov.br/ccivil_03/constituicao/emendas/emc/emc29.htm

Cooper, M., & Nguyen, Q. T. (2020). Multinational enterprises and corporate tax planning: A review of literature and suggestions for a future research agenda. *International Business Review*, 29(3), 101692. DOI: 10.1016/j.ibusrev.2020.101692

Correia, I. (2005). *BANCO DE PORTUGAL Economic Research Department CONSUMPTION TAXES AND REDISTRIBUTION Consumption Taxes and Redistribution*.

Correia, S., & Martins, A. (2018). *Preços de Transferência, Litigância e Arbitragem Fiscal* [Transfer Pricing, Litigation and Tax Arbitration]. Petrony.

Costa, T., Lopes, S., Fernández-Llimós, F., Amante, M. J., & Lopes, P. F. (2012). A bibliometria e a avaliação da produção científica. ACTAS – Congresso Nacional de Bibliotecários. *Arquivistas e Documentalistas*, 11, 1–7.

Council Resolution on a Strategic Framework for European Cooperation in Education and Training towards the European Education Area and beyond (2021-2030), Official Journal of the European Union (2021).

Court of Audit. (2019). *Report on the execution of budget 2019 Morocco.* https://www.courdescomptes.ma/en/publication/report-on-the-execution-of-the-finance-law-for-the-year-2019/

Cropley, A. J. (2022). *Qualitative research methods: A practice-oriented introduction.* Bucharest: Editura Intaglio. https://doi:DOI: 10.13140/RG.2.1.3095.6888/1

Croushore, D. (1993). Money in the utility function: Functional equivalence to a shopping-time model. *Journal of Macroeconomics*, 15(1), 175–182. DOI: 10.1016/0164-0704(93)90060-Y

Cruz, S. R., & Soares, C. (2022). Use of the tax benefit of conventional remuneration of share capital by Portuguese companies. *Revista Contabilidade & Finanças*, 33(90), e1587. Advance online publication. DOI: 10.1590/1808-057x20221587.en

Cugova, A., & Cug, J. (2019, Apr 10-11). News and Changes in Slovak Transfer Pricing Rules. [Education excellence and innovation management through vision 2020]. 33rd International-Business-Information-Management-Association (IBIMA) Conference, Granada, SPAIN.

Cutler, D. M. (1995). Cutting costs and improving health: Making reform work. *Health Affairs (Project Hope)*, 14(1), 161–172. DOI: 10.1377/hlthaff.14.1.161 PMID: 7657201

Czarnitzki, D., Hanel, P., & Rosa, J. M. (2011). Evaluating the impact of R&D tax credits on innovation: A microeconometric study on Canadian firms. *Research Policy*, 40(2), 217–229. DOI: 10.1016/j.respol.2010.09.017

Czerwonka, L., & Jaworski, J. (2017). Capital Structure Determinants of Industrial: Companies Listed on the Warsaw Stock Exchange. *11th International Scientific Conference on Financial Management of Firms and Financial Institutions*, 157–164.

d'Andria, D., DeBacker, J., Evans, R. W., Pycroft, J., & Zachlod-Jelec, M. (2021). Taxing income or consumption: macroeconomic and distributional effects for Italy (No. 13/2021). JRC Working Papers on Taxation and Structural Reforms.

da Cunha, R. S. (2018). A Legisprudência na Construção de Uma Teoria Normativa da Legislação em Timor-Leste.

da Fonseca, P. V., Jucá, M. N., & Nakamura, W. T. (2020). Debt Tax Benefits in a High Tax Emerging Market: Evidence from Brazil. In *International Journal of Economics and Business Administration: Vol. VIII* (Issue 2).

Dabrowski, M., & Tomczynska, M. (2001). Tax reforms in transition economies - A mixed record and a complex future agenda. *SSRN*, (231). Advance online publication. DOI: 10.2139/ssrn.1440219

Dacian, C. D. (2010). The relationship between accounting and taxation: A brief international literature review. *Faculty of Economics and Business Administration*, 1(1), 496–502.

Dadzie, J., Runeson, G., & Ding, G. (2018). Sustainable Technologies as Determinants of Energy Efficient Upgrade of Existing Buildings. *2018 International Conference on Smart Grid and Clean Energy Technologies (ICSGCE)*, 145–149. DOI: 10.1109/ICSGCE.2018.8556688

Dagan, N., Serrano, R., & Volij, O. (1999). Feasible implementation of taxation methods. *Review of Economic Design*, 4(1), 57–72. DOI: 10.1007/s100580050026

Dagar, V., Ahmed, F., Waheed, F., Bojnec, Š., Khan, M. K., & Shaikh, S. (2022). Testing the Pollution Haven Hypothesis with the Role of Foreign Direct Investments and Total Energy Consumption. *Energies*, 15(11), 4046. DOI: 10.3390/en15114046

Dahl, G. B., & Lochner, L. (2012). The impact of family income on child achievement: Evidence from the earned income tax credit. *The American Economic Review*, 102(5), 1927–1956. DOI: 10.1257/aer.102.5.1927

Das, P. (2022). India's evolving tax system: Its successes and challenges. *RESEARCH REVIEW International Journal of Multidisciplinary*, 7(7), 118–124. DOI: 10.31305/rrijm.2022.v07.i07.016

Das, S. (2017). Some concerns regarding the goods and services tax. *Economic and Political Weekly*, 52(9), 107–124.

De Cesare, C. M., Fernandes, C. E., & Cavalcanti, C. B. (2015). Imposto sobre a Propriedade Predial e Territorial Urbana (Vol. 3). Ministério das Cidades https://www.caubr.gov.br/wp-content/uploads/2017/10/CAPACIDADES3.pdf

de Hek, P. A. (2006). On taxation in a two-sector endogenous growth model with endogenous labour supply. *Journal of Economic Dynamics & Control*, 30(4), 655–685. DOI: 10.1016/j.jedc.2005.02.006

De Lange, D., & Dodds, R. (2017). Increasing sustainable tourism through social entrepreneurship. *International Journal of Contemporary Hospitality Management*, 29(7), 1977–2002. DOI: 10.1108/IJCHM-02-2016-0096

de Oliveira, D. B. (2014). "IPTU Verde": Uma perspectiva legislativa no município de Pelotas. *Revista da Faculdade de Direito de Pelotas*, 1(1), 159–182.

de Prato, G., & Simon, J. P. (2016). Global trends in mobile: A new global landscape for supply and demand. In *Emerging perspectives on the mobile content evolution* (pp. 1–31). IGI Global. DOI: 10.4018/978-1-4666-8838-4.ch001

Deb, R. (2024). Tax Administration Reform: End of Tax Disputes in India?. *MDIM Journal of Management Review*, 46.

Deb, R. (2018). Tax Reforms and GST: A Systematic Literature Review. *Journal of Commerce and Accounting Research*, 7(1), 40.

Delgado, F. J., Freire-González, J., & Presno, M. J. (2022). Environmental taxation in the European Union: Are there common trends? *Economic Analysis and Policy*, 73, 670–682. DOI: 10.1016/j.eap.2021.12.019

Desai, B. H., & Desai, J. B. (2024). The Climate Change Conundrum: A Case for Course Correction in the Global Regulatory Approach. *Environmental Policy and Law*, 54(1), 3–14. DOI: 10.3233/EPL-239028

Deshmukh, A. K., Mohan, A., & Mohan, I. (2022). Goods and services tax (GST) implementation in India: A SAP–LAP–Twitter analytic perspective. *Global Journal of Flexible Systems Managment*, 23(2), 165–183. DOI: 10.1007/s40171-021-00297-3 PMID: 37522093

Destination Sustainability Movement & Group Nao. (2020). *Tourism taxes by design white paper: Destination funding and the impact of tourism taxes on European cities and urban communities* (BTRP-ID: 2701).

Devkota, N., Paudel, U. R., & Bhandari, U. (2020). Tourism entrepreneurs' expectation from the provincial government in touristic city–Pokhara, Nepal. *Journal of Hospitality and Tourism Insights*, 3(3), 329–351. DOI: 10.1108/JHTI-06-2019-0082

Deyganto, K. O. (2022). The effect of tax incentives practices on the sustainability of micro, small and medium enterprises in Ethiopia during the outbreak of corona virus pandemic. *Journal of Innovation and Entrepreneurship*, 11(1), 8. DOI: 10.1186/s13731-022-00194-8 PMID: 35106268

DGE Division of Graduate Education. (2022). *NSF Award Search Award # 2224769 - Training Scientists to Tackle Grand Challenge Societal Problems through Convergent Action in Transdisciplinary Teams*. https://www.nsf.gov/awardsearch/showAward?AWD_ID=2224769

DGO. (2023) Report state budget for 2024 of 16 october 2023 available at https://www.dgo.gov.pt/politicaorcamental/OrcamentodeEstado/2024/Proposta%20do%20Or%C3%A7amento/Documentos%20do%20OE/OE2024_doc16_Relatorio.pdf (05/09/2024)

Diakomichalis, N.-M., & Diakomihalis, M. (2024). Sustainable Tourism Within the Boundaries of Carrying Capacity and Tourism Satellite Account. Em *Palgrave. Stud. Cross-Discip. Bus. Res. Association. EuroMed. Acad. Bus.: Vol. Part F1799* (pp. 45–72). Palgrave Macmillan. DOI: 10.1007/978-3-031-37365-7_3

Dias, A. C. G. (2024). *Preços de Transferência [Transfer Pricing]*. Ordem dos Contabilistas Certificados.

Dias, S. L., & Ribeiro, J. S. (2023). Taxation Policies as an Environmental Protection Instrument: The Portuguese Case. In Taking on Climate Change Through Green Taxation (pp. 265–281). IGI Global. DOI: 10.4018/978-1-6684-8592-7.ch011

Dinis, A. A., Carvalho, A., & Dias, S. L. (2023). Sustainable Taxi Fleet: An Approach to the Contribution of Green Taxation. In A. A. Dinis, F. David, L. Pereira, & S. L. Dias (Eds.), *Taking on Climate Change Through Green Taxation* (pp. 241–264). IGI Global. DOI: 10.4018/978-1-6684-8592-7.ch010

Dinis, A. A. (2024). Promoting Fiscal Incentives for Urban Regeneration: Local Government Digital Presence. In Rocha, Á., Adeli, H., Dzemyda, G., Moreira, F., & Poniszewska-Marańda, A. (Eds.), *Good Practices and New Perspectives in Information Systems and Technologies* (Vol. 990, pp. 335–343). Springer Nature Switzerland., DOI: 10.1007/978-3-031-60328-0_34

Dinis, A. A., & Pereira, L. (2022). Tax Incentives for Tourism: The Case of Portuguese Municipalities. In Costa, V., & Costa, C. (Eds.), *Advances in Hospitality, Tourism, and the Services Industry* (pp. 95–118). IGI Global., DOI: 10.4018/978-1-7998-9285-4.ch004

Dinis, A., Carvalho, A., & Pereira, L. (2024). Forest Protection Tax Policy in the Context of Portuguese Societies. *Portuguese Review of Regional Studies*, 68(68), 68. Advance online publication. DOI: 10.59072/rper.vi68.584

Dispatch n.º 7516-A/2016, of June 6 from the Office of the Assistant Secretary of State for Health. Diário da República: II série, nº 108, 1º Suplemento (2016). https://diariodarepublica.pt/dr/detalhe/despacho/7516-a-2016-74604818

Dispatch n.º 8127/2021, of August 17 from the Office of the Assistant Secretary of State for Health. Diário da República: II série, nº 159 (2021) https://diariodarepublica.pt/dr/detalhe/despacho/8127-2021-169689544

Ditz, X., & Nowotny, C. (2022). Internationale Verrechnungspreise – Vergleich der deutschen VWG Verrechnungspreise mit den österreichischen Verrechnungspreis-Richtlinien. *IStR Internationales Steuerrecht*, (18), 669–678.

do Amaral, D. F. (2017). *Manual de Introdução ao Direito* [Handbook of Introduction to Law]. Vol. I). Almedina.

Dodds, R., & Holmes, M. (2011). Sustainability in Canadian B&Bs: Comparing the East Versus West. *International Journal of Tourism Research*, 13(5), 482–495. DOI: 10.1002/jtr.822

Doghmi, H. (2020). *The capacity to mobilize tax revenue in Morocco.*

Domonkos, S. (2016). Who wants a progressive income tax? Determinants of tax policy preferences in post-socialist Eastern Europe. *Eastern European Politics and Societies*, 30(2), 423–448. DOI: 10.1177/0888325415602055

Donaldson, E. A., Cohen, J. E., Rutkow, L., Villanti, A. C., Kanarek, N. F., & Barry, C. L. (2015). Public support for a sugar-sweetened beverage tax and pro-tax messages in a Mid-Atlantic US state. *Public Health Nutrition*, 18(12), 2263–2273. DOI: 10.1017/S1368980014002699 PMID: 25430945

Donthu, N., Kumar, S., Mukherjee, D., Pandey, N., & Lim, W. M. (2021). How to conduct a bibliometric analysis: An overview and guidelines. *Journal of Business Research*, 133, 285–296. DOI: 10.1016/j.jbusres.2021.04.070

Dourado, A. P. (2018). *Governação Fiscal Global* [Global Tax Governance]. 2nd ed.). Almedina.

Dourado, A. P. (2019). *Direito fiscal* [Tax Law]. 4th ed.). Almedina.

Duncan, D., & Peter, K. S. (2010). Does labour supply respond to a flat tax? *Economics of Transition*, 18(2), 365–404. DOI: 10.1111/j.1468-0351.2009.00383.x

Durán-Román, J. L., Pulido-Fernández, J. I., Rey-Carmona, F. J., & Núñez-Tabales, J. M. (2022). Willingness to Pay by Tourist Companies for Improving Sustainability and Competitiveness in a Mature Destination. *Leisure Sciences*, 1–22. Advance online publication. DOI: 10.1080/01490400.2022.2123072

Durán-Román, J., Cárdenas-García, P., & Pulido-Fernández, J. (2021a). Tourist Tax to Improve Sustainability and the Experience in Mass Tourism Destinations: The Case of Andalusia (Spain). *Sustainability (Basel)*, 13(1), 42. Advance online publication. DOI: 10.3390/su13010042

Durán-Román, J., Cárdenas-García, P., & Pulido-Fernández, J. (2021b). Tourists' willingness to pay to improve sustainability and experience at destination. *Journal of Destination Marketing & Management*, 19, 100540. Advance online publication. DOI: 10.1016/j.jdmm.2020.100540

EC (European Commission) (2020). Revue of the VAT Rules for Financial and Insurance Services. Combined Evaluation Roadmap/Inception Impact Assessment, Ares (2020)5770956.

ECLAC. (2022). "Fiscal Policy and Climate Change: Recent Experiences of Latin American and Caribbean Countries". Santiago: United Nations. https://repositorio.cepal.org/handle/11362/47913

Economic Commission for Latin America and the Caribbean (ECLAC). (2019). The Climate Change Emergency in Latin America and the Caribbean: Do We Still Have Time? https://repositorio.cepal.org/handle/11362/44969

Economidou, M., Todeschi, V., Bertoldi, P., D'Agostino, D., Zangheri, P., & Castellazzi, L. (2020). Review of 50 years of EU energy efficiency policies for buildings. *Energy and Building*, 225, 110322. DOI: 10.1016/j.enbuild.2020.110322

Edelmann, N., Müller, A., Steen, T., Gerhardter, B., & Holzbauer, T. (2022). Sustainable Co-Creation in the Public Sector: A Case Study in the Lower Austrian Federal Government. Em L. Amaral, D. Soares, & L. Zheng (Eds.), *KU Leuven* (WOS:001098408200016; pp. 111–118). DOI: 10.1145/3560107.3560126

Eden, L. (2023). Pillar One Amount B: Simplifying the Arm's Length Principle for Baseline Distribution Activities (Submission to the OECD/Inclusive Framework on 1 September 2023 in Response to the 12 July 2023 Public Consultation Document on Pillar One Amount B). SSRN *Electronic Journal*, 1–11. DOI: 10.2139/ssrn.4560131

Eissa, N., & Hoynes, H. W. (2004). Taxes and the labor market participation of married couples: The earned income tax credit. *Journal of Public Economics*, 88(9–10), 1931–1958. DOI: 10.1016/j.jpubeco.2003.09.005

Ellegaard, O., & Wallin, J. A. (2015). The bibliometric analysis of scholarly production: How great is the impact? *Scientometrics*, 105(3), 1809–1831. DOI: 10.1007/s11192-015-1645-z PMID: 26594073

Elliott, R., & Timulak, L. (2021). Why a generic approach to descriptive-interpretive qualitative research? In Elliott, R., & Timulak, L. (Eds.), *Essentials of descriptive-interpretive qualitative research: A generic approach* (pp. 3–14). American Psychological Association., DOI: 10.1037/0000224-001

Ellwood, D. T. (2000). The Impact of the Earned Income Tax Credit and Social Policy Reforms on Work, Marriage, and Living Arrangements. Https://Doi.Org/10.17310/Ntj.2000.4S1.03, *53*(4 PART 2), 1063–1103. DOI: 10.17310/ntj.2000.4S1.03

Ensslin, L., Dutra, A., Ensslin, S. R., Chaves, L. C., Dezem, V., Ensslin, L., Dutra, A., Ensslin, S. R., Chaves, L. C., & Dezem, V. (2015). Research Process for Selecting a Theoretical Framework and Bibliometric Analysis of a Theme: Illustration for the Management of Customer Service in a Bank. *Modern Economy*, 6(6), 782–796. DOI: 10.4236/me.2015.66074

Eom, T. H., Duncombe, W., Nguyen-Hoang, P., & Yinger, J. (2014). The unintended consequences of property tax relief: New york's star program. *Education Finance and Policy*, 9(4), 446–480. DOI: 10.1162/EDFP_a_00143

Esteller-Moré, A., Rizzo, L., & Secomandi, R. (2021). The role of tax system complexity on foreign direct investment [Article]. *Applied Economics*, 53(45), 5208–5220. DOI: 10.1080/00036846.2021.1922587

EU - European Union. (2000). *Charter of Fundamental Rights of the European Union*. Available in: https://www.europarl.europa.eu/charter/pdf/text_en.pdf [Accessed in January 2024].

EU - European Union. (2012). *Treaty on the Functioning of the European Union*. Available in: https://eur-lex.europa.eu/legal-content/EN/TXT/PDF/?uri=CELEX:12012E/TXT [Accessed in January 2024].

European Commission. (2020). *Taxation in support of green transition: an overview and assessment of existing tax practices to reduce greenhouse gas emissions Final Report*. DOI: 10.2778/343194

European Commission. (2020). Working document: EU Building Renovation Strategy. https://ec.europa.eu/energy/sites/ener/files/eu_renovation_wave_strategy.pdf

European Commission. (2022). https://taxation-customs.ec.europa.eu/taxation-1/value-added-tax-vat_en

European Commission. (2023). *Proposal for a Council Directive on transfer pricing*

Eurostat (2024, May 24). *Self-perceived health by sex, age and income quintile*. DOI: 10.2908/HLTH_SILC_10

Evans, A. J., & Aligica, P. D. (2008). The spread of the flat tax in eastern europe: A comparative study. *Eastern European Economics*, 46(3), 49–67. DOI: 10.2753/EEE0012-8775460303

Ewald, J., Sterner, T., & Sterner, E. (2022). Understanding the resistance to carbon taxes: Drivers and barriers among the general public and fuel-tax protesters. *Resource and Energy Economics*, 70, 101331. Advance online publication. DOI: 10.1016/j.reseneeco.2022.101331

Faccio, M., & Xu, J. (2015). Taxes and Capital Structure. *Journal of Financial and Quantitative Analysis*, 50(3), 277–300. DOI: 10.1017/S0022109015000174

Fajriyati, I., Afiff, A. Z., Gayatri, G., & Hati, S. R. H. (2020). Generic and Islamic attributes for non-Muslim majority destinations: Application of the three-factor theory of customer satisfaction. *Heliyon*, 6(6), e04324. DOI: 10.1016/j.heliyon.2020.e04324 PMID: 32637707

Farooq, U., Haider Subhani, B., Nouman Shafiq, M., & Gillani, S. (2023). Assessing the environmental impacts of environmental tax rate and corporate statutory tax rate: Empirical evidence from industry-intensive economies. *Energy Reports*, 9, 6241–6250. DOI: 10.1016/j.egyr.2023.05.254

Fehling, D. (2022). Addressing Base Erosion and Profit Shifting: The Implementation of the ATAD in Germany [Article]. *Intertax*, 50(10), 721–729. https://www.scopus.com/inward/record.uri?eid=2-s2.0-85138153176&partnerID=40&md5=7b9a5267579ff94eff9bd99ccbbf8237. DOI: 10.54648/TAXI2022076

Feigin, S. V., Wiebers, D. O., Lueddeke, G., Morand, S., Lee, K., Knight, A., Brainin, M., Feigin, V. L., Whitfort, A., Marcum, J., Shackelford, T. K., Skerratt, L. F., & Winkler, A. S. (2023). Proposed solutions to anthropogenic climate change: A systematic literature review and a new way forward. *Heliyon*, 9(10), e20544. Advance online publication. DOI: 10.1016/j.heliyon.2023.e20544 PMID: 37867892

Feldstein, M. (1995). Behavioral responses to tax rates: Evidence from the tax reform act of 1986. *The American Economic Review*, 85(2), 170–174. https://search.proquest.com/scholarly-journals/behavioral-responses-tax-rates-evidence-reform/docview/233022407/se-2?accountid=38384 PMID: 10160509

Feng, P., Lu, H., Li, W., & Wang, X. (2022). Tax Policies of Low Carbon in China: Effectiveness Evaluation, System Design and Prospects. *Frontiers in Environmental Science*, 10, 953512. DOI: 10.3389/fenvs.2022.953512

Feng, Y., Tan, X., & Wang, R. (2022). The value of higher education to entrepreneurial performance: Evidence from higher education expansion in China. *China Economic Review*, 73, 101789. Advance online publication. DOI: 10.1016/j.chieco.2022.101789

Fernandes, F. V. (2022). *Direito Fiscal do Terceiro Setor*. AAFDL Editora.

Fernandez Morales, A., & Mayorga Toledano, M. C. (2018). Seasonality of cruise tourism in Spanish ports. A multivariate approach. *Pasos (El Sauzal)*, 16(1), 253–264. DOI: 10.25145/j.pasos.2018.16.016

Fernández, C., & Villar, L. (2023). Informality and labor market policies in Colombia. *Labour Economics*, 81, 102310. DOI: 10.1016/j.labeco.2022.102310

Fernandez, P. (2004). The value of tax shields is NOT equal to the present value of tax shields. *Journal of Financial Economics*, 73(1), 145–165. DOI: 10.1016/j.jfineco.2002.10.001

Ferreira, A. (2020). IVA e Preços de Transferência [VAT and Transfer Pricing]. *Revista Electrónica de Fiscalidade da AFP, 2*(II).

Ferreira, A. (2023). *6 doenças associadas à obesidade.* Lusíadas. https://www.lusiadas.pt/blog/sintomas-tratamentos/doencas/6-doencas-associadas-obesidade

Ferreiro Lapatza, J. J. (1984). Financiación de las Comunidades Autónomas. In González Encinar, J.J. (Coord.), *Diccionario del sistema político español* (326-337). Akal.

Figueira, M., Bica, M., Vicente, B., Gaspar, M., & Gregório, M. (2023). *Exposição das crianças portuguesas ao marketing digital de alimentos e bebidas: estudo piloto da ferramenta click da OMS Europa.* Direção Geral da Saúde. https://nutrimento.pt/activeapp/wp-content/uploads/2023/05/DGS_PNPAS_MarketingDigital-2.pdf

Finance Law for the 2024 Financial Year (2024).

Finkelstein, E. A., Zhen, C., Bilger, M., Nonnemaker, J., Farooqui, A. M., & Todd, J. E. (2013). Implications of a sugar-sweetened beverage (SSB) tax when substitutions to non-beverage items are considered. *Journal of Health Economics*, 32(1), 219–239. DOI: 10.1016/j.jhealeco.2012.10.005 PMID: 23202266

Fiorillo, C. A. P., & Ferreira, R. M. (2010). Direito ambiental tributário (3o ed). Saraiva Publisher

Fischer, D.-H., & Ferraro, S. (2019). A proposal for a simple average-based progressive taxation system. *Public Sector Economics*, 43(2), 141–165. DOI: 10.3326/pse.43.2.2

Fossen, F. M. (2009). Would a flat-rate tax stimulate entrepreneurship in Germany? A behavioural microsimulation analysis allowing for risk. *Fiscal Studies*, 30(2), 179–218. DOI: 10.1111/j.1475-5890.2009.00093.x

Friedman, M. (1962). *Capitalism and Freedom.* University of Chicago Press.

Fuest, C., Peichl, A., & Schaefer, T. (2008). Does a simpler income tax yield more equity and efficiency? *CESifo Economic Studies*, 54(1), 73–97. DOI: 10.1093/cesifo/ifn003

Fuest, C., Peichl, A., & Schaefer, T. (2008). Is a flat tax reform feasible in a grown-up democracy of Western Europe? A simulation study for Germany. *International Tax and Public Finance*, 15(5), 620–636. DOI: 10.1007/s10797-008-9071-2

Gago, A., Labandeira, X., Picos, F., & Rodríguez, M. (2009). Specific and general taxation of tourism activities. Evidence from Spain. *Tourism Management*, 30(3), 381–392. DOI: 10.1016/j.tourman.2008.08.004

Gainsbury, M., S., Hing, N., Delfabbro, P. H., & King, D. L. (. (2014). A taxonomy of gambling and casino games via social media and online technologies. *International Gambling Studies*, 14(2), 196–213. DOI: 10.1080/14459795.2014.890634

Galarza, R.; Cuji, C. (2022). "Optimal Energy Management in a Gradual and Controlled Process to Contribute to the Decarbonization of the Electricity Sector". Technical Journal "energy". No. 19, Issue I, Pp. 71-84 ISSN On-line: 2602-8492 - ISSN Print: 1390-5074. Doi:DOI: 10.37116/revistaenergia.v19.n1.2022.518

Gale, W. G., & Potter, S. R. (2002). An economic evaluation of the Economic Growth and Tax Relief Reconciliation Act of 2001. *National Tax Journal*, 55(1), 133–177. DOI: 10.17310/ntj.2002.1.08

Gallato, C. G., Gallato-Reamillo, K. A., Valdez, N. P., Warokka, A., & Hilman, H. (2012). Eco-tourism in the Philippines: Educational and recreational value of the Alayan cave systems. *Journal for Global Business Advancement, 5*(2), 169–178. *Scopus.* Advance online publication. DOI: 10.1504/JGBA.2012.049509

Gallego, J. A., Hoffmann, B., Ibarrarán, P., Medina, M. P., Pecha, C., Romero, O., Stampini, M., Vargas, D., & Vera-Cossio, D. A. (2021). Impacts of the Solidarity Income program in the face of the COVID-19 crisis in Colombia. *World Development*, 149, 105316. DOI: 10.1016/j.worlddev.2020.105316

Gallo, P., Dobrovic, J., Cabinova, V., Partlova, P., Strakova, J., & Mihalcova, B. (2021). Increasing the Efficiency of Enterprises in Tourism Sector Using Innovative Management Methods and Tools. *Social Sciences (Basel, Switzerland)*, 10(4), 132. DOI: 10.3390/socsci10040132

García Martínez, A., & Herrera Molina, P. M. (2001). Europa: El Derecho comunitario como límite a la cesión del IVA a las Comunidades Autónomas. *Revista Valenciana de Economía y Hacienda*, 2, 167–195.

García Novoa, C. (2008). Reflexiones sobre los impuestos propios de carácter medioambiental en el ámbito de la tributación autonómica. In Aneiros Pereira, J. (Coord.), *La financiación autonómica en los Estatutos de Autonomía* (411-461). Marcial Pons.

García Novoa, C. (1998). Financiación autonómica y Derecho Comunitario. *Crónica Tributaria*, 85, 119–144.

García Prats, F. A. (2011). Spain. In Bizioli, G. & Sacchetto, C. (Coords), *Tax Aspects of Fiscal Federalism. A Comparative Analysis* (361-402). IBFD.

Garfield, E. (1955). Citation indexes for science. *Science*, 122(3159), 108–111. DOI: 10.1126/science.122.3159.108 PMID: 14385826

Gathergood, J. (2012). Self-control, financial literacy and consumer over-indebtedness. *Journal of Economic Psychology*, 33(3), 590–602. DOI: 10.1016/j.joep.2011.11.006

Gautam, M. (2023). Federalism and National Security in India After Liberalisation. *Global Journal for Research Analysis*.

Ghazouani, A., Xia, W., Ben Jebli, M., & Shahzad, U. (2020). Exploring the Role of Carbon Taxation Policies on CO2 Emissions: Contextual Evidence from Tax Implementation and Non-Implementation European Countries. *Sustainability (Basel)*, 12(20), 8680. DOI: 10.3390/su12208680

Ghuge, N. R., & Katdare, V. V. (2015). Indian tax structure-An analytical perspective. *International Journal of Management and Social Sciences*, 3(9), 242–252.

Gil, A. C. (2019). *Métodos e técnicas de pesquisa social*. Atlas Ltda Publisher.

Glänzel, W., & Leuven, K. U. (2003). *Bibliometrics as a research field: A course on theory and application of bibliometric indicators Topic identification challenge View project*. https://www.researchgate.net/publication/242406991

Glass, L.-M., & Newig, J. (2019). Governance for achieving the Sustainable Development Goals: How important are participation, policy coherence, reflexivity, adaptation and democratic institutions? *Earth System Governance*, 2, 100031. DOI: 10.1016/j.esg.2019.100031

Goel, M. (2022). Evolution of Indian Tax System-Tax Policy, e-initiatives and administrative reforms. *Special Education*, 2(43).

Göktaş, L. S., & Çetin, G. (2023). Tourist tax for sustainability: Determining willingness to pay. *European Journal of Tourism Research, 35.European Journal of Tourism Research*, 35, 3503. Advance online publication. DOI: 10.54055/ejtr.v35i.2813

Gomes, P., Teixeira, C., & Azevedo, G. (2023). Debate: Integrating new perspectives in public sector accounting education (PSAE). *Public Money & Management*, 43(7), 727–728. DOI: 10.1080/09540962.2023.2248409

Gómez-Sabaini, J. C., & Morán, D. (2021). Fiscal policy and the SDGs: From theory to practice in Latin America and the Caribbean. In *United Nations, Recover better: Economic and social challenges and opportunities* (pp. 165–184). United Nations., DOI: 10.18356/9789210054980c011

Gonçalves, R. da R., Oliveira, C. de R. de, Carvalho, A. B., & Santos, R. Á. (2019). O impacto da política pública de IPTU Verde no município de Curitiba. Revibec. *Revista de la Red Iberoamericana de Economia Ecológica*, 30(1), 120–137.

Gonçalves, T., Dias, J., & Barros, V. (2022). Sustainability Performance and the Cost of Capital. *International Journal of Financial Studies*, 10(3), 63. DOI: 10.3390/ijfs10030063

González González, A. I. (2018). Una nueva reforma de la financiación autonómica: Entre la suficiencia financiera y la autonomía tributaria. *Documentos-Instituto de Estudios Fiscales*, 12/2018, 177–189.

Gonzalo Escribano, Lara Lázaro & Ignacio Urbasos. (2022). The development of hydrogen: strategies and policies in Europe and Spain. International review of economic policy. DOI: 10.7203/IREP.4.2.25807

Gore, T., Urios, J., & Karamperi, M. (2022). Green and fair taxation in the EU - Green EU tax systems tend to also be more progressive. *Institute for European Environmental Policy*. https://ieep.eu/publications/green-and-fair-taxation-in-the-eu/

Gorsky, M., & Mold, A. (2020). Documentary analysis. *Qualitative Research in Health Care*, 83–96.

Gössling, S., Peeters, P., Ceron, J.-P., Dubois, G., Patterson, T., & Richardson, R. B. (2005). The eco-efficiency of tourism. *Ecological Economics*, 54(4), 417–434. DOI: 10.1016/j.ecolecon.2004.10.006

Gouveia, M., & Oliver, D. (1995). Voting over flat taxes in an endowment economy. *Economics Letters*, 50(2), 251–258. DOI: 10.1016/0165-1765(95)00749-0

Grabowski, M. (2005). Reforms of Tax Systems in Transition Countries. *Transition Studies Review*, 12(2), 293–312. DOI: 10.1007/s11300-005-0063-y

Graça, P., Gregório, M. J., Santos, A., & Sousa, S. (2016). *Redução do consumo de açúcar em Portugal: evidência que justifica ação*. https://alimentacaosaudavel.dgs.pt/activeapp2020/wp-content/uploads/2020/01/Redução-do-Consumo-de-Açúcar-em-Portugal-Evidência-que-Justifica-Ação.pdf

Graci, S. (2013). Collaboration and Partnership Development for Sustainable Tourism. *Tourism Geographies*, 15(1), 25–42. DOI: 10.1080/14616688.2012.675513

Graham, J. R. (2000). How big are the tax benefits of debt? *The Journal of Finance*, 55(5), 1901–1941. DOI: 10.1111/0022-1082.00277

Graham, J. R., Raedy, J. S., & Shackelford, D. A. (2012). Research in accounting for income taxes. *Journal of Accounting and Economics*, 53(1–2), 412–434. DOI: 10.1016/j.jacceco.2011.11.006

Graham, J. R., & Rogers, D. A. (2002). Do firms hedge in response to tax incentives? *The Journal of Finance*, 57(2), 815–839. DOI: 10.1111/1540-6261.00443

Graham, J. R., & Smith, C. W. (1999). Tax Incentives to Hedge. *The Journal of Finance*, 54(6), 2241–2262. DOI: 10.1111/0022-1082.00187

Gregova, E., Smrcka, L., Michalkova, L., & Svabova, L. (2021). Impact of tax benefits and earnings management on capital structures across V4 countries. *Acta Polytechnica Hungarica*, 18(3), 221–244. DOI: 10.12700/APH.18.3.2021.3.12

Greil, S. (2021). The arm's length principle in the 21st century - a literature overview. *Journal of Tax Administration*, 6(2), 148–198.

Gribnau, H. (2015). Corporate social responsibility and tax planning: Not by rules alone. *Social & Legal Studies*, 24(2), 225–250. DOI: 10.1177/0964663915575053

Grillini, G., Streifeneder, T., Sacchi, G., & Fischer, C. (2024). Comparative analysis of alpine agritourism in Trentino, Tyrol, and South Tyrol: Regional variations and prospects. *Open Agriculture*, 9(1), 20220281. Advance online publication. DOI: 10.1515/opag-2022-0281

Grinenko, J., Melnychuk, D., Mykhalchyshyna, L., Belei, S., & Yevtushenko, N. (2021, May). IMPROVING TRANSFER PRICING IN UKRAINE USING AMERICAN EXPERIENCE [Article]. *Independent Journal of Management & Production*, 12(3), S205–S231. DOI: 10.14807/ijmp.v12i3.1524

Groote, O., Valdez, R. M., & Contreras-Araneda, S. J. (2021). Cash transfers for mitigating the social costs of climate change. *Environment Systems & Decisions*, 41, 5–15. DOI: 10.1007/s10669-021-09815-7

Grubb, M., Drummond, P., Poncia, A., McDowall, W., Popp, D., Samadi, S., & Patt, A. (2021). Induced innovation in energy technologies and systems: A review of evidence and potential implications for CO2 mitigation. *Environmental Research Letters*, 16(4), 043007. DOI: 10.1088/1748-9326/abde07

Grytsevych, V. S., Podvirna, K. Y., & Senkiv, M. I. (2019). Motor transport network of western region of Ukraine as a factor of development of tourism industry. *Вісник Харківського національного університету імені ВН Каразіна.Серія: Геологія. Географія. Екологія*, 50, 91–100. DOI: 10.26565/2410-7360-2019-50-07

Guo, B., Wang, Y., Feng, Y., Liang, C., Tang, L., Yao, X., & Hu, F. (2022). The effects of environmental tax reform on urban air pollution: A quasi-natural experiment based on the Environmental Protection Tax Law. *Frontiers in Public Health*, 10, 967524. DOI: 10.3389/fpubh.2022.967524 PMID: 36033767

Guo, Y., & Li, X. (2024). Regional inequality in China's educational development: An urban-rural comparison. *Heliyon*, 10(4), e26249. Advance online publication. DOI: 10.1016/j.heliyon.2024.e26249 PMID: 38379968

Gupta, S., & Jalles, J. T. (2022). Can COVID-19 induce governments to implement tax reforms in developing countries? *Applied Economics*, 54(20), 2288–2301. DOI: 10.1080/00036846.2021.1987380

Gurnak, A.V. (2018). Problems and prospects of Indian tax system development: industrial context Section: Macroeconomic and regional problems of industrial development.

Guruswamy, M., & Singh, Z. D. (2008). *Chasing the dragon: Will India catch up with China?* Pearson Education India.

Gu, Y., Onggo, B., Kunc, M., & Bayer, S. (2022). Small Island Developing States (SIDS) COVID-19 post-pandemic tourism recovery: A system dynamics approach. *Current Issues in Tourism*, 25(9), 1481–1508. DOI: 10.1080/13683500.2021.1924636

Hafez, F. S., Sa'di, B., Safa-Gamal, M., Taufiq-Yap, Y. H., Alrifaey, M., Seyedmahmoudian, M., Stojcevski, A., Horan, B., & Mekhilef, S. (2023). Energy Efficiency in Sustainable Buildings: A Systematic Review with Taxonomy, Challenges, Motivations, Methodological Aspects, Recommendations, and Pathways for Future Research. *Energy Strategy Reviews*, 45, 101013. DOI: 10.1016/j.esr.2022.101013

Hagenaars, L. L., Jeurissen, P. P. T., & Klazinga, N. S. (2017). The taxation of unhealthy energy-dense foods (EDFs) and sugar-sweetened beverages (SSBs): An overview of patterns observed in the policy content and policy context of 13 case studies. *Health Policy (Amsterdam)*, 121(8), 887–894. DOI: 10.1016/j.healthpol.2017.06.011 PMID: 28711301

Halim, M. A., & Rahman, M. M. (2022). The effect of taxation on sustainable development goals: Evidence from emerging countries. *Heliyon*, 8(9), e10512. DOI: 10.1016/j.heliyon.2022.e10512 PMID: 36105472

Hall, R. E., & Rabushka, A. (1983). *Low tax, simple tax, flat tax*. McGraw-Hill Companies.

Hall, R. E., & Rabushka, A. (2013). *The flat tax*. Hoover Press.

Hamilton, M. A. (1994). Discussion and decisions: A proposal to replace the myth of self-rule with an attorneyship model of representation. *NYUL Rev.*, 69, 477.

Han, H., & Lee, T. (2023). Varieties of Green Stimulus Policies: Comparative Analysis of the Green Growth and Green New Deal Policies in South Korea. *Journal of Environment & Development*, 32(1), 61–82. DOI: 10.1177/10704965221139303

Hanlon, M., & Heitzman, S. (2010). A review of tax research. In *Journal of Accounting and Economics* (Vol. 50, Issues 2–3, pp. 127–178). DOI: 10.1016/j.jacceco.2010.09.002

Hariram, N. P., Mekha, K. B., Suganthan, V., & Sudhakar, K. (2024). Decoding the epics of sustainable world: Sustainalism. *Social Sciences & Humanities Open*, 10, 100958. Advance online publication. DOI: 10.1016/j.ssaho.2024.100958

Hasan, A. A.-T. (2024). Theory of sustainable consumption behavior (TSCB) to predict renewable energy consumption behavior: A case of eco-tourism visitors of Bangladesh. *Management of Environmental Quality: An International Journal, 35*(1), 101–118. *Scopus*. Advance online publication. DOI: 10.1108/MEQ-05-2023-0146

Hassan, M., Oueslati, W., & Rousselière, D. (2020). Environmental taxes, reforms and economic growth: An empirical analysis of panel data. *Economic Systems*, 44(3), 100806. DOI: 10.1016/j.ecosys.2020.100806

Hayek, F. (1960). *The constitution of liberty*. University of Chicago Press.

Heath, A. (2006). *Flat tax: Towards a british model*. Stockholm Network.

Heide, M., Dudka, K. M., & Hauschild, M. Z. (2023). Absolute sustainable CO2-limits for buildings should reflect their function. A case study of four building typologies. *Developments in the Built Environment*, 15, 100175. DOI: 10.1016/j.dibe.2023.100175

Heidenthaler, D., Deng, Y., Leeb, M., Grobbauer, M., Kranzl, L., Seiwald, L., Mascherbauer, P., Reindl, P., & Bednar, T. (2023). Automated energy performance certificate based urban building energy modelling approach for predicting heat load profiles of districts. *Energy*, 278, 128024. DOI: 10.1016/j.energy.2023.128024

Hemling, L., Plesner Rossing, J. C., & Hoffjan, A. (2022). The use of information technology for international transfer pricing in multinational enterprises. *International Journal of Accounting Information Systems*, 44, 100546. DOI: 10.1016/j.accinf.2021.100546

Hepburn, C., O'Callaghan, B., Stern, N., Stiglitz, J., & Zenghelis, D. (2020). Will COVID-19 fiscal recovery packages confront climate change? *Oxford Review of Economic Policy*, 36(Supplement_1), S359–S381. DOI: 10.1093/oxrep/graa015

Herbert, W. E., Nwarogu, I. A., & Nwabueze, C. C. (2018). Tax reforms and Nigeria's economic stability. *International Journal of Applied Economics. Finance and Accounting*, 3(2), 74–87.

Hernádi, P., & Ormos, M. (2012). Capital structure and its choice in Central and Eastern Europe. *Acta Oeconomica*, 62(2), 229–263. DOI: 10.1556/aoecon.62.2012.2.5

He, Y., & Liu, R. (2023). The impact of the level of green finance development on corporate debt financing capacity. *Finance Research Letters*, 52, 103552. DOI: 10.1016/j.frl.2022.103552

High-Quality Data. (n.d.). Retrieved from Elsevier: https://www.elsevier.com/solutions/scopus/how-scopus-works/high-quality-data

Higinbotham, H., Srinivasan, N., Starkov, V., Mert-Beydilli, N., & Eden, L. (2021). Amount B: Facts and Circumstances Matter – Even for Routine Distributors. *Tax Management International Journal, 50*(2), 90–97. https://ssrn.com/abstract=3780374

Hirsch, J. E. (2005). *An index to quantify an individual's scientific research output*. www.pnas.orgcgidoi10.1073pnas.0507655102

Hirsch, J. E., & Cardona, M. (2007). Does the h index have predictive power? In *PNAS December* (Vol. 4). www.pnas.orgcgidoi10.1073pnas.0707962104

Hirsch, J., & Buela-Casal, G. (2014). The meaning of the h-index. *International Journal of Clinical and Health Psychology*, 14(2), 161–164. DOI: 10.1016/S1697-2600(14)70050-X

Houle, F. (2006). Regulatory history material as an extrinsic aid to interpretation: An empirical study on the use of RIAs by the Federal Court of Canada. Canadian journal of administrative law and practice, 19, 151-189.

House, C. L., & Shapiro, M. D. (2008). Temporary Investment Tax Incentives: Theory with Evidence from Bonus Depreciation. *The American Economic Review*, 98(3), 737–768. DOI: 10.1257/aer.98.3.737

Hoynes, H., Miller, D., & Simon, D. (2015). Income, the Earned Income Tax Credit, and Infant Health. *American Economic Journal. Economic Policy*, 7(1), 172–211. DOI: 10.1257/pol.20120179

Hruby, A., & Hu, F. B. (2015). The epidemiology of obesity: A big picture. *PharmacoEconomics*, 33(7), 673–689. DOI: 10.1007/s40273-014-0243-x PMID: 25471927

Hua, L. (2024). The impact of environmental taxation on the structure and performance of industrial symbiosis networks: An agent-based simulation study. *Heliyon*, 10(3), e25675. Advance online publication. DOI: 10.1016/j.heliyon.2024.e25675 PMID: 38356598

Iannaccone, L. (2023). *Introdução à economia da religião*. Available in: https://www.researchgate.net/publication/376014586_Introducao_a_economia_da_religiao [Accessed in January 2024].

Ibragimov, M. Y., Ibragimov, R. M., Sinnikova, Y. M., & Tufetulov, A. M. (2014). About progressive tax systems of labor remuneration in Russia. *Asian Social Science*, 10(23), 28–35. DOI: 10.5539/ass.v10n23p28

ICC - International Criminal Court. (2021). *Rome Statute of the International Criminal Court.* Available in: https://www.icc-cpi.int/sites/default/files/2024-05/Rome-Statute-eng.pdf [Accessed in January 2024].

Ignat, L., & Tache, M. (2023, October). Transfer Pricing System of EU Countries: An Analysis in the Context of SDGS [Article]. *Transylvanian Review of Administrative Sciences*, (70E), 45–66. DOI: 10.24193/tras.70E.3

Ilgov, V., Gardanova, Z., & Nikitina, N. (2021). Sustainable development of the universities in the 21stcentury. *E3S Web of Conferences, 250*. DOI: 10.1051/e3sconf/202125004010

IMF (2010). A fair and substantial contribution by the financial sector. *Financial Sector Taxation: The IMF's Report to the G-20 and Background Material.*

IMF (2018), 'Managing Public Wealth' Fiscal Monitor, October 2018 Mandelkern Report on the Improvement of Legislative Quality – published in Lisboa, Ministério da Reforma do Estado e da Administração Pública, volume 1, March 2002 [also in Legislação. Cadernos de Ciência de Legislação, 29, Oct.-Dez. 2000}

IMF. (2023). *Morocco: 2022 Article IV Consultation-Press Release and Staff Report; IMF Country Report No. 23/42; December 16, 2022*. http://www.imf.org

Inquérito Alimentar Nacional e de Atividade Física. (2016). *O inquérito alimentar nacional e de atividade física, IAN-AF 2015-2016.*https://ian-af.up.pt/sites/default/files/IAN-AF%20Brochura%20de%20resultados.pdf

Instituto de Estudios Fiscales. (2022). *Libro Blanco sobre la Reforma Tributaria*, Ministerio de Hacienda y Función Pública. https://www.ief.es/docs/investigacion/comiteexpertos/LibroBlancoReformaTributaria_2022.pdf

Instituto Nacional de Estatística. (2023, September 15). Óbitos (n.º) por causa de morte (lista sucinta europeia) e mês (óbito); Anual - INE, Óbitos por causas de morte. https://www.ine.pt/xportal/xmain?xpid=INE&xpgid=ine_indicadores&indOcorrCod=0010082&contexto=bd&selTab=tab2

Instituto Nacional de Estatística. (2024, February 9). Consumo humano de açúcar per capita (kg/ hab.). https://www.ine.pt/xportal/xmain?xpid=INE&xpgid=ine_indicadores&indOcorrCod=0000198&contexto=bd&selTab=tab2&xlang=pt

International Energy Agency (IEA). (2021). Energy taxes for a sustainable future. https://www.iea.org/reports/taxing-energy-use-2019

International Labour Organization (ILO). (2022). Just transition to environmentally sustainable economies and resilient societies. https://www.ilo.org/global/topics/green-jobs/publications/WCMS_828094/lang--es/index.htm

International Monetary Fund. (2021). Fiscal Monitor: Strengthening the Credibility of Public Finances. https://www.imf.org/en/Publications/FM/Issues/2021/10/13/fiscal-monitor-october-2021

IRENA. (2021). World Energy Transitions Outlook 2021. International Renewable Energy Agency. https://irena.org/publications/2021/March/World-Energy-Transitions-Outlook

Ispriyarso, B., & Wibawa, K. C. S. (2023). Reconstruction of the national economy post-covid-19 pandemic: Critical study of tax reforms in Indonesia. *Cogent Social Sciences*, 9(1), 2174517. DOI: 10.1080/23311886.2023.2174517

Istok, M., Solilová, V., & Brychta, K. (2022, December). Challenges in transfer pricing: A concept of safe harbours for financial transactions [Article]. *Financial Internet Quarterly*, 18(4), 23–34. DOI: 10.2478/fiqf-2022-0025

Ivanovic, O. M., & Golusin, M. (2012). Environmental Taxation as a Tool for Sustainable Development Policy-State Comparison of Serbia and Application of Ecological Taxation Reform in European Union. *Economic Analysis*, 45, 32–44.

Jack, W. (2000). The treatment of financial services under a broad-based consumption tax. *National Tax Journal*, 53(4), 841–851. DOI: 10.17310/ntj.2000.4.03

Jacob, R., Binu, K., & Anjana, P. B. (2024). A Comprehensive Study on Goods and Services Tax in India. *International Journal of Engineering and Management Research*, 14(1), 58–64.

Jacobson, M. F. (2005). Liquid candy: how soft drinks are harming americans' health. *Center For Science in the Public Interest Washington, D.C.*https://www.cspinet.org/sites/default/files/attachment/liquid_candy_final_w_new_supplement.pdf

Jain, S. (2018). Strengthening Financial and Taxation Regulatory Framework in India: A Review of Recent Legislations. *VISION: Journal of Indian Taxation.*

Jamal, T., & Watt, E. (2011). Climate change pedagogy and performative action: Toward community-based destination governance. *Journal of Sustainable Tourism*, 19(4–5), 571–588. DOI: 10.1080/09669582.2011.575227

Jha, R. (2013). Indirect Tax Reform and Fiscal Federalism in India. *Public Economics: National Government Expenditures & Related Policies eJournal.*

Jiang, H.-D., Hao, W.-T., Xu, Q.-Y., & Liang, Q.-M. (2020). Socio-economic and environmental impacts of the iron ore resource tax reform in China: A CGE-based analysis. *Resources Policy*, 68, 101775. DOI: 10.1016/j.resourpol.2020.101775

Ji, C., Hong, T., Kim, H., & Yeom, S. (2022). Effect of building energy efficiency certificate on reducing energy consumption of non-residential buildings in South Korea. *Energy and Building*, 255, 111701. DOI: 10.1016/j.enbuild.2021.111701

John, W., & Ii, C. (2000). Welfare and optimum dynamic taxation of consumption and income. [). www.elsevier.nl/locate/econbase]. *Journal of Public Economics*, 76, •••.

Jones, T., Huggett, S., & Kamalski, J. (2011). Finding a Way Through the Scientific Literature: Indexes and Measures. *World Neurosurgery*, 76(1–2), 36–38. DOI: 10.1016/j.wneu.2011.01.015 PMID: 21839937

Jonkutė, G., Norvaišienė, R., Banionis, K., Monstvilas, E., & Bliūdžius, R. (2021). Analysis of carbon dioxide emissions in residential buildings through energy performance certification in Lithuania. *Energy Sources. Part B, Economics, Planning, and Policy*, 16(2), 198–215. DOI: 10.1080/15567249.2020.1773581

Jornal Oficial da União Europeia. (2010, October 29). Bebidas, líquidos alcoólicos e vinagres. https://dev.anceve.pt/wp-content/uploads/2017/12/Nomenclatura-Combinada.pdf

Josep Pons-Vives, P., Morro-Ribot, M., Mulet-Forteza, C., & Valero, O. (2022). An Application of Ordered Weighted Averaging Operators to Customer Classification in Hotels. *Mathematics*, 10(12), 1987. DOI: 10.3390/math10121987

Joumard, I., Thomas, A., & Morgavi, H. (2017). *Making Income and Property Taxes More Growth-Friendly and Redistributive in India*. OECD Publications.

Junior, P. C., & De Cesare, C. (2022). Who pays the property tax? Evidence from Brazil. *Land Use Policy*, 120, 106235. DOI: 10.1016/j.landusepol.2022.106235

Juodis, A., Karavias, Y., & Sarafidis, V. (2021). A homogeneous approach to testing for Granger noncausality in heterogeneous panels. *Empirical Economics*, 60(1), 93–112. DOI: 10.1007/s00181-020-01970-9

Jurigova, Z. (2016). Tourism industry analysis with the Czech Republic as the focal point. *Procedia Economics and Finance*, 39, 305–312. DOI: 10.1016/S2212-5671(16)30328-8

Kalra, A., & Afzal, M. N. I. (2023). Transfer pricing practices in multinational corporations and their effects on developing countries' tax revenue: A systematic literature review. *International Trade. Politics and Development*, 7(3), 172–190. DOI: 10.1108/ITPD-04-2023-0011

Kamath, N., Shrivastava, A., & Shekar, R. S. (2021). Emerging from the shadows: The evolving legal treatment of fantasy sports in India. *The International Sports Law Journal*, 21(3), 188–202. DOI: 10.1007/s40318-021-00190-2

Kapoor, S., & Singh, A. (2023). *Development of Indian Tax System: Pre and Post-Colonial Influences*. FIIB Business Review.

Karim, R., Muhammad, F., Serafino, L., Latip, N. A., & Marzuki, A. (2020). Integration of pro-poor tourism activities in community-based development initiatives: A case study in high mountain areas of Pakistan. *International Journal of Scientific and Technology Research*, 9(4), 848–852.

Keen, M., Kim, Y., & Varsano, R. (2008). The "flat tax (es)": Principles and experience. *International Tax and Public Finance*, 15(6), 712–751. DOI: 10.1007/s10797-007-9050-z

Kemsley, D., & Nissim, D. (2002). Valuation of the debt tax shield. *The Journal of Finance*, 57(5), 2045–2073. DOI: 10.1111/0022-1082.00488

Kent, M., Newnham, R., & Essex, S. (2002). Tourism and sustainable water supply in Mallorca: A geographical analysis. *Applied Geography (Sevenoaks, England)*, 22(4), 351–374. DOI: 10.1016/S0143-6228(02)00050-4

Keune, M., Payton, N., Been, W., Green, A., Mathieu, C., Postels, D., ... & Wright, S. (2018). –Innovation and Job Quality in the Games Industry in Germany, the Netherlands, Sweden and the UK. *Virtuous circles between innovations, job quality and employment in Europe? Case study evidence from the manufacturing sector, private and public service sector*, 234.

Khan, R., & Khan, S. (2022). Reform of Indirect Taxes in India through the Plexus of Goods and Services Tax (GST); A post-COVID 19 Fiscal Stimulus. *International Journal of Multidisciplinary: Applied Business and Education Research*, 3(6), 1011–1016. DOI: 10.11594/ijmaber.03.06.06

Khoo-Lattimore, C., & Prideaux, B. (2014). ZMET: A psychological approach to understanding unsustainable tourism mobility. Em *Underst. And Gov. Sustainable Tourism Mobil.: Psychological and Behavioural Approaches* (pp. 88–103). Taylor and Francis. https://doi.org/DOI: 10.4324/9780203771501-15

Kim, K., Križnik, B., & Kamvasinou, K. (2021). Between the state and citizens: Changing governance of intermediary organisations for inclusive and sustainable urban regeneration in Seoul. *Land Use Policy*, 105, 105433. DOI: 10.1016/j.landusepol.2021.105433

Kingdom of Morocco (2024).

Kingdom of Morocco. (2021). *Framework Law 69-19 on Tax Reform.*

Kingdom of Morocco. (2023). *Finance Law.*

Klenert, D., Mattauch, L., & Narassima, V. (2023). Progressive carbon taxation. *European Economic Review*, 151, 104382. DOI: 10.1016/j.euroecorev.2023.104382

Kluza, K., Ziolo, M., & Postula, M. (2024). Climate policy development and implementation from the Sustainable Development Goals perspective. Evidence from the European Union countries. *Energy Strategy Reviews*, 52, 101321. DOI: 10.1016/j.esr.2024.101321

Kobbi-Fakhfakh, S., & Bougacha, F. (2023). The impact of the COVID-19 pandemic on corporate tax avoidance: Evidence from S&P 500 firms. *Journal of Financial Reporting and Accounting*, 21(4), 847–866. DOI: 10.1108/JFRA-06-2022-0216

Kougias, K., & Efstathopoulos, J. (2020). The Operational Framework of the Greek Educational System as an Obstacle to the Implementation of Sustainable School. *Frontiers in Education*, 5, 142. Advance online publication. DOI: 10.3389/feduc.2020.00142

Krämer, R. (2015). Taxation and Capital Structure Choice: The Role of Ownership. *The Scandinavian Journal of Economics*, 117(3), 957–982. DOI: 10.1111/sjoe.12107

Krautheim, S., & Schmidt-Eisenlohr, T. (2011). 2011-01-01). Heterogeneous firms, 'profit shifting' FDI and international tax competition. *Journal of Public Economics*, 95(1), 122–133. DOI: 10.1016/j.jpubeco.2010.10.008

Krishnan, M. S., Ramaswamy, V., Meyer, M. C., & Damien, P. (1999). Customer satisfaction for financial services: The role of products, services, and information technology. *Management Science*, 45(9), 1194–1209. DOI: 10.1287/mnsc.45.9.1194

Krishnaswamy, H. (2021). Do The Indian Tax Enactments & Fiscal Policies? Incentivise & Facilitate Tax Evasion?-A Critical Study.

Kronenberg, K., & Fuchs, M. (2022). The socio-economic impact of regional tourism: An occupation-based modelling perspective from Sweden. *Journal of Sustainable Tourism*, 30(12), 2785–2805. DOI: 10.1080/09669582.2021.1924757

Krushna, A. V. (2015). Tax buoyancy of India: An empirical analysis. *International Journal of Research in Management. Economics & Commerce*, 5(12), 46–55.

Kühnhenrich, D. (2023). The German Environmental Tax Reform: A difference-in-differences analysis of its impacts in European comparison. *Environmental Economics and Policy Studies*. Advance online publication. DOI: 10.1007/s10018-023-00375-z

Kumar, S., Pandey, N., Lim, W. M., Chatterjee, A. N., & Pandey, N. (2021). What do we know about transfer pricing? Insights from bibliometric analysis. *Journal of Business Research*, 134, 275–287. DOI: 10.1016/j.jbusres.2021.05.041

Kuner, C. (2010). Data protection law and international jurisdiction on the Internet (part 1). *International Journal of Law and Information Technology*, 18(2), 176–193. DOI: 10.1093/ijlit/eaq002

Kuropka, K. (2020). Advance Pricing Arrangements as a Tax Strategy Tool for Related Entities. *European Financial and Accounting Journal*, 15(2), 31–44. DOI: 10.18267/j.efaj.240

Laddha, H. (2017). Is India Ready for BEPS?: Foreseeable Problems and Suggestions [Article]. *Intertax, 45*(12), 828-840. <Go to ISI>://WOS:000426266600008

Laffer, A. B. (2019). Reflections on economic policy. *Business Economics (Cleveland, Ohio)*, 55(1), 41–44. DOI: 10.1057/s11369-019-00150-7

Laffitte, S., Martin, J., Parenti, M., Souillard, B., & Toubal, F. (2020). International corporate taxation after COVID-19: Minimum taxation as the new normal. *CEPII Policy Briefs*, 30, 1–6.

Lafuente-Lechuga, M., Cifuentes-Faura, J., & Faura-Martínez, Ú. (2024). Teaching sustainability in higher education by integrating mathematical concepts. *International Journal of Sustainability in Higher Education*, 25(1), 62–77. DOI: 10.1108/IJSHE-07-2022-0221

Lago Montero, J. M. (2017). Los impuestos propios en el sistema de financiación autonómica. In *Sanz Gómez, R. (coord.), Tributos propios de las Comunidades Autónomas* (pp. 15–43). Tirant lo Blanch.

Lago Peñas, S. (2019). Tax decentralisation in Spain: Significant progress and remaining challenges. *Funcas SEFO, Vol. 8, N. 5,* 51-58. https://www.funcas.es/wp-content/uploads/Migracion/Articulos/FUNCAS_SEFO/045art07.pdf

Lagos, R., Rocheteau, G., & Wright, R. (2017). Liquidity: A new monetarist perspective. *Journal of Economic Literature*, 55(2), 371–440. DOI: 10.1257/jel.20141195

Laires, R. (2012). *O IVA nas actividades culturais, educativas, recreativas, desportivas e de assistência médica ou social – Cadernos IDEFF N.º 14*. Almedina.

Laporte, A., Vandentorren, S., Détrez, M. A., Douay, C., Le Strat, Y., Le Méner, E., & Chauvin, P.Samenta Research Group. (2018). Prevalence of mental disorders and addictions among homeless people in the greater Paris area, France. *International Journal of Environmental Research and Public Health*, 15(2), 241. DOI: 10.3390/ijerph15020241 PMID: 29385053

Lasarte Álvarez, F. J. (1979). La financiación de las Comunidades Autónomas. *Documentación Administrativa*, 181, 413–443.

Lasarte López, R. (2017). Principios y límites rectores en la creación de tributos propios tras la modificación del artículo 6 de la LOFCA. In Sanz Gómez, R. (Coord.), *Tributos propios de las Comunidades Autónomas* (179-205). Tirant lo Blanch.

Law n.º 30/2019, of April 23rd of the Assembly of the Republic, Diário da República: I série, nº 79 (2019). https://diariodarepublica.pt/dr/detalhe/lei/30-2019-122151046

Law n.º 42/2016, of December 28 of the Assembly of the Republic, Diário da República: I série, nº 248 (2016). https://diariodarepublica.pt/dr/detalhe/lei/42-2016-105637672

Law n.º 82/2023, of December 29 of the Assembly of the Republic, Diário da República: I série, nº 250 (2023). https://diariodarepublica.pt/dr/detalhe/lei/82-2023-835864042

Law, No. 10.257, of July 10th, 2001, 10,257 (2001). http://www.planalto.gov.br/ccivil_03/leis/LEIS_2001/L10257.htm

Law, No. 3.686, of November 11th, 2003, 3.686 (2003). https://jales.siscam.com.br/arquivo?id=24777

Law, No. 5.172, of October 25th, 1966 (1966). https://www.planalto.gov.br/ccivil_03/leis/l5172compilado.htm

Law, No. 7.186, of December 27th, 2006, 7.186 (2006). http://leismunicipa.is/ekbmt

Law, No. 8.474, of October 2nd, 2013 (2013). http://leismunicipa.is/mktgd

Law, No. 8.953, of December 25th, 2015, 8.953 (2015). http://leismunicipa.is/qgoul

Law, No. 9.069, of June 30th, 2016 (2016). http://leismunicipa.is/cjuot Organic Law of the Municipality of Salvador/BA (2024).https://www.cms.ba.gov.br/lei-organica

Leal, M. V. O., Oliveira, J. R. S., Azevedo, T. C., & Conceição, M. G. (November 1st, 2022). Características dos programas de IPTU Verde em municípios baianos. Anais do XXIV ENGEMA 2022. Encontro Internacional sobre Gestão Empresarial e Meio Ambiente (ENGEMA), São Paulo https://engemausp.submissao.com.br/24/anais/arquivos/319.pdf?v=1716844002

Lei, Z., Huang, L., & Cai, Y. (2022). Can environmental tax bring strong porter effect? Evidence from Chinese listed companies. *Environmental Science and Pollution Research International*, 29(21), 32246–32260. DOI: 10.1007/s11356-021-17119-9 PMID: 35013959

Leland, H. E., & Toft, K. B. (1996). Optimal capital structure, endogenous bankruptcy, and the term structure of credit spreads. *The Journal of Finance*, 51(3), 987–1019. DOI: 10.1111/j.1540-6261.1996.tb02714.x

Lenaerts, K. (2012), 'The European Court of Justice and Process-Oriented Review', Yearbook of European Law, pages 3–16. DOI: 10.1093/yel/yes009

Leuven, E., & Oosterbeek, H. (2004). Evaluating the effect of tax deductions on training. *Journal of Labor Economics*, 22(2), 461–488. DOI: 10.1086/381257

Levaggi, R., & Panteghini, P. M. (2023). Environmental taxation and profit-shifting activities. In *Ecological Economics* (Vol. 214). Elsevier B.V., DOI: 10.1016/j.ecolecon.2023.107972

Liberati, A., Altman, D. G., Tetzlaff, J., Mulrow, C., Gøtzsche, P. C., Ioannidis, J. P., Clarke, M., Devereaux, P. J., Kleijnen, J., & Moher, D. (2009). The PRISMA statement for reporting systematic reviews and meta-analyses of studies that evaluate healthcare interventions: Explanation and elaboration. *Journal of Clinical Epidemiology*, 62(10), 1–34. DOI: 10.1016/j.jclinepi.2009.06.006 PMID: 19631507

Lima, J. M., Borsatto, S., Marcolin, C. B., Cardoso Abdalla, E., & Dutra Amaral, F. (2024). Aligning community outreach initiatives with SDGs in a higher education institution with artificial intelligence. *Cleaner and Responsible Consumption*, 12, 100160. DOI: 10.1016/j.clrc.2023.100160

Lin, B.-H., Smith, T. A., Lee, J.-Y., & Hall, K. D. (2011). Measuring weight outcomes for obesity intervention strategies: The case of a sugar-sweetened beverage tax. *Economics and Human Biology*, 9(4), 329–341. DOI: 10.1016/j.ehb.2011.08.007 PMID: 21940223

Lin, K. Z. (2006). The impact of tax holidays on earnings management: An empirical study of corporate reporting behavior in a developing-economy framework. *The International Journal of Accounting*, 41(2), 163–175. DOI: 10.1016/j.intacc.2006.04.006

Li, Q., Li, S., Hu, J., Zhang, S., & Hu, J. (2018). Tourism Review Sentiment Classification Using a Bidirectional Recurrent Neural Network with an Attention Mechanism and Topic-Enriched Word Vectors. *Sustainability (Basel)*, 10(9), 3313. DOI: 10.3390/su10093313

Liu, Y. C. (2009). The slicing approach to valuing tax shields. *Journal of Banking & Finance*, 33(6), 1069–1078. DOI: 10.1016/j.jbankfin.2008.12.002

Liu, Y., & Mao, J. (2019). How Do Tax Incentives Affect Investment and Productivity? Firm-Level Evidence from China. *American Economic Journal. Economic Policy*, 11(3), 261–291. DOI: 10.1257/pol.20170478

Liu, Y., Sang, M., Xu, X., Shen, L., & Bao, H. (2023). How Can Urban Regeneration Reduce Carbon Emissions? A Bibliometric Review. *Land (Basel)*, 12(7), 1328. DOI: 10.3390/land12071328

Li, Z., & Zhou, Z. (2022). Research on the Impact Mechanism of Fiscal and Tax Policies on Carbon Emissions under the Dual Carbon Goals. *Frontiers in Business. Economics and Management*, 6(2), 32–37. DOI: 10.54097/fbem.v6i2.2637

Lobo, C. B. (2019). *Finanças e Fiscalidade do Ambiente e da Energia* (S. A. Edições Almedina, Ed.; Vol. 1).

Lockwood, B., & Yerushalmi, E. (2019). How should payment services be taxed? *Social Choice and Welfare*, 53(1), 21–47. DOI: 10.1007/s00355-019-01178-6

Loganathan, N., Shahbaz, M., & Taha, R. (2014). The link between green taxation and economic growth on CO2 emissions: Fresh evidence from Malaysia. *Renewable & Sustainable Energy Reviews*, 38, 1083–1091. DOI: 10.1016/j.rser.2014.07.057

Lompo, M. L., & Ouoba, M. M. (2024). Taxes and social instability: How large corporations and wealthy taxpayers hide taxable money? *Economic Analysis Letters*, 3(1), 36–45. DOI: 10.58567/eal03010005

Lopes, C., Oliveira, A., Afonso, L., Moreira, T., Durão, C., Severo, M., Vilela, S., Ramos, E., & Barros, H. (2014). *Consumo alimentar e nutricional de crianças em idade pré-escolar: resultados da coorte geração 21.* Instituto de Saúde Pública da Universidade do Porto. https://ispup.up.pt/wp-content/uploads/2023/09/2_PDFsam_RelConsG212014.pdf

López Díaz, A. (2013). Tributación medioambiental en España a nivel subcentral: CCAA y CCLL. *Dereito*, 22, 225–244.

López Laborda, J., Martínez Vázquez, J., & Monasterio Escudero, C. (2023). Spain. In Tremblay, J.-F. (Ed.), *The Forum of Federations Handbook on Fiscal Federalism* (pp. 341–382). Palgrave Macmillan. DOI: 10.1007/978-3-030-97258-5_9

Lopez, G. W., Kao, J., & Ritchie, L. (2010). To what extent have sweetened beverages contributed to the obesity epidemic? *Public Health Nutrition*, 14(3), 499–509. DOI: 10.1017/S1368980010002375 PMID: 20860886

López-Laborda, J., & Peña, G. (2018). A new method for applying VAT to financial services. *National Tax Journal*, 71(1), 155–182. DOI: 10.17310/ntj.2018.1.05

López-Laborda, J., & Peña, G. (2022). Financial VAT may improve trade openness. *Applied Economics*, 54(19), 2148–2160. DOI: 10.1080/00036846.2021.1985072

Lora, E., & Mejía, L. F. (2022). Reforming for a post-COVID world. *Bulletin of Latin American Research*, 41(1), 34–49. DOI: 10.1111/blar.13294

Lotka, A. J. (1926). The frequency distribution of scientific productivity. In *Source. Journal of the Washington Academy of Sciences*, 16(12), •••.

Lu, C. H., Ueng, K. L. G., & Chang, J. J. (2022). Consumption indivisibility and the optimal tax mix. *Economic Modelling*, 112, 105845. Advance online publication. DOI: 10.1016/j.econmod.2022.105845

Lucas Durán, M. (2020). Beneficios fiscales con requisitos territoriales, normativa tributaria autonómica y libre circulación de personas y capitales: Reflexiones desde el derecho de la UE, la constitución española y el bloque de constitucionalidad. *Nueva Fiscalidad*, 3, 127–177.

Lunina, I., Bilousova, O., & Frolova, N. (2020). Tax Reforms for the Development of Fiscal Space. *Baltic Journal of Economic Studies*, 6(3), 48–58. DOI: 10.30525/2256-0742/2020-6-3-48-58

Lupu, M. (2023, Mar 23-25 Jul 1). International Cooperation and Solving Transfer Pricing Disputes: A Discussion about Mutual Agreement Procedures. [Proceedings of the international conference on business excellence]. 17th Edition of the International Conference on Business Excellence (ICBE), Romania.

Luque-Martínez, T. (2023). Sensibilidad y elasticidad de las universidades españolas a los indicadores del Ranking de Shanghái (ARWU) Enhanced Reader. *Revista Española de Documentación Científica*, 45(1), e350. Advance online publication. DOI: 10.3989/redc.2023.1.1947

Lusa (2016, October 11). *OMS apela à tributação de bebidas açucaradas para reduzir obesidade.* Diário de Notícias. https://www.dn.pt/sociedade/oms-apela-a-tributacao-de-bebidas-acucaradas-para-reduzir-obesidade-5435705.html

Lutz, B., & Levell, P. (2021). Green Taxation and Employment: Evidence from Germany's Ecological Tax Reform. *Journal of Environmental Economics and Management*, 107, 102442. DOI: 10.1016/j.jeem.2021.102442

Lu, X. B., & Landry, P. F. (2014, August). Show Me the Money: Interjurisdiction Political Competition and Fiscal Extraction in China [Article]. *The American Political Science Review*, 108(3), 706–722. DOI: 10.1017/S0003055414000252

Mack, N., Woodsong, C., Macqueen, K. M., Guest, G., & Namey, E. (2005). *Qualitative Research Methods: A Data Collector's Field Guide.* Available in: https://www.fhi360.org/wp-content/uploads/2024/01/Qualitative-Research-Methods-A-Data-Collectors-Field-Guide.pdf [Accessed in January 2024].

Maddern, H., Maull, R., Smart, A., & Baker, P. (2007). Customer satisfaction and service quality in UK financial services. *International Journal of Operations & Production Management*, 27(9), 999–1019. DOI: 10.1108/01443570710775838

Maillo, M. Á. G. (2016). Usos y abusos en la fiscalidad ambiental. Congreso Salamanca/FMU: Derecho Ambiental Contemporâneo España/Brasil, Salamanca (España).

Makin, A. J., & Layton, A. (2021). The global fiscal response to COVID-19: Risks and repercussions. *Economic Analysis and Policy*, 69, 340–349. DOI: 10.1016/j.eap.2020.12.016

Maleki, F., Bararzadeh Ledari, M., & Fani, M., & kamelizadeh, D. (. (2024). Sustainable hydrogen supply chain development for low-carbon transportation in a fossil-based port region: A case study in a tourism hub. *International Journal of Hydrogen Energy, 65*, 95–111. *Scopus*. Advance online publication. DOI: 10.1016/j.ijhydene.2024.03.362

Mananyi, A. (1998). Optimal management of ecotourism. *Tourism Economics*, 4(2), 147–169. DOI: 10.1177/135481669800400203

Manjunatha, N. (2019). Descriptive Research. *Journal of Emerging Technologies and Innovative Research*, 6(6), 863–867. https://www.jetir.org/papers/JETIR1908597.pdf

Mansfield, C.Y. (1987). Tax Administration in Developing Countries: An Economic Perspective. *Political Economy (Topic).*

Manta, A. G., Doran, N. M., Bădîrcea, R. M., Badareu, G., & ăran, A. M. (2023). Does the implementation of a Pigouvian tax be considered an effective approach to address climate change mitigation? *Economic Analysis and Policy*, 80, 1719–1731. DOI: 10.1016/j.eap.2023.11.002

Manzano Silva, E. (2005). Proceso de integración europea *versus* autonomía financiera autonómica. *Nueva Fiscalidad*, 1, 47–102.

Mardones, C. (2022). Pigouvian taxes to internalize environmental damages from Chilean mining–A computable general equilibrium analysis. *Journal of Cleaner Production*, 362, 132359. DOI: 10.1016/j.jclepro.2022.132359

Mardones, C., & Baeza, N. (2018). Economic and environmental effects of a CO2 tax in Latin American countries. *Energy Policy*, 114, 262–273. DOI: 10.1016/j.enpol.2017.12.001

Martini, M. H., & Tandon, S. (2023). A review of India approaches to Cooperative Compliance in light of the International Tax Practice and the OECD Framework. *Intertax*, 51(10).

Martins, A. (2022). *Valorização de intangíveis e preços de transferência* [Valuation of Intangibles and Transfer Pricing]. Almedina.

Martins, A., & Duarte, F. (2024). *Acordos Prévios sobre Preços de Transferência* [Advance Pricing Agreement]. Petrony.

Marx, K., & Engels, F. (1848). The communist manifesto.

Matta, A. M. (1979). Search and Seizure Under Income-Tax Law. *Journal of the Indian Law Institute*, 21(4), 575–591.

Maxim, M. R., & Zander, K. K. (2020). Green tax reform in Australia in the presence of improved environment-induced productivity gain: Does it offer sustainable recovery from a post-COVID-19 recession? *Sustainability (Basel)*, 12(16), 6514. DOI: 10.3390/su12166514

Maxwell, J. A. (1992). Understanding and validity in qualitative research. *Harvard Educational Review*, 62(3), 279–300. DOI: 10.17763/haer.62.3.8323320856251826

Ma, Y., He, F. J., Yin, Y., Hashem, K. M., & MacGregor, G. A. (2016). Gradual reduction of sugar in soft drinks without substitution as a strategy to reduce overweight, obesity, and type 2 diabetes: A modelling study. *The Lancet. Diabetes & Endocrinology*, 4(2), 105–114. DOI: 10.1016/S2213-8587(15)00477-5 PMID: 26777597

Maydew, E. L. (2001). Empirical tax research in accounting: A discussion $. In *Journal of Accounting and Economics* (Vol. 31).

Mazilu, M., Toma, E., Lazar, I., & SGEM. (2014). The Economic Complex Tourism Relationship. *University of Craiova*, 711–718.

McCowan, T. (2023). The crosscutting impact of higher education on the Sustainable Development Goals. *International Journal of Educational Development*, 103, 102945. Advance online publication. DOI: 10.1016/j.ijedudev.2023.102945

McGreal, S., Berry, J., Lloyd, G., & McCarthy, J. (2002). Tax-based Mechanisms in Urban Regeneration: Dublin and Chicago Models. *Urban Studies (Edinburgh, Scotland)*, 39(10), 1819–1831. DOI: 10.1080/0042098022000002975

McKenzie, M., Benavot, A., & Redman, A. (2024). Global indicators of progress on climate change education: Non-state actor data collaboration for SDG 4. *International Journal of Educational Development*, 104, 102968. Advance online publication. DOI: 10.1016/j.ijedudev.2023.102968

Meer, F. V., Laan, L., Eiben, G., Lissner, L., Wolters, M., Rach, S., Herrmann, M., Erhard, P., Molnar, D., Orsi, G., Viergever, M. A., Adan, R. A. H., Smeets, P. A. M., & Consortium, I. F. (2019). Development and body mass inversely affect children's brain activation in dorsolateral prefrontal cortex during food choice. *NeuroImage, 201*. Academic Press Inc. DOI: 10.1016/j.neuroimage.2019.116016

Meira, D. (2013). A Lei de Bases da Economia Social Portuguesa: do projeto ao texto final. *CIRIEC-España, Revista jurídica de economía social y cooperativa (number 24/2013)*. Pp. 21-52.

Meira, D., Aguiar, N., & Raquel, S. (2016). Estudio sobre la eficácia del régimen fiscal cooperativo português. *REVESCO, n.º 121*. Pp. 7-32.

Meireles, M., Robaina, M., & Magueta, D. (2021). The Effectiveness of Environmental Taxes in Reducing CO2 Emissions in Passenger Vehicles: The Case of Mediterranean Countries. *International Journal of Environmental Research and Public Health*, 18(10), 5442. DOI: 10.3390/ijerph18105442 PMID: 34069643

Melo, S., Silva, M., Melo, F., & Vo-Thanh, T. (2022). The practice of (un)sustainable tourism in a National Park: An empirical study focusing on structural elements. *Journal of Outdoor Recreation and Tourism*, 39, 100548. Advance online publication. DOI: 10.1016/j.jort.2022.100548

Melubo, K., Lovelock, B., & Filep, S. (2019). Motivations and barriers for corporate social responsibility engagement: Evidence from the Tanzanian tourism industry. *Tourism and Hospitality Research*, 19(3), 284–295. DOI: 10.1177/1467358417742685

Menéndez Moreno, A. (2010). La nueva financiación de las Comunidades Autónomas. *Lex nova: La revista, 59,* 7.

Menéndez Moreno, A. (2023). ¿Qué fue de la reforma del sistema de financiación de las Comunidades Autónomas? *Quincena Fiscal*, 9, 9–20.

Menon, S. P., & KP, A. (2022). An Analytical Perspective of the Indian Tax Structure. *Issue 6 Indian JL & Legal Rsch., 4*, 1.

Merino Jara, I. (2017). Los impuestos autonómicos sobre grandes establecimientos comerciales desde la perspectiva de las libertades de la Unión Europea y del régimen de ayudas de Estado. In Sanz Gómez, R. (Coord.), *Tributos propios de las Comunidades Autónomas* (207-232). Tirant lo Blanch.

Merlin, L. V. D. C. T., & Vasconcelos, J. A. S. (2020). Tributação predial e territorial urbana no município de Afuá. Revista Científica do UniRios, 282

Merriam, S. B. (2009). *Qualitative research: A guide to design and implementation* (3rd ed.). Jossey-Bass.

Meyer, B. D., & Rosenbaum, D. T. (2001). Welfare, the earned income tax credit, and the labor supply of single mothers. *The Quarterly Journal of Economics*, 116(3), 1063–1114. DOI: 10.1162/00335530152466313

MF - Ministério das Finanças. (1990). *Decreto-Lei n.º 20/90, 13.01.1990 – Prevê a restituição de IVA à Igreja Católica e às instituições particulares de solidariedade social.* Available in: https://files.diariodarepublica.pt/1s/1990/01/01100/01990201.pdf [Accessed in January 2024].

Miao, Z., Beghin, J. C., & Jensen, H. H. (2011). Taxing sweets: Sweetener input tax or final consumption tax? *Contemporary Economic Policy*, 30(3), 344–361. DOI: 10.1111/j.1465-7287.2011.00278.x

Mikulic, J., Seric, M., & Kresic, D. (2023). Asymmetric effects of wellness destination and wellness facility attributes on tourist satisfaction. *Tourism Review*, 79(4), 969–980. Advance online publication. DOI: 10.1108/TR-12-2022-0635

Mill, J. S. (1848). Principles of political economy.

Milligan, K. (2005). Subsidizing the Stork: New Evidence on Tax Incentives and Fertility. *The Review of Economics and Statistics*, 87(3), 539–555. DOI: 10.1162/0034653054638382

Milligan, K., & Stabile, M. (2011). Do child tax benefits affect the well-being of children? Evidence from Canadian child benefit expansions. *American Economic Journal. Economic Policy*, 3(3), 175–205. DOI: 10.1257/pol.3.3.175

Milman, A., Okumus, F., & Dickson, D. (2010). The contribution of theme parks and attractions to the social and economic sustainability of destinations. *Worldwide Hospitality and Tourism Themes*, 2(3), 338–345. DOI: 10.1108/17554211011052249

Mingers, J., & Leydesdorff, L. (2015). A review of theory and practice in scientometrics. In *European Journal of Operational Research* (Vol. 246, Issue 1, pp. 1–19). Elsevier B.V. DOI: 10.1016/j.ejor.2015.04.002

Ministerio de Hacienda y Función Pública. (2021). *Las Haciendas Autonómicas en cifras*. https://www.hacienda.gob.es/CDI/Sist%20Financiacion%20y%20Deuda/Informaci%C3%B3nCCAA/Las-Haciendas-Autonomicas-en-cifras-2021.pdf

Ministry of Economy and Finance. (2019). *National Tax Forum*. https://www.finances.gov.ma/fr/Pages/detail-actualite.aspx?fiche=4431

Miranda, J. (2000). *Manual de Direito Constitucional, Tomo IV, Direitos Fundamentais*. Coimbra Editora.

Miranda, J. (2023). Liberdade Religiosa e Constituição. In *Marujo, A. (2023). Os Caminhos da Liberdade Religiosa em Portugal. Catálogo da exposição na Assembleia da República*. Edições Assembleia da República.

Mishra, C. (2011). Determinants of Capital Structure-A Study of Manufacturing Sector PSUs in India. *2011 International Conference on Financial Management and Economics*.

Mitić, P., Fedajev, A., & Kojić, M. (2023). Exploring the Economy – Environment Interactions in the Western Balkans. *Economic Analysis*, 56(1), 43–56. DOI: 10.28934/ea.23.56.1.pp43-56

MNE - Ministério dos Negócios Estrangeiros (2006). *Decreto n.º 11/2006, 11.03.2006 - Protocolo de Cooperação entre o Governo da República Portuguesa e o Imamat Ismaili e respectiva lista de compromissos existentes e iniciativas adicionais*. Available in: https://files.diariodarepublica.pt/1s/2006/03/053a00/18581870.pdf [Accessed in January 2024].

MNE - Ministério dos Negócios Estrangeiros (2024). *Relações de Portugal com a Santa Sé*. Available in: https://santase.embaixadaportugal.mne.gov.pt/pt/sobre-a-santa-se/relações-com-portugal [Accessed in January 2024].

Moallemi, E. A., Malekpour, S., Hadjikakou, M., Raven, R., Szetey, K., Ningrum, D., Dhiaulhaq, A., & Bryan, B. A. (2020). Achieving the Sustainable Development Goals Requires Transdisciplinary Innovation at the Local Scale. In *One Earth* (Vol. 3, Issue 3, pp. 300–313). Cell Press. DOI: 10.1016/j.oneear.2020.08.006

Moher, D., Shamseer, L., Clarke, M., Ghersi, D., Liberati, A., Petticrew, M., Shekelle, P., & Stewart, L. A. (2015). Preferred reporting items for systematic review and meta-analysis protocols (PRISMA-P) 2015 statement. *Systematic Reviews*, 4(1), 1. Advance online publication. DOI: 10.1186/2046-4053-4-1 PMID: 25554246

Moinuddin, S., & Moinuddin, S. (2021). Mapping digital political economy in India. *Digital Shutdowns and Social Media: Spatiality, Political Economy and Internet Shutdowns in India*, 1-34.

Monika chhatwani, D., & Asthana, P.K. (2023). A Study Of Impact Of GST On Indian Economy.

Montes-Vergara, F. J., Arango-Miranda, R., & Rojano, R. (2022). A review of carbon pricing instruments implementation: Lessons for the Colombian case. *Energies*, 15(9), 3303. DOI: 10.3390/en15093303

Montfort, K. V., Masurel, E., & Rijn, I. V. (2000). Service satisfaction: An empirical analysis of consumer satisfaction in financial services. *Service Industries Journal*, 20(3), 80–94. DOI: 10.1080/02642060000000033

Morais, R. (2009). Preços de Transferência - "O Sistema Fiscal no Fio da Navalha [Transfer Pricing - "The Tax System on the Razor's Edge]. *Revista de Finanças Públicas e Direito Fiscal, 2*(1).

Moreno-Pino, F. M., Jiménez-fontana, R., Domingo, J. M. C., & Goded, P. A. (2022). Training in Mathematics Education from a Sustainability Perspective: A Case Study of University Teachers' Views. *Education Sciences*, 12(3), 199. Advance online publication. DOI: 10.3390/educsci12030199

Mpofu, F. Y. (2022). Green Taxes in Africa: Opportunities and Challenges for Environmental Protection, Sustainability, and the Attainment of Sustainable Development Goals. *Sustainability (Basel)*, 14(16), 10239. DOI: 10.3390/su141610239

MPP - Ministério Público Portugal. (2004). *Concordata entre a República Portuguesa e a Santa Sé*. Available in: https://gddc.ministeriopublico.pt/sites/default/files/documentos/instrumentos/concordata_santa_se.pdf [Accessed in January 2024].

Mukherjee, S. (2017). Changing Tax Capacity and Tax Effort of Indian States in the Era of High Economic Growth, 2001-2014.

Mukherjee, D., Lim, W. M., Kumar, S., & Donthu, N. (2022). Guidelines for advancing theory and practice through bibliometric research. *Journal of Business Research*, 148, 101–115. DOI: 10.1016/j.jbusres.2022.04.042

Mukherjee, S. (2022). *Videogames in the Indian Subcontinent: Development, culture (s) and Representations*. Bloomsbury Publishing. DOI: 10.5040/9789354359637

Mullee, A., Romaguera, D., Pearson-Stuttard, J., Viallon, V., Stepien, M., Freisling, H., Fagherazzj, G., Mancini, F., Boutron-Ruault, M., Kuhn, T., Kaaks, R., Boeing, H., Aleksandrova, K., Tionneland, A., Halkjaer, J., Overvad, K., Weiderpass, E., Skeie, G., Parr, C., & Murphy, N. (2019). Association between soft drink consumption and mortality in 10 european countries. *JAMA Internal Medicine*, 179(11), 1479–1490. DOI: 10.1001/jamainternmed.2019.2478 PMID: 31479109

Muller, A., & Kolk, A. (2015). Responsible Tax as Corporate Social Responsibility: The Case of Multinational Enterprises and Effective Tax in India [Article]. *Business & Society*, 54(4), 435–463. DOI: 10.1177/0007650312449989

Mundy, K. (2023). SDG4 and state capacity: The missing link. *International Journal of Educational Development*, 103, 102937. Advance online publication. DOI: 10.1016/j.ijedudev.2023.102937

Municipal Decree No. 25.157, of April 18th, 2016 (2016). http://leismunicipa.is/noaru

Muñoz Barriga, A. (2017). Tourism Management Perceptions in two Ecuadorian Biosphere Reserves: Galapagos and Sumaco. *Investigaciones Geográficas*, 2017(93), 110–125. DOI: 10.14350/rig.47805

Musgrave, R. A., & Musgrave, P. B. (1989). *Public finance in theory and practice* (International Editions). McGraw-Hill.

Mutanga, C. N., & Gandiwa, E. (2024). Contemporary Issues Affecting Wildlife Tourism: Crises and Disasters. Em *Geogr. Tour. Glob. Chang.: Vol. Part F2881* (pp. 167–180). Springer Nature; DOI: 10.1007/978-3-031-57252-4_12

Nabais, J. C. (2019). *Direito Fiscal [Tax Law]* (Reimpressão 2023 - 11ª ed.). Almedina.

Nabais, J. C. (2021). *Direito Fiscal*. Almedina.PINHEIRO. Alexandre Sousa; LOURENÇO, Paula Meira (2006) Manual de Feitura das Leis, CPLP, Lisboa.

Nassaji, H. (2015). Qualitative and descriptive research: Data type versus data analysis. *Language Teaching Research*, 19(2), 129–132. DOI: 10.1177/1362168815572747

National Environmental Education Act 1. (2022). In *Public Law 101–619*.

National Environmental Policy Act of 1969. (2023). In *Public Law 91–190*.

Nayudu, A. (2019). Tax Revenue Efficiency in India States: The case of Stamp Duty and Registration Fees.

Neher, T. P., Soupir, M. L., & Kanwar, R. S. (2021). Lake atitlan: A review of the food, energy, and water sustainability of a mountain lake in guatemala. *Sustainability (Switzerland), 13*(2), 1–15. *Scopus*. Advance online publication. DOI: 10.3390/su13020515

Neog, Y., & Gaur, A. K. (2020). Tax structure and economic growth: A study of selected Indian states. *Journal of Economic Structures*, 9(1), 9. DOI: 10.1186/s40008-020-00215-3

Ngwu, R. O., Onodugo, V. A., Monyei, F. E., Ukpere, W. I., Onyekwelu, P. N., & Mmamel, U. G. (2023). The Nexus between Industrial Parks and the Sustainability of Small and Medium-Scaled Ventures. *Sustainability (Switzerland), 15*(12). *Sustainability (Basel)*, 15(12), 9529. Advance online publication. DOI: 10.3390/su15129529

Nobanee, H., & Ullah, S. (2023). Mapping green tax: A bibliometric analysis and visualization of relevant research. *Sustainable Futures : An Applied Journal of Technology, Environment and Society*, 6, 100129. DOI: 10.1016/j.sftr.2023.100129

Nofita, E., Nuryanah, S., Mulyono, K. B., Rahman, Y. A., & Astuti, D. P. (2021, Jul 27-28). Benefit Test Analysis on Intra-Group Services Transactions in Indonesia. *EAI Computing and Communication in Emerging Regions* [Ice-bees 2021]. 4th International Conference on Economics, Business and Economic Education Science (ICE-BEES), Semarang, INDONESIA.

Noubissi Domguia, E. (2023). Taxing for a better life? The impact of environmental taxes on income distribution and inclusive education. *Heliyon*, 9(11), e21443. DOI: 10.1016/j.heliyon.2023.e21443 PMID: 38027993

Novovic Buric, M., Jaksic Stojanovic, A., Lalevic Filipovic, A., & Kascelan, L. (2022). Research of Attitudes toward Implementation of Green Accounting in Tourism Industry in Montenegro-Practices, and Challenges. *Sustainability (Basel)*, 14(3), 1725. DOI: 10.3390/su14031725

Nunes, P., Lerer, M. M., & Carrilho da Graça, G. (2013). Energy certification of existing office buildings: Analysis of two case studies and qualitative reflection. *Sustainable Cities and Society*, 9, 81–95. DOI: 10.1016/j.scs.2013.03.003

Núñez, J., Olivieri, S., Parra, J., & Pico, J. (2022). The distributive impact of taxes and expenditures in Colombia. *Cuadernos de Economía y Dirección de la Empresa*, 25(1), 100005. DOI: 10.1016/j.cesjef.2021.100005

Ocampo-Rodríguez, K. V., Ávila-Díaz, A. J., & Soto-Paz, J. (2023). Effect of environmental taxes on innovation and sustainable development in Colombia. *Sustainability*, 15(3), 2054. DOI: 10.3390/su15032054

OECD Guiding Principles for Regulatory Quality and Performance. (2005), available at em https://www.oecd.org/fr/reformereg/34976533.pdf (05/09/2024)

OECD Recommendations of the Council for Regulatory Policy and Governance. (2012) available at https://www.oecd.org/gov/regulatory-policy/49990817.pdf (05/09/2024)

OECD. (2001). *Environmentally Related Taxes in OECD Countries: Issues and Strategies*. OECD., DOI: 10.1787/9789264193659-

OECD. (2013). *Addressing Base Erosion and Profit Shifting [Combate à Erosão da Base Tributária e à Transferência de Lucros].*

OECD. (2014). *Action Plan on Base Erosion and Profit Shifting [Plano de ação para o combate à erosão da base tributária e à transferência de lucros].*

OECD. (2014). *OECD Tourism trends and policies 2014*. OECD Publishing., DOI: 10.1787/tour-2014-6-

OECD. (2015). *Aligning Transfer Pricing Outcomes with Value Creation, Actions 8-10 - 2015 Final Reports*. OECD Publishing., DOI: 10.1787/9789264241244-

OECD. (2015). *Transfer Pricing Documentation and Country-by-Country Reporting, Action 13 - 2015 Final Report.*

OECD. (2019). *Model Tax Convention on Income and on Capital 2017 (Full Version)*. OECD Publishing.

OECD. (2021). *OECD/G20 Base Erosion and Profit Shifting Project: Two-Pillar Solution to Address the Tax Challenges Arising from the Digitalisation of the Economy*. https://www.oecd.org/tax/beps/brochure-two-pillar-solution-to-address-the-tax-challenges-arising-from-the-digitalisation-of-the-economy-october-2021.pdf

OECD. (2022). https://www.oecd.org/tax/consumption/vat-gst-rates-historical-tax-database.xlsx

OECD. (2022). *OECD Transfer Pricing Guidelines for Multinational Enterprises and Tax Administrations 2022.*

OECD. (2022a). *OECD Transfer Pricing Guidelines for Multinational Enterprises and Tax Administrations 2022*. OECD Publishing., DOI: 10.1787/0e655865-

OECD. (2022b). *Public Consultation Document: Pillar One - Amount B: 8 December 2022 - 25 January 2023*. https://web-archive.oecd.org/2022-12-08/645900-public-consultation-document-pillar-one-amount-b-2022.pdf

OECD. (2023). "Taxing Energy Use for Sustainable Development: Opportunities for energy tax and subsidy reform in selected developing and emerging economies". https://www.oecd.org/tax/tax-policy/taxing-energy-use-for-sustainable-development.htm

OECD. (2023). *Public Consultation Document: Pillar One – Amount B: 17 July 2023 - 1 September 2023*. https://www.oecd.org/tax/beps/public-consultation-document-pillar-one-amount-b-2023.pdf

OECD. (2023). *Revenue Statistics 2023 – Spain*. https://www.oecd.org/content/dam/oecd/en/topics/policy-sub-issues/global-tax-revenues/revenue-statistics-spain.pdf

OECD. (2023). *Tax Administration 2023: Comparative Information on OECD and Other Advanced and Emerging Economies.*

OECD. (2024). *Pillar One - Amount B: Inclusive Framework on BEPS, OECD/G20 Base Erosion and Profit Shifting Project*. OECD Publishing., DOI: 10.1787/21ea168b-

OECD. (2024). *The International Tax Reform Journey: Past — Present — Future*.

Ogunoye, A. A., Ibitoye, O. J., & Kleynhans, E. P. J. (2023, Mar). Manipulation of transfer prices by multi-national companies in Nigeria [Article]. *South African Journal of Economic and Management Sciences, 26*(1), 7, Article a4657. https://doi.org/DOI: 10.4102/sajems.v26i1.4657

Oguttu, A. W. (2020). Challenges of Applying the Comparability Analysis in Curtailing Transfer Pricing: Evaluating the Suitability of Some Alternative Approaches in Africa [Article]. *Intertax, 48*(1), 74-102. <Go to ISI>://WOS:000584419900006

Ohlendorf, N., Jakob, M., Minx, J. C., Schröder, C., & Steckel, J. C. (2021). Distributional impacts of carbon pricing: A meta-analysis. *Environmental and Resource Economics*, 78(1), 1–42. DOI: 10.1007/s10640-020-00521-1

Ojha, A., Chouriya, I., & Anute, N. (2022). Impact of Indirect Tax Reforms in India. *Journal of Accounting Research, Business and Finance Management*.

Olcina, J., & Morote, Á. F. (2023). Climate Change and Sustainable Development Goals (SDG): Adaptation and Education as main Challenges in the Mediterranean Area. *Finisterra*, 58(122), 39–61. DOI: 10.18055/Finis28898

Oliveira, E. R., & Ferreira, P. (2014). *Métodos de investigação: Da interrogação à descoberta científica*. Vida Económica.

Oliveira, I. T., & Poiatti, N. D. (2022). The importance of Higher Education for Innovation: the Chinese Example. *Educacao e Sociedade, 43*. https://doi.org/DOI: 10.1590/ES.234975

Onifade, S., & Haouas, I. (2023). Assessing environmental sustainability in top Middle East travel destinations: Insights on the multifaceted roles of air transport amidst other energy indicators. *Environmental Science and Pollution Research International*, 30(45), 101911–101926. DOI: 10.1007/s11356-023-29183-4 PMID: 37653199

Organization for Economic Cooperation and Development (OECD). (2022). Environmental Taxes: A Policy Approach. https://doi.org/DOI: 10.1787/638fe8c4-es

Orgeira Pillai, N., Van den Boogaard, V., & Prichard, W. (2024). The politics of taxation and tax reform in times of crisis: Covid-19 and attitudes towards taxation in Sierra Leone. *The Journal of Development Studies*, 60(2), 196–216. DOI: 10.1080/00220388.2023.2255717

Ortiz, A. C. T. D. T., Brandao, L. P., Rabelo, J. S., Gama, L. U., & Malvestio, A. C. (2022). Tax incentives as an instrument of environmental policy: An analysis of the green IPTU on municipalities of Minas Gerais. *Urbe. Revista Brasileira de Gestão Urbana*, 14, e20210181. DOI: 10.1590/2175-3369.014.e20210181

Osberg, L. (1995). The equity/efficiency trade-off in retrospect. Canadian Business Economics, 3, 5-19. Retrieved from http://hdl.handle.net/10222/34134

Osorio-Andrade, C. F., Pastrana, C. A. A., & Orejuela, A. R. (2023). Evolution of scientific research on electronic word of mouth in the tourism industry: A bibliometric analysis. *Estudios Gerenciales*, 39(166), 110–123. DOI: 10.18046/j.estger.2023.166.5415

Oueslati, W. (2014). Environmental tax reform: Short-term versus long-term macroeconomic effects. *Journal of Macroeconomics*, 40, 190–201. DOI: 10.1016/j.jmacro.2014.02.004

Ozel, M. (2022). Corporate Sustainability Practices of the European Commission in Higher Education. *Professional Studies: Theory and Practice*, 25(1), 66–75. DOI: 10.56131/pstp.2022.25.1

Özgit, H., & Uludağ, O. (2022). A unique destination and transportation: Current issues and possible solutions. *Worldwide Hospitality and Tourism Themes*, 14(4), 365–373. DOI: 10.1108/WHATT-03-2022-0034

Paczkowski, K., & Totzek, A. (2024). Kapitel 6: Operationalisierung von Verrechnungspreisen: a) Konzeptionelle Produktgestaltung. In Vögele, A., Borstell, T., & van der Ham, S. (Eds.), *Verrechnungspreise. C. H. Beck* (subsec. 163–167). Subsec.

Palanichamy, A. P. (2011). Fiscal policy reforms in India â€“ Overviews. *International Multidisciplinary Research Journal,*, 1.

Palma, C. C. (2015). *Introdução ao Imposto Sobre o Valor Acrescentado* (6th ed.). Almedina.

Palma, C. C. (2016). *A interpretação das normas de isenção de IVA pelo Tribunal de Justiça da União Europeia – Algumas notas. Temas de Direito Tributário – IRC.* IVA e IRS, Centro de Estudos Judiciários.

Panfiluk, E. (2021). Innovativeness of Tourism Enterprises: Example of Poland. *Sustainability (Basel)*, 13(3), 1024. DOI: 10.3390/su13031024

Pang, Q., & Zhang, M. (2021). Evolutionary game analysis of land income distribution in tourism development. *Tourism Economics*, 27(4), 670–687. DOI: 10.1177/1354816619898078

Pántya, J., Kovács, J., Kogler, C., & Kirchler, E. (2016). Work performance and tax compliance in flat and progressive tax systems. *Journal of Economic Psychology*, 56, 262–273. DOI: 10.1016/j.joep.2016.08.002

Panzina, J. P. (2016). *Direito Fiscal das Religiões.* Available in: https://repositorio-aberto.up.pt/handle/10216/86804 [Accessed in January 2024].

Pardo Martínez, C. I., & Alfonso, W. H. (2023). Environmental taxes as a tool to foster sustainability in Colombia. *Sustainability*, 15(6), 5263. DOI: 10.3390/su15065263

Parry, I. W. H., & Bento, A. M. (2000). Tax deductions, environmental policy, and the "double dividend" hypothesis. *Journal of Environmental Economics and Management*, 39(1), 67–96. DOI: 10.1006/jeem.1999.1093

Passos, A. B. da M., & Pozzetti, V. C. (2012). IPTU VERDE: Extrafiscalidade aplicada a proteção ambiental do cenário urbano brasileiro. Hiléia: Revista do Direito Ambiental da Amazônia, 18(jan-jun/2012) http://periodicos.uea.edu.br/index.php/Hileia/article/view/151

Patel, S. K., & Jhalani, P. (2024). Formulation of variables of environmental taxation: A bibliometric analysis of Scopus database (2001–2022). *Environment, Development and Sustainability*, 26(3), 7687–7714. DOI: 10.1007/s10668-023-03027-0

Pathania, R. (2019). Estimation of Central Tax Buoyancy in India. *Journal of Global Economics*, 15, 158–166.

Paulus, A., & Peichl, A. (2009). Effects of flat tax reforms in Western Europe. *Journal of Policy Modeling*, 31(5), 620–636. DOI: 10.1016/j.jpolmod.2009.06.001

Paz, M. S., Azevedo, T. C., Conceição, M. G., & Oliveira, J. R. S. (2023). Práticas e medidas sustentáveis como instrumento de política pública local ambiental e os ODS para as cidades: um estudo das estratégias adotadas nos municípios baianos. Revista de Administração e Contabilidade da FAT, 14(3).

PCM - Presidência do Conselho de Ministros. (1983). *Decreto-Lei n.º 130/83, 16.03.1983, Autoriza a Fundação Aga Kahn a desenvolver a sua actividade em Portugal.* Available in: https://files.diariodarepublica.pt/gratuitos/1s/1983/03/06200.pdf [Accessed in January 2024].

Peeters, P., Gössling, S., & Becken, S. (2006). Innovation towards tourism sustainability: Climate change and aviation. *International Journal of Innovation and Sustainable Development*, 1(3), 184–200. DOI: 10.1504/IJISD.2006.012421

Peichl, A. (2009). The benefits and problems of linking micro and macro models - Evidence from a flat tax analysis. *Journal of Applied Econometrics*, 12(2), 301–329. DOI: 10.1016/S1514-0326(09)60017-9

Peña, G. (2022). Optimal VAT on Financial Services: A Theoretical Model of Financial VAT. In Handbook of Research on Challenges in Public Economics in the Era of Globalization (pp. 279-318). IGI Global.

Peña, G. (2019). Efficient treatment of banking services under VAT. *Economics and Business Letters*, 8(2), 115–121. DOI: 10.17811/ebl.8.2.2019.115-121

Peña, G. (2020). A new trading algorithm with financial applications. *Quantitative Finance and Economics*, 4(4), 596–607. DOI: 10.3934/QFE.2020027

Peña, G., & López-Laborda, J. (2022). Financial VAT may improve trade openness, Harvard-Dataverse, DOI: 10.7910/DVN/WEW6EU

Pence, K. M. (2006). The Role of Wealth Transformations: An Application to Estimating the Effect of Tax Incentives on Saving. *The B.E. Journal of Economic Analysis & Policy*, 5(1), 000010151515380645l430. Advance online publication. DOI: 10.1515/1538-0645.1430

Pereira, E. (2024), "Incentivo Fiscal à Investigação Científica e Inovação". *In Vida Económica*, pages 21 et ff., available at https://www.occ.pt/sites/default/files/public/2024-02/109744423.pdf

Pereira, M. F. (2014). *Fiscalidade* (5th ed.). Almedina.

Pereira, P. T., Afonso, A., Arcanjo, M., & Santos, J. C. G. (2016). *Economia e Finanças Públicas*. Escolar Editora.

Perles-Ribes, J. F., Ivars-Baidal, J. A., Ramon-Rodriguez, A. B., & Vera-Rebollo, J. F. (2020). The typological classification of tourist destinations: The region of Valencia, a case study. *Tourism Economics*, 26(5), 764–773. DOI: 10.1177/1354816619838413

Peters, C. (2022, Jan). Critical Analysis of the General Court's 'EU Arm's Length Tool': Beware of the Reflexivity of Transfer Pricing Law! [Review]. *Ec Tax Review, 31*(1), 30-49. <Go to ISI>://WOS:000754866100004

Philander, K. S. (2013). A normative analysis of gambling tax policy. *UNLV Gaming Research & Review Journal*, 17(2), 2.

Picas, S., Reis, P., Pinto, A., & Abrantes, J. L. (2021). Does Tax, Financial, and Government Incentives Impact Long-Term Portuguese SMEs' Sustainable Company Performance? *Sustainability (Basel)*, 13(21), 11866. DOI: 10.3390/su132111866

Piga, C. (2003). Territorial planning and tourism development tax. *Annals of Tourism Research*, 30(4), 886–905. DOI: 10.1016/S0160-7383(03)00061-6

Pigato, M. A. (Ed.). (2019). Fiscal Policies for Development and Climate Action. World Bank Publications. https://doi.org/. This book provides a comprehensive analysis of green fiscal policies in developing countries, which could offer valuable insights for the Colombian context. On the other hand, the information related toDOI: 10.1596/978-1-4648-1358-0

Pires, J. A. R. (2006). *Os Preços de Transferência* [Transfer Pricing]. Grupo Editorial Vida Económica.

Pirotta, E., & Lusseau, D. (2015). Managing the wildlife tourism commons. *Ecological Applications*, 25(3), 729–741. DOI: 10.1890/14-0986.1 PMID: 26214918

Pita Grandal, A. M. (2003). Incidencia del Derecho comunitario europeo en el poder financiero autonómico. In Pita Grandal, A.M. (Dir.), *Hacienda autonómica y local. III Seminario Iberoamericano de Derecho Tributario* (149-168). Tórculo Edicións.

Pita Grandal, A. M. (1987). Reflexiones en torno a los límites de la previsión contenida en el art. 6,3 de la LOFCA. *Impuestos: Revista de doctrina, legislación y jurisprudencia. Year*, 3(2), 136–146.

Poddar, S., & Ahmad, E. (2009). GST reforms and intergovernmental considerations in India. *Government of India, Ministry of Finance, Department of Economic Affairs. Working Paper*, 1, 2009.

Poddar, S., & English, M. (1997). Taxation of Financial Services under a Value-Added Tax: Applying the Cash-Flow Approach. *National Tax Journal*, 50(1), 89–111. DOI: 10.1086/NTJ41789244

Pogátsa, Z. (2009). Tatra tiger: Growth miracle or belated recovery? *Acta Oeconomica*, 59(4), 377–390. DOI: 10.1556/aoecon.59.2009.4.1

Poirson, H. (2006). The Tax System in India: Could Reform Spur Growth? *Corporate Finance: Valuation.*

Poledna, S., & Thurner, S. (2016). Elimination of systemic risk in financial networks by means of a systemic risk transaction tax. *Quantitative Finance*, 16(10), 1599–1613. DOI: 10.1080/14697688.2016.1156146

Popescu, C. R. G., & Šebestová, J. D. (2022). Fiscally Responsible Businesses as a Result of COVID-19 Pandemic Shock: Taking Control of Countries' Tax Systems by Putting an End to Corporate Tax Evasion and Tax Havens. In *Handbook of Research on Changing Dynamics in Responsible and Sustainable Business in the Post-COVID-19 Era* (pp. 161–192). IGI Global.

Popescu, M. E., Militaru, E., Stanila, L., Vasilescu, M. D., & Cristescu, A. (2019). Flat-rate versus progressive taxation? An impact evaluation study for the case of Romania. *Sustainability (Basel)*, 11(22), 6405–6421. DOI: 10.3390/su11226405

Porto, N., Dowbley, V., & Ines Garcia, C. (2020). Tactics for the tourism game in groups of municipalities from Buenos Aires Province: A classification for the development of sports tourism. *Revista Brasileira de Pesquisa em Turismo*, 14(3), 134–157. DOI: 10.7784/rbtur.v14i3.1915

Portugal. Ministério da Saúde. (2022). *Programa nacional para a promoção da alimentação saudável 2022-2030* (M. da G. Freitas & R. Mestre, Eds.). Direção-Geral da Saúde. https://nutrimento.pt/activeapp/wp-content/uploads/2022/10/PNPAS2022_2030_VF.pdf

Poterba, J. M., & Rotemberg, J. J. (1986). Money in the utility function: An empirical implementation, *NBER Working Papers.*

Powell, L. M., Chriqui, J. F., Tamkeen, K., Wada, R., & Chaloupka, F. J. (2013). Assessing the potential effectiveness of food and beverage taxes and subsidies for improving public health: A systematic review of prices, demand and body weight outcomes. *National Institutes of Health, 14*(2), 110–128. DOI: 10.1111/obr.12002

Powell, L. M., & Chaloupka, F. J. (2009). Food prices and obesity: Evidence and policy implications for taxes and subsidies. *The Milbank Quarterly*, 87(1), 229–257. DOI: 10.1111/j.1468-0009.2009.00554.x PMID: 19298422

Price, D. J. D. S. (1963). *Little Science, Big Science*. Columbia University Press., https://doi.org/doi:10.7312/pric91844 DOI: 10.7312/pric91844

Price, D. J. de S. (1961). *Science Since Babylon* (Vol. 67). Yale University Press.

Qiu, L. D., Zhou, M., & Wei, X. (2018). Regulation, innovation, and firm selection: The porter hypothesis under monopolistic competition. *Journal of Environmental Economics and Management*, 92, 638–658. DOI: 10.1016/j.jeem.2017.08.012

Qiu, Y., & Kahn, M. E. (2019). Impact of voluntary green certification on building energy performance. *Energy Economics*, 80, 461–475. DOI: 10.1016/j.eneco.2019.01.035

Qi, Y., Zhang, J., & Chen, J. (2023). Tax incentives, environmental regulation and firms' emission reduction strategies: Evidence from China. *Journal of Environmental Economics and Management*, 117, 102750. DOI: 10.1016/j.jeem.2022.102750

Qorraj, G., Krasniqi, B., & Jusufi, G. (2022). Academic freedom and higher education governance in the Western Balkans: The case of Kosovo. *Issues in Educational Research*, 32(3), 1092–1110.

Rahman, M. H., Tanchangya, T., Rahman, J., Aktar, M. A., & Majumder, S. C. (2024). Corporate social responsibility and green financing behavior in Bangladesh: Towards sustainable tourism. *Innovation and Green Development*, 3(3), 100133. Advance online publication. DOI: 10.1016/j.igd.2024.100133

Raimi, L., & Aljadani, A. (2020). Sustainability of public finance of rentier states. Em *Recent Advancements in Sustainable Entrepreneurship and Corporate soc. Responsibility* (pp. 88–113). IGI Global. DOI: 10.4018/978-1-7998-2347-6.ch005

Raimi, L., & Aljadani, A. (2022). Sustainability of public finance of rentier states. Em *Res. Anthology on Macroecon. And the Achiev. Of Global Stability* (pp. 1028–1047). IGI Global. DOI: 10.4018/978-1-6684-7460-0.ch055

Raimundo, A. M., Sousa, A. M., & Oliveira, A. V. M. (2023). Assessment of Energy, Environmental and Economic Costs of Buildings' Thermal Insulation–Influence of Type of Use and Climate. *Buildings*, 13(2), 279. DOI: 10.3390/buildings13020279

Raji, S. A., & Demehin, M. O. (2023). "Long walk to 2030": A bibliometric and systematic review of research trends on the UN sustainable development goal 3. *Dialogues in Health*, 2, 100132. Advance online publication. DOI: 10.1016/j.dialog.2023.100132 PMID: 38515499

Ramon-Cardona, J., Dolores Sanchez-Fernandez, M., Duran-Sanchez, A., & Alvarez-Garcia, J. (2022). Music as an Element of Tourism Innovation: Types of Nightlife Premises in Ibiza (Spain). *Frontiers in Psychology*, 13, 890847. DOI: 10.3389/fpsyg.2022.890847 PMID: 35795411

Ramos Prieto, J. (2017). La importancia presupuestaria de los tributos propios de las Comunidades Autónomas. Análisis comparativo. In Sanz Gómez, R. (Coord.), *Tributos propios de las Comunidades Autónomas* (45-82). Tirant lo Blanch.

Ramos Prieto, J., García Martínez, A., Martín Rodríguez, J.M. & Macarro Osuna, J.M. (2019). A propósito de la reforma del sistema de financiación de las Comunidades Autónomas de régimen general. Problemas y propuestas. *Documentos- IEF, 2,* 1-51.

Ramos, S., & Naranjo, E. (2014). *Metodologia da investigação científica*. Escolar Editora.

Rangel, A. C. L. D. C., Aranha, K. C., & Da Silva, M. C. B. C. (2015). Os telhados verdes nas políticas ambientais como medida indutora para a sustentabilidade. *Desenvolvimento e Meio Ambiente*, 35. Advance online publication. DOI: 10.5380/dma.v35i0.39177

Rani, V. (2014). Tax reforms in India since 1991: An overview. *VISION: Journal of Indian Taxation*, 1(1), 36–54.

Rao, M. G. (2016). Tyranny of the status quo: The challenges of reforming the Indian tax system. In *Indian Policy Forum 2015* (Vol. 16, No. 12, pp. 47-101).

Rao, M. G., & Rao, R. K. (2010Tax System Reform in India. In *Taxation in Developing Countries: Six Case Studies and Policy Implications* (pp. 109-152). Columbia University Press.

Rao, M. G. (2000). Tax reform in India: Achievements and challenges. *Asia-Pacific Development Journal*, 7(2), 59–74.

Rao, M. G. (2005). Tax system reform in India: Achievements and challenges ahead §. *Journal of Asian Economics*, 16(6), 993–1011. DOI: 10.1016/j.asieco.2005.10.003

Rawls, J. (1971). *A theory of justice*. Belknap Press/ Harvard University Press. DOI: 10.4159/9780674042605

Recanati, A. M. (2023). *AI Battle Royale: How to Protect Your Job from Disruption in the 4th Industrial Revolution*. Springer Nature. DOI: 10.1007/978-3-031-19278-4

Ren, G., & Hong, T. (2017). Investigating Online Destination Images Using a Topic-Based Sentiment Analysis Approach. *Sustainability (Basel)*, 9(10), 1765. DOI: 10.3390/su9101765

REPORTS. CoA (2022) Parecer sobre a Conta Geral do Estado 2022, available at https://www.tcontas.pt/pt-pt/ProdutosTC/PareceresTribunalContas/ParecerCGE/Documents/2022/pcge2022.pdf (05/09/2024)

Revenue Service, I. (2023). *Guidance on Requirements for Home Energy Audits for Purposes of the Energy Efficient Home Improvement Credit under Section 25C.*

Ribeiro, D., Machado, L. P., & Henriques, P. (2022). Tourism Economics—Tourists' Perception of the Tourist Tax in Oporto. In Vujicic, M. D., Kasim, A., Kostopoulou, S., Chica Olmo, J., & Aslam, M. (Eds.), *Adv. Sci. Tech. Inno* (pp. 135–141). Springer Nature., DOI: 10.1007/978-3-031-07819-4_12

Ribeiro, F. M., & Santos, S. F. (2013). *A Fiscalidade e as Organizações de Economia Social*. Vida Económica.

Ribes Ribes, A. (2018). Los retos del nuevo modelo de financiación autonómica: Reflexiones y propuestas. *Documentos-Instituto de Estudios Fiscales*, 12/2018, 209–221.

Ricardo, D. (1817). *Principles of political economy and taxation.*

Rocha, A. P. (2023). The Portuguese Tax Regime applicable to the Environmental Non-Governmental Organizations. In *Dinis, Ana et al (Coord.): Taking on Climate Change Through Green Taxation* (pp. 82–100). IGI Global. DOI: 10.4018/978-1-6684-8592-7.ch004

Rocha, A. P. (2024). A tributação da Economia Social em Portugal. *CIRIEC-España. Revista Jurídica de Economía Social y Cooperativa*, (44), 349–386.

Rodríguez Márquez, J. (2008). Aspectos controvertidos en el futuro sistema de financiación autonómica. In Aneiros Pereira, J. (Coord.), *La financiación autonómica en los Estatutos de Autonomía* (239-257). Marcial Pons.

Rodríguez, D., & Ávila, F. (2023). Fiscal policy and income redistribution in Latin America: Challenging the conventional wisdom. *The Journal of Development Studies*, 59(5), 816–833. DOI: 10.1080/00220388.2022.2161688

Rodríguez, M., Robaina, M., & Teotónio, C. (2019). Sectoral effects of a Green Tax Reform in Portugal. *Renewable & Sustainable Energy Reviews*, 104, 408–418. DOI: 10.1016/j.rser.2019.01.016

Rogers, H., & Oats, L. (2022). Transfer pricing: Changing views in changing times. *Accounting Forum*, 46(1), 83–107. DOI: 10.1080/01559982.2021.1926778

Roldan-Valadez, E., Salazar-Ruiz, S. Y., Ibarra-Contreras, R., & Rios, C. (2019). Current concepts on bibliometrics: A brief review about impact factor, Eigenfactor score, CiteScore, SCImago Journal Rank, Source-Normalised Impact per Paper, H-index, and alternative metrics. *Irish Journal of Medical Science*, 188(3), 939–951. DOI: 10.1007/s11845-018-1936-5 PMID: 30511320

Román, J. L. D., Fernández, J. I. P., & García, P. J. C. (2020). Delimitación de ingresos públicos aplicables en los destinos turísticos españoles. *Investigaciones Regionales Journal of Regional Research*, 47, 179–199. DOI: 10.38191/iirr-jorr.20.016

Romero, G., Álvarez, F., & Caldentey, E. P. (2022). The political economy of environmental taxes in Latin America: Carbon taxes and distributional impacts. *Ecological Economics*, 193, 107318. DOI: 10.1016/j.ecolecon.2022.107318

Romero-Jordán, D., del Río, P., & Peñasco, C. (2022). An analysis of the factors influencing CO2 emissions in developing countries: The role of renewable energy and environmental taxes. *Energy Economics*, 114, 105990. DOI: 10.1016/j.eneco.2022.105990

Roper, P. (2024). *Amount B: more sticky situation than honey sweet: Amount B of Pillar One: game changing for low-capacity jurisdictions but no buzz from multinational enterprises.* https://kpmg.com/uk/en/home/insights/2024/02/tmd-amount-b-more-sticky-situation-than-honey-sweet.html

Rosário, A. T., & Raimundo, R. (2024). Sustainable Entrepreneurship Education: A Systematic Bibliometric Literature Review. *Sustainability (Basel)*, 16(2), 784. Advance online publication. DOI: 10.3390/su16020784

Ruíz Almendral, V. (2012). Sharing Taxes and Sharing the Deficit in Spanish Fiscal Federalism. *eJournal of Tax Research, Vol. 10, No. 1*, 88-125.

Ruíz Almendral, V. (2017). La imposición propia autonómica ante el Derecho de la Unión Europea. In Sanz Gómez, R. (Coord.), *Tributos propios de las Comunidades Autónomas* (83-118). Tirant lo Blanch.

Ruíz Almendral, V. (2002). Fiscal Federalism in Spain: The Assignment of Taxation Powers to the Autonomous Communities. *European Taxation*, 42(11), 467–475.

Ruíz Almendral, V. (2013). The Spanish Legal Framework for Curbing the Public Debt and the Deficit. *European Constitutional Law Review*, 9(2), 189–204. DOI: 10.1017/S1574019612001113

Ruíz Almendral, V. (2022a). Una reforma tributaria para España. *Actualidad Jurídica Uría Menéndez*, 58, 7–26.

Ruíz Almendral, V. (2022b). Tax decentralization and tax reform in the EU context. *Revista General de Derecho Europeo*, 57, 3.

Runge, W. (2014). *Gameforge AG. Technology entrepreneurship: A treatise on entrepreneurs and entrepreneurship for and in technology ventures.* KIT Scientific Publishing.

Run, K., Cévaër, F., & Dubé, J.-F. (2023). Does energy-efficient renovation positively impact thermal comfort and air quality in university buildings? *Journal of Building Engineering*, 78, 107507. DOI: 10.1016/j.jobe.2023.107507

Rupa, R. (2017). GST in India: An Overview. *International Education and Research Journal*,, 3.

Sabitova, N. M., & Dyudina, M. P. (2015). Income taxation as a took of income redistribution. Mediterranean Journal of Social Sciences, 6(1 S3), 174-178. DOI: 10.5901/mjss.2015.v6n1s3p174

Sachs, J. (2015). *The age of sustainable development.* Columbia University Press. DOI: 10.7312/sach17314

Sackitey, G. L. (2023). Do environmental taxes affect energy consumption and energy intensity? An empirical analysis of OECD countries. *Cogent Economics & Finance*, 11(1), 2156094. DOI: 10.1080/23322039.2022.2156094

Sainsbury, T., & Breunig, R. (2020). The urgent need for Tax Reform in Australia in the COVID-19 World. *Australian Journal of Labour Economics*, 23(2), 211–230.

Saka, C., Oshika, T., & Jimichi, M. (2020). Does Tax Avoidance Diminish Firms' Sustainability? *Journal Global Policy and Governance*, 8(2). Advance online publication. DOI: 10.14666/2194-7759-8-2-005

Salassa Boix, R. (2022). Los impuestos autonómicos propios: ¿una especie en peligro de extinción? *Crónica Tributaria*, 187(2), 67–105. DOI: 10.47092/CT.23.2.3

Salassa Boix, R. (2023). Cláusula de compensación en favor de las Comunidades Autónomas: Desafíos de una medida excepcional cada vez más habitual. *Nueva Fiscalidad*, 2(2-2023), 227–262. DOI: 10.14679/2089

Salvador, (Municipality). (2024). Incentivos tributários. https://www2.sefaz.salvador.ba.gov.br/transparencia/incentivos-tributarios

SAMANTARA. D. (2021). Tax reforms in India: A critical analysis. *Journal Homepage:*http://ijmr. net. *in, 9*(1).

Sandelowski, M. (2000). Whatever Happened to Qualitative Description? *Research in Nursing & Health*, 23(4), 334–340. DOI: 10.1002/1098-240X(200008)23:4<334::AID-NUR9>3.0.CO;2-G PMID: 10940958

Sandelowski, M. (2010). What's in a name? Qualitative description revisited. *Research in Nursing & Health*, 33(1), 77–84. DOI: 10.1002/nur.20362 PMID: 20014004

Santos, J. A. (1989). A Fiscalidade: Medição e Limites. *Estudes de Economia, IX, n.º4*, 393–426. http://hdl.handle.net/10400.5/9582

Santos, M. C., & Cordeiro, F. R. (2016). *A Introdução das fat taxes em Portugal: Algumas considerações*. Observatório de Taxas e Contribuições, CEDIPRE- Centro de Estudos de Direito Público e Regulação, Faculdade de Direito da Universidade de Coimbra. https://www.fd.uc.pt/cedipre/observatorio/publicacoes/estudos_1.pdf

Saraiva, R. N. C. e G., & Nylander, V. G. R. (2023). Ways of Using the Tribute for Environmental Protection. *Taking on Climate Change Through Green Taxation*, 16, 350–371. DOI: 10.4018/978-1-6684-8592-7.ch016

Sarigiannidis, C., Halkiopoulos, C., & Boutsinas, B. (2024). An Environmental Management Accounting System for Sustainable Tourism Based on Business Intelligence. In Katsoni, V., & Cassar, G. (Eds.), *Springer Proc. Bus. Econ* (pp. 543–556). Springer Nature., DOI: 10.1007/978-3-031-54338-8_31

Saw, S. M., & Rajan, U. (1997, March). The epidemiology of obesity: A review. *Annals of the Academy of Medicine, Singapore*, 39(1), 1–7. DOI: 10.47102/annals-acadmedsg.V35N1p1 PMID: 9395816

Sayta, J. (2012). Legality of Poker and Other Games of Skill: A Critical Analysis of India's Gaming Laws. *NUJS L. Rev.*, 5, 93.

Schanzenbach, D. W., & Strain, M. R. (2021). Employment effects of the earned income tax credit: Taking the long view. In *Tax Policy and the Economy* (Vol. 35, Issue 1, pp. 87–129). University of Chicago Press. DOI: 10.1086/713494

Scharf, K., & Smith, S. (2015). The price elasticity of charitable giving: Does the form of tax relief matter? *International Tax and Public Finance*, 22(2), 330–352. DOI: 10.1007/s10797-014-9306-3

Schubert, S., & Schamel, G. (2021). Sustainable tourism development: A dynamic model incorporating resident spillovers. *Tourism Economics*, 27(7), 1561–1587. DOI: 10.1177/1354816620934552

Scopus - Content Coverage Guide. (n.d.). Retrieved from Elsevier: https://www.elsevier.com/?a=69451&fbclid=IwAR2WBehEx2U6n9VoMkyyVzm00gWEFD1RtsvgjXpKtdew4_pLVcbhbUsZtMo

Scrioşteanu, A., Barbu, C. M., & Criveanu, M. M. (2022). Sustainable tourism in the current European context. In *Managing risk and decision making in times of economic distress, 108* (Vol. B, pp. 17–36). Emerald Publishing Limited., DOI: 10.1108/S1569-37592022000108B031

Sebele-Mpofu, F., Mashiri, E., & Schwartz, S. C. (2021, Jan). An exposition of transfer pricing motives, strategies and their implementation in tax avoidance by MNEs in developing countries [Article]. *Cogent Business & Management, 8*(1), 25, Article 1944007. https://doi.org/DOI: 10.1080/23311975.2021.1944007

Sedai, A., & Medda, F. (2021). Complex tourism dynamics and fiscal sustainability. Em *Handb. On Entropy, Complexity and Spatial Dynamics: A Rebirth of Theory?* (pp. 321–341). Edward Elgar Publishing Ltd. https://www.scopus.com/inward/record.uri?eid=2-s2.0-85130158234&partnerID=40&md5=804e662904ac273db777de8065189e73

Sedur, Secretaria de Desenvolvimento Urbano do Munícipio de Salvador. (Mucniciplaity). IPTU Verde: número de beneficiados pelo incentivo tributário cresce 235% em 2024. https://sedur.salvador.ba.gov.br/noticias/852-iptu-verde-numero-de-beneficiados-pelo-incentivo-tributario-cresce-235-em-2024

Şen, H., & Kaya, A. (2023). Do revenue-neutral tax swaps boost growth? *Journal of Economic Policy Reform*, •••, 1–20.

Sepulveda, C. F. (2021). Time-saving goods, time inequalities and optimal commodity taxation. *International Tax and Public Finance*, •••, 1–26.

Shackelford, D. A., & Shevlin, T. (2001). Empirical tax research in accounting $. In *Journal of Accounting and Economics* (Vol. 31). DOI: 10.1016/S0165-4101(01)00022-2

Shao-ke, C. (2012). On the Reform Approach of China's Tax System under the Circumstances of the Transformation of the Pattern of Economy Development.

Shen, J., Wei, B., & Yan, H. (2021). Financial intermediation chains in an over-the-counter market. *Management Science*, 67(7), 4623–4642. DOI: 10.1287/mnsc.2020.3687

Shen, Y., & Zhang, X. (2022). Study on the Impact of Environmental Tax on Industrial Green Transformation. *International Journal of Environmental Research and Public Health*, 19(24), 16749. DOI: 10.3390/ijerph192416749 PMID: 36554630

Sherraden, M. (1990). Stakeholding: Notes on a theory of welfare based on assets. *The Social Service Review*, 64(4), 580–601. DOI: 10.1086/603797

Siddiqua, A., Hahladakis, J. N., & Al-Attiya, W. A. K. A. (2022). An overview of the environmental pollution and health effects associated with waste landfilling and open dumping. In *Environmental Science and Pollution Research* (Vol. 29, Issue 39, pp. 58514–58536). Springer Science and Business Media Deutschland GmbH. DOI: 10.1007/s11356-022-21578-z

Silva, R. (2021, February 1). *Imposto sobre bebidas açucaradas "funciona" e pode tornar Portugal um exemplo contra a obesidade.* TSF. https://www.tsf.pt/portugal/economia/imposto-sobre-bebidas-acucaradas-funciona-e-pode-tornar-portugal-um-exemplo-contra-a-obesidade-13300793.html

Silva, A.-I. S., Alves, M.-C. G., & Estevão, C. (2022). Tourism and Sustainability in Natural Parks: A Survey. *International Journal of Social Ecology and Sustainable Development*, 13(1), 1–17. Advance online publication. DOI: 10.4018/IJSESD.287879

Silva, B. V. F., Holm-Nielsen, J. B., Sadrizadeh, S., Teles, M. P. R., Kiani-Moghaddam, M., & Arabkoohsar, A. (2024). Sustainable, green, or smart? Pathways for energy-efficient healthcare buildings. *Sustainable Cities and Society*, 100, 105013. DOI: 10.1016/j.scs.2023.105013

Silva, F. B., Barranco, R., Proietti, P., Pigaiani, C., & Lavalle, C. (2021). A new European regional tourism typology based on hotel location patterns and geographical criteria. *Annals of Tourism Research*, 89, 103077. DOI: 10.1016/j.annals.2020.103077

Silva, L. F. D., Azevedo, T. C., & Oliveira, J. R. S. (2022). Panorama da legislação sobre tributação ecológica em países Latino-Americanos. Research. *Social Development*, 11(7), e3711729566. DOI: 10.33448/rsd-v11i7.29566

Silva, S. T., & Soares, C. D. (2015). *Regime Fiscal das Entidades da Economia Social e Civil.* Vida Económica.

Singh, A., & Jaiswal, K. S. (2021). Post Implementation Issues of Goods and Services Tax in India. *Management Insight*, 17(02), 81–87. DOI: 10.21844/mijia.17.2.9

Singh, N., Srinivasan, T.N., Aziz, J., Cashin, P., Chaudhuri, S., Nair, M.R., Govinda Rao, M., Reddy, Y.V., Sahay, R., Towe, C.M., & Bhandari, L., Aarti, & Federalism, I. (2002). Indian Federalism, Economic Reform and Globalization. *The Developing Economies*.

Situmorang, V., Elyani, T., Tambunan, R., & Gulto, Y. (2019). Applying opinion mining technique on tourism study case: Lake Toba. *Journal of Physics: Conference Series*, 1175(1), 012091. Advance online publication. DOI: 10.1088/1742-6596/1175/1/012091

Sivesan, S. (2019). Impact of Service Quality on Customer Satisfaction in Life Insurance Companies in Sri Lanka. *Global Journal of Management and Business Research: E-Marketing*, 19(5), 50–55.

Skipper, D. W., & Burton, H. A. (2008). Ramifications of a flat tax - Shifting the burden to the middle class. *International Advances in Economic Research*, 14(4), 460–471. DOI: 10.1007/s11294-008-9168-5

Smith, T. A., Lin, B., & Lee, J. (2010, July). Taxing caloric sweetened beverages: Potential effects on beverage consumption, calorie intake, and obesity. *Economic Research Service*. https://www.ers.usda.gov/webdocs/publications/44732/8311_err100_1_.pdf?v=0

Smith, A. (1776). *The wealth of nations*.

Soku, M. G., Amidu, M., & William, C. (2023). Environmental tax, carbon emmission and female economic inclusion. *Cogent Business and Management*, 10(2), 2210355. Advance online publication. DOI: 10.1080/23311975.2023.2210355

Solilová, V., Nerudová, D., Bohušová, H., & Svoboda, P. (2017). Compliance Costs of Transfer Pricing in Case of SMEs: Czech Case. *European Financial and Accounting Journal*, 12(1), 35–50. DOI: 10.18267/j.efaj.176

Soliman, K. S. (Ed.). (2017). Proceedings of the 29th International Business Information Management Association Conference—Education Excellence and Innovation Management through Vision 2020: From Regional Development Sustainability to Global Economic Growth. Em *Proc. Int. Bus. Inf. Manag. Assoc. Conf. - Educ. Excell. Innov. Manag. Vis.: Reg. Dev. Sustain. Glob. Econ. Growth*. International Business Information Management Association, IBIMA. https://www.scopus.com/inward/record.uri?eid=2-s2.0-85029738713&partnerID=40&md5=faa8180944d03c1a87a26fb3bd3cf916

Somohano-Rodríguez, F. M., David, F., & Azevedo, T. C. (2023). Spanish business commitment to the 2030 Agenda in uncertain times. *AIMS Environmental Science*, 10(2), 246–266. DOI: 10.3934/environsci.2023015

Song, M., Wang, S., & Zhang, H. (2020). Could environmental regulation and R&D tax incentives affect green product innovation? *Journal of Cleaner Production*, 258, 120849. DOI: 10.1016/j.jclepro.2020.120849

Sousa, M., & Baptista, C. (2011). *Como fazer investigação, dissertação, teses e relatórios: Segundo Bolonha*. PACTOR.

Srivastava, S., Sultan, A., & Chashti, N. (2017). Influence of innovation competence on firm level competitiveness: An exploratory study. *Asia Pacific Journal of Innovation and Entrepreneurship*, 11(1), 63–75. DOI: 10.1108/APJIE-04-2017-021

Stabler, M. (2003). THE ECONOMIC EVALUATION OF THE ROLE OF CONSERVATION AND TOURISM IN THE REGENERATION OF HISTORIC URBAN DESTINATIONS. Em *Embrac. And Managing Change in Tourism: International case studies* (pp. 239–266). Taylor and Francis. https://doi.org/DOI: 10.4324/9780203360491-25

Stahel, W. R. (2013). Policy for material efficiency—sustainable taxation as a departure from the throwaway society. *Philosophical Transactions of the Royal Society A: Mathematical, Physical and Engineering Sciences, 371*(1986), 20110567.

Sterner, T., Barbier, E. B., Bateman, I., van den Bijgaart, I., Crépin, A. S., Edenhofer, O., & Robinson, A. (2022). Policy design for the Anthropocene. *Nature Sustainability*, 5(1), 5–13. DOI: 10.1038/s41893-021-00755-x

Stewart, D. D., & Soong, S. (2024). *An Update on Pillar 1 Amount B*.https://www.taxnotes.com/tax-notes-live/tax-notes-talk/update-pillar-1-amount-b/7j9r1?s=03

Stockholm Environment Institute. Climate Analytics, E3G, the International Institute for Sustainable Development, and the United Nations Environment Programme (UNEP) (2023). The production gap. https://www.un.org/es/climatechange/reports#:~:text=El%20informe%202023%20concluye%20que,que%20ser%C3%ADa%20con%202%20%C2%BAC

Strully, K. W., Rehkopf, D. H., & Xuan, Z. (2010). Effects of Prenatal Poverty on Infant Health: State Earned Income Tax Credits and Birth Weight. *American Sociological Review*, 75(4), 534–562. DOI: 10.1177/0003122410374086 PMID: 21643514

Suess, C., & Mody, M. (2016). Gaming can be sustainable too! Using Social Representation Theory to examine the moderating effects of tourism diversification on residents' tax paying behavior. *Tourism Management*, 56, 20–39. DOI: 10.1016/j.tourman.2016.03.022

Suhardono, S., Fitria, L., Suryawan, I., Septiariva, I., Mulyana, R., Sari, M., Ulhasanah, N., & Prayogo, W. (2024). Human activities and forest fires in Indonesia: An analysis of the Bromo incident and implications for conservation tourism. *Trees, Forests and People*, 15, 100509. Advance online publication. DOI: 10.1016/j.tfp.2024.100509

Sun, M., & Sun, W. (2022). A Study to Explore Environmental Education in the Curriculum Development in China. *International Journal for Cross-Disciplinary Subjects in Education*, 13(2), 4685–4691. DOI: 10.20533/ijcdse.2042.6364.2022.0576

Su, S., Qamruzzaman, M., & Karim, S. (2023). Charting a Sustainable Future: The Impact of Economic Policy, Environmental Taxation, Innovation, and Natural Resources on Clean Energy Consumption. *Sustainability (Basel)*, 15(18), 13585. DOI: 10.3390/su151813585

Tachinakis, P. (2022). Tax benefits determinants and earnings management: Results from the eurozone countries. *International Journal of Computational Economics and Econometrics*, 12(3), 263–274. DOI: 10.1504/IJCEE.2022.122831

Tamir, O., Cohen-Yogev, T., Furman-Assaf, S., & Endevelt, R. (2018). Taxation of sugar sweetened beverages and unhealthy foods: A qualitative study of key opinion leaders' views. *Israel Journal of Health Policy Research*, 7(1), 43. DOI: 10.1186/s13584-018-0240-1 PMID: 30064503

Tang, Y., & Chen, Y. (2017). Protecting the Biodiversity in the Fast Urbanization Age—An Ecotourism Zone in Hainan, China. *Procedia Engineering*, 198, 419–427. DOI: 10.1016/j.proeng.2017.07.097

Tan, Z., Wu, Y., Gu, Y., Liu, T., Wang, W., & Liu, X. (2022). An overview on implementation of environmental tax and related economic instruments in typical countries. In *Journal of Cleaner Production* (Vol. 330). Elsevier Ltd., DOI: 10.1016/j.jclepro.2021.129688

Taranu, V., & Verbeeck, G. (2022). Property tax as a policy against urban sprawl. *Land Use Policy*, 122, 106335. DOI: 10.1016/j.landusepol.2022.106335

Taxe Justice Network (TJN). (2023). *State of Tax Justice 2023*. https://taxjustice.net/reports/the-state-of-tax-justice-2023/

TEDH - Tribunal Europeu dos Direitos do Homem (1950). *European Convention on Human Rights, for the Projection of Human Rights and Fundamental Freedoms*. Available in: https://gddc.ministeriopublico.pt/sites/default/files/convention_por.pdf [Accessed in January 2024].

Teixeira, G. (2023). *Preços de Transferência [Transfer Pricing]*. Editora D'Ideias.

Teixeira, G. (2021). *Glossário Fiscal* [Tax Glossary]. Almedina.

Tejerizo López, J. M. (2005). La financiación de las Comunidades Autónomas. Notas para un balance. In Varona Alabern, J.E. (Ed.), *25 años de financiación autonómica* (21-38). Editorial de la Universidad de Cantabria.

Tekwani, K., & Pabla, C. K. (2021). Goods and Services Tax in India and Other Countries: A Comparative Study. *The Management Accountant Journal*, 56(7), 40–44. DOI: 10.33516/maj.v56i7.40-44p

Tetiana, V., Samusevych, Y., Babenko, V., Bestuzheva, S., Bondarenko, S. A., & Nesterenko, I. (2023). Environmental Taxation: Role in Promotion of the Pro-Environmental Behaviour. *WSEAS Transactions On Business And Economics*, 20, 410–427. DOI: 10.37394/23207.2023.20.38

Thaçi, L., & Gërxhaliu, A. (2018). Tax Structure and Developing Countries. *European Journal of Economics and Business Studies*, 4(1), 213–220. DOI: 10.26417/ejes.v10i1.p220-227

Thanh, N. V., & Van Toan, N. (2023). Building awareness of environmental protection among university students in Vietnam. *Perspektivy Nauki i Obrazovania*, 63(3), 160–174. DOI: 10.32744/pse.2023.3.10

Thow, A. M., Downs, S. M., & Jan, S. (2014). A systematic review of the effectiveness of food taxes and subsidies to improve diets: Understanding the recent evidence. *Nutrition Reviews*, 72(9), 551–565. DOI: 10.1111/nure.12123 PMID: 25091552

Tjahyanto, A., & Sisephaputra, B. (2017). The utilization of filter on object-based opinion mining in tourism product reviews. *Procedia Computer Science, 124*, 38-45. Elsevier Science Bv. DOI: 10.1016/j.procs.2017.12.127

Tobin, J. (1980). Discussion. In Kareken, J. H., & Wallace, N. (Eds.), *Models of Monetary Economies*. Federal Reserve Bank of Minneapolis.

Tovar, B., Boto-García, D., & Pino, J. (2024). Meeting externalities: The effects of educational training on support for tourism activities. *Tourism Economics*, 30(3), 785–805. DOI: 10.1177/13548166231185897

Tracana, D., & Dias, C. C. (2020). Tributação do Setor Cooperativista em Portugal: Análise dos principais aspetos e questões em aberto. *Revista Eletrónica de Fiscalidade da Associação Fiscal Portuguesa*, II, 2.

Treidler, O. (2020). *Transfer Pricing in One Lesson*. Springer International Publishing., DOI: 10.1007/978-3-030-25085-0

Trutescu, M.-N. (2020). Satisfaction of Generations X and Baby Boomers with tourist services in resorts from the Subcarpathians of Oltenia, in line with sustainable tourism destination development. *Balneo Research Journal*, 11(1), 64–73. DOI: 10.12680/balneo.2020.318

Tullock, G. (1967). The welfare costs of tariffs, monopolies, and theft. *Economic Inquiry*, 5(3), 224–232. DOI: 10.1111/j.1465-7295.1967.tb01923.x

Uddin, K. M. K., Rahman, M. M., & Saha, S. (2023). The impact of green tax and energy efficiency on sustainability: Evidence from Bangladesh. *Energy Reports*, 10, 2306–2318. DOI: 10.1016/j.egyr.2023.09.050

Uljens, M., & Elo, J. (2024). Grounding Higher Education Leadership Research in Non-affirmative Education Theory. In *Educational Governance Research* (Vol. 25, pp. 1–44). Springer Science and Business Media B.V., DOI: 10.1007/978-3-031-55116-1_1

Ulyanchenko, O., Borysova, O., Akhmedova, O. O., Sysoieva, S., Sheludko, R. M., Stankevych, S., Kovalova, T., Khalmuradov, B. D., & Kharlamova, Y. Y. (2020). Prospective use of ecological tourism in Ukraine and integrative view of international experience. *Ukrainian Journal of Ecology*, 10(1), 49–54. DOI: 10.15421/2020_8

UN - United Nations. (1948). *Universal Declaration of Human Rights.* Available in: https://www.un.org/en/about-us/universal-declaration-of-human-rights [Accessed in January 2024]..

UN - United Nations. (1967a). *International Covenant on Economic, Social and Cultural Rights.* Available in: https://treaties.un.org/doc/Treaties/1976/01/19760103%2009-57%20PM/Ch_IV_03.pdf [Accessed in January 2024].

UN - United Nations. (1967b). *International Covenant on Civil and Political Rights.* Available in: https://treaties.un.org/doc/Treaties/1976/03/19760323%2006-17%20AM/Ch_IV_04.pdf [Accessed in January 2024].

UN - United Nations. (1981). *Declaration on the Elimination of All Forms of Intolerance and of Discrimination Based on Religion or Belief.* Available in: https://www.ohchr.org/en/instruments-mechanisms/instruments/declaration-elimination-all-forms-intolerance-and-discrimination [Accessed in January 2024].

UNCTAD's BioTrade Initiative. (2007). Biotrade Principles and Criteria. United Nations Conference on Trade and Development. BioTrade Initiative (pp. 6-14). Geneva, Switzerland: UNCTAD. http://www.asocam.org/sites/default/files/publicaciones/files/2807acffecd17b29a5d3ee02ca4395a5.pdf

Unesda (2024, abril). *Sales and consumption.*https://www.unesda.eu/sales-and-consumption/

United Nations Development Programme (UNDP). (2018). Environmental taxation and equity in Latin America. https://www.undp.org/es/latin-america/publications/environmental-taxation-and-equity-latin-america

United Nations Environment Programme. (2023). Emissions Gap Report 2023: Broken Record – Temperatures hit new highs, yet world fails to cut emissions (again). https://wedocs.unep.org/20.500.11822/43922

United Nations World Tourism Organization [UNWTO]. (1998). *Tourism taxation. Striking a fair deal.* World Tourism Organization, Madrid, Spain.

United Nations World Tourism Organization [UNWTO]. (2003). *Sustainable development of tourism: Concepts and definitions*, World Tourism Organization, Madrid, Spain.

United Nations. (2015). Transforming our world: The 2030 Agenda for Sustainable Development, 70/1. https://documents.un.org/doc/undoc/gen/n15/291/89/pdf/n1529189.pdf?token=TtFoPNjXD5KjtHiSdb&fe=true

United Nations. (2022). 2021 Emissions Disparity Report. https://www.unep.org/emissions-gap-report-2021

University of North Carolina. (2022). *Sugary drink taxes around the world.*https://www.globalfoodresearchprogram.org/wp-content/uploads/2022/02/Sugary_Drink_Tax_maps_2022_02.pdf

Vaid, B. (1972). Tax Policy and Tax Administration in India. *The Indian Journal of Public Administration*, 18(3), 426–435. DOI: 10.1177/0019556119720308

Vail, D., & Heldt, T. (2000). Institutional factors influencing the size and structure of tourism: Comparing Dalarma (Sweden) and Maine (USA). *Current Issues in Tourism, 3(4)*, 283–324. *Scopus.* Advance online publication. DOI: 10.1080/13683500008667876

Valdagni, R., Scardino, P. T., & Denis, L. (2009). The 2008 European School of Oncology Inside Track Conference, «Predictive Modeling in Prostate Cancer». *Cancer*, 115(13), 3035–3038. DOI: 10.1002/cncr.24342 PMID: 19544554

van der Ham, S. (2023). Das neue OECD-Konsultationspapier zu Amount B – Verrechnungspreise einfach gemacht? *IStR Internationales Steuerrecht*, (21), 785–792.

van der Hoeven, R., & Vos, R. (2022). Reforming the international financial and fiscal system for better COVID-19 and post-pandemic crisis responsiveness. In *Covid-19 and international development* (pp. 9–27). Springer. DOI: 10.1007/978-3-030-82339-9_2

Van Gestel, R., & De Poorter, J. (2016). Putting evidence-based law making to the test: Judicial review of legislative rationality. *The Theory and Practice of Legislation*, 4(2), 155–185.

Vanistendael, F. (2011). The European Union. In Bizioli, G. & Sacchetto, C. (Co-ords), *Tax Aspects of Fiscal Federalism. A Comparative Analysis* (581-646). IBFD.

Vaquero, P. (2020). Buildings Energy Certification System in Portugal: Ten years later. *Energy Reports*, 6, 541–547. DOI: 10.1016/j.egyr.2019.09.023

Vargas-Chaves, I., Luna-Galván, M., & Franco-Gántiva, A. M. (2022). Circular economy and environmental taxation in Colombia: An analysis from sustainable development. *Sustainability*, 14(11), 6572. DOI: 10.3390/su14116572

Vaz, P. F. A. C. (2013). *O Contributo do Código Aduaneiro Comunitário nos Preços de Transferência* [The Contribution of the Community Customs Code to Transfer Pricing]. Universidade do Porto.

Vázquez, F. M. (2011). Técnica Legislativa y seguridad jurídica:¿ Hacia el control constitucional de la calidad de las Leyes? *Teoría y Realidad Constitucional*, (28), 681.

Venkataraman, S., & Urmi, A. (2017). The impact of taxation on economic growth in India: A disaggregated approach using the ARDL bounds test to co-integration. *International Journal of Accounting and Economics Studies*, 5(1), 19–21. DOI: 10.14419/ijaes.v5i1.7040

Ventosa, I. P., Forn, M. C., Sora, M. J., & Sanz, E. S. (2015). Estado actual de la fiscalidad ambiental en España y perspectivas de futuro. In *F. A. Martínez (Org.), Fiscalidad ambiental en España: Situación actual y perspectivas de futuro*. Arazandi.

Ventura, G. (1999). Flat tax reform: A quantitative exploration. *Journal of Economic Dynamics & Control*, 23(9-10), 1425–1458. DOI: 10.1016/S0165-1889(98)00079-7

Vianna, G., Meekan, M., Pannell, D., Marsh, S., & Meeuwig, J. (2012). Socio-economic value and community benefits from shark-diving tourism in Palau: A sustainable use of reef shark populations. *Biological Conservation*, 145(1), 267–277. DOI: 10.1016/j.biocon.2011.11.022

Vijayakumar, J., Rasheed, A. A., & Krishnan, V. (2005). Corruption and taxation: Lessons from the indian experience. *Journal of Public Budgeting, Accounting & Financial Management*, 17(3), 398–419. DOI: 10.1108/JPBAFM-17-03-2005-B007

Vijayanand, K. (2022). Regulation of E-Sports in India: Can Online Gaming Be Brought under the Purview of Cyber Laws in India? *Jus Corpus LJ*, 3, 1050.

Voinea, L. (2013). Revisiting crisis generators in romania and other new EU member states. *Review of International Political Economy*, 20(4), 979–1008. DOI: 10.1080/09692290.2012.733315

Vujicic, M. D., Kasim, A., Kostopoulou, S., Chica Olmo, J., & Aslam, M. (Eds.). (2022). *Cultural Sustainable Tourism, CST 2020. Advances in Science, Technology and Innovation*. Springer.

VV.AA. (2014). *Informe de la Comisión de Expertos para la reforma del sistema tributario español. Ministerio de Hacienda y Administraciones Públicas.*https://www.hacienda.gob.es/es-ES/Prensa/En%20Portada/2014/Documents/Informe%20expertos.pdf

VV.AA. (2017). *Informe de la Comisión de Expertos para la revisión del modelo de financiación autonómica*. Ministerio de Hacienda y Función Pública._https://www.hacienda.gob.es/CDI/sist%20financiacion%20y%20deuda/informaci%C3%B3nccaa/informe_final_comisi%C3%B3n_reforma_sfa.pdf

Waldron, J. (2003). *A dignidade da legislação*. Trad. Luís Carlos Borges. São Paulo: Martins Fontes, 2003.

Wang, J., Shen, G., & Tang, D. (2021). Does tax deduction relax financing constraints? Evidence from China's value-added tax reform. *China Economic Review*, 67, 101619. DOI: 10.1016/j.chieco.2021.101619

Wang, Z., Zhu, N., Wang, J., Hu, Y., & Nkana, M. (2022). The impact of environmental taxes on economic benefits and technology innovation input of heavily polluting industries in China. *Frontiers in Environmental Science*, 10, 959939. DOI: 10.3389/fenvs.2022.959939

Watrin, C., & Ullmann, R. (2008). Comparing direct and indirect taxation: The influence of framing on tax compliance. *The European Journal of Comparative Economics*, 5(1), 33–56.

Webster, G. R., & Webster, R. H. (2004). Taxing issues: Geography, politics and the 2003 tax reform referendum in Alabama. *Southeastern Geographer*, 44(2), 190–215. DOI: 10.1353/sgo.2004.0031

Weninger, M. (2009). *Uma Europa sem Deus? A União Europeia e o diálogo com religiões, igrejas e comunidades confessionais*. Coimbra: Edições 70.

Whait, R. B., Christ, K. L., Ortas, E. B., & Burritt, R. L. (2018). What do we know about tax agressiveness and corporate social responsability? An integrative review. *Journal of Cleaner Production*, 204, 542–522. DOI: 10.1016/j.jclepro.2018.08.334

Why choose Scopus. (n.d.). Retrieved from Elsevier: https://www.elsevier.com/solutions/scopus/why-choose-scopus?fbclid=IwAR3h_5tDC9qSJL3jcHIX2EE6N1fNos4Nd-zxiuxULoaGAxsD3pGFqf7Auhc

Wilson, D. J. (2009). Beggar Thy Neighbor? The In-State, Out-of-State, and Aggregate Effects of R&D Tax Credits. *The Review of Economics and Statistics*, 91(2), 431–436. DOI: 10.1162/rest.91.2.431

Wintgens, L. J. (2016). Legitimacy and legitimation from the legisprudential perspective. In *Legislation in context: Essays in legisprudence* (pp. 17–68). Routledge.

Working Group. (2019) Grupo de Trabalho para o Estudo dos Benefícios Fiscais, os Benefícios Fiscais em Portugal, Available at https://www.portugal.gov.pt/pt/gc21/comunicacao/documento?i=estudo-dos-beneficios-fiscais-em-portugal (27/06/2024)

World Bank. (2020). Fiscal Policies for an Inclusive Green Economy

World Bank. (2022). Electrification and Electric Mobility. https://www.worldbank.org/en/topic/transport/brief/electrification-and-electric-mobility

World Bank. (2023). "State and Trends of Carbon Pricing 2023". Washington, DC: World Bank. https://openknowledge.worldbank.org/handle/10986/39551

World Health Organization. (2015). Using price policies to promote healthier diets. DOI: 10.13140/RG.2.1.4853.3923

World Health Organization. (2020, December 9). *The top 10 causes of death.*https://www.who.int/news-room/fact-sheets/detail/the-top-10-causes-of-death

World Health Organization. (2021, June 9). *Obesity and overweight.*https://www.who.int/news-room/fact-sheets/detail/obesity-and-overweight

World Health Organization. (2022). *Who european regional obesity.* https://www.who.int/europe/publications/i/item/9789289057738

Wu, W., Hu, Y., & Wu, Q. (2023). Subsidies and tax incentives - Does it make a difference on TFP? Evidences from China's photovoltaic and wind listed companies. *Renewable Energy*, 208, 645–656. DOI: 10.1016/j.renene.2023.03.080

Wu, W., Wu, C., Zhou, C., & Wu, J. (2012). Political connections, tax benefits and firm performance: Evidence from China. *Journal of Accounting and Public Policy*, 31(3), 277–300. DOI: 10.1016/j.jaccpubpol.2011.10.005

Wyczykier, G. (2023). Trails of the Energy Transition: Green Hydrogen in the Era of Climate Change. Revista temas sociológicos n°31, pp. 453-484 DOI: 10.29344/07196458.31.3164

Xiao, J., Karavias, Y., Juodis, A., Sarafidis, V., & Ditzen, J. (2023). Improved tests for Granger noncausality in panel data. *The Stata Journal*, 23(1), 230–242. DOI: 10.1177/1536867X231162034

Xu, H., & Lv, Y. (2022). Mining and Application of Tourism Online Review Text Based on Natural Language Processing and Text Classification Technology. *Wireless Communications and Mobile Computing*, 2022(2), 9905114. DOI: 10.1155/2022/9905114

Ya, D., Quddus, A., Feng, M., Ullah, E., & Ameer, W. (2024). Assessing the impact of fiscal policy and natural resources on environmental degradation in BRICS countries: A resource management perspective. *Resources Policy*, 90, 104792. Advance online publication. DOI: 10.1016/j.resourpol.2024.104792

Yang, L., Zhou, Y., Meng, B., Li, H., Zhan, J., Xiong, H., Zhao, H., Cong, W., Wang, X., Zhang, W., Lakshmanan, P., Deng, Y., Shi, X., Chen, X., & Zhang, F. (2022). Reconciling productivity, profitability and sustainability of small-holder sugarcane farms: A combined life cycle and data envelopment analysis. *Agricultural Systems*, 199, 103392. DOI: 10.1016/j.agsy.2022.103392

Yang, X., & Tang, W. (2023). Additional social welfare of environmental regulation: The effect of environmental taxes on income inequality. *Journal of Environmental Management*, 330, 117095. DOI: 10.1016/j.jenvman.2022.117095 PMID: 36584467

Yan, S., Lv, C., & Yao, L. (2024). Social welfare and equality equilibrium based carbon tax subsidy incentive approach for biomass-coal co-firing towards carbon emissions. *Energy*, 291, 130282. Advance online publication. DOI: 10.1016/j.energy.2024.130282

Yassaghi, H., & Hoque, S. (2019). An Overview of Climate Change and Building Energy: Performance, Responses and Uncertainties. *Buildings*, 9(7), 166. DOI: 10.3390/buildings9070166

Yi, Y., Wei, Z., & Fu, C. (2021). An optimal combination of emissions tax and green innovation subsidies for polluting oligopolies. *Journal of Cleaner Production*, 284, 124693. DOI: 10.1016/j.jclepro.2020.124693

Zabaloy, M. F., Guzowski, C., & Recalde, M. Y. (2023). Public policies for the Argentine energy transition: Past, present and future. Rev. *Est. de Políticas Públicas*, 9(1). Advance online publication. DOI: 10.5354/0719-6296.2023.69379

Zemla, S., Zemla, N., & Gelo, F. (2020). FACTORS INFLUENCING TOURISM GROWTH IN CROATIA. Em M. Benazic, S. Buric, L. Tijanic, S. Laporsek, & T. Wolowiec (Eds.), *University of Juraj Dobrila Pula* (WOS:000835726900001; pp. 5–35).

Zhang, J., & Zhang, Y. (2020). Low-carbon tourism system in an urban destination. *Current Issues in Tourism*, 23(13), 1688–1704. DOI: 10.1080/13683500.2019.1641473

Zhang, Y., Sun, J., Yang, Z., & Wang, Y. (2020). Critical success factors of green innovation: Technology, organization and environment readiness. *Journal of Cleaner Production*, 264, 121701. DOI: 10.1016/j.jclepro.2020.121701

Zhang, Y., Teoh, B. K., & Zhang, L. (2023). Exploring driving force factors of building energy use and GHG emission using a spatio-temporal regression method. *Energy*, 269, 126747. DOI: 10.1016/j.energy.2023.126747

Zhouxiang, L. (2022). *A history of competitive gaming*. Routledge. DOI: 10.4324/9781003095859

Zhou, Z., Zhang, W., Pan, X., Hu, J., & Pu, G. (2019). Environmental Tax Reform and the "Double Dividend" Hypothesis in a Small Open Economy. *International Journal of Environmental Research and Public Health*, 17(1), 217. DOI: 10.3390/ijerph17010217 PMID: 31892259

Zimmerhackel, J., Kragt, M., Rogers, A., Ali, K., & Meekan, M. (2019). Evidence of increased economic benefits from shark-diving tourism in the Maldives. *Marine Policy*, 100, 21–26. DOI: 10.1016/j.marpol.2018.11.004

About the Contributors

Ana Dinis is a Researcher in Taxation in the Research Centre on Accounting and Taxation (IPCA, Portugal). PhD in Business Management from the Faculty of Economics of the University of Coimbra (2020). Master in Accounting and Corporate Taxation (2013) and Postgraduate in Accounting and Corporate Taxation (2009) from the Coimbra Business School (ISCAC). Postgraduate in Taxation (2010) by APEU / FEUC - Association for University Extension of the University of Coimbra. Invited Adjunct Teacher at the Polytechnic University of Cávado and Ave (IPCA), in the Accounting and Taxation Department of the School of Management, Barcelos, in the area of Taxation since 2014. Chartered Accountant, since 2003. Author and co-author in scientific papers, in national and international scientific journals, in the tax area.

Fátima David is an Accounting and Finance Professor in the School of Technology and Management - Polytechnic of Guarda, Portugal, since 1991, and Certified Accountant, since 1993. She received her PhD Degree in Accounting and Taxation from the University of Salamanca, Spain (2007). Her PhD is registred at NOVA University of Lisbon, Portugal (2008). She is a effective member of the Ethics Committee of the Polytechnic of Guarda, since 2018. She develops activities with Social Responsibility Research Network (SRRN) and Research Centre on Accounting and Taxation (IPCA-CICF); her research has been published in several journals, and she participates in several conferences and meetings.

Liliana Pereira completed in April 2015 a PhD in "Basic Principles and Categories of Internal and International Taxation. The Tax procedures" by the University of Santiago de Compostela. Degree in Taxation in July 2005 by the Polytechnic University of Cávado and Ave and Bachelor Professor at Polytechnic University of Cávado and Ave in the area(s) of Social Sciences with an emphasis on Economics and Management with an emphasis on Organization and Management companies. In his Science Vitae curriculum, the most frequent terms in the context of scientific, technological and artistic-cultural production are: taxation; tax law; taxes; tax education; State aid; VAT; income taxation.

Sara Dias is a PhD in Law (University of Santiago de Compostela). Master in Tax Law (University of Minho). Law Degree (Law Faculty of Porto University). Lawyer (partner) at Yolanda Busse, Oehen Mendes & Associados, S.P., R.L. Assistant Professor at the Polytechnic University of Cávado and Ave and at the Portucalense University (tax law, insolvency law and corporate law). Trainer at Regional Council of Porto of the Portuguese Bar Association and in several advanced training courses in the area of Tax Law, organized by UNIFOJ - Centre for Social Studies of the University of Coimbra. Member of the Portuguese Tax Association (AFP) and the International Fiscal Association (IFA). External reviewer of Portuguese Law Lagazines (Revista Jurídica Portucalense and RED - Revista Electrónica de Direito). Participation, as a speaker, in several conferences/seminars and publication of several articles in magazines and books in the areas of Tax Law and Insolvency Law.

* * *

Susana Aldeia is a full-time Assistant Professor at the Portucalense University (UPT) and a part-time Associated Professor at the Polytechnic Institute of Cávado and Ave (IPCA). She holds a Phd with mention in Tax Law and a DEA from the Vigo University (Spain); a postgraduation in taxation from the IPCA and a degree in Accounting, also from the IPCA. Currently, she teaches in 1st and 2nd cycle courses in the areas of accounting, taxation and management simulation. She is a researcher at Research on Economics, Management and Information Technologies (REMIT), Portucalense Institute for Legal Research (IJP), Research Centre on Accounting and Taxation (CICF). She develops research activities on income, consumption and property taxation, but particularly on income taxation and its relationship with accounting. She has been a chartered accountant since 2003 in exercise and is a member of the Income Tax College of Portuguese Chartered Accountants Association (OCC).

El Houssan Attak holds a PhD in Business Administration from Aix-Marseille University and a Master's degree in Research from the University Paris-Panthéon-Assas. He is a professor at the National School of Business and Management at Cadi Ayyad University in Marrakesh. Dr. Attak has published papers in Scopus-indexed journals and contributed chapters to Scopus-indexed books.

Tania Cristina Azevedo is an Accountant, Master in Accounting and PhD in Territorial Planning and Social Development, with an Abroad Internship at the University of Salamanca (USAL)/Spain. Professor at the State University of Feira de Santana and University Federal de Bahia. Partner and manager of the Silveira Accounting Organization. Urban socio-environmental sustainability researcher, with emphasis on economic and tax instruments of urban policy; green taxes and environmental taxation with a view to tax extrafiscality. And urban policies integrated with the Sustainable Development Goals of the 2030/UN Agenda.

Rida Belahouaoui is a PhD researcher specializing in digital taxation, tax compliance, and tax avoidance at Cadi Ayyad University. He has established himself as an expert in the field of taxation with a keen focus on compliance and avoidance strategies. His academic endeavors are directed towards unraveling the complexities of tax legislation and the mechanisms to curb tax avoidance.

Anna Białek-Jaworska, PhD, is dealing with issues of Financial Accounting, Taxation and Financial Reporting. She has published in economics, taxation and finance; she is an author of research concerning profit shifting, international financial reporting standards and corporate finance. She conducts research for the Ministry of Finance on tax analysis and the effects of regulations.

André Carvalho is a master's student in Taxation at the Polytechnic Institute of Cávado and Ave (IPCA) and a Research Fellow at the Research Center on Accounting and Taxation (CICF)/Polytechnic Institute of Cávado and Ave (IPCA). Degree in Public Management from the Polytechnic Institute of Cávado and Ave (IPCA) and Postgraduate in Accounting and Corporate Taxation from Coimbra Business School (ISCAC). Author and co-author of scientific articles on green taxation.

Saurabh Chandra is an accomplished legal scholar and currently serves as an Associate Professor at the School of Law, Bennett University, India. With a robust academic foundation, he earned his Bachelor of Arts and Bachelor of Laws (B.A. LL.B.) from the prestigious Aligarh Muslim University (AMU). He further specialized in Business Laws, completing his Master of Laws (LL.M.) at the renowned National Law School of India University (NLSIU), Bangalore. Dr. Chandra's academic journey culminated in a Doctorate in Law (Ph.D.) from the esteemed National Law University. In addition to his impressive legal education from some of India's most prestigious institutions, Dr. Saurabh Chandra also holds a master's degree in Management with a specialization in Human Resources in Management and another in Journalism and Mass Communication. With 16 years of teaching experience, he has established himself as an expert in Business and Corporate Law, with numerous publications to his credit. Dr. Chandra brings a wealth of experience in Academic Administration, having successfully held various key administrative positions.

Vânia Costa has a PhD in Economics from the University of Vigo, with the thesis "Regional Portuguese Airports, Local Economy and Tourism Development", a MSc in Industrial Economics and Business from University of Minho and a degree in Economics from University of Minho. She is an Assistent Professor in the School of Hospitality and Tourism of Polytechnic Institute of Cávado and Ave (Barcelos, Portugal). She is a Researcher at CiTUR - Centre for Research, Development and Innovation in Tourism, Portugal; Member of the research unit GOVCOPP - Research Unit on Governance, Competitiveness and Public Policies, University of Aveiro, Portugal; and also Researcher of the UNIAG - Applied Management Research Unit. Her current research interests include Tourism Research, Tourism and Economic Development, Investment Projects in Tourism, Competitiveness and Corporate Finance of Hospitality and Tourism, Human Capital in Tourism, Health and Wellness Tourism and Transports.

Sérgio Cruz is Adjunct Professor at the University of Aveiro (ISCA-UA). PhD in Accounting and researcher in the field of taxation with scientific publications in books and journals subject to peer review.

Ricardo Sousa da Cunha is a Law Professor at the Law Department of the Management School of IPCA. The Author holds a PhD in Public Law by the Law School of University of Minho, a Master Degree in Public Law by the Law School of the University of Coimbra and a Master Degree in International Law by the Law School of the University of Macau. The author has taught at different Universities, in Portugal, at the Law School of UMinho, and abroad, namely the Universidade Nacional de Timor-Lorosa'e; is the author of many publications on national and foreign journals an labels (books, articles and reports), besides having worked as a legal consultant for national and foreign companies and Governments, most notably the Government of Timor-Leste and the Government of the Macau SAR, PRC.

Paulo Dias is a PhD in Accounting and MBA in Management, by ISCTE-IUL, Post-Graduate in Finance, by CEMAF-ISCTE and Graduate in Management, by UML. He is coordinator of Courses of Taxation, Business Taxation, Company Tax Management, Principles and Procedures of Tax Litigation and Taxation of Non-Residents. He is Executive Director of the Executive MBA and Director of Post-Graduation in Tax Management at INDEG-ISCTE.

Mónica García Freiría is a Researcher in Taxation and a Tax Law Profesor at the University of Vigo. She received her PhD Degree in Taxation by the University of Vigo, Spain (2021). With the defense of her doctoral thesis "Qualification in tax matters. A study from the perspective of Spanish Law and the EU" she received the extraordinary Doctoral Award from the UVigo. She teaches in various degrees (Law, Labor Relations, Commerce,...) at the University of Vigo since 2017. She has participated in different collective works. She has published in some relevants magazines such as Quincena Fiscal, Revista española de Derecho financiero, Crónica tributaria... Currently she has published two books: "La calificación jurídica en materia tributaria" and "Criterios para la aplicación de los Convenios de Doble Imposición Internacional".

Siddharth Kanojia is an Asst. Professor of Law at O.P Jindal Global University. He is also a visiting professor at Indian Institute of Management Amritsar and Sirmaur. He holds a Ph.D in Corporate Law & Governance, LL.M in International Business and Commercial Law, LL.B and BBS in Finance. Before commencing the academic stints, he was associated with U.K Intellectual Property Management Company as Legal Consultant and Manchester based Start-up Company as Legal Advisor. Till date, he has various publication in the SCOPUS and WoS indexed journals. He has authored a book which was published by Thomson Reuters and he is the editor of the book titled 'Bridging Health, Environment and Legalities: A Holistic Approach' published by IGI Global. He is also an active member in Human Development and Capability Association, USA and Development Studies Association, U.K.

Pascal René Marcel Kubin is a transfer pricing consultant. Prior to this, he was a research associate at the University of Speyer. His research focuses on decentralized systems, information asymmetries, digital innovation, as well as individualism. Apart from that, he analyzes new developments in the field of taxation (particularly in the area of transfer pricing and with regard to the taxation of crypto assets). From a technological perspective, he is interested in distributed ledger technologies as well as technologies used for transfer pricing.

Hélder Lopes is, since 2008, a Catholic Priest from the Diocese of Guarda, Portugal. Since 2021 has been in the Pontificio Collegio Portoghese, Italy. Graduated in Theology from the Catholic University of Portugal (2007). Graduated in Moral Theology from the Accademia Alfonsiana - Università Pontificia Lateranense, Italy (2023). Master in Management - Accounting speciality from the Guarda Polytechnic Institute, Portugal (2024). PhD student in Neuroetic and Moral Theology at the Accademia Alfonsiana, Italy.

Bhumika Muchan is a distinguished legal professional known for her unwavering commitment to bridging the gap between legal theory and practical application. Her academic journey commenced with the completion of a Bachelor in Law degree from the Guru Gobind Singh Indraprastha University. She has obtained a Master of Laws degree in Business and Corporate Laws (from Symbiosis International (Deemed University, Pune). She is currently practising at Delhi District Courts and Delhi High Court.

Shane O'Sullivan is a Senior Lecturer in the Department of Applied Social Sciences; and researcher within the Sustainable Development Research Institute at the Technological University of the Shannon - Midlands Midwest (TUS).

Raquel Pereira is an Assistant Professor at the School of Hospitality and Tourism of the Polytechnic Institute of Cavado and Ave in Barcelos, Portugal. She holds a PhD in Theory and History of Education from the University of Santiago de Compostela and a Master's in Adult Education from the University of Minho. She is also a researcher at CiTUR - Centre for Research, Development and Innovation in Tourism, Portugal. Her primary research interests include tourism research, tourism and well-being, human capital in tourism, and foreign languages in tourism. Additionally, she is also interested in teaching second languages and critical pedagogy.

Maria Helena Pernadas is a Tax and Customs Inspector since 1987, with the position of Director of Finance for the Guard District. Teacher of taxation in the School of Technology and Management - Polytechnic of Guarda, Portugal. Graduated in Audit (ISCAL, Portugal). MBA in Business Administration (ISCTE, Portugal).

Franz Rodríguez Franky is a professional with more than 15 years of experience, with more than 8 years in University Teaching. Research professor recognized by Minciencias. Master's Degree in Environmental Management and Auditing, Specialist in Administration and Management of Quality Systems from the University of Santo Tomas in agreement with ICONTEC, and Agricultural Engineer. Professional with the ability to integrate technical, administrative, economic and human resources of the field, educational, virtual LMS, Moodle and others. Knowledge of ISO, 9001, 14001 and 45001 Standards.

Sílvia Santos is a PhD student in Business Management at Technological University of the Shannon: Midlands Midwest (TUS) and Doctoral fellow at Research Centre on Accounting and Taxation (CICF)/Polytechnic Institute of Cávado and Ave (IPCA). Master's degree in Solicitors at the Polytechnic Institute of Cávado and Ave (IPCA) and a degree in Accounting and Administration at the Polytechnic

Institute of Porto (IPP). Chartered Accountant, since 2013. Author and co-author in scientific papers in the green taxation area.

Index

A

Arm's Length Principle 424, 425, 426, 427, 438, 440, 443, 444, 446, 448, 450, 469
Autonomic financial system 76, 90

B

BEPS 362, 363, 372, 385, 423, 425, 426, 435, 437, 441, 449, 458, 459, 468, 469, 470, 472
Bibliometric 64, 65, 211, 212, 213, 217, 218, 220, 239, 240, 244, 324, 448, 450, 473, 475, 477, 478, 479, 481, 502, 504, 505, 507, 510, 515, 517, 525, 531, 532, 555
bibliometric analysis 65, 211, 212, 213, 217, 239, 240, 244, 324, 448, 450, 473, 475, 477, 478, 479, 481, 502, 504, 510, 525

C

change behaviors 194
Compliance Costs 40, 278, 379, 423, 424, 425, 426, 449, 459, 460, 522
Concordat 115, 116, 117, 121, 122, 124, 128, 129, 130, 131, 132, 133, 134, 139
Corporate patronage 400, 403, 404, 406
Covid-19 178, 179, 181, 204, 212, 213, 215, 231, 233, 234, 237, 280, 359, 361, 363, 364, 365, 366, 367, 368, 376, 377, 379, 380, 381, 382, 383, 384, 433

D

destination management 244
Digitalization 365, 366, 379, 382, 384, 426, 441, 451, 509
Direct Tax 275, 276, 278, 282, 290, 302, 377, 511, 519, 553
drinks 101, 142, 143, 144, 145, 146, 147, 148, 149, 150, 151, 152, 153, 154, 155, 156, 157, 158, 159, 160, 161, 166, 167, 169, 192, 193

E

Ecological Taxation 39, 63, 341
Economic recovery 364, 365, 366, 368, 379, 380
Energy Efficiency 34, 36, 37, 41, 43, 44, 53, 54, 56, 58, 60, 62, 63, 68, 183, 185, 189, 195, 198, 209, 325, 341
Environmental Law 40, 303, 320, 327
Environmental Taxation 34, 35, 37, 38, 40, 41, 42, 61, 63, 66, 84, 94, 199, 206, 207, 303, 322, 323, 324, 327, 340
e-Sports 409, 410, 420, 421
European integration 90, 94, 100
European Union 34, 35, 37, 61, 63, 64, 71, 72, 74, 76, 91, 92, 94, 95, 96, 108, 112, 113, 124, 136, 153, 198, 249, 251, 255, 257, 267, 304, 312, 313, 321, 326, 387, 388, 389, 391, 392, 393, 395, 396, 401, 403, 407, 415, 457, 459, 462, 524

F

Fantasy Sports 410, 411, 419, 421
Financial Services 1, 2, 3, 4, 5, 6, 7, 8, 9, 10, 16, 17, 21, 23, 24, 25, 26, 27, 28, 29, 30, 31
Fiscal Federalism 75, 76, 105, 106, 107, 108, 110, 279, 298, 299
flat tax 370, 371, 382, 383, 385, 515, 516, 517, 518, 521, 522, 523, 524, 525, 526, 527, 528, 529, 530, 531, 532, 534, 538, 541, 544, 547, 548, 549, 550, 551, 552, 553, 554, 555, 556, 557, 558, 559, 560, 561, 562
food 144, 146, 147, 149, 150, 151, 156, 157, 160, 161, 162, 163, 164, 167, 168, 169, 239, 304, 307, 363, 394, 397
Functions 10, 40, 69, 111, 118, 119, 120, 127, 128, 133, 203, 260, 290, 291, 424, 426, 428, 438, 439, 440, 442, 444, 456
Funds 59, 72, 80, 88, 89, 90, 103, 111, 188, 189, 195, 212, 214, 216, 274, 281, 296,

308, 312, 320, 343, 377, 518

G

Goods and Service Tax 278
Government Measures 303, 306, 309, 313, 315, 318, 327
green business 186
Greenhouse Gas Emissions 33, 35, 37, 40, 42, 45, 50, 53, 54, 58, 60, 172, 174, 175, 176, 185, 189, 197, 209, 304, 321
Green tax 38, 40, 41, 60, 65, 66, 68, 174, 175, 176, 179, 180, 182, 191, 192, 194, 196, 213, 239, 308, 309, 310, 311, 325, 327, 340, 365, 366, 383, 512
Green Taxation 35, 38, 40, 41, 42, 61, 62, 64, 68, 172, 173, 174, 175, 176, 177, 178, 187, 188, 189, 190, 191, 192, 193, 195, 197, 200, 201, 205, 208, 209, 211, 212, 213, 216, 218, 231, 232, 244, 303, 304, 305, 306, 307, 308, 309, 310, 311, 312, 313, 315, 316, 317, 318, 319, 320, 321, 322, 323, 325, 327, 405

H

health professionals 142, 158, 159, 161, 162
HEI 312, 319
Higher Education Curricula 303, 310, 312, 327
Household Behavior 26

I

Indirect Tax 1, 16, 22, 25, 275, 279, 282, 283, 284, 287, 290, 291, 299, 300, 302, 373, 377, 519
International Tax 29, 300, 360, 362, 363, 364, 365, 366, 372, 383, 424, 437, 458, 459, 468, 470, 484, 485, 508, 545, 546, 556, 560
Ismaili Imamat 115, 117, 122, 123, 124, 127, 128, 131, 132, 133, 134, 139

L

Legislation 82, 139, 147, 247, 248, 249, 250, 251, 252, 253, 254, 255, 256, 257, 258, 260, 266, 267, 270, 278, 290, 291, 292, 296, 306, 331, 332, 334, 335, 337, 338, 341, 343, 344, 345, 346, 347, 348, 349, 350, 372, 387, 388, 389, 392, 393, 394, 396, 398, 400, 402, 403, 404, 407, 412, 454, 458, 460, 462, 465, 466, 467
LOFCA 77, 78, 79, 81, 82, 83, 84, 85, 88, 95, 98, 101, 106, 107, 110, 112

M

Morocco 150, 359, 360, 361, 365, 366, 368, 372, 375, 376, 377, 378, 379, 380, 381, 382, 383
Multinational Enterprises 362, 423, 424, 425, 426, 427, 433, 434, 435, 437, 442, 445, 446, 447, 448, 449, 450, 457, 470, 471
Municipal Property Tax 33, 42, 44, 129, 130, 310
Municipal Property Transfer Tax 33, 42, 44, 129, 130

N

Non-profit Sector 387, 388, 389, 401, 403
nutrition education 169

O

OECD 10, 16, 17, 25, 29, 30, 39, 40, 41, 65, 66, 73, 74, 107, 111, 177, 196, 205, 207, 208, 209, 214, 239, 249, 251, 252, 267, 269, 271, 289, 300, 351, 362, 363, 366, 368, 383, 423, 424, 425, 426, 427, 428, 429, 430, 431, 435, 437, 438, 439, 440, 441, 442, 443, 444, 445, 448, 449, 450, 453, 454, 455, 457, 458, 459, 460, 461, 462, 463, 464, 466, 467, 470, 471, 492
Online Games 409, 410, 411, 412, 413, 416, 417, 418, 421

Own Taxes 73, 75, 78, 80, 81, 82, 83, 86, 87, 94, 96, 98, 100, 101, 110, 112

P

Portugal 15, 33, 35, 37, 38, 41, 42, 48, 54, 57, 66, 67, 115, 116, 117, 118, 120, 121, 123, 127, 128, 129, 131, 134, 135, 136, 137, 138, 139, 141, 142, 143, 144, 145, 148, 149, 152, 153, 156, 157, 158, 159, 161, 162, 163, 165, 167, 168, 184, 185, 186, 211, 247, 248, 249, 250, 252, 253, 257, 260, 261, 262, 264, 265, 266, 270, 272, 303, 318, 340, 387, 388, 393, 395, 401, 402, 403, 404, 405, 406, 453, 454, 455, 462, 463, 466, 468, 473, 503, 515
Portuguese tax regime 115, 117, 389, 393, 398, 405
Profit Shifting 362, 385, 401, 426, 449, 455, 456, 458, 459, 466, 467, 469, 470, 471, 472
Property Tax 33, 42, 44, 69, 129, 130, 310, 330, 331, 333, 334, 335, 336, 337, 338, 340, 341, 342, 343, 345, 346, 347, 348, 349, 350, 353, 355, 504, 513
Public Policies 34, 172, 191, 207, 214, 270, 330, 338, 339, 351, 355, 360, 378

Q

quality of life 142, 162, 177, 183, 184, 185, 189, 245, 330, 334, 340, 341, 342

R

Reform 18, 29, 38, 39, 41, 61, 62, 63, 65, 66, 67, 71, 72, 73, 74, 80, 81, 84, 85, 86, 92, 95, 97, 100, 102, 103, 104, 108, 164, 171, 172, 173, 174, 175, 180, 182, 192, 193, 197, 202, 203, 205, 207, 248, 252, 254, 258, 265, 271, 273, 274, 276, 277, 278, 279, 280, 282, 283, 285, 288, 296, 298, 299, 301, 320, 322, 359, 360, 361, 362, 363, 364, 365, 366, 367, 369, 370, 371, 372, 373, 374, 375, 376, 378, 379, 380, 381, 382, 383, 384, 414, 420, 459, 495, 508, 516, 521, 522, 527, 528, 529, 530, 539, 541, 547, 549, 550, 551, 552, 553, 554, 556, 558, 559, 560, 562
Regulatory Impact Assessment 247, 248, 249, 250, 262, 263, 265, 266, 267, 270
Religious Freedom Law 115, 116, 120, 124, 128, 131, 132, 133, 139
Risks 84, 208, 258, 319, 362, 364, 383, 424, 426, 427, 428, 433, 437, 444, 446, 451, 459, 510

S

Salvador 329, 331, 332, 341, 342, 343, 344, 345, 346, 347, 348, 349, 350, 352, 353, 354
SGDs 327
Social Economy 127, 378, 387, 388, 389, 390, 391, 392, 393, 394, 395, 396, 397, 398, 399, 400, 401, 402, 403, 404, 406, 407
Standardization 361, 445
State Budget 81, 247, 248, 249, 258, 259, 260, 261, 262, 263, 264, 265, 267, 269, 270, 466
subsidies 41, 57, 67, 147, 148, 167, 168, 169, 172, 190, 194, 195, 196, 199, 200, 294, 305, 308, 312, 392, 399, 495, 496, 512
sugar 142, 143, 144, 145, 146, 150, 151, 152, 153, 154, 155, 156, 159, 160, 161, 162, 164, 165, 166, 167, 168, 169
sustainability 33, 34, 35, 36, 37, 38, 39, 40, 41, 42, 43, 44, 51, 55, 56, 57, 58, 60, 61, 62, 65, 66, 67, 68, 69, 73, 80, 96, 100, 127, 174, 175, 176, 178, 179, 180, 182, 191, 192, 197, 200, 205, 206, 207, 208, 211, 212, 213, 214, 215, 216, 218, 219, 220, 221, 223, 224, 225, 227, 228, 230, 231, 232, 233, 234, 235, 236, 238, 239, 240, 241, 242, 244, 264, 303, 305, 307, 308, 309, 311, 313, 315, 317, 318, 320, 323, 324, 325, 326, 327, 328,

338, 340, 341, 342, 344, 345, 346, 349, 350, 355, 356, 359, 363, 365, 379, 380, 383, 467, 474, 499, 501, 502, 527, 561
Sustainable Development 34, 35, 36, 39, 40, 41, 44, 56, 58, 59, 62, 63, 64, 65, 68, 69, 172, 173, 176, 179, 181, 186, 187, 191, 200, 202, 205, 206, 207, 208, 209, 212, 213, 214, 216, 221, 224, 230, 231, 232, 233, 240, 242, 243, 279, 303, 304, 305, 306, 309, 311, 313, 314, 316, 317, 318, 319, 320, 322, 323, 324, 326, 327, 328, 329, 330, 331, 336, 338, 339, 340, 341, 346, 348, 350, 354, 355, 356, 363, 364, 365, 367, 368, 377, 380, 381, 509

T

Tax 1, 2, 4, 5, 8, 9, 10, 15, 16, 18, 19, 20, 23, 24, 25, 26, 28, 29, 30, 33, 34, 35, 38, 39, 40, 41, 42, 43, 44, 45, 46, 47, 48, 49, 50, 51, 52, 53, 54, 55, 56, 57, 58, 60, 61, 62, 63, 64, 65, 66, 67, 68, 69, 70, 71, 72, 73, 74, 75, 76, 79, 80, 81, 82, 83, 84, 85, 86, 87, 88, 89, 91, 92, 93, 94, 95, 96, 97, 98, 99, 100, 101, 102, 103, 104, 105, 106, 107, 108, 110, 111, 113, 115, 116, 117, 121, 122, 123, 125, 126, 127, 128, 129, 130, 131, 132, 133, 134, 139, 140, 141, 142, 144, 145, 146, 147, 148, 149, 152, 153, 154, 155, 156, 157, 158, 159, 160, 161, 162, 163, 165, 166, 167, 169, 171, 172, 174, 175, 176, 177, 178, 179, 180, 181, 182, 183, 184, 185, 186, 187, 188, 190, 191, 192, 193, 194, 195, 196, 197, 198, 199, 200, 202, 203, 205, 207, 212, 213, 214, 215, 216, 221, 224, 225, 227, 228, 229, 230, 231, 232, 235, 236, 239, 240, 241, 242, 244, 247, 248, 249, 259, 260, 261, 262, 263, 264, 265, 266, 267, 270, 271, 273, 274, 275, 276, 277, 278, 279, 280, 281, 282, 283, 284, 285, 286, 287, 288, 289, 290, 291, 292, 293, 294, 295, 296, 297, 298, 299, 300, 301, 302, 306, 308, 309, 310, 311, 320, 321, 322, 323, 325, 326, 327, 328, 329, 330, 331, 332, 333, 334, 335, 336, 337, 338, 340, 341, 342, 343, 344, 345, 346, 347, 348, 349, 350, 351, 353, 354, 355, 356, 359, 360, 361, 362, 363, 364, 365, 366, 367, 368, 369, 370, 371, 372, 373, 374, 375, 376, 377, 378, 379, 380, 381, 382, 383, 384, 385, 387, 388, 389, 390, 391, 392, 393, 394, 395, 396, 397, 398, 399, 400, 401, 402, 403, 404, 405, 406, 407, 411, 412, 413, 414, 415, 416, 417, 418, 419, 420, 423, 424, 425, 426, 427, 434, 435, 437, 438, 441, 442, 443, 444, 445, 446, 448, 449, 450, 453, 454, 455, 456, 457, 458, 459, 460, 461, 462, 463, 464, 465, 466, 467, 468, 469, 470, 471, 472, 473, 474, 475, 476, 477, 479, 480, 481, 482, 483, 484, 485, 487, 488, 490, 491, 492, 493, 494, 495, 496, 497, 498, 499, 500, 501, 502, 503, 504, 505, 506, 507, 508, 509, 510, 511, 512, 513, 515, 516, 517, 518, 519, 520, 521, 522, 523, 524, 525, 526, 527, 528, 529, 530, 531, 532, 534, 538, 539, 541, 544, 545, 546, 547, 548, 549, 550, 551, 552, 553, 554, 555, 556, 557, 558, 559, 560, 561, 562, 563
taxation 2, 3, 6, 18, 24, 25, 27, 28, 29, 30, 33, 34, 35, 37, 38, 39, 40, 41, 42, 61, 62, 63, 64, 66, 68, 69, 75, 76, 78, 82, 84, 91, 93, 94, 97, 98, 99, 100, 102, 107, 116, 117, 126, 128, 130, 131, 135, 139, 140, 142, 147, 148, 155, 157, 160, 161, 165, 168, 171, 172, 173, 174, 175, 176, 177, 178, 181, 187, 188, 189, 190, 191, 192, 193, 195, 197, 198, 199, 200, 201, 202, 205, 206, 207, 208, 209, 211, 212, 213, 214, 215, 216, 217, 218, 219, 221, 228, 231, 232, 234, 236, 243, 244, 247, 248, 260, 261, 262, 270, 275, 277, 278, 281, 282, 283, 286,

287, 288, 289, 291, 292, 293, 295, 296, 298, 299, 301, 302, 303, 304, 305, 306, 307, 308, 309, 310, 311, 312, 313, 315, 316, 317, 318, 319, 320, 321, 322, 323, 324, 325, 326, 327, 332, 336, 339, 340, 341, 342, 345, 351, 356, 360, 361, 362, 365, 366, 369, 370, 375, 378, 382, 383, 384, 385, 387, 388, 389, 390, 391, 392, 394, 395, 396, 397, 398, 399, 400, 401, 402, 403, 405, 407, 409, 413, 414, 415, 417, 418, 420, 421, 424, 425, 426, 427, 436, 437, 441, 442, 443, 446, 448, 455, 456, 458, 459, 460, 461, 462, 466, 469, 471, 472, 473, 474, 475, 476, 477, 485, 488, 497, 501, 503, 504, 506, 515, 516, 517, 518, 519, 520, 521, 524, 527, 528, 529, 530, 549, 551, 553, 554, 556, 558, 559, 561, 562
Taxation of religions 139
Tax autonomy 73, 74, 85, 92, 97, 98
Tax benefits 41, 42, 43, 48, 49, 50, 87, 93, 98, 99, 100, 115, 125, 126, 127, 129, 134, 140, 183, 184, 185, 192, 197, 198, 247, 248, 249, 262, 263, 264, 265, 266, 267, 310, 329, 331, 332, 334, 336, 337, 340, 344, 345, 346, 349, 350, 387, 388, 393, 394, 395, 399, 400, 401, 402, 403, 404, 407, 473, 474, 475, 476, 477, 479, 480, 482, 483, 484, 487, 490, 491, 492, 494, 495, 496, 497, 498, 499, 500, 501, 502, 504, 505, 507, 508, 509, 510, 512
Tax Credits 282, 375, 391, 399, 483, 490, 491, 492, 493, 494, 495, 496, 497, 498, 503, 508, 509, 510, 511, 512
Tax Deductions 80, 293, 498, 506, 507, 510, 513, 524
Tax exemption 129, 130, 131, 132, 140, 336, 348, 371, 375, 399, 402, 404, 407
Tax Holidays 477, 480, 499, 503, 506, 510, 513
Tax incentives 33, 34, 35, 38, 40, 41, 42, 44, 45, 46, 47, 48, 49, 50, 51, 52, 53, 54, 55, 56, 57, 58, 61, 62, 65, 67, 68, 86, 127, 181, 182, 188, 191, 198, 199, 214, 294, 308, 310, 311, 327, 329, 331, 332, 335, 338, 340, 341, 344, 345, 346, 347, 348, 349, 350, 351, 354, 356, 365, 366, 369, 391, 392, 399, 490, 491, 492, 493, 494, 495, 496, 497, 498, 501, 505, 506, 507, 508, 509, 510, 511
Tax justice 72, 87, 104, 384, 394, 407
Tax obligations 117, 134, 140, 296, 372, 374, 375, 376, 384
Tax policy 38, 48, 61, 179, 181, 188, 190, 196, 207, 247, 248, 260, 274, 275, 276, 277, 290, 295, 296, 298, 299, 302, 306, 308, 311, 330, 341, 359, 361, 364, 365, 366, 368, 369, 380, 381, 384, 419, 508, 509, 528, 550, 554, 559
Tax reform 18, 38, 39, 61, 62, 63, 65, 66, 67, 73, 74, 80, 92, 108, 171, 172, 174, 175, 180, 182, 192, 193, 197, 202, 203, 205, 273, 274, 277, 279, 283, 296, 298, 299, 301, 320, 322, 359, 360, 361, 362, 363, 364, 365, 366, 367, 369, 370, 372, 375, 376, 379, 380, 381, 382, 383, 384, 414, 420, 495, 508, 516, 521, 522, 527, 528, 529, 530, 539, 541, 547, 549, 550, 551, 552, 553, 554, 556, 558, 559, 560, 562
Tax Reliefs 510
Tax revenues mobilization 376
Tax Shields 498, 505, 506, 510, 512, 513
tourism destinations 211, 212, 213, 214, 217, 219, 220, 228, 231, 232, 234, 235, 245
tourism taxes 211, 212, 213, 214, 215, 216, 230, 235, 245
Two-Pillar Solution 362, 363, 425, 426, 449, 451

U

unhealthy products 147, 148, 160, 161
Urban Policy 330, 331, 333, 336, 338, 339, 341, 342, 343, 344, 345, 356
Urban Real Estate 330, 331, 333, 334, 342
Urban Rehabilitation 33, 36, 38, 42, 43, 44, 45, 46, 47, 48, 49, 50, 51, 53, 56, 57, 58, 69, 70

Utility Function 1, 2, 3, 4, 5, 6, 7, 8, 9, 10, 24, 25, 26, 28, 29

V

Value Added Tax 1, 10, 30, 41, 42, 43, 128, 302, 360, 393, 395, 563

W

weighting factors 147
World Health Organization 143, 168, 169, 212

www.ingramcontent.com/pod-product-compliance
Lightning Source LLC
LaVergne TN
LVHW080616300926
849162LV00005B/1178
* 9 7 9 8 3 6 9 3 3 9 0 8 4 *